THE HERO DEFINED

MAGE ™

VOLUME TWO

WRITTEN & ILLUSTRATED
MATT WAGNER

COLORED BY
JEROMY COX

LETTERED BY
SEAN KONOT

MAGE, VOL. 2: THE HERO DEFINED, July 2005. Published by Image Comics, Inc., Office of publication: 1942 University Avenue, Suite 305, Berkeley, California 94704, Copyright © 2005 Erik Larsen. All rights reserved. Mage™ (including all prominent characters featured in this issue), the Mage™ logo and allMage™ character likenesses are trademarks of Matt Wagner, unless otherwise noted. Image Comics® is a trademark of Image Comics, Inc. All rights reserved. No part of this publication may be reproduced or transmitted, in any form or by any means (except for for short excerpts for review purposes) without the express written permission of Image Comics, Inc. All names, characters, events and locales in this publication are entirely fictional. Any resemblance to actual persons (living or dead), events or places, without satiric intent, is coincidental. PRINTED IN CANADA

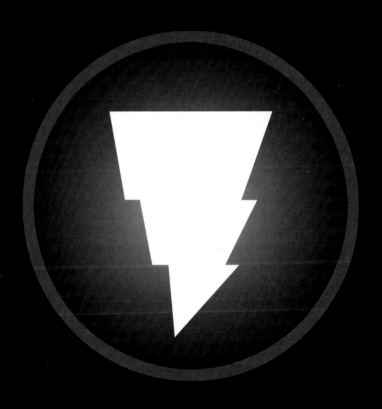

FOR IMAGE COMICS
Erik Larsen - Publisher
Todd McFarlane - President
Marc Silvestri - CEO
Jim Valentino - Vice-President

Eric Stephenson - Managing Editor
Missie Miranda - Controller
Brett Evans - Production Manager
Jim Demonakos - PR & Marketing Coordinator
Allen Hui - Production Artist
Joe Keatinge - Traffic Manager
Mia MacHatton - Administrative Assistant
Jonathan Chan - Production Assistant

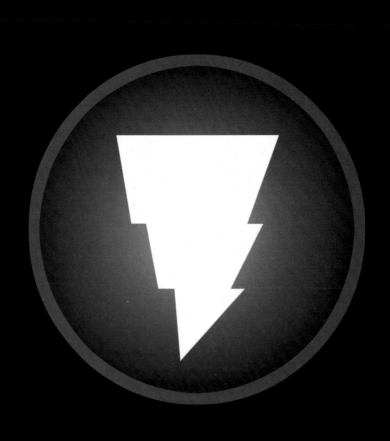

TABLE OF CONTENTS

To my darling wife,
who utterly enchanted me so many
years ago. Even after all our time
together, I still live under your spell.

second interlude

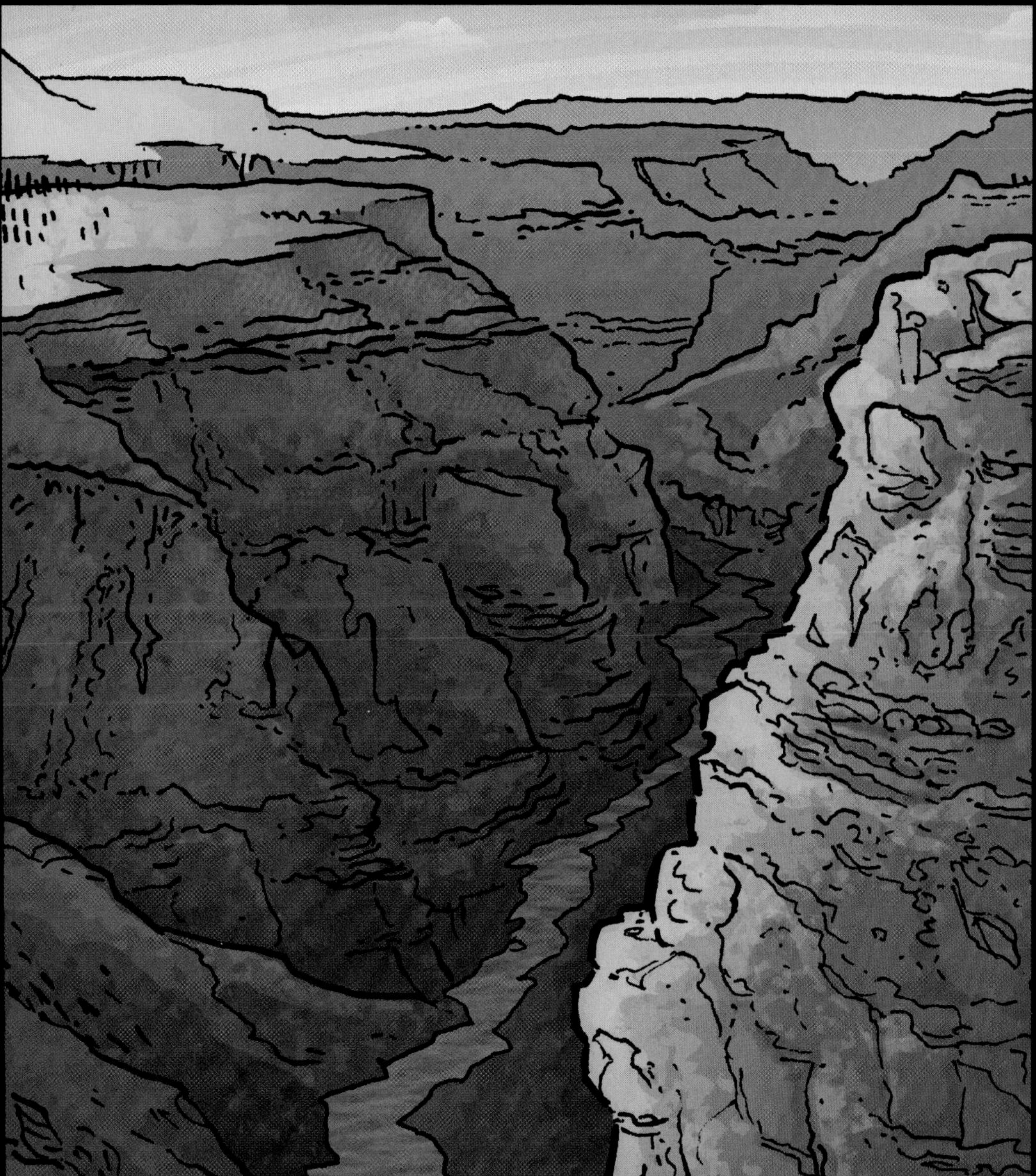

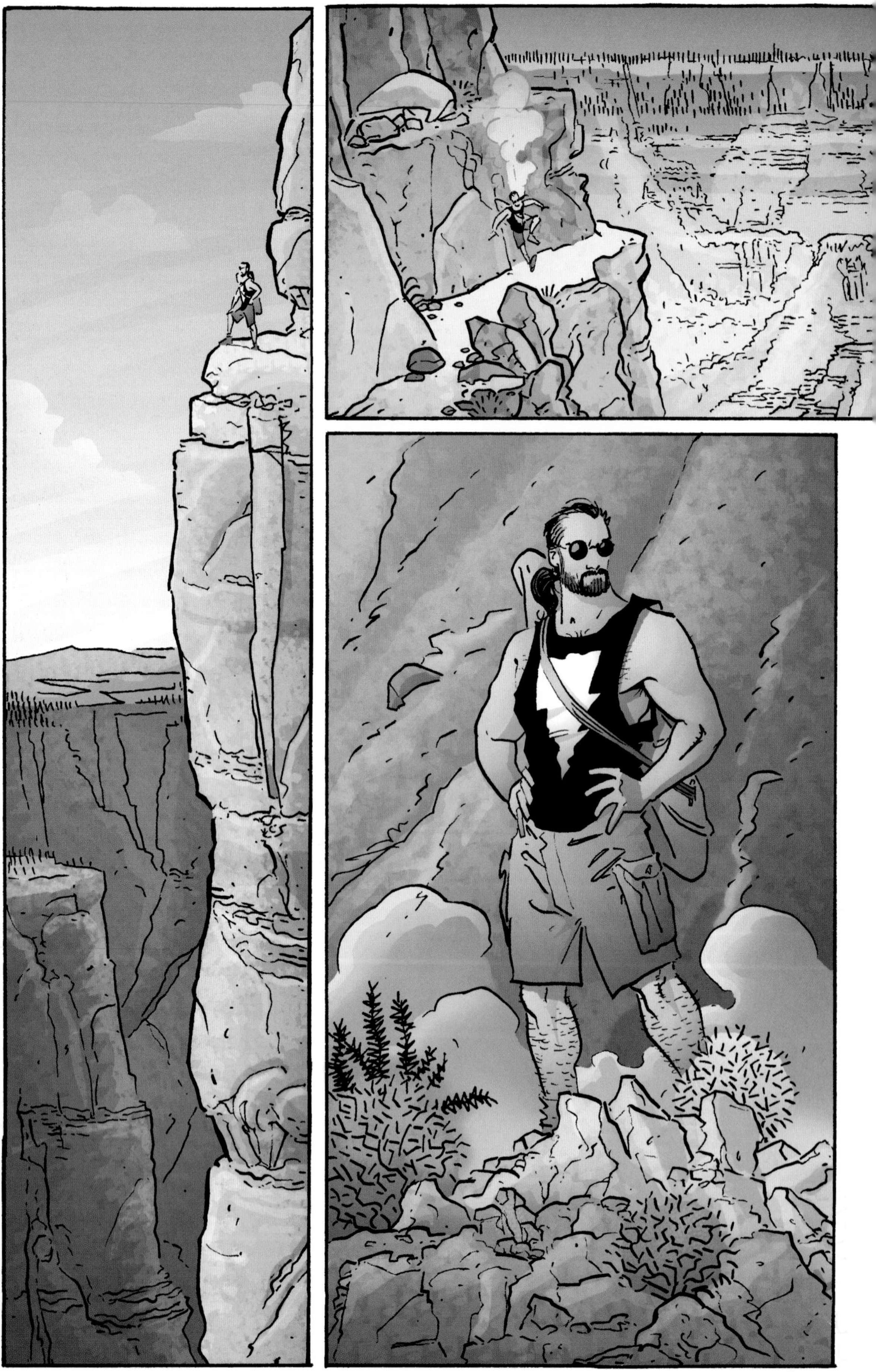

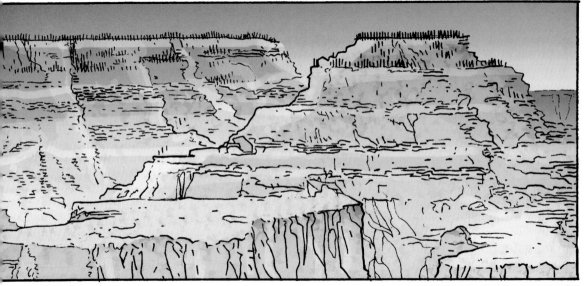

YUP, IT'S FRESH. I FOUND ANOTHER ONE 'BOUT A HUNDRED YARDS SOUTH.

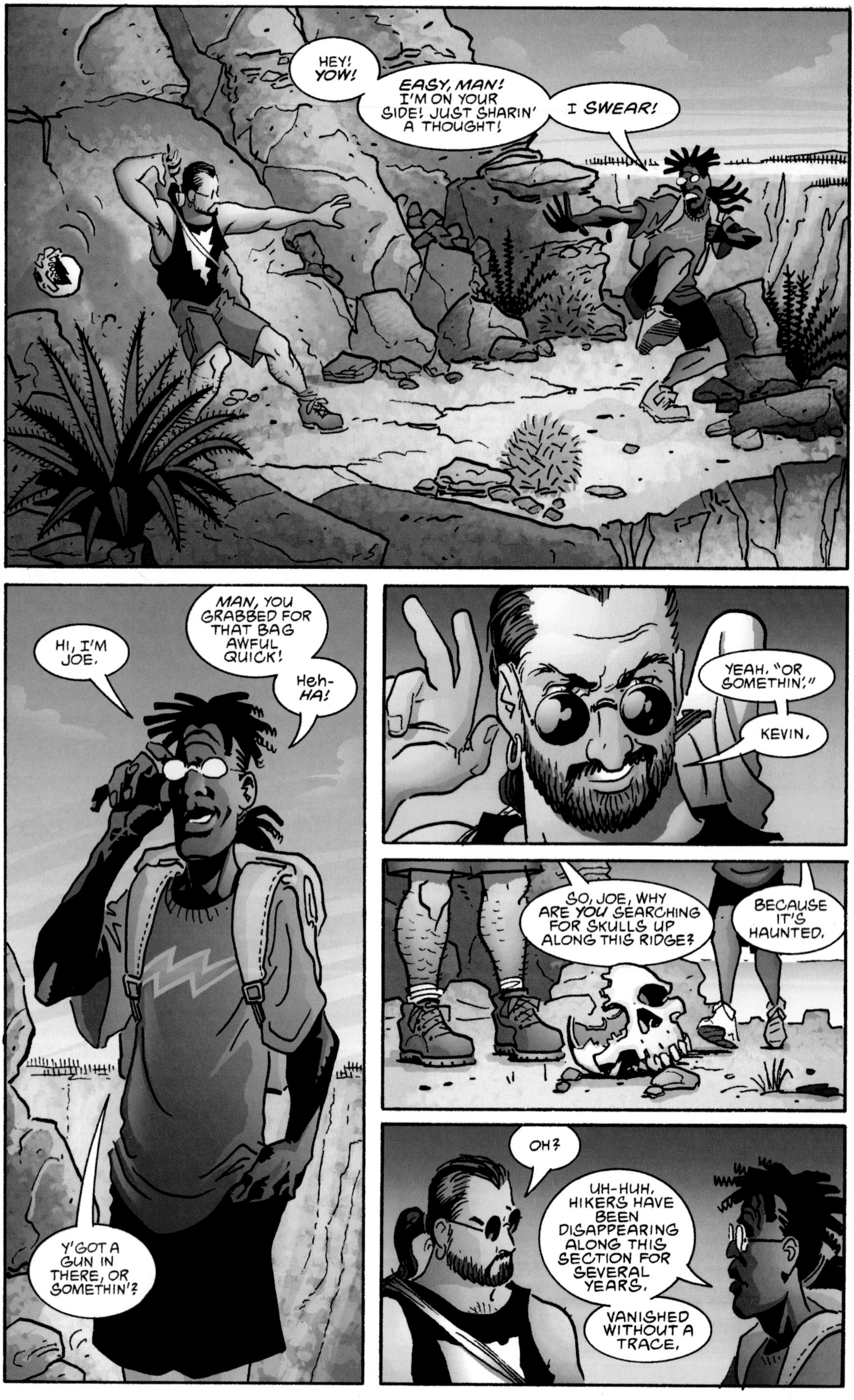
HEY! YOW!
EASY, MAN! I'M ON YOUR SIDE! JUST SHARIN' A THOUGHT!
I SWEAR!
HI, I'M JOE.
MAN, YOU GRABBED FOR THAT BAG AWFUL QUICK!
Heh-HA!
Y'GOT A GUN IN THERE, OR SOMETHIN'?
YEAH. "OR SOMETHIN'."
KEVIN.
SO, JOE, WHY ARE YOU SEARCHING FOR SKULLS UP ALONG THIS RIDGE?
BECAUSE IT'S HAUNTED.
OH?
UH-HUH. HIKERS HAVE BEEN DISAPPEARING ALONG THIS SECTION FOR SEVERAL YEARS.
VANISHED WITHOUT A TRACE.

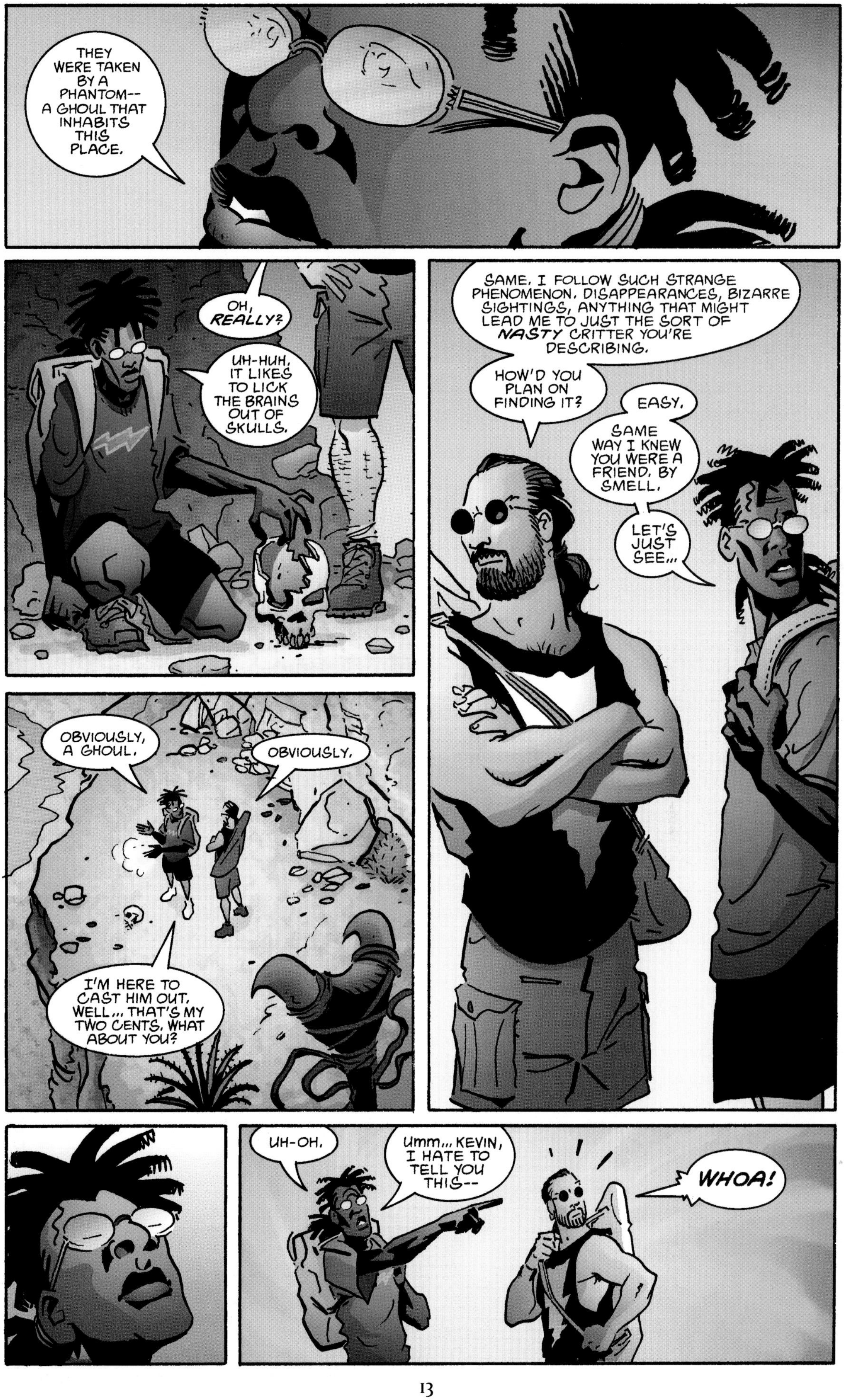
THEY WERE TAKEN BY A PHANTOM-- A GHOUL THAT INHABITS THIS PLACE.
OH, *REALLY?*
UH-HUH, IT LIKES TO LICK THE BRAINS OUT OF SKULLS.
OBVIOUSLY, A GHOUL.
OBVIOUSLY.
I'M HERE TO CAST HIM OUT. WELL... THAT'S MY TWO CENTS. WHAT ABOUT YOU?
SAME. I FOLLOW SUCH STRANGE PHENOMENON. DISAPPEARANCES, BIZARRE SIGHTINGS, ANYTHING THAT MIGHT LEAD ME TO JUST THE SORT OF *NASTY* CRITTER YOU'RE DESCRIBING.
HOW'D YOU PLAN ON FINDING IT?
EASY.
SAME WAY I KNEW YOU WERE A FRIEND. BY SMELL.
LET'S JUST SEE...
UH-OH.
UMM... KEVIN, I HATE TO TELL YOU THIS--
WHOA!

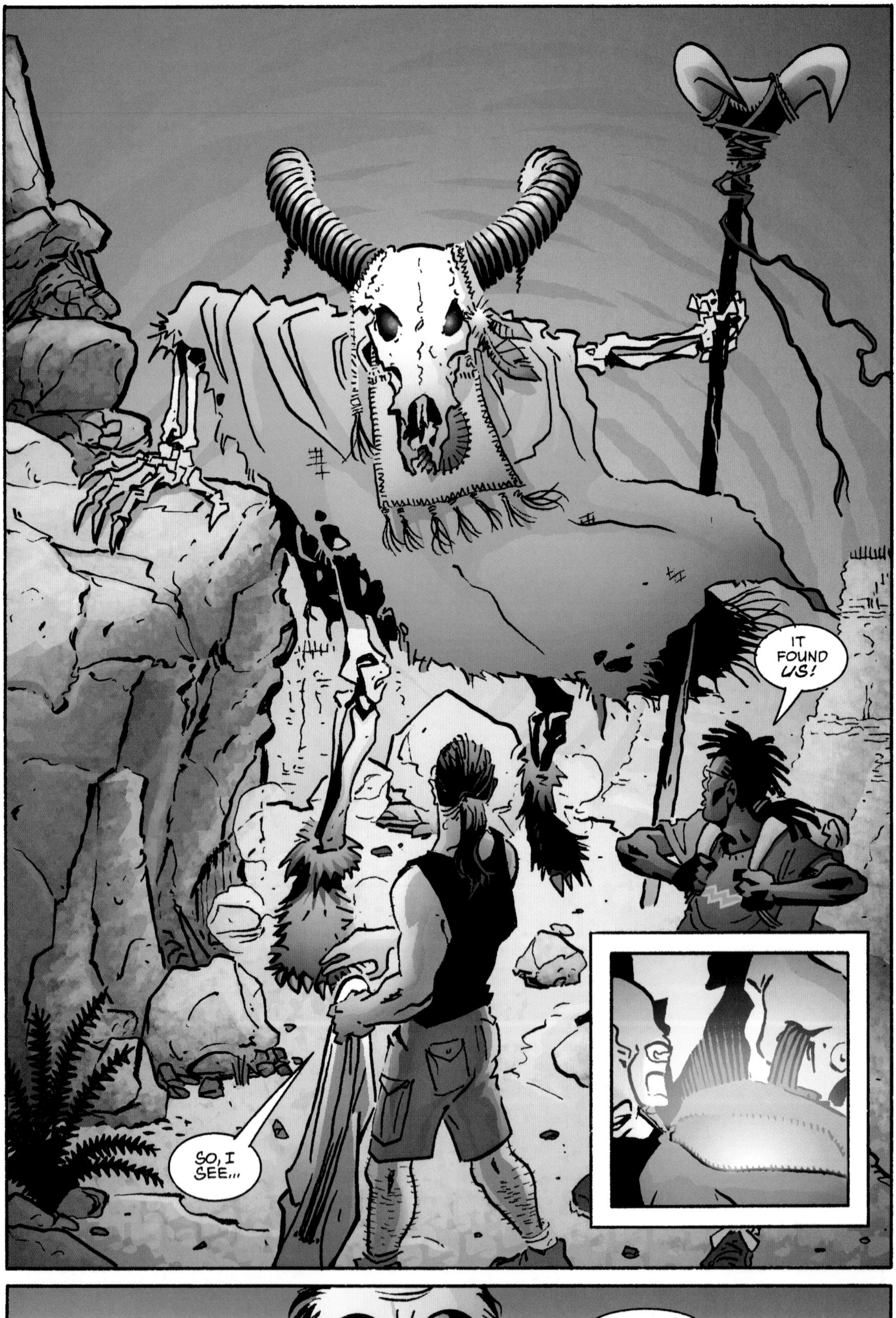
IT FOUND US!
SO, I SEE...

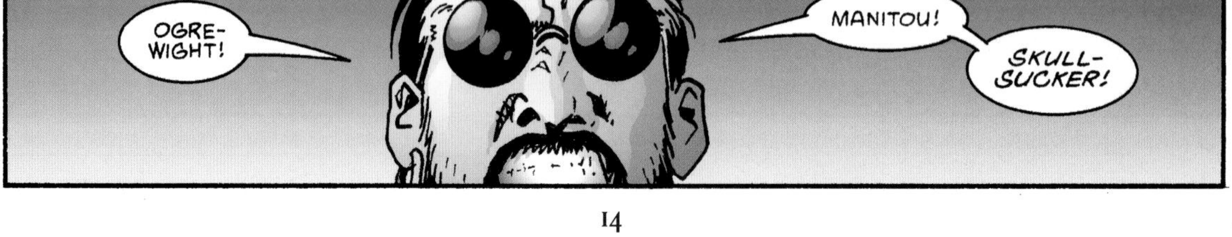
OGRE-WIGHT!
MANITOU!
SKULL-SUCKER!

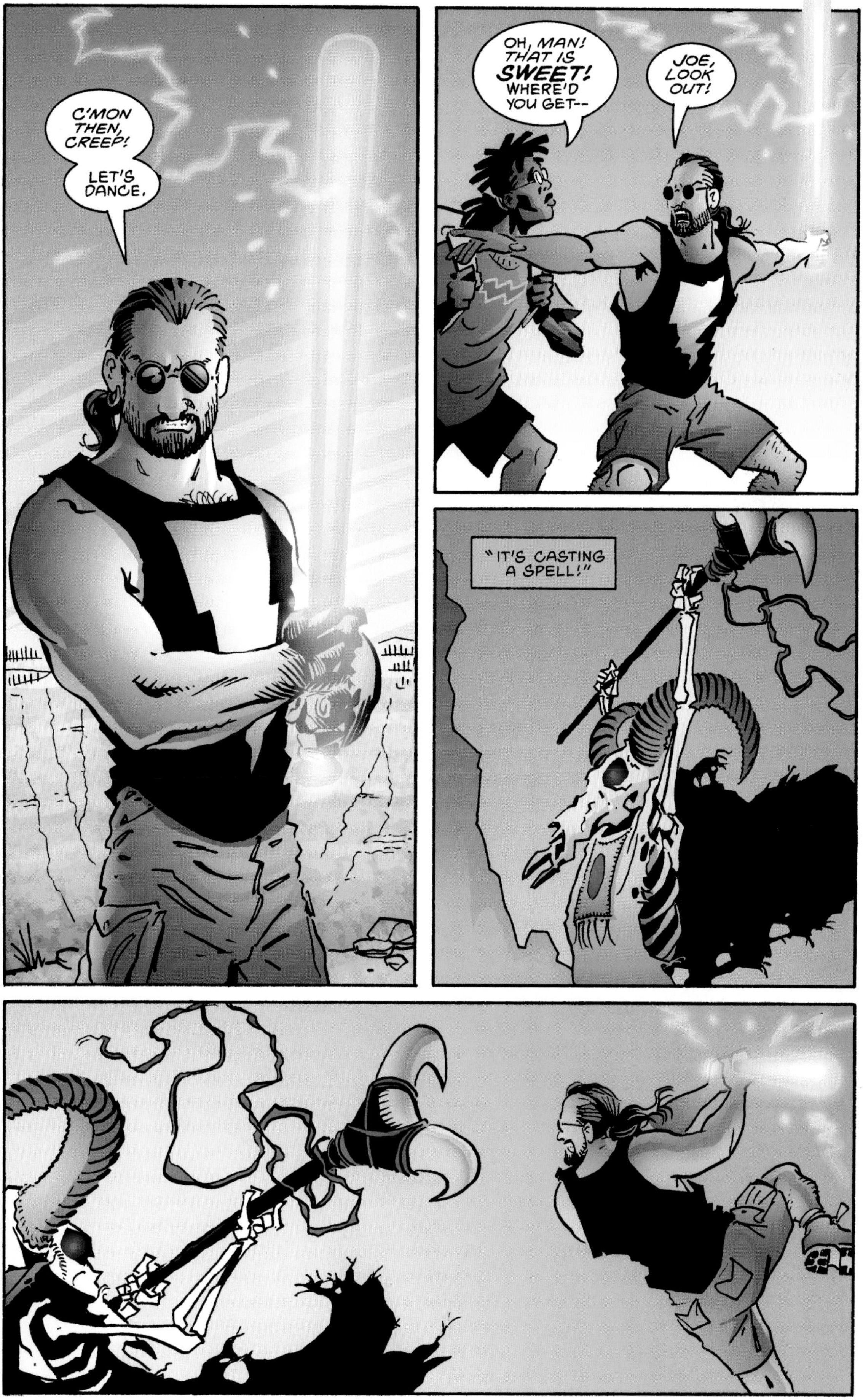
C'MON THEN, CREEP!
LET'S DANCE.
OH, MAN! THAT IS SWEET! WHERE'D YOU GET--
JOE, LOOK OUT!
"IT'S CASTING A SPELL!"

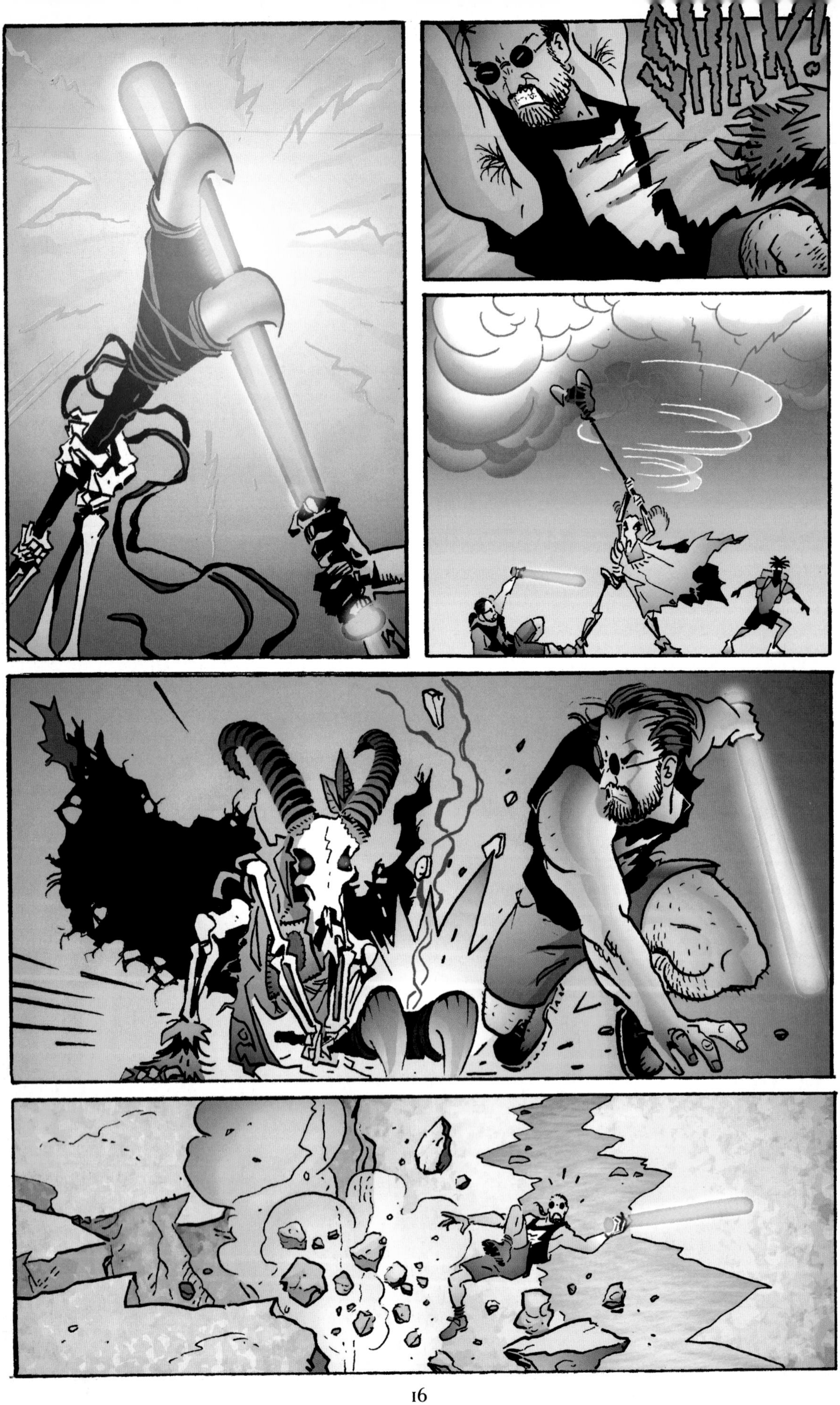
SHAK!

UH-OH!

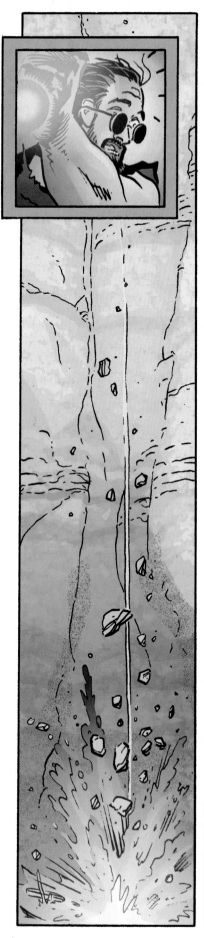

JESUS, THAT WAS *SOME* DROP! AND YOU'RE STILL OKAY?!

Y-YEAH... THE BAT--

PROTECTS ME...

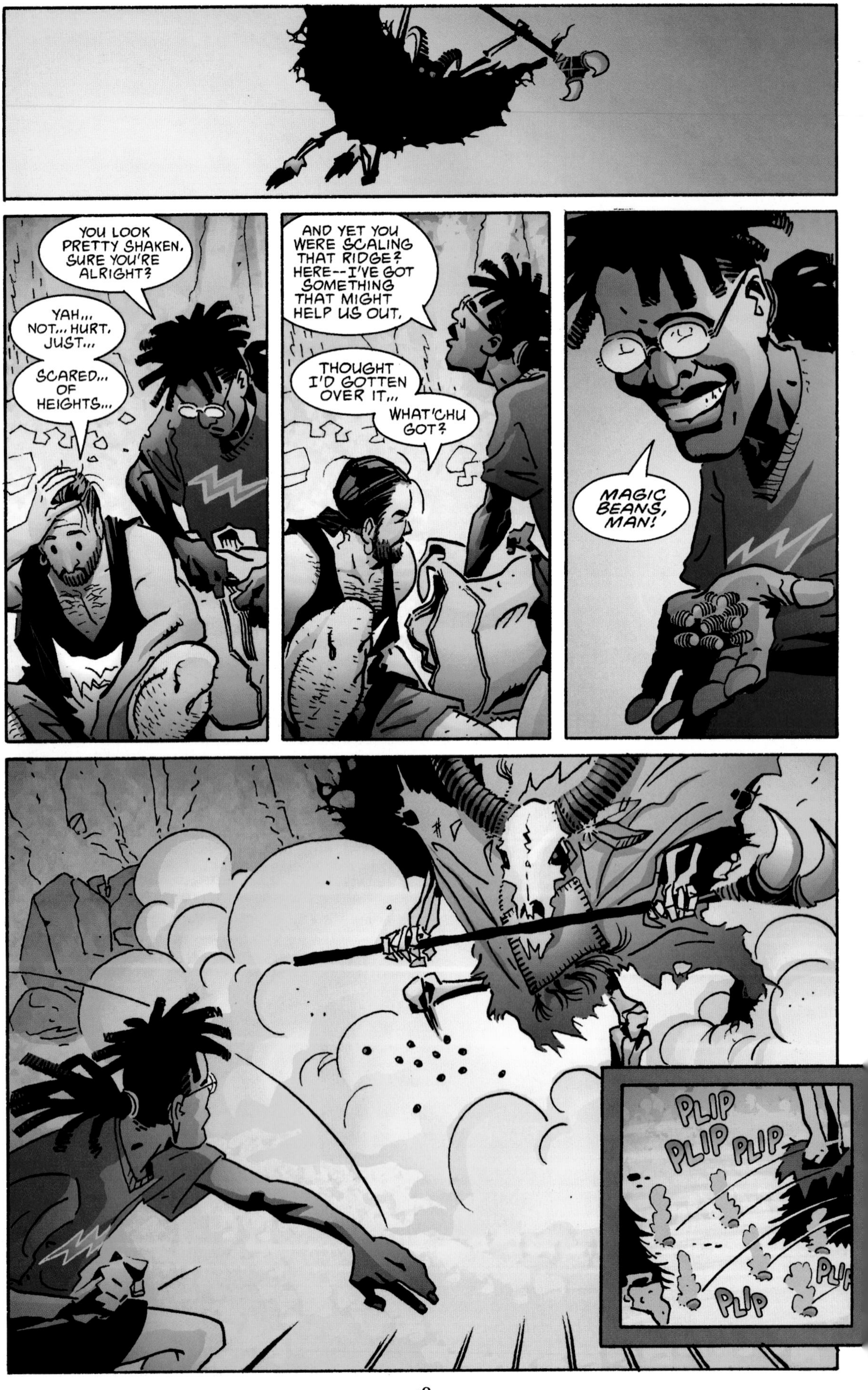
YOU LOOK PRETTY SHAKEN, SURE YOU'RE ALRIGHT?
YAH... NOT... HURT, JUST...
SCARED... OF HEIGHTS...
AND YET YOU WERE SCALING THAT RIDGE? HERE--I'VE GOT SOMETHING THAT MIGHT HELP US OUT.
THOUGHT I'D GOTTEN OVER IT...
WHAT'CHU GOT?
MAGIC BEANS, MAN!
PLIP
PLIP PLIP
PLIP
PLIP

JEEZ, WHAT A RIP!

THE GUY I STOL... uh, GOT THOSE BEANS FROM SWORE THOSE VINES WOULD REACH TEN FOOT! MINIMUM!!

FWAK

UH-OH.

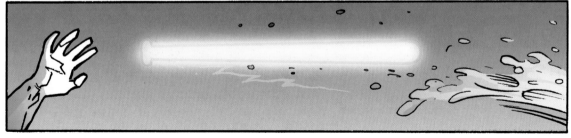

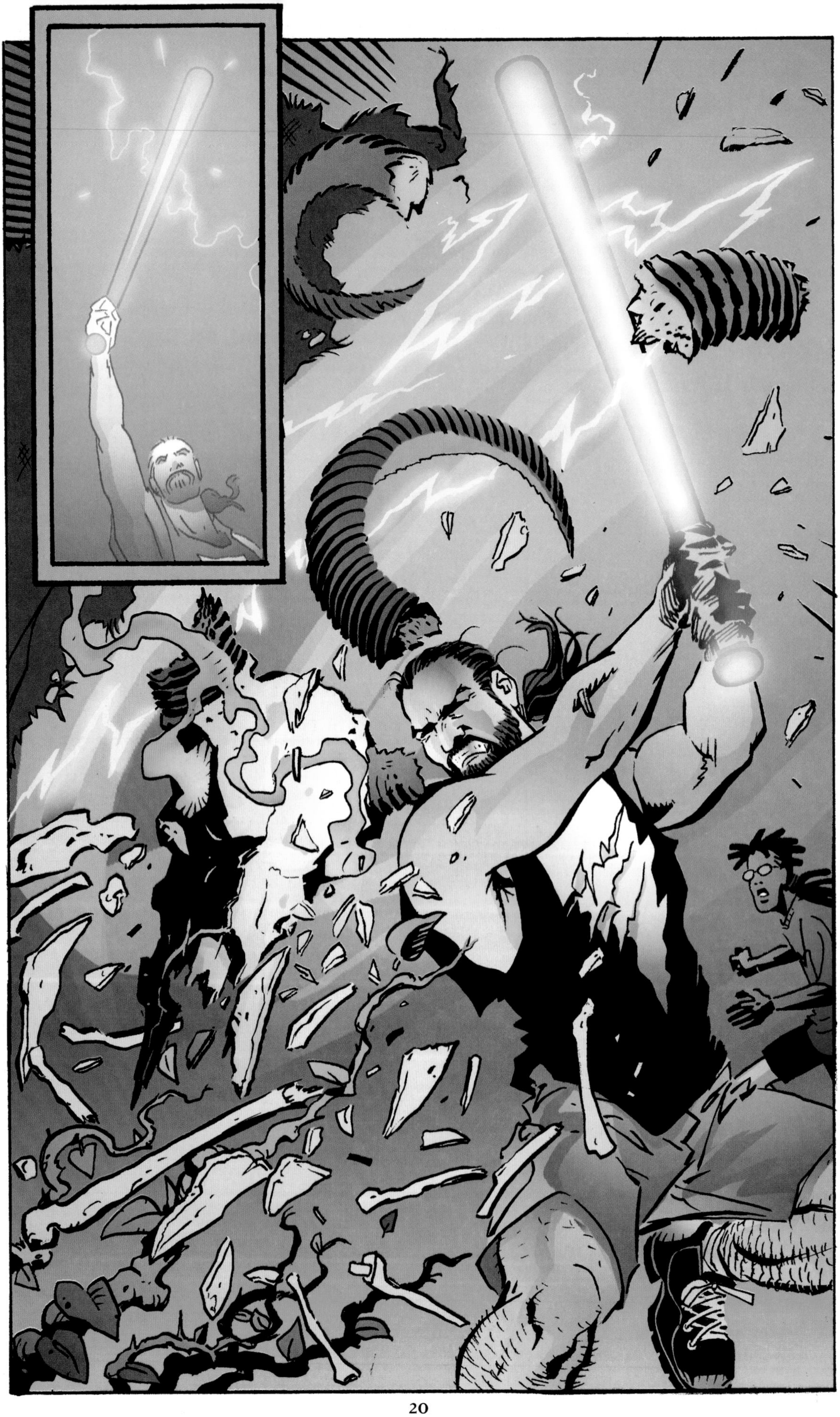

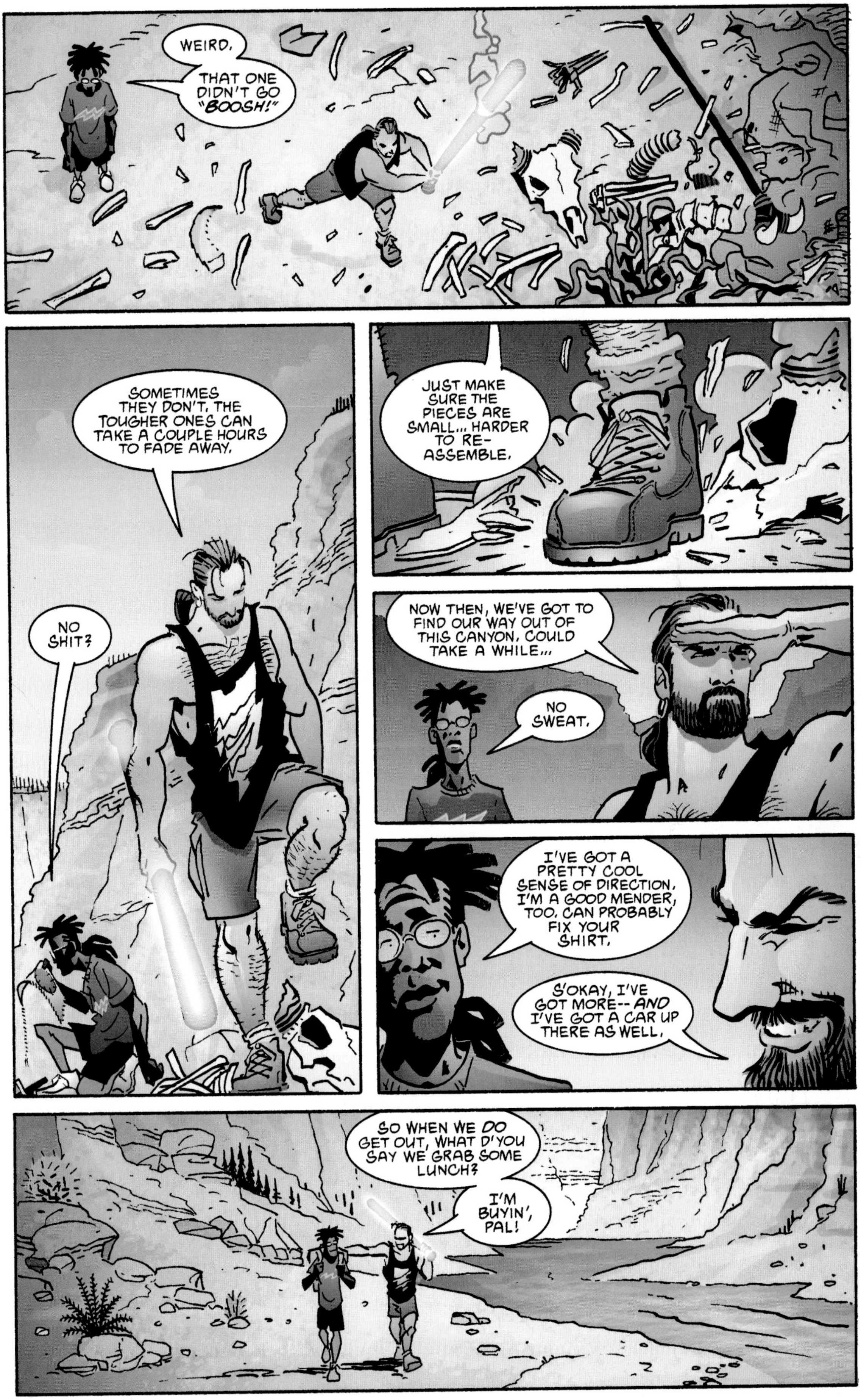
WEIRD.
THAT ONE DIDN'T GO "BOOSH!"
SOMETIMES THEY DON'T. THE TOUGHER ONES CAN TAKE A COUPLE HOURS TO FADE AWAY.
NO SHIT?
JUST MAKE SURE THE PIECES ARE SMALL... HARDER TO RE-ASSEMBLE.
NOW THEN, WE'VE GOT TO FIND OUR WAY OUT OF THIS CANYON. COULD TAKE A WHILE...
NO SWEAT.
I'VE GOT A PRETTY COOL SENSE OF DIRECTION. I'M A GOOD MENDER, TOO. CAN PROBABLY FIX YOUR SHIRT.
S'OKAY, I'VE GOT MORE-- AND I'VE GOT A CAR UP THERE AS WELL.
SO WHEN WE DO GET OUT, WHAT D'YOU SAY WE GRAB SOME LUNCH?
I'M BUYIN', PAL!

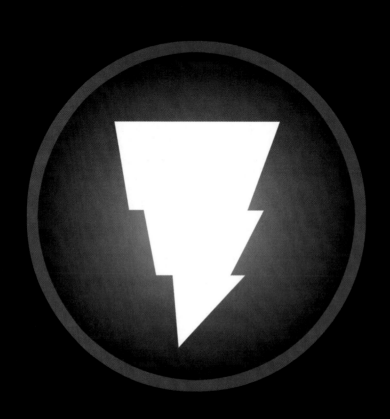

THE HERO DEFINED

MAGE

chapter

1

"The Handle
Towards My Hand"

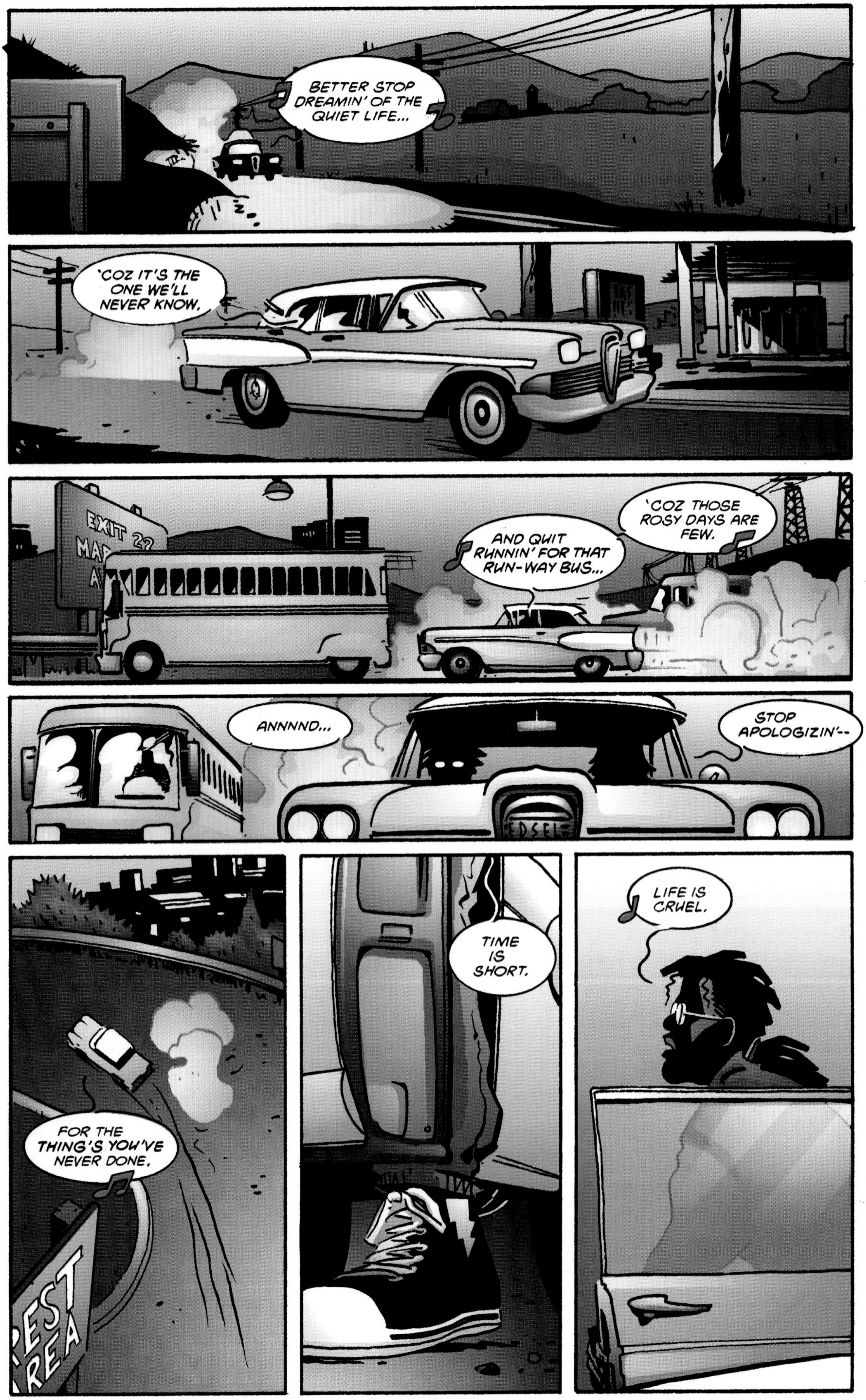
BETTER STOP DREAMIN' OF THE QUIET LIFE...
'COZ IT'S THE ONE WE'LL NEVER KNOW.
EXIT 22
AND QUIT RUNNIN' FOR THAT RUN-WAY BUS...
'COZ THOSE ROSY DAYS ARE FEW.
ANNNND...
STOP APOLOGIZIN'--
EDSEL
FOR THE THING'S YOU'VE NEVER DONE.
REST AREA
TIME IS SHORT.
LIFE IS CRUEL.

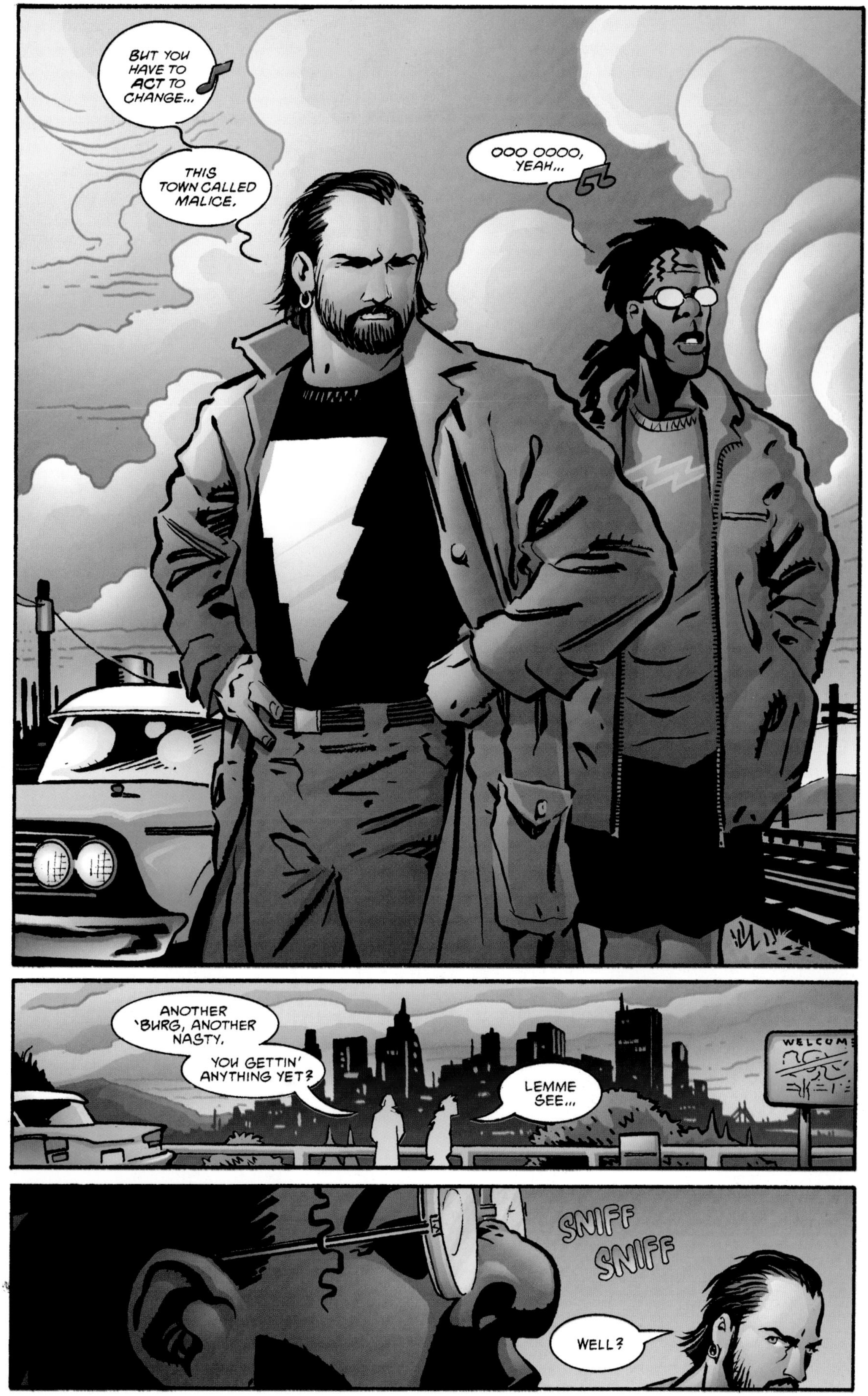
BUT YOU HAVE TO ACT TO CHANGE...
THIS TOWN CALLED MALICE.
OOO OOOO, YEAH...
ANOTHER 'BURG, ANOTHER NASTY.
YOU GETTIN' ANYTHING YET?
LEMME SEE...
WELCOM
SNIFF SNIFF
WELL?

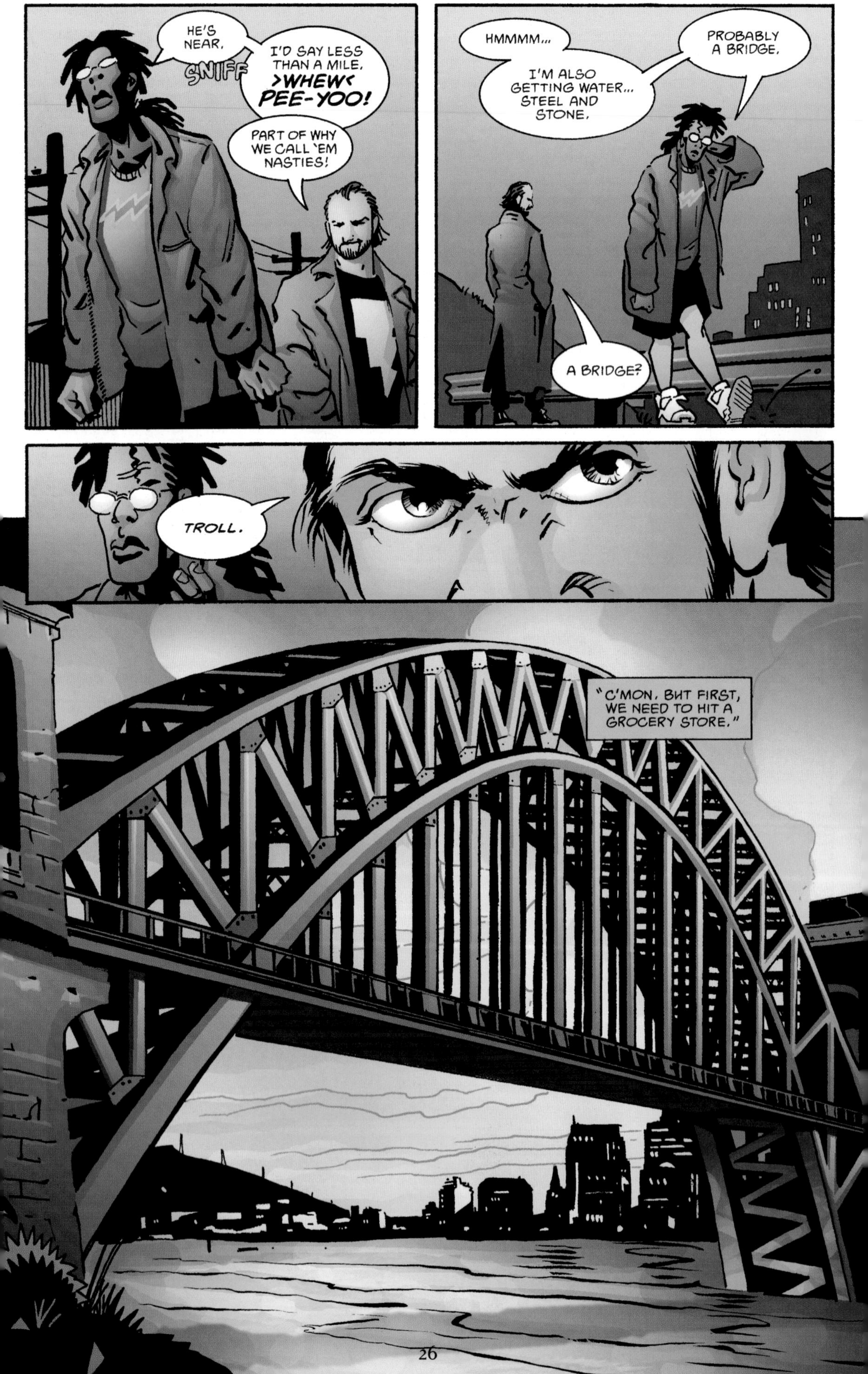
HE'S NEAR.
SNIFF
I'D SAY LESS THAN A MILE. >WHEW< PEE-YOO!
PART OF WHY WE CALL 'EM NASTIES!
HMMMM...
I'M ALSO GETTING WATER... STEEL AND STONE.
PROBABLY A BRIDGE.
A BRIDGE?
TROLL.
"C'MON. BUT FIRST, WE NEED TO HIT A GROCERY STORE."

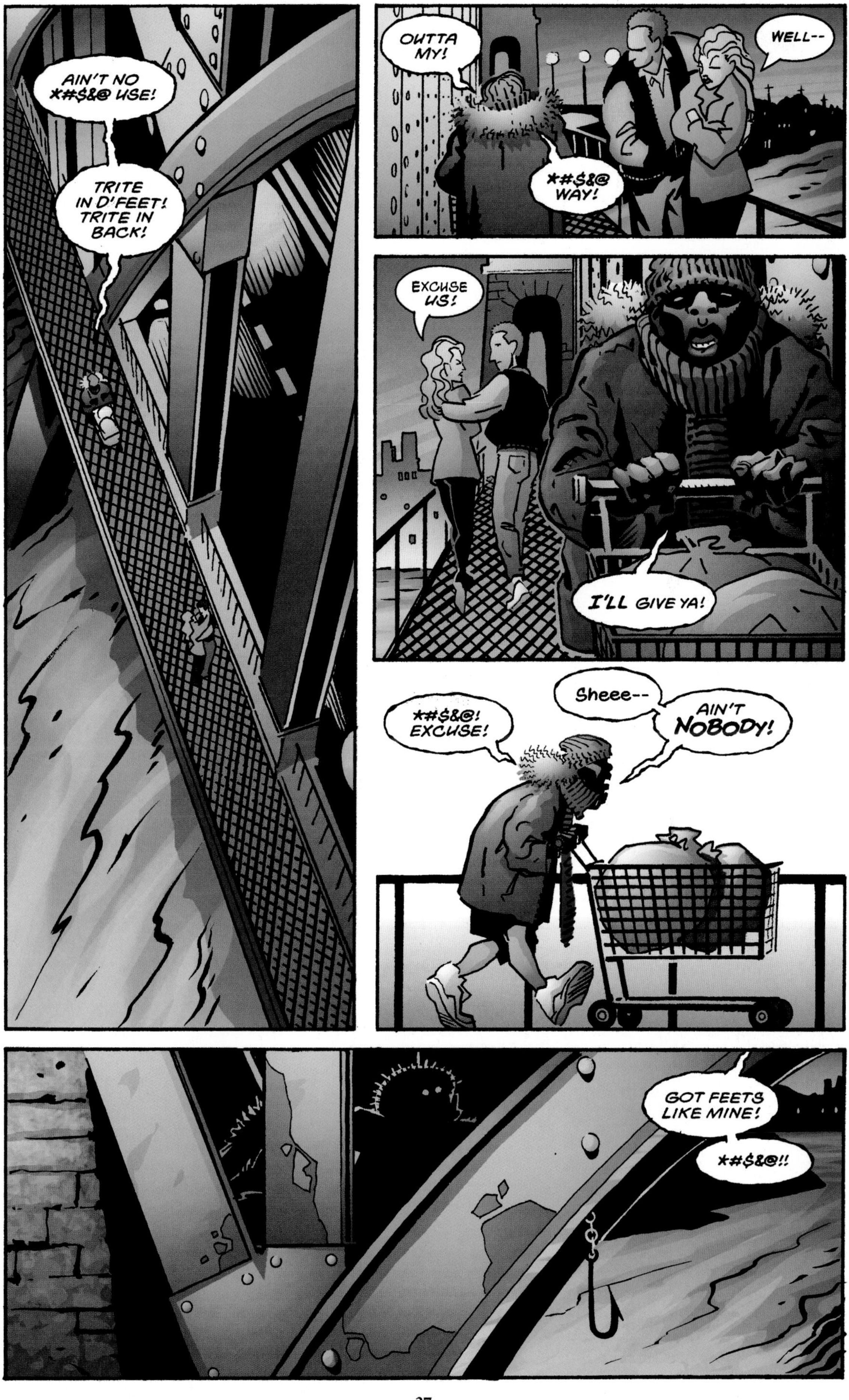
AIN'T NO *#$&@ USE!
TRITE IN D'FEET! TRITE IN BACK!
OUTTA MY!
*#$&@ WAY!
WELL--
EXCUSE US!
I'LL GIVE YA!
*#$&@! EXCUSE!
Sheee--
AIN'T NOBODY!
GOT FEETS LIKE MINE!
*#$&@!!

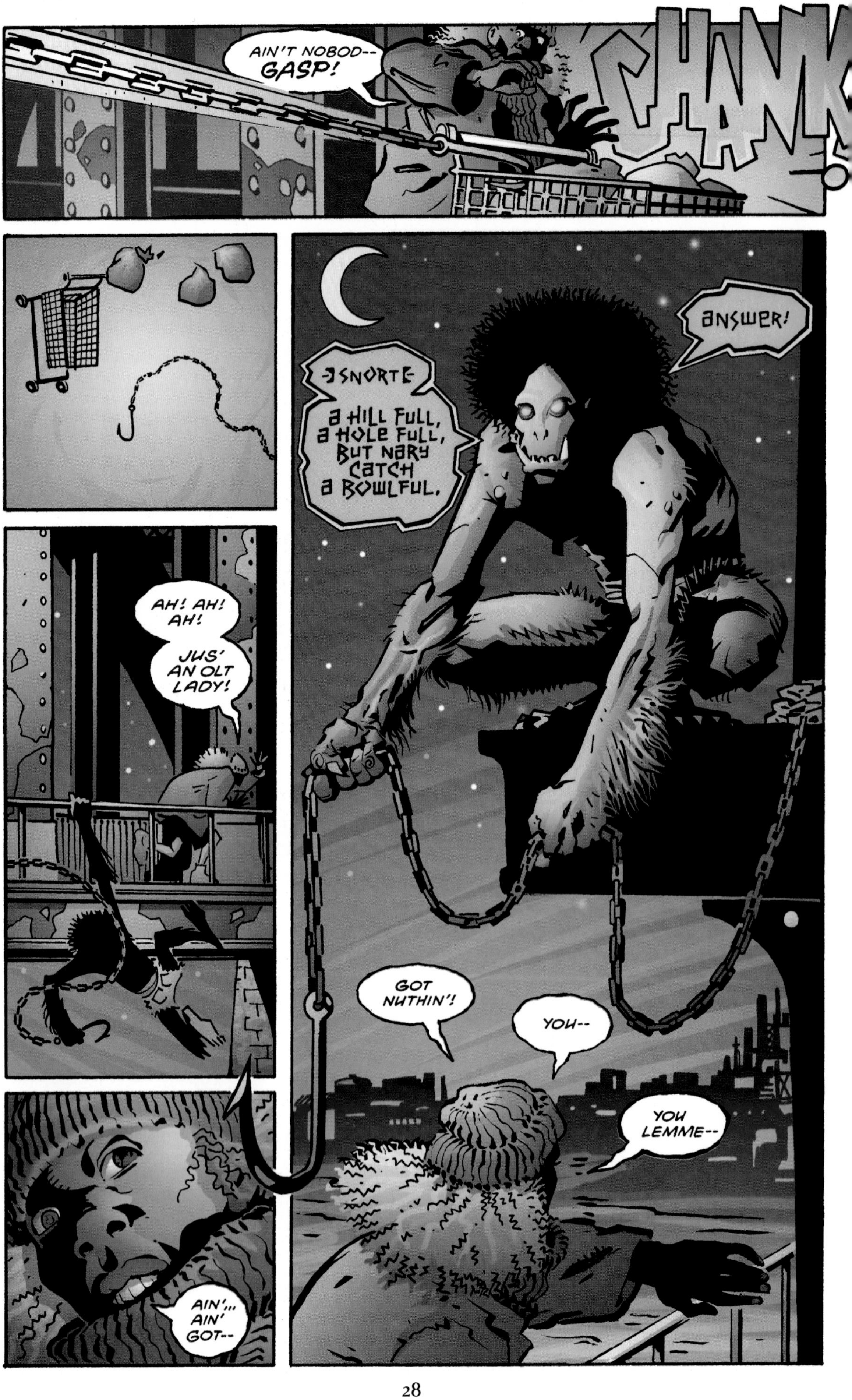

AIN'T NOBOD-- GASP!
CHANK
AH! AH! AH!
JUS' AN OLT LADY!
AIN'... AIN' GOT--
SNORT
A HILL FULL, A HOLE FULL, BUT NARY CATCH A BOWLFUL.
ANSWER!
GOT NUTHIN'!
YOU--
YOU LEMME--

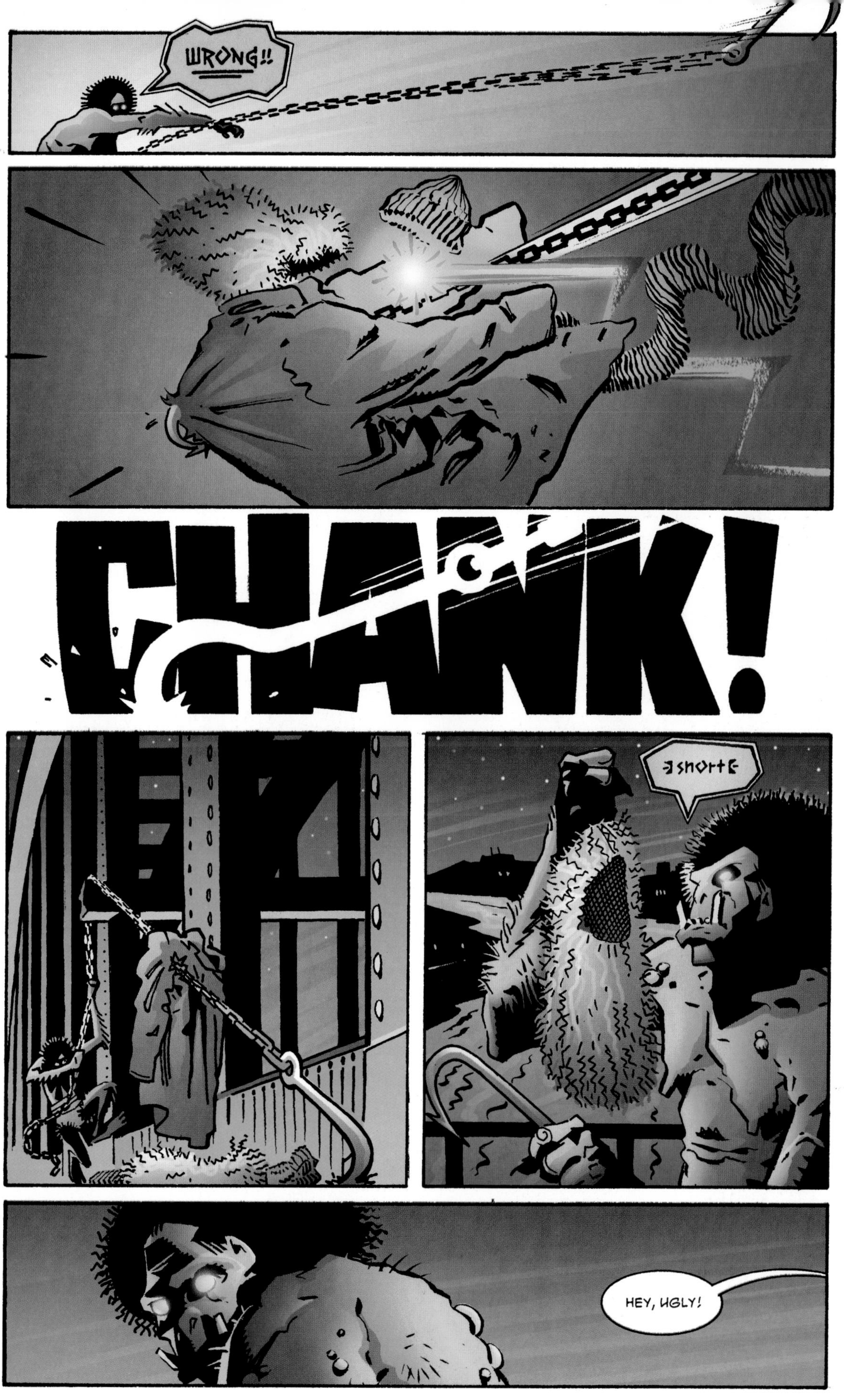
WRONG!!
CHANK!
≡snort≡
HEY, UGLY!

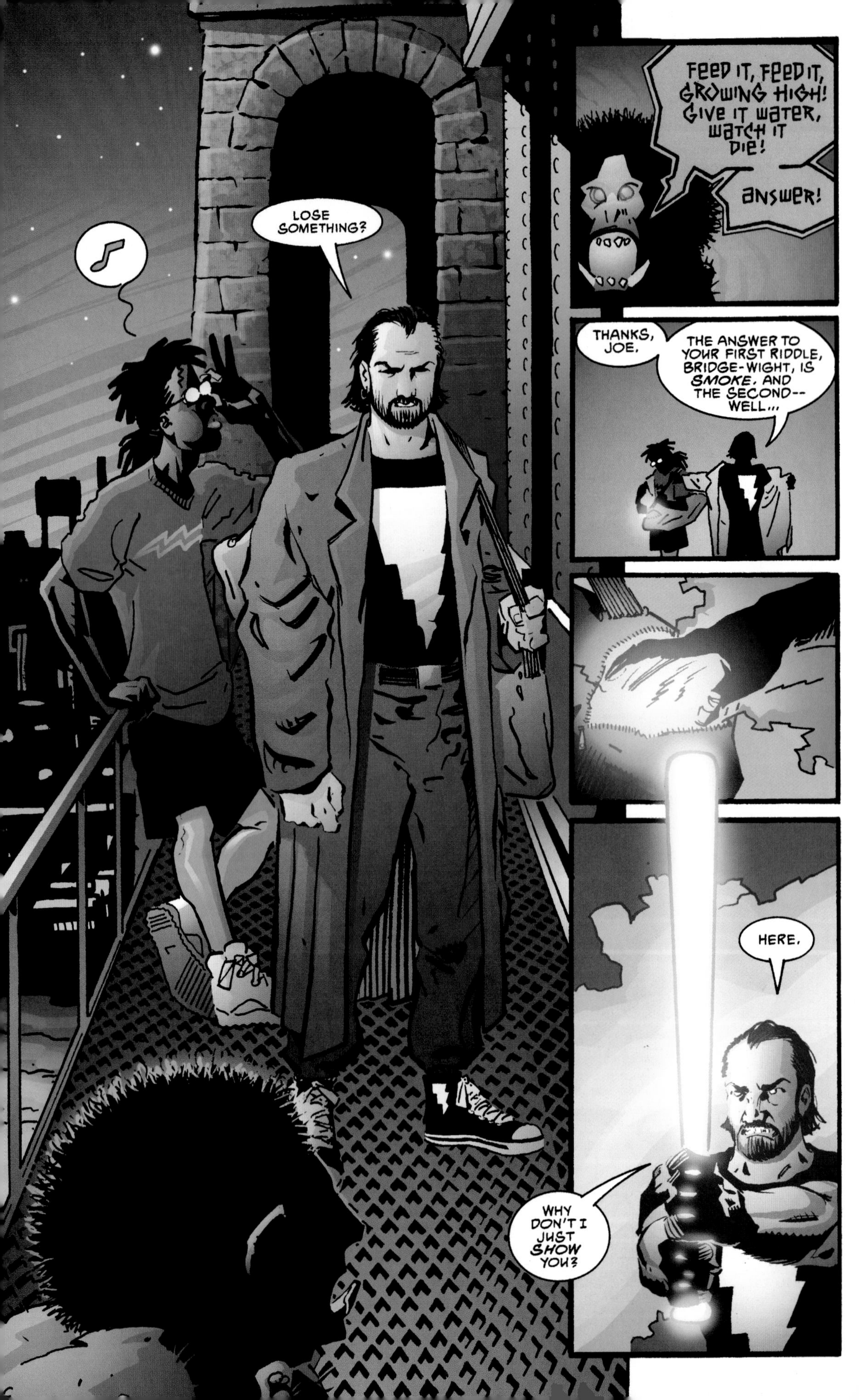
♪
LOSE SOMETHING?
FEED IT, FEED IT, GROWING HIGH! GIVE IT WATER, WATCH IT DIE!
ANSWER!
THANKS, JOE.
THE ANSWER TO YOUR FIRST RIDDLE, BRIDGE-WIGHT, IS SMOKE. AND THE SECOND-- WELL...
HERE.
WHY DON'T I JUST SHOW YOU?

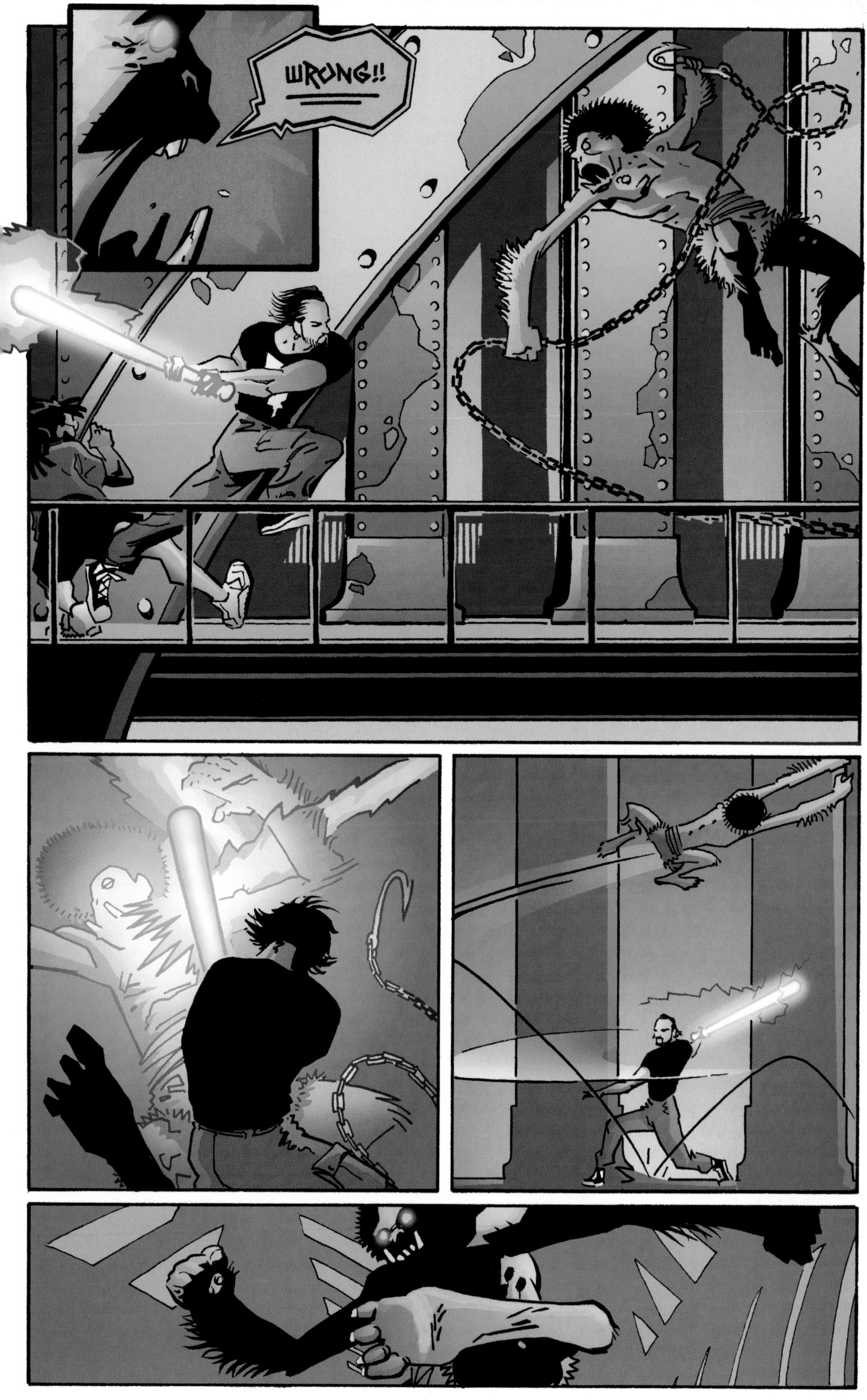
WRONG!!

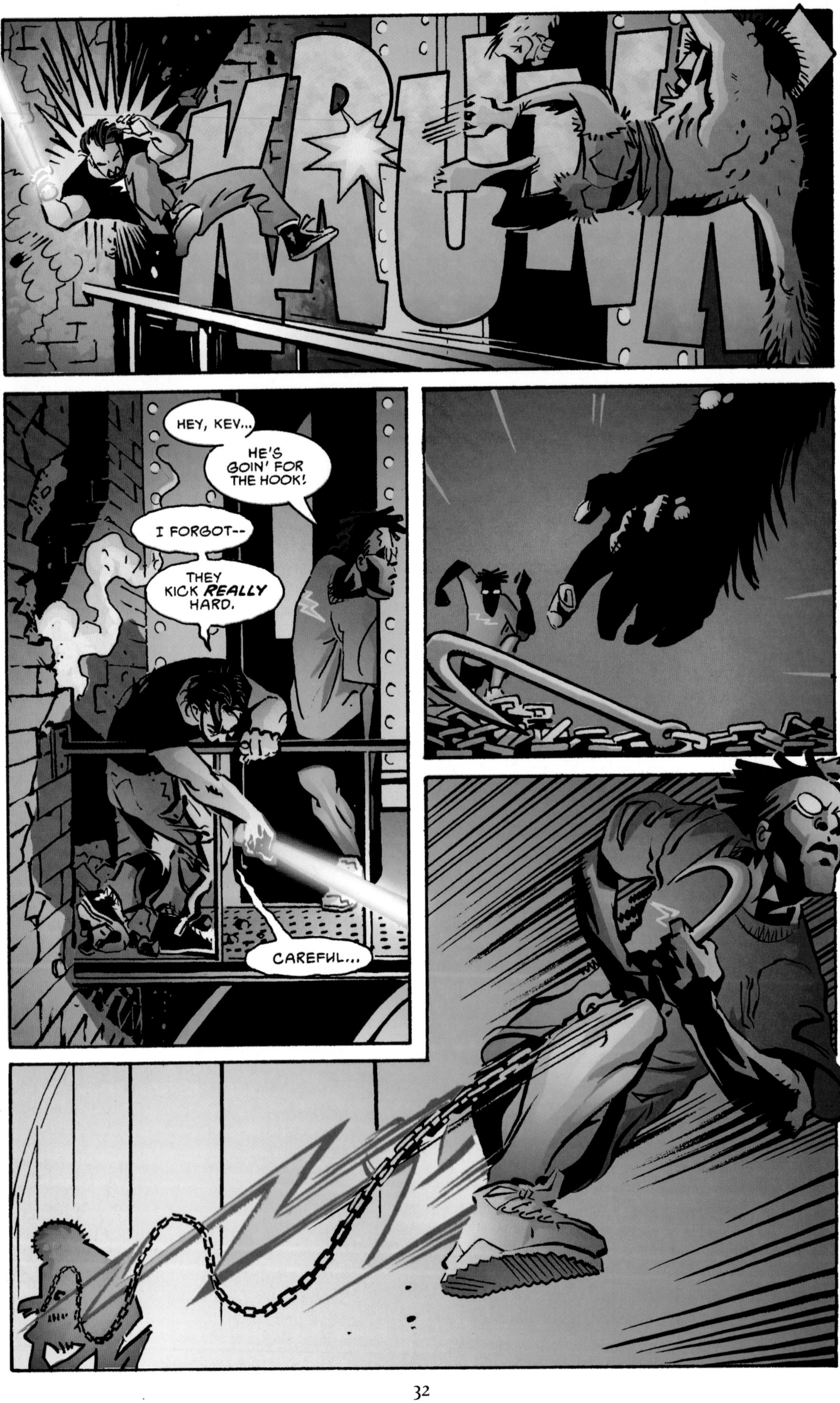

KRUNK
HEY, KEV...
HE'S GOIN' FOR THE HOOK!
I FORGOT--
THEY KICK **REALLY** HARD.
CAREFUL...

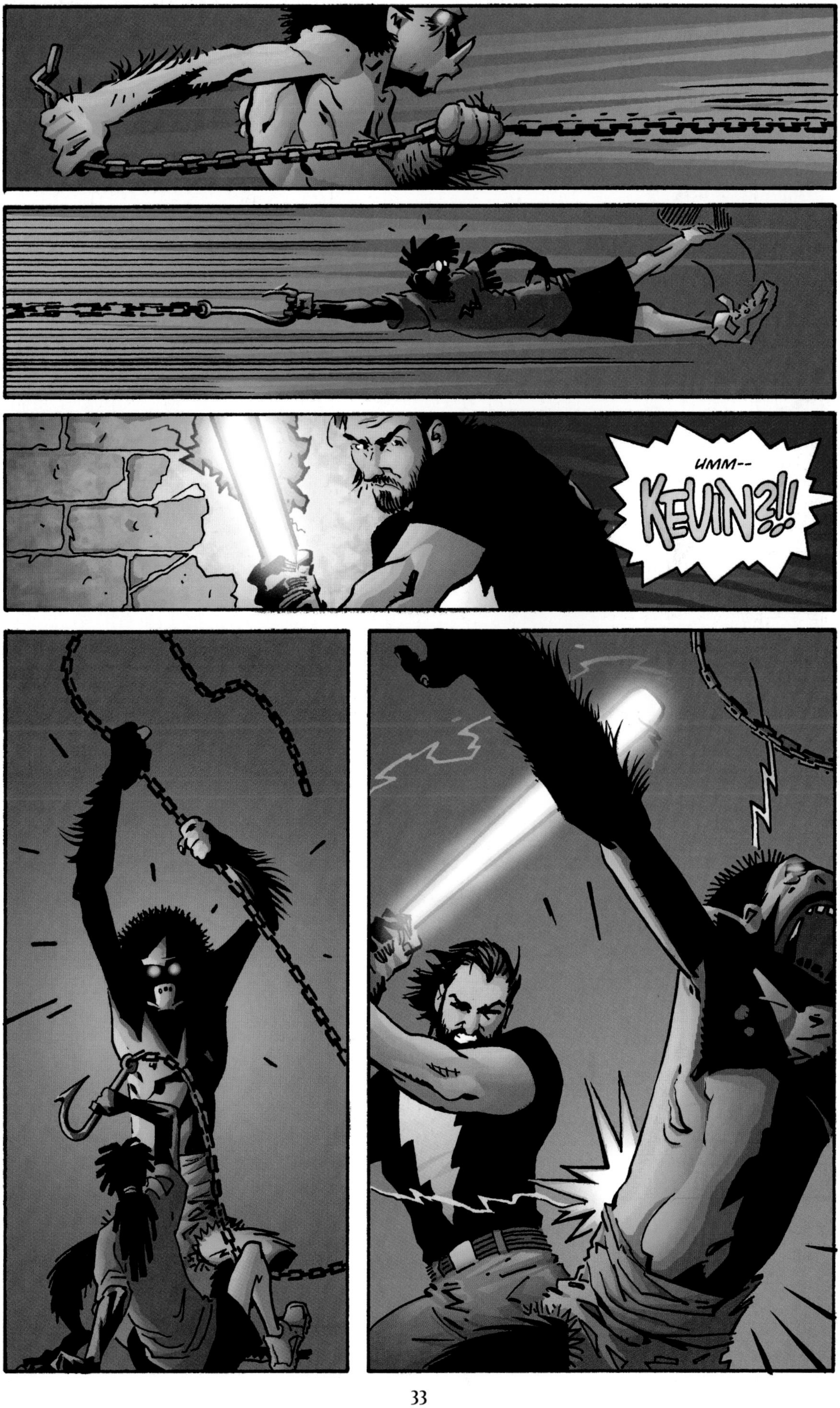
UMM--
KEVIN?!!

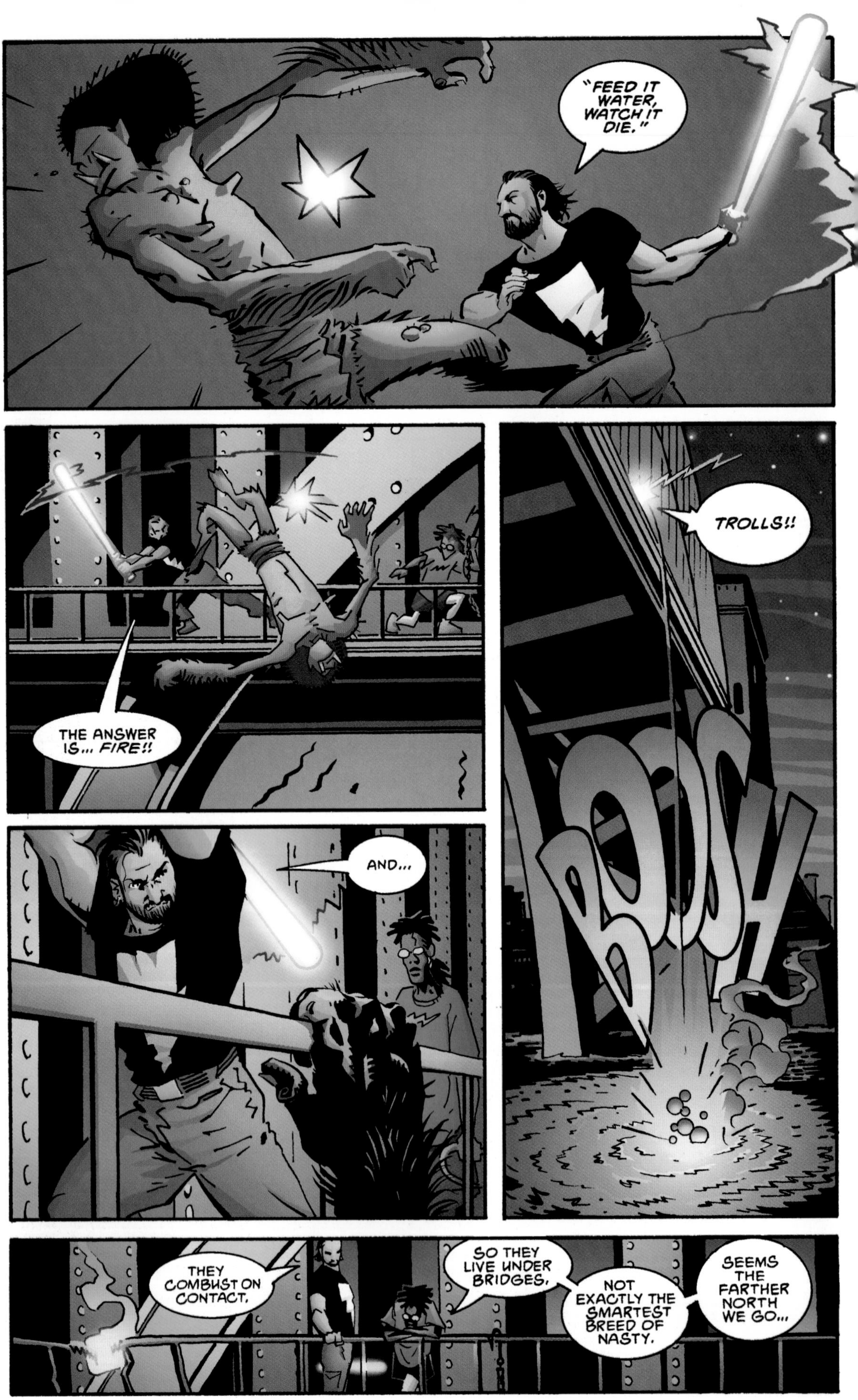
"FEED IT WATER, WATCH IT DIE."
THE ANSWER IS... FIRE!!
TROLLS!!
BOOSH
AND...
THEY COMBUST ON CONTACT.
SO THEY LIVE UNDER BRIDGES,
NOT EXACTLY THE SMARTEST BREED OF NASTY.
SEEMS THE FARTHER NORTH WE GO...

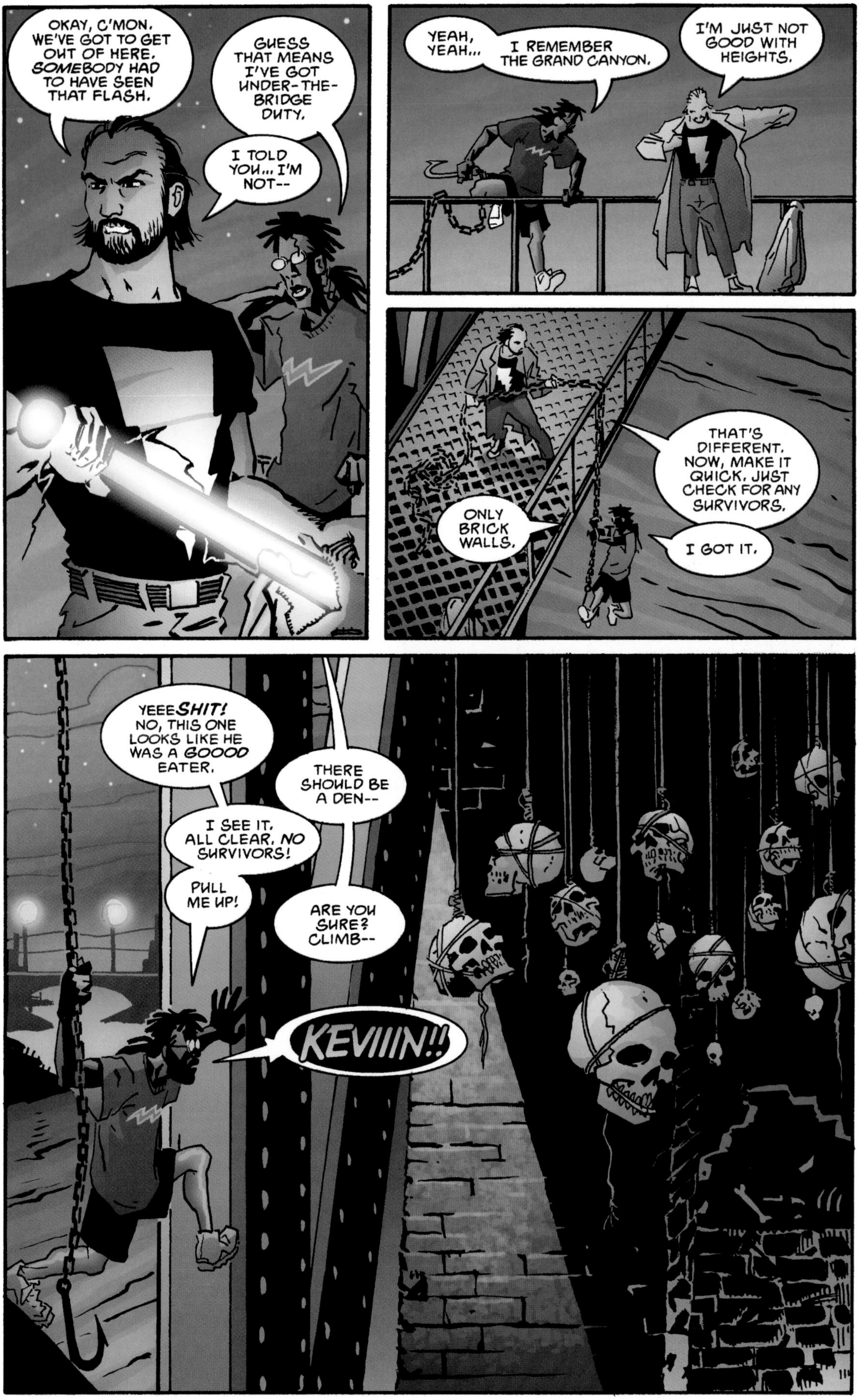

OKAY, C'MON. WE'VE GOT TO GET OUT OF HERE. SOMEBODY HAD TO HAVE SEEN THAT FLASH.
GUESS THAT MEANS I'VE GOT UNDER-THE-BRIDGE DUTY.
I TOLD YOU... I'M NOT--
YEAH, YEAH...
I REMEMBER THE GRAND CANYON.
I'M JUST NOT GOOD WITH HEIGHTS.
THAT'S DIFFERENT. NOW, MAKE IT QUICK. JUST CHECK FOR ANY SURVIVORS.
ONLY BRICK WALLS.
I GOT IT.
YEEESHIT! NO, THIS ONE LOOKS LIKE HE WAS A GOOOD EATER.
THERE SHOULD BE A DEN--
I SEE IT. ALL CLEAR. NO SURVIVORS!
PULL ME UP!
ARE YOU SURE? CLIMB--
KEVIIIN!!

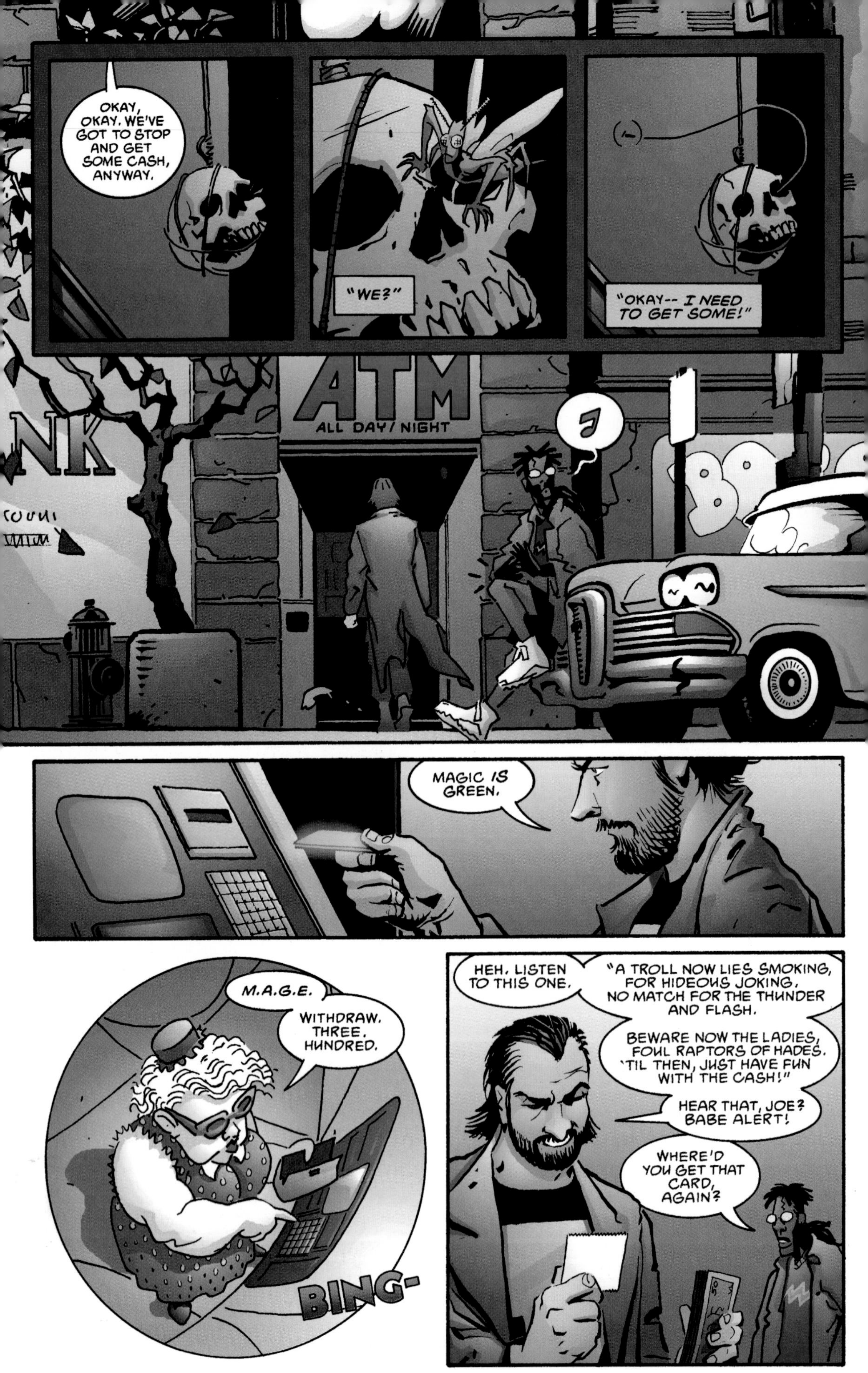
OKAY, OKAY. WE'VE GOT TO STOP AND GET SOME CASH, ANYWAY.
"WE?"
(–)
"OKAY-- I NEED TO GET SOME!"
ATM
ALL DAY/ NIGHT
NK
MAGIC IS GREEN.
M.A.G.E.
WITHDRAW. THREE. HUNDRED.
BING-
HEH. LISTEN TO THIS ONE.
"A TROLL NOW LIES SMOKING, FOR HIDEOUS JOKING, NO MATCH FOR THE THUNDER AND FLASH.
BEWARE NOW THE LADIES, FOUL RAPTORS OF HADES. 'TIL THEN, JUST HAVE FUN WITH THE CASH!"
HEAR THAT, JOE? BABE ALERT!
WHERE'D YOU GET THAT CARD, AGAIN?

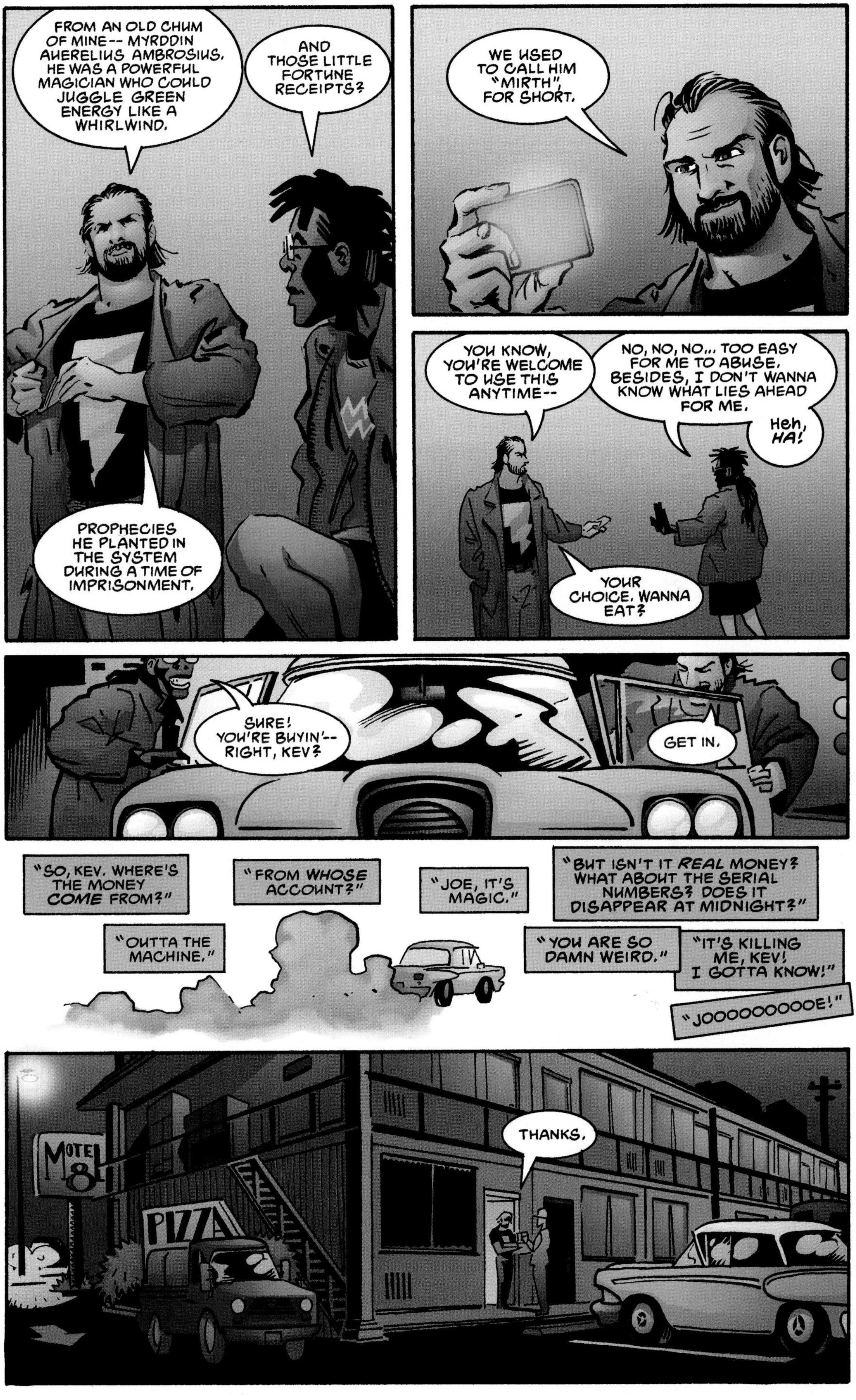
FROM AN OLD CHUM OF MINE-- MYRDDIN AURELIUS AMBROSIUS. HE WAS A POWERFUL MAGICIAN WHO COULD JUGGLE GREEN ENERGY LIKE A WHIRLWIND.
AND THOSE LITTLE FORTUNE RECEIPTS?
PROPHECIES HE PLANTED IN THE SYSTEM DURING A TIME OF IMPRISONMENT.
WE USED TO CALL HIM "MIRTH", FOR SHORT.
YOU KNOW, YOU'RE WELCOME TO USE THIS ANYTIME--
NO, NO, NO... TOO EASY FOR ME TO ABUSE. BESIDES, I DON'T WANNA KNOW WHAT LIES AHEAD FOR ME.
Heh, *HA!*
YOUR CHOICE. WANNA EAT?
SURE! YOU'RE BUYIN'-- RIGHT, KEV?
GET IN.
"SO, KEV. WHERE'S THE MONEY *COME* FROM?"
"OUTTA THE MACHINE."
"FROM *WHOSE* ACCOUNT?"
"JOE, IT'S MAGIC."
"BUT ISN'T IT *REAL* MONEY? WHAT ABOUT THE SERIAL NUMBERS? DOES IT DISAPPEAR AT MIDNIGHT?"
"YOU ARE SO DAMN WEIRD."
"IT'S KILLING ME, KEV! I GOTTA KNOW!"
"JOOOOOOOOOE!"
MOTEL 8
PIZZA
THANKS.

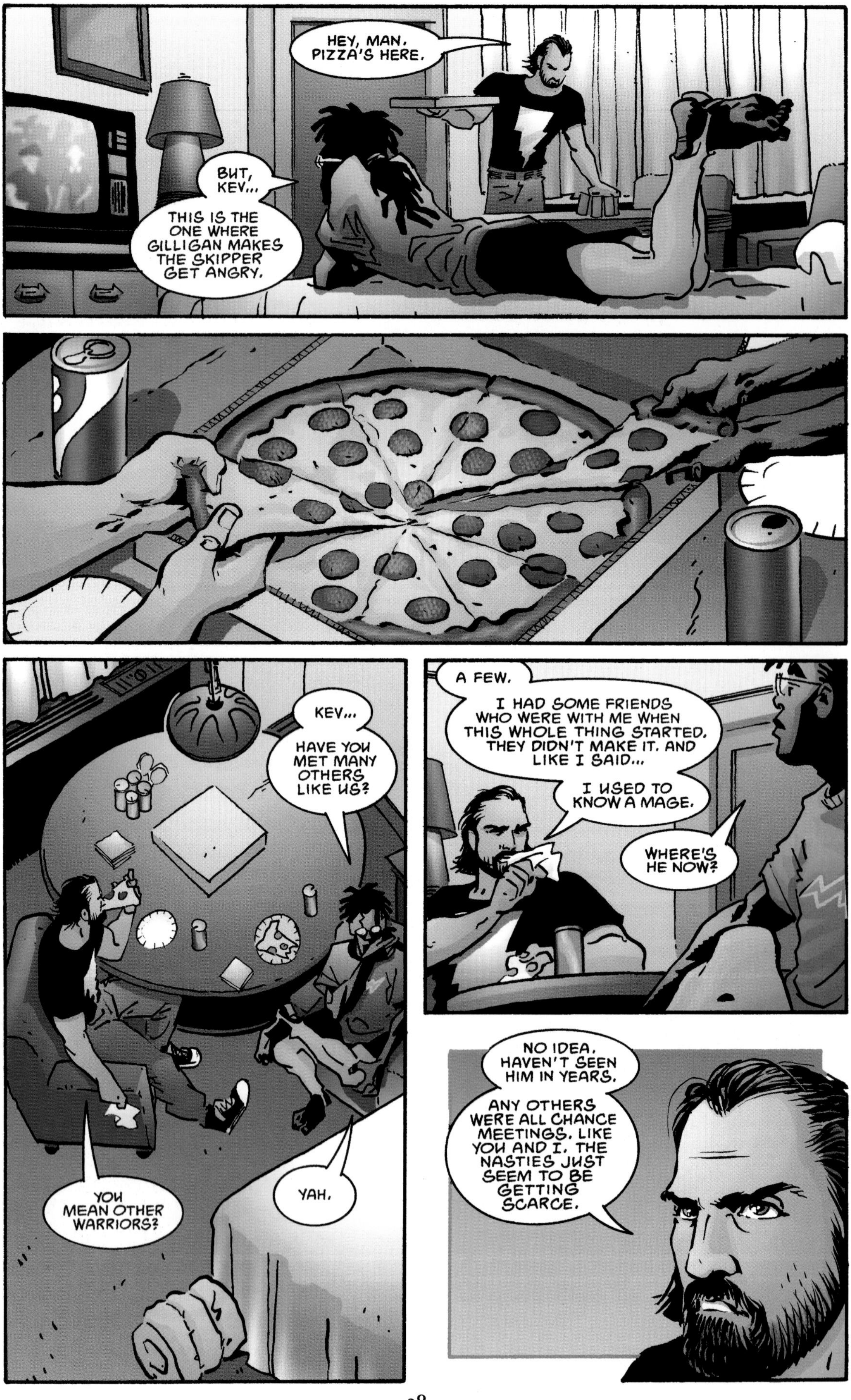
HEY, MAN, PIZZA'S HERE.
BUT, KEV...
THIS IS THE ONE WHERE GILLIGAN MAKES THE SKIPPER GET ANGRY.
KEV...
HAVE YOU MET MANY OTHERS LIKE US?
YOU MEAN OTHER WARRIORS?
YAH.
A FEW.
I HAD SOME FRIENDS WHO WERE WITH ME WHEN THIS WHOLE THING STARTED. THEY DIDN'T MAKE IT. AND LIKE I SAID...
I USED TO KNOW A MAGE.
WHERE'S HE NOW?
NO IDEA. HAVEN'T SEEN HIM IN YEARS.
ANY OTHERS WERE ALL CHANCE MEETINGS, LIKE YOU AND I. THE NASTIES JUST SEEM TO BE GETTING SCARCE.

TIMES ARE CHANGIN'...

LOOK AT THIS -- YOU CAN EVEN GET CHERRY COKE IN A CAN NOW!

CRAZY THING IS, I'VE EVEN HEARD SUCH ENCOUNTERS CAN LEAD TO IN-FIGHTING OVER WHO GETS THE MONSTER.

DAMN!!

WHOSE SIDE ARE THESE GUYS ON, ANYWAY?

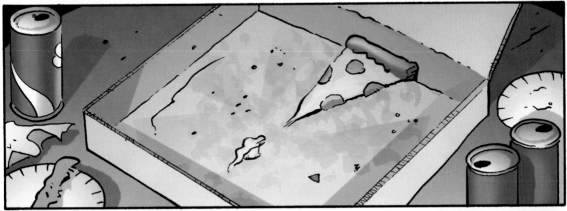

YOU KNOW, I WISH YOU'D LET ME PAY FOR AN EXTRA BED.

YOU WOULDN'T HAVE TO SLEEP ON THE FLOOR.

I DON'T MIND.

BESIDES, YOU KNOW MY MOTTO...

"WASTE NOT, WANT NOT." THAT MONEY COULD BE SPENT ON *FOOD!!*

Heh, *HA!*

KEV?

OHHH, PROFESSOR, THE SKIPPER'S GONNA *KILL* ME WHEN HE FINDS OUT--

39

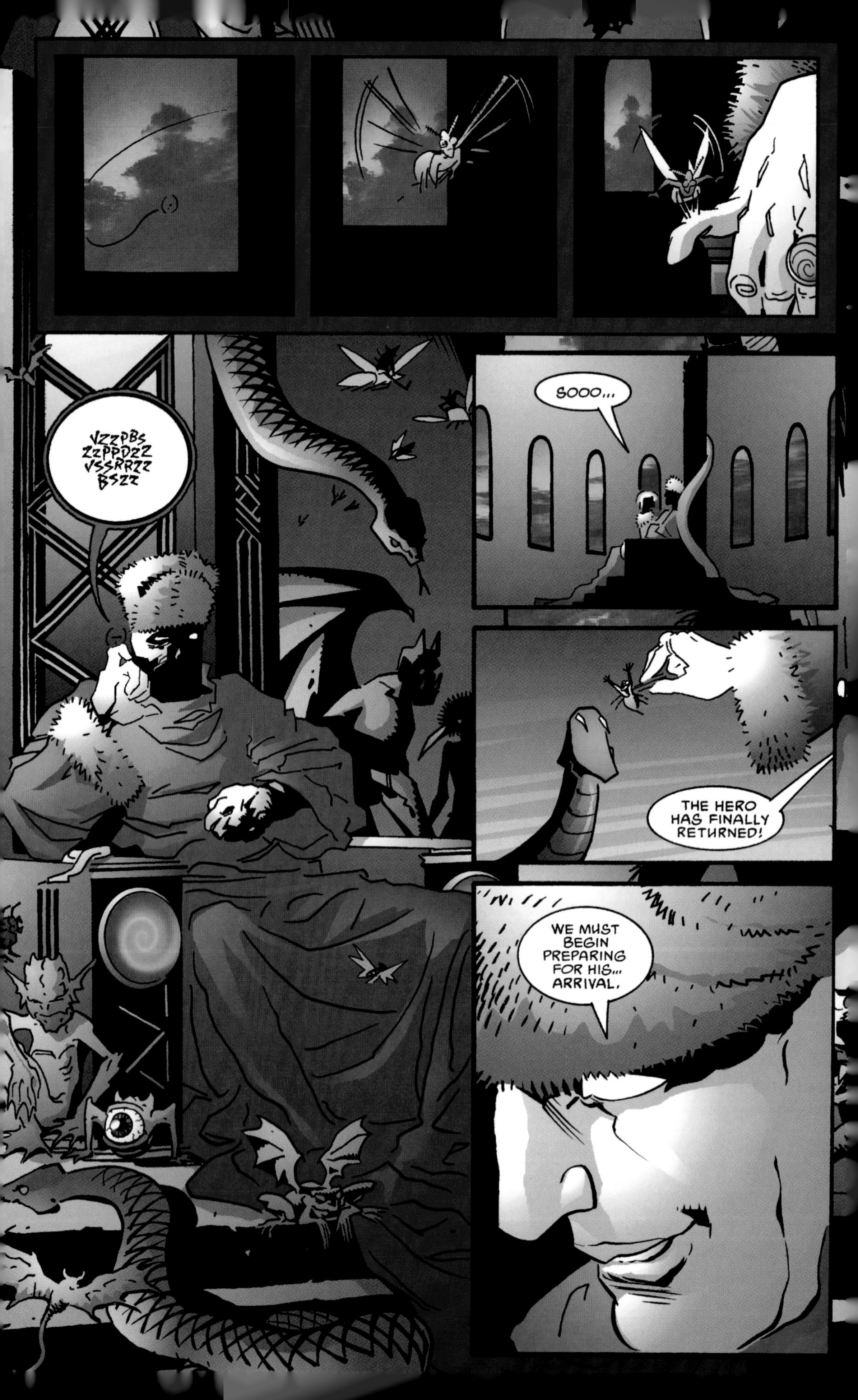
VZZPBS ZZPPDZZ VSSRRZZ BSZZ
SOOO...
THE HERO HAS FINALLY RETURNED!
WE MUST BEGIN PREPARING FOR HIS... ARRIVAL.

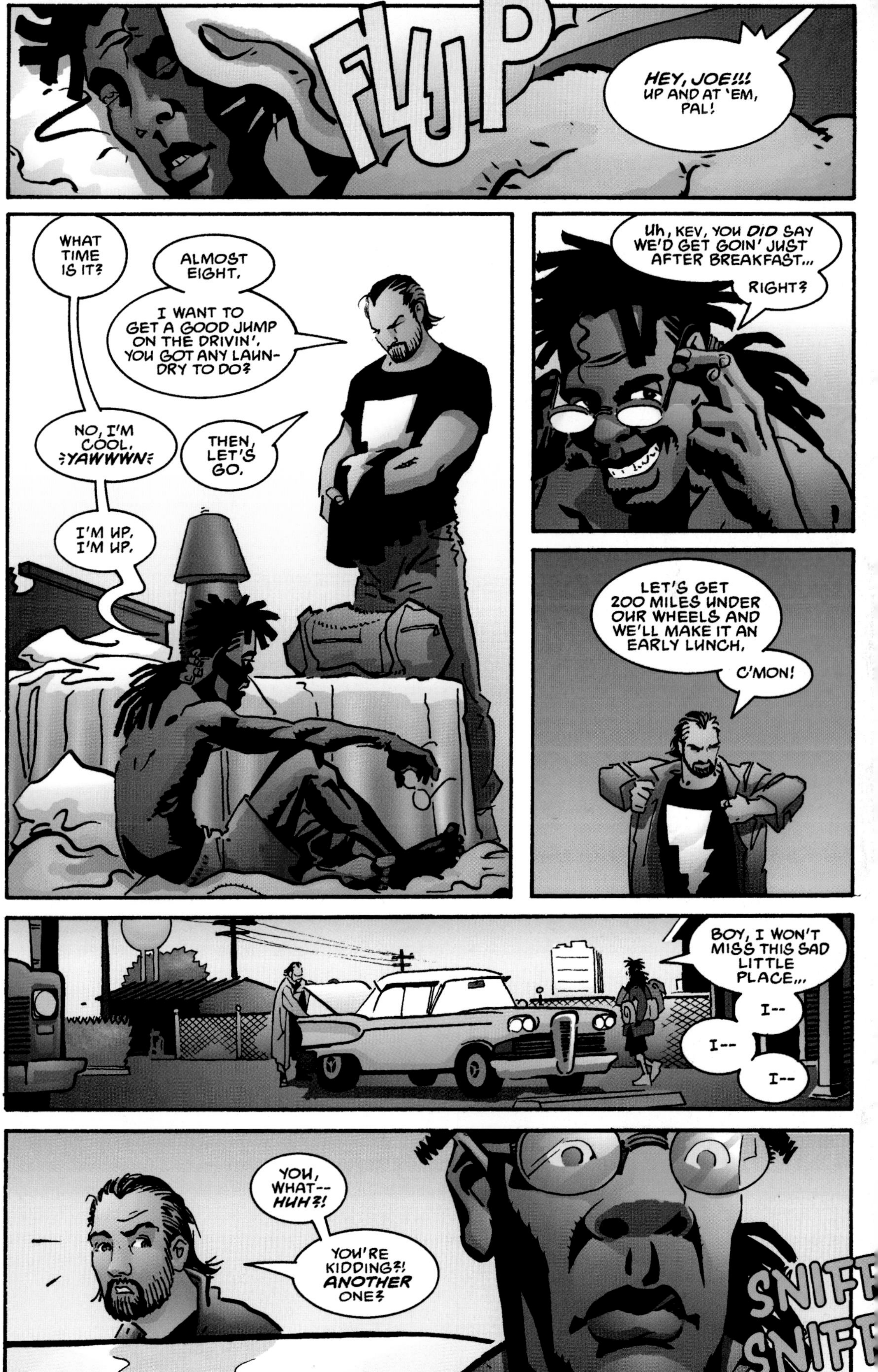
FLUP
HEY, JOE!!! UP AND AT 'EM, PAL!
WHAT TIME IS IT?
ALMOST EIGHT.
I WANT TO GET A GOOD JUMP ON THE DRIVIN'. YOU GOT ANY LAUNDRY TO DO?
NO, I'M COOL. ;YAWWWN;
THEN, LET'S GO.
I'M UP, I'M UP.
UH, KEV, YOU DID SAY WE'D GET GOIN' JUST AFTER BREAKFAST...
RIGHT?
LET'S GET 200 MILES UNDER OUR WHEELS AND WE'LL MAKE IT AN EARLY LUNCH.
C'MON!
BOY, I WON'T MISS THIS SAD LITTLE PLACE...
I--
I--
I--
YOU, WHAT-- HUH?!
YOU'RE KIDDING?! ANOTHER ONE?
SNIFF
SNIFF

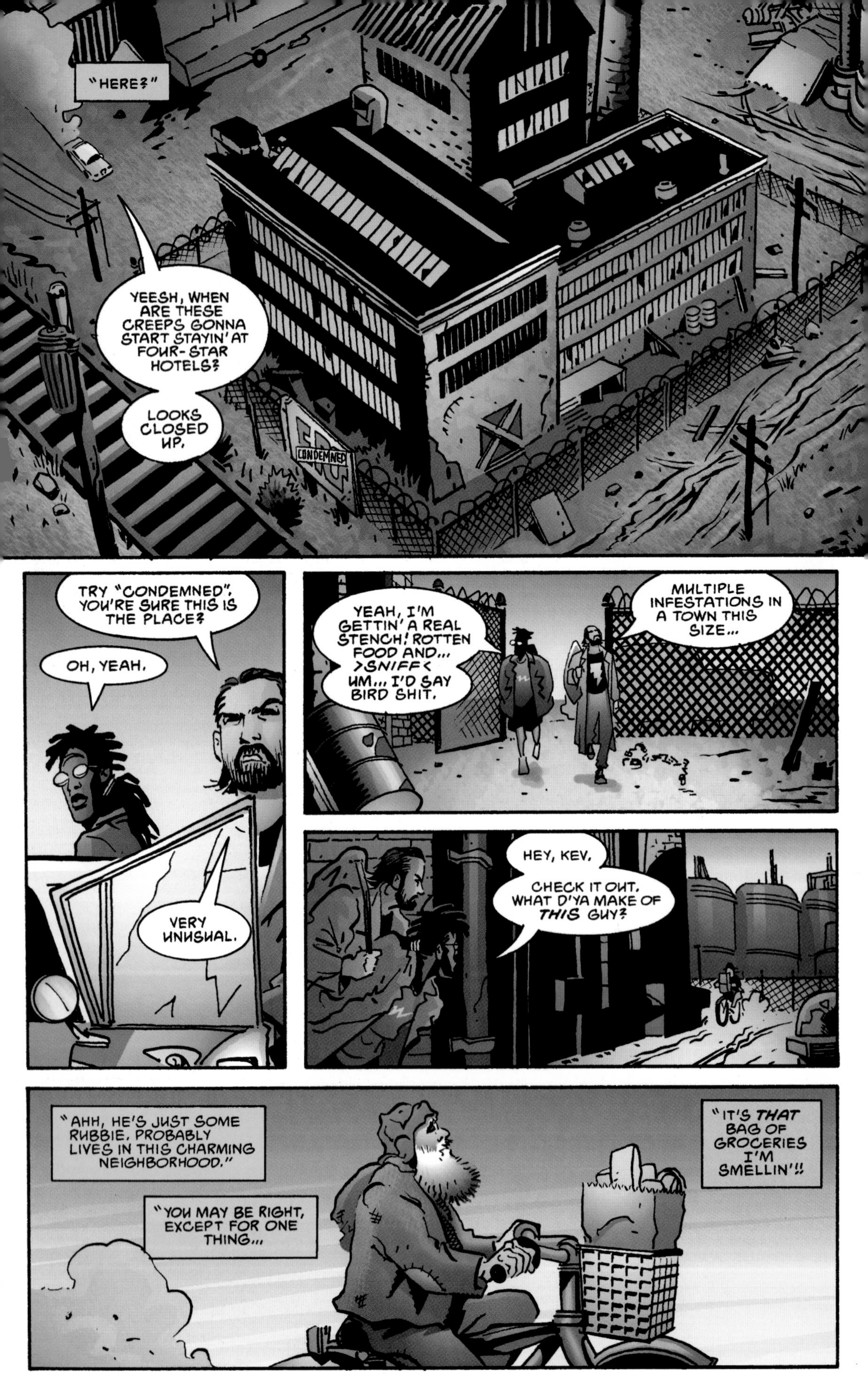
"HERE?"
YEESH, WHEN ARE THESE CREEPS GONNA START STAYIN' AT FOUR-STAR HOTELS?
LOOKS CLOSED UP.
CONDEMNED
TRY "CONDEMNED". YOU'RE SURE THIS IS THE PLACE?
OH, YEAH.
VERY UNUSUAL.
YEAH, I'M GETTIN' A REAL STENCH! ROTTEN FOOD AND... >SNIFF< UM... I'D SAY BIRD SHIT.
MULTIPLE INFESTATIONS IN A TOWN THIS SIZE...
HEY, KEV.
CHECK IT OUT. WHAT D'YA MAKE OF *THIS* GUY?
"AHH, HE'S JUST SOME RUBBIE. PROBABLY LIVES IN THIS CHARMING NEIGHBORHOOD."
"YOU MAY BE RIGHT, EXCEPT FOR ONE THING...
"IT'S *THAT* BAG OF GROCERIES I'M SMELLIN'!!

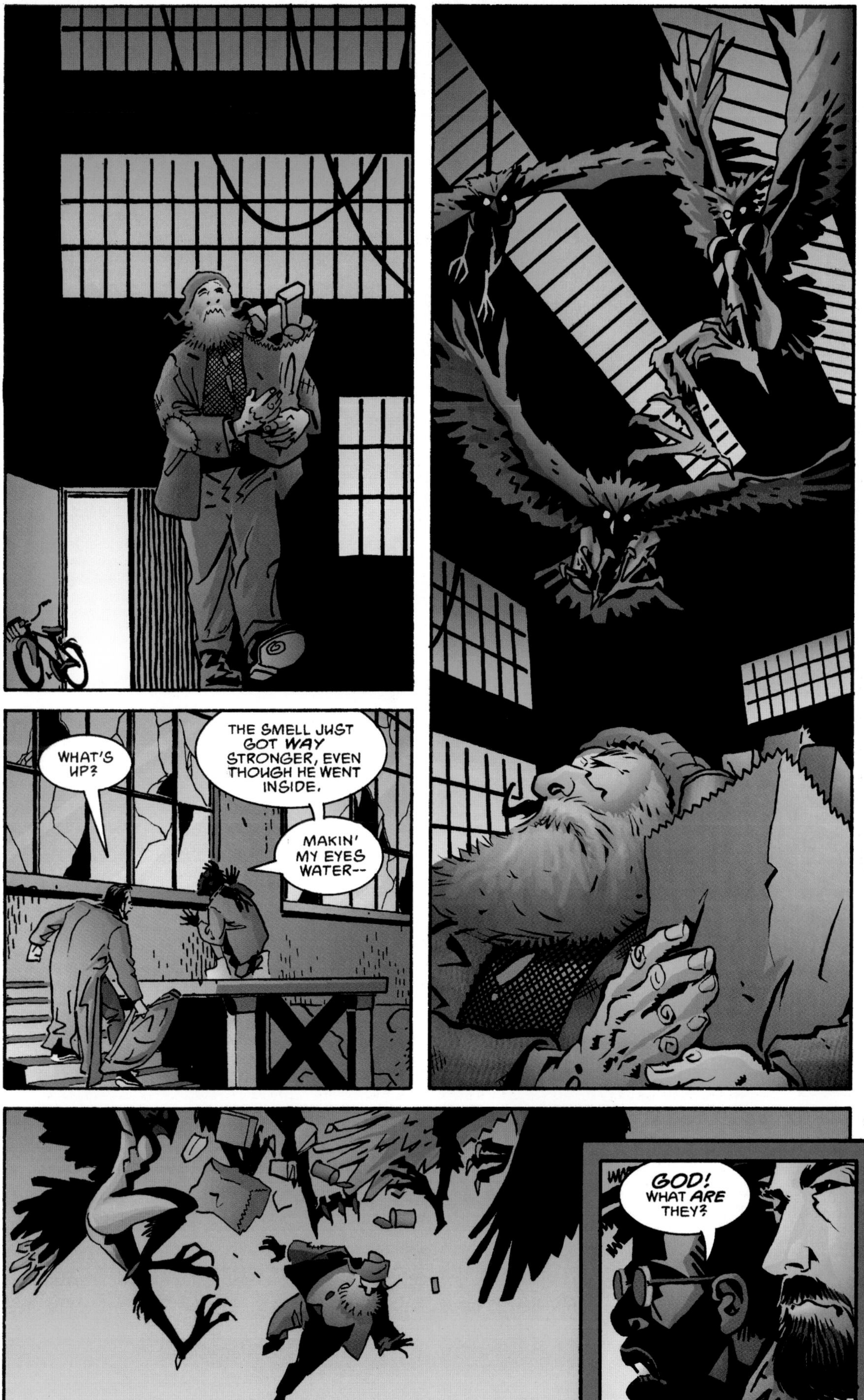
WHAT'S UP?
THE SMELL JUST GOT WAY STRONGER, EVEN THOUGH HE WENT INSIDE.
MAKIN' MY EYES WATER--
GOD! WHAT ARE THEY?

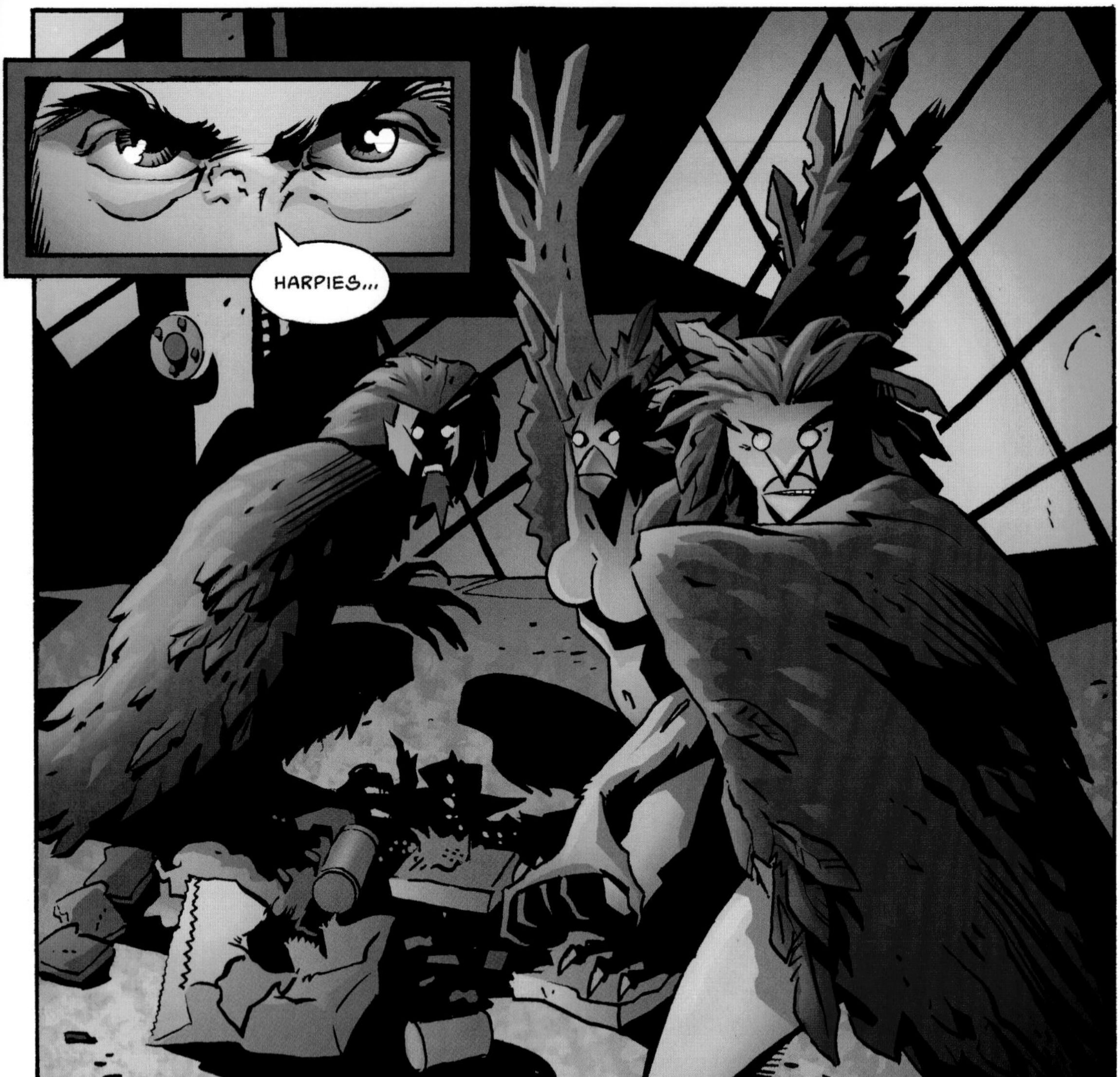
HARPIES...

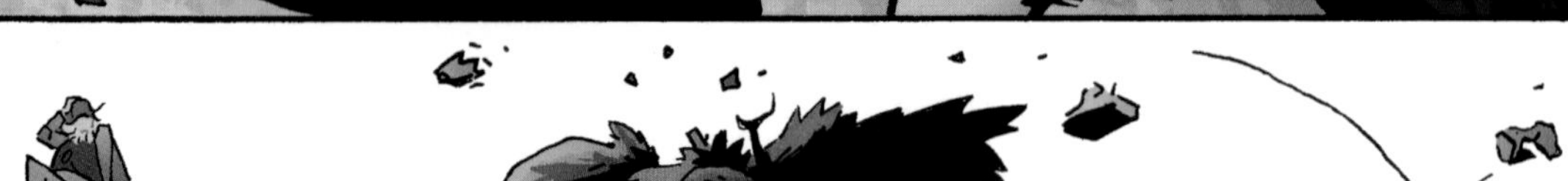

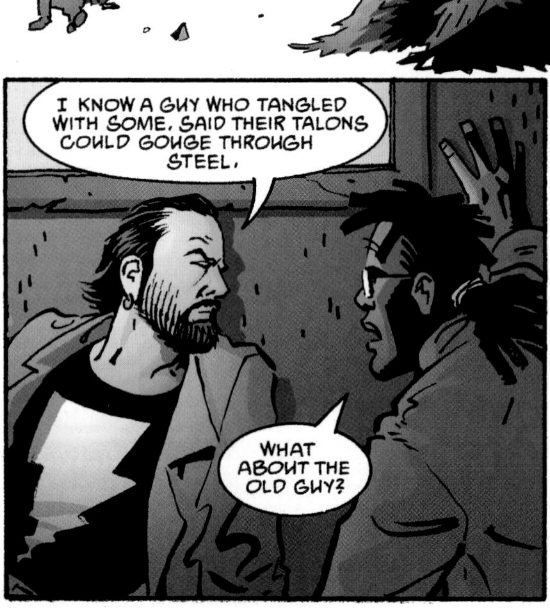
I KNOW A GUY WHO TANGLED WITH SOME. SAID THEIR TALONS COULD GOUGE THROUGH STEEL.
WHAT ABOUT THE OLD GUY?

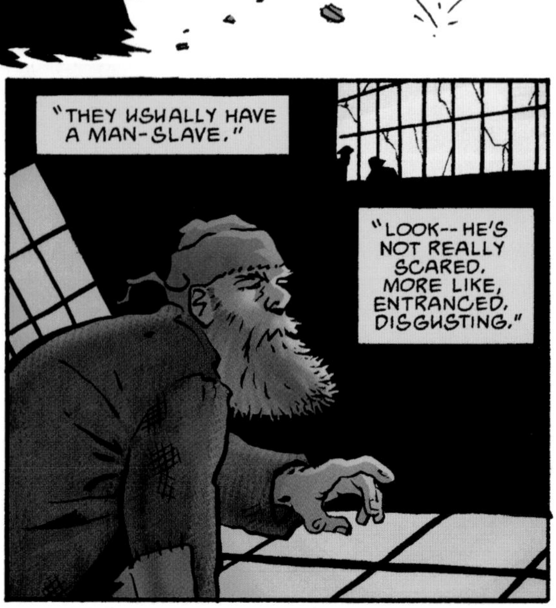
"THEY USUALLY HAVE A MAN-SLAVE."
"LOOK--HE'S NOT REALLY SCARED. MORE LIKE, ENTRANCED. DISGUSTING."

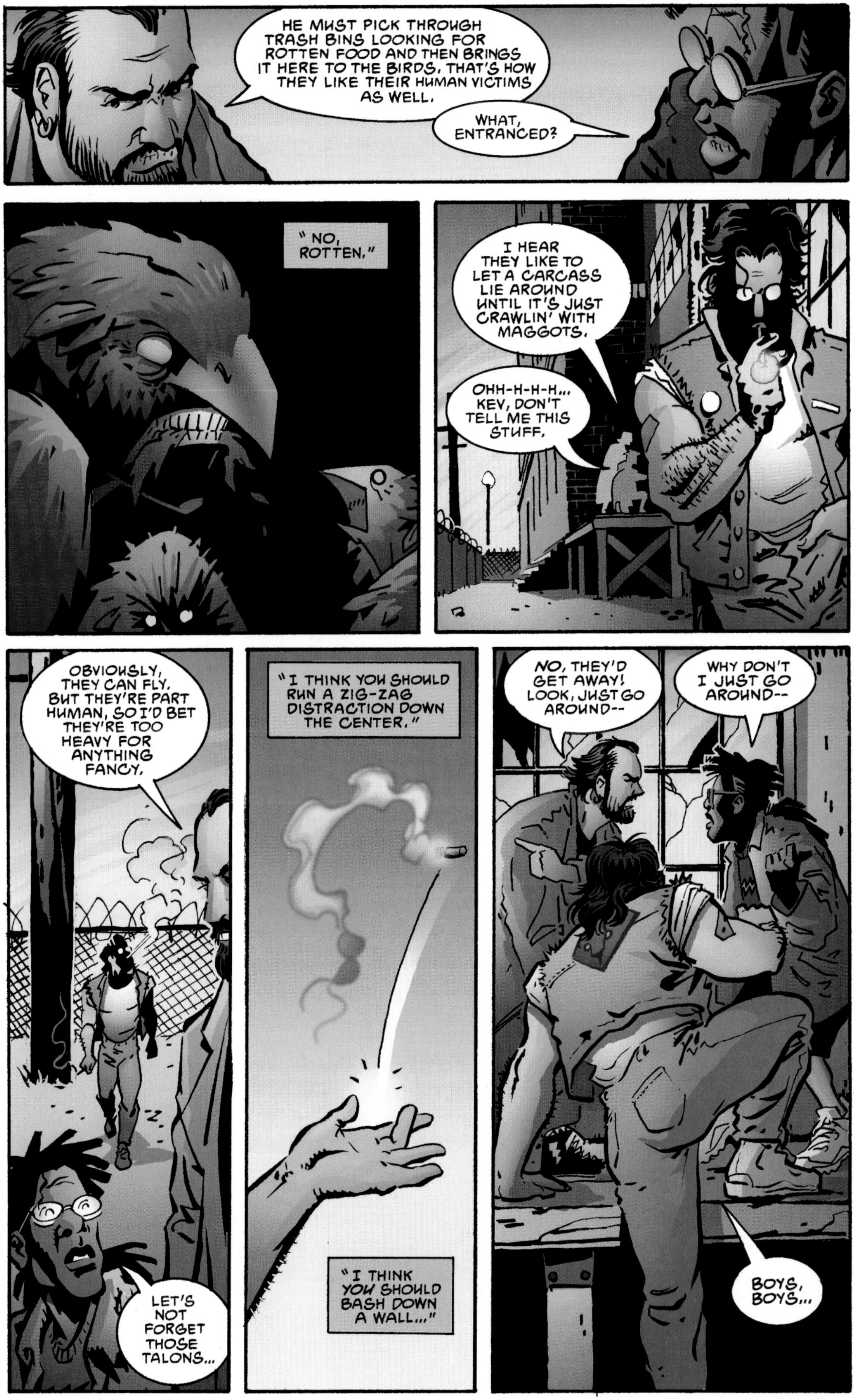
HE MUST PICK THROUGH TRASH BINS LOOKING FOR ROTTEN FOOD AND THEN BRINGS IT HERE TO THE BIRDS. THAT'S HOW THEY LIKE THEIR HUMAN VICTIMS AS WELL.
WHAT, ENTRANCED?
"NO, ROTTEN."
I HEAR THEY LIKE TO LET A CARCASS LIE AROUND UNTIL IT'S JUST CRAWLIN' WITH MAGGOTS.
OHH-H-H-H... KEV, DON'T TELL ME THIS STUFF.
OBVIOUSLY, THEY CAN FLY. BUT THEY'RE PART HUMAN, SO I'D BET THEY'RE TOO HEAVY FOR ANYTHING FANCY.
LET'S NOT FORGET THOSE TALONS...
"I THINK YOU SHOULD RUN A ZIG-ZAG DISTRACTION DOWN THE CENTER."
"I THINK *YOU* SHOULD BASH DOWN A WALL..."
NO, THEY'D GET AWAY! LOOK, JUST GO AROUND--
WHY DON'T I JUST GO AROUND--
BOYS, BOYS...

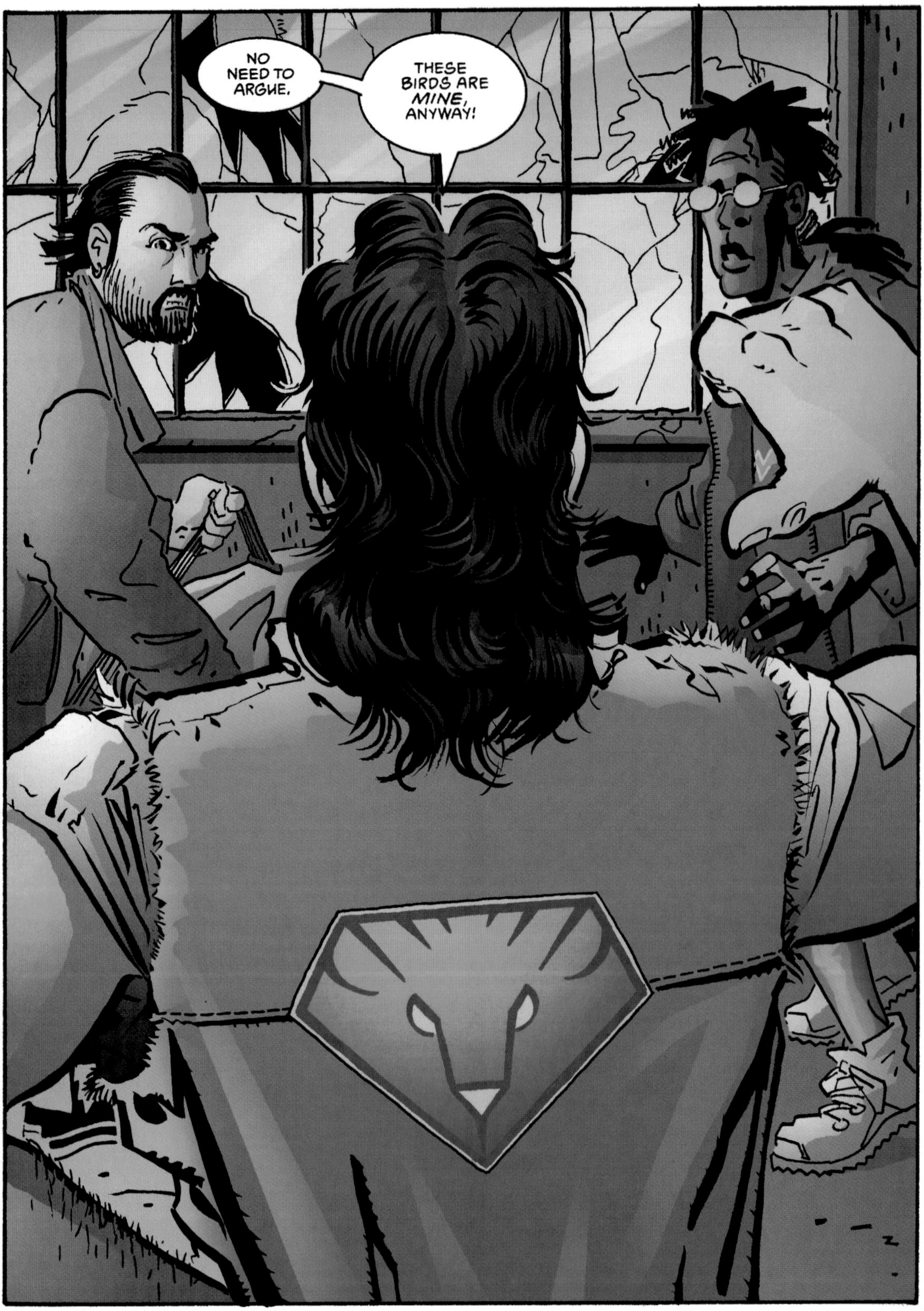
NO NEED TO ARGUE.
THESE BIRDS ARE *MINE*, ANYWAY!

THE HERO DEFINED
MAGE®

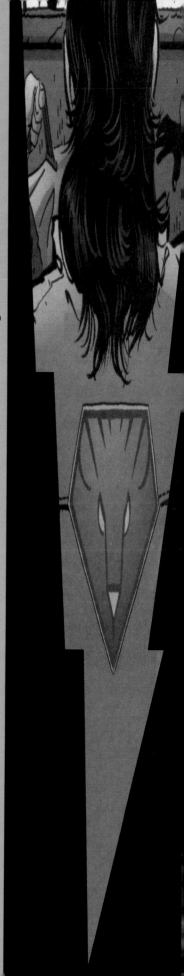

chapter
2

"When We Three
Shall Meet"

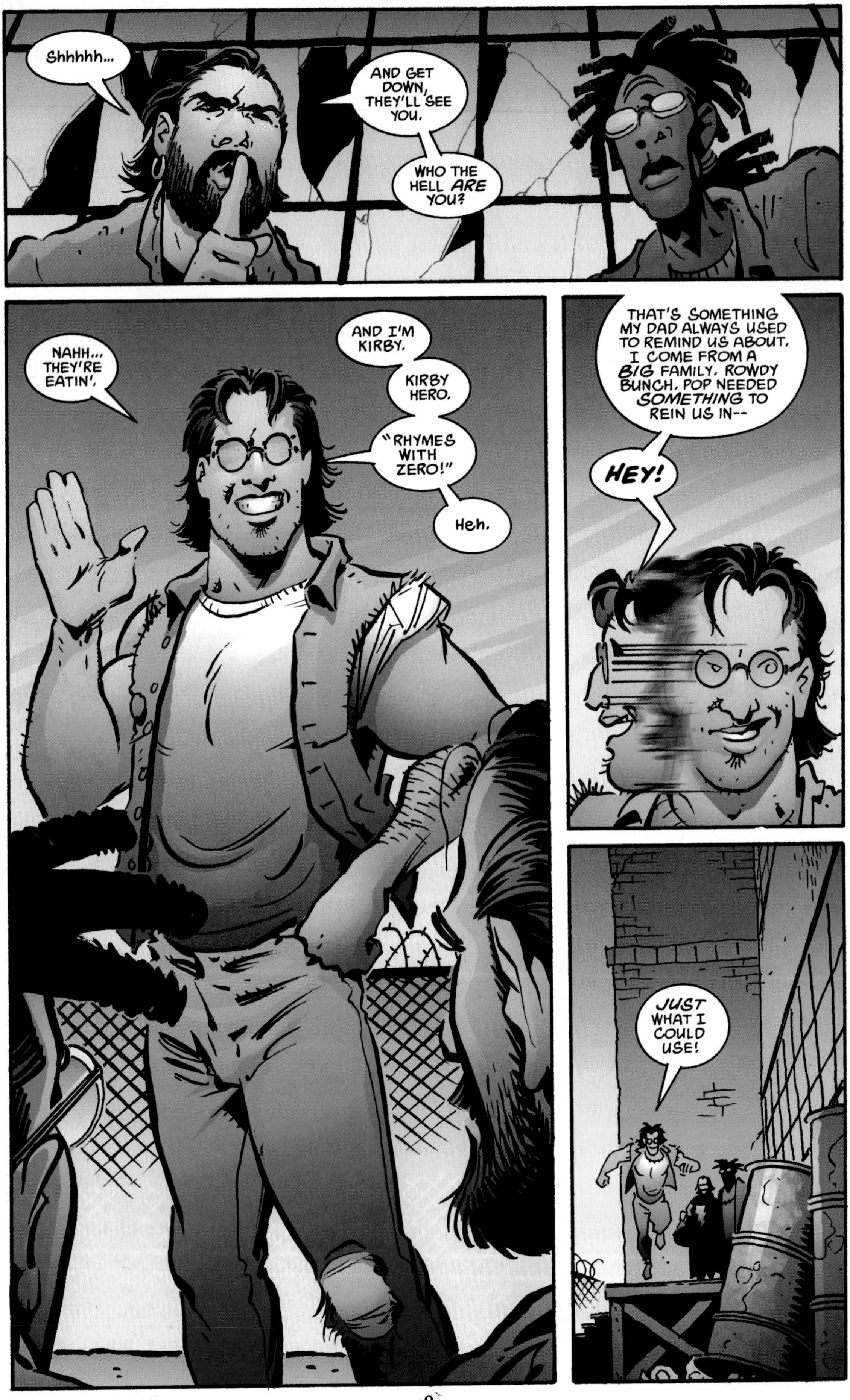
Shhhhh...
AND GET DOWN, THEY'LL SEE YOU.
WHO THE HELL ARE YOU?
NAHH... THEY'RE EATIN'.
AND I'M KIRBY.
KIRBY HERO.
"RHYMES WITH ZERO!"
Heh.
THAT'S SOMETHING MY DAD ALWAYS USED TO REMIND US ABOUT. I COME FROM A BIG FAMILY. ROWDY BUNCH. POP NEEDED SOMETHING TO REIN US IN--
HEY!
JUST WHAT I COULD USE!

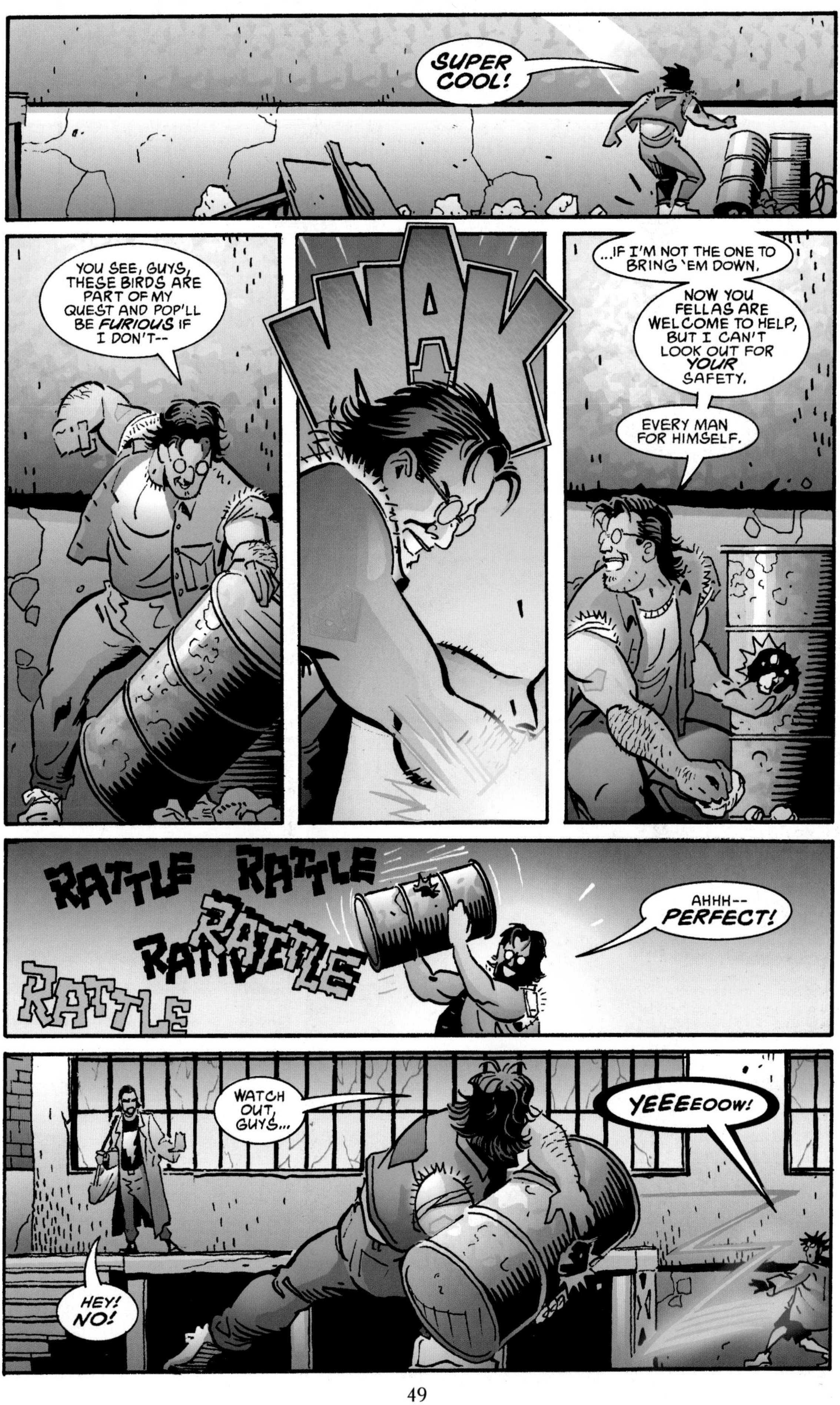
SUPER COOL!
YOU SEE, GUYS, THESE BIRDS ARE PART OF MY QUEST AND POP'LL BE *FURIOUS* IF I DON'T--
WAK
...IF I'M NOT THE ONE TO BRING 'EM DOWN.
NOW YOU FELLAS ARE WELCOME TO HELP, BUT I CAN'T LOOK OUT FOR *YOUR* SAFETY.
EVERY MAN FOR HIMSELF.
RATTLE RATTLE
RATTLE
RATTLE
RATTLE
AHHH-- *PERFECT!*
WATCH OUT, GUYS...
YEEEEOOW!
HEY! NO!

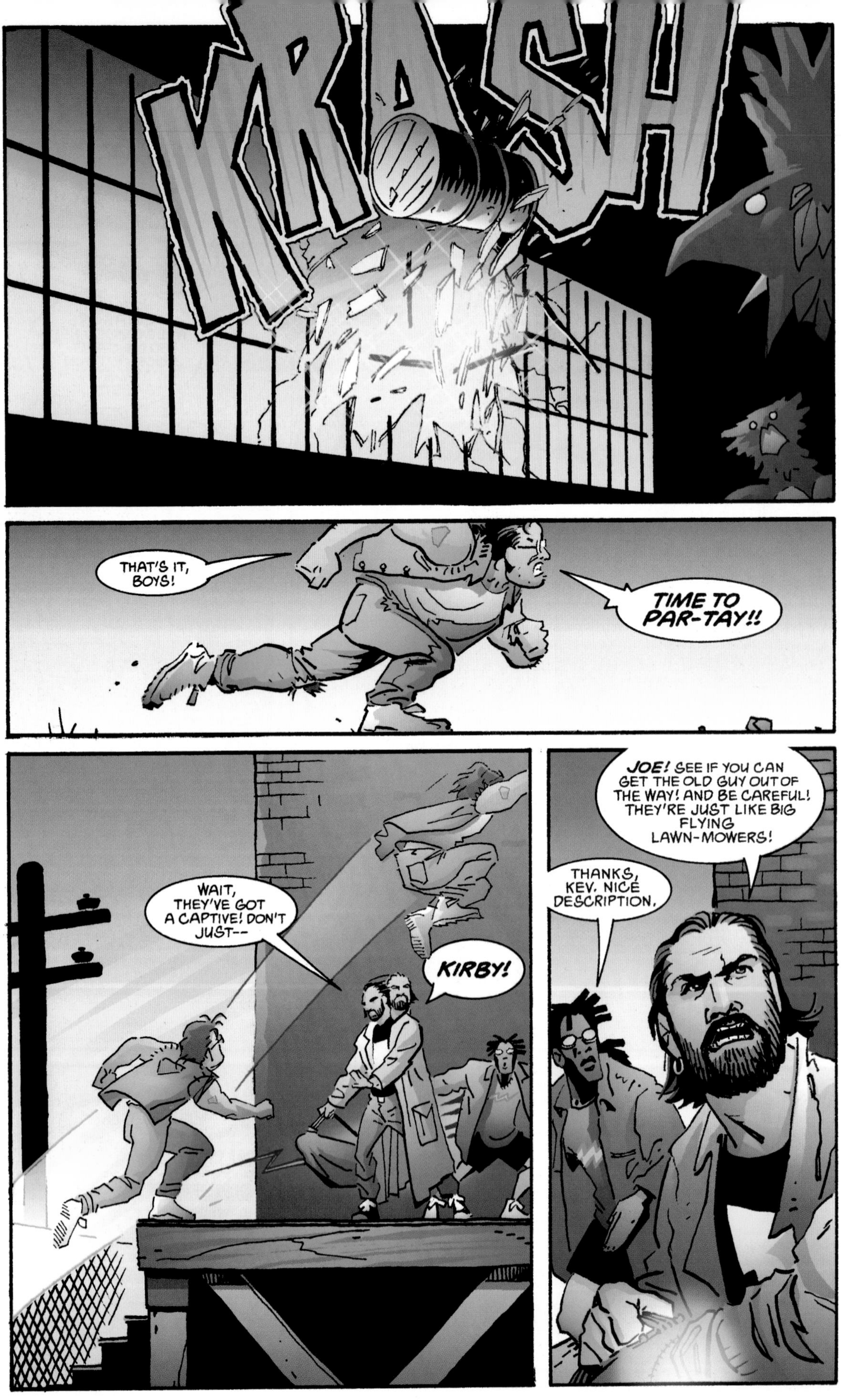
KRASH
THAT'S IT, BOYS!
TIME TO PAR-TAY!!
WAIT, THEY'VE GOT A CAPTIVE! DON'T JUST--
KIRBY!
JOE! SEE IF YOU CAN GET THE OLD GUY OUT OF THE WAY! AND BE CAREFUL! THEY'RE JUST LIKE BIG FLYING LAWN-MOWERS!
THANKS, KEV. NICE DESCRIPTION.

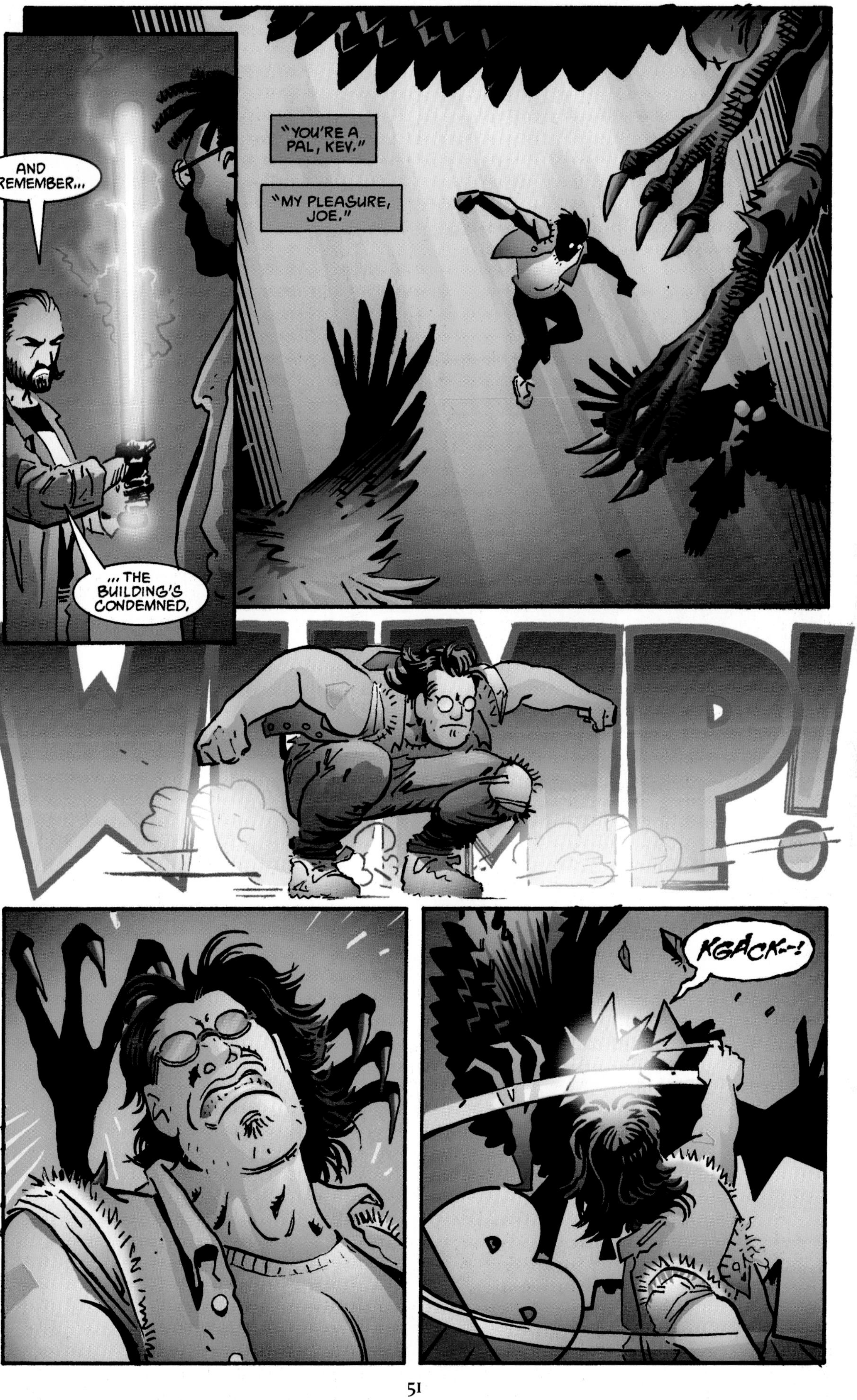

AND REMEMBER...
...THE BUILDING'S CONDEMNED.
"YOU'RE A PAL, KEV."
"MY PLEASURE, JOE."
KGACK--!

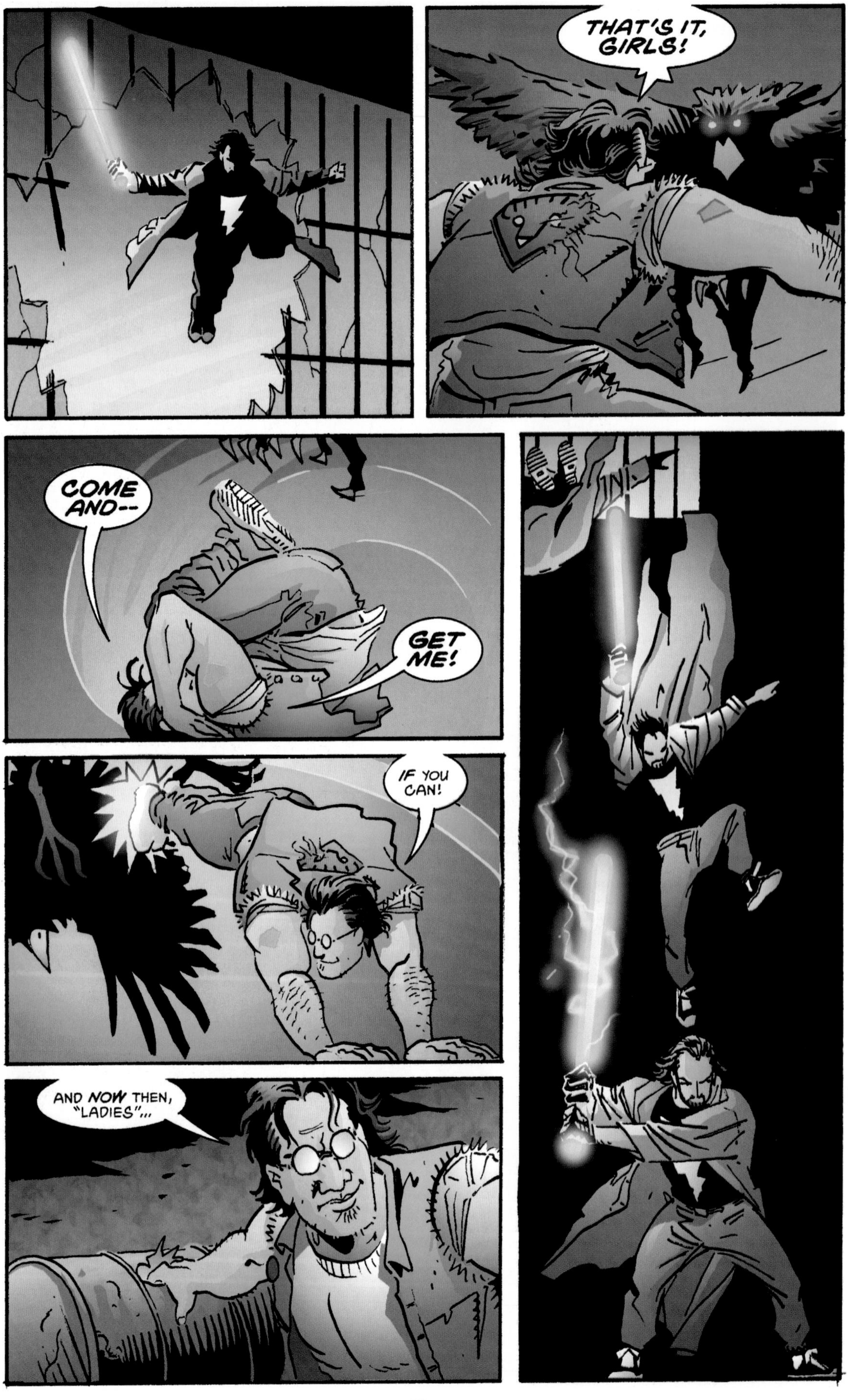
THAT'S IT, GIRLS!
COME AND--
GET ME!
IF YOU CAN!
AND NOW THEN, "LADIES"...

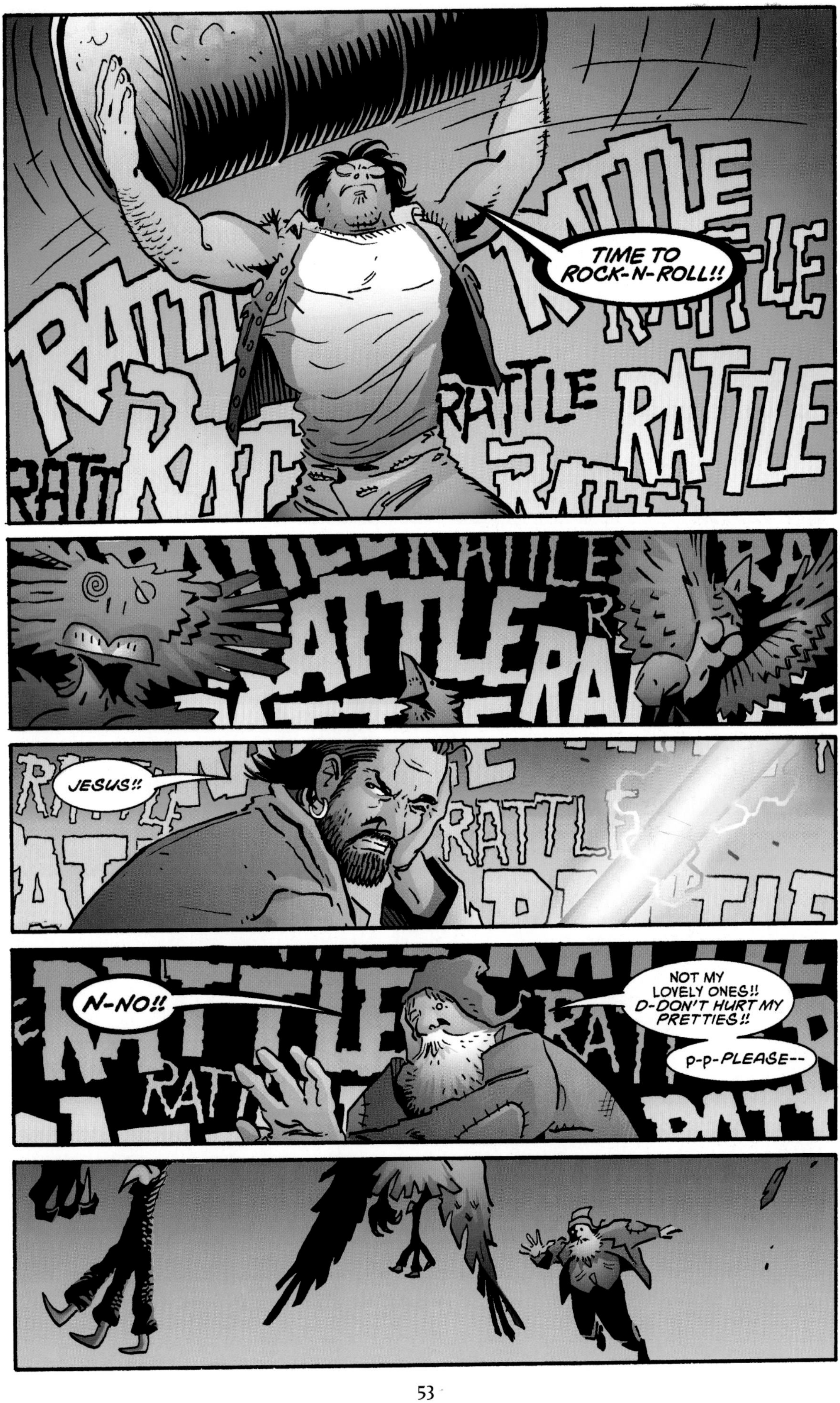
RATTLE
TIME TO ROCK-N-ROLL!!
RATTLE
RATTLE
JESUS!!
RATTLE
N-NO!!
NOT MY LOVELY ONES!! D-DON'T HURT MY PRETTIES!!
P-P-PLEASE--

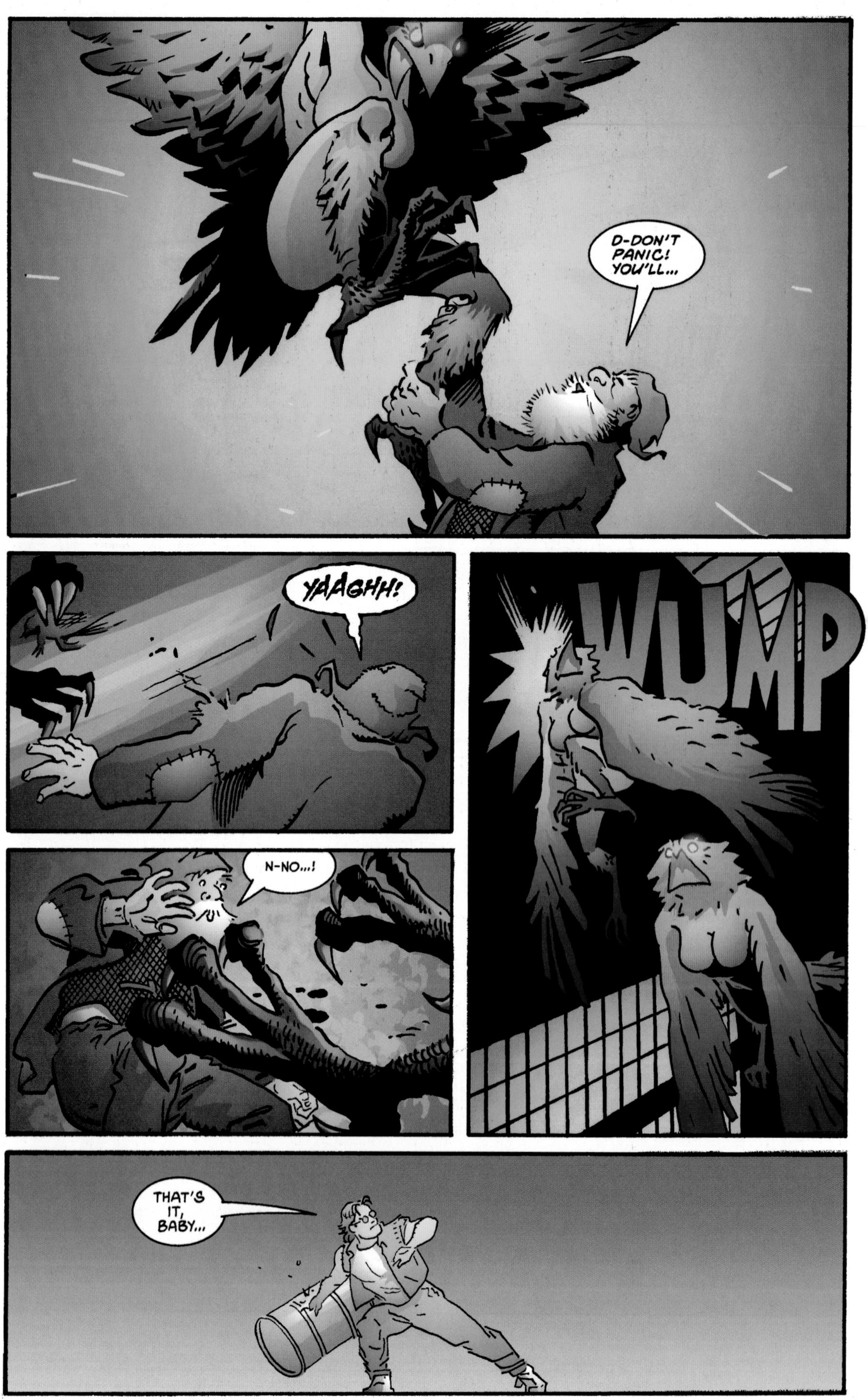
D-DON'T PANIC! YOU'LL...
YAAGHH!
N-NO...!
WUMP
THAT'S IT, BABY...

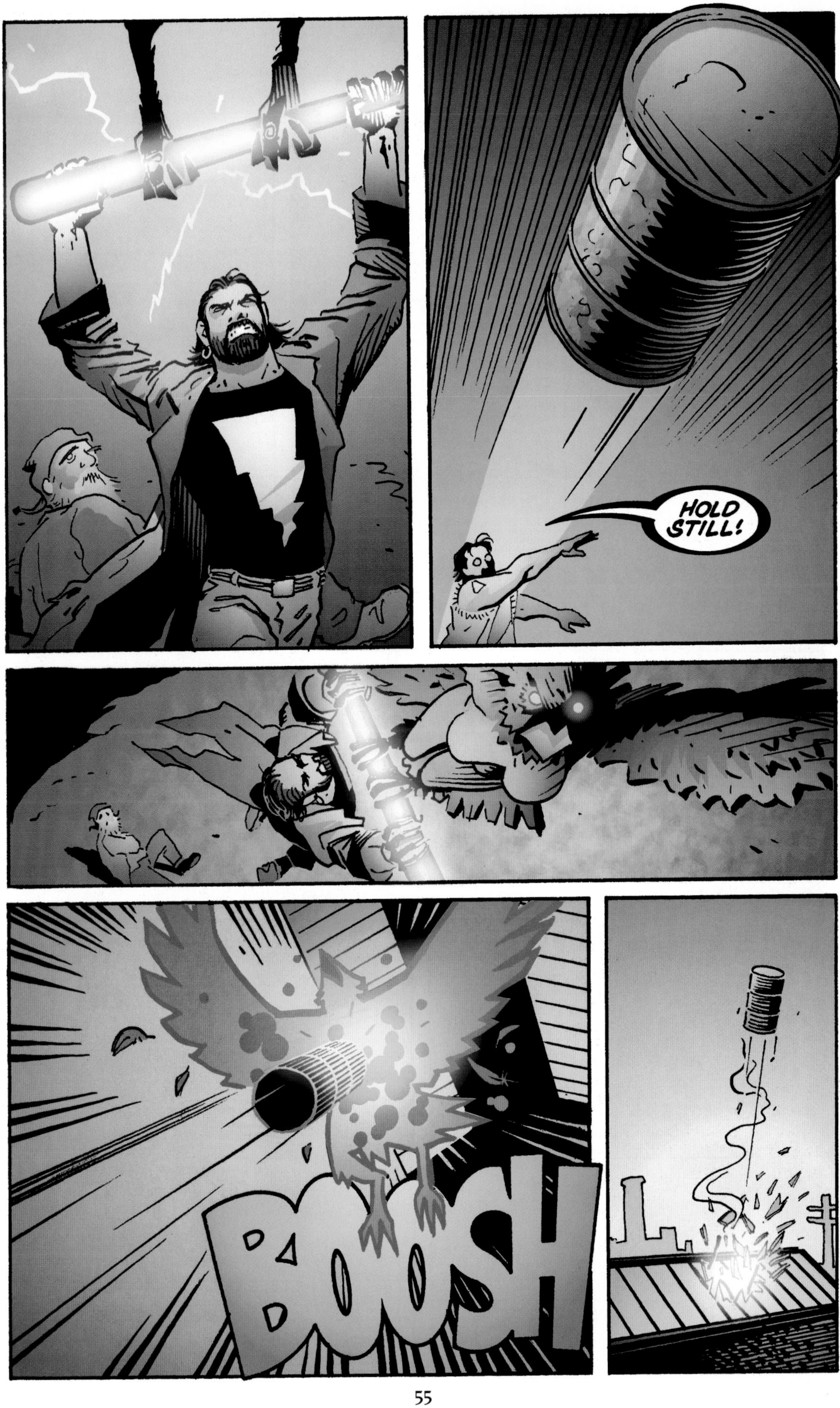
HOLD STILL!
BOOSH!

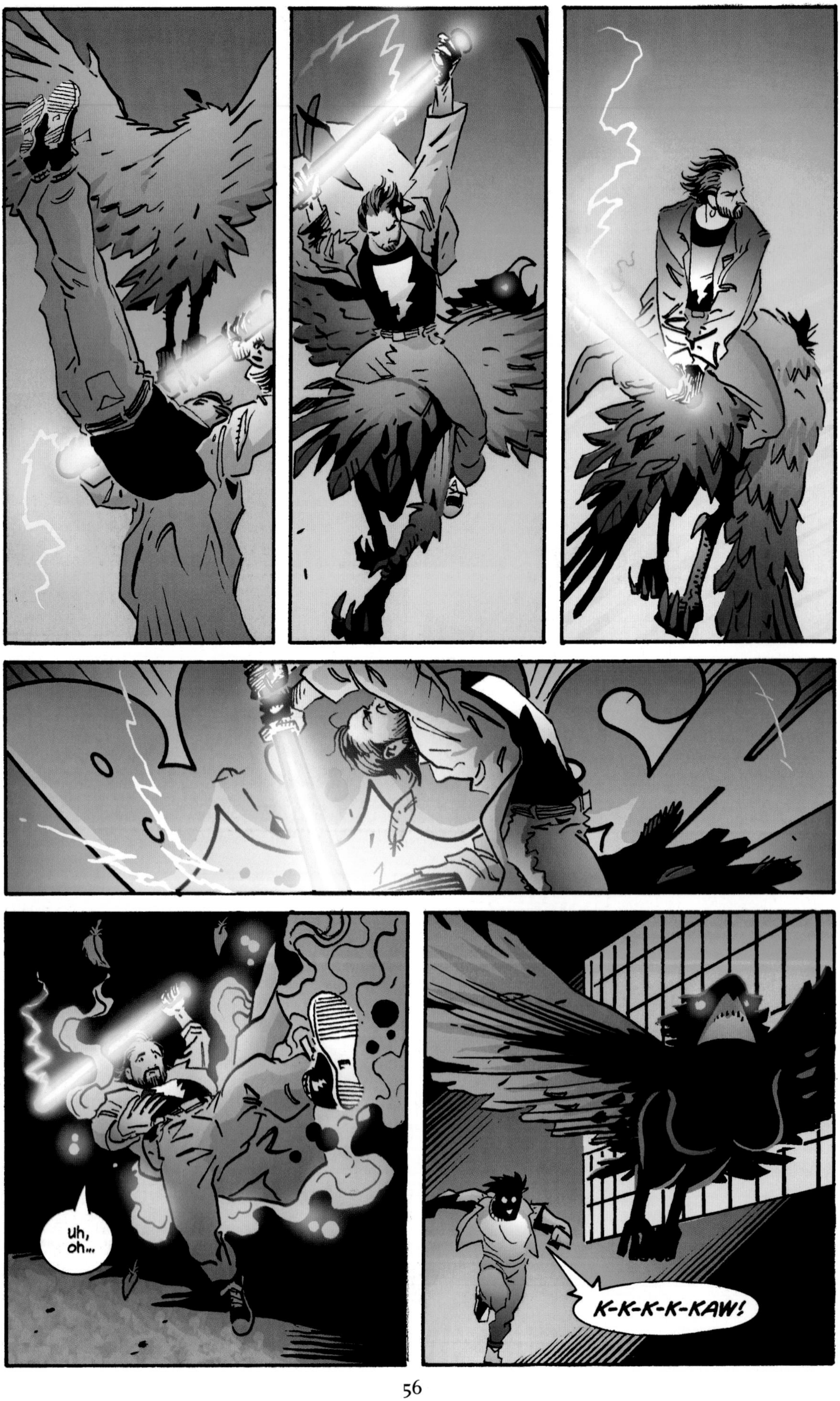
uh, oh...
K-K-K-K-KAW!

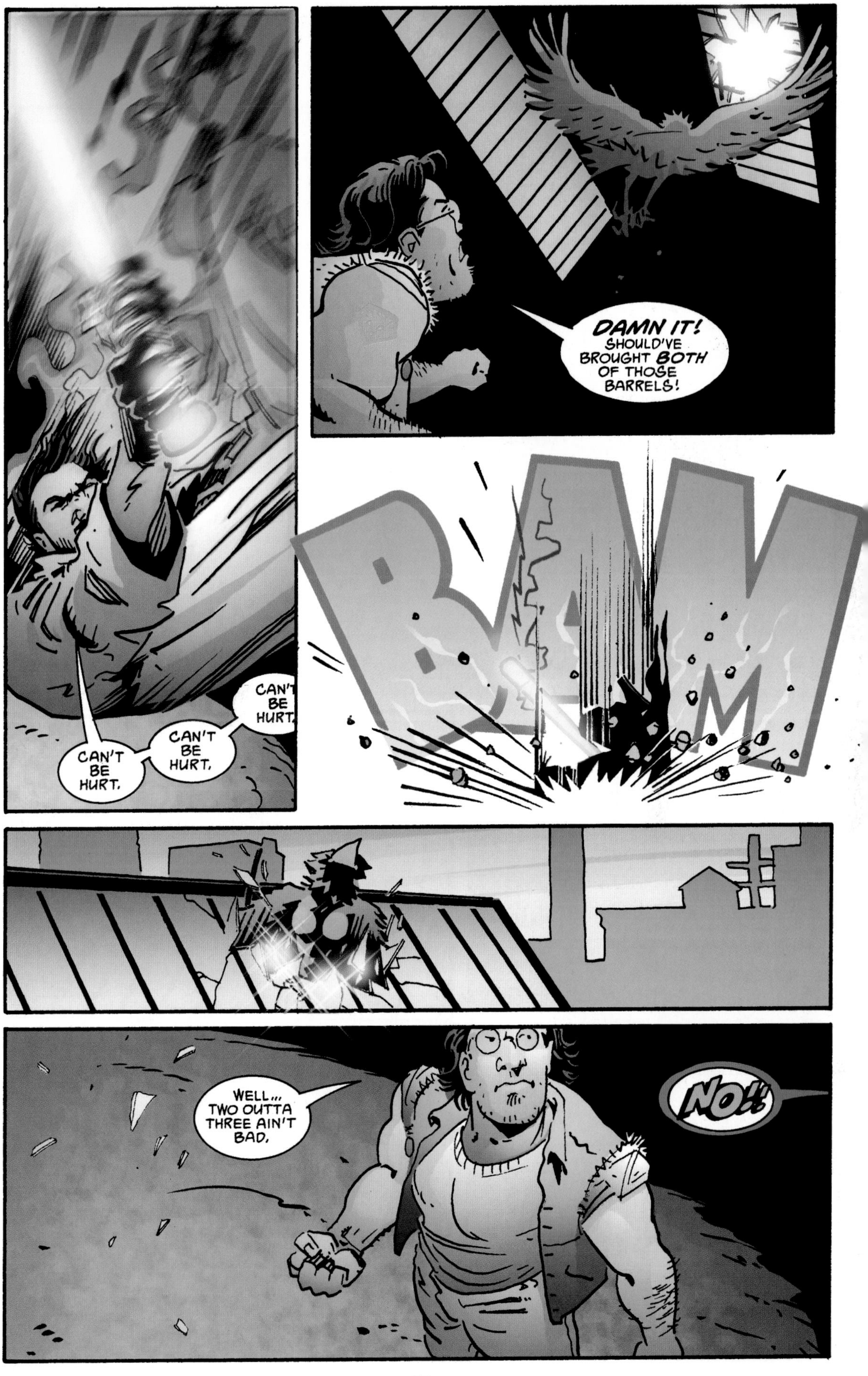
CAN'T BE HURT.
CAN'T BE HURT.
CAN'T BE HURT.
DAMN IT! SHOULD'VE BROUGHT BOTH OF THOSE BARRELS!
BAM
WELL... TWO OUTTA THREE AIN'T BAD.
NO!!

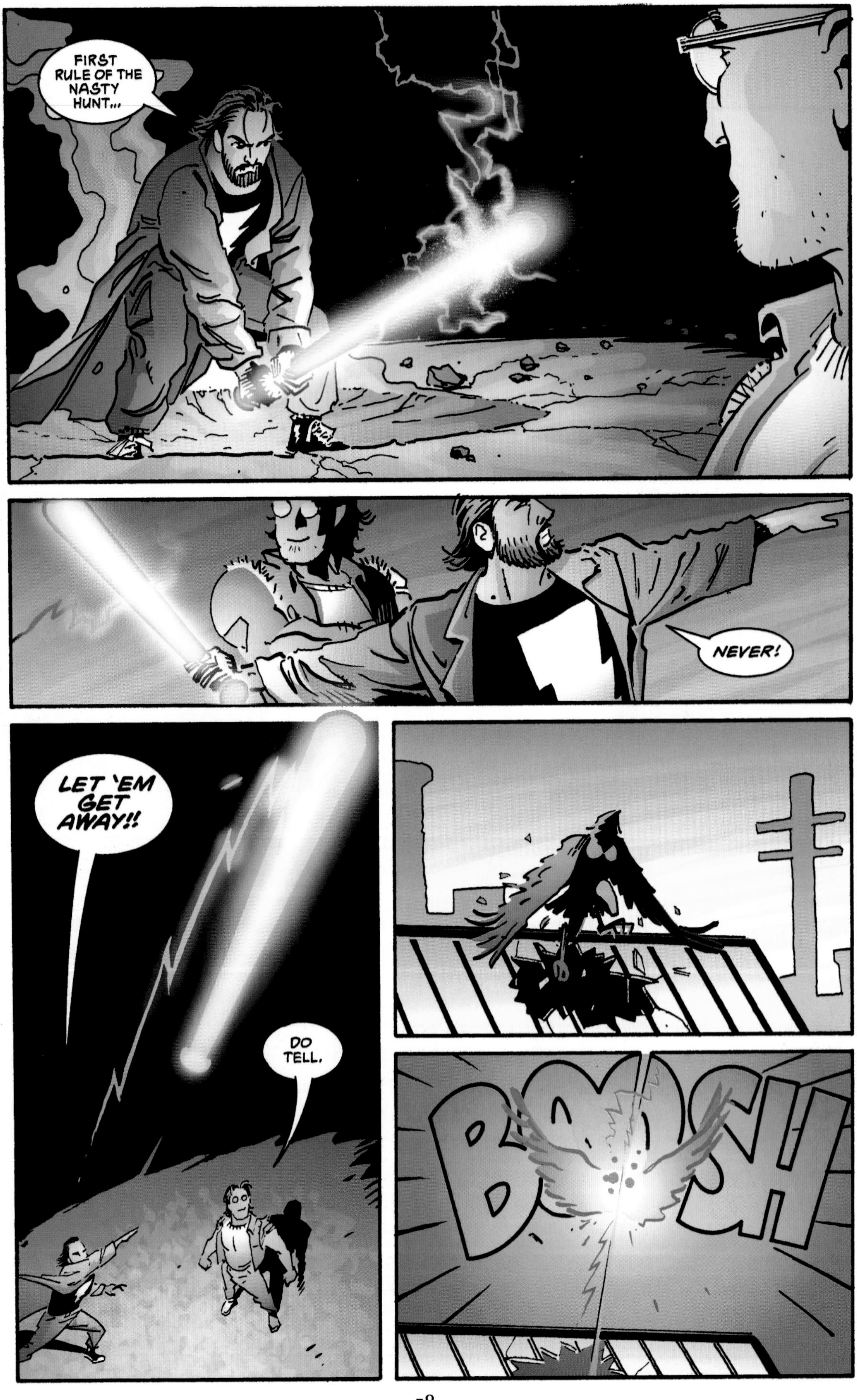
FIRST RULE OF THE NASTY HUNT...
NEVER!
LET 'EM GET AWAY!!
DO TELL.
BOOSH

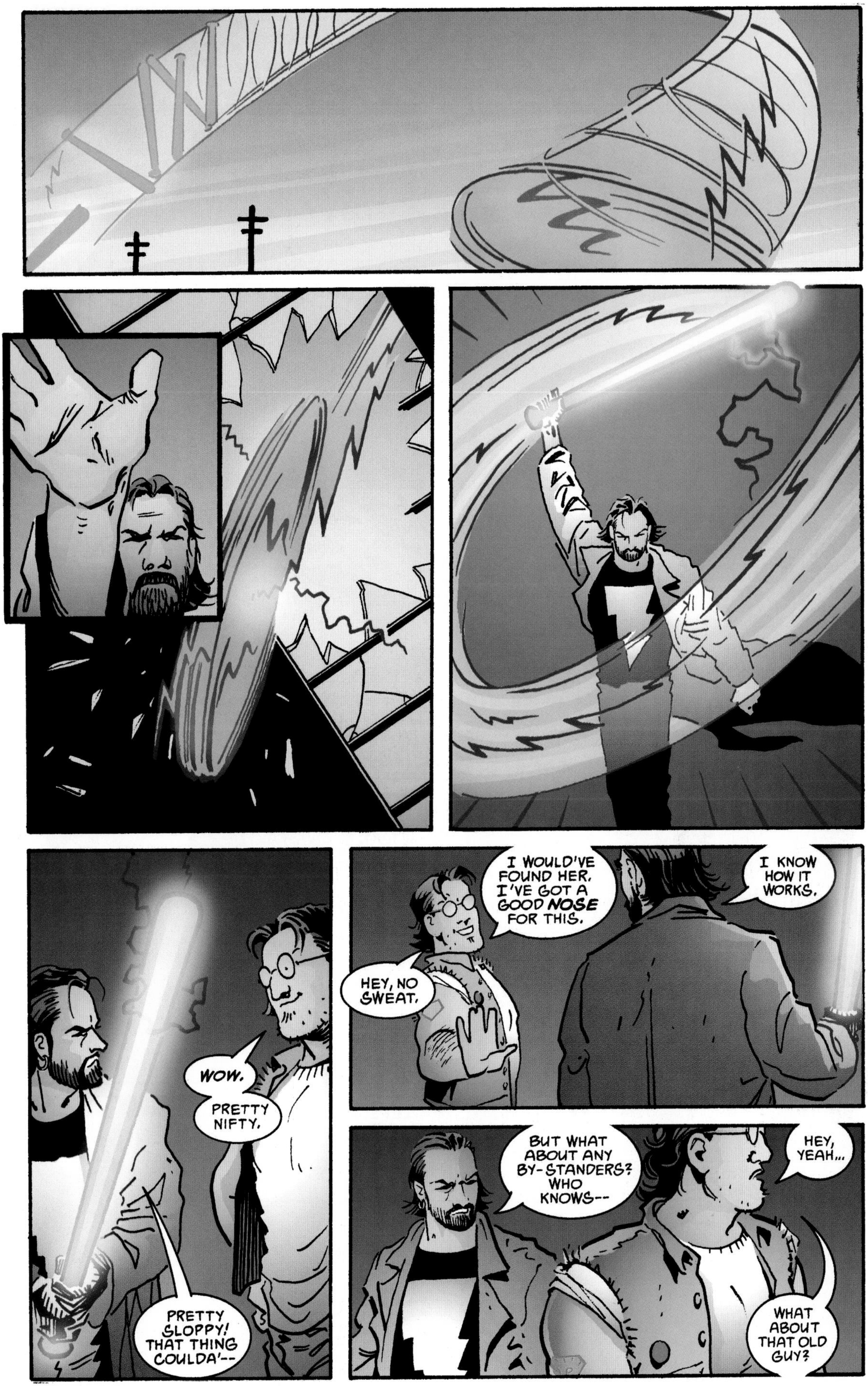
WOW.
PRETTY NIFTY.
PRETTY SLOPPY! THAT THING COULDA'--
I WOULD'VE FOUND HER. I'VE GOT A GOOD NOSE FOR THIS.
I KNOW HOW IT WORKS.
HEY, NO SWEAT.
BUT WHAT ABOUT ANY BY-STANDERS? WHO KNOWS--
HEY, YEAH...
WHAT ABOUT THAT OLD GUY?

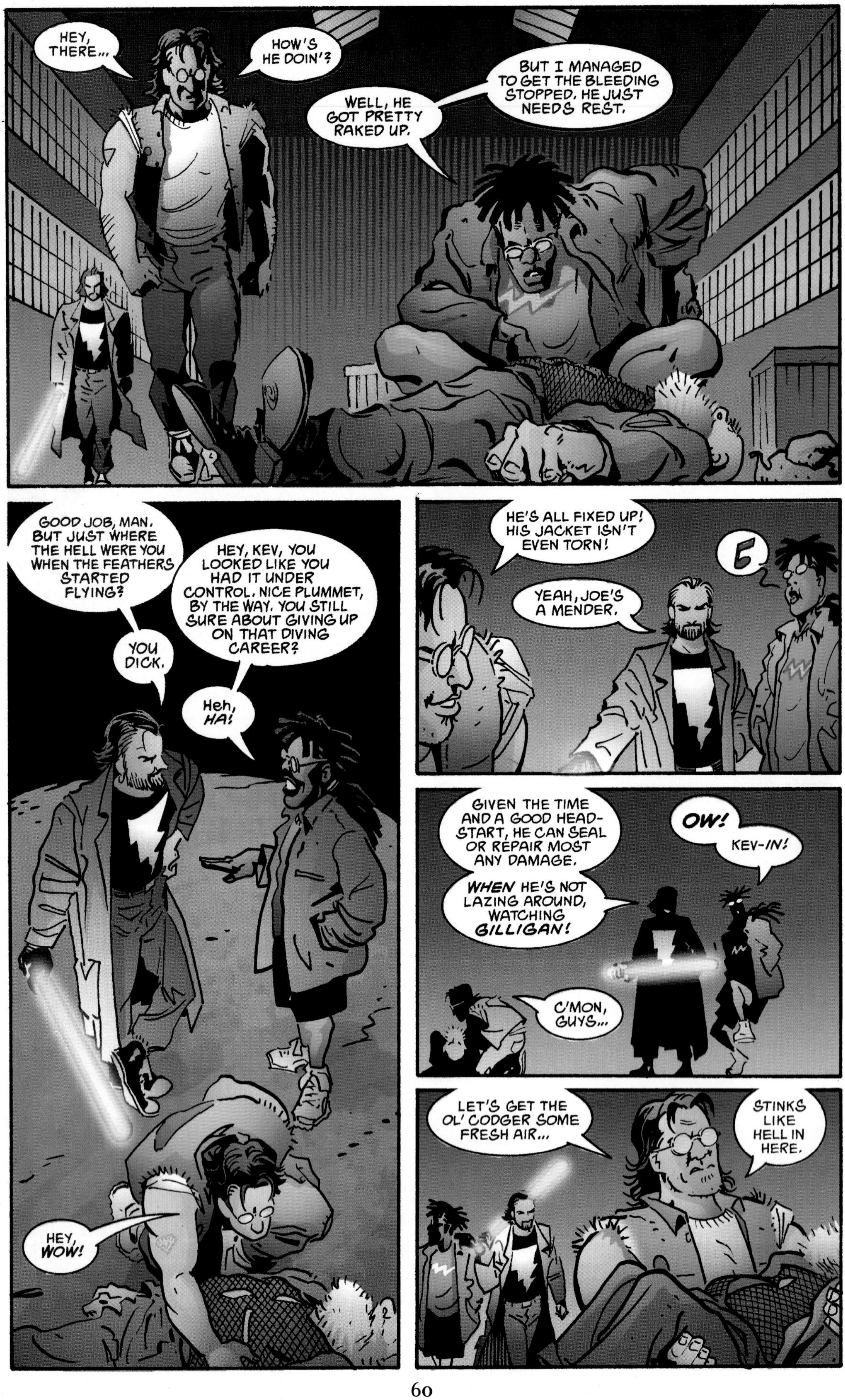
HEY, THERE...
HOW'S HE DOIN'?
WELL, HE GOT PRETTY RAKED UP.
BUT I MANAGED TO GET THE BLEEDING STOPPED. HE JUST NEEDS REST.
GOOD JOB, MAN. BUT JUST WHERE THE HELL WERE YOU WHEN THE FEATHERS STARTED FLYING?
YOU DICK.
HEY, KEV, YOU LOOKED LIKE YOU HAD IT UNDER CONTROL. NICE PLUMMET, BY THE WAY. YOU STILL SURE ABOUT GIVING UP ON THAT DIVING CAREER?
Heh, HA!
HEY, WOW!
HE'S ALL FIXED UP! HIS JACKET ISN'T EVEN TORN!
YEAH, JOE'S A MENDER.
GIVEN THE TIME AND A GOOD HEAD-START, HE CAN SEAL OR REPAIR MOST ANY DAMAGE.
WHEN HE'S NOT LAZING AROUND, WATCHING GILLIGAN!
OW!
KEV-IN!
C'MON, GUYS...
LET'S GET THE OL' CODGER SOME FRESH AIR...
STINKS LIKE HELL IN HERE.

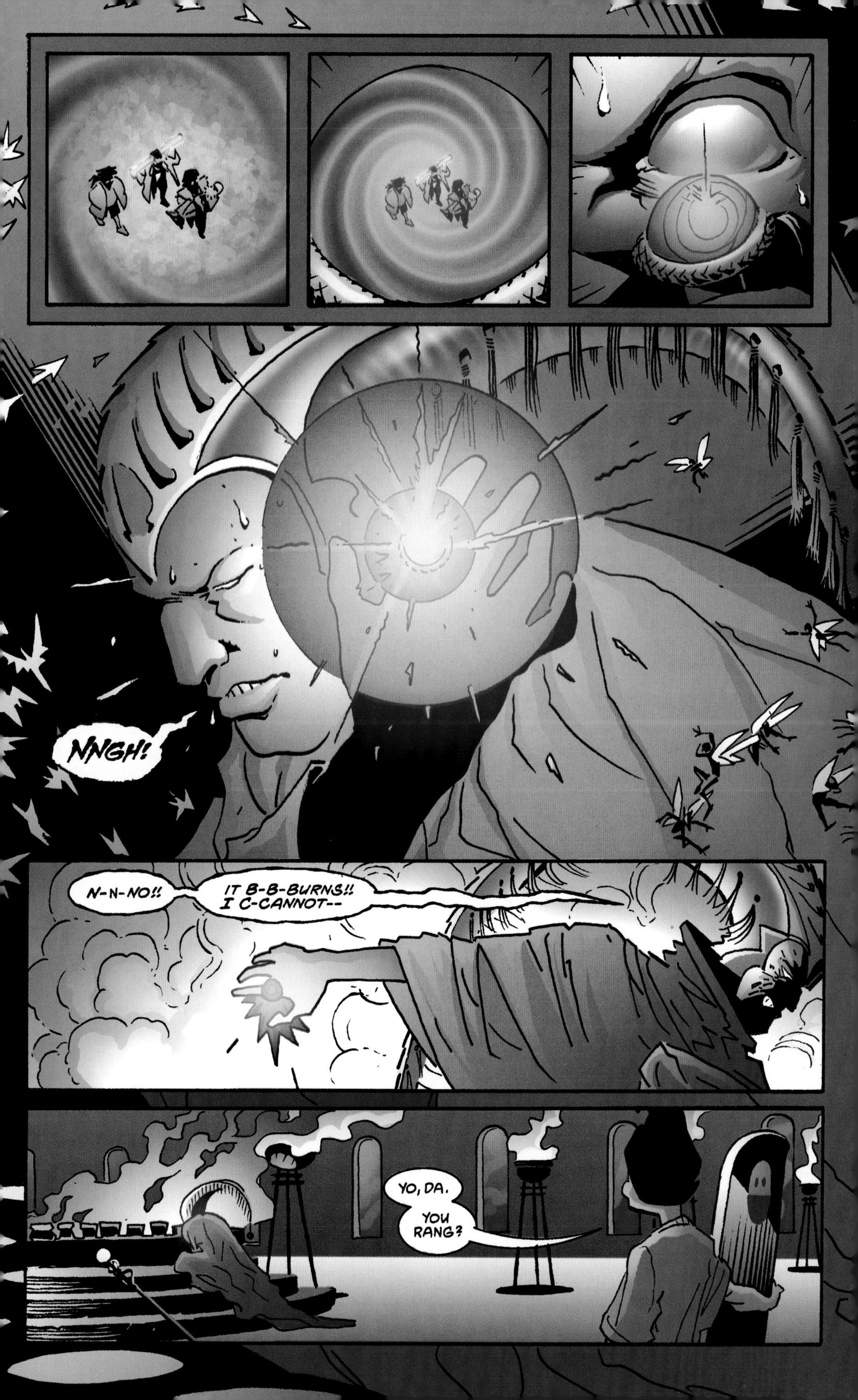
NNGH!
N-N-NO!!
IT B-B-BURNS!! I C-CANNOT--
YO, DA.
YOU RANG?

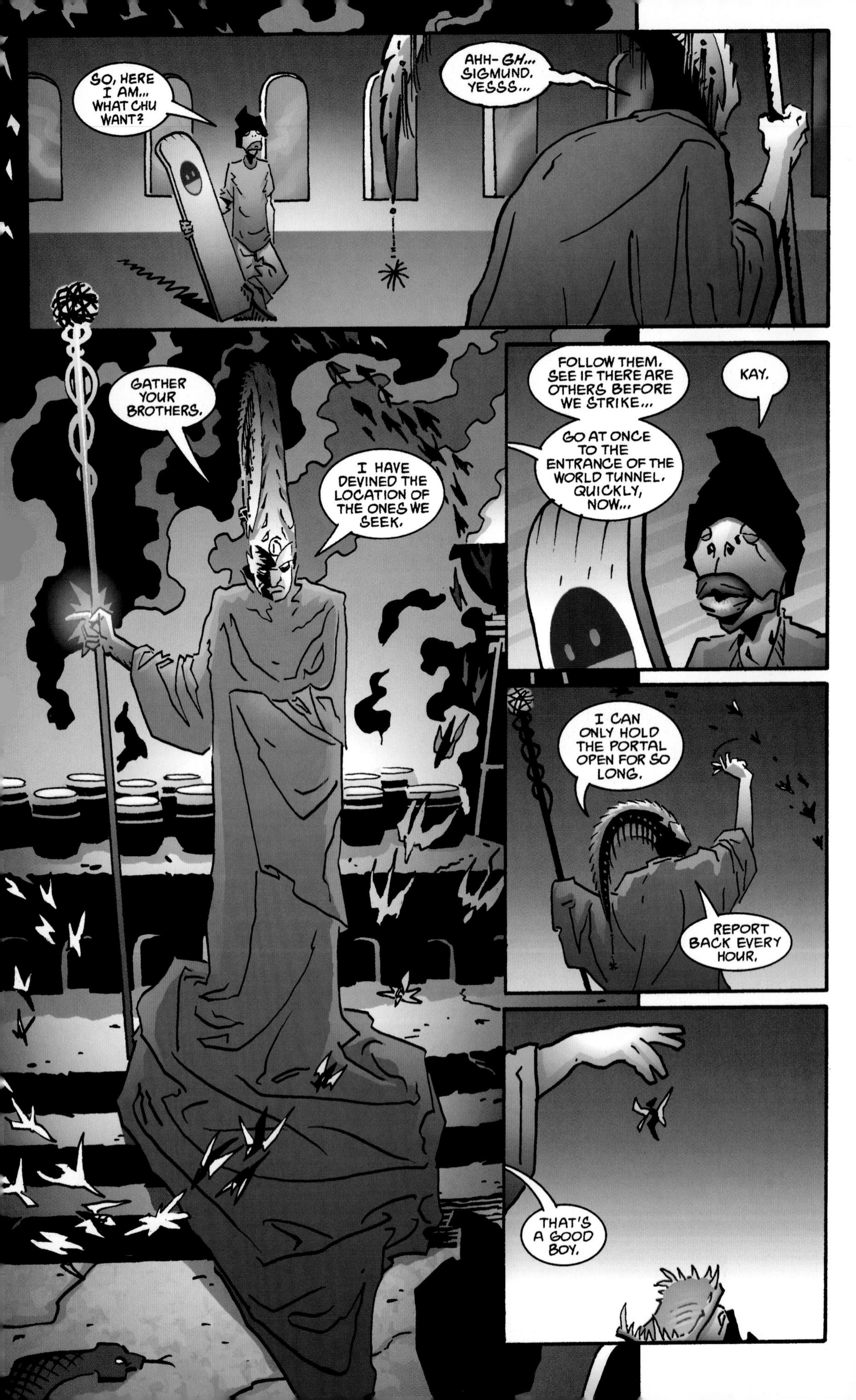
SO, HERE I AM... WHAT CHU WANT?
AHH-GH... SIGMUND. YESSS...
GATHER YOUR BROTHERS.
I HAVE DEVINED THE LOCATION OF THE ONES WE SEEK.
FOLLOW THEM. SEE IF THERE ARE OTHERS BEFORE WE STRIKE...
KAY.
GO AT ONCE TO THE ENTRANCE OF THE WORLD TUNNEL. QUICKLY, NOW...
I CAN ONLY HOLD THE PORTAL OPEN FOR SO LONG.
REPORT BACK EVERY HOUR.
THAT'S A GOOD BOY.

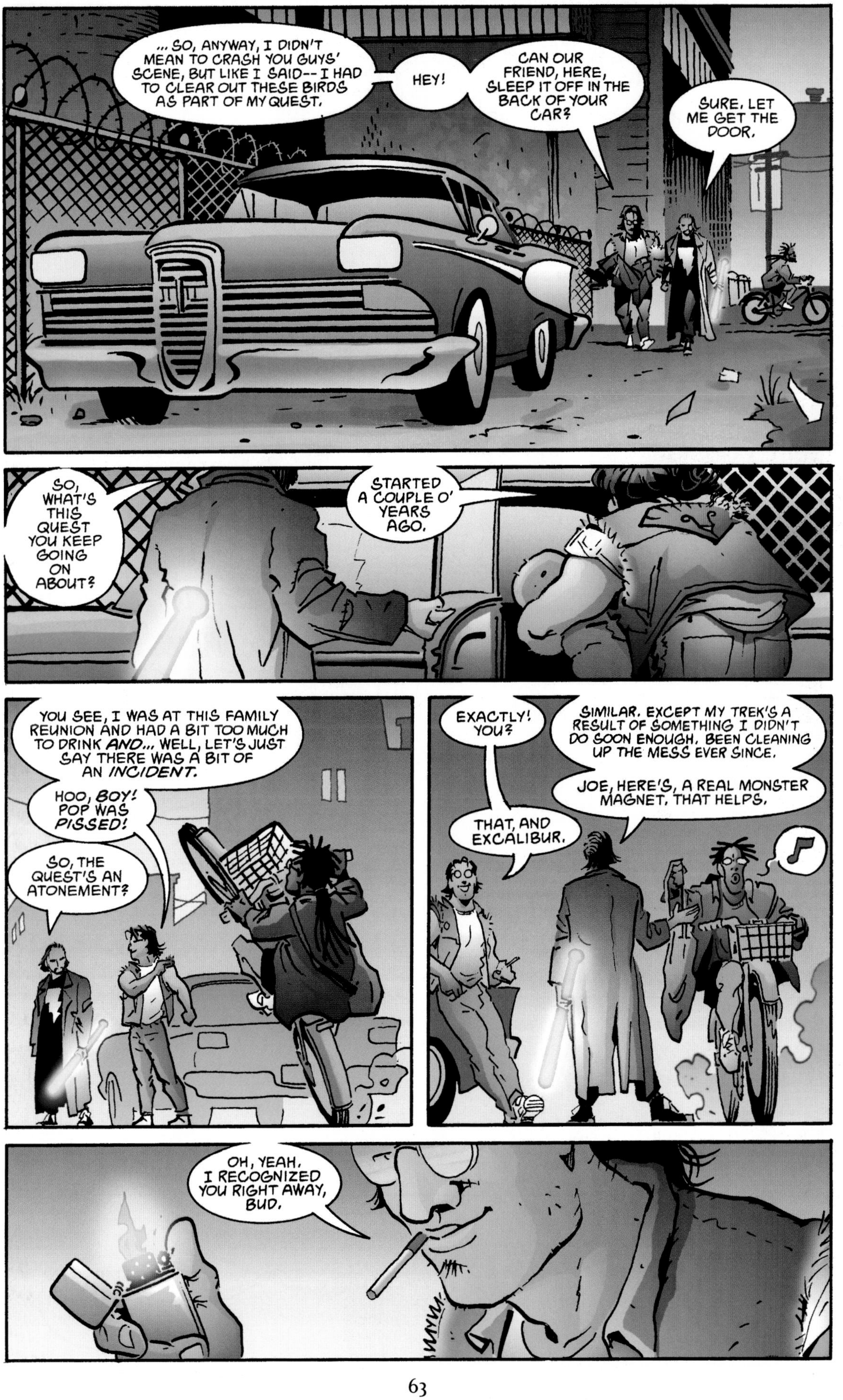
...SO, ANYWAY, I DIDN'T MEAN TO CRASH YOU GUYS' SCENE, BUT LIKE I SAID-- I HAD TO CLEAR OUT THESE BIRDS AS PART OF MY QUEST.
HEY!
CAN OUR FRIEND, HERE, SLEEP IT OFF IN THE BACK OF YOUR CAR?
SURE. LET ME GET THE DOOR.
SO, WHAT'S THIS QUEST YOU KEEP GOING ON ABOUT?
STARTED A COUPLE O' YEARS AGO.
YOU SEE, I WAS AT THIS FAMILY REUNION AND HAD A BIT TOO MUCH TO DRINK *AND*... WELL, LET'S JUST SAY THERE WAS A BIT OF AN *INCIDENT*.
HOO, *BOY*! POP WAS *PISSED*!
SO, THE QUEST'S AN ATONEMENT?
EXACTLY! YOU?
SIMILAR. EXCEPT MY TREK'S A RESULT OF SOMETHING I DIDN'T DO SOON ENOUGH. BEEN CLEANING UP THE MESS EVER SINCE.
JOE, HERE'S, A REAL MONSTER MAGNET. THAT HELPS.
THAT, AND EXCALIBUR.
OH, YEAH. I RECOGNIZED YOU RIGHT AWAY, BUD.

YOU'RE KEVIN MATCHSTICK, *THE PENDRAGON.*

GUILTY AS CHARGED.

WORD GETS AROUND, EH?

YEAH, I RAN INTO A GUY 'BOUT A YEAR AGO, TOLD ME ABOUT YOU AND THAT BAT.

SO WHAT HAPPENS AFTER THIS BIG "CLEAN UP"?

DON'T KNOW YET. WHEN I FIRST FELT THE CALL, I WAS TUTORED BY A GUIDE-- THE *WORLD-MAGE.*

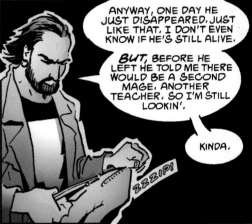

ANYWAY, ONE DAY HE JUST DISAPPEARED. JUST LIKE THAT. I DON'T EVEN KNOW IF HE'S STILL ALIVE.

BUT, BEFORE HE LEFT HE TOLD ME THERE WOULD BE A SECOND MAGE, ANOTHER TEACHER. SO I'M STILL LOOKIN'.

KINDA.

ZZZIP!

OKAY, YOUR TURN.

MOI?!

I, BUD, AM *THE OLYMPIAN!*

THE LADIES FEINT! THE CROWD GOES WILD!

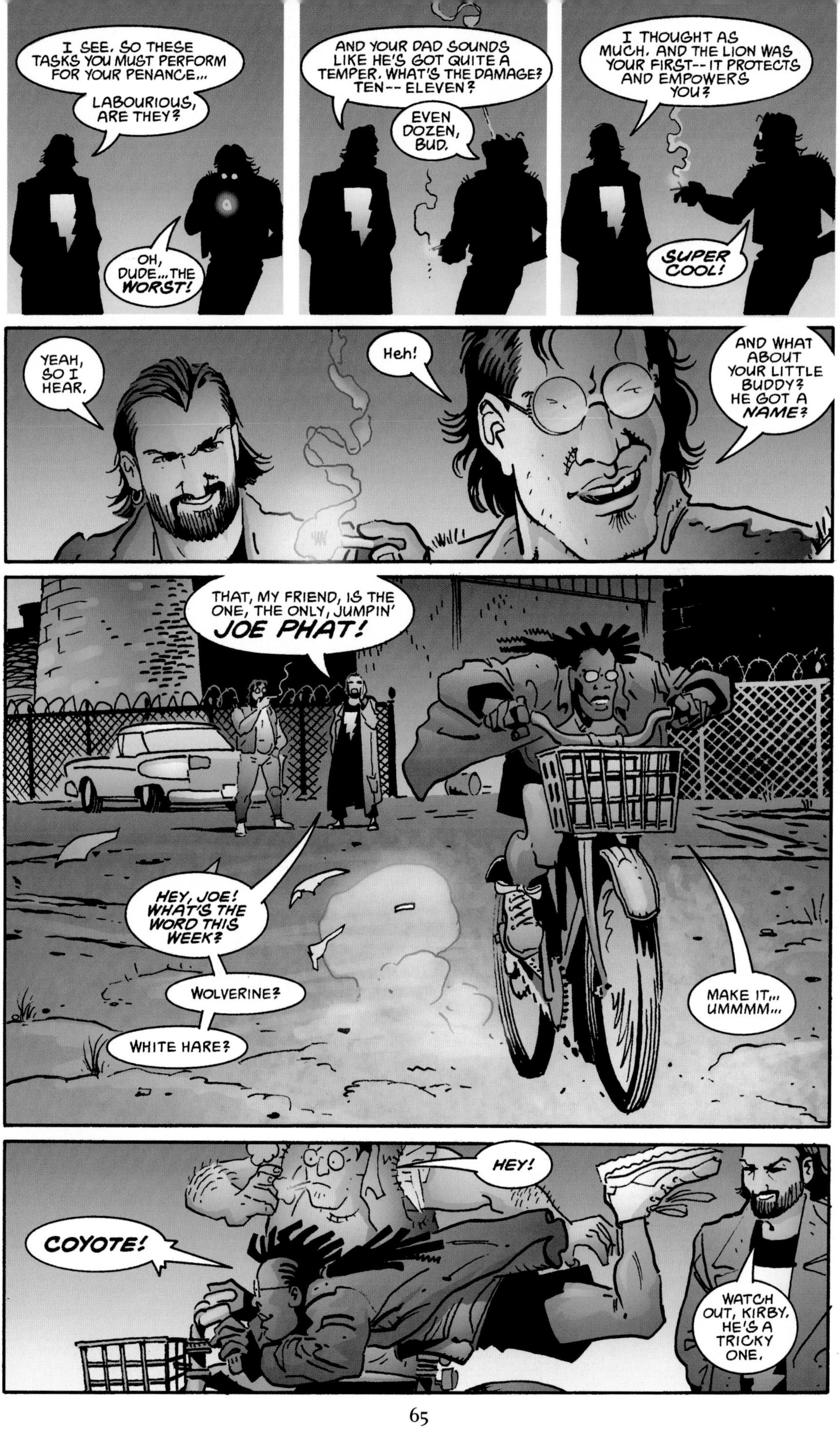
I SEE. SO THESE TASKS YOU MUST PERFORM FOR YOUR PENANCE...
LABOURIOUS, ARE THEY?
OH, DUDE...THE WORST!
AND YOUR DAD SOUNDS LIKE HE'S GOT QUITE A TEMPER. WHAT'S THE DAMAGE? TEN-- ELEVEN?
EVEN DOZEN, BUD.
I THOUGHT AS MUCH. AND THE LION WAS YOUR FIRST-- IT PROTECTS AND EMPOWERS YOU?
SUPER COOL!
YEAH, SO I HEAR.
Heh!
AND WHAT ABOUT YOUR LITTLE BUDDY? HE GOT A NAME?
THAT, MY FRIEND, IS THE ONE, THE ONLY, JUMPIN' JOE PHAT!
HEY, JOE! WHAT'S THE WORD THIS WEEK?
WOLVERINE?
WHITE HARE?
MAKE IT... UMMMM...
HEY!
COYOTE!
WATCH OUT, KIRBY. HE'S A TRICKY ONE.

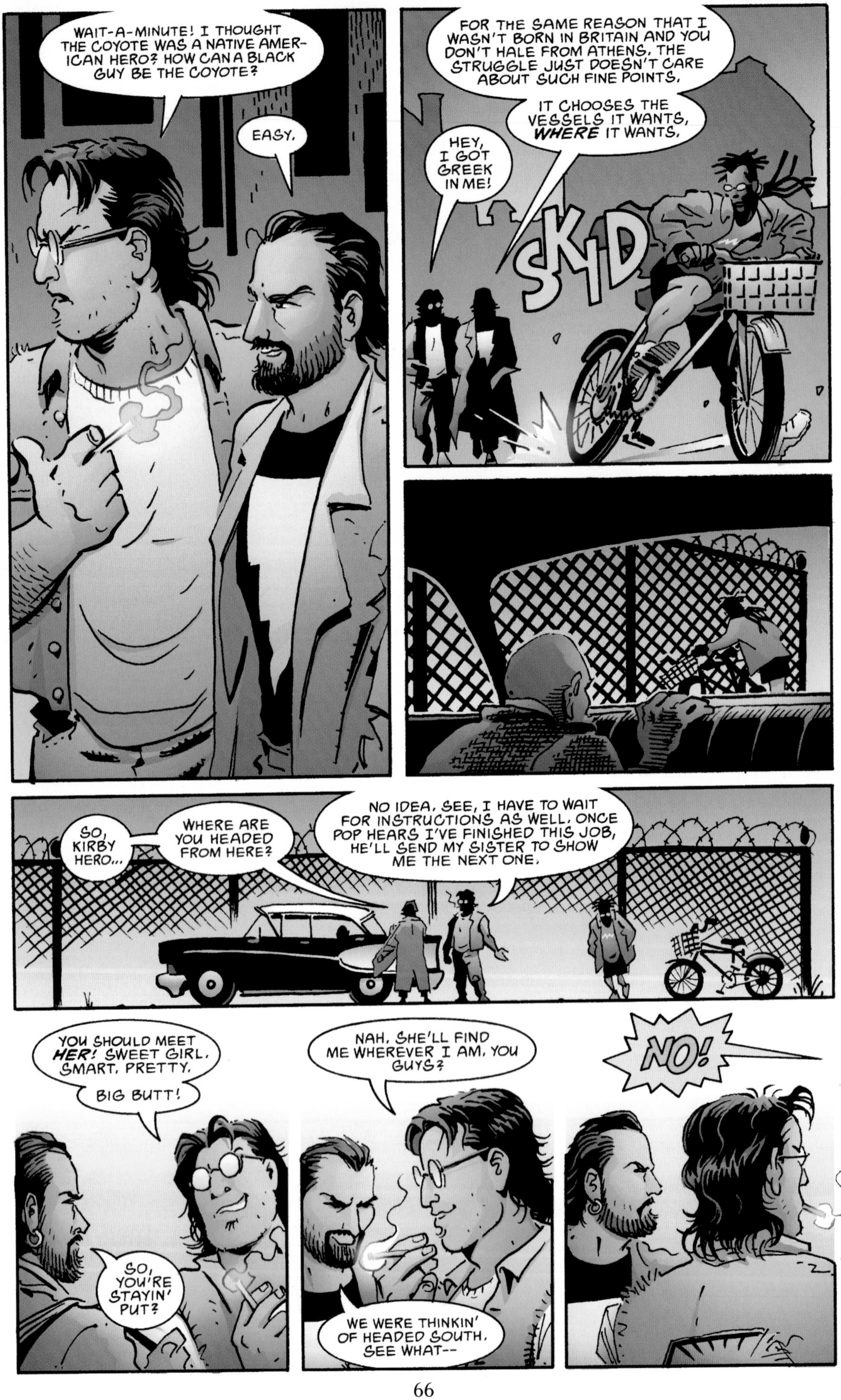
WAIT-A-MINUTE! I THOUGHT THE COYOTE WAS A NATIVE AMERICAN HERO? HOW CAN A BLACK GUY BE THE COYOTE?
EASY.
FOR THE SAME REASON THAT I WASN'T BORN IN BRITAIN AND YOU DON'T HALE FROM ATHENS, THE STRUGGLE JUST DOESN'T CARE ABOUT SUCH FINE POINTS.
IT CHOOSES THE VESSELS IT WANTS, *WHERE* IT WANTS.
HEY, I GOT GREEK IN ME!
SKYD
SO, KIRBY HERO...
WHERE ARE YOU HEADED FROM HERE?
NO IDEA. SEE, I HAVE TO WAIT FOR INSTRUCTIONS AS WELL. ONCE POP HEARS I'VE FINISHED THIS JOB, HE'LL SEND MY SISTER TO SHOW ME THE NEXT ONE.
YOU SHOULD MEET *HER!* SWEET GIRL. SMART. PRETTY.
BIG BUTT!
SO, YOU'RE STAYIN' PUT?
NAH, SHE'LL FIND ME WHEREVER I AM. YOU GUYS?
WE WERE THINKIN' OF HEADED SOUTH. SEE WHAT--
NO!

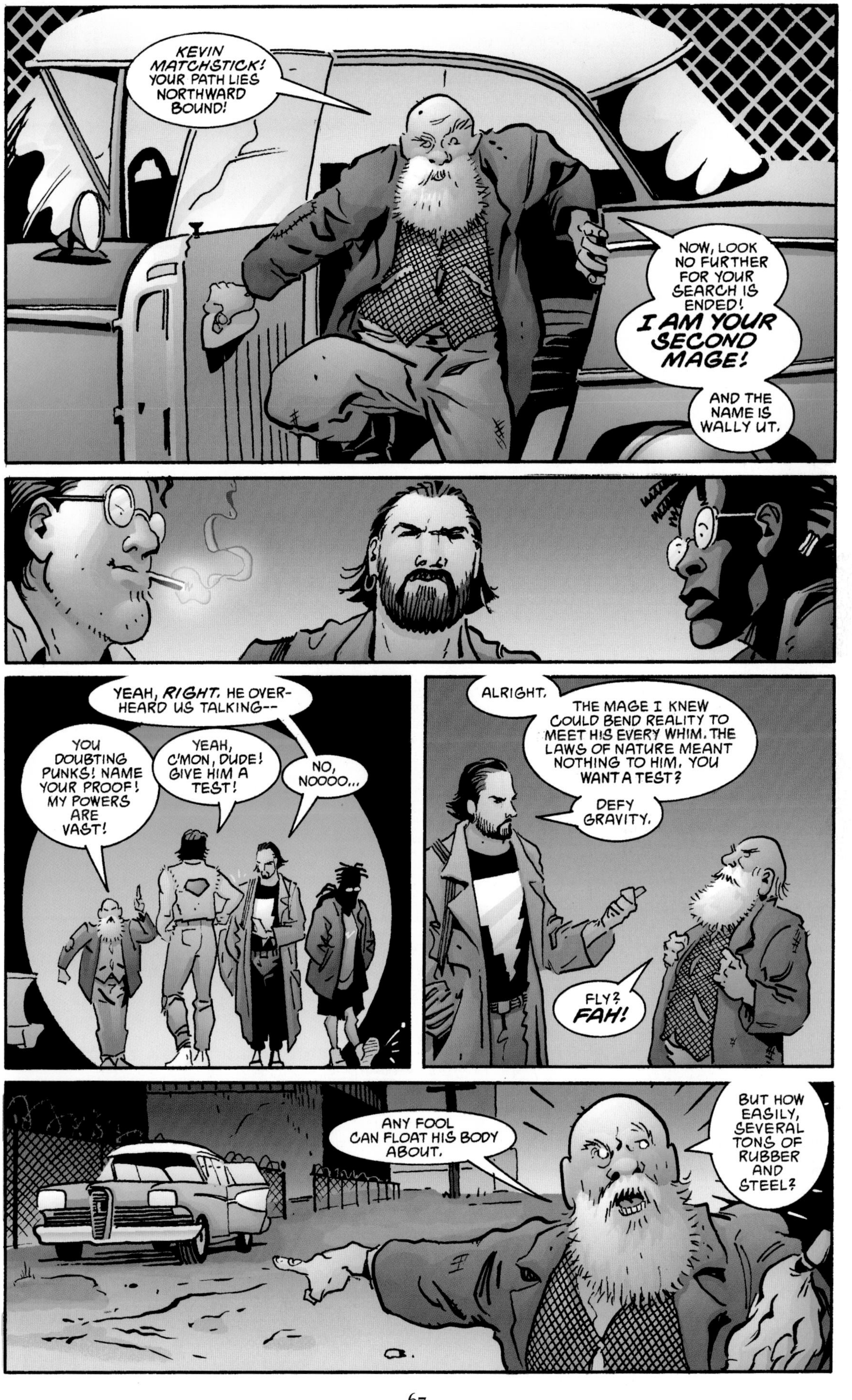
KEVIN MATCHSTICK! YOUR PATH LIES NORTHWARD BOUND!
NOW, LOOK NO FURTHER FOR YOUR SEARCH IS ENDED! I AM YOUR SECOND MAGE!
AND THE NAME IS WALLY UT.
YEAH, RIGHT. HE OVERHEARD US TALKING--
YOU DOUBTING PUNKS! NAME YOUR PROOF! MY POWERS ARE VAST!
YEAH, C'MON, DUDE! GIVE HIM A TEST!
NO, NOOOO...
ALRIGHT.
THE MAGE I KNEW COULD BEND REALITY TO MEET HIS EVERY WHIM. THE LAWS OF NATURE MEANT NOTHING TO HIM. YOU WANT A TEST?
DEFY GRAVITY.
FLY? FAH!
ANY FOOL CAN FLOAT HIS BODY ABOUT.
BUT HOW EASILY, SEVERAL TONS OF RUBBER AND STEEL?

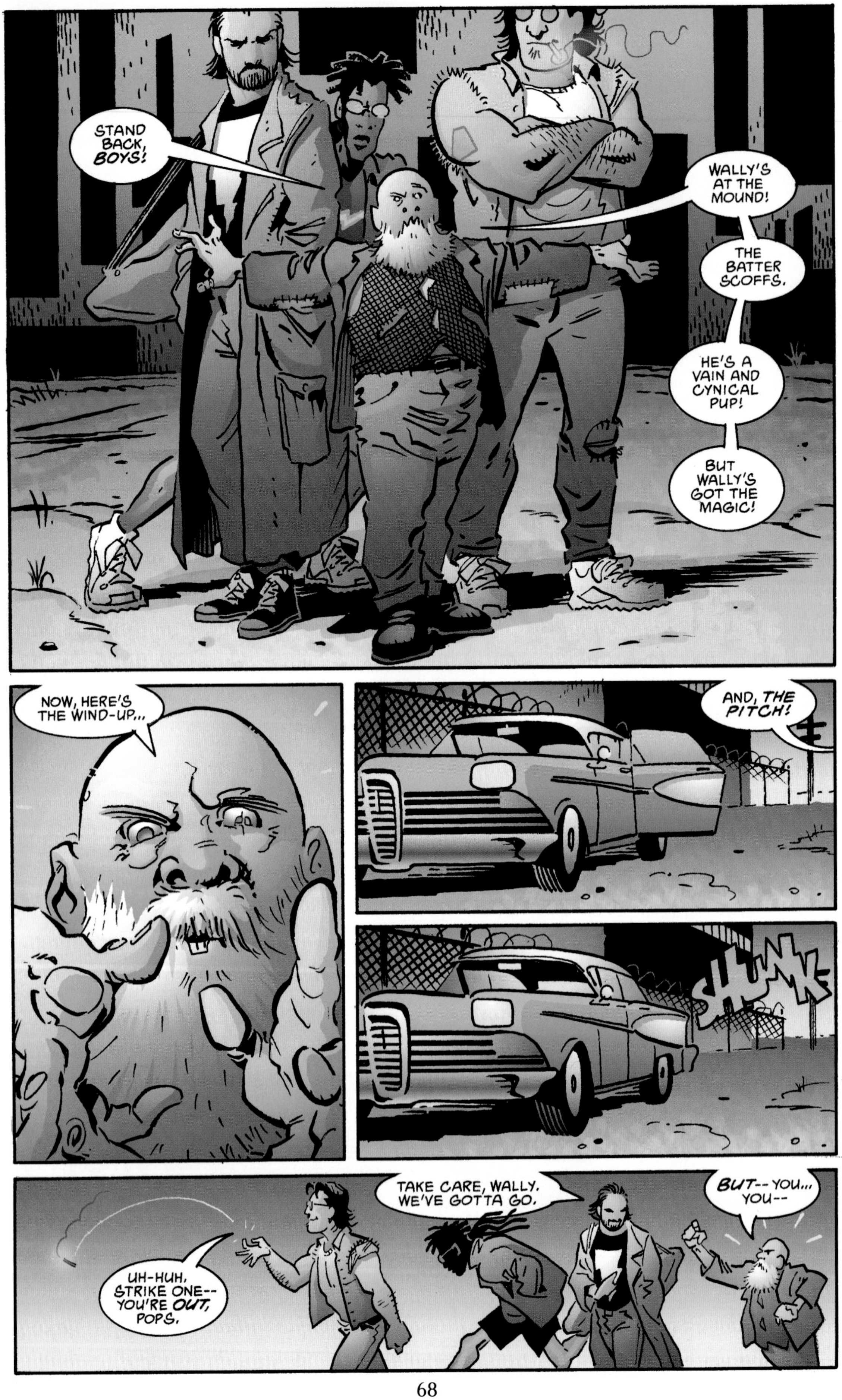
STAND BACK, BOYS!
WALLY'S AT THE MOUND!
THE BATTER SCOFFS.
HE'S A VAIN AND CYNICAL PUP!
BUT WALLY'S GOT THE MAGIC!
NOW, HERE'S THE WIND-UP...
AND, THE PITCH!
SHUNK
UH-HUH, STRIKE ONE-- YOU'RE OUT, POPS.
TAKE CARE, WALLY. WE'VE GOTTA GO.
BUT-- YOU... YOU--

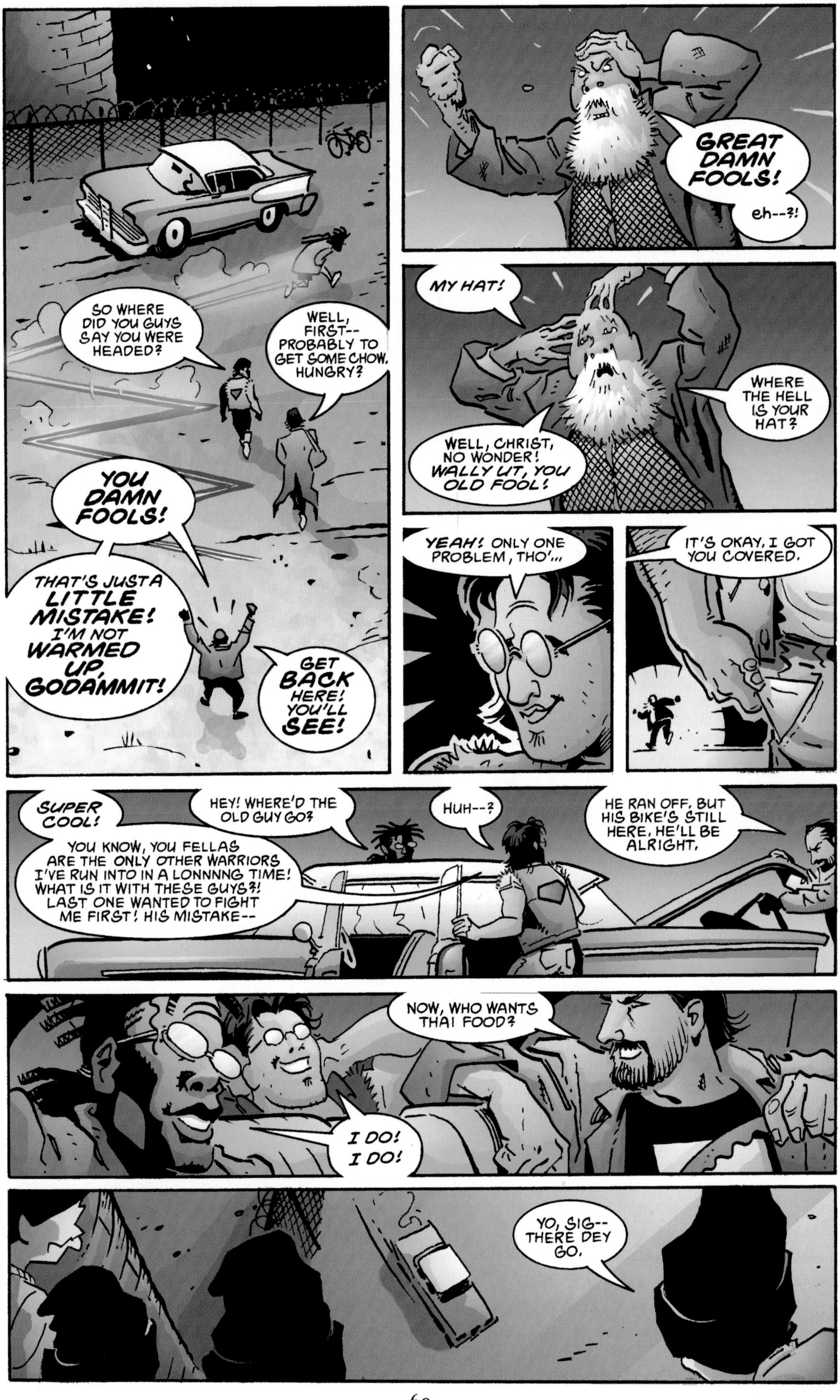
SO WHERE DID YOU GUYS SAY YOU WERE HEADED?
WELL, FIRST-- PROBABLY TO GET SOME CHOW. HUNGRY?
YOU DAMN FOOLS!
THAT'S JUST A LITTLE MISTAKE! I'M NOT WARMED UP, GODAMMIT!
GET BACK HERE! YOU'LL SEE!
GREAT DAMN FOOLS!
eh--?!
MY HAT!
WHERE THE HELL IS YOUR HAT?
WELL, CHRIST, NO WONDER! WALLY UT, YOU OLD FOOL!
YEAH! ONLY ONE PROBLEM, THO'...
IT'S OKAY, I GOT YOU COVERED.
SUPER COOL!
YOU KNOW, YOU FELLAS ARE THE ONLY OTHER WARRIORS I'VE RUN INTO IN A LONNNNG TIME! WHAT IS IT WITH THESE GUYS?! LAST ONE WANTED TO FIGHT ME FIRST! HIS MISTAKE--
HEY! WHERE'D THE OLD GUY GO?
HUH--?
HE RAN OFF, BUT HIS BIKE'S STILL HERE. HE'LL BE ALRIGHT.
NOW, WHO WANTS THAI FOOD?
I DO! I DO!
YO, SIG-- THERE DEY GO.

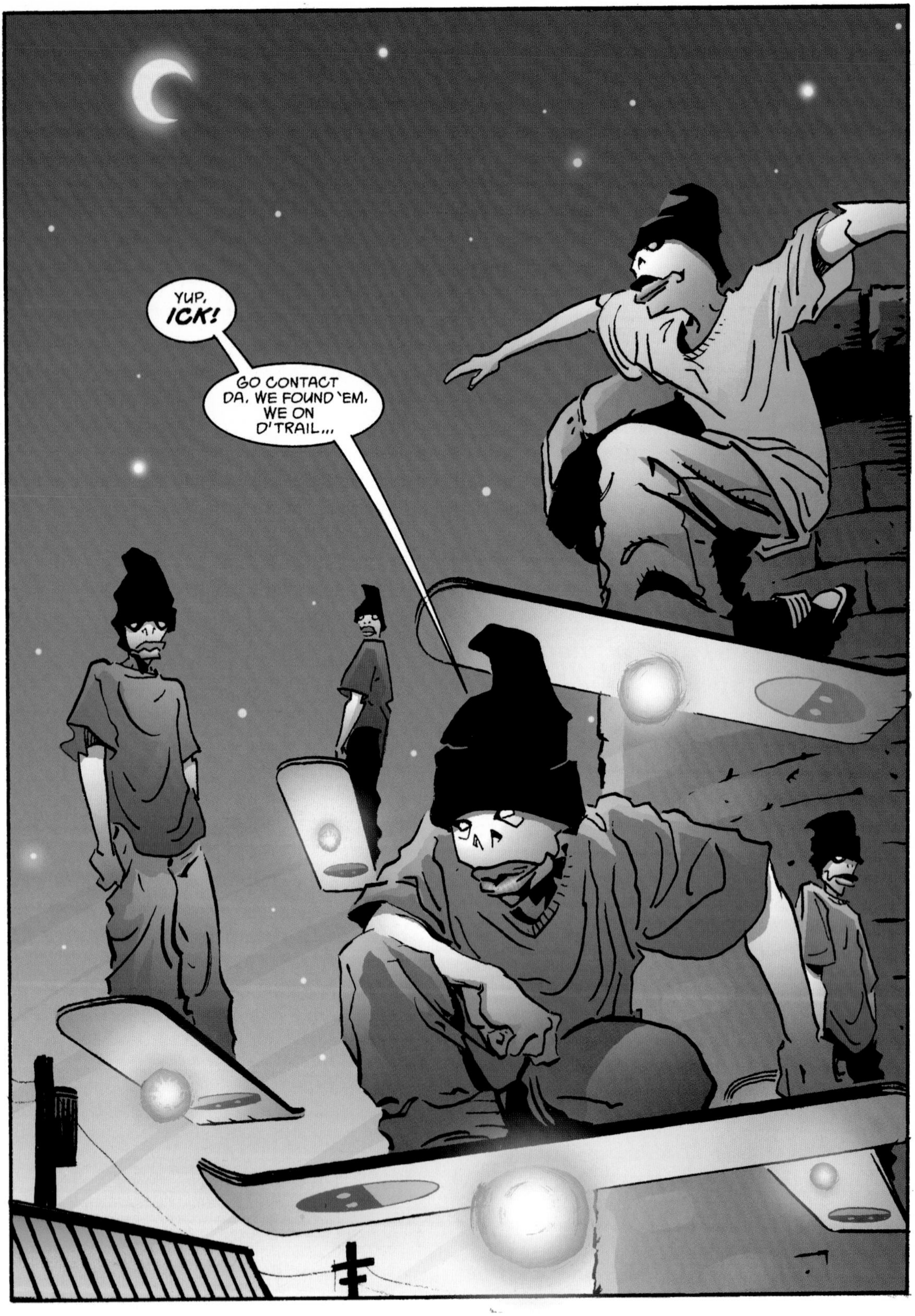
YUP, ICK!
GO CONTACT DA. WE FOUND 'EM. WE ON D'TRAIL...

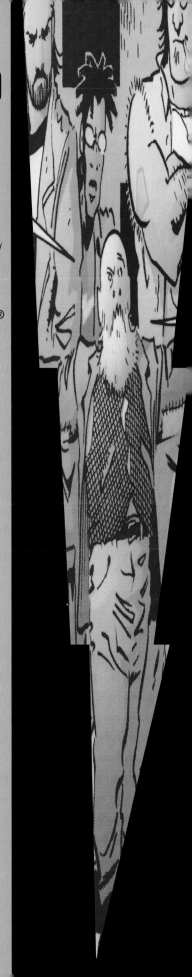

THE HERO DEFINED

MAGE

®

chapter

3

"Two Truths
Are Told"

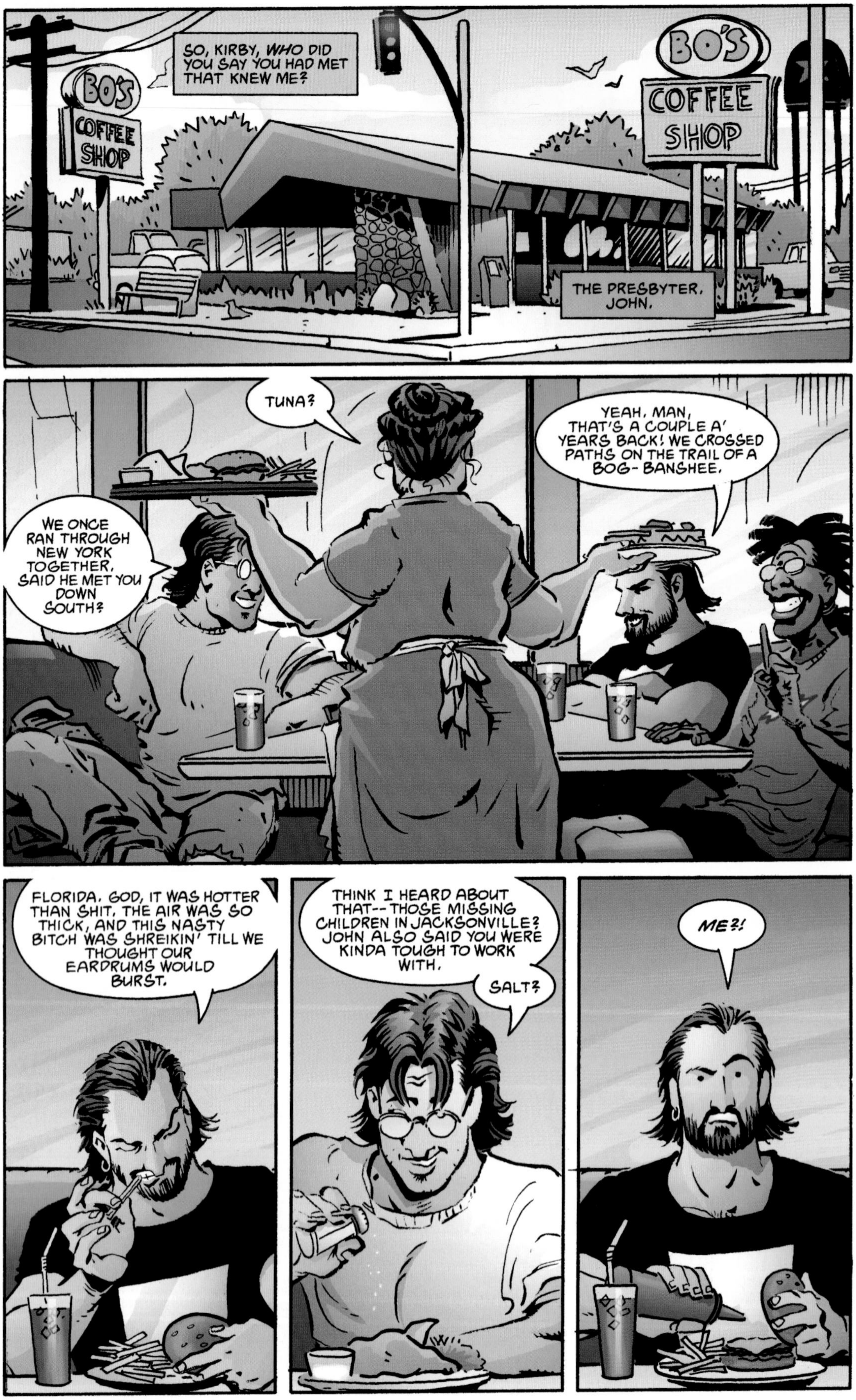
SO, KIRBY, WHO DID YOU SAY YOU HAD MET THAT KNEW ME?
BO'S
COFFEE SHOP
BO'S
COFFEE SHOP
THE PRESBYTER. JOHN.
TUNA?
YEAH, MAN, THAT'S A COUPLE A' YEARS BACK! WE CROSSED PATHS ON THE TRAIL OF A BOG-BANSHEE.
WE ONCE RAN THROUGH NEW YORK TOGETHER. SAID HE MET YOU DOWN SOUTH?
FLORIDA. GOD, IT WAS HOTTER THAN SHIT. THE AIR WAS SO THICK, AND THIS NASTY BITCH WAS SHREIKIN' TILL WE THOUGHT OUR EARDRUMS WOULD BURST.
THINK I HEARD ABOUT THAT-- THOSE MISSING CHILDREN IN JACKSONVILLE? JOHN ALSO SAID YOU WERE KINDA TOUGH TO WORK WITH.
SALT?
ME?!

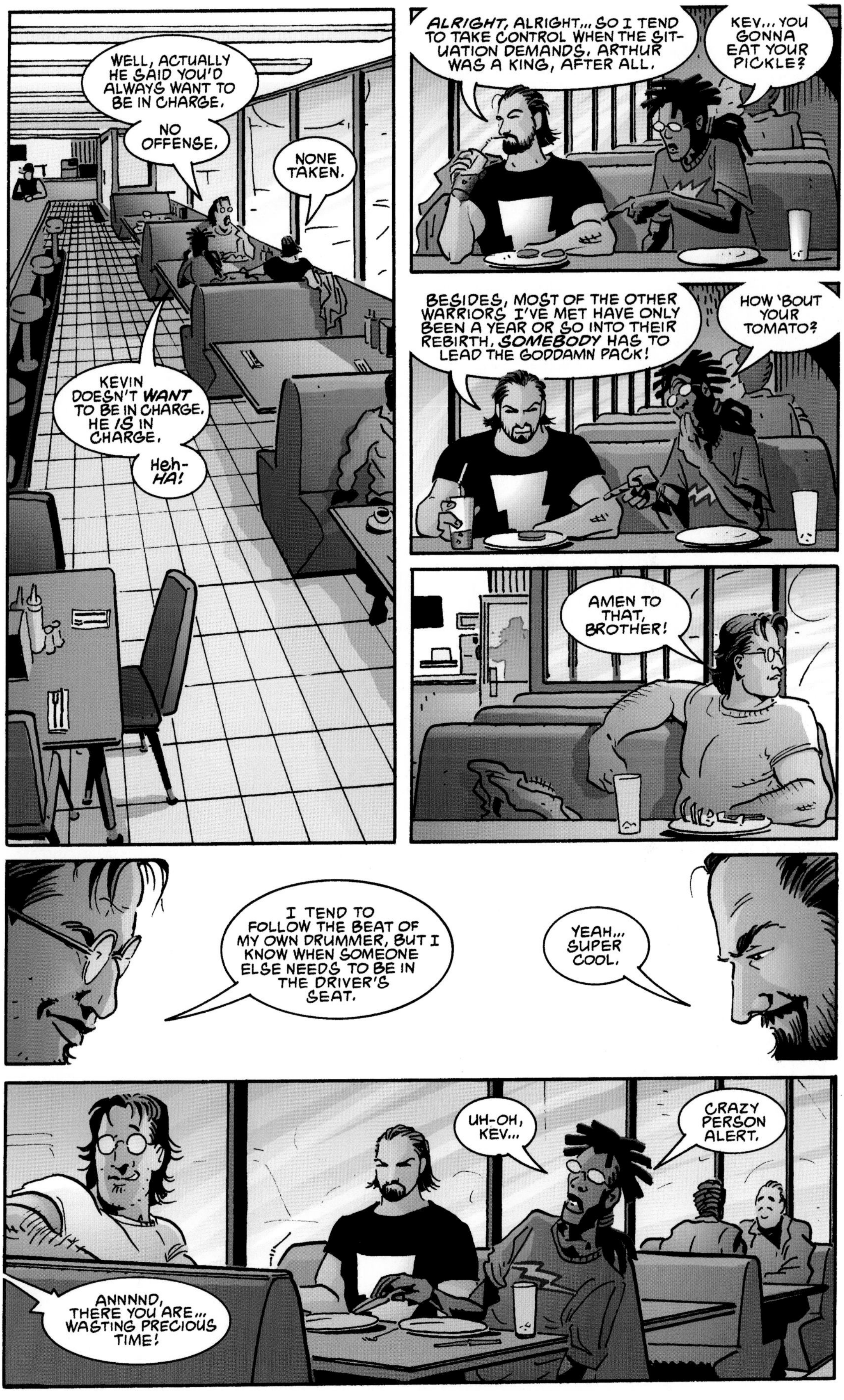
WELL, ACTUALLY HE SAID YOU'D ALWAYS WANT TO BE IN CHARGE.
NO OFFENSE.
NONE TAKEN.
KEVIN DOESN'T WANT TO BE IN CHARGE. HE IS IN CHARGE.
Heh-HA!
ALRIGHT, ALRIGHT... SO I TEND TO TAKE CONTROL WHEN THE SIT-UATION DEMANDS. ARTHUR WAS A KING, AFTER ALL.
KEV... YOU GONNA EAT YOUR PICKLE?
BESIDES, MOST OF THE OTHER WARRIORS I'VE MET HAVE ONLY BEEN A YEAR OR SO INTO THEIR REBIRTH. SOMEBODY HAS TO LEAD THE GODDAMN PACK!
HOW 'BOUT YOUR TOMATO?
AMEN TO THAT, BROTHER!
I TEND TO FOLLOW THE BEAT OF MY OWN DRUMMER, BUT I KNOW WHEN SOMEONE ELSE NEEDS TO BE IN THE DRIVER'S SEAT.
YEAH... SUPER COOL.
ANNNND, THERE YOU ARE... WASTING PRECIOUS TIME!
UH-OH, KEV...
CRAZY PERSON ALERT.

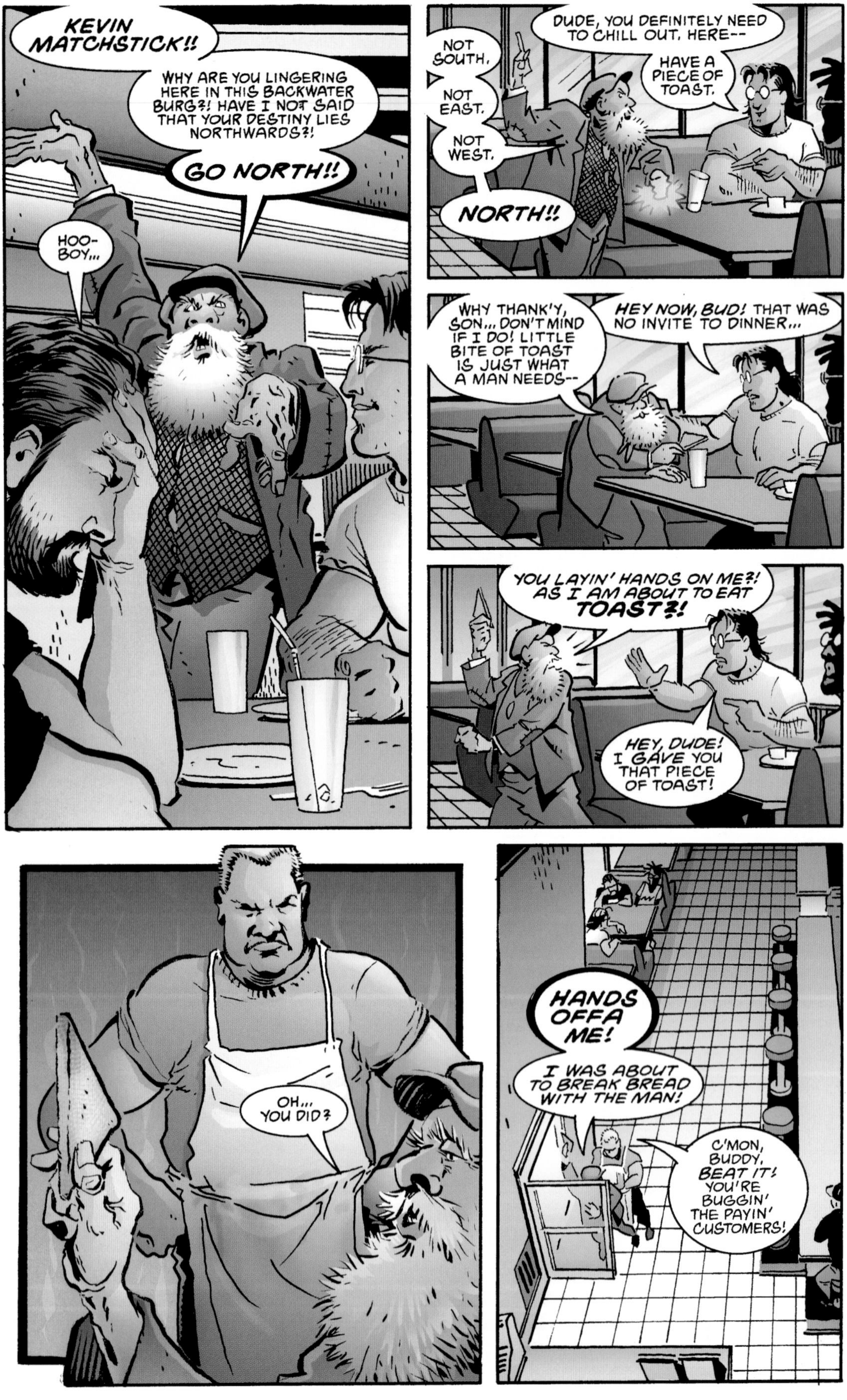
KEVIN MATCHSTICK!!
WHY ARE YOU LINGERING HERE IN THIS BACKWATER BURG?! HAVE I NOT SAID THAT YOUR DESTINY LIES NORTHWARDS?!
GO NORTH!!
HOO-BOY...
NOT SOUTH.
NOT EAST.
NOT WEST.
NORTH!!
DUDE, YOU DEFINITELY NEED TO CHILL OUT. HERE--
HAVE A PIECE OF TOAST.
WHY THANK'Y, SON... DON'T MIND IF I DO! LITTLE BITE OF TOAST IS JUST WHAT A MAN NEEDS--
HEY NOW, BUD! THAT WAS NO INVITE TO DINNER...
YOU LAYIN' HANDS ON ME?! AS I AM ABOUT TO EAT TOAST?!
HEY, DUDE! I GAVE YOU THAT PIECE OF TOAST!
OH... YOU DID?
HANDS OFFA ME!
I WAS ABOUT TO BREAK BREAD WITH THE MAN!
C'MON, BUDDY, BEAT IT! YOU'RE BUGGIN' THE PAYIN' CUSTOMERS!

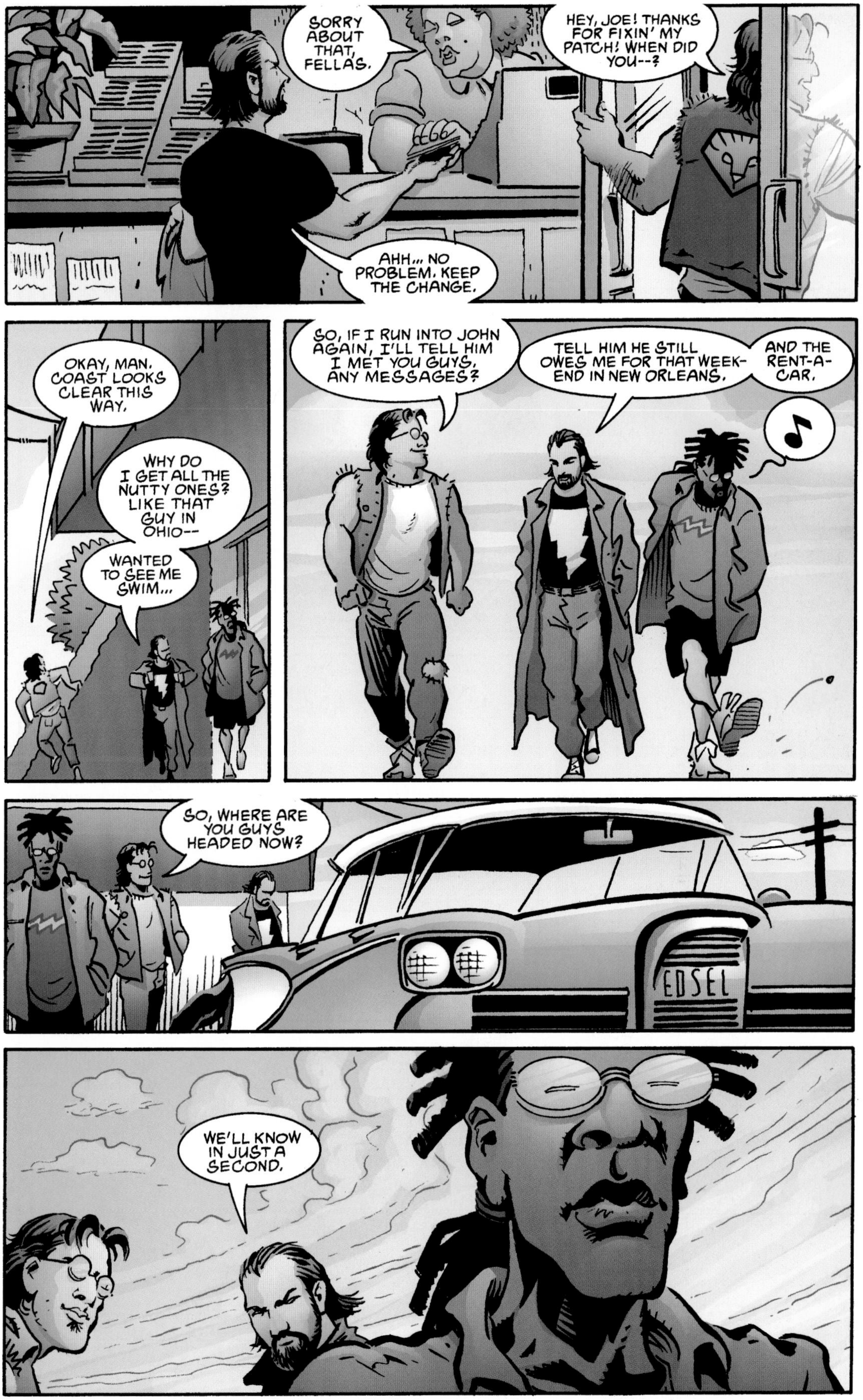
SORRY ABOUT THAT, FELLAS.
HEY, JOE! THANKS FOR FIXIN' MY PATCH! WHEN DID YOU--?
AHH... NO PROBLEM. KEEP THE CHANGE.
OKAY, MAN. COAST LOOKS CLEAR THIS WAY.
WHY DO I GET ALL THE NUTTY ONES? LIKE THAT GUY IN OHIO--
WANTED TO SEE ME SWIM...
SO, IF I RUN INTO JOHN AGAIN, I'LL TELL HIM I MET YOU GUYS. ANY MESSAGES?
TELL HIM HE STILL OWES ME FOR THAT WEEK-END IN NEW ORLEANS.
AND THE RENT-A-CAR.
♪
SO, WHERE ARE YOU GUYS HEADED NOW?
EDSEL
WE'LL KNOW IN JUST A SECOND.

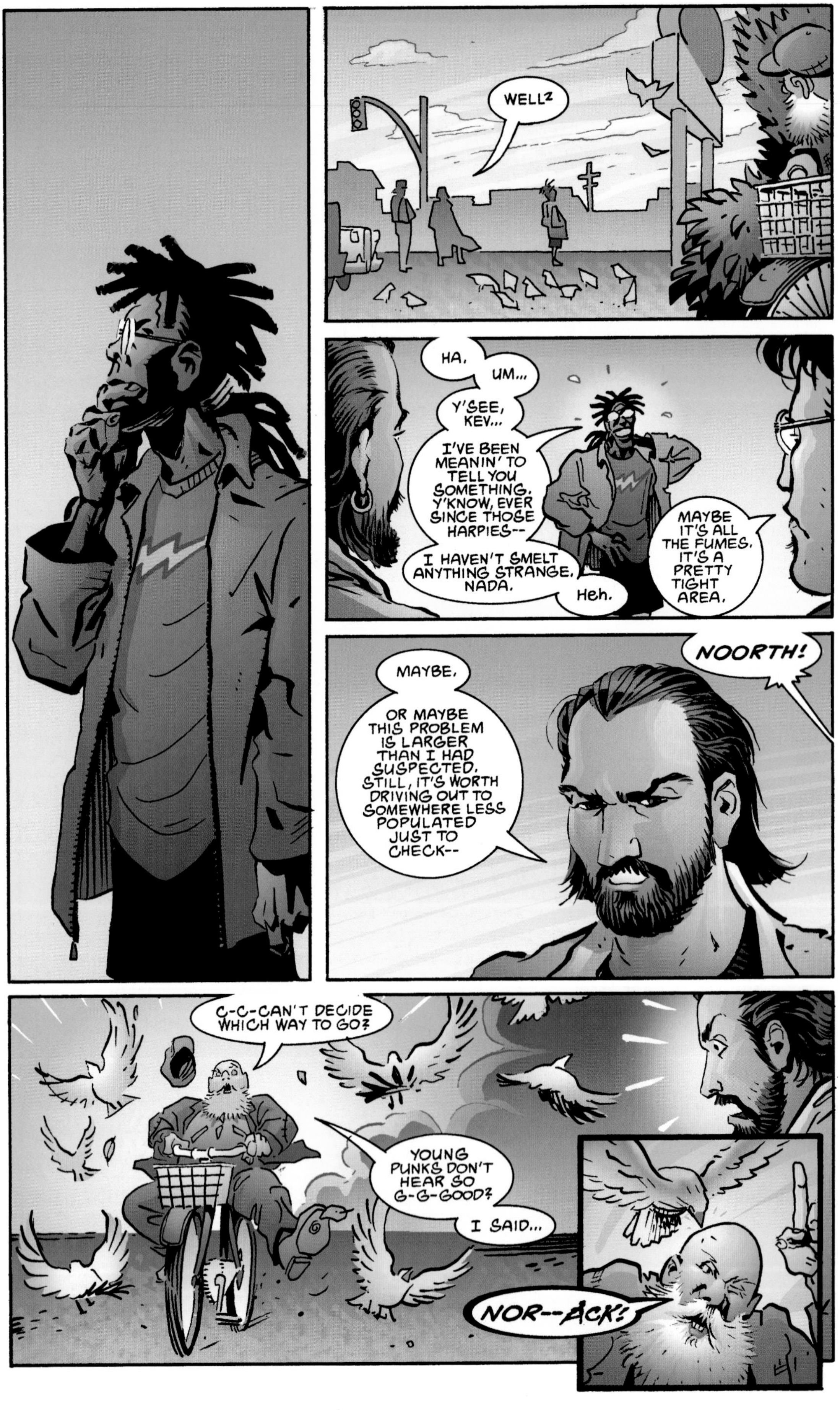
WELL?
HA.
UM...
Y'SEE, KEV...
I'VE BEEN MEANIN' TO TELL YOU SOMETHING. Y'KNOW, EVER SINCE THOSE HARPIES--
I HAVEN'T SMELT ANYTHING STRANGE. NADA.
Heh.
MAYBE IT'S ALL THE FUMES. IT'S A PRETTY TIGHT AREA.
MAYBE.
OR MAYBE THIS PROBLEM IS LARGER THAN I HAD SUSPECTED. STILL, IT'S WORTH DRIVING OUT TO SOMEWHERE LESS POPULATED JUST TO CHECK--
NOORTH!
C-C-CAN'T DECIDE WHICH WAY TO GO?
YOUNG PUNKS DON'T HEAR SO G-G-GOOD?
I SAID...
NOR--ACK!

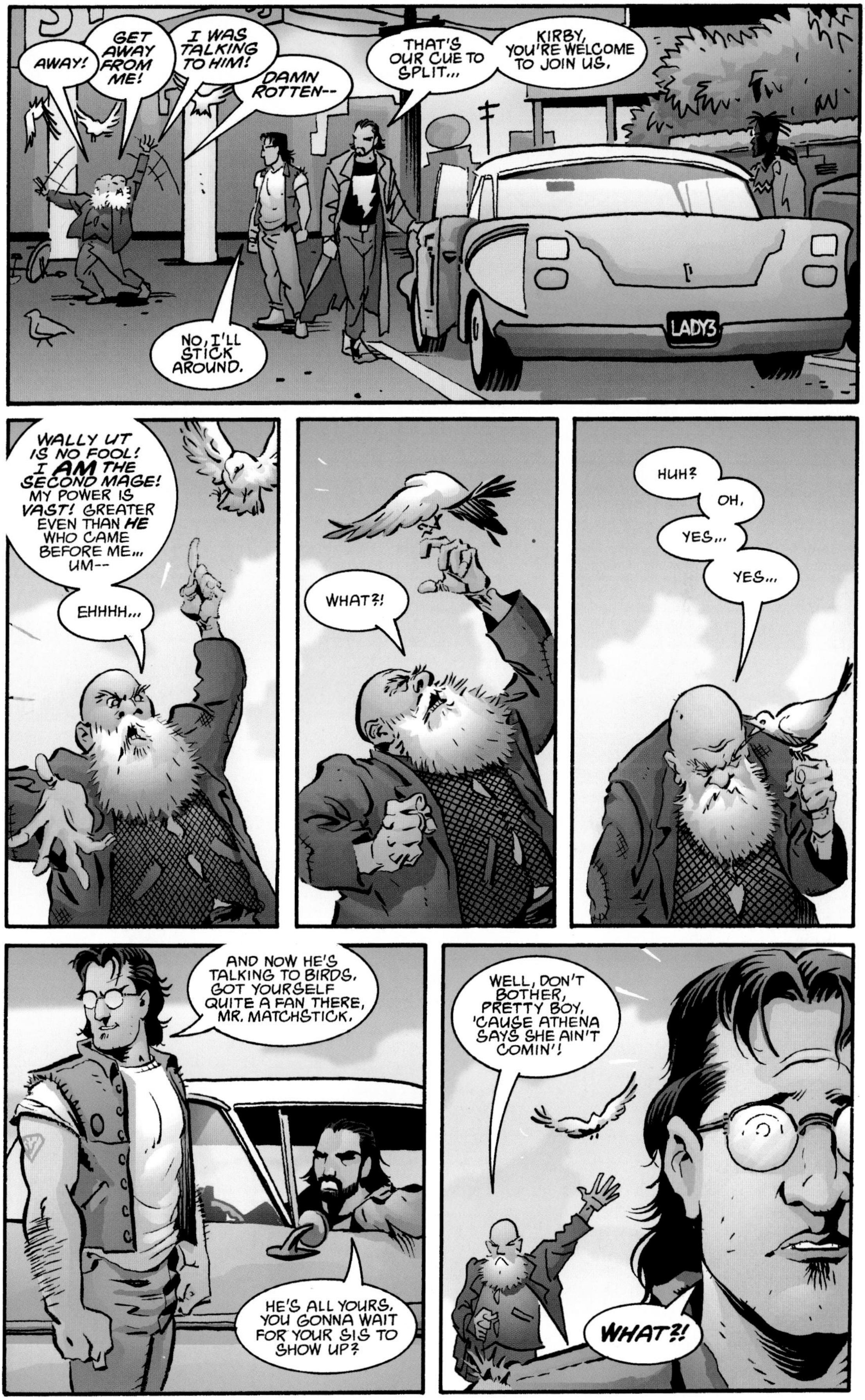
AWAY!
GET AWAY FROM ME!
I WAS TALKING TO HIM!
DAMN ROTTEN--
THAT'S OUR CUE TO SPLIT...
KIRBY, YOU'RE WELCOME TO JOIN US.
NO, I'LL STICK AROUND.
LADY3
WALLY UT IS NO FOOL! I AM THE SECOND MAGE! MY POWER IS VAST! GREATER EVEN THAN HE WHO CAME BEFORE ME... UM--
EHHHH...
WHAT?!
HUH?
OH,
YES...
YES...
AND NOW HE'S TALKING TO BIRDS. GOT YOURSELF QUITE A FAN THERE, MR. MATCHSTICK.
HE'S ALL YOURS. YOU GONNA WAIT FOR YOUR SIS TO SHOW UP?
WELL, DON'T BOTHER, PRETTY BOY, 'CAUSE ATHENA SAYS SHE AIN'T COMIN'!
WHAT?!

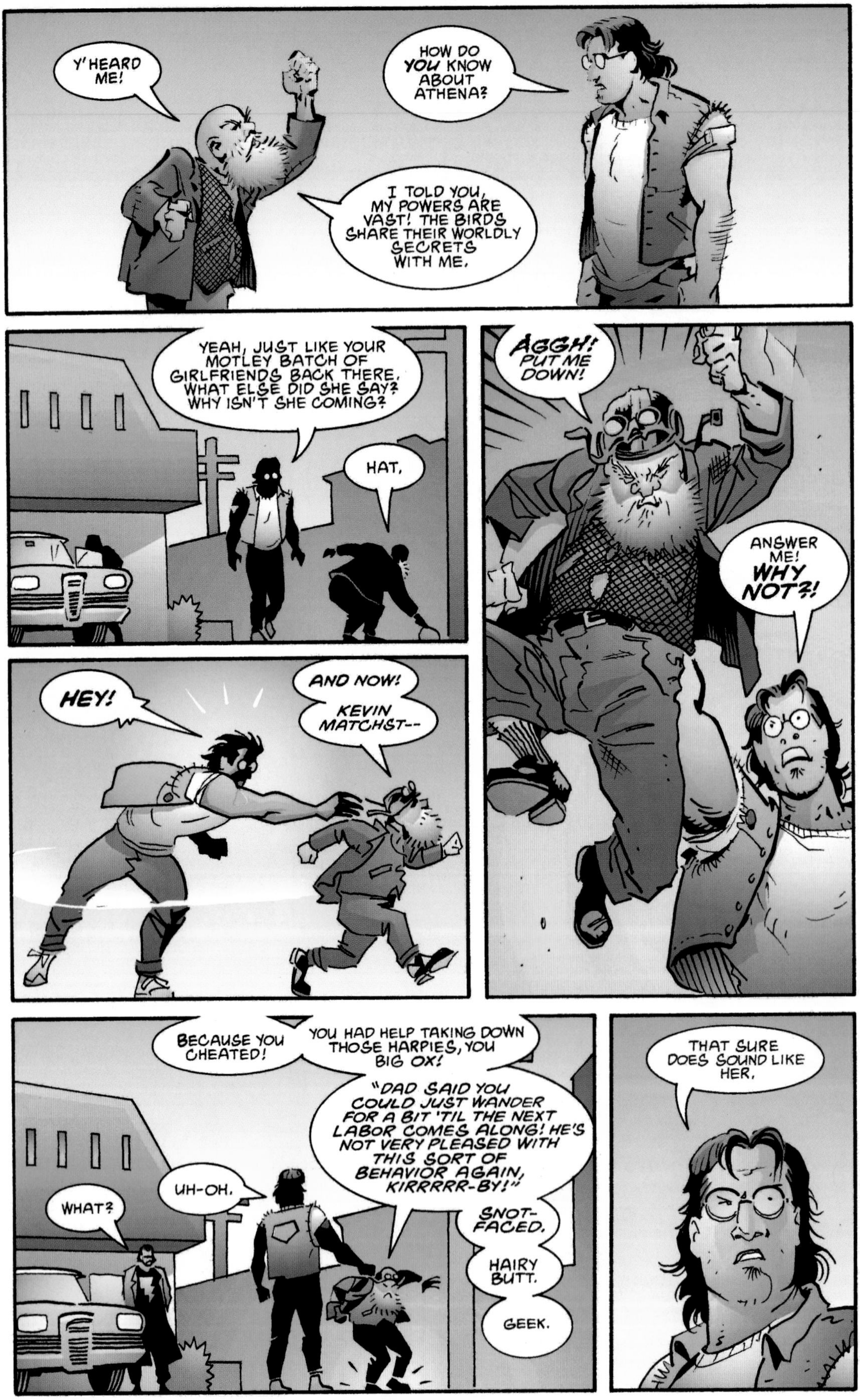
Y'HEARD ME!
HOW DO YOU KNOW ABOUT ATHENA?
I TOLD YOU, MY POWERS ARE VAST! THE BIRDS SHARE THEIR WORLDLY SECRETS WITH ME.
YEAH, JUST LIKE YOUR MOTLEY BATCH OF GIRLFRIENDS BACK THERE. WHAT ELSE DID SHE SAY? WHY ISN'T SHE COMING?
HAT.
AGGH! PUT ME DOWN!
ANSWER ME! WHY NOT?!
HEY!
AND NOW!
KEVIN MATCHST--
BECAUSE YOU CHEATED!
YOU HAD HELP TAKING DOWN THOSE HARPIES, YOU BIG OX!
"DAD SAID YOU COULD JUST WANDER FOR A BIT 'TIL THE NEXT LABOR COMES ALONG! HE'S NOT VERY PLEASED WITH THIS SORT OF BEHAVIOR AGAIN, KIRRRRR-BY!"
SNOT-FACED.
HAIRY BUTT.
GEEK.
WHAT?
UH-OH.
THAT SURE DOES SOUND LIKE HER.

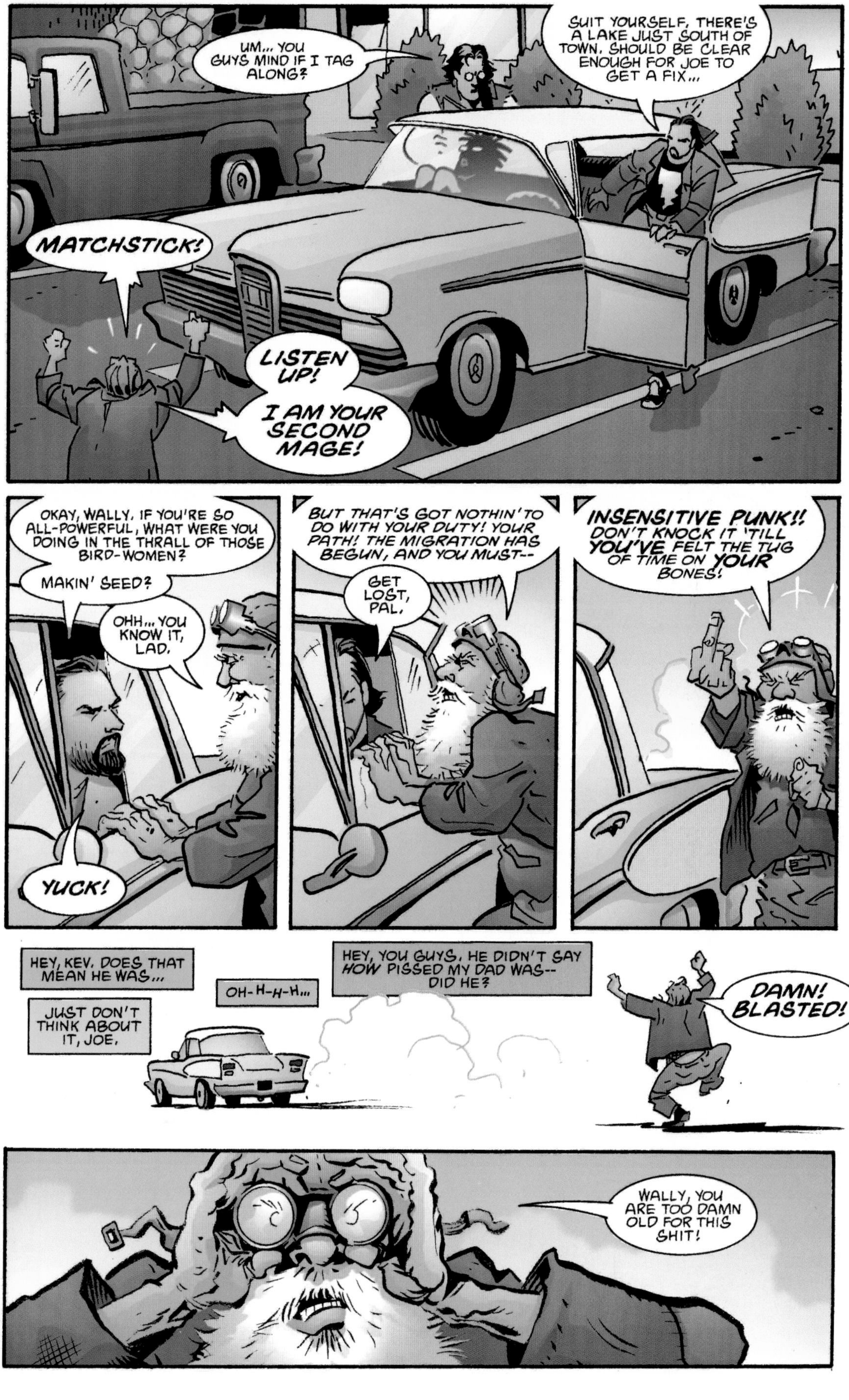
UM... YOU GUYS MIND IF I TAG ALONG?
SUIT YOURSELF, THERE'S A LAKE JUST SOUTH OF TOWN, SHOULD BE CLEAR ENOUGH FOR JOE TO GET A FIX...
MATCHSTICK!
LISTEN UP!
I AM YOUR SECOND MAGE!
OKAY, WALLY, IF YOU'RE SO ALL-POWERFUL, WHAT WERE YOU DOING IN THE THRALL OF THOSE BIRD-WOMEN?
MAKIN' SEED?
OHH... YOU KNOW IT, LAD.
YUCK!
BUT THAT'S GOT NOTHIN' TO DO WITH YOUR DUTY! YOUR PATH! THE MIGRATION HAS BEGUN, AND YOU MUST--
GET LOST, PAL.
INSENSITIVE PUNK!! DON'T KNOCK IT 'TILL YOU'VE FELT THE TUG OF TIME ON YOUR BONES!
HEY, KEV. DOES THAT MEAN HE WAS...
JUST DON'T THINK ABOUT IT, JOE.
OH-H-H-H...
HEY, YOU GUYS. HE DIDN'T SAY HOW PISSED MY DAD WAS--DID HE?
DAMN! BLASTED!
WALLY, YOU ARE TOO DAMN OLD FOR THIS SHIT!

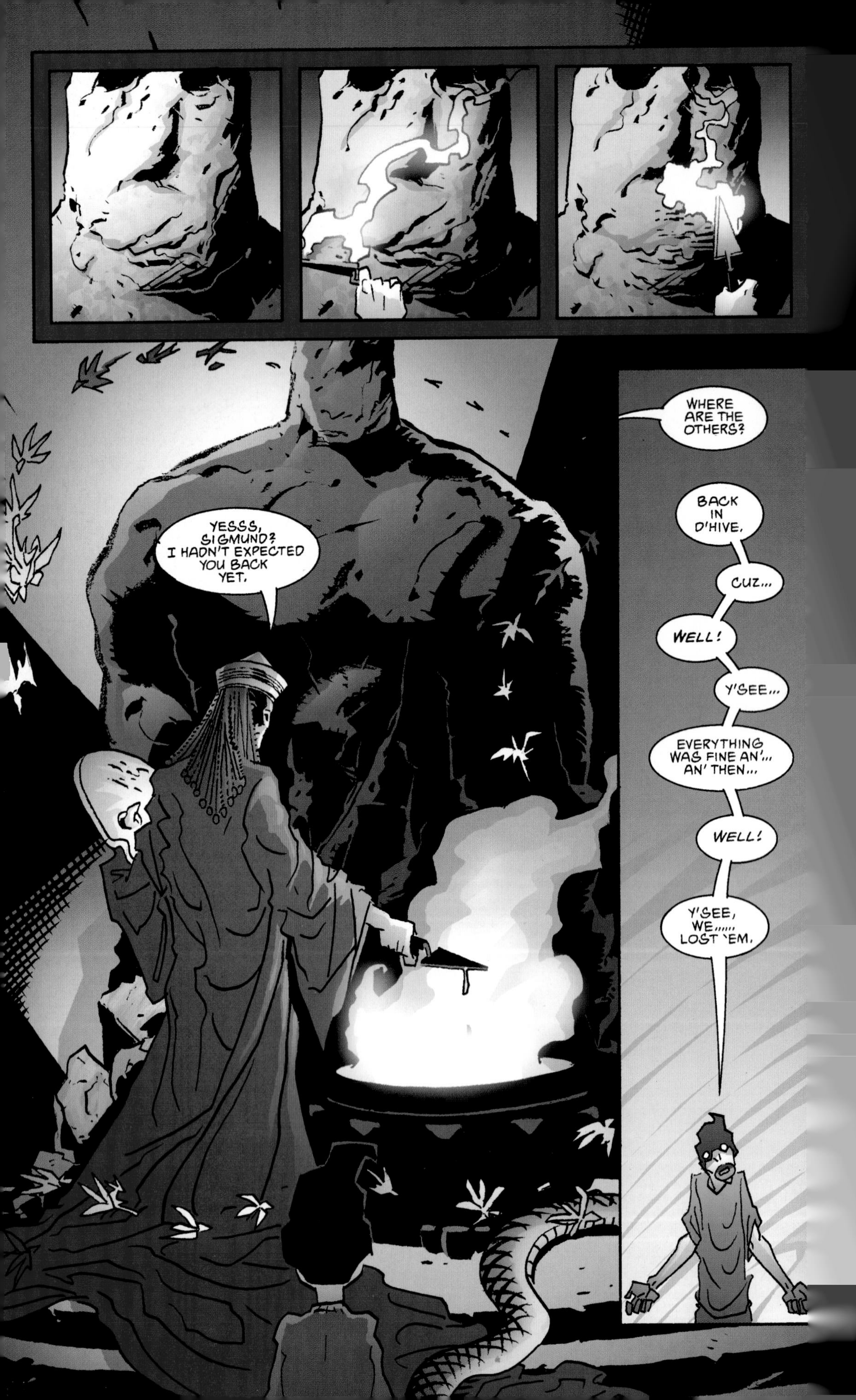
YESSS, SIGMUND? I HADN'T EXPECTED YOU BACK YET.
WHERE ARE THE OTHERS?
BACK IN D'HIVE.
CUZ...
WELL!
Y'SEE...
EVERYTHING WAS FINE AN'... AN' THEN...
WELL!
Y'SEE, WE...... LOST 'EM.

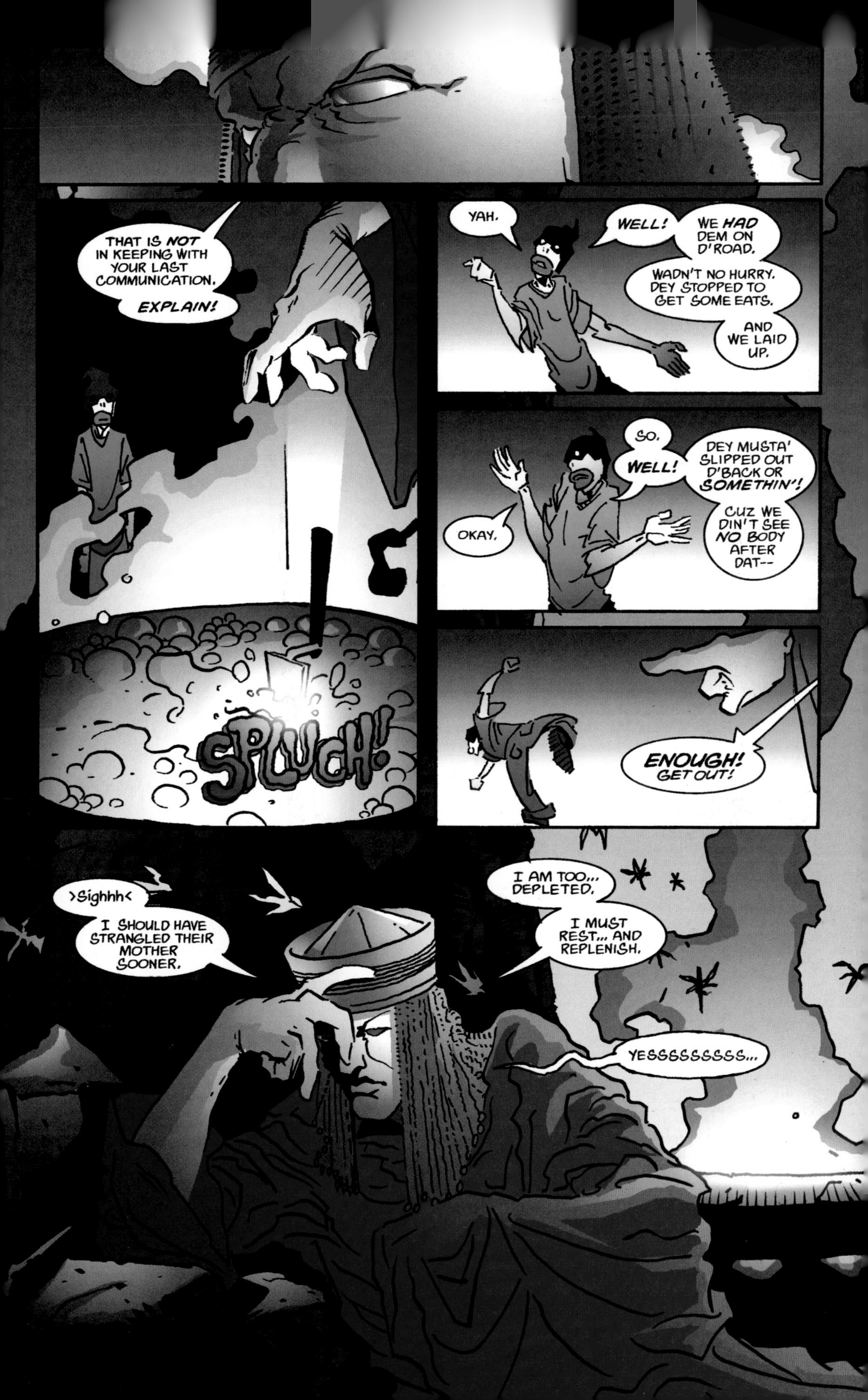
THAT IS NOT IN KEEPING WITH YOUR LAST COMMUNICATION.
EXPLAIN!
YAH.
WELL!
WE HAD DEM ON D'ROAD.
WADN'T NO HURRY. DEY STOPPED TO GET SOME EATS.
AND WE LAID UP.
SO,
WELL!
DEY MUSTA' SLIPPED OUT D'BACK OR SOMETHIN'!
OKAY.
CUZ WE DIN'T SEE NO BODY AFTER DAT--
SPLUCH!
ENOUGH! GET OUT!
>Sighhh<
I SHOULD HAVE STRANGLED THEIR MOTHER SOONER.
I AM TOO... DEPLETED.
I MUST REST... AND REPLENISH.
YESSSSSSSSS...

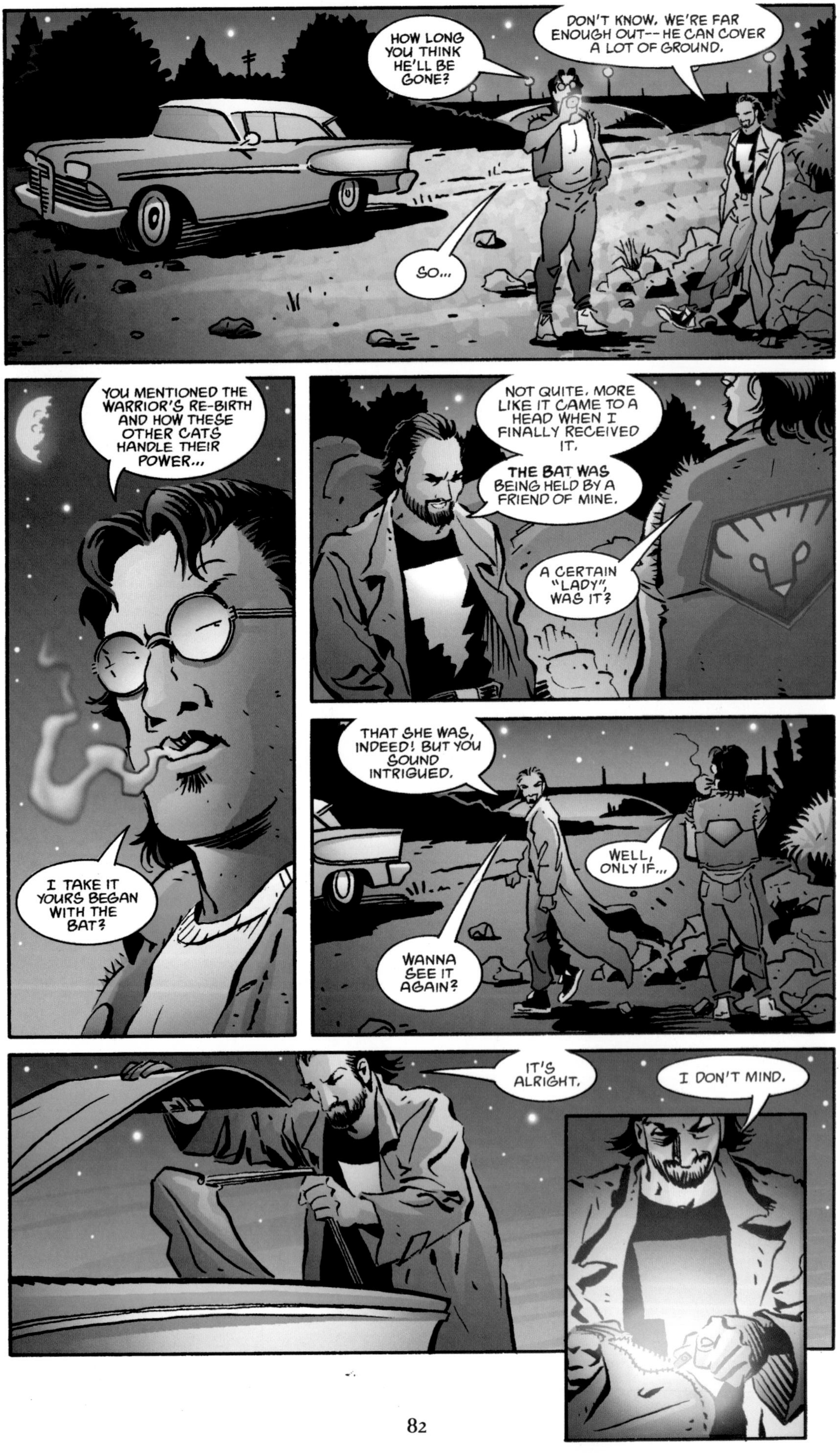
HOW LONG YOU THINK HE'LL BE GONE?
DON'T KNOW. WE'RE FAR ENOUGH OUT-- HE CAN COVER A LOT OF GROUND.
SO...
YOU MENTIONED THE WARRIOR'S RE-BIRTH AND HOW THESE OTHER CATS HANDLE THEIR POWER...
I TAKE IT YOURS BEGAN WITH THE BAT?
NOT QUITE. MORE LIKE IT CAME TO A HEAD WHEN I FINALLY RECEIVED IT.
THE BAT WAS BEING HELD BY A FRIEND OF MINE.
A CERTAIN "LADY", WAS IT?
THAT SHE WAS, INDEED! BUT YOU SOUND INTRIGUED.
WELL, ONLY IF...
WANNA SEE IT AGAIN?
IT'S ALRIGHT.
I DON'T MIND.

WELL, AS YOU'VE ALREADY SEEN, IT'LL RETURN TO MY HAND WHEN THROWN.

AND SO LONG AS I'M IN IT'S GENERAL VICINITY, I'M FAIRLY RESISTANT TO HARM. MORE SO, IF IT'S IN-HAND.

NORMALLY, I'M RIGHT-HANDED BUT-- WITH THE BAT -- MY AIM AND DEXTERITY ARE FLAWLESS.

MY BALANCE AND AGILITY, PRECISE.

NOW...

GET A LOAD OF *THIS* ONE.

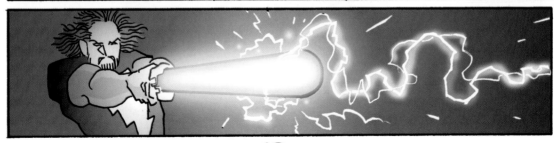

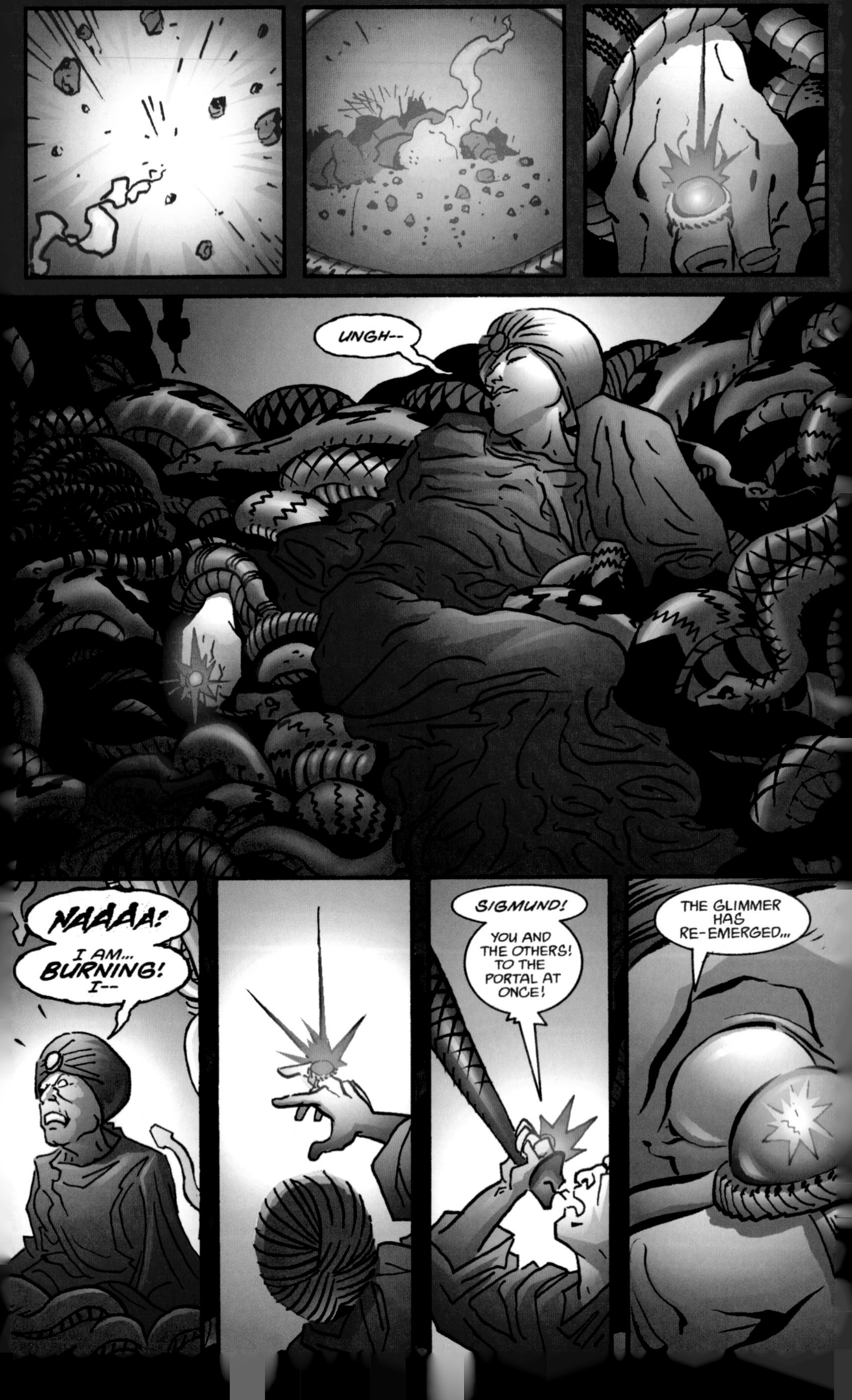
UNGH--
NAAAA!
I AM... BURNING! I--
SIGMUND!
YOU AND THE OTHERS! TO THE PORTAL AT ONCE!
THE GLIMMER HAS RE-EMERGED...

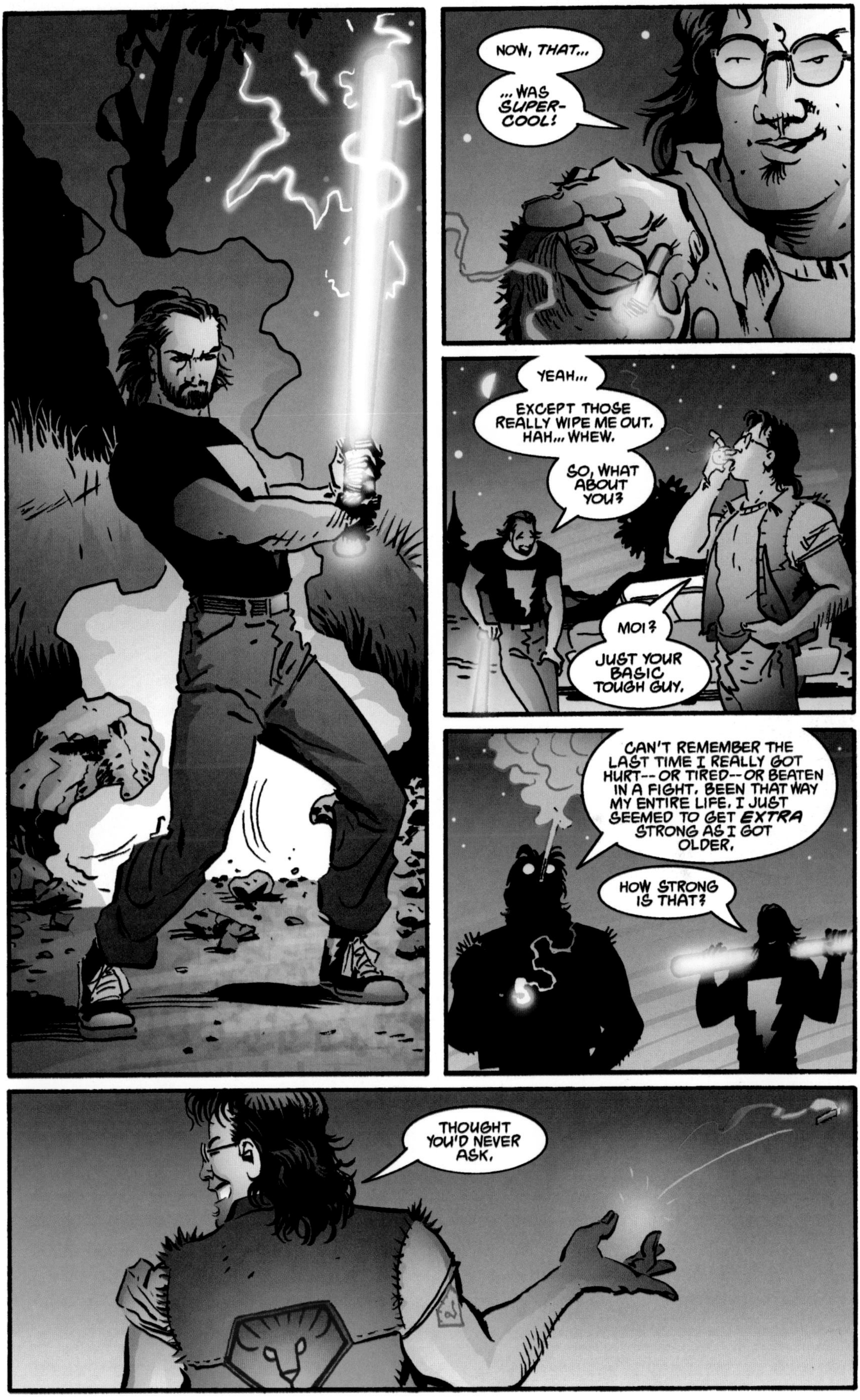
NOW, THAT...
...WAS SUPER-COOL!
YEAH...
EXCEPT THOSE REALLY WIPE ME OUT. HAH... WHEW.
SO, WHAT ABOUT YOU?
MOI?
JUST YOUR BASIC TOUGH GUY.
CAN'T REMEMBER THE LAST TIME I REALLY GOT HURT-- OR TIRED-- OR BEATEN IN A FIGHT. BEEN THAT WAY MY ENTIRE LIFE. I JUST SEEMED TO GET EXTRA STRONG AS I GOT OLDER.
HOW STRONG IS THAT?
THOUGHT YOU'D NEVER ASK.

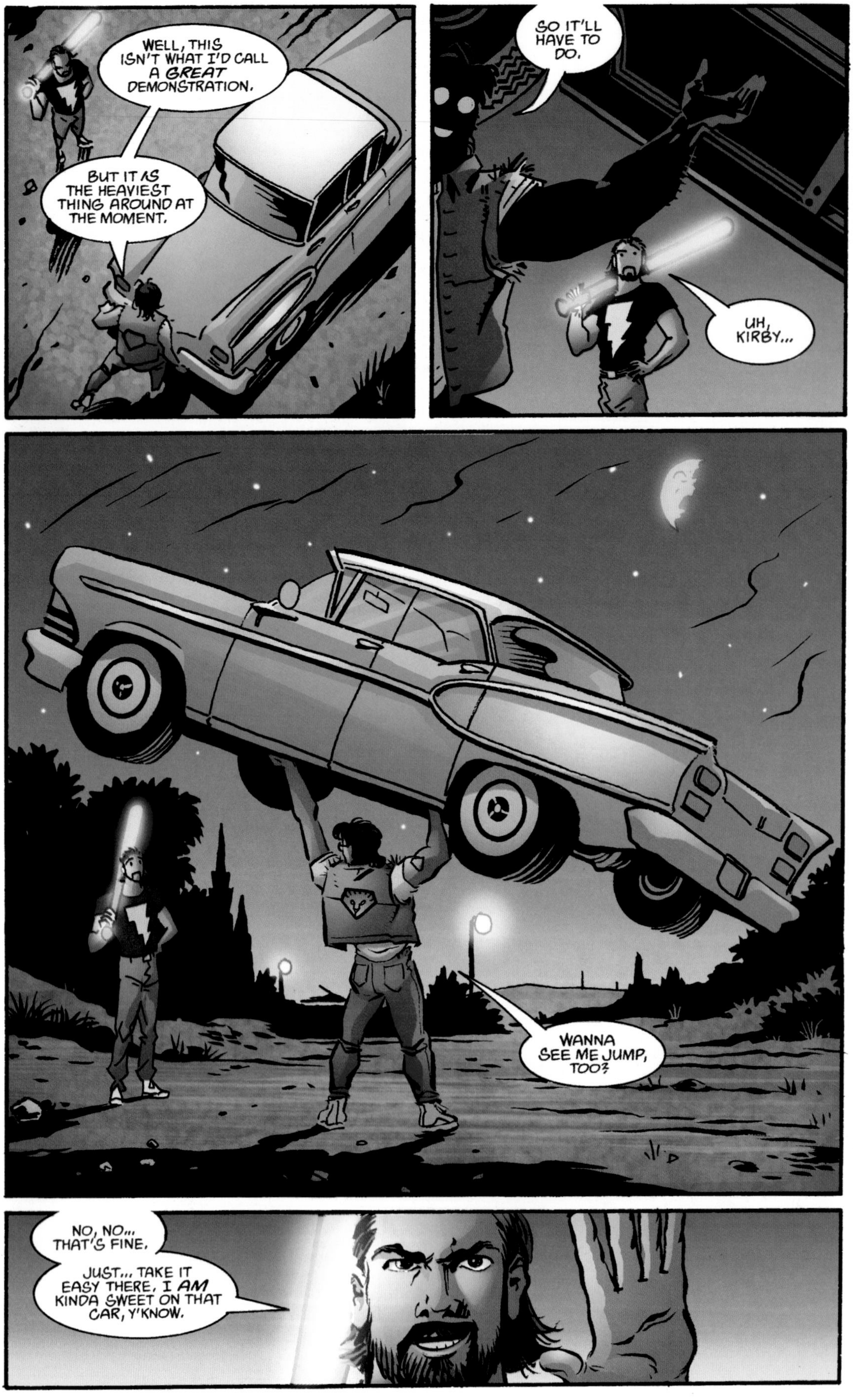
WELL, THIS ISN'T WHAT I'D CALL A *GREAT* DEMONSTRATION.
BUT IT IS THE HEAVIEST THING AROUND AT THE MOMENT.
SO IT'LL HAVE TO DO.
UH, KIRBY...
WANNA SEE ME JUMP, TOO?
NO, NO... THAT'S FINE.
JUST... TAKE IT EASY THERE. I *AM* KINDA SWEET ON THAT CAR, Y'KNOW.

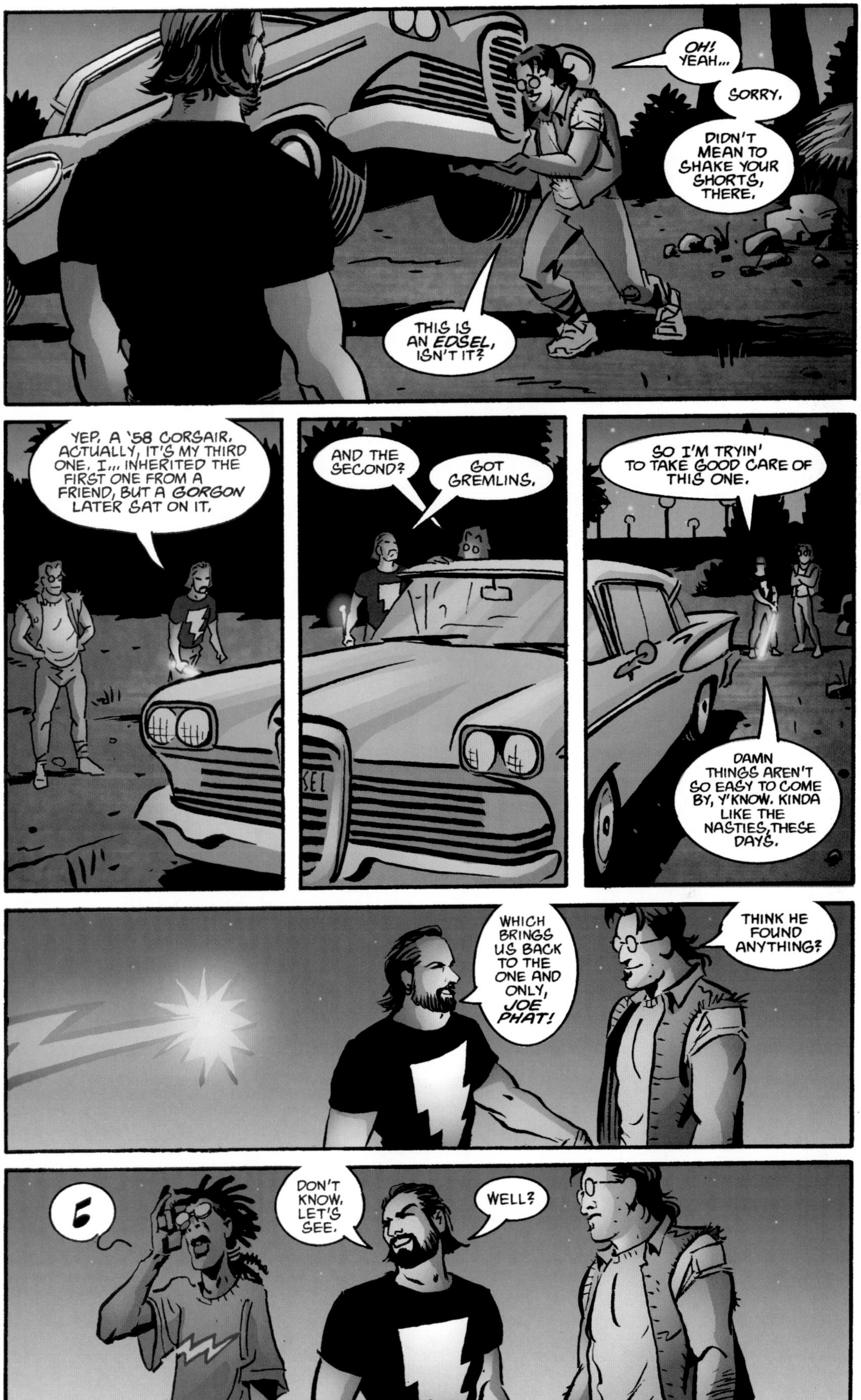
OH! YEAH...
SORRY.
DIDN'T MEAN TO SHAKE YOUR SHORTS, THERE.
THIS IS AN *EDSEL*, ISN'T IT?
YEP. A '58 CORSAIR, ACTUALLY. IT'S MY THIRD ONE. I... INHERITED THE FIRST ONE FROM A FRIEND, BUT A *GORGON* LATER SAT ON IT.
AND THE SECOND?
GOT GREMLINS.
SO I'M TRYIN' TO TAKE GOOD CARE OF THIS ONE.
DAMN THINGS AREN'T SO EASY TO COME BY, Y'KNOW. KINDA LIKE THE NASTIES, THESE DAYS.
WHICH BRINGS US BACK TO THE ONE AND ONLY, *JOE PHAT!*
THINK HE FOUND ANYTHING?
DON'T KNOW. LET'S SEE.
WELL?

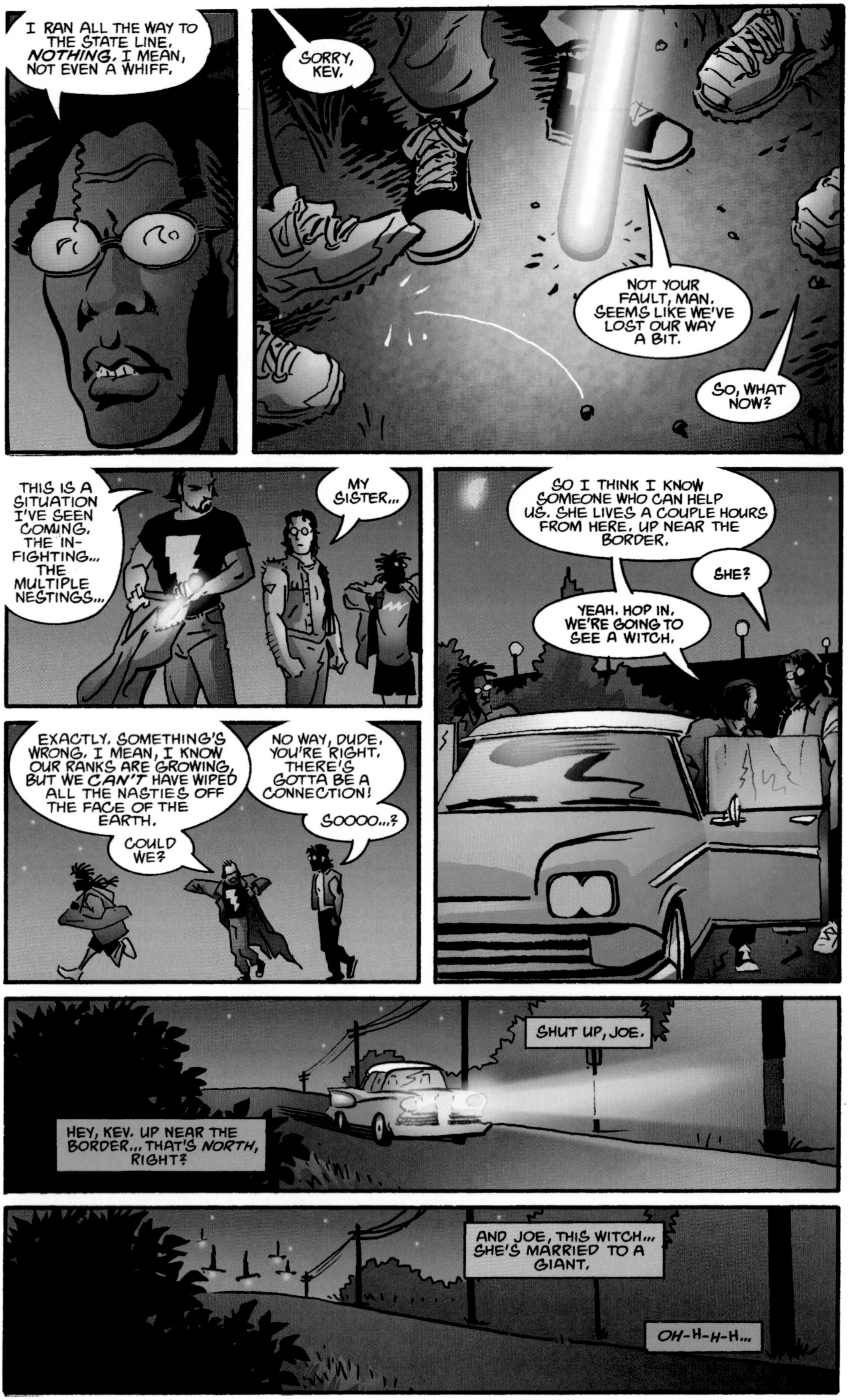
I RAN ALL THE WAY TO THE STATE LINE. *NOTHING.* I MEAN, NOT EVEN A WHIFF.
SORRY, KEV.
NOT YOUR FAULT, MAN. SEEMS LIKE WE'VE LOST OUR WAY A BIT.
SO, WHAT NOW?
THIS IS A SITUATION I'VE SEEN COMING. THE IN-FIGHTING... THE MULTIPLE NESTINGS...
MY SISTER...
SO I THINK I KNOW SOMEONE WHO CAN HELP US. SHE LIVES A COUPLE HOURS FROM HERE, UP NEAR THE BORDER.
SHE?
YEAH. HOP IN. WE'RE GOING TO SEE A WITCH.
EXACTLY. SOMETHING'S WRONG. I MEAN, I KNOW OUR RANKS ARE GROWING, BUT WE *CAN'T* HAVE WIPED ALL THE NASTIES OFF THE FACE OF THE EARTH.
COULD WE?
NO WAY, DUDE, YOU'RE RIGHT. THERE'S GOTTA BE A CONNECTION!
SOOOO...?
HEY, KEV. UP NEAR THE BORDER... THAT'S *NORTH,* RIGHT?
SHUT UP, JOE.
AND JOE, THIS WITCH... SHE'S MARRIED TO A GIANT.
OH-H-H-H...

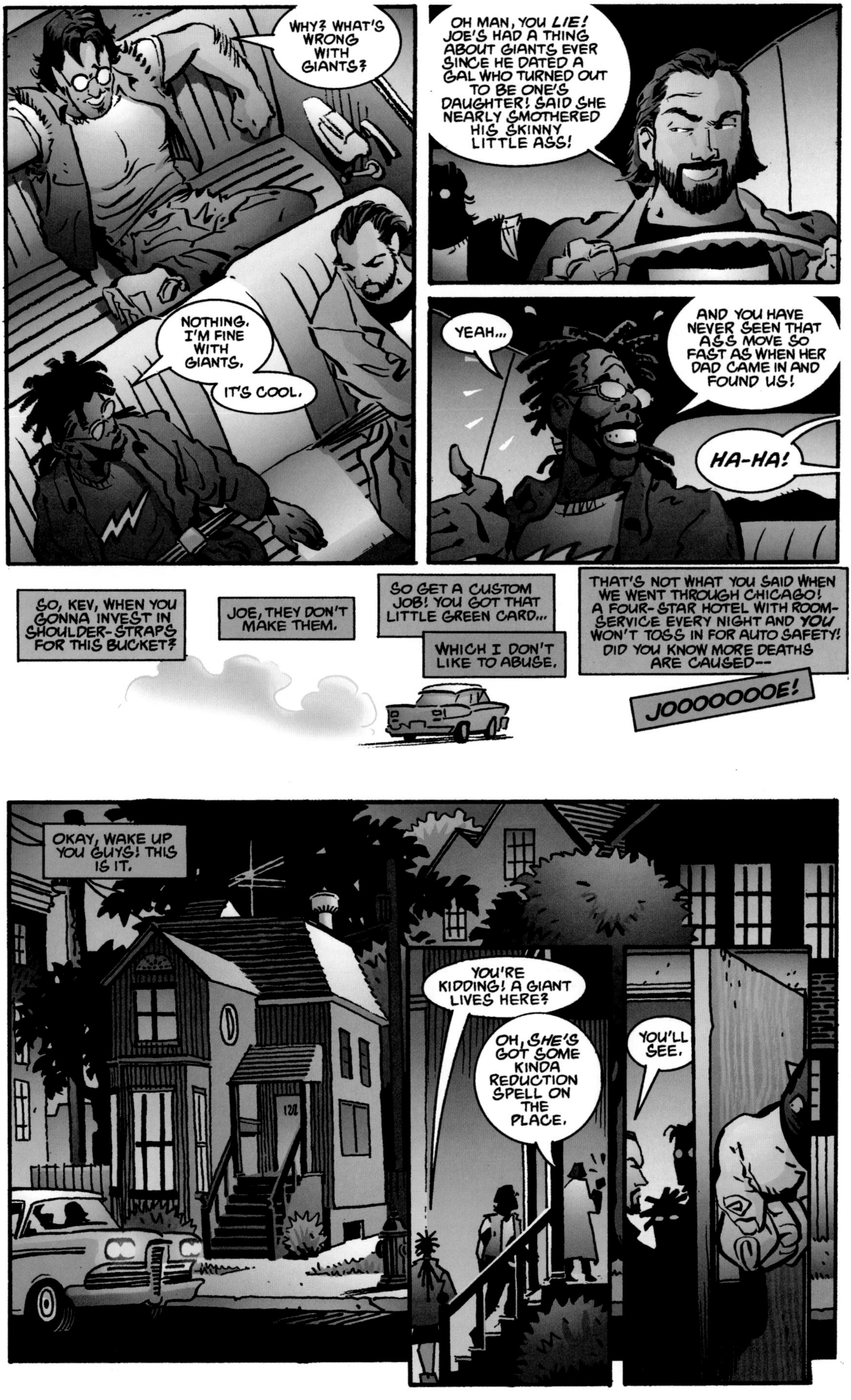
WHY? WHAT'S WRONG WITH GIANTS?
NOTHING. I'M FINE WITH GIANTS.
IT'S COOL.
OH MAN, YOU LIE! JOE'S HAD A THING ABOUT GIANTS EVER SINCE HE DATED A GAL WHO TURNED OUT TO BE ONE'S DAUGHTER! SAID SHE NEARLY SMOTHERED HIS SKINNY LITTLE ASS!
YEAH...
AND YOU HAVE NEVER SEEN THAT ASS MOVE SO FAST AS WHEN HER DAD CAME IN AND FOUND US!
HA-HA!
SO, KEV, WHEN YOU GONNA INVEST IN SHOULDER-STRAPS FOR THIS BUCKET?
JOE, THEY DON'T MAKE THEM.
SO GET A CUSTOM JOB! YOU GOT THAT LITTLE GREEN CARD...
WHICH I DON'T LIKE TO ABUSE.
THAT'S NOT WHAT YOU SAID WHEN WE WENT THROUGH CHICAGO! A FOUR-STAR HOTEL WITH ROOM-SERVICE EVERY NIGHT AND YOU WON'T TOSS IN FOR AUTO SAFETY! DID YOU KNOW MORE DEATHS ARE CAUSED--
JOOOOOOOE!
OKAY, WAKE UP YOU GUYS! THIS IS IT.
YOU'RE KIDDING! A GIANT LIVES HERE?
OH, SHE'S GOT SOME KINDA REDUCTION SPELL ON THE PLACE.
YOU'LL SEE.

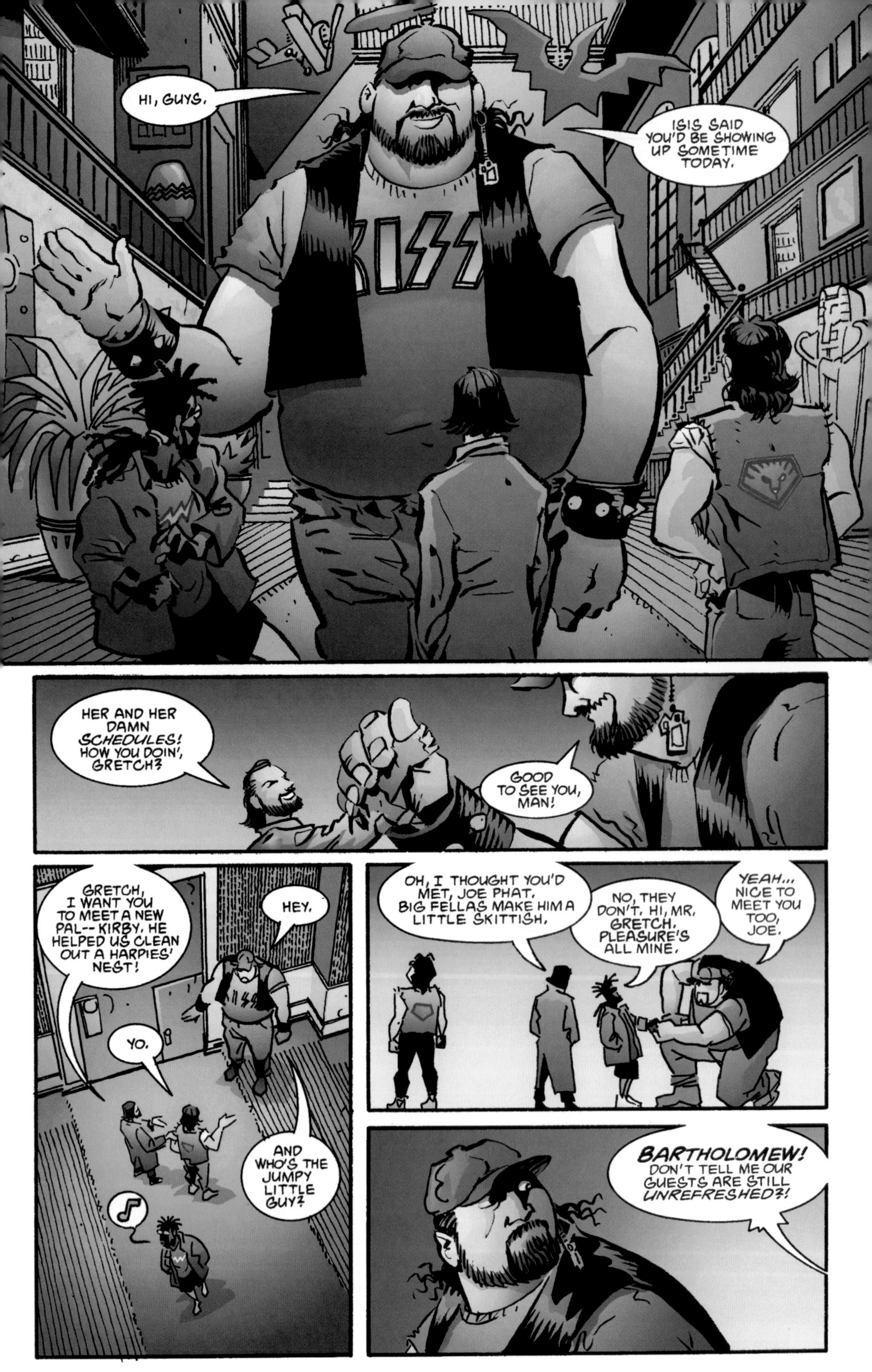
HI, GUYS.
ISIS SAID YOU'D BE SHOWING UP SOMETIME TODAY.
HER AND HER DAMN SCHEDULES! HOW YOU DOIN', GRETCH?
GOOD TO SEE YOU, MAN!
GRETCH, I WANT YOU TO MEET A NEW PAL-- KIRBY. HE HELPED US CLEAN OUT A HARPIES' NEST!
HEY.
YO.
AND WHO'S THE JUMPY LITTLE GUY?
OH, I THOUGHT YOU'D MET, JOE PHAT. BIG FELLAS MAKE HIM A LITTLE SKITTISH.
NO, THEY DON'T. HI, MR. GRETCH. PLEASURE'S ALL MINE.
YEAH... NICE TO MEET YOU TOO, JOE.
BARTHOLOMEW! DON'T TELL ME OUR GUESTS ARE STILL UNREFRESHED?!

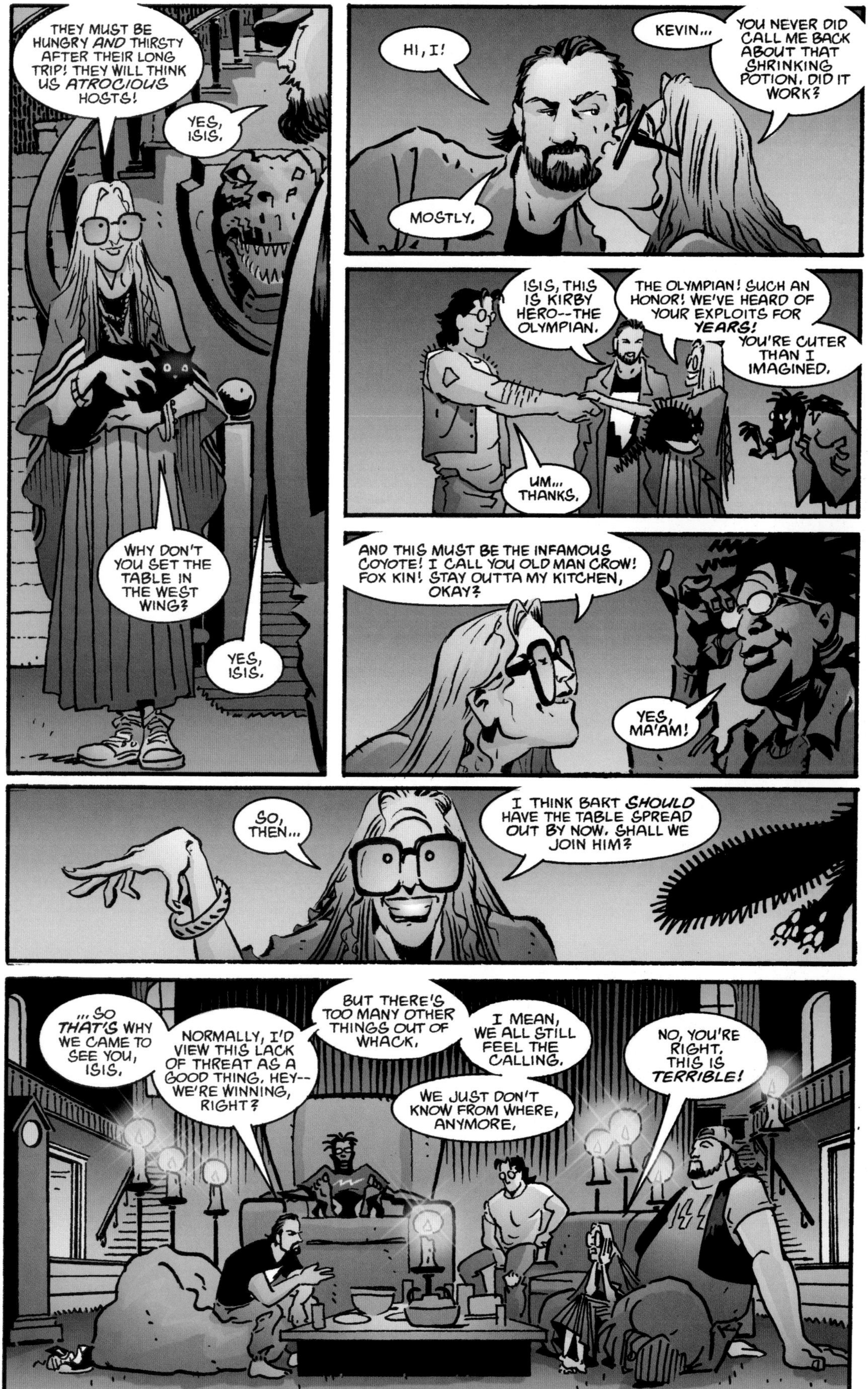

THEY MUST BE HUNGRY AND THIRSTY AFTER THEIR LONG TRIP! THEY WILL THINK US ATROCIOUS HOSTS!
YES, ISIS.
WHY DON'T YOU SET THE TABLE IN THE WEST WING?
YES, ISIS.
HI, I!
KEVIN...
YOU NEVER DID CALL ME BACK ABOUT THAT SHRINKING POTION. DID IT WORK?
MOSTLY.
ISIS, THIS IS KIRBY HERO--THE OLYMPIAN.
THE OLYMPIAN! SUCH AN HONOR! WE'VE HEARD OF YOUR EXPLOITS FOR YEARS!
YOU'RE CUTER THAN I IMAGINED.
UM... THANKS.
AND THIS MUST BE THE INFAMOUS COYOTE! I CALL YOU OLD MAN CROW! FOX KIN! STAY OUTTA MY KITCHEN, OKAY?
YES, MA'AM!
SO, THEN...
I THINK BART SHOULD HAVE THE TABLE SPREAD OUT BY NOW. SHALL WE JOIN HIM?
...SO THAT'S WHY WE CAME TO SEE YOU, ISIS.
NORMALLY, I'D VIEW THIS LACK OF THREAT AS A GOOD THING. HEY-- WE'RE WINNING, RIGHT?
BUT THERE'S TOO MANY OTHER THINGS OUT OF WHACK.
I MEAN, WE ALL STILL FEEL THE CALLING.
WE JUST DON'T KNOW FROM WHERE, ANYMORE.
NO, YOU'RE RIGHT. THIS IS TERRIBLE!

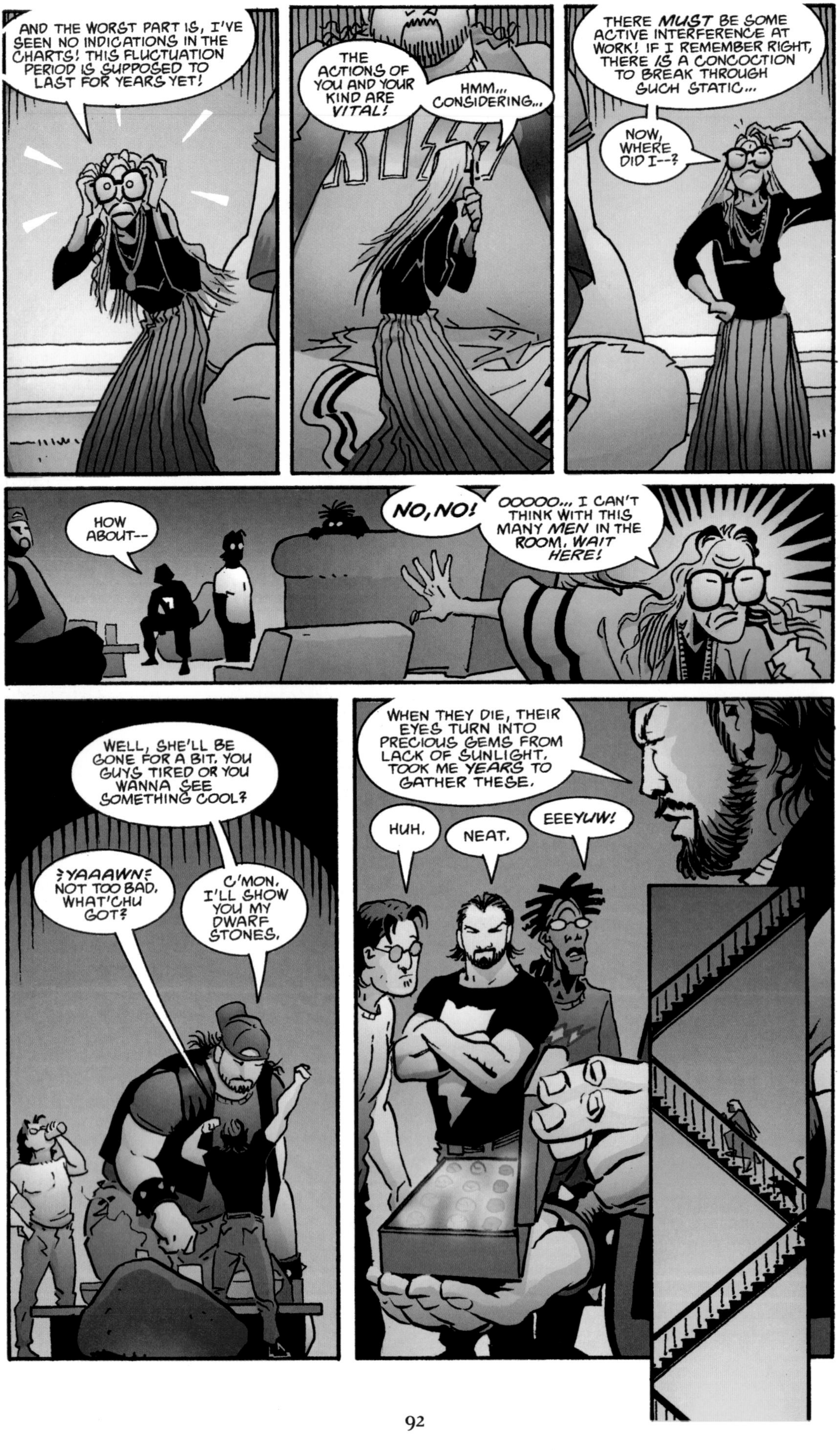
AND THE WORST PART IS, I'VE SEEN NO INDICATIONS IN THE CHARTS! THIS FLUCTUATION PERIOD IS SUPPOSED TO LAST FOR YEARS YET!
THE ACTIONS OF YOU AND YOUR KIND ARE *VITAL!*
HMM... CONSIDERING...
THERE *MUST* BE SOME ACTIVE INTERFERENCE AT WORK! IF I REMEMBER RIGHT, THERE *IS* A CONCOCTION TO BREAK THROUGH SUCH STATIC...
NOW, WHERE DID I--?
HOW ABOUT--
NO, NO!
OOOOO... I CAN'T THINK WITH THIS MANY *MEN* IN THE ROOM. *WAIT HERE!*
WELL, SHE'LL BE GONE FOR A BIT. YOU GUYS TIRED OR YOU WANNA SEE SOMETHING COOL?
YAAAWN NOT TOO BAD. WHAT'CHU GOT?
C'MON. I'LL SHOW YOU MY DWARF STONES.
WHEN THEY DIE, THEIR EYES TURN INTO PRECIOUS GEMS FROM LACK OF SUNLIGHT. TOOK ME *YEARS* TO GATHER THESE.
HUH.
NEAT.
EEEYUW!

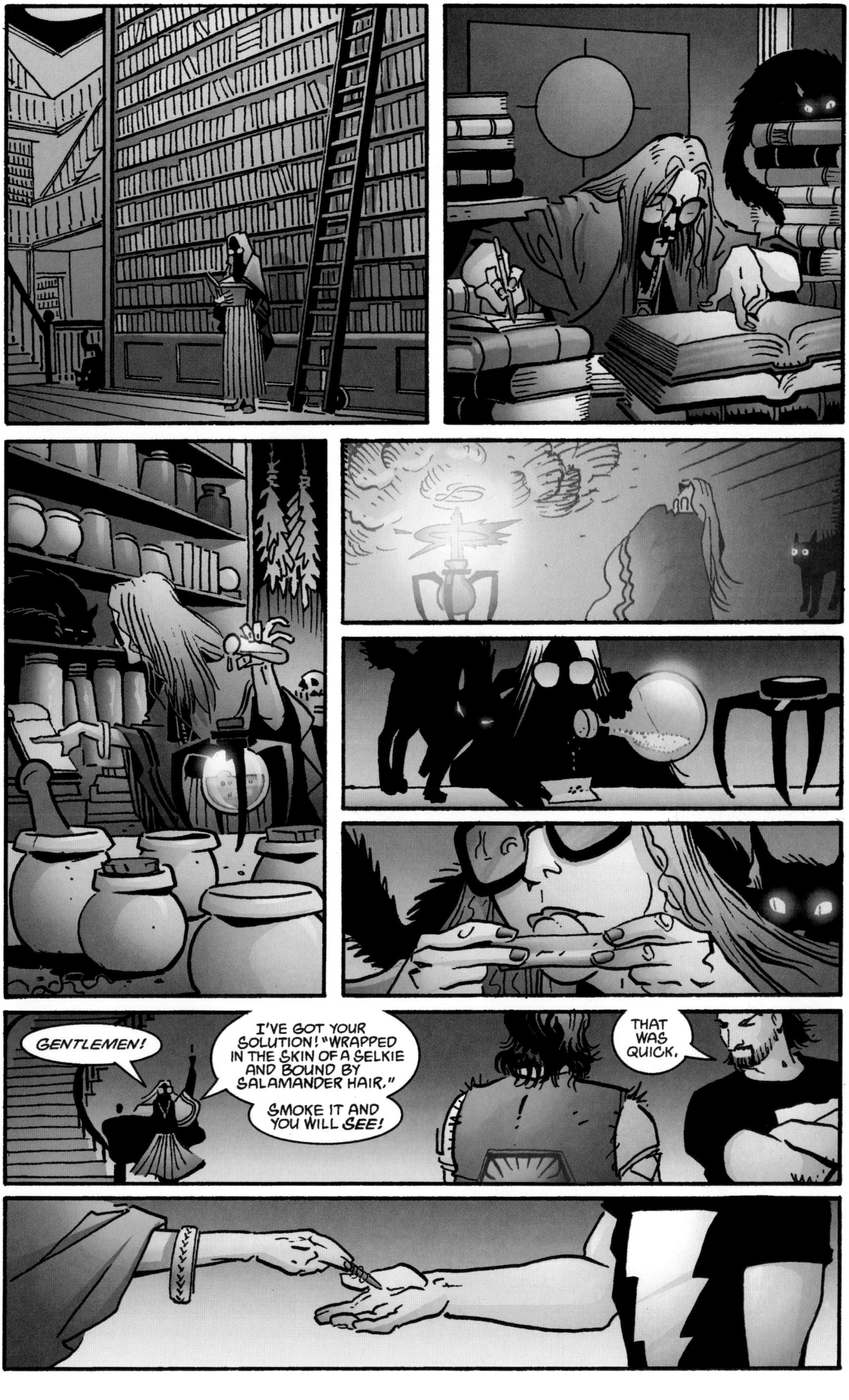
GENTLEMEN!
I'VE GOT YOUR SOLUTION! "WRAPPED IN THE SKIN OF A SELKIE AND BOUND BY SALAMANDER HAIR."
SMOKE IT AND YOU WILL SEE!
THAT WAS QUICK.

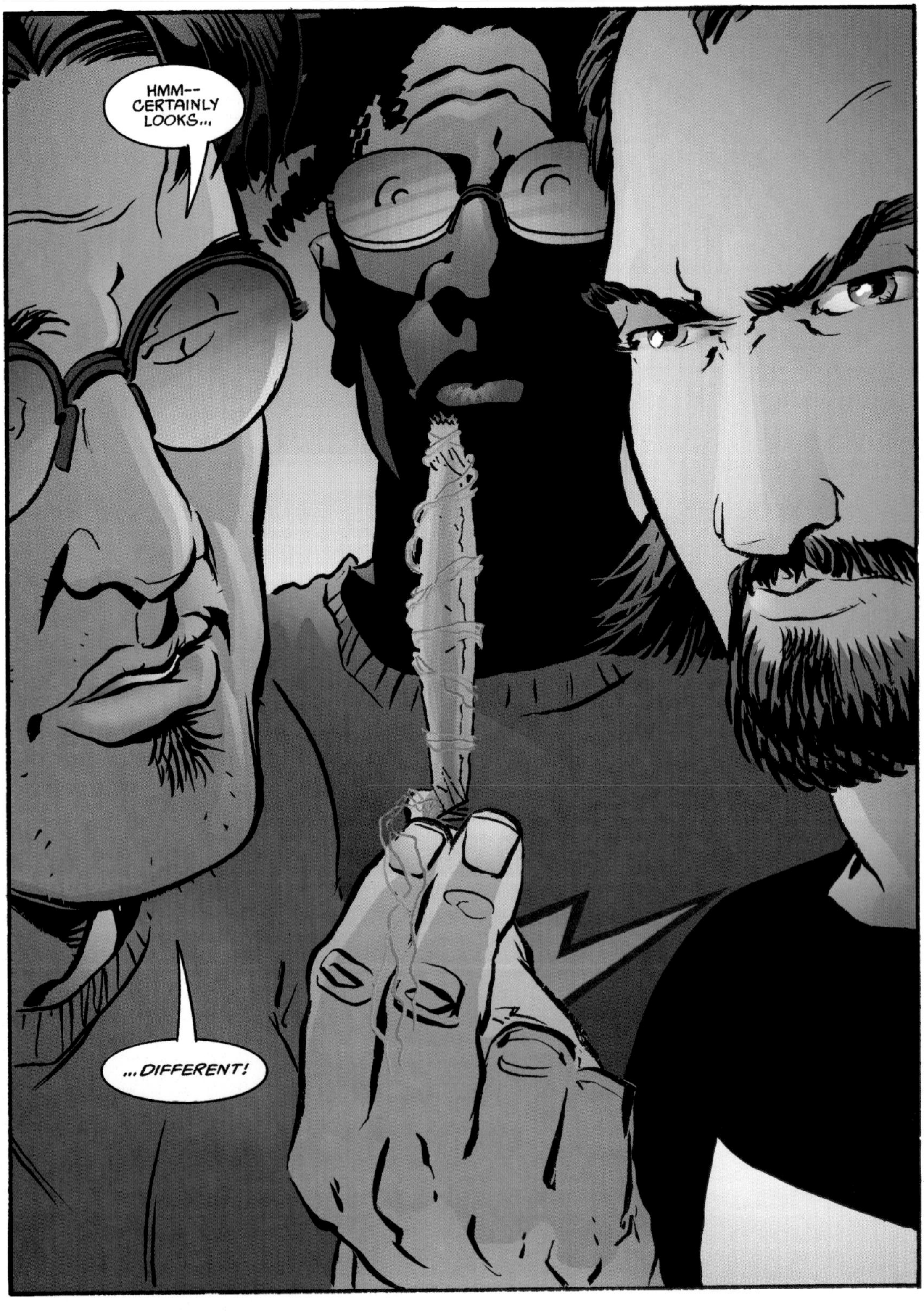
HMM-- CERTAINLY LOOKS...
...DIFFERENT!

THE HERO DEFINED
MAGE ®

chapter

4

"Bubble, Bubble
Toil and Trouble"

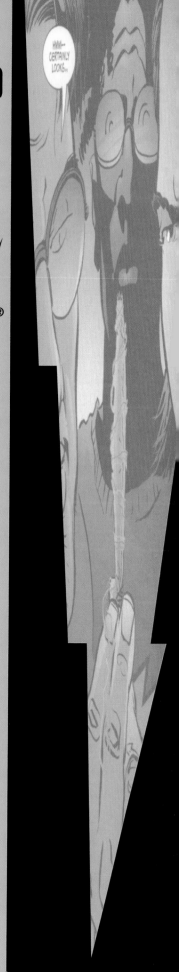

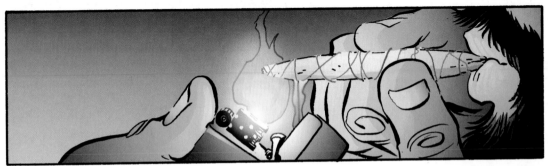

NOTHING YET?

NOT EVEN A SINGE. REGULAR FLAME DOESN'T SEEM TO HAVE ANY EFFECT. MAGIC... CONFUSING AS EVER.

I'M SURPRISED ISIS DIDN'T GIVE US A LIST OF INSTRUCTIONS WITH THIS THING. SHE'S OBSESSIVELY EFFICIENT.

BIZARRO,

MAYBE I SHOULD GET THE BAT.

HERE, KEV. TRY THIS.

JOE, THAT'S NOT GOING TO WORK. REGULAR FLAME WON'T--

SHE TOLD US TO SMOKE IT IN THIS ROOM. MAYBE THOSE WERE THE INSTRUCTIONS.

EH--?

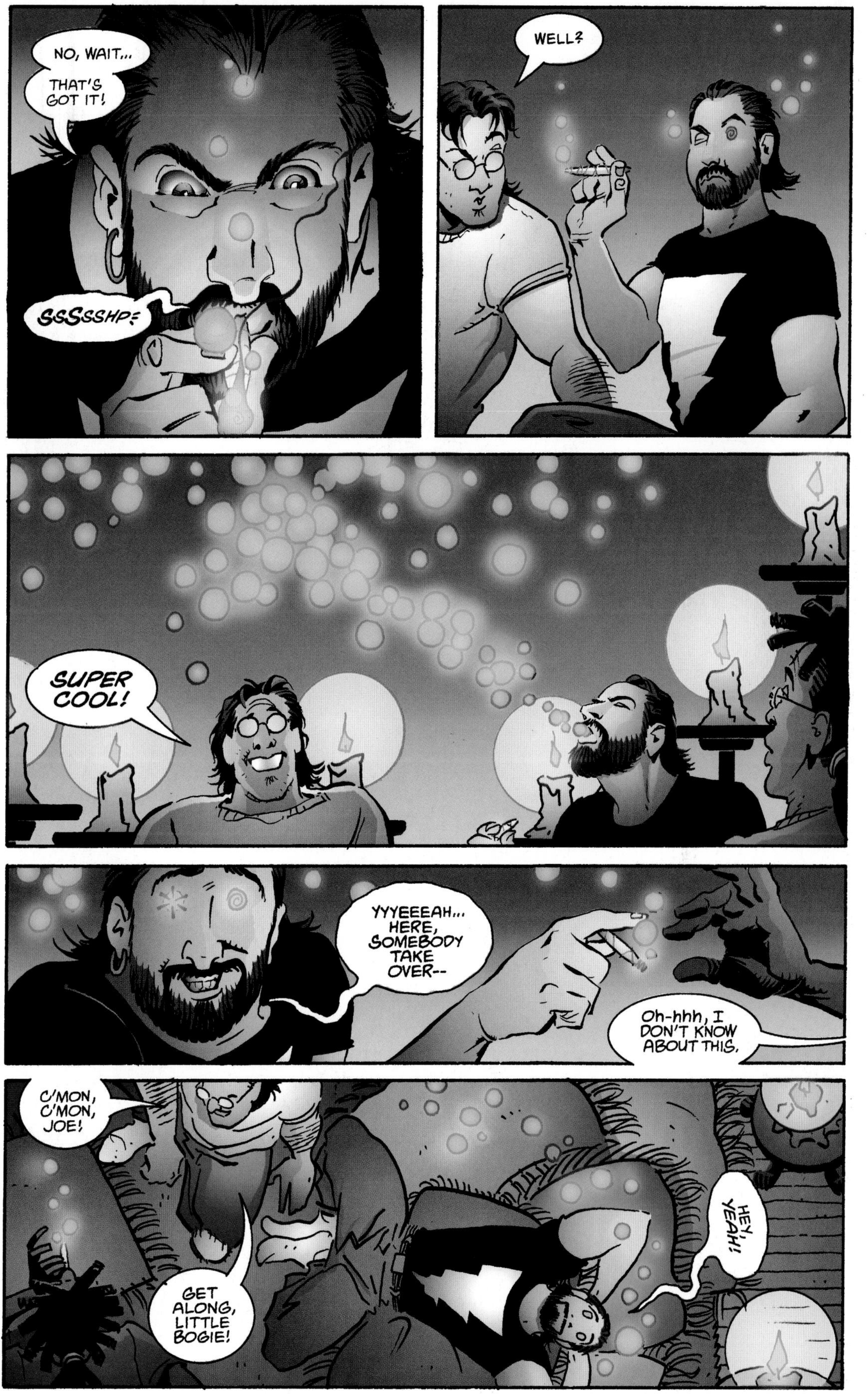
NO, WAIT...
THAT'S GOT IT!
SSSSSHP=
WELL?
SUPER COOL!
YYYEEEAH... HERE, SOMEBODY TAKE OVER--
Oh-hhh, I DON'T KNOW ABOUT THIS,
C'MON, C'MON, JOE!
GET ALONG, LITTLE BOGIE!
HEY, YEAH!

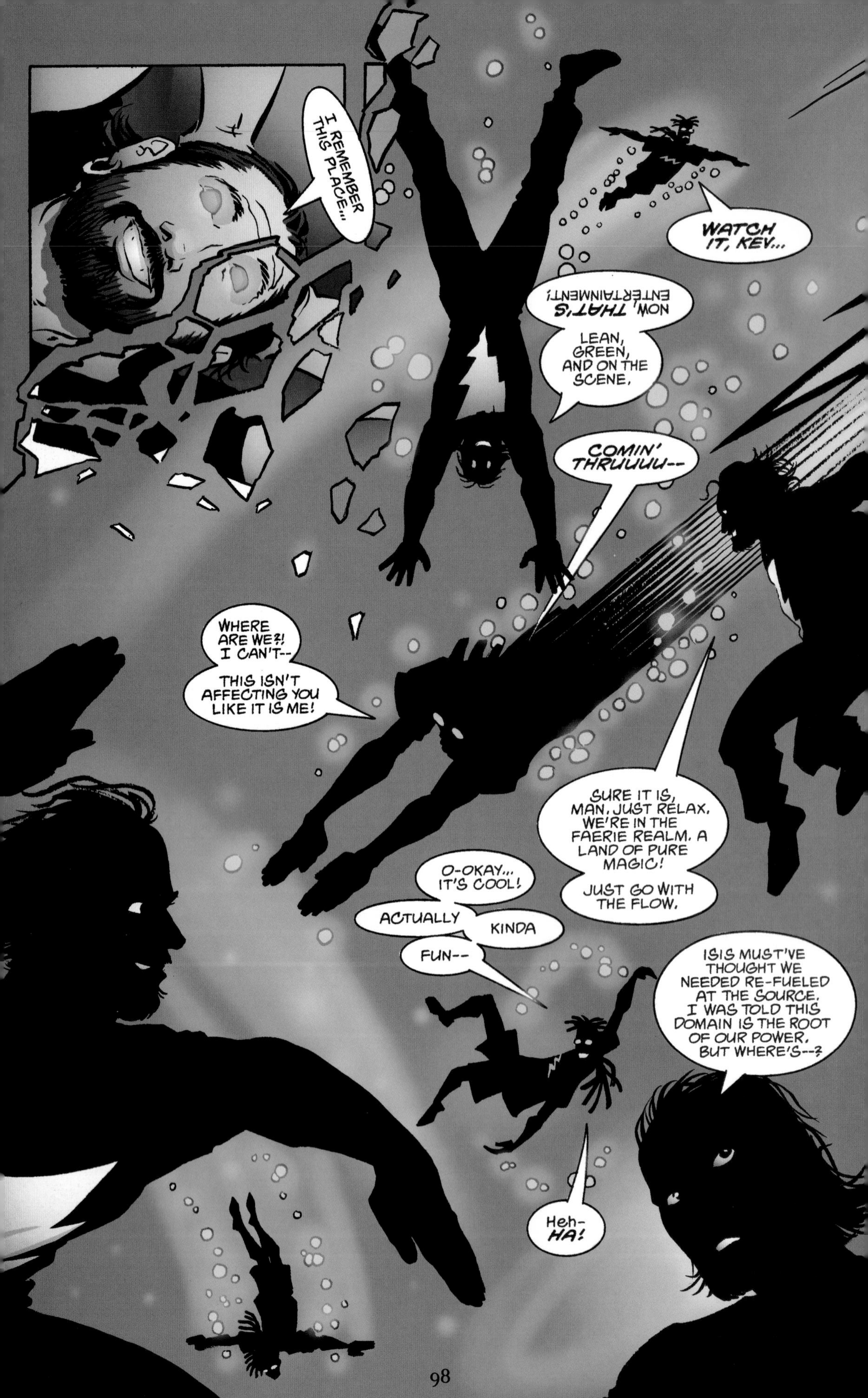
I REMEMBER THIS PLACE...
WATCH IT, KEV...
NOW, THAT'S ENTERTAINMENT!
LEAN, GREEN, AND ON THE SCENE.
COMIN' THRUUUU--
WHERE ARE WE?! I CAN'T--
THIS ISN'T AFFECTING YOU LIKE IT IS ME!
SURE IT IS, MAN. JUST RELAX. WE'RE IN THE FAERIE REALM. A LAND OF PURE MAGIC!
JUST GO WITH THE FLOW.
O-OKAY... IT'S COOL!
ACTUALLY
KINDA
FUN--
ISIS MUST'VE THOUGHT WE NEEDED RE-FUELED AT THE SOURCE. I WAS TOLD THIS DOMAIN IS THE ROOT OF OUR POWER. BUT WHERE'S--?
Heh-HA!

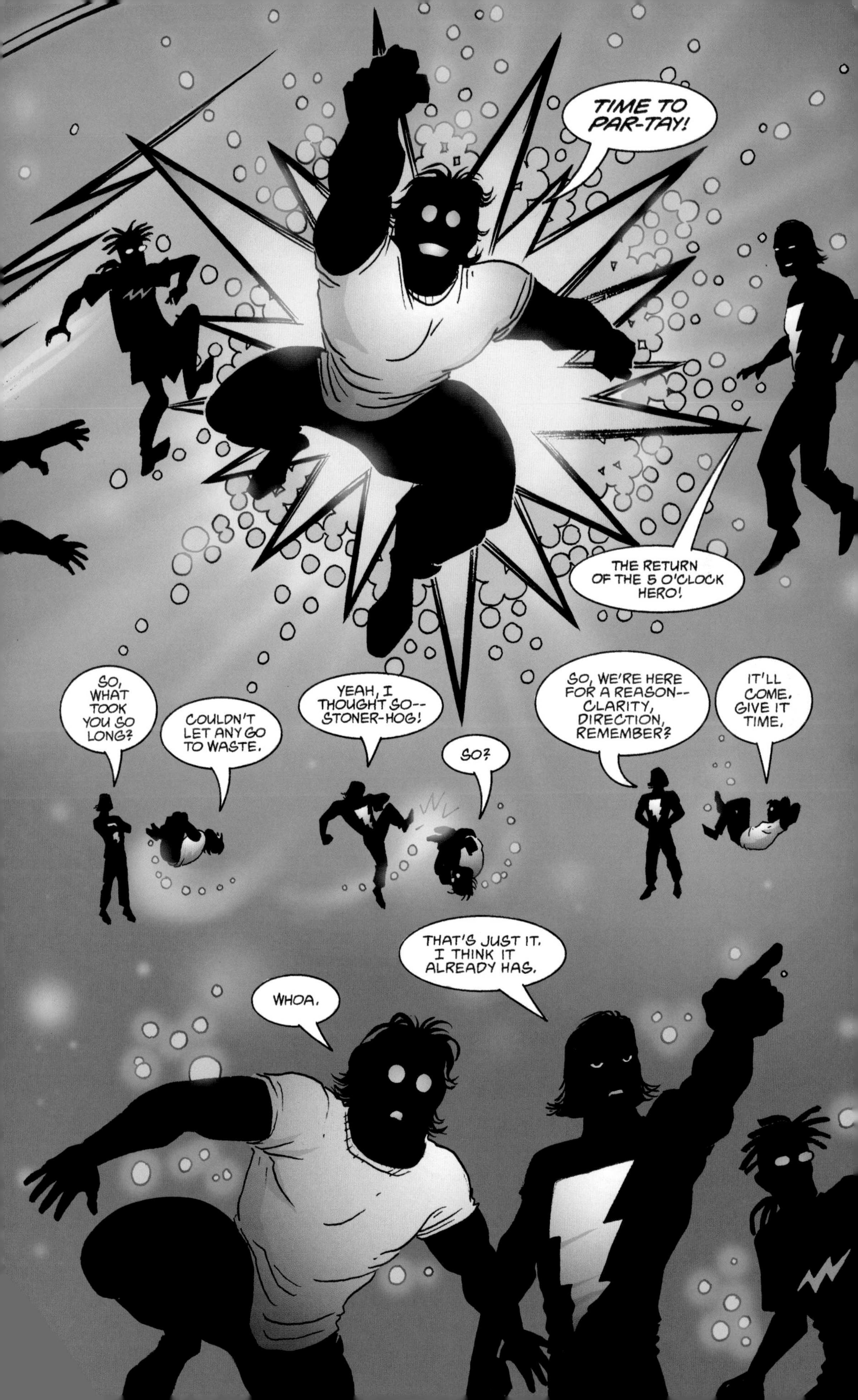
TIME TO PAR-TAY!
THE RETURN OF THE 5 O'CLOCK HERO!
SO, WHAT TOOK YOU SO LONG?
COULDN'T LET ANY GO TO WASTE.
YEAH, I THOUGHT SO-- STONER-HOG!
SO?
SO, WE'RE HERE FOR A REASON-- CLARITY, DIRECTION, REMEMBER?
IT'LL COME. GIVE IT TIME.
WHOA.
THAT'S JUST IT. I THINK IT ALREADY HAS.

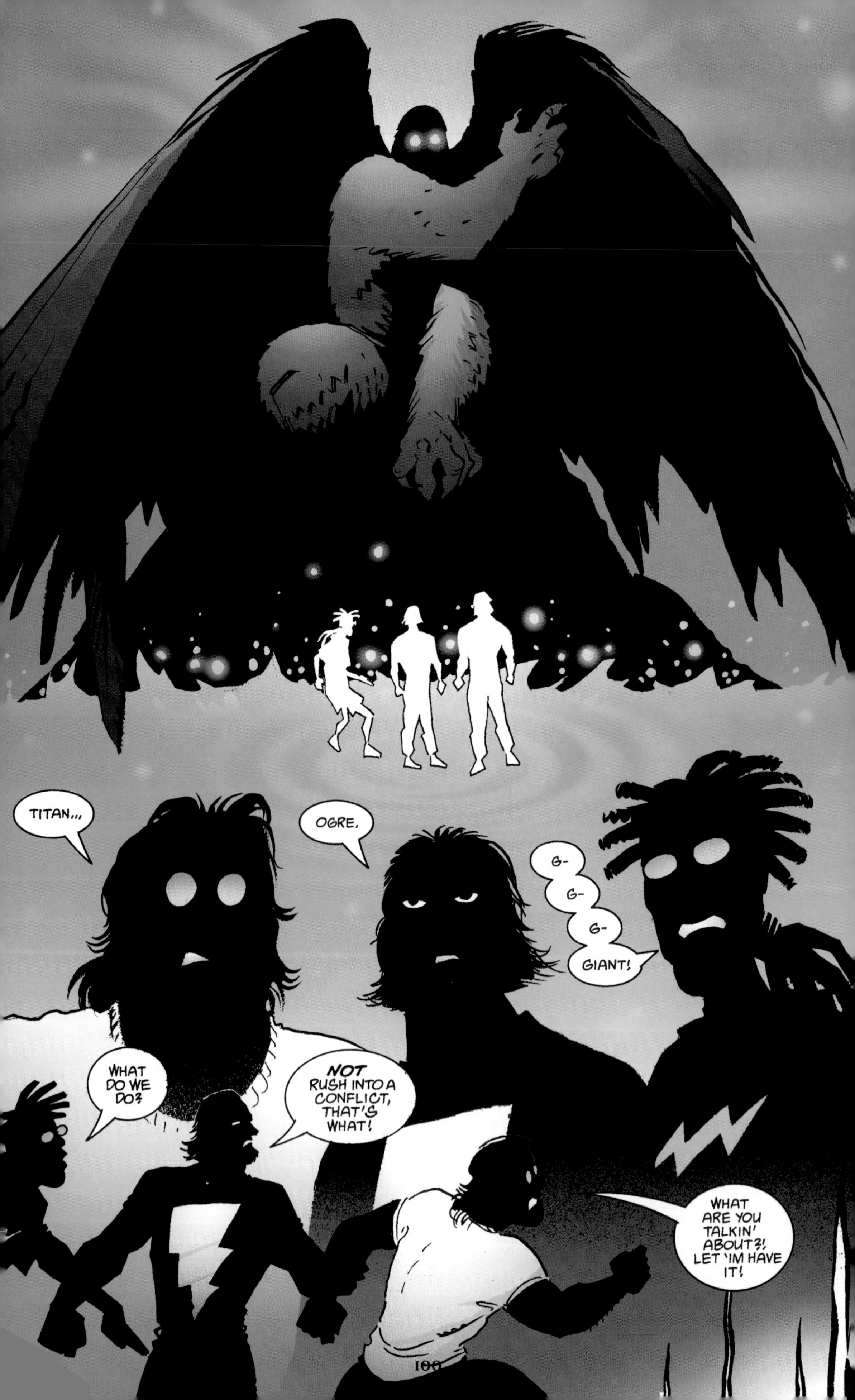
TITAN...
OGRE.
G-
G-
G-
GIANT!
WHAT DO WE DO?
NOT RUSH INTO A CONFLICT, THAT'S WHAT!
WHAT ARE YOU TALKIN' ABOUT?! LET 'IM HAVE IT!

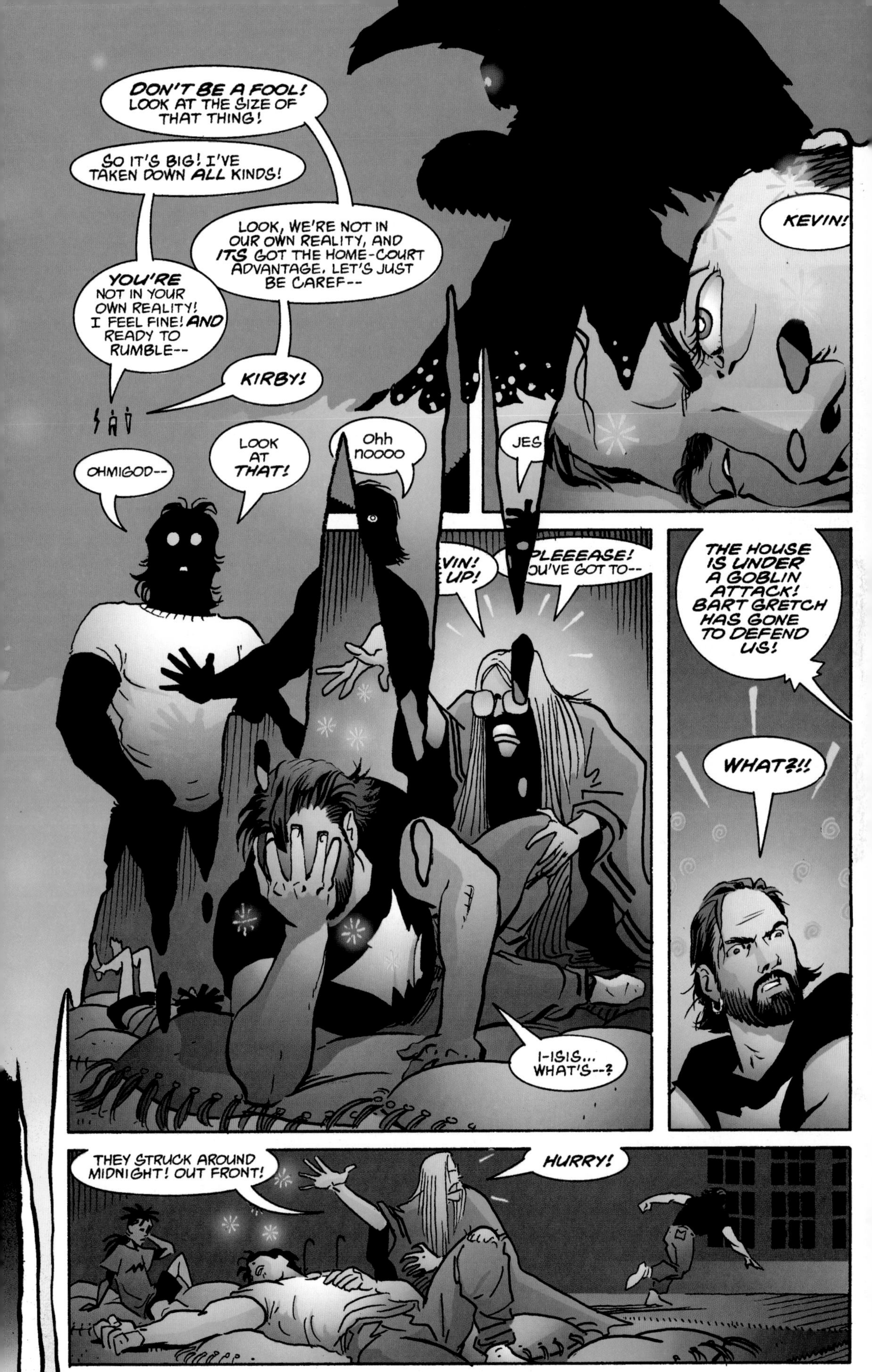
DON'T BE A FOOL! LOOK AT THE SIZE OF THAT THING!
SO IT'S BIG! I'VE TAKEN DOWN ALL KINDS!
LOOK, WE'RE NOT IN OUR OWN REALITY, AND ITS GOT THE HOME-COURT ADVANTAGE. LET'S JUST BE CAREF--
YOU'RE NOT IN YOUR OWN REALITY! I FEEL FINE! AND READY TO RUMBLE--
KIRBY!
KEVIN!
OHMIGOD--
LOOK AT THAT!
Ohh noooo
JES
EVIN! E UP!
PLEEEASE! OU'VE GOT TO--
I-ISIS... WHAT'S--?
THE HOUSE IS UNDER A GOBLIN ATTACK! BART GRETCH HAS GONE TO DEFEND US!
WHAT?!!
THEY STRUCK AROUND MIDNIGHT! OUT FRONT!
HURRY!

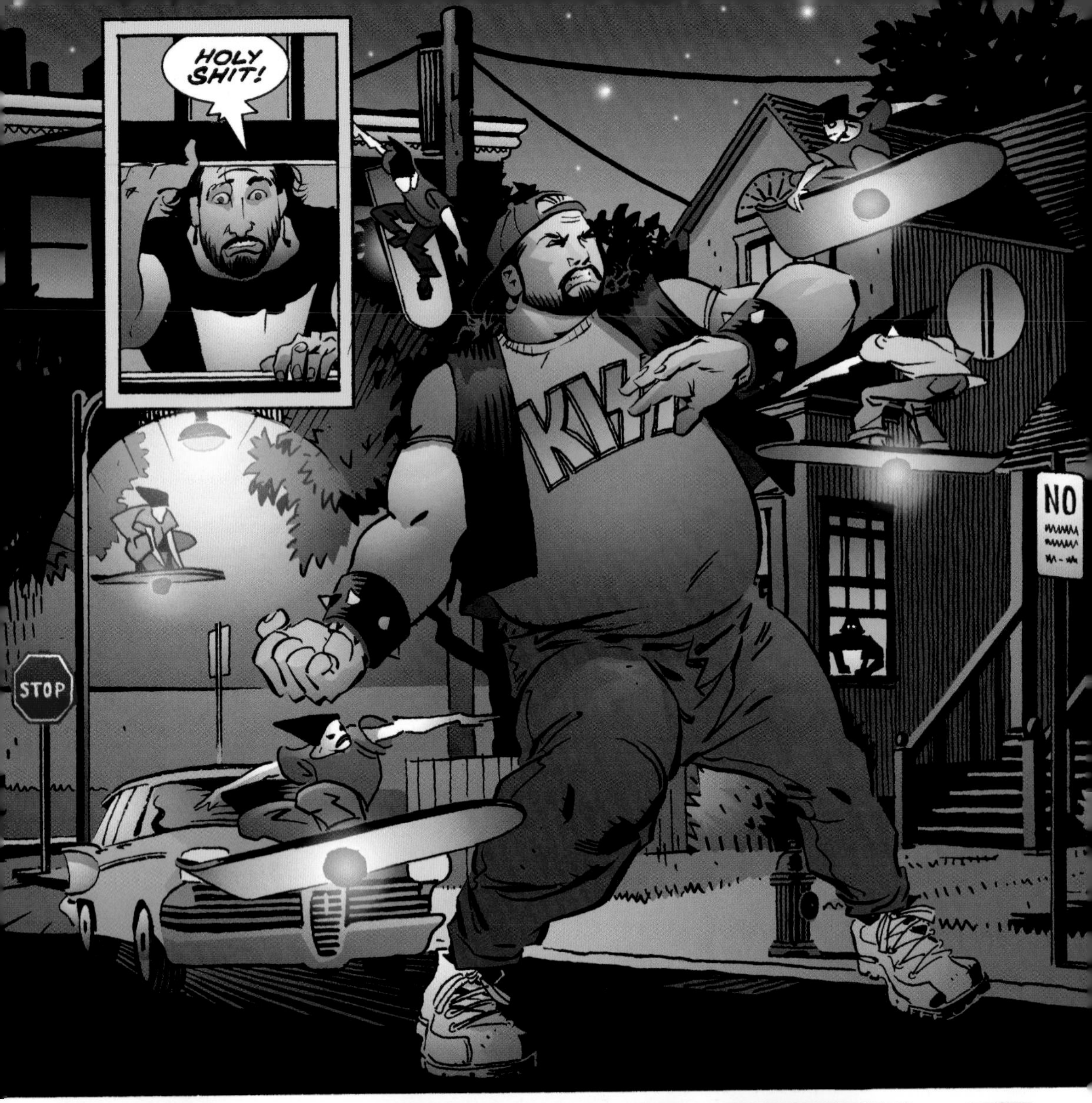
HOLY SHIT!
STOP
NO

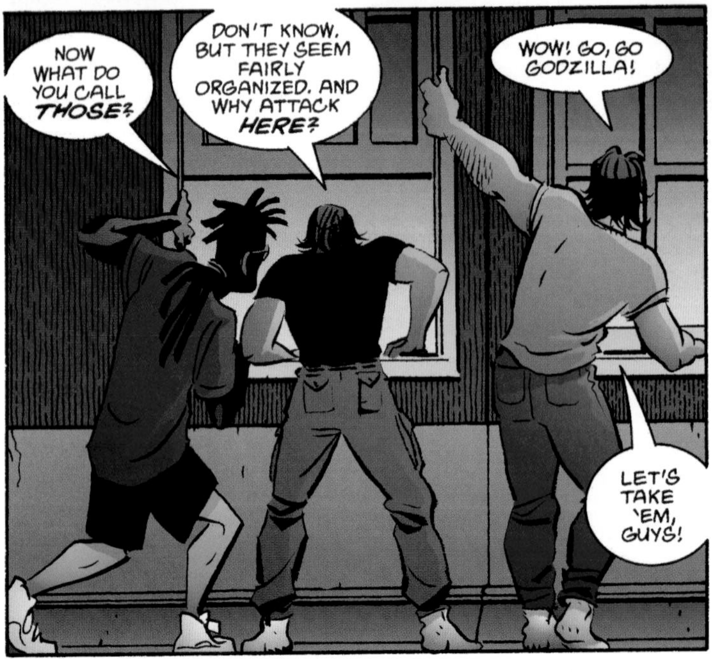
NOW WHAT DO YOU CALL *THOSE*?
DON'T KNOW. BUT THEY SEEM FAIRLY ORGANIZED. AND WHY ATTACK *HERE*?
WOW! GO, GO GODZILLA!
LET'S TAKE 'EM, GUYS!

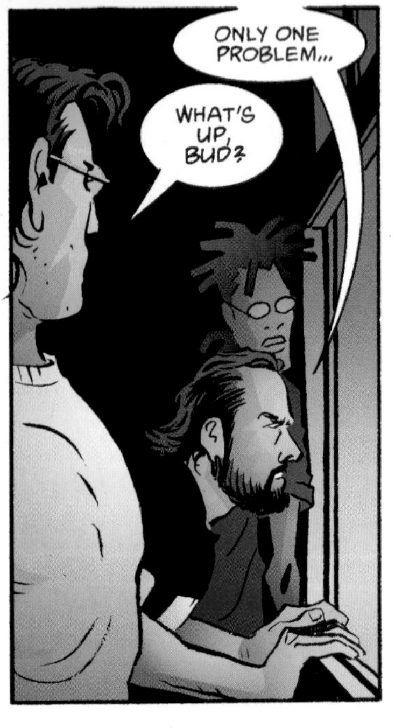
ONLY ONE PROBLEM...
WHAT'S UP, BUD?

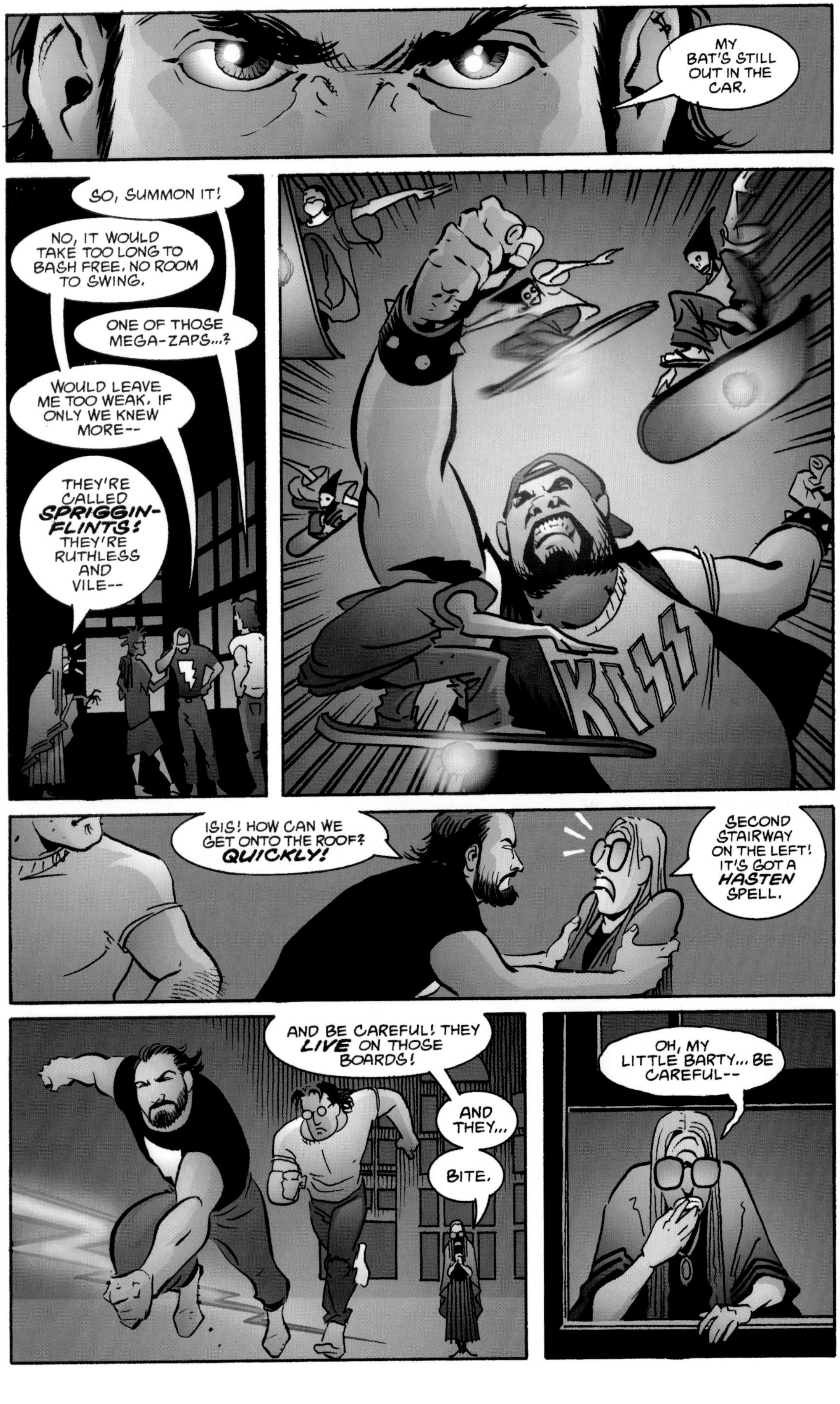
MY BAT'S STILL OUT IN THE CAR.
SO, SUMMON IT!
NO, IT WOULD TAKE TOO LONG TO BASH FREE. NO ROOM TO SWING.
ONE OF THOSE MEGA-ZAPS...?
WOULD LEAVE ME TOO WEAK. IF ONLY WE KNEW MORE--
THEY'RE CALLED **SPRIGGIN-FLINTS!** THEY'RE RUTHLESS AND VILE--
ISIS! HOW CAN WE GET ONTO THE ROOF? **QUICKLY!**
SECOND STAIRWAY ON THE LEFT! IT'S GOT A **HASTEN** SPELL.
AND BE CAREFUL! THEY **LIVE** ON THOSE BOARDS!
AND THEY...
BITE.
OH, MY LITTLE BARTY... BE CAREFUL--

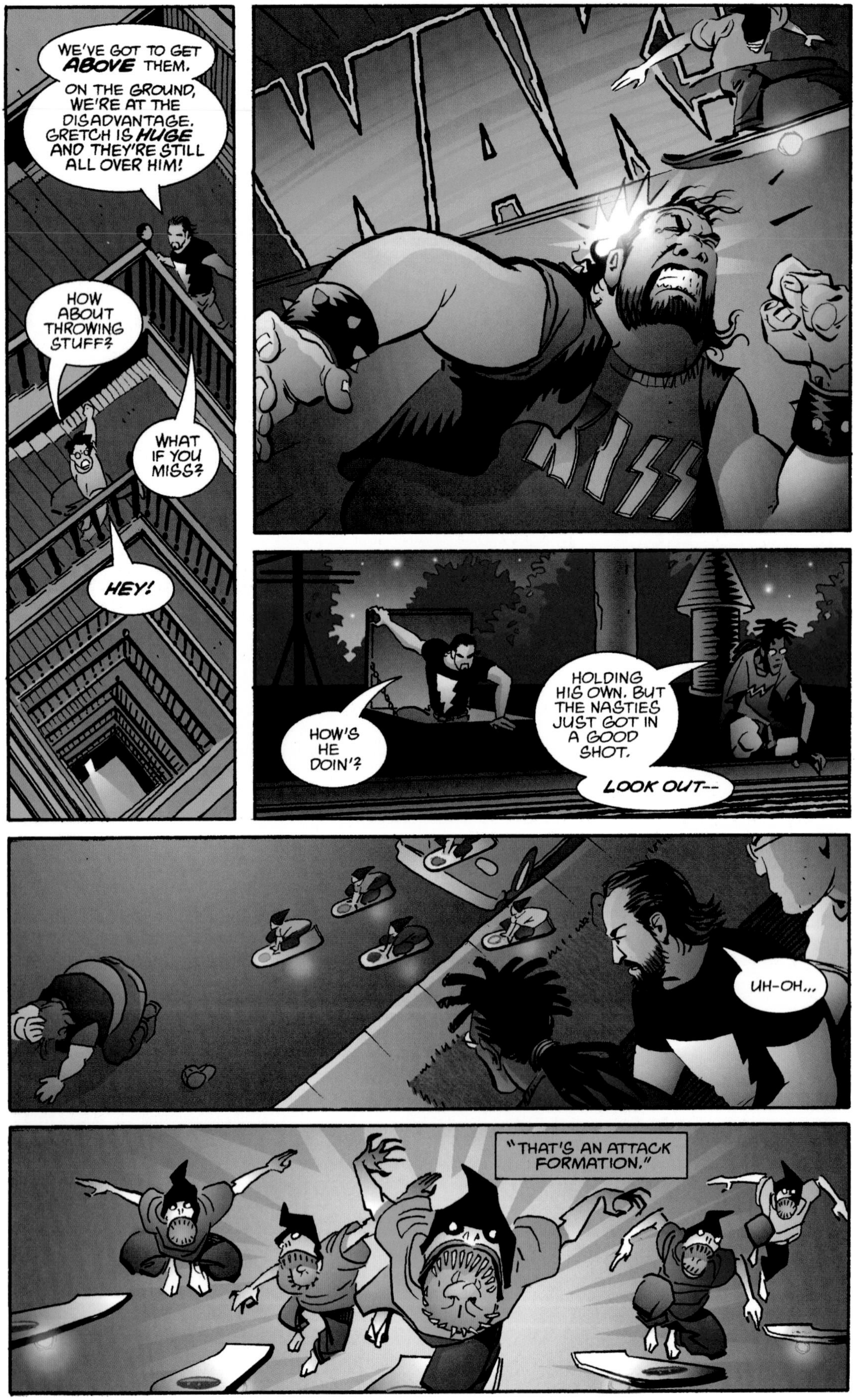
WE'VE GOT TO GET ABOVE THEM.
ON THE GROUND, WE'RE AT THE DISADVANTAGE. GRETCH IS HUGE AND THEY'RE STILL ALL OVER HIM!
HOW ABOUT THROWING STUFF?
WHAT IF YOU MISS?
HEY!
HOW'S HE DOIN'?
HOLDING HIS OWN. BUT THE NASTIES JUST GOT IN A GOOD SHOT.
LOOK OUT--
UH-OH...
"THAT'S AN ATTACK FORMATION."

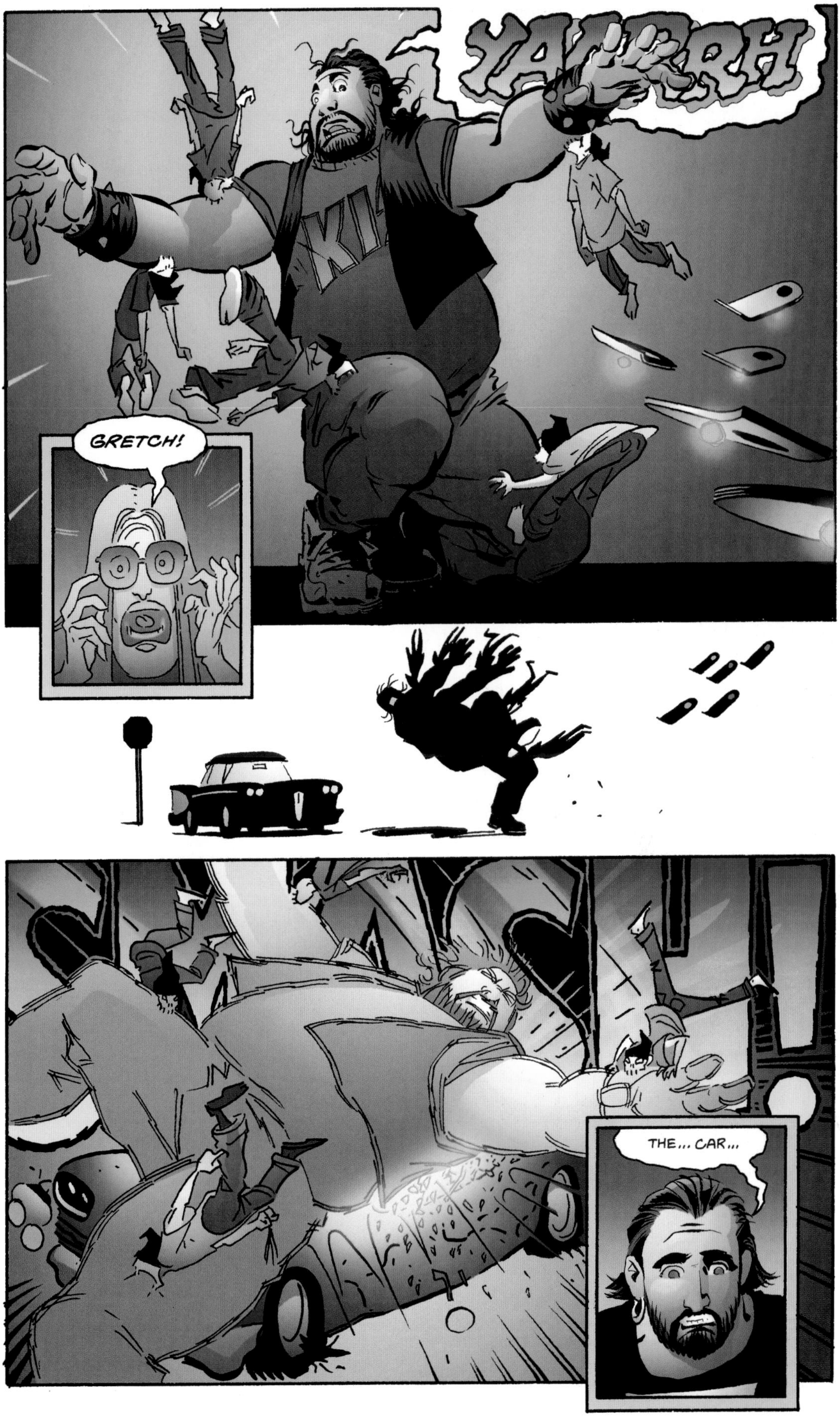
GRETCH!
THE... CAR...

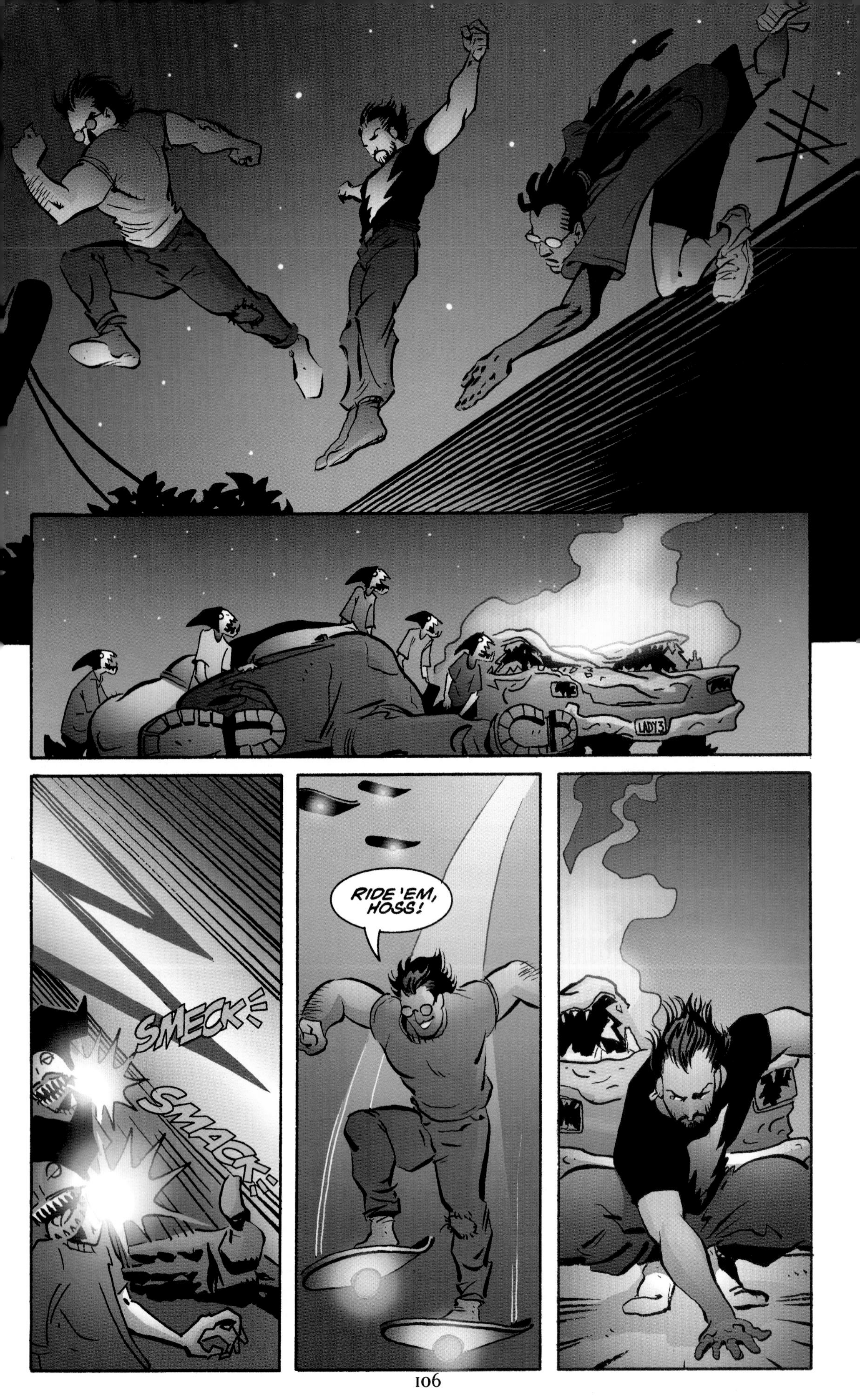
LADY3
SMECK!
SMACK!
RIDE 'EM, HOSS!

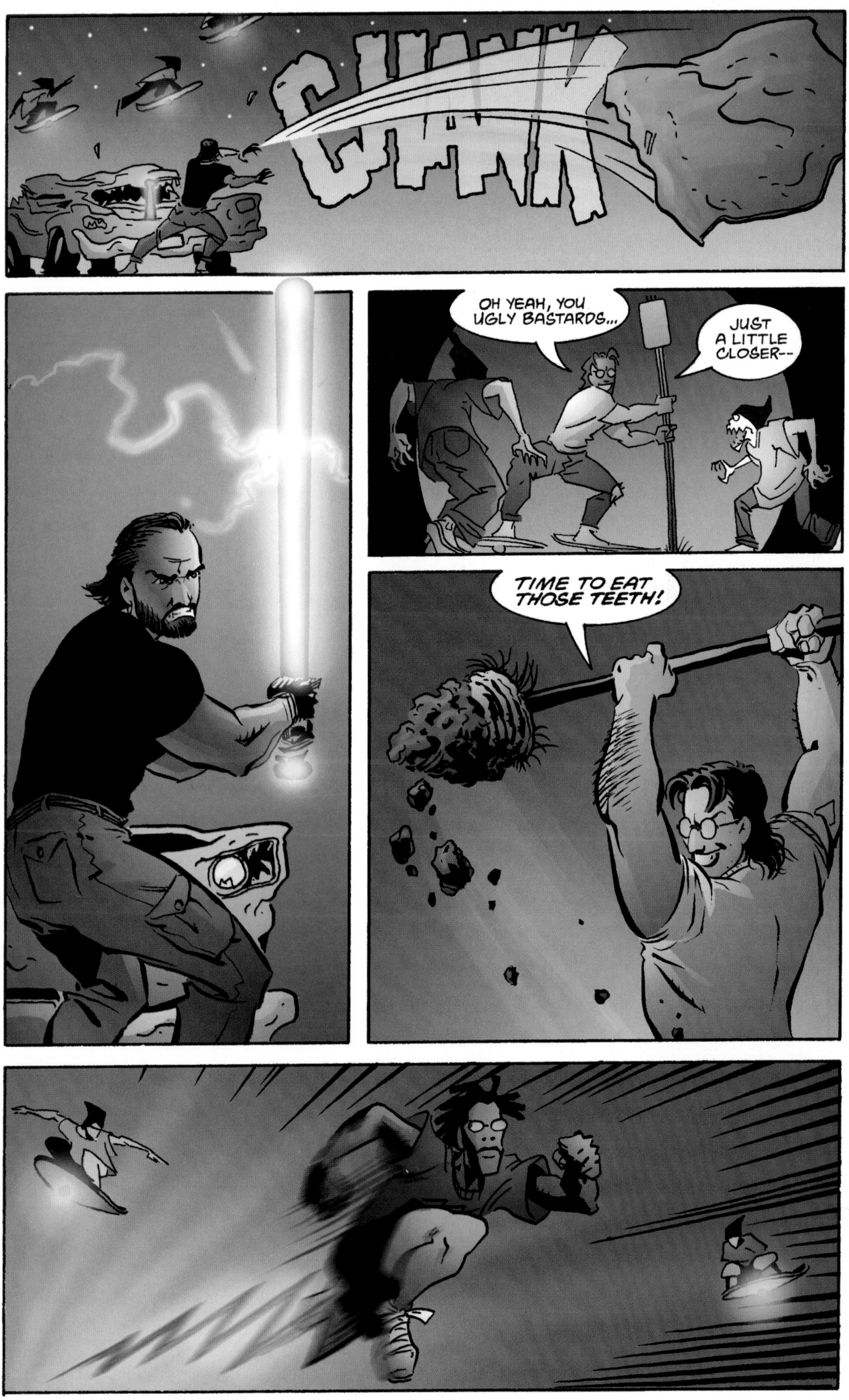
CHANK
OH YEAH, YOU UGLY BASTARDS...
JUST A LITTLE CLOSER--
TIME TO EAT THOSE TEETH!

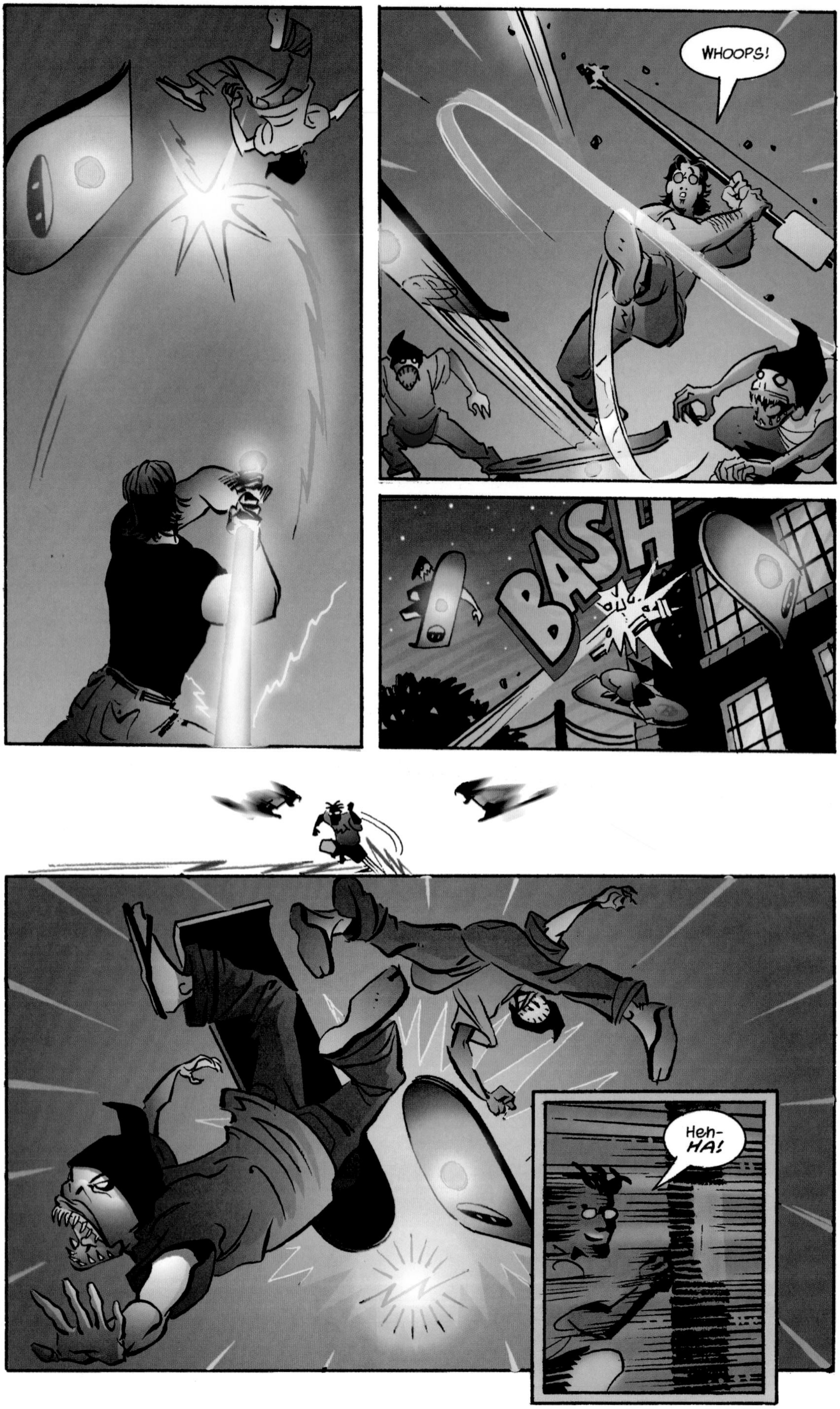
WHOOPS!
BASH
Heh-
HA!

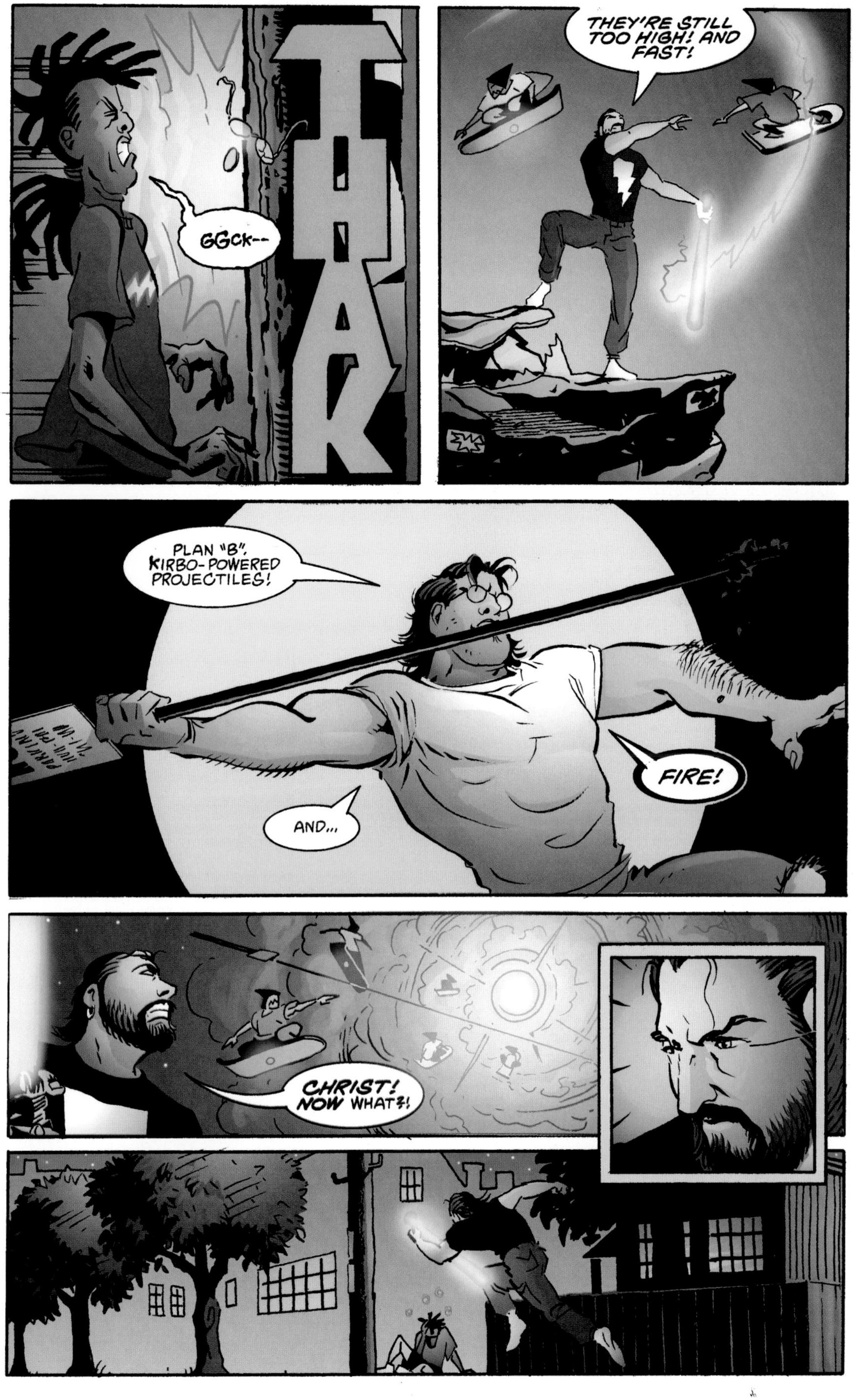
GGck--
THAK
THEY'RE STILL TOO HIGH! AND FAST!
PLAN "B". KIRBO-POWERED PROJECTILES!
AND...
FIRE!
CHRIST! NOW WHAT?!

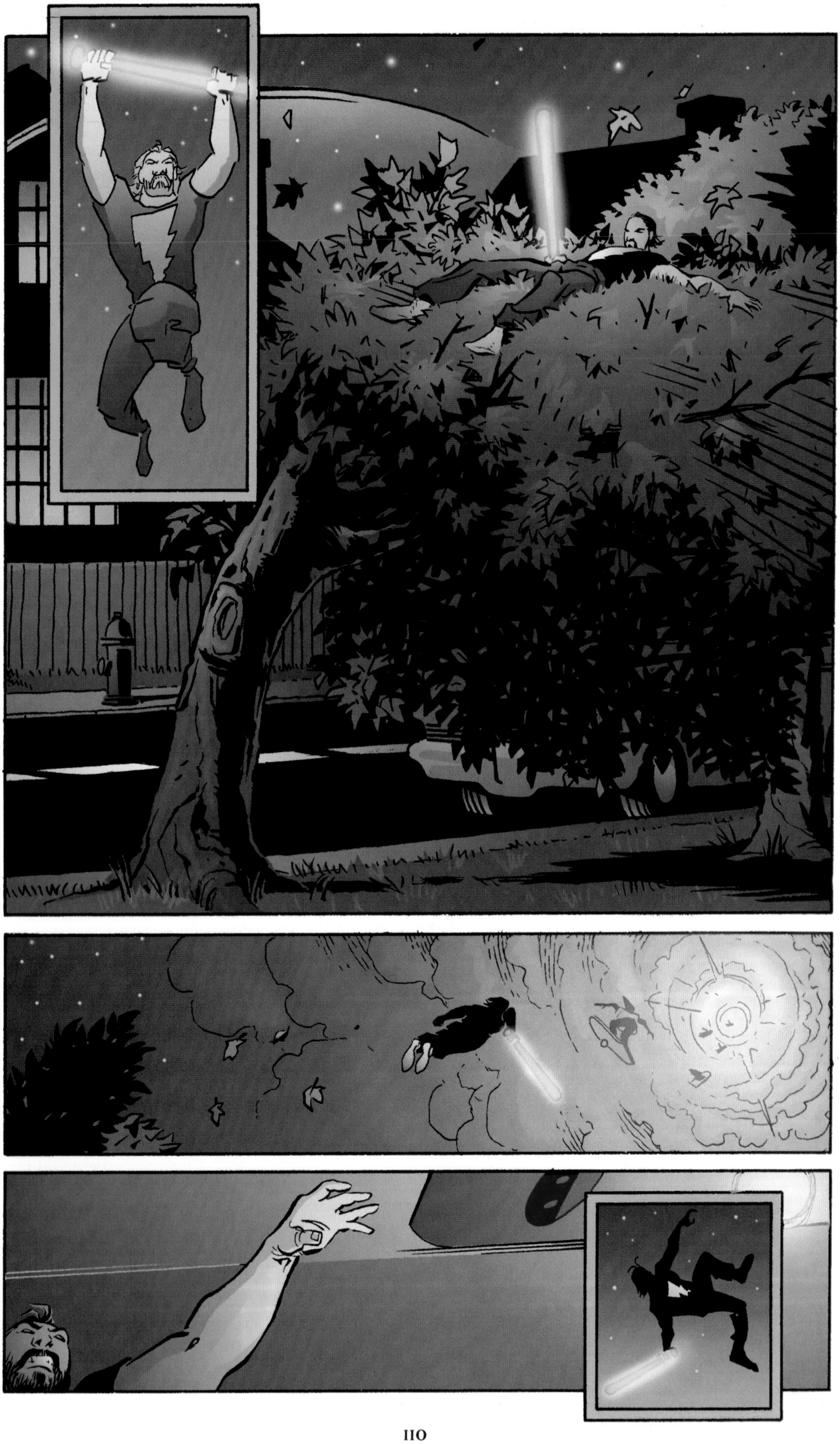

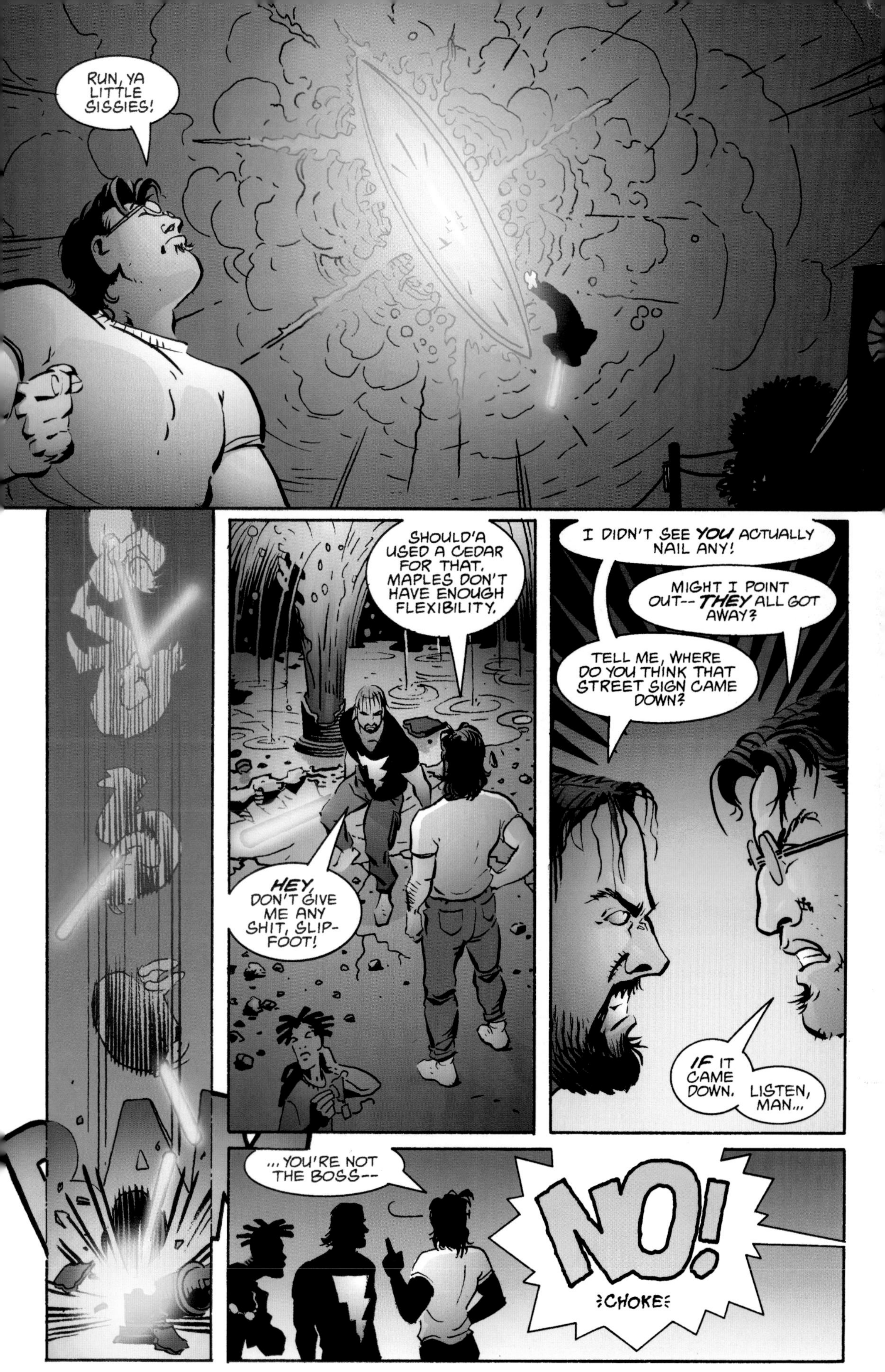
RUN, YA LITTLE SISSIES!
SHOULD'A USED A CEDAR FOR THAT. MAPLES DON'T HAVE ENOUGH FLEXIBILITY.
HEY, DON'T GIVE ME ANY SHIT, SLIP-FOOT!
I DIDN'T SEE YOU ACTUALLY NAIL ANY!
MIGHT I POINT OUT--THEY ALL GOT AWAY?
TELL ME, WHERE DO YOU THINK THAT STREET SIGN CAME DOWN?
IF IT CAME DOWN.
LISTEN, MAN...
...YOU'RE NOT THE BOSS--
NO!
CHOKE

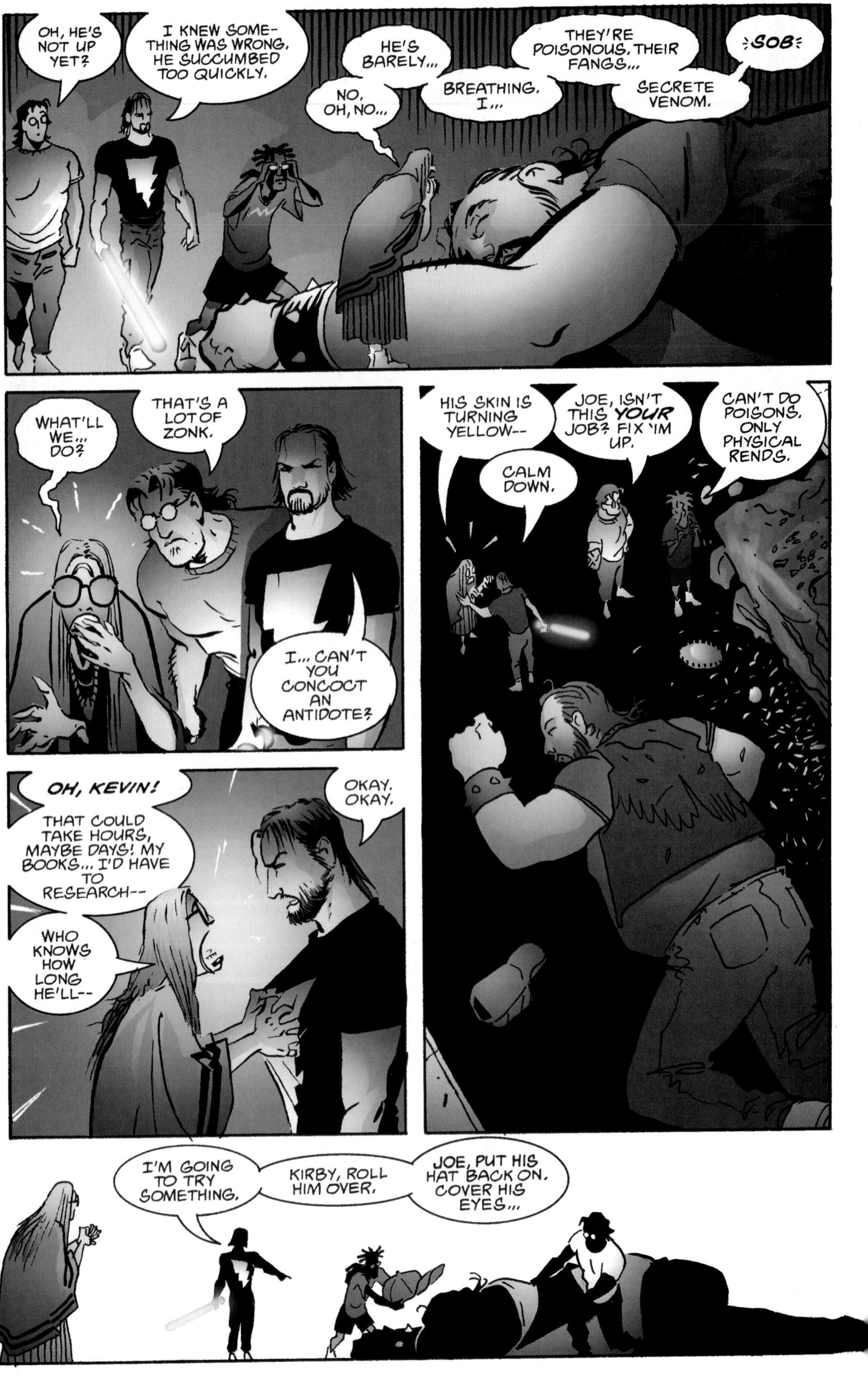
OH, HE'S NOT UP YET?
I KNEW SOMETHING WAS WRONG. HE SUCCUMBED TOO QUICKLY.
HE'S BARELY...
NO, OH, NO...
BREATHING. I...
THEY'RE POISONOUS, THEIR FANGS...
SECRETE VENOM.
SOB
WHAT'LL WE... DO?
THAT'S A LOT OF ZONK.
I... CAN'T YOU CONCOCT AN ANTIDOTE?
OH, KEVIN!
THAT COULD TAKE HOURS, MAYBE DAYS! MY BOOKS... I'D HAVE TO RESEARCH--
WHO KNOWS HOW LONG HE'LL--
OKAY. OKAY.
HIS SKIN IS TURNING YELLOW--
CALM DOWN.
JOE, ISN'T THIS YOUR JOB? FIX 'IM UP.
CAN'T DO POISONS. ONLY PHYSICAL RENDS.
I'M GOING TO TRY SOMETHING.
KIRBY, ROLL HIM OVER.
JOE, PUT HIS HAT BACK ON. COVER HIS EYES...

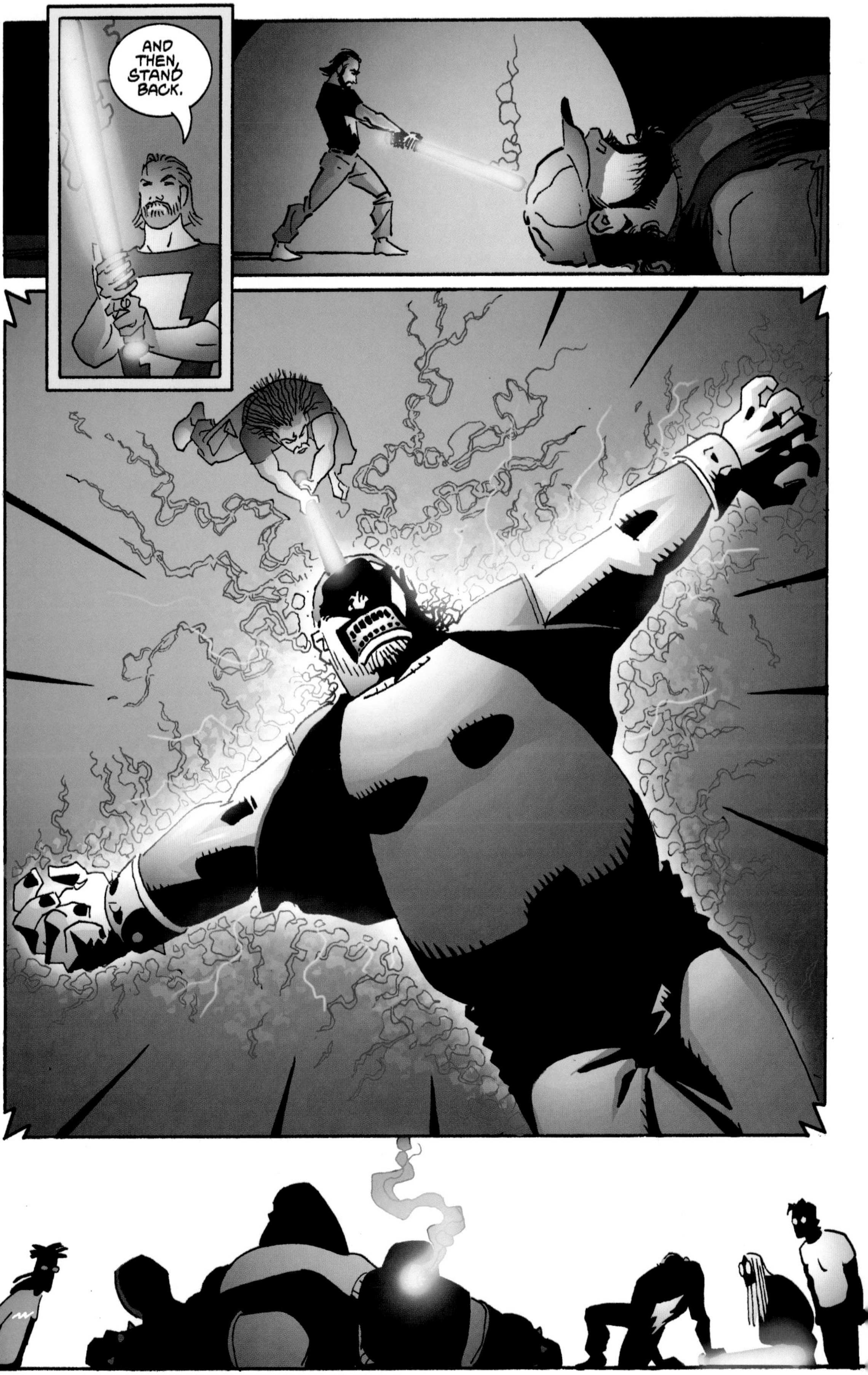
AND THEN, STAND BACK.

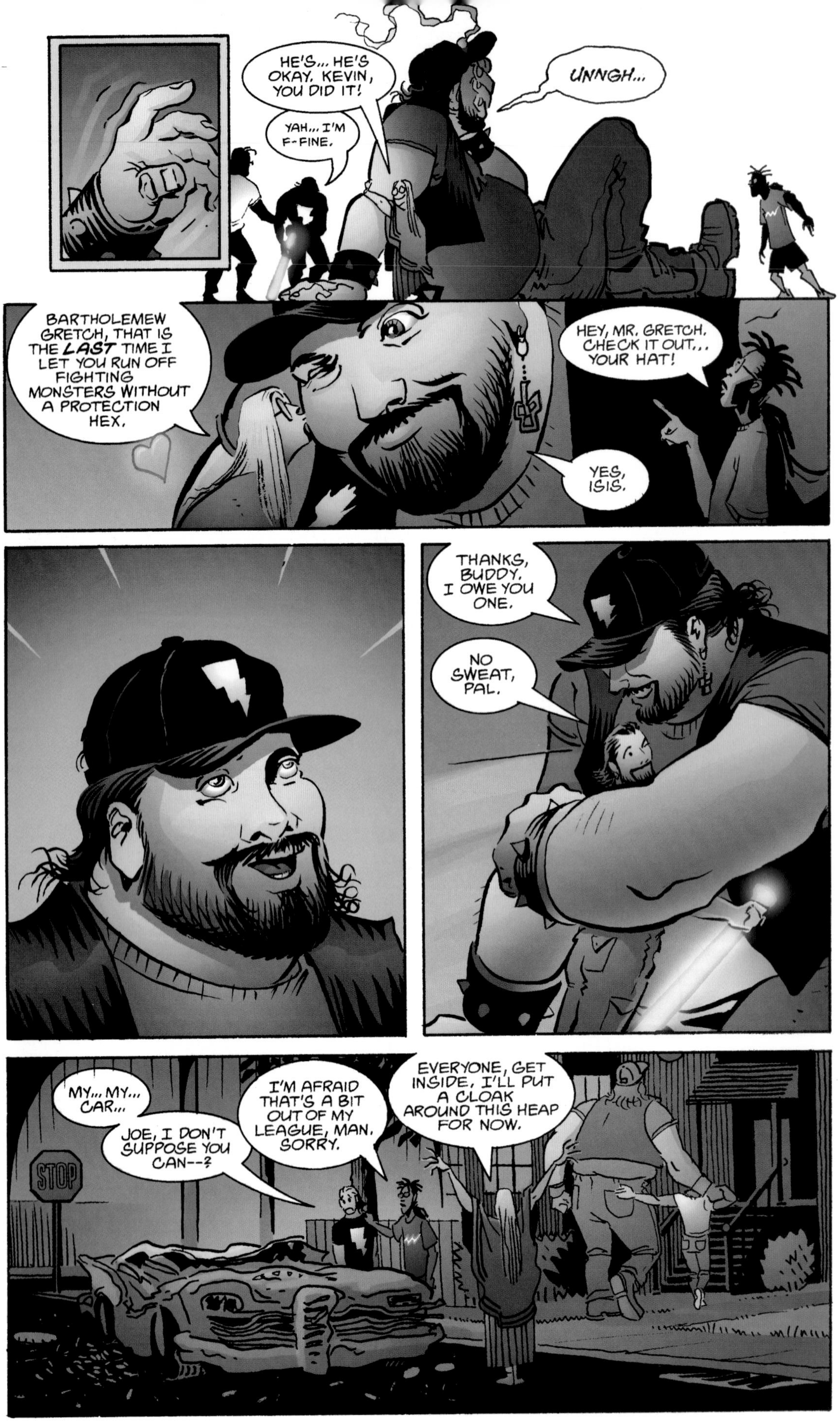
HE'S... HE'S OKAY, KEVIN, YOU DID IT!
YAH... I'M F-FINE.
UNNGH...
BARTHOLEMEW GRETCH, THAT IS THE *LAST* TIME I LET YOU RUN OFF FIGHTING MONSTERS WITHOUT A PROTECTION HEX.
YES, ISIS.
HEY, MR. GRETCH, CHECK IT OUT... YOUR HAT!
THANKS, BUDDY, I OWE YOU ONE.
NO SWEAT, PAL.
MY... MY... CAR...
JOE, I DON'T SUPPOSE YOU CAN--?
I'M AFRAID THAT'S A BIT OUT OF MY LEAGUE, MAN. SORRY.
EVERYONE, GET INSIDE, I'LL PUT A CLOAK AROUND THIS HEAP FOR NOW.
STOP

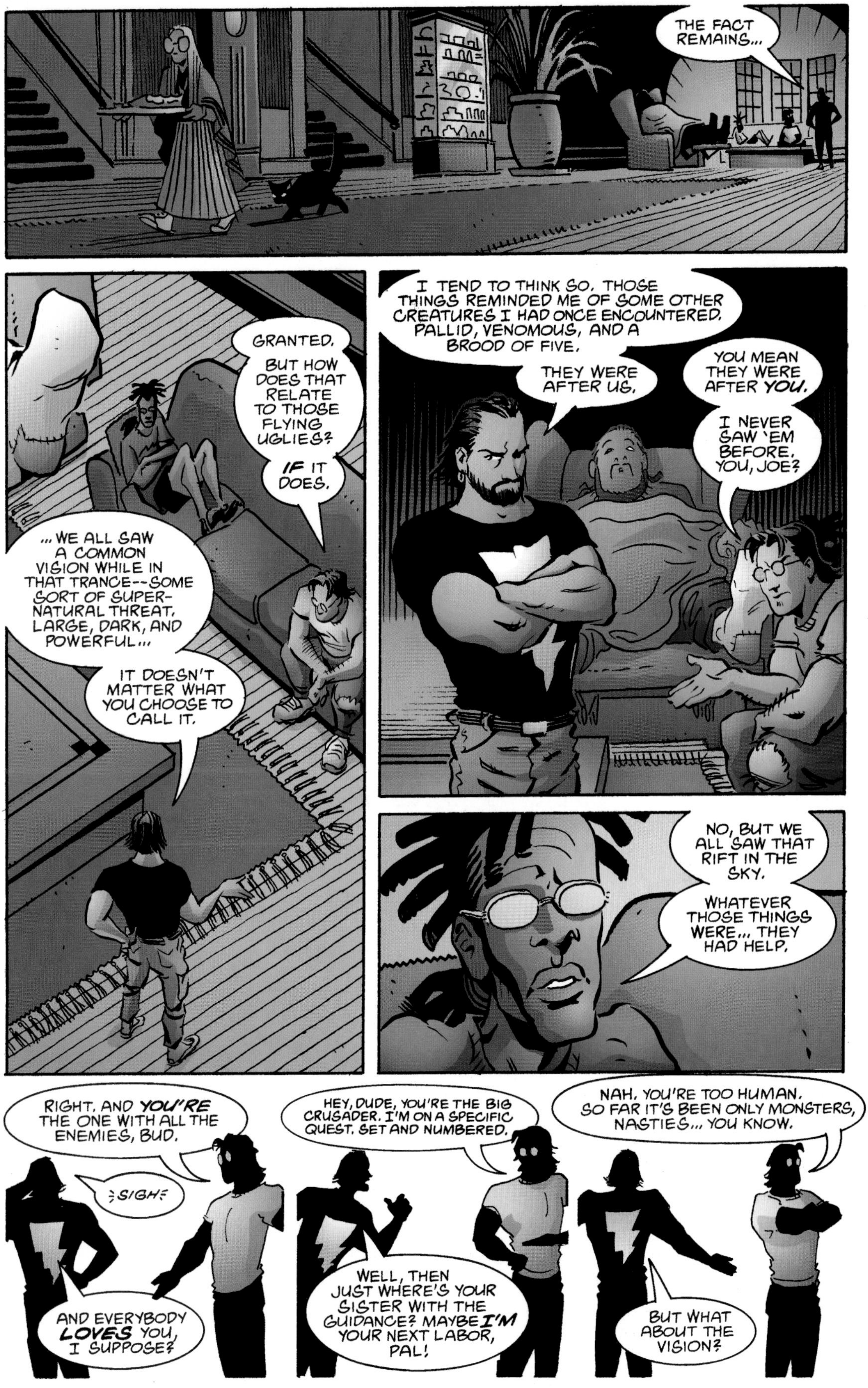
THE FACT REMAINS...
GRANTED. BUT HOW DOES THAT RELATE TO THOSE FLYING UGLIES?
IF IT DOES.
...WE ALL SAW A COMMON VISION WHILE IN THAT TRANCE--SOME SORT OF SUPER-NATURAL THREAT. LARGE, DARK, AND POWERFUL...
IT DOESN'T MATTER WHAT YOU CHOOSE TO CALL IT.
I TEND TO THINK SO. THOSE THINGS REMINDED ME OF SOME OTHER CREATURES I HAD ONCE ENCOUNTERED. PALLID, VENOMOUS, AND A BROOD OF FIVE.
THEY WERE AFTER US.
YOU MEAN THEY WERE AFTER YOU.
I NEVER SAW 'EM BEFORE. YOU, JOE?
NO, BUT WE ALL SAW THAT RIFT IN THE SKY.
WHATEVER THOSE THINGS WERE... THEY HAD HELP.
RIGHT. AND YOU'RE THE ONE WITH ALL THE ENEMIES, BUD.
SIGH
AND EVERYBODY LOVES YOU, I SUPPOSE?
HEY, DUDE, YOU'RE THE BIG CRUSADER. I'M ON A SPECIFIC QUEST. SET AND NUMBERED.
WELL, THEN JUST WHERE'S YOUR SISTER WITH THE GUIDANCE? MAYBE I'M YOUR NEXT LABOR, PAL!
NAH. YOU'RE TOO HUMAN. SO FAR IT'S BEEN ONLY MONSTERS, NASTIES... YOU KNOW.
BUT WHAT ABOUT THE VISION?

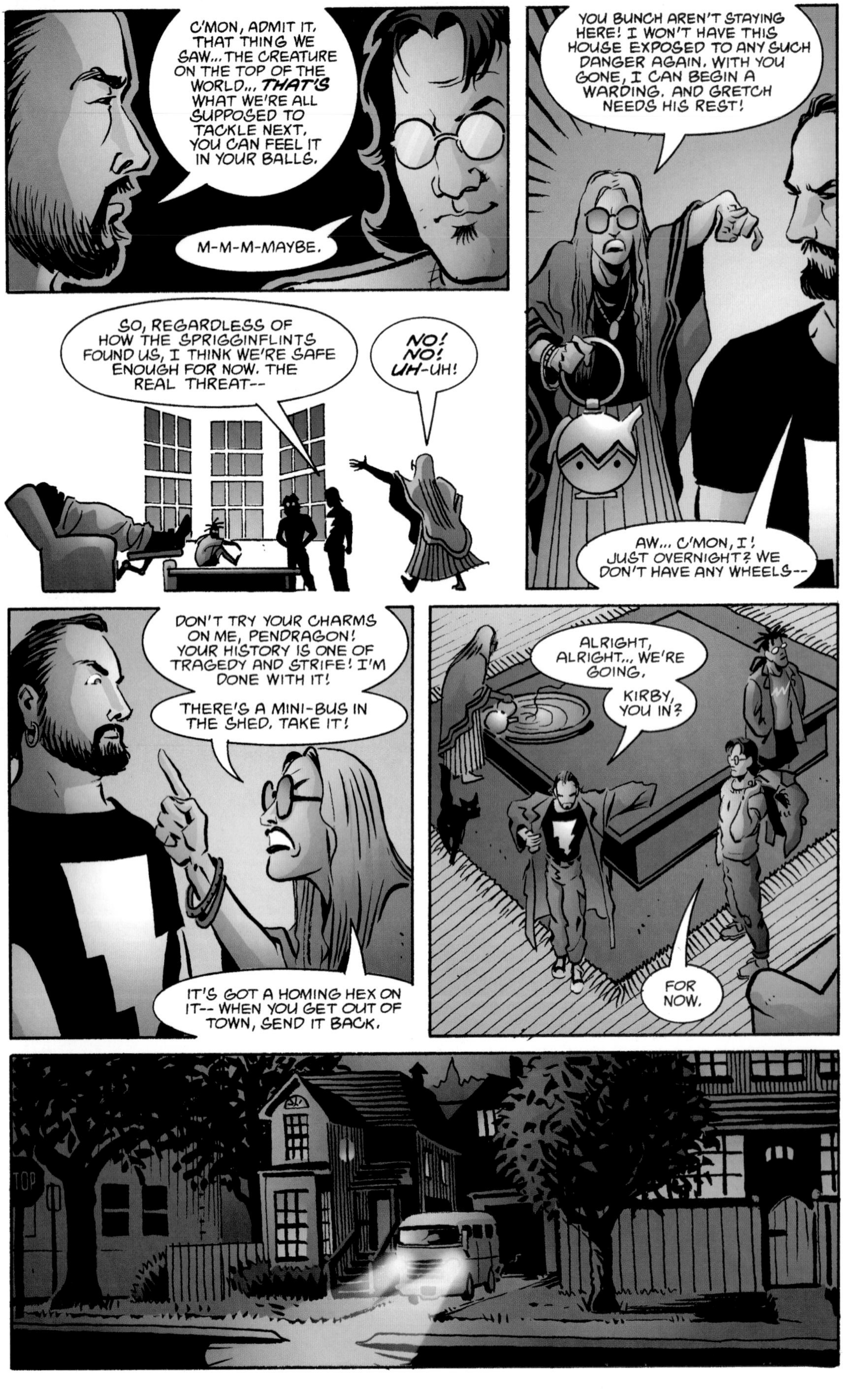
C'MON, ADMIT IT. THAT THING WE SAW... THE CREATURE ON THE TOP OF THE WORLD... *THAT'S* WHAT WE'RE ALL SUPPOSED TO TACKLE NEXT. YOU CAN FEEL IT IN YOUR BALLS.
M-M-M-MAYBE.
YOU BUNCH AREN'T STAYING HERE! I WON'T HAVE THIS HOUSE EXPOSED TO ANY SUCH DANGER AGAIN. WITH YOU GONE, I CAN BEGIN A WARDING. AND GRETCH NEEDS HIS REST!
SO, REGARDLESS OF HOW THE SPRIGGINFLINTS FOUND US, I THINK WE'RE SAFE ENOUGH FOR NOW. THE REAL THREAT--
NO! NO! UH-UH!
AW... C'MON, I! JUST OVERNIGHT? WE DON'T HAVE ANY WHEELS--
DON'T TRY YOUR CHARMS ON ME, PENDRAGON! YOUR HISTORY IS ONE OF TRAGEDY AND STRIFE! I'M DONE WITH IT!
THERE'S A MINI-BUS IN THE SHED. TAKE IT!
IT'S GOT A HOMING HEX ON IT-- WHEN YOU GET OUT OF TOWN, SEND IT BACK.
ALRIGHT, ALRIGHT... WE'RE GOING.
KIRBY, YOU IN?
FOR NOW.
STOP

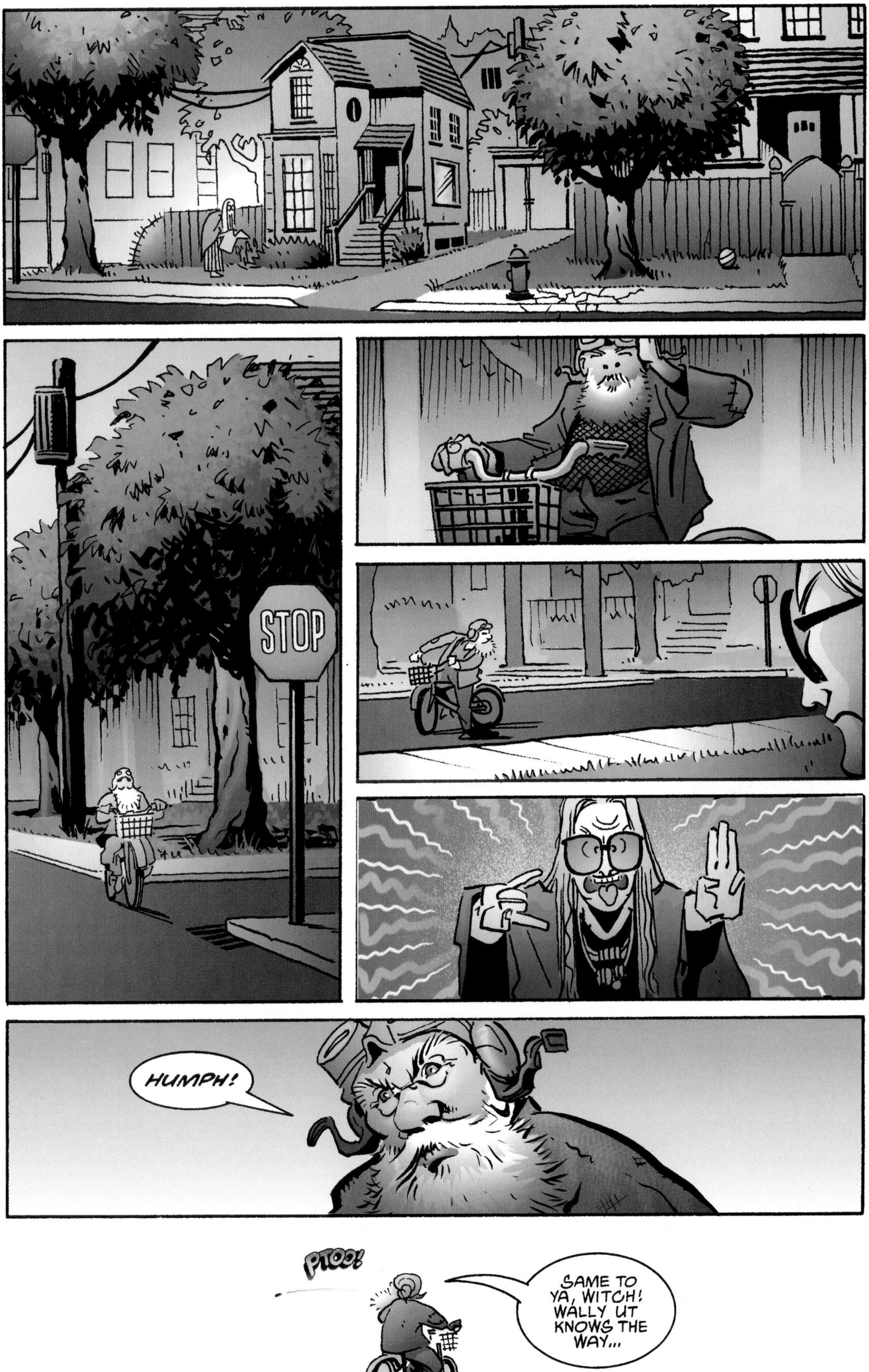
STOP
HUMPH!
PTOO!
SAME TO YA, WITCH! WALLY UT KNOWS THE WAY...

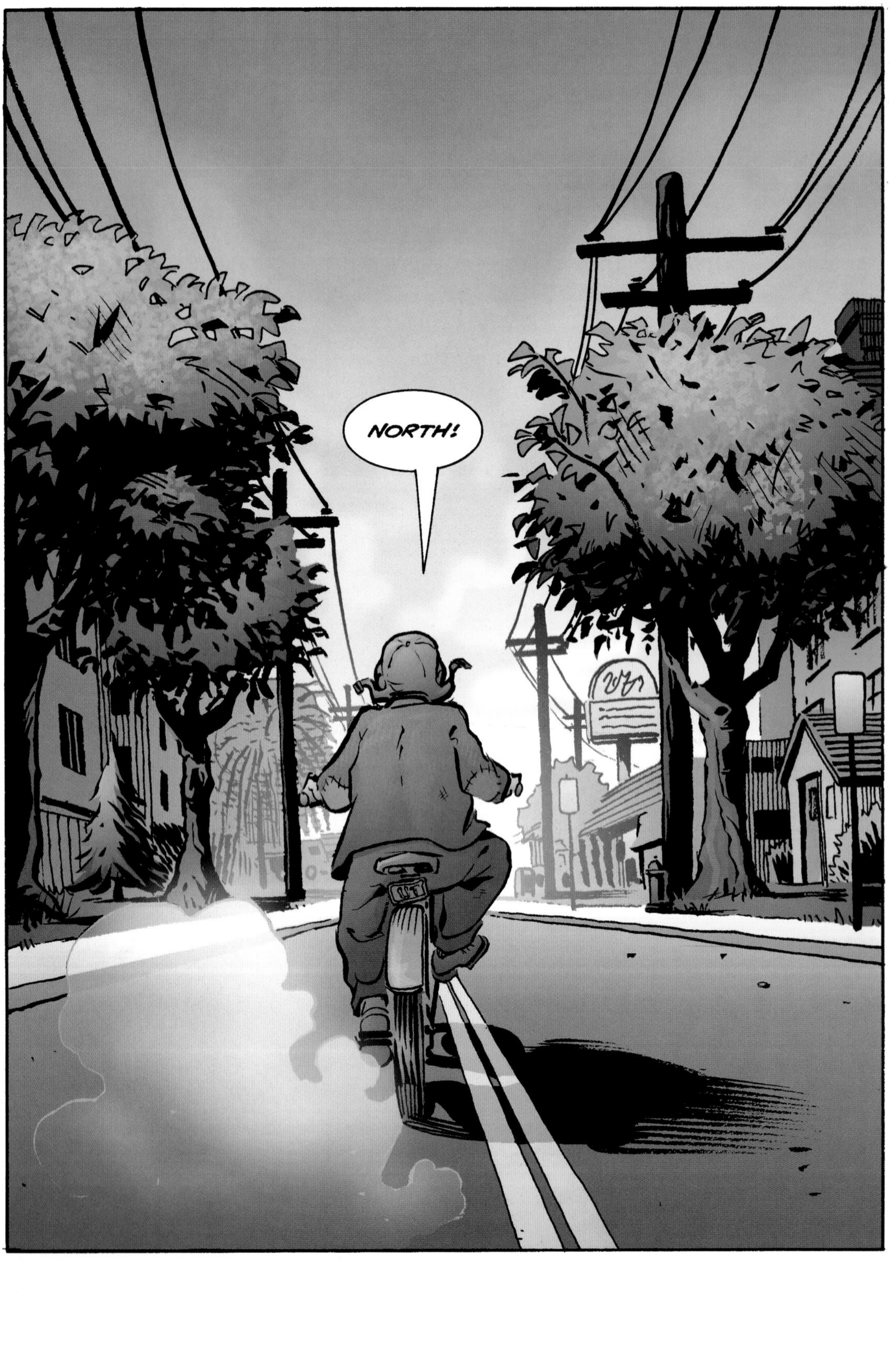
NORTH!

THE HERO DEFINED

MAGE®

chapter 5

"Come What Come May"

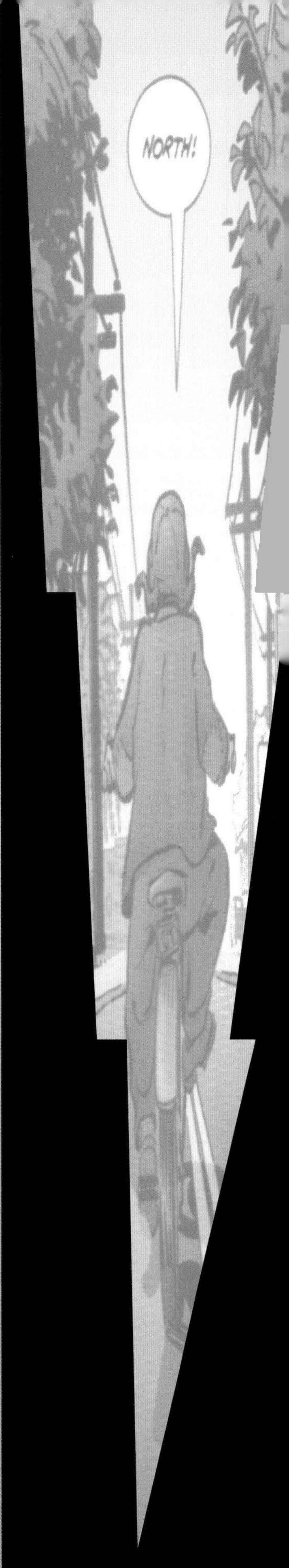
NORTH!

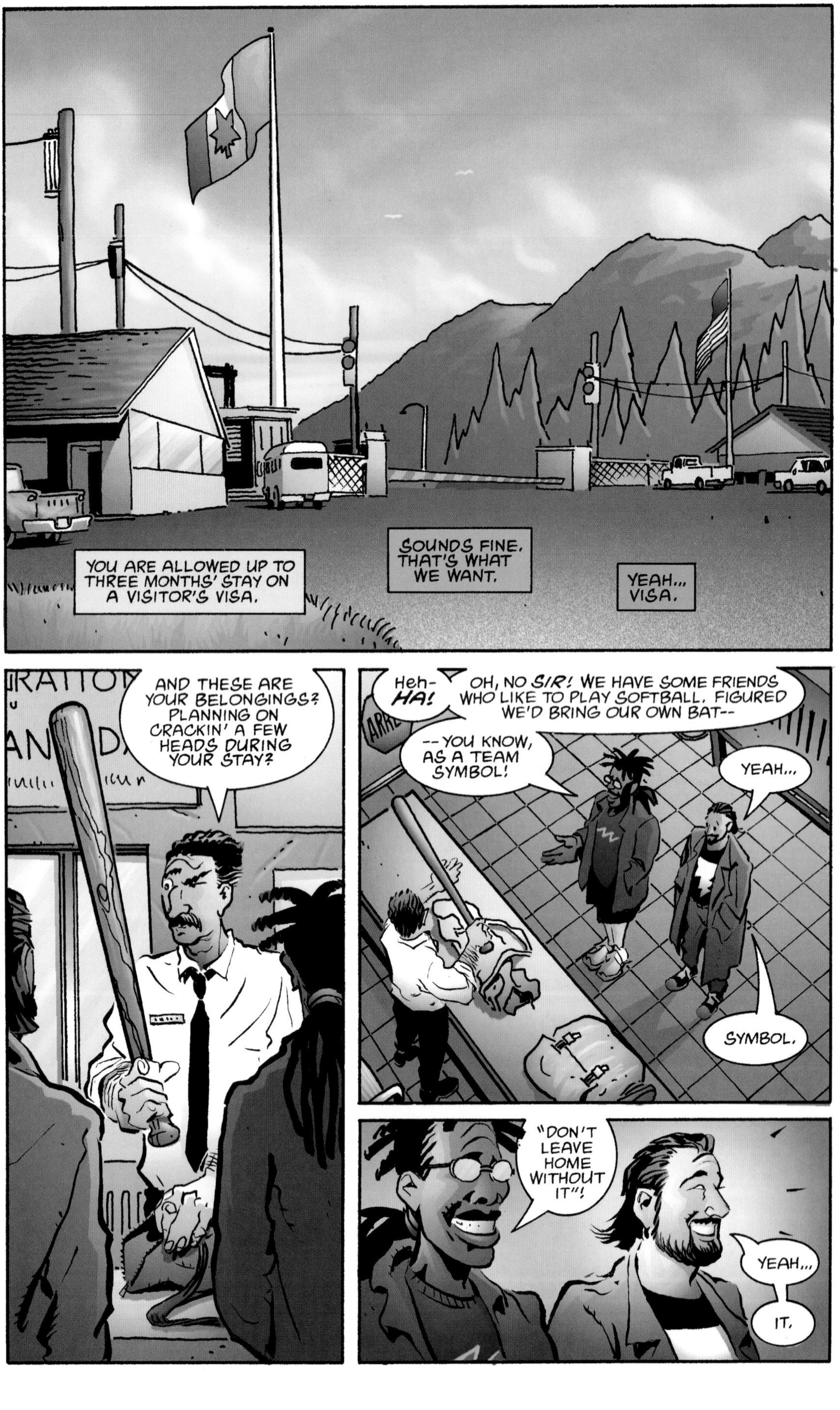
YOU ARE ALLOWED UP TO THREE MONTHS' STAY ON A VISITOR'S VISA.
SOUNDS FINE. THAT'S WHAT WE WANT.
YEAH... VISA.
AND THESE ARE YOUR BELONGINGS? PLANNING ON CRACKIN' A FEW HEADS DURING YOUR STAY?
Heh-HA!
OH, NO SIR! WE HAVE SOME FRIENDS WHO LIKE TO PLAY SOFTBALL. FIGURED WE'D BRING OUR OWN BAT--
--YOU KNOW, AS A TEAM SYMBOL!
YEAH...
SYMBOL.
"DON'T LEAVE HOME WITHOUT IT"!
YEAH...
IT.

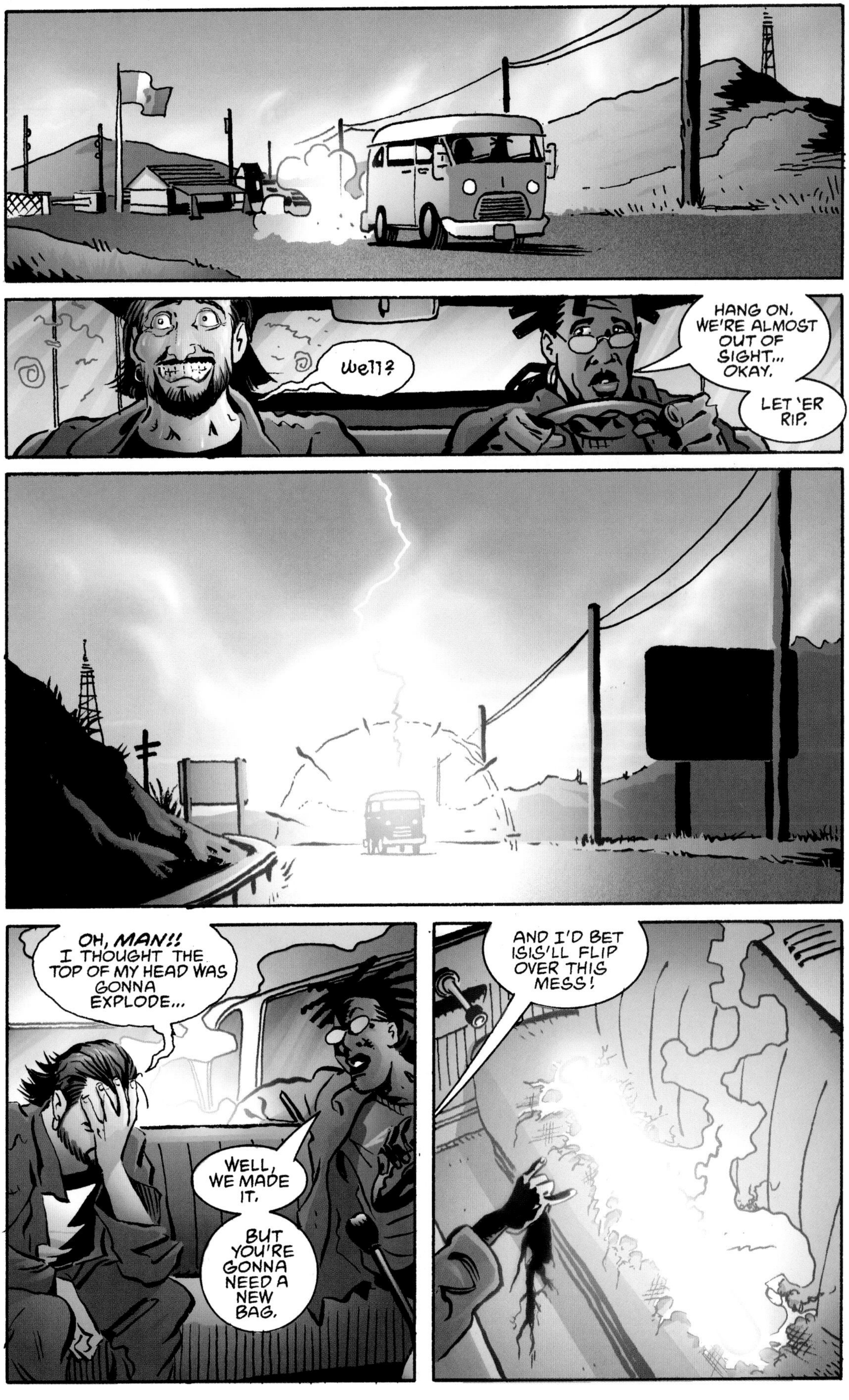
Well?
HANG ON. WE'RE ALMOST OUT OF SIGHT... OKAY.
LET 'ER RIP.
OH, MAN!! I THOUGHT THE TOP OF MY HEAD WAS GONNA EXPLODE...
WELL, WE MADE IT.
BUT YOU'RE GONNA NEED A NEW BAG.
AND I'D BET ISIS'LL FLIP OVER THIS MESS!

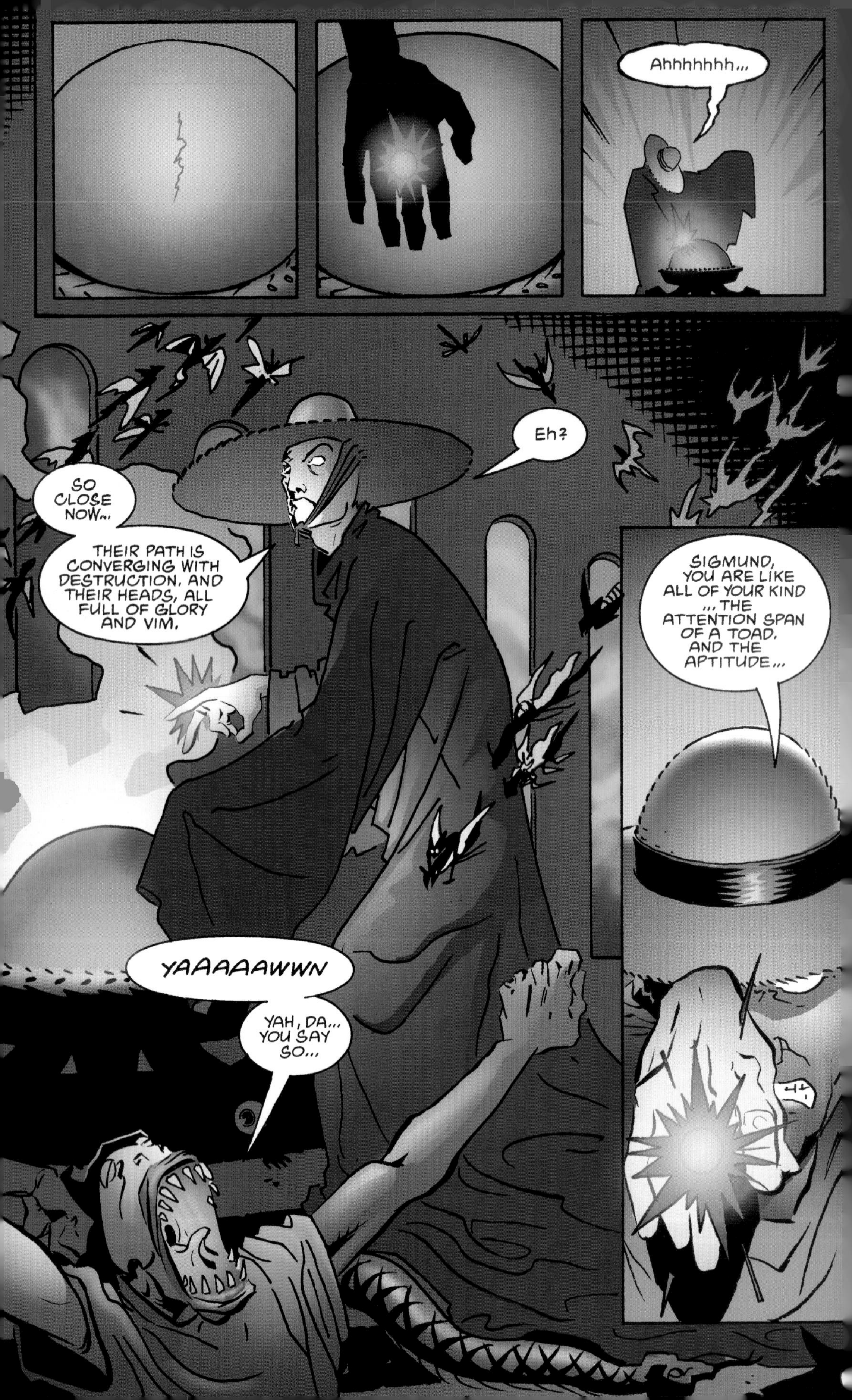
Ahhhhhhh...
SO CLOSE NOW...
THEIR PATH IS CONVERGING WITH DESTRUCTION. AND THEIR HEADS, ALL FULL OF GLORY AND VIM.
Eh?
YAAAAAWWN
YAH, DA... YOU SAY SO...
SIGMUND, YOU ARE LIKE ALL OF YOUR KIND ...THE ATTENTION SPAN OF A TOAD. AND THE APTITUDE...

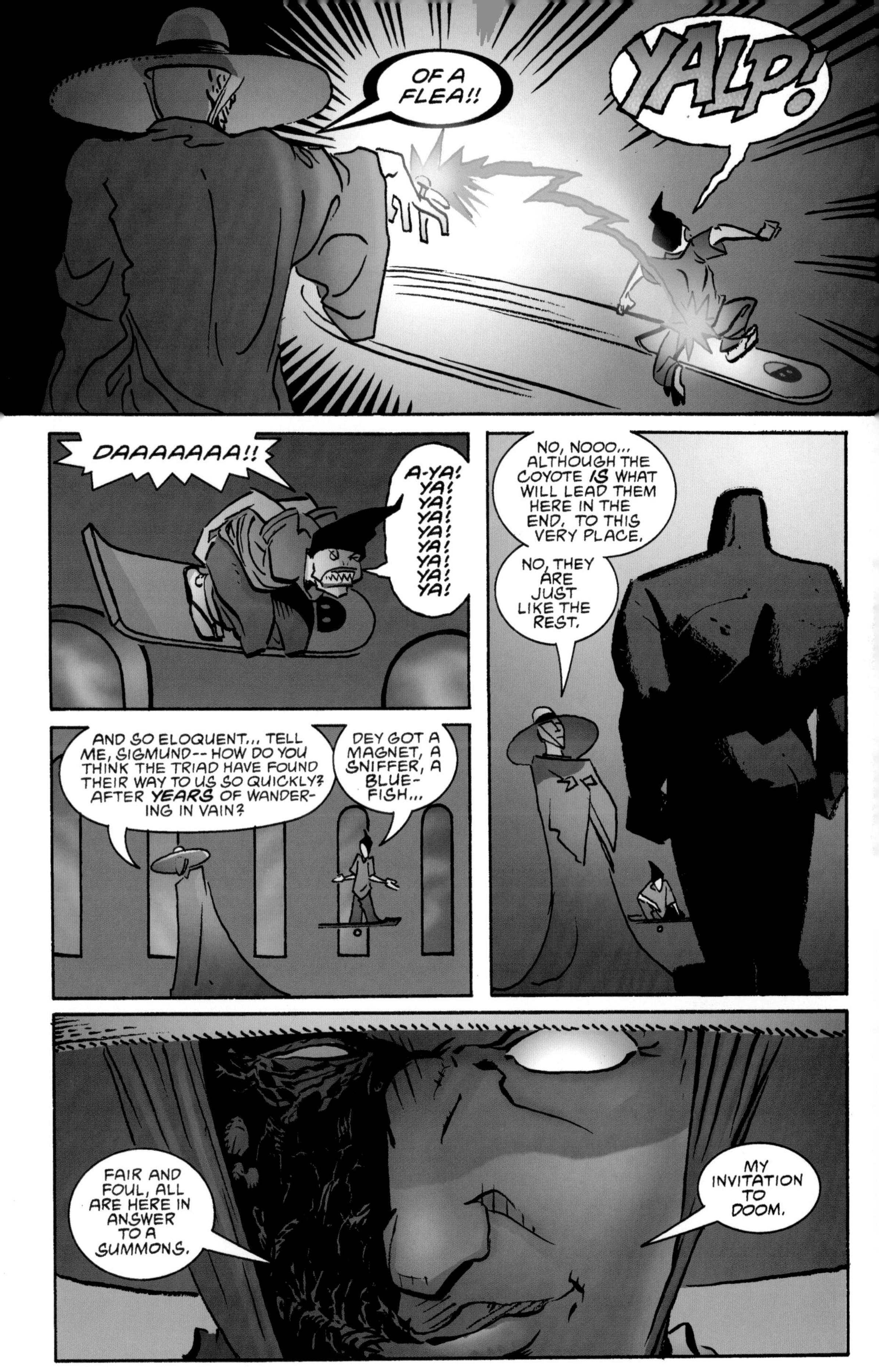
OF A FLEA!!
YALP!
DAAAAAAA!!
A-YA! YA! YA! YA! YA! YA! YA! YA! YA!
AND SO ELOQUENT... TELL ME, SIGMUND-- HOW DO YOU THINK THE TRIAD HAVE FOUND THEIR WAY TO US SO QUICKLY? AFTER YEARS OF WANDERING IN VAIN?
DEY GOT A MAGNET, A SNIFFER, A BLUE-FISH...
NO, NOOO... ALTHOUGH THE COYOTE IS WHAT WILL LEAD THEM HERE IN THE END, TO THIS VERY PLACE.
NO, THEY ARE JUST LIKE THE REST.
FAIR AND FOUL, ALL ARE HERE IN ANSWER TO A SUMMONS.
MY INVITATION TO DOOM.

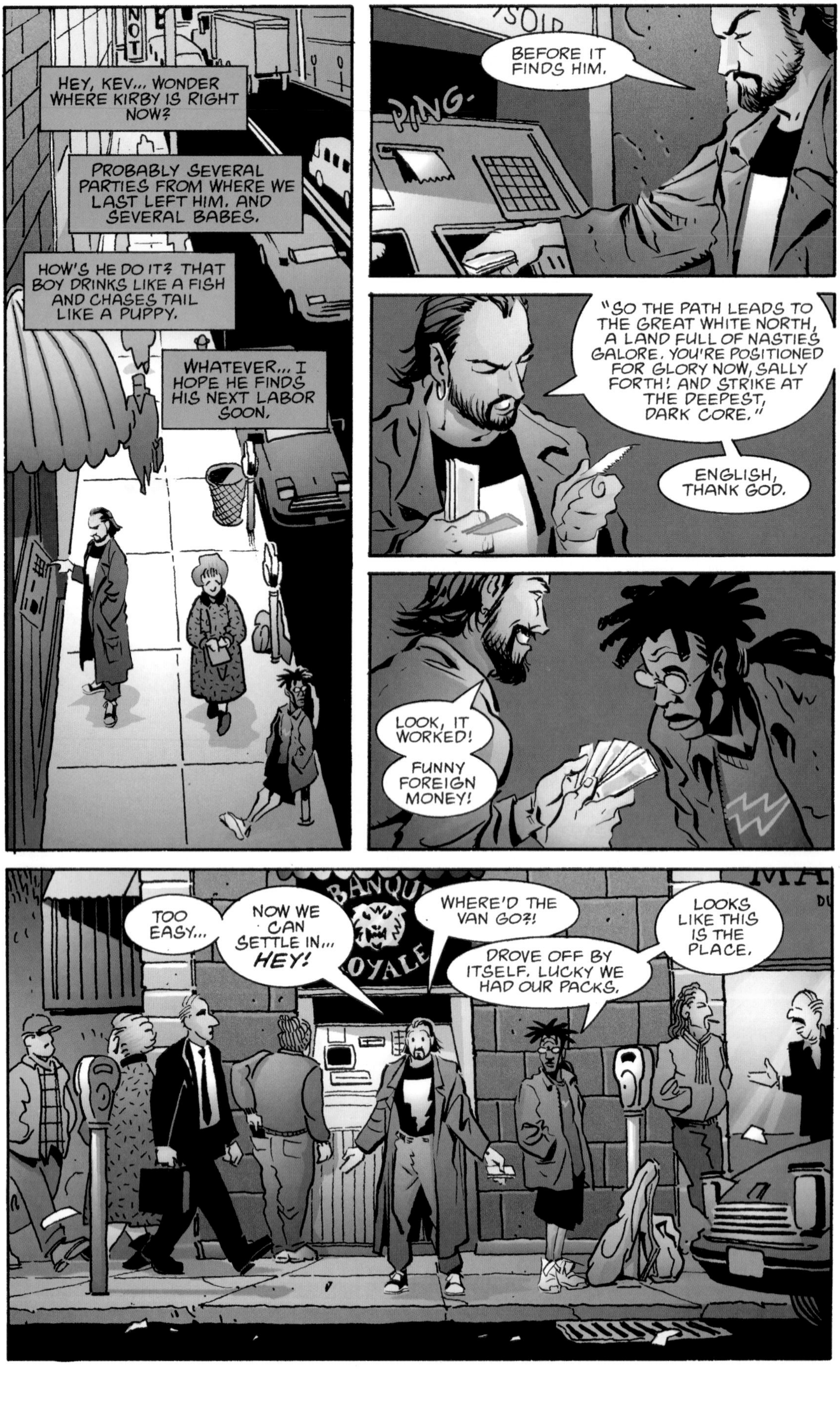
HEY, KEV... WONDER WHERE KIRBY IS RIGHT NOW?
PROBABLY SEVERAL PARTIES FROM WHERE WE LAST LEFT HIM. AND SEVERAL BABES.
HOW'S HE DO IT? THAT BOY DRINKS LIKE A FISH AND CHASES TAIL LIKE A PUPPY.
WHATEVER... I HOPE HE FINDS HIS NEXT LABOR SOON.
BEFORE IT FINDS HIM.
PING-
"SO THE PATH LEADS TO THE GREAT WHITE NORTH, A LAND FULL OF NASTIES GALORE. YOU'RE POSITIONED FOR GLORY NOW, SALLY FORTH! AND STRIKE AT THE DEEPEST, DARK CORE."
ENGLISH, THANK GOD.
LOOK, IT WORKED!
FUNNY FOREIGN MONEY!
TOO EASY...
NOW WE CAN SETTLE IN... HEY!
WHERE'D THE VAN GO?!
DROVE OFF BY ITSELF. LUCKY WE HAD OUR PACKS.
LOOKS LIKE THIS IS THE PLACE.

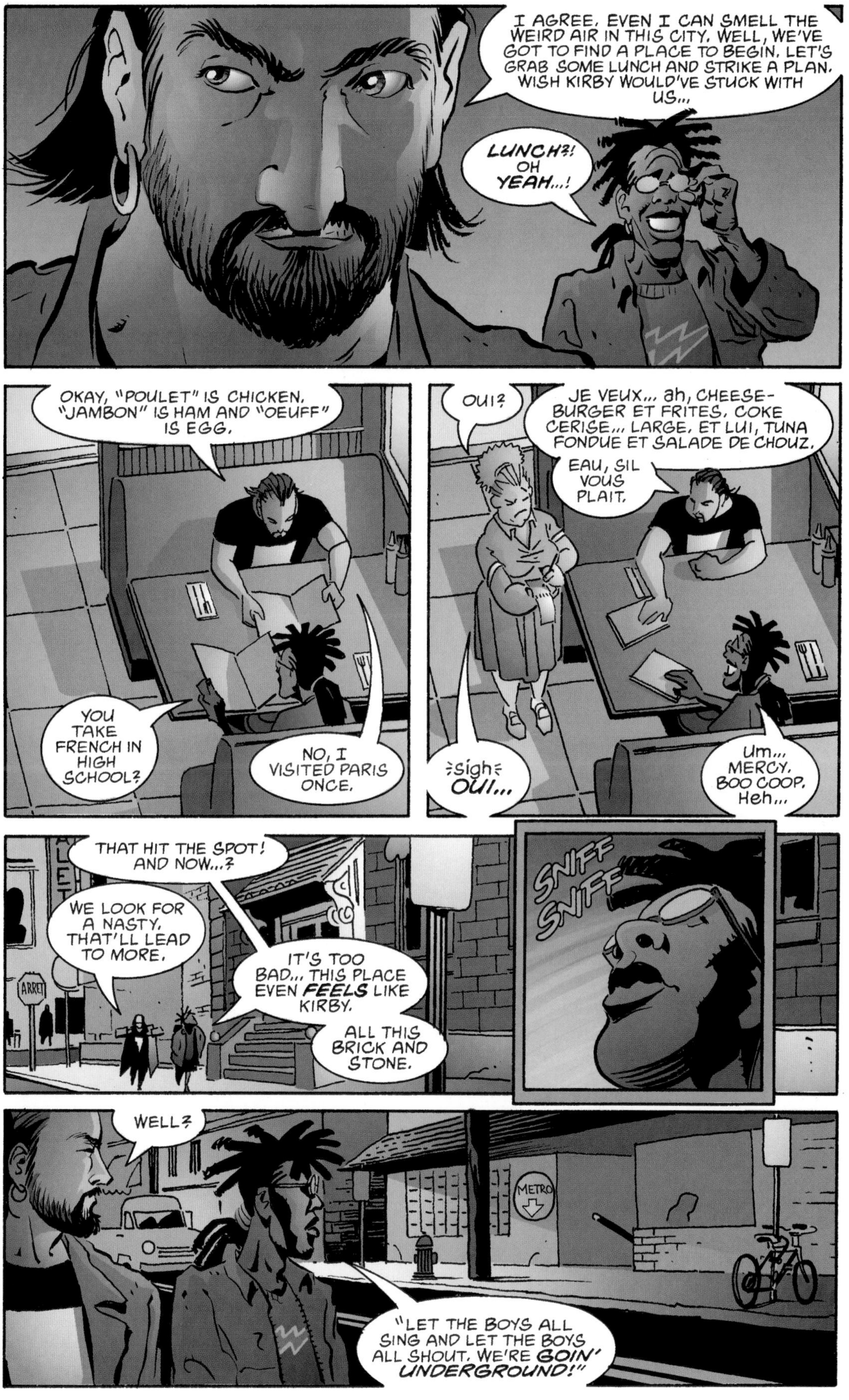
I AGREE. EVEN I CAN SMELL THE WEIRD AIR IN THIS CITY. WELL, WE'VE GOT TO FIND A PLACE TO BEGIN. LET'S GRAB SOME LUNCH AND STRIKE A PLAN. WISH KIRBY WOULD'VE STUCK WITH US...
LUNCH?! OH YEAH...!
OKAY, "POULET" IS CHICKEN. "JAMBON" IS HAM AND "OEUFF" IS EGG.
YOU TAKE FRENCH IN HIGH SCHOOL?
NO, I VISITED PARIS ONCE.
OUI?
JE VEUX... ah, CHEESE-BURGER ET FRITES. COKE CERISE... LARGE. ET LUI, TUNA FONDUE ET SALADE DE CHOUZ.
EAU, SIL VOUS PLAIT.
sigh OUI...
Um... MERCY. BOO COOP. Heh...
THAT HIT THE SPOT! AND NOW...?
WE LOOK FOR A NASTY. THAT'LL LEAD TO MORE.
IT'S TOO BAD... THIS PLACE EVEN FEELS LIKE KIRBY.
ALL THIS BRICK AND STONE.
ARRET
SNIFF SNIFF
WELL?
METRO
"LET THE BOYS ALL SING AND LET THE BOYS ALL SHOUT. WE'RE GOIN' UNDERGROUND!"

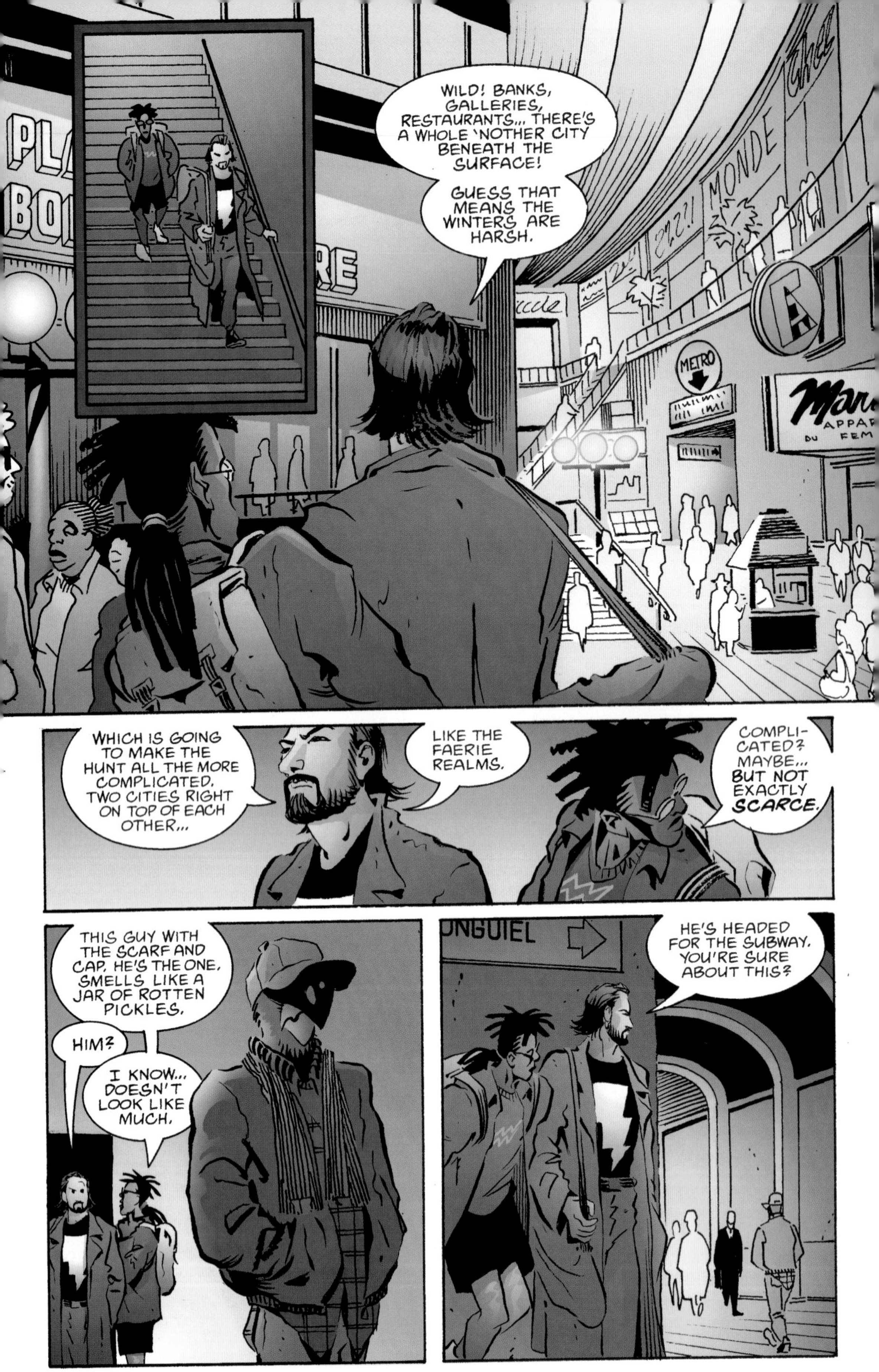
WILD! BANKS, GALLERIES, RESTAURANTS... THERE'S A WHOLE 'NOTHER CITY BENEATH THE SURFACE!
GUESS THAT MEANS THE WINTERS ARE HARSH.
MONDE
METRO
WHICH IS GOING TO MAKE THE HUNT ALL THE MORE COMPLICATED. TWO CITIES RIGHT ON TOP OF EACH OTHER...
LIKE THE FAERIE REALMS.
COMPLI-CATED? MAYBE... BUT NOT EXACTLY SCARCE.
THIS GUY WITH THE SCARF AND CAP. HE'S THE ONE. SMELLS LIKE A JAR OF ROTTEN PICKLES.
HIM?
I KNOW... DOESN'T LOOK LIKE MUCH.
HE'S HEADED FOR THE SUBWAY. YOU'RE SURE ABOUT THIS?

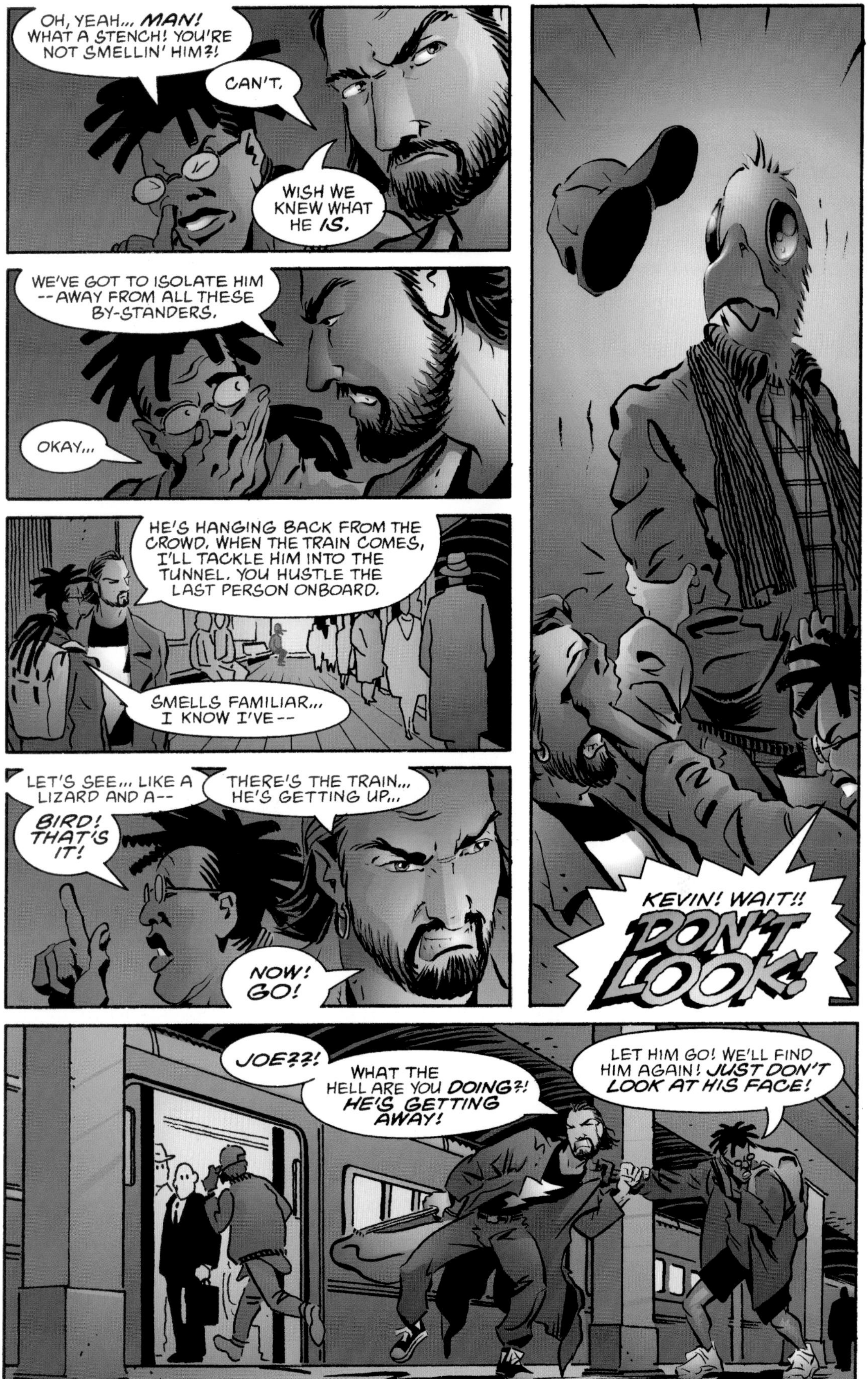
OH, YEAH... MAN! WHAT A STENCH! YOU'RE NOT SMELLIN' HIM?!
CAN'T.
WISH WE KNEW WHAT HE IS.
WE'VE GOT TO ISOLATE HIM --AWAY FROM ALL THESE BY-STANDERS.
OKAY...
HE'S HANGING BACK FROM THE CROWD. WHEN THE TRAIN COMES, I'LL TACKLE HIM INTO THE TUNNEL. YOU HUSTLE THE LAST PERSON ONBOARD.
SMELLS FAMILIAR... I KNOW I'VE--
LET'S SEE... LIKE A LIZARD AND A--
THERE'S THE TRAIN... HE'S GETTING UP...
BIRD! THAT'S IT!
NOW! GO!
KEVIN! WAIT!! DON'T LOOK!
JOE?!
WHAT THE HELL ARE YOU DOING?! HE'S GETTING AWAY!
LET HIM GO! WE'LL FIND HIM AGAIN! JUST DON'T LOOK AT HIS FACE!

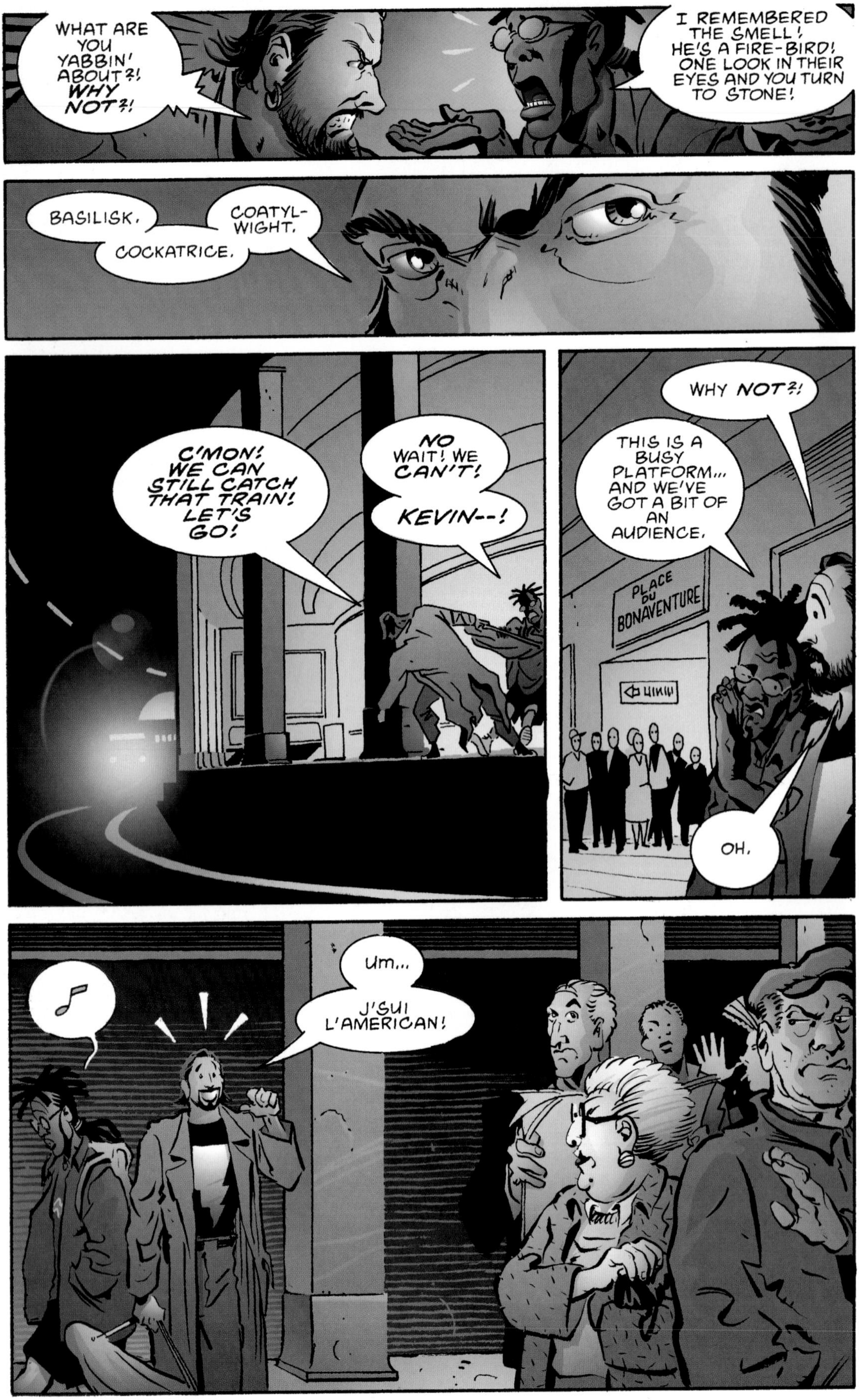
WHAT ARE YOU YABBIN' ABOUT?! WHY NOT?!
I REMEMBERED THE SMELL! HE'S A FIRE-BIRD! ONE LOOK IN THEIR EYES AND YOU TURN TO STONE!
BASILISK.
COCKATRICE.
COATYL-WIGHT.
C'MON! WE CAN STILL CATCH THAT TRAIN! LET'S GO!
NO WAIT! WE CAN'T!
KEVIN--!
WHY NOT?!
THIS IS A BUSY PLATFORM... AND WE'VE GOT A BIT OF AN AUDIENCE.
PLACE DU BONAVENTURE
OH.
♪
UM...
J'SUI L'AMERICAN!

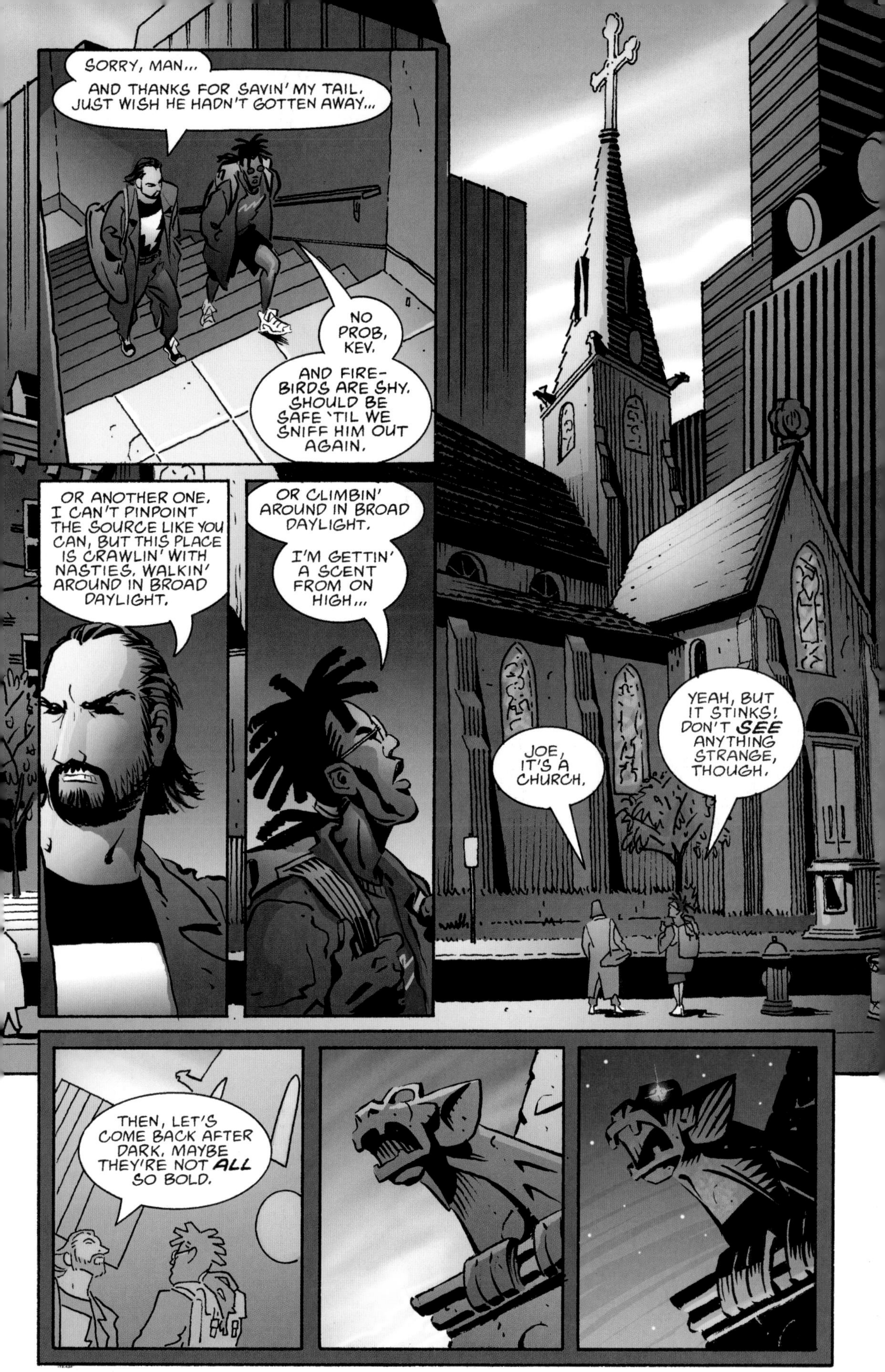
SORRY, MAN...
AND THANKS FOR SAVIN' MY TAIL. JUST WISH HE HADN'T GOTTEN AWAY...
NO PROB, KEV.
AND FIRE-BIRDS ARE SHY. SHOULD BE SAFE 'TIL WE SNIFF HIM OUT AGAIN.
OR ANOTHER ONE. I CAN'T PINPOINT THE SOURCE LIKE YOU CAN, BUT THIS PLACE IS CRAWLIN' WITH NASTIES. WALKIN' AROUND IN BROAD DAYLIGHT.
OR CLIMBIN' AROUND IN BROAD DAYLIGHT.
I'M GETTIN' A SCENT FROM ON HIGH...
JOE, IT'S A CHURCH.
YEAH, BUT IT STINKS! DON'T SEE ANYTHING STRANGE, THOUGH.
THEN, LET'S COME BACK AFTER DARK. MAYBE THEY'RE NOT ALL SO BOLD.

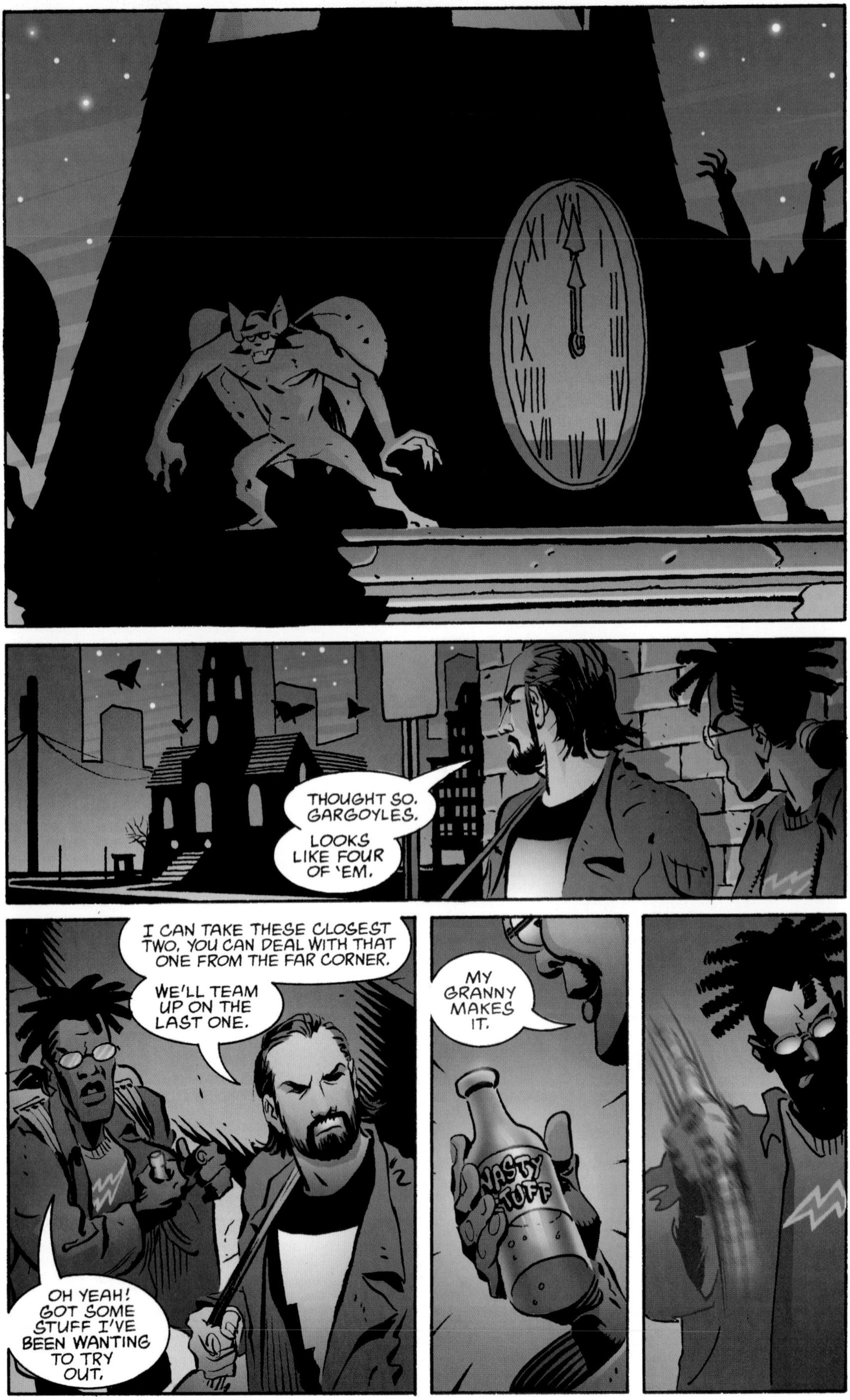
THOUGHT SO. GARGOYLES.
LOOKS LIKE FOUR OF 'EM.
I CAN TAKE THESE CLOSEST TWO, YOU CAN DEAL WITH THAT ONE FROM THE FAR CORNER.
WE'LL TEAM UP ON THE LAST ONE.
OH YEAH! GOT SOME STUFF I'VE BEEN WANTING TO TRY OUT.
MY GRANNY MAKES IT.
NASTY STUFF

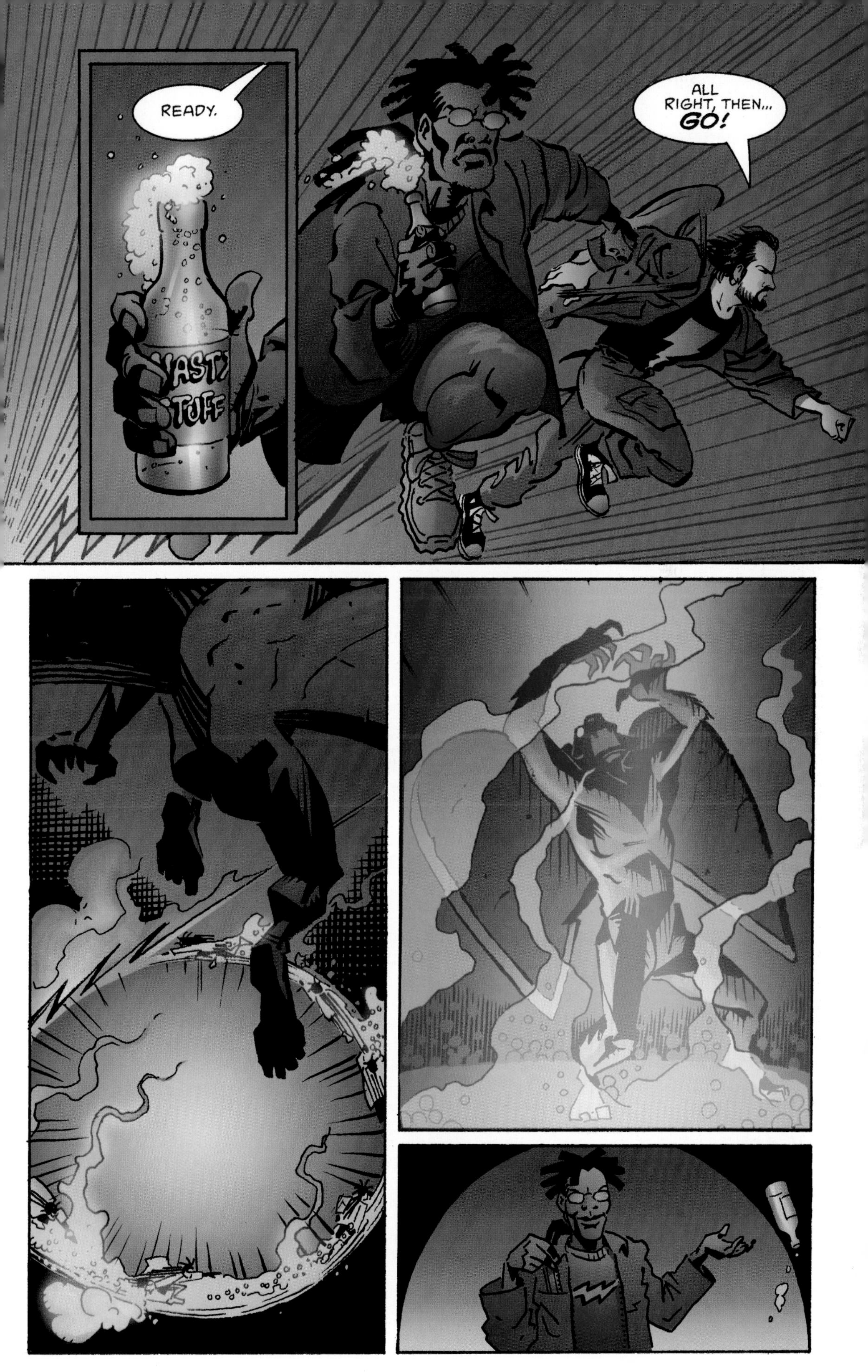
READY.
ALL RIGHT, THEN... GO!

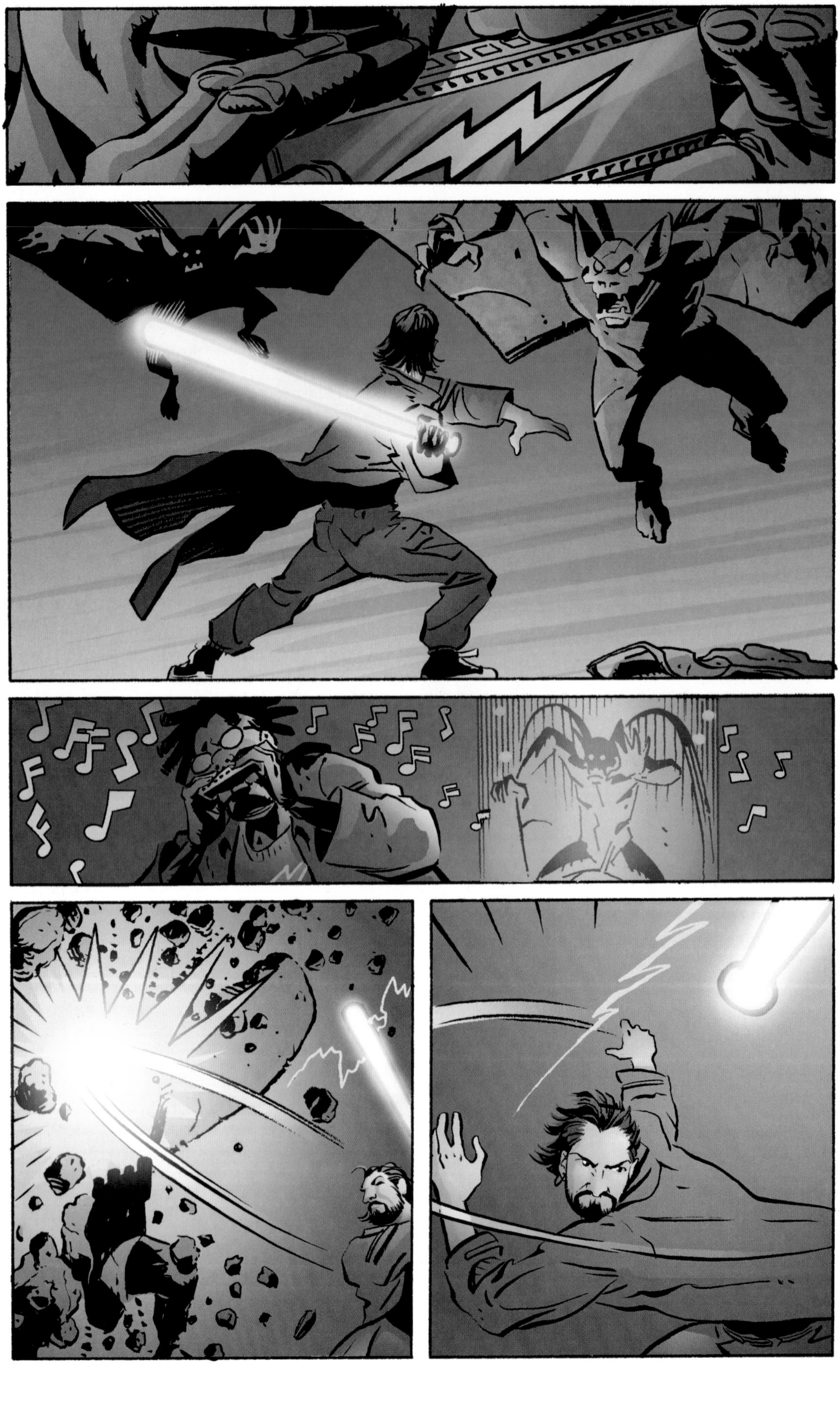

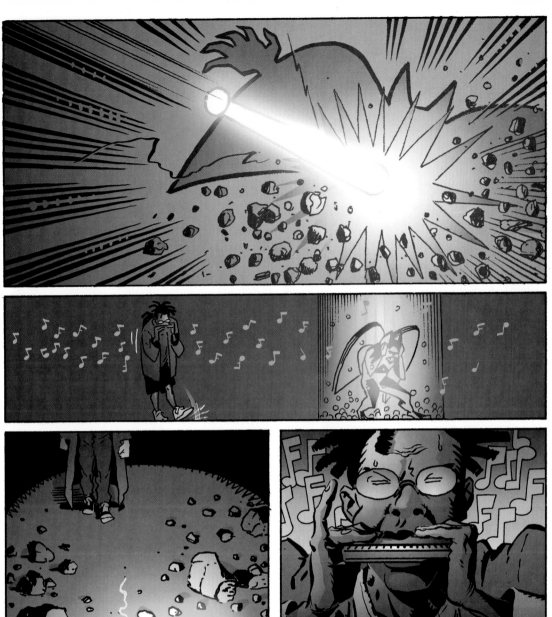

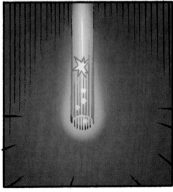

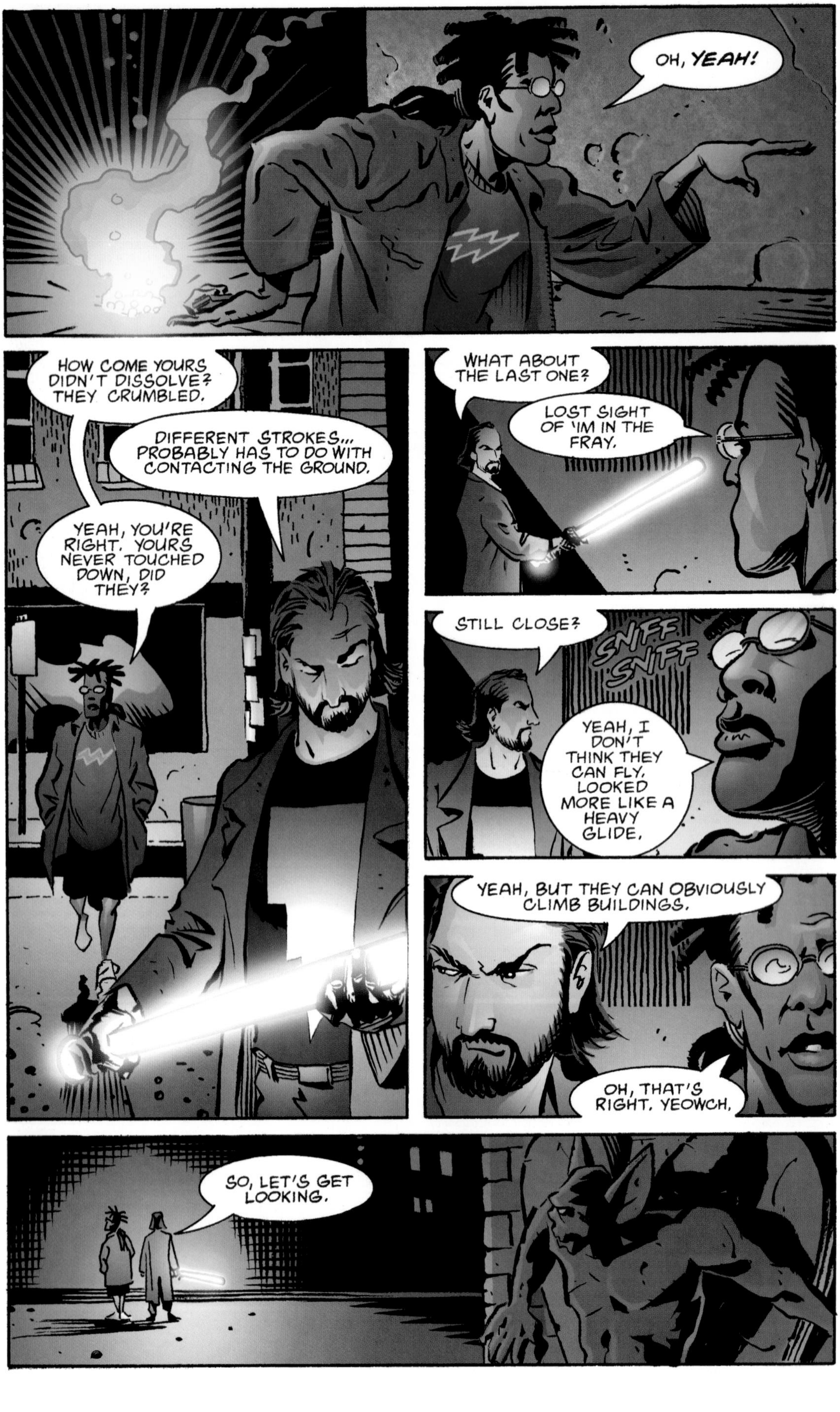
OH, YEAH!
HOW COME YOURS DIDN'T DISSOLVE? THEY CRUMBLED.
DIFFERENT STROKES... PROBABLY HAS TO DO WITH CONTACTING THE GROUND.
YEAH, YOU'RE RIGHT. YOURS NEVER TOUCHED DOWN, DID THEY?
WHAT ABOUT THE LAST ONE?
LOST SIGHT OF 'IM IN THE FRAY.
STILL CLOSE?
SNIFF SNIFF
YEAH, I DON'T THINK THEY CAN FLY. LOOKED MORE LIKE A HEAVY GLIDE.
YEAH, BUT THEY CAN OBVIOUSLY CLIMB BUILDINGS.
OH, THAT'S RIGHT. YEOWCH.
SO, LET'S GET LOOKING.

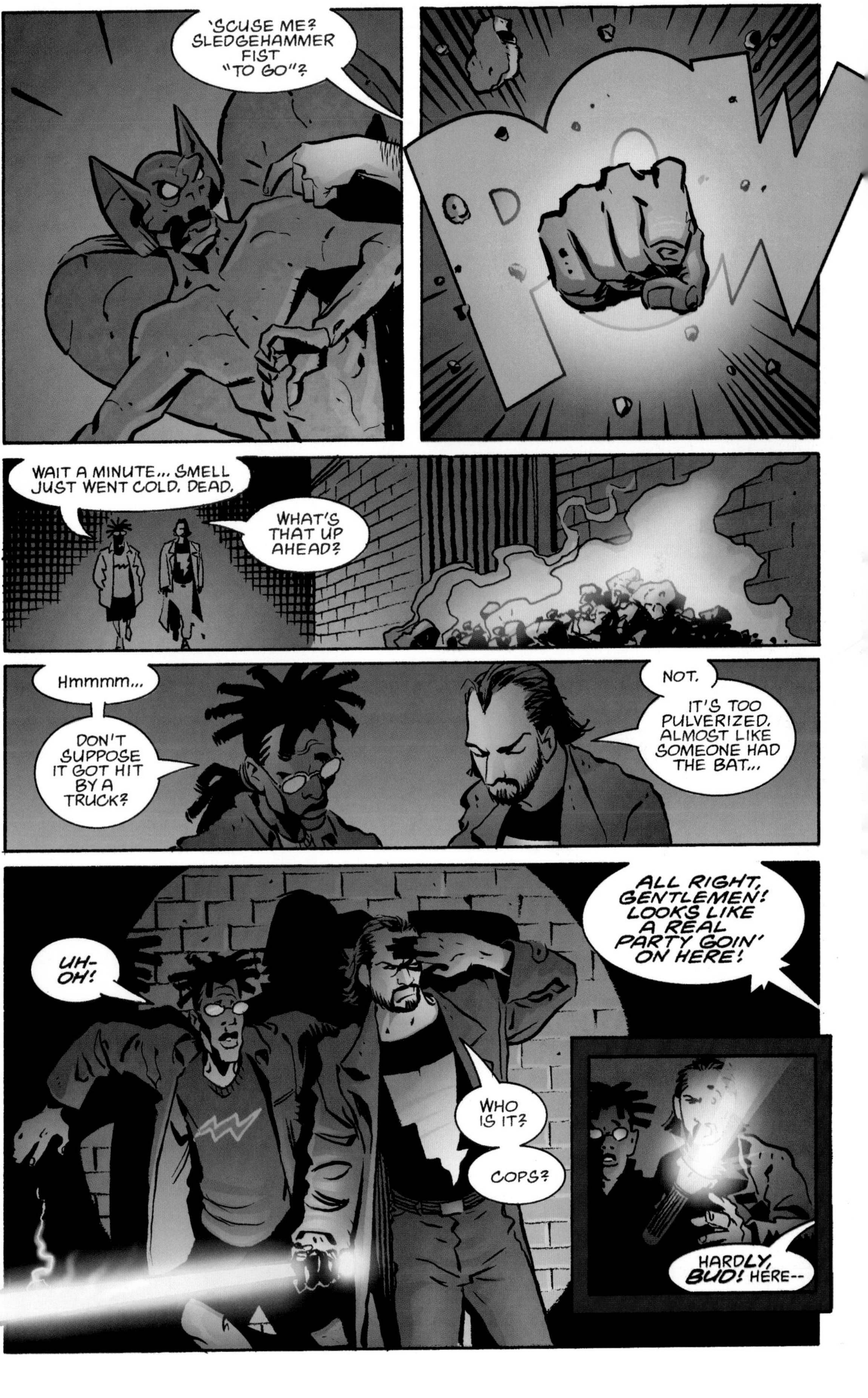

'SCUSE ME? SLEDGEHAMMER FIST "TO GO"?
POW
WAIT A MINUTE... SMELL JUST WENT COLD. DEAD.
WHAT'S THAT UP AHEAD?
Hmmmm...
DON'T SUPPOSE IT GOT HIT BY A TRUCK?
NOT.
IT'S TOO PULVERIZED. ALMOST LIKE SOMEONE HAD THE BAT...
UH-OH!
ALL RIGHT, GENTLEMEN! LOOKS LIKE A REAL PARTY GOIN' ON HERE!
WHO IS IT?
COPS?
HARDLY, BUD! HERE--

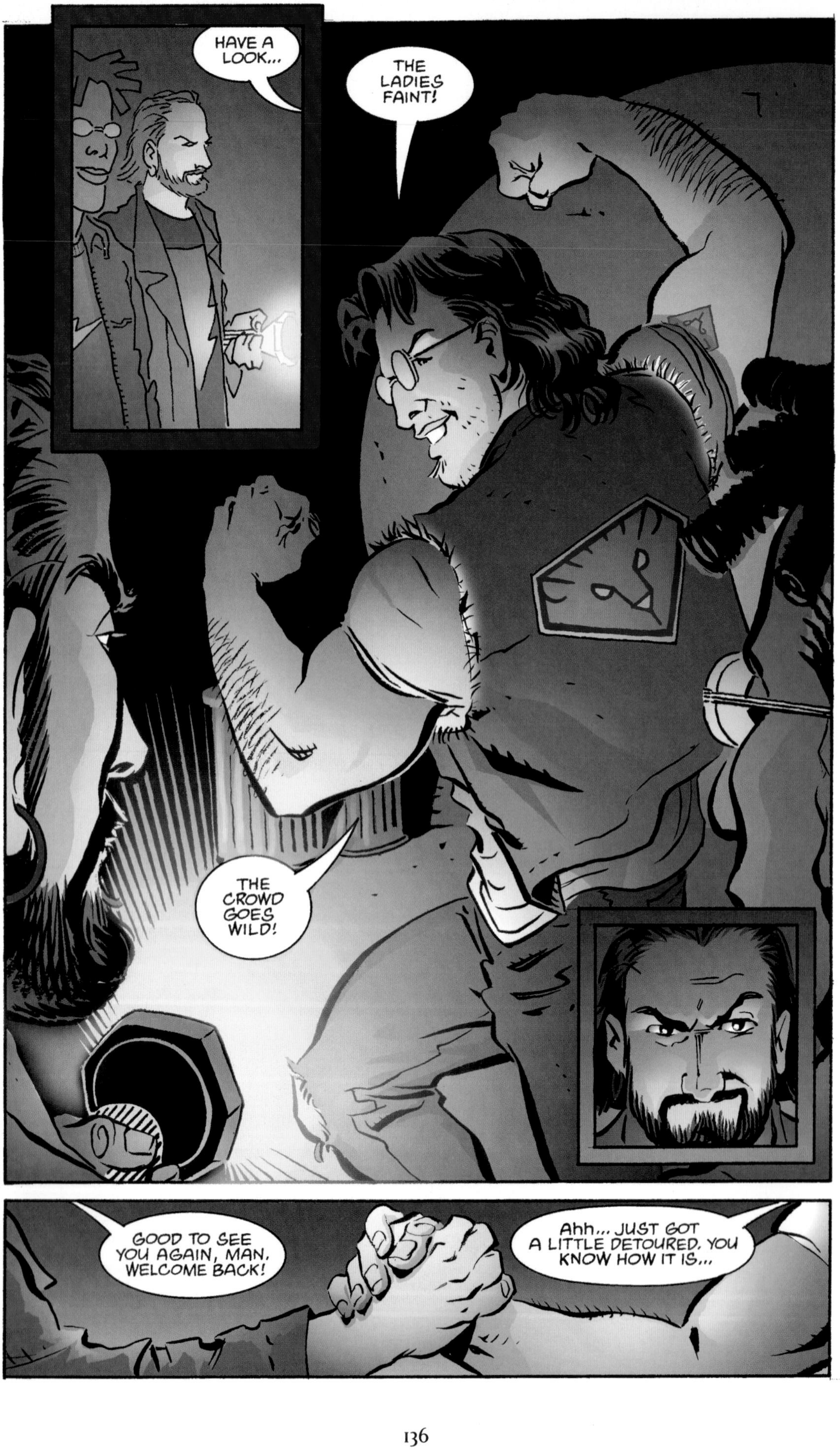
HAVE A LOOK...
THE LADIES FAINT!
THE CROWD GOES WILD!
GOOD TO SEE YOU AGAIN, MAN. WELCOME BACK!
Ahh... JUST GOT A LITTLE DETOURED. YOU KNOW HOW IT IS...

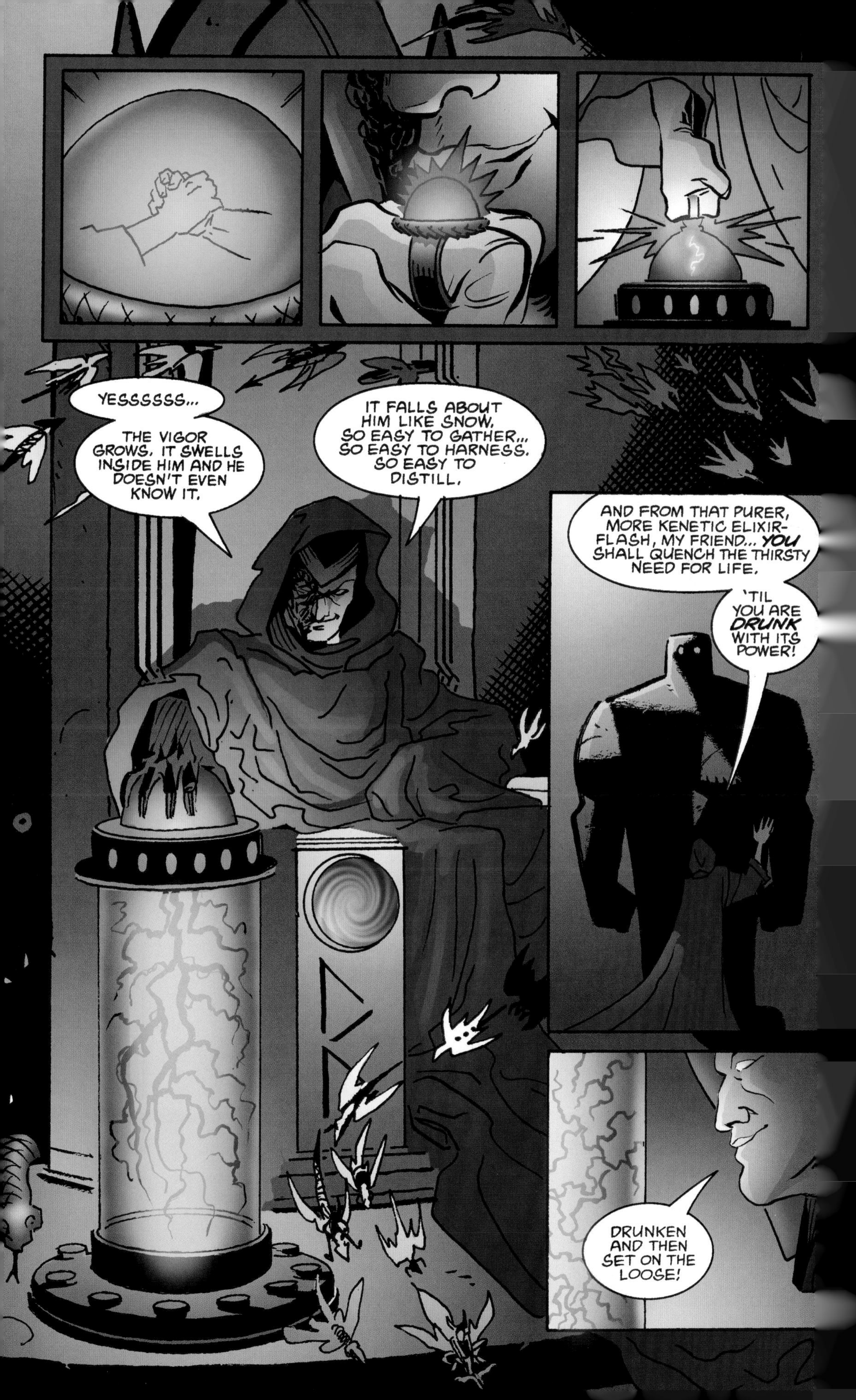
YESSSSSS...
THE VIGOR GROWS. IT SWELLS INSIDE HIM AND HE DOESN'T EVEN KNOW IT.
IT FALLS ABOUT HIM LIKE SNOW. SO EASY TO GATHER... SO EASY TO HARNESS. SO EASY TO DISTILL.
AND FROM THAT PURER, MORE KENETIC ELIXIR-FLASH, MY FRIEND... YOU SHALL QUENCH THE THIRSTY NEED FOR LIFE.
'TIL YOU ARE DRUNK WITH ITS POWER!
DRUNKEN AND THEN SET ON THE LOOSE!

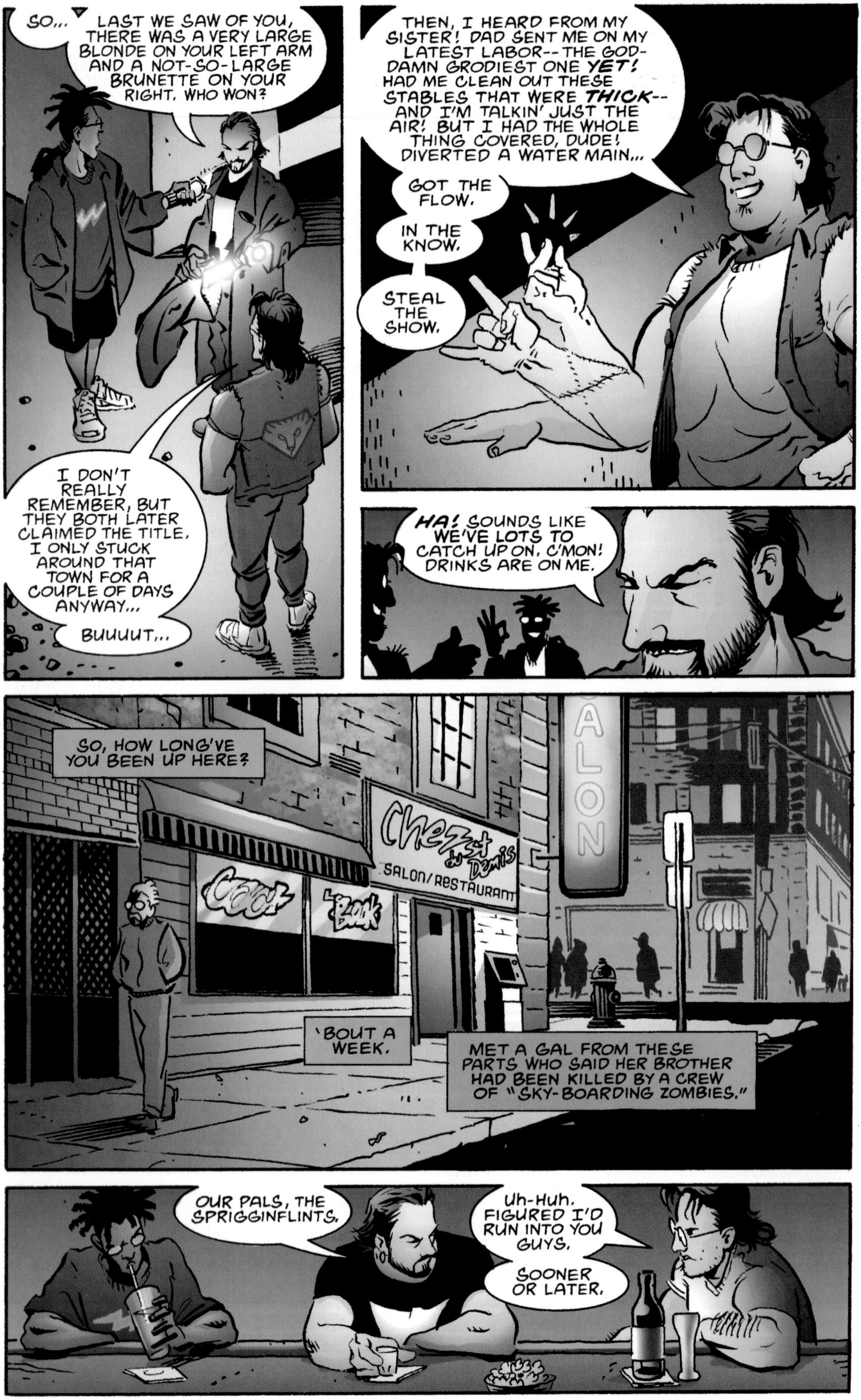
SO...
LAST WE SAW OF YOU, THERE WAS A VERY LARGE BLONDE ON YOUR LEFT ARM AND A NOT-SO-LARGE BRUNETTE ON YOUR RIGHT. WHO WON?
I DON'T REALLY REMEMBER, BUT THEY BOTH LATER CLAIMED THE TITLE. I ONLY STUCK AROUND THAT TOWN FOR A COUPLE OF DAYS ANYWAY...
BUUUUT...
THEN, I HEARD FROM MY SISTER! DAD SENT ME ON MY LATEST LABOR-- THE GOD-DAMN GRODIEST ONE YET! HAD ME CLEAN OUT THESE STABLES THAT WERE THICK-- AND I'M TALKIN' JUST THE AIR! BUT I HAD THE WHOLE THING COVERED, DUDE! DIVERTED A WATER MAIN...
GOT THE FLOW.
IN THE KNOW.
STEAL THE SHOW.
HA! SOUNDS LIKE WE'VE LOTS TO CATCH UP ON. C'MON! DRINKS ARE ON ME.
SO, HOW LONG'VE YOU BEEN UP HERE?
SALON
SALON/RESTAURANT
'BOUT A WEEK.
MET A GAL FROM THESE PARTS WHO SAID HER BROTHER HAD BEEN KILLED BY A CREW OF "SKY-BOARDING ZOMBIES."
OUR PALS, THE SPRIGGINFLINTS.
Uh-Huh. FIGURED I'D RUN INTO YOU GUYS.
SOONER OR LATER.

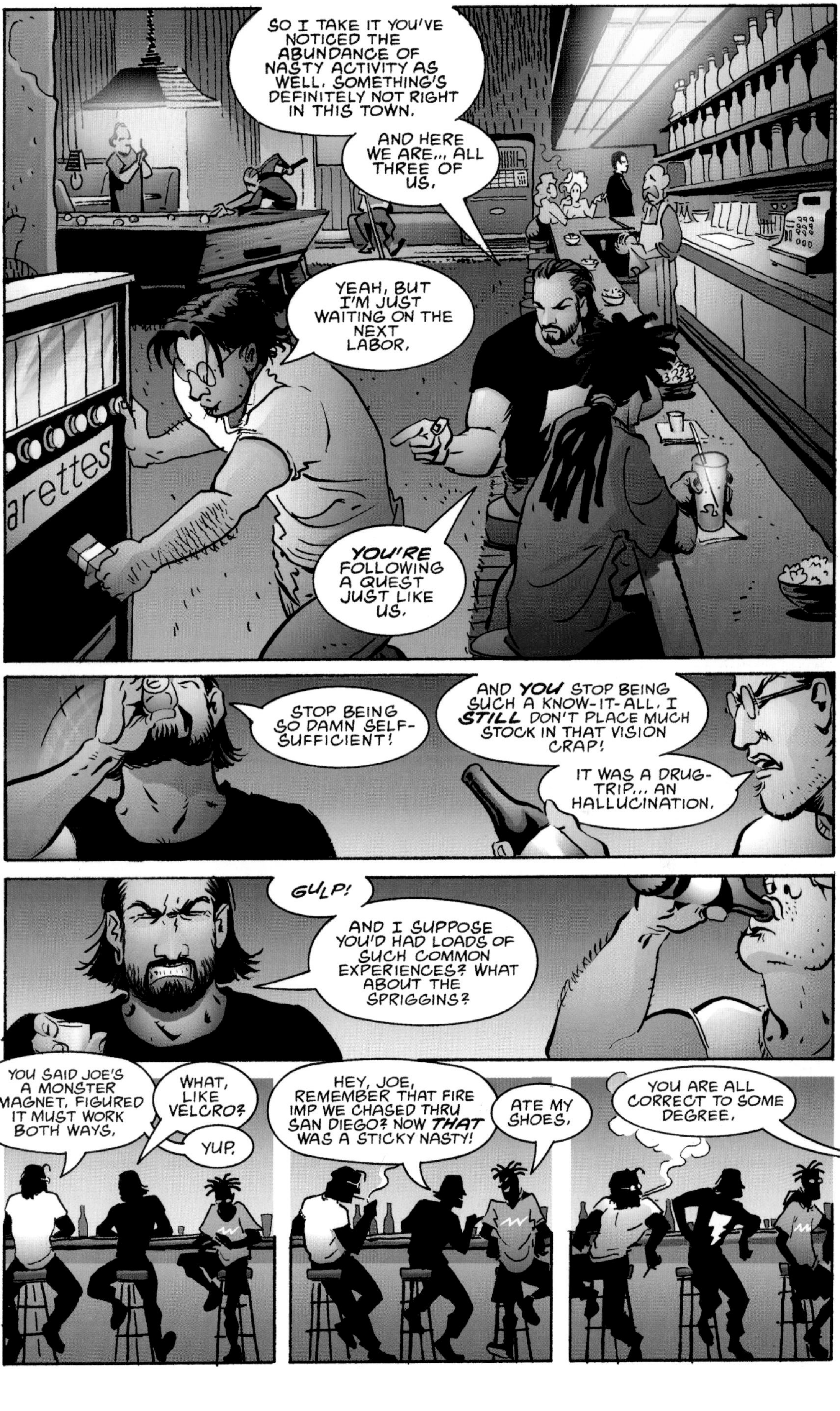
SO I TAKE IT YOU'VE NOTICED THE ABUNDANCE OF NASTY ACTIVITY AS WELL. SOMETHING'S DEFINITELY NOT RIGHT IN THIS TOWN.
AND HERE WE ARE... ALL THREE OF US.
YEAH, BUT I'M JUST WAITING ON THE NEXT LABOR.
arettes
YOU'RE FOLLOWING A QUEST JUST LIKE US.
STOP BEING SO DAMN SELF-SUFFICIENT!
AND YOU STOP BEING SUCH A KNOW-IT-ALL. I STILL DON'T PLACE MUCH STOCK IN THAT VISION CRAP!
IT WAS A DRUG-TRIP... AN HALLUCINATION.
GULP!
AND I SUPPOSE YOU'D HAD LOADS OF SUCH COMMON EXPERIENCES? WHAT ABOUT THE SPRIGGINS?
YOU SAID JOE'S A MONSTER MAGNET, FIGURED IT MUST WORK BOTH WAYS.
WHAT, LIKE VELCRO?
YUP.
HEY, JOE, REMEMBER THAT FIRE IMP WE CHASED THRU SAN DIEGO? NOW THAT WAS A STICKY NASTY!
ATE MY SHOES.
YOU ARE ALL CORRECT TO SOME DEGREE.

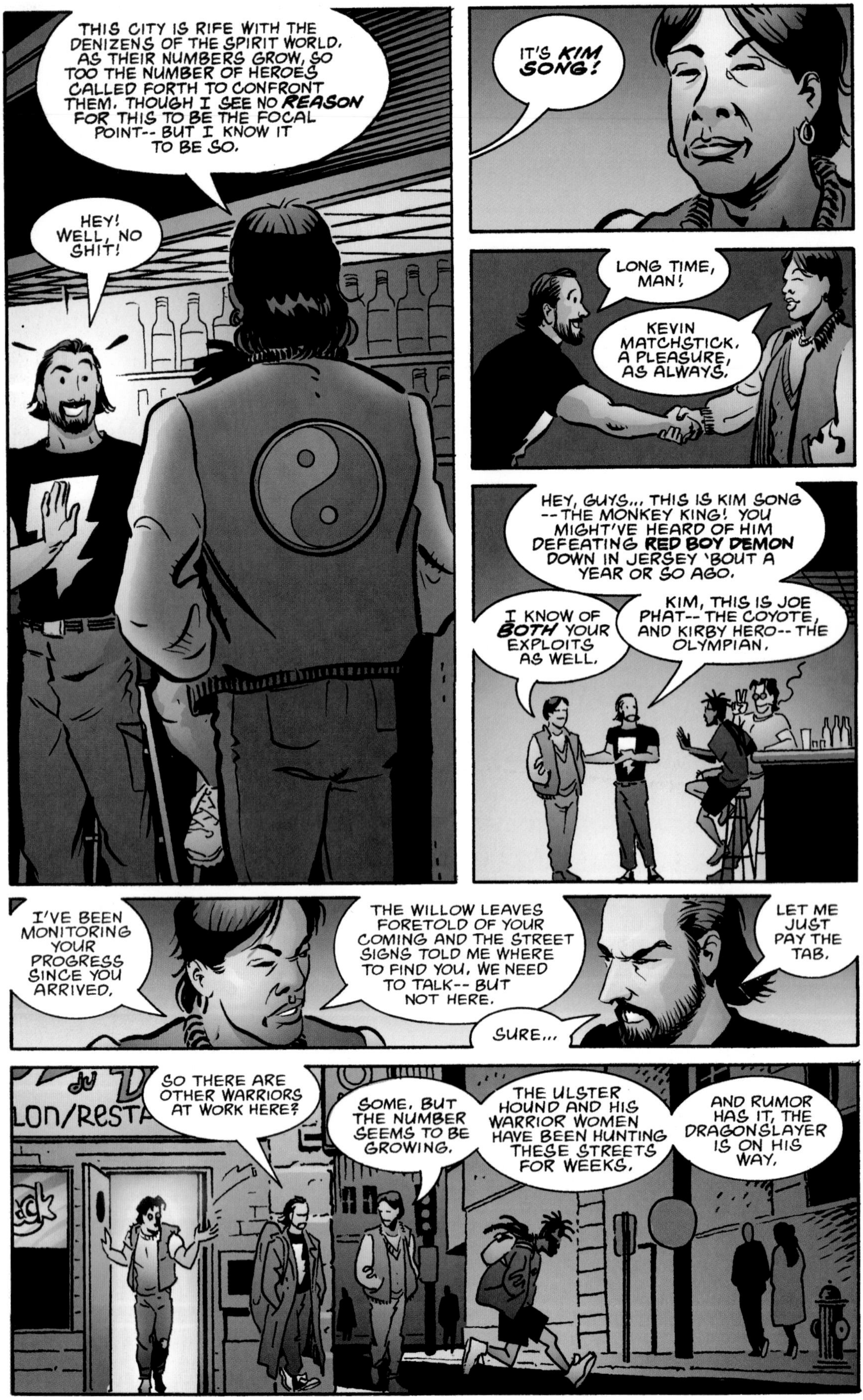
THIS CITY IS RIFE WITH THE DENIZENS OF THE SPIRIT WORLD. AS THEIR NUMBERS GROW, SO TOO THE NUMBER OF HEROES CALLED FORTH TO CONFRONT THEM. THOUGH I SEE NO REASON FOR THIS TO BE THE FOCAL POINT-- BUT I KNOW IT TO BE SO.
HEY! WELL, NO SHIT!
IT'S KIM SONG!
LONG TIME, MAN!
KEVIN MATCHSTICK. A PLEASURE, AS ALWAYS.
HEY, GUYS... THIS IS KIM SONG --THE MONKEY KING! YOU MIGHT'VE HEARD OF HIM DEFEATING RED BOY DEMON DOWN IN JERSEY 'BOUT A YEAR OR SO AGO.
KIM, THIS IS JOE PHAT-- THE COYOTE, AND KIRBY HERO-- THE OLYMPIAN.
I KNOW OF BOTH YOUR EXPLOITS AS WELL.
I'VE BEEN MONITORING YOUR PROGRESS SINCE YOU ARRIVED.
THE WILLOW LEAVES FORETOLD OF YOUR COMING AND THE STREET SIGNS TOLD ME WHERE TO FIND YOU. WE NEED TO TALK-- BUT NOT HERE.
SURE...
LET ME JUST PAY THE TAB.
SO THERE ARE OTHER WARRIORS AT WORK HERE?
SOME. BUT THE NUMBER SEEMS TO BE GROWING.
THE ULSTER HOUND AND HIS WARRIOR WOMEN HAVE BEEN HUNTING THESE STREETS FOR WEEKS.
AND RUMOR HAS IT, THE DRAGONSLAYER IS ON HIS WAY.

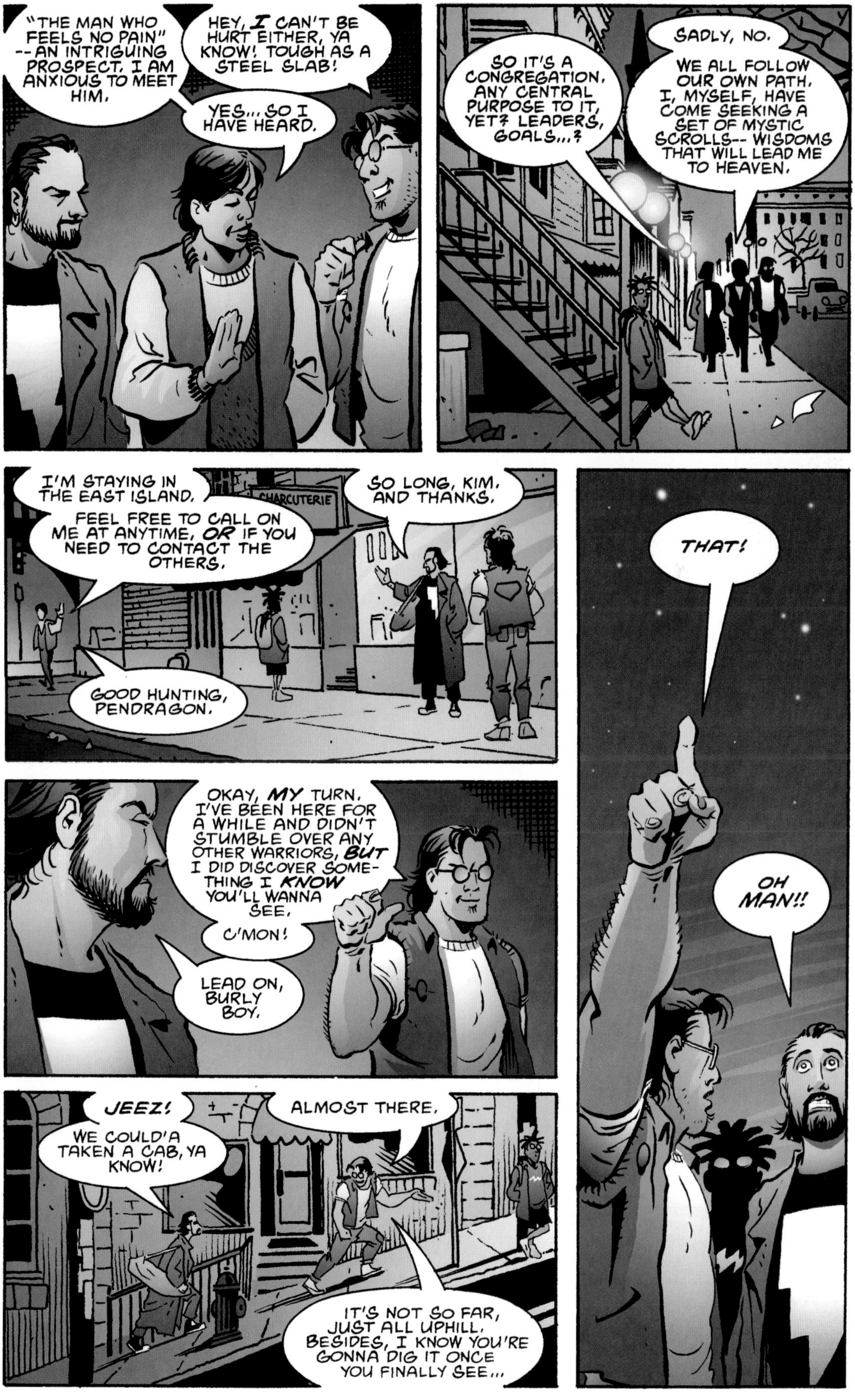
"THE MAN WHO FEELS NO PAIN" --AN INTRIGUING PROSPECT. I AM ANXIOUS TO MEET HIM.
HEY, I CAN'T BE HURT EITHER, YA KNOW! TOUGH AS A STEEL SLAB!
YES... SO I HAVE HEARD.
SO IT'S A CONGREGATION. ANY CENTRAL PURPOSE TO IT, YET? LEADERS, GOALS...?
SADLY, NO.
WE ALL FOLLOW OUR OWN PATH. I, MYSELF, HAVE COME SEEKING A SET OF MYSTIC SCROLLS-- WISDOMS THAT WILL LEAD ME TO HEAVEN.
I'M STAYING IN THE EAST ISLAND.
FEEL FREE TO CALL ON ME AT ANYTIME, OR IF YOU NEED TO CONTACT THE OTHERS.
CHARCUTERIE
SO LONG, KIM. AND THANKS.
GOOD HUNTING, PENDRAGON.
OKAY, MY TURN. I'VE BEEN HERE FOR A WHILE AND DIDN'T STUMBLE OVER ANY OTHER WARRIORS, BUT I DID DISCOVER SOME-THING I KNOW YOU'LL WANNA SEE.
C'MON!
LEAD ON, BURLY BOY.
JEEZ!
WE COULD'A TAKEN A CAB, YA KNOW!
ALMOST THERE.
IT'S NOT SO FAR, JUST ALL UPHILL. BESIDES, I KNOW YOU'RE GONNA DIG IT ONCE YOU FINALLY SEE...
THAT!
OH MAN!!

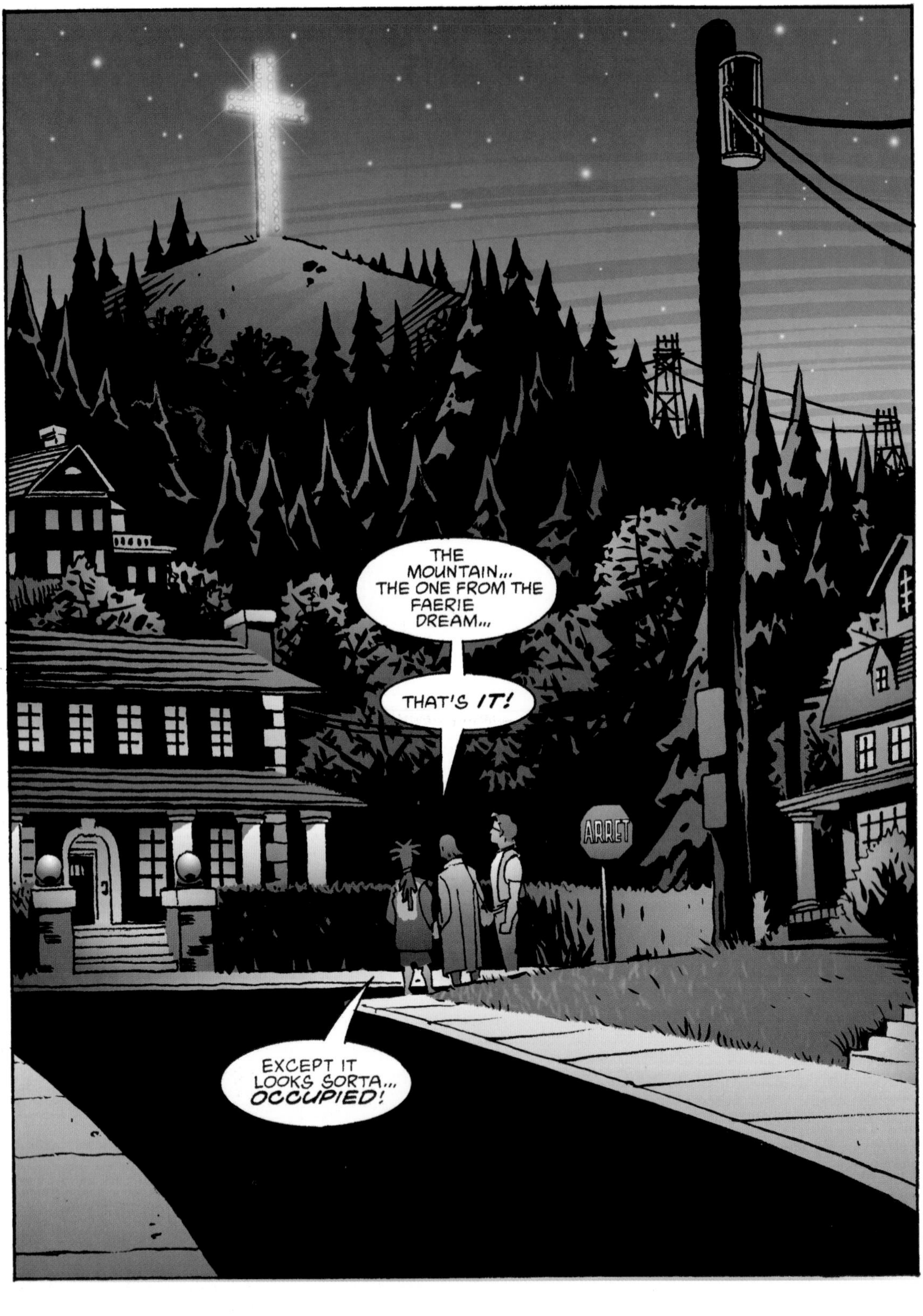
THE MOUNTAIN... THE ONE FROM THE FAERIE DREAM...
THAT'S *IT!*
EXCEPT IT LOOKS SORTA... ***OCCUPIED!***
ARRET

THE HERO DEFINED

MAGE®

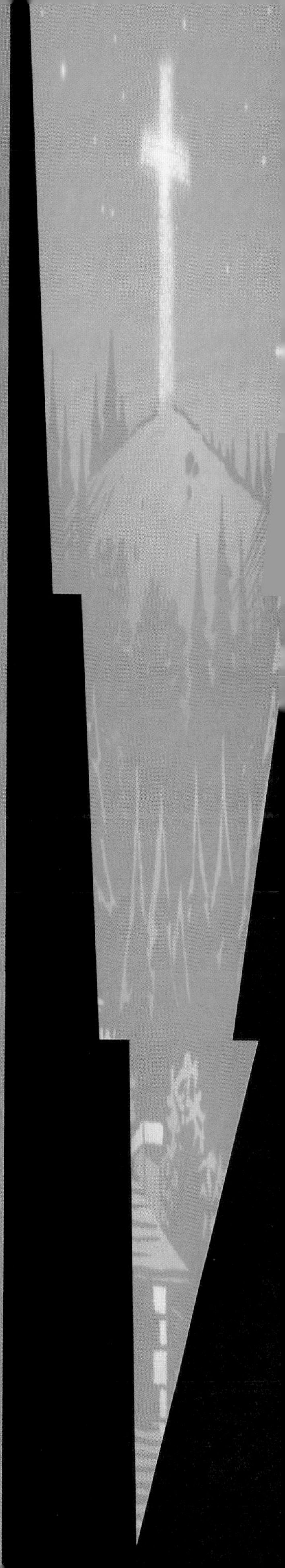

chapter 6

"Lay On Macduff"

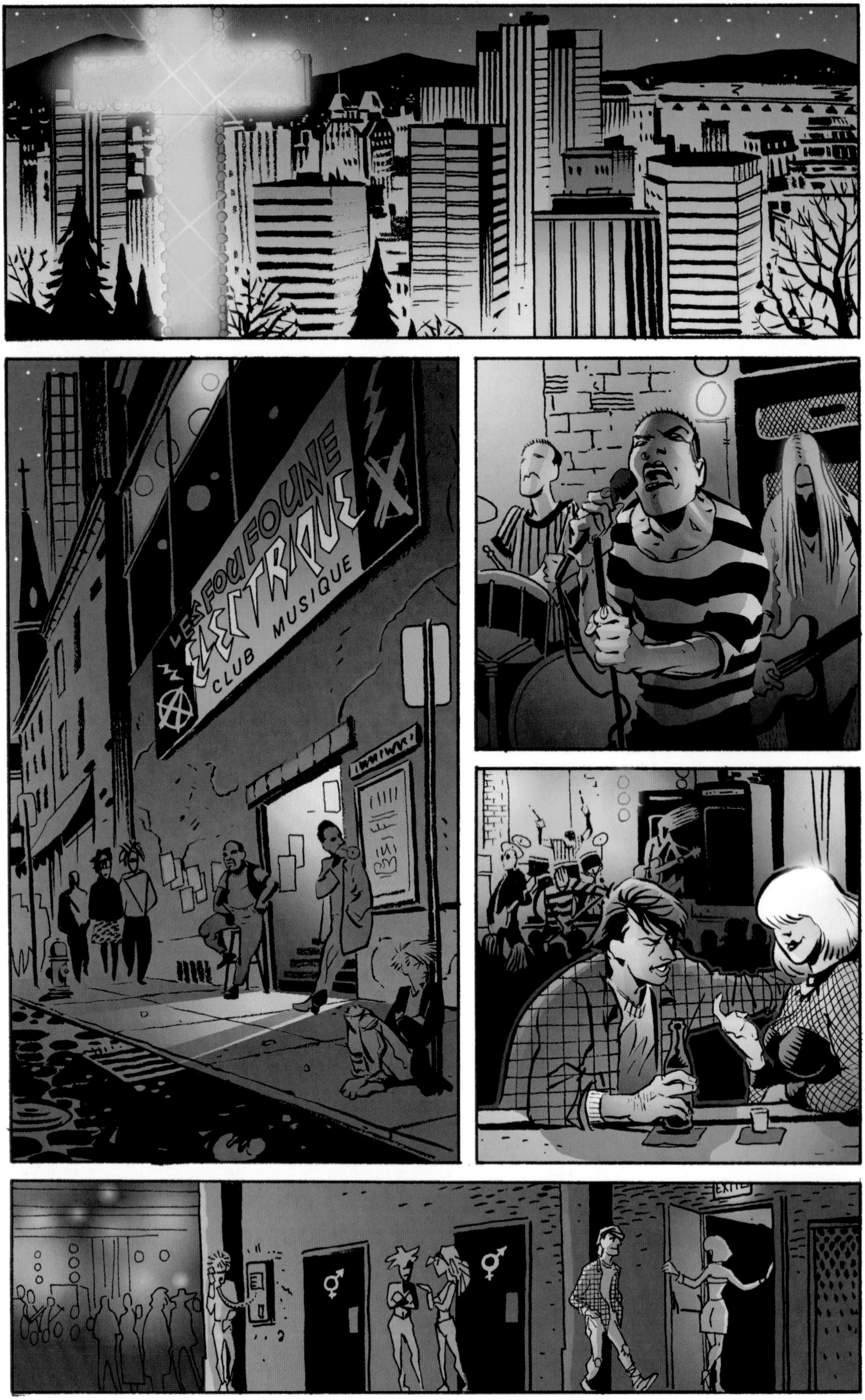
LES FOUFOUNE
ELECTRIQUE
CLUB MUSIQUE
EXIT

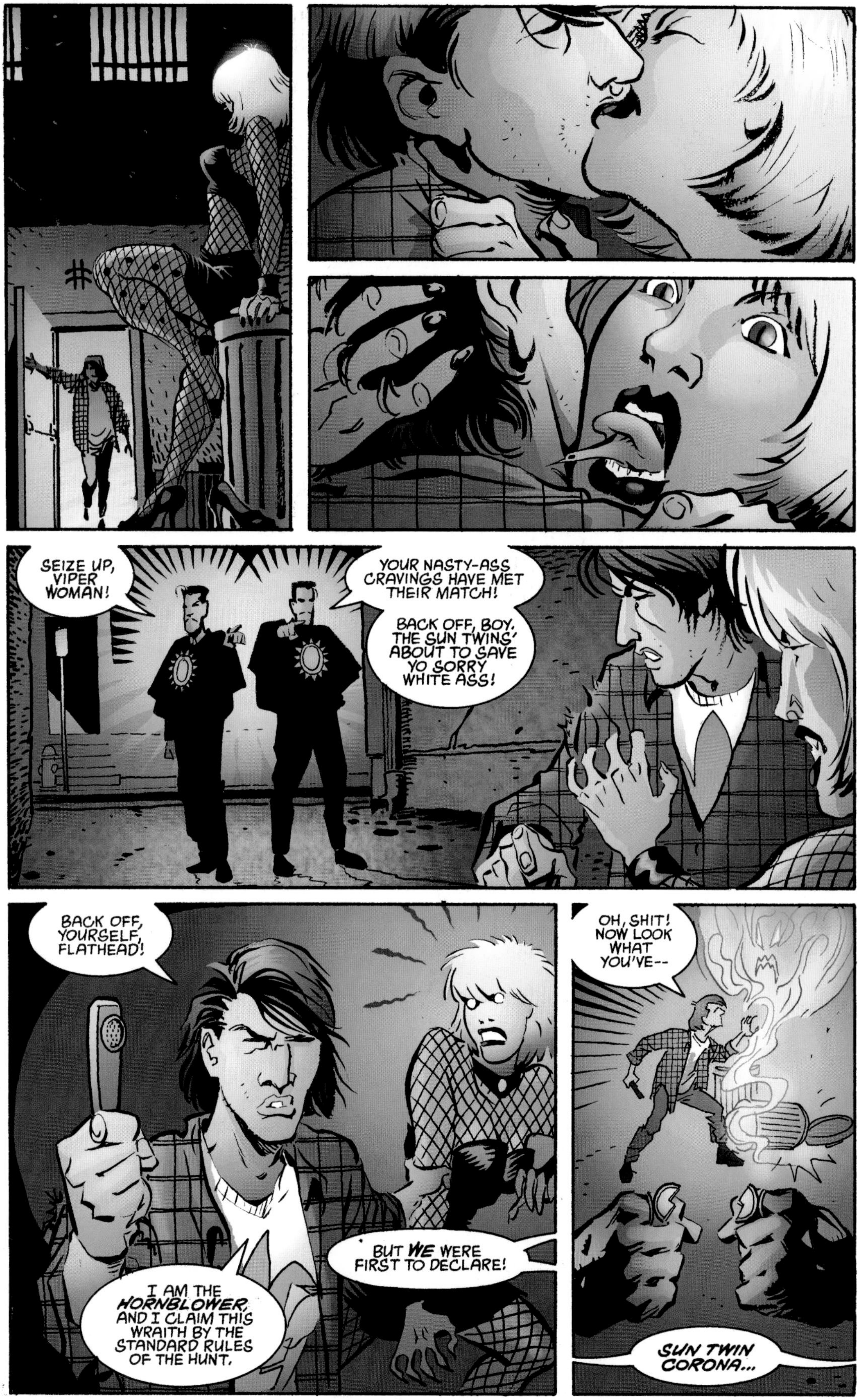
SEIZE UP, VIPER WOMAN!
YOUR NASTY-ASS CRAVINGS HAVE MET THEIR MATCH!
BACK OFF, BOY. THE SUN TWINS' ABOUT TO SAVE YO SORRY WHITE ASS!
BACK OFF, YOURSELF, FLATHEAD!
I AM THE HORNBLOWER, AND I CLAIM THIS WRAITH BY THE STANDARD RULES OF THE HUNT.
BUT WE WERE FIRST TO DECLARE!
OH, SHIT! NOW LOOK WHAT YOU'VE--
SUN TWIN CORONA...

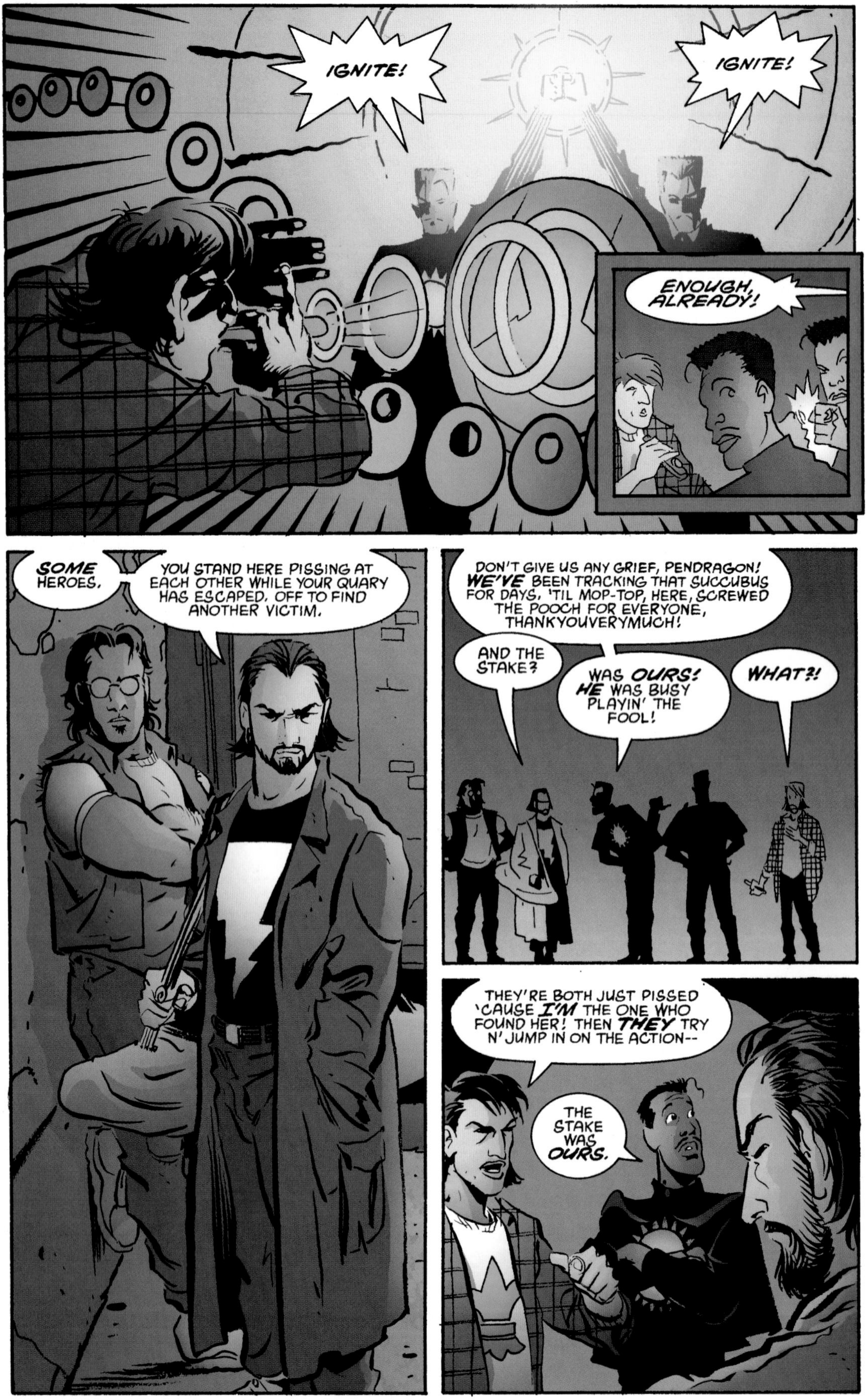
IGNITE!
IGNITE!
ENOUGH, ALREADY!
SOME HEROES.
YOU STAND HERE PISSING AT EACH OTHER WHILE YOUR QUARY HAS ESCAPED, OFF TO FIND ANOTHER VICTIM.
DON'T GIVE US ANY GRIEF, PENDRAGON! WE'VE BEEN TRACKING THAT SUCCUBUS FOR DAYS, 'TIL MOP-TOP, HERE, SCREWED THE POOCH FOR EVERYONE, THANKYOUVERYMUCH!
AND THE STAKE?
WAS OURS! HE WAS BUSY PLAYIN' THE FOOL!
WHAT?!
THEY'RE BOTH JUST PISSED 'CAUSE I'M THE ONE WHO FOUND HER! THEN THEY TRY N' JUMP IN ON THE ACTION--
THE STAKE WAS OURS.

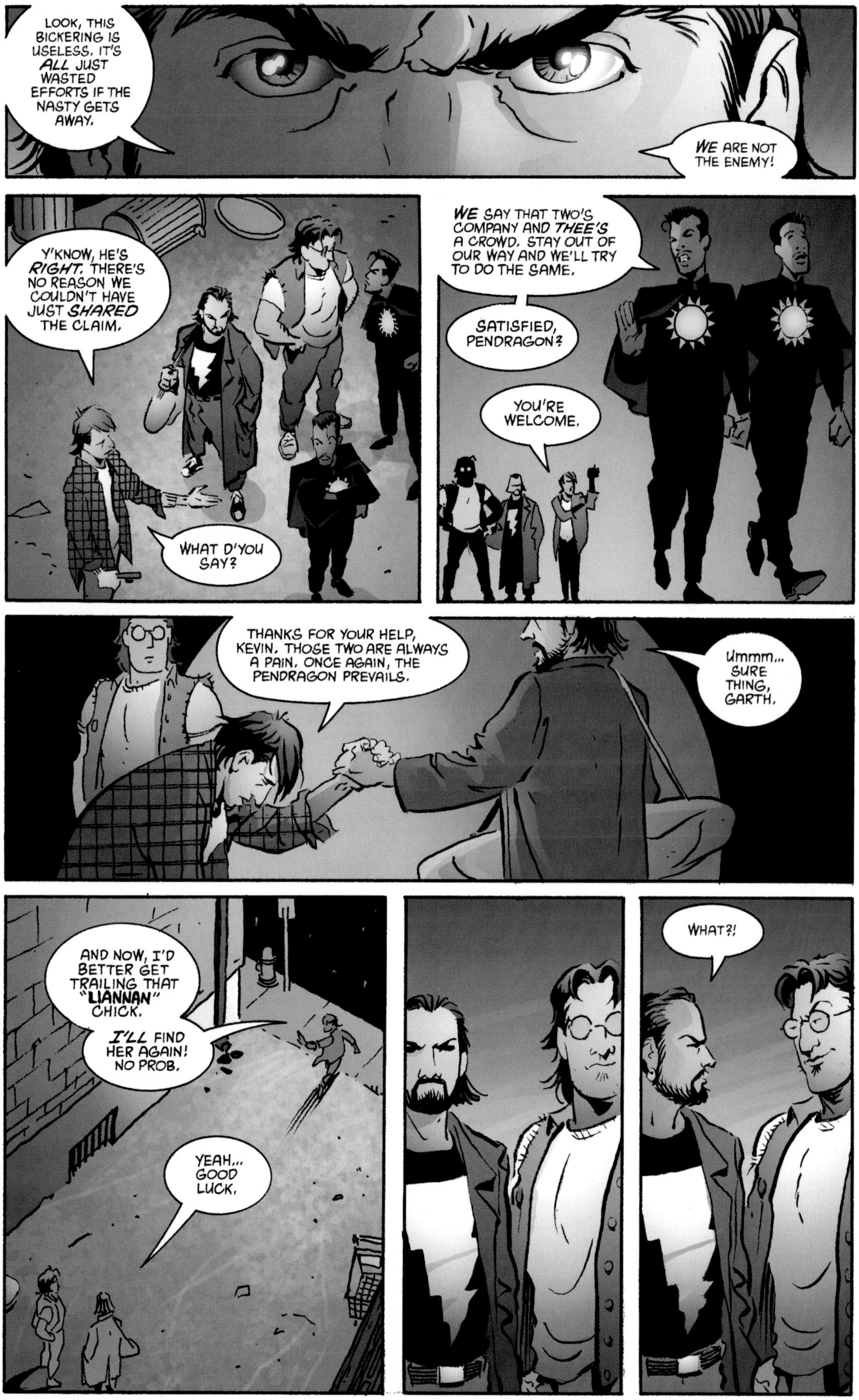
LOOK, THIS BICKERING IS USELESS. IT'S ALL JUST WASTED EFFORTS IF THE NASTY GETS AWAY.
WE ARE NOT THE ENEMY!
Y'KNOW, HE'S RIGHT. THERE'S NO REASON WE COULDN'T HAVE JUST SHARED THE CLAIM.
WHAT D'YOU SAY?
WE SAY THAT TWO'S COMPANY AND THEE'S A CROWD. STAY OUT OF OUR WAY AND WE'LL TRY TO DO THE SAME.
SATISFIED, PENDRAGON?
YOU'RE WELCOME.
THANKS FOR YOUR HELP, KEVIN. THOSE TWO ARE ALWAYS A PAIN. ONCE AGAIN, THE PENDRAGON PREVAILS.
Ummm... SURE THING, GARTH.
AND NOW, I'D BETTER GET TRAILING THAT "LIANNAN" CHICK.
I'LL FIND HER AGAIN! NO PROB.
YEAH... GOOD LUCK.
WHAT?!

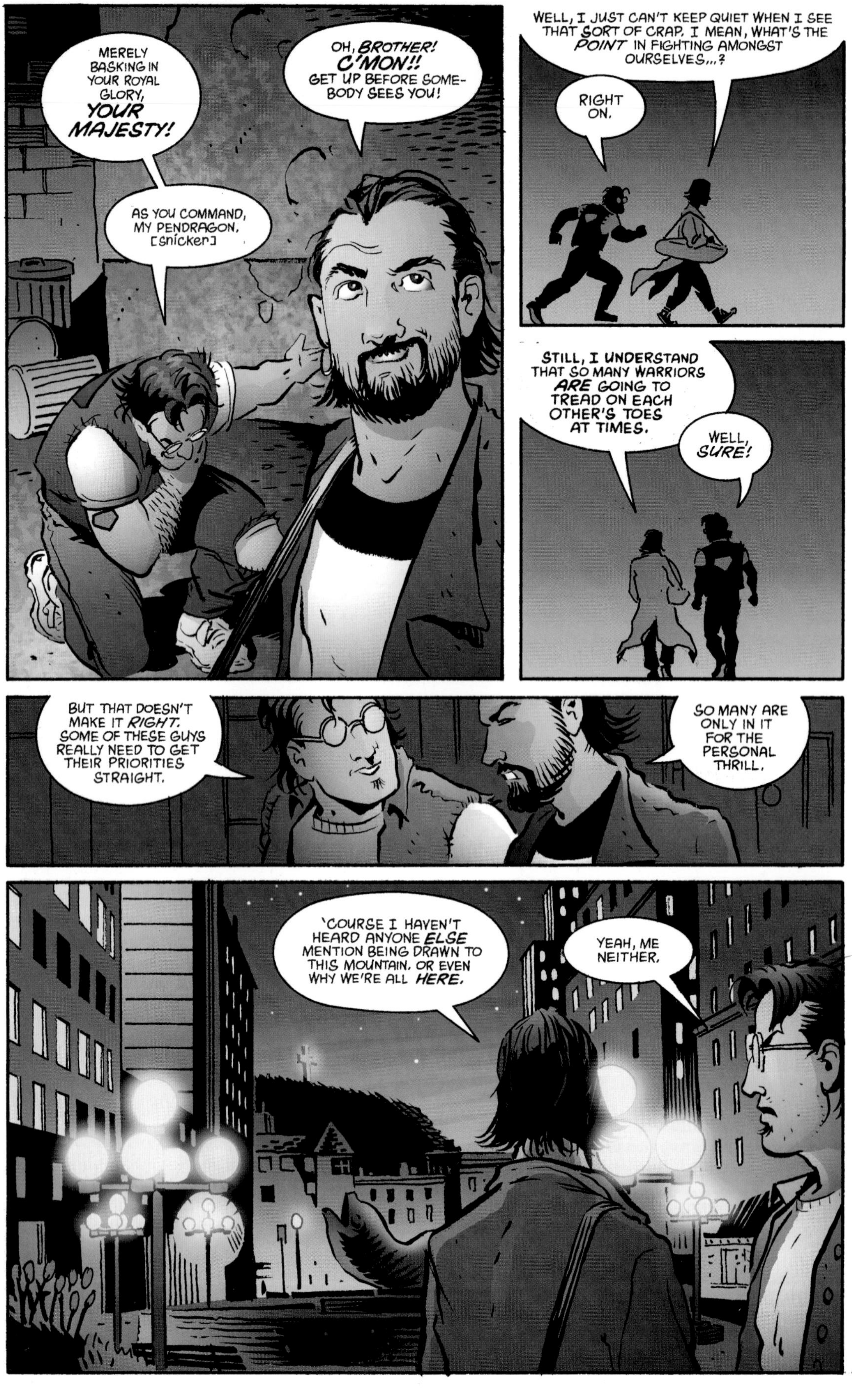
MERELY BASKING IN YOUR ROYAL GLORY, YOUR MAJESTY!
AS YOU COMMAND, MY PENDRAGON. [snicker]
OH, BROTHER! C'MON!! GET UP BEFORE SOMEBODY SEES YOU!
WELL, I JUST CAN'T KEEP QUIET WHEN I SEE THAT SORT OF CRAP. I MEAN, WHAT'S THE POINT IN FIGHTING AMONGST OURSELVES...?
RIGHT ON.
STILL, I UNDERSTAND THAT SO MANY WARRIORS ARE GOING TO TREAD ON EACH OTHER'S TOES AT TIMES.
WELL, SURE!
BUT THAT DOESN'T MAKE IT RIGHT. SOME OF THESE GUYS REALLY NEED TO GET THEIR PRIORITIES STRAIGHT.
SO MANY ARE ONLY IN IT FOR THE PERSONAL THRILL.
'COURSE I HAVEN'T HEARD ANYONE ELSE MENTION BEING DRAWN TO THIS MOUNTAIN. OR EVEN WHY WE'RE ALL HERE.
YEAH, ME NEITHER.

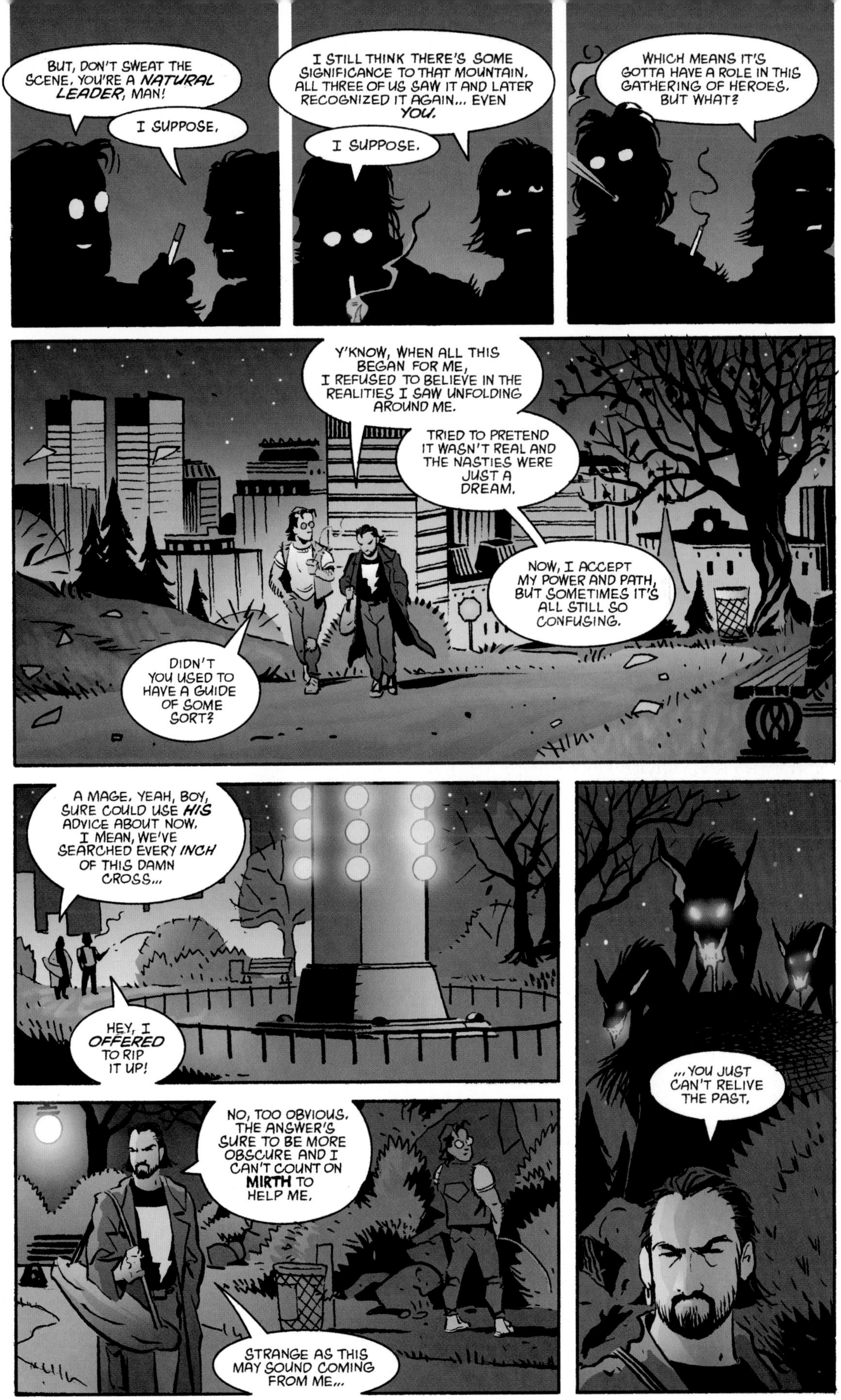

BUT, DON'T SWEAT THE SCENE. YOU'RE A NATURAL LEADER, MAN!
I SUPPOSE.
I STILL THINK THERE'S SOME SIGNIFICANCE TO THAT MOUNTAIN. ALL THREE OF US SAW IT AND LATER RECOGNIZED IT AGAIN... EVEN YOU.
I SUPPOSE.
WHICH MEANS IT'S GOTTA HAVE A ROLE IN THIS GATHERING OF HEROES. BUT WHAT?
Y'KNOW, WHEN ALL THIS BEGAN FOR ME, I REFUSED TO BELIEVE IN THE REALITIES I SAW UNFOLDING AROUND ME.
TRIED TO PRETEND IT WASN'T REAL AND THE NASTIES WERE JUST A DREAM.
NOW, I ACCEPT MY POWER AND PATH, BUT SOMETIMES IT'S ALL STILL SO CONFUSING.
DIDN'T YOU USED TO HAVE A GUIDE OF SOME SORT?
A MAGE. YEAH, BOY, SURE COULD USE HIS ADVICE ABOUT NOW. I MEAN, WE'VE SEARCHED EVERY INCH OF THIS DAMN CROSS...
HEY, I OFFERED TO RIP IT UP!
NO, TOO OBVIOUS. THE ANSWER'S SURE TO BE MORE OBSCURE AND I CAN'T COUNT ON MIRTH TO HELP ME.
STRANGE AS THIS MAY SOUND COMING FROM ME...
...YOU JUST CAN'T RELIVE THE PAST.

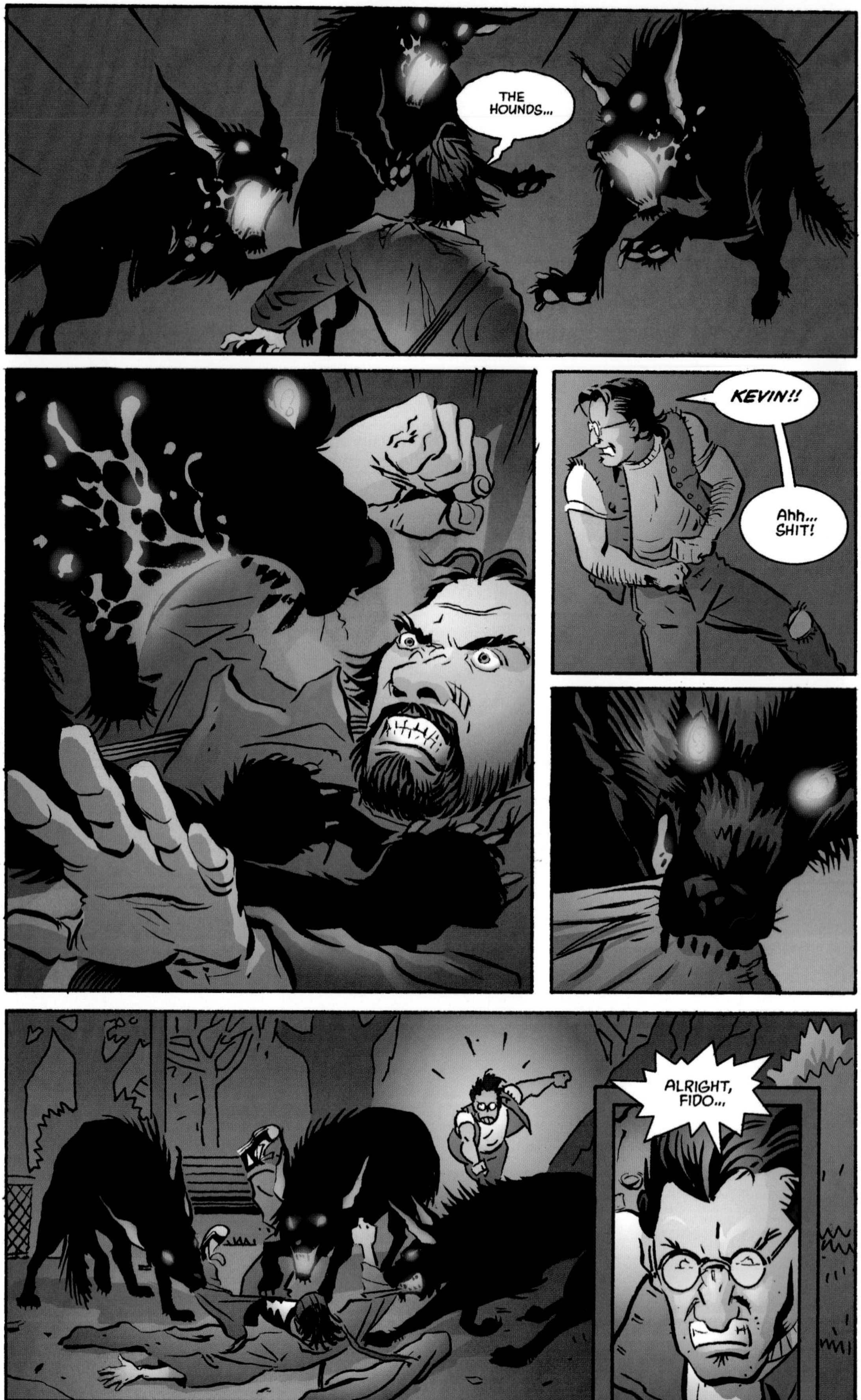
THE HOUNDS...
KEVIN!!
Ahh... SHIT!
ALRIGHT, FIDO...

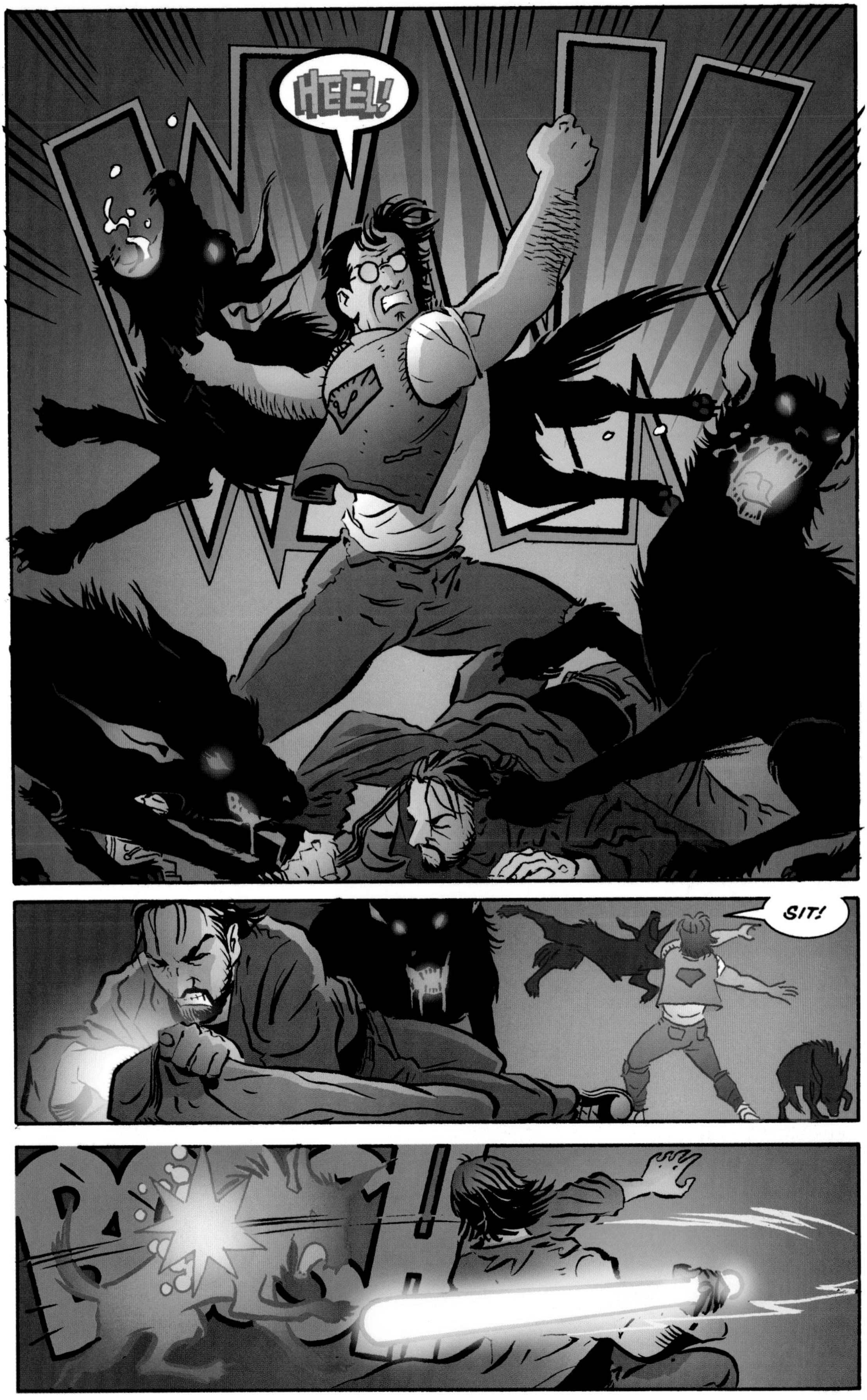
HEEL!
SIT!

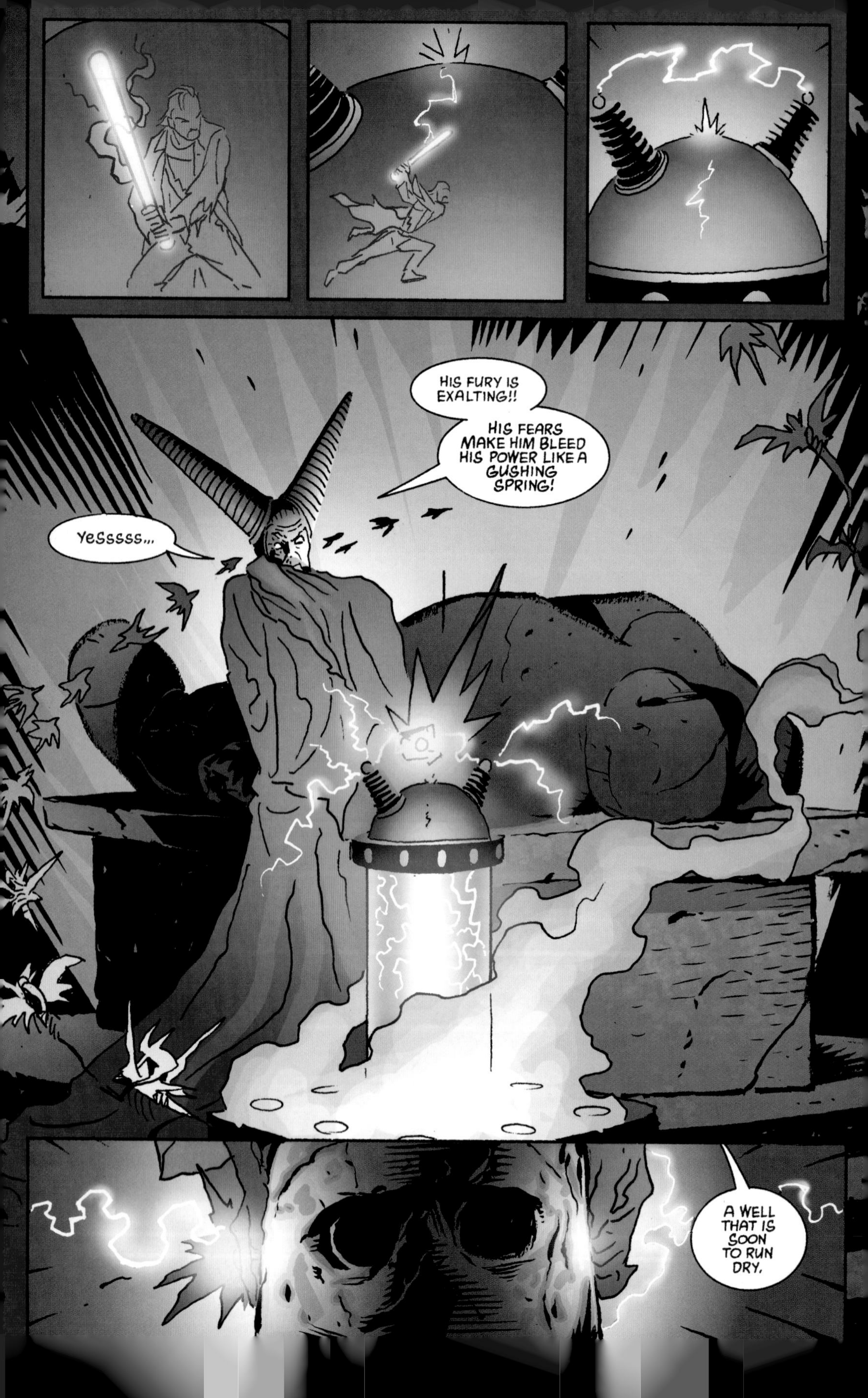
HIS FURY IS EXALTING!!
HIS FEARS MAKE HIM BLEED HIS POWER LIKE A GUSHING SPRING!
YeSSSSS...
A WELL THAT IS SOON TO RUN DRY.

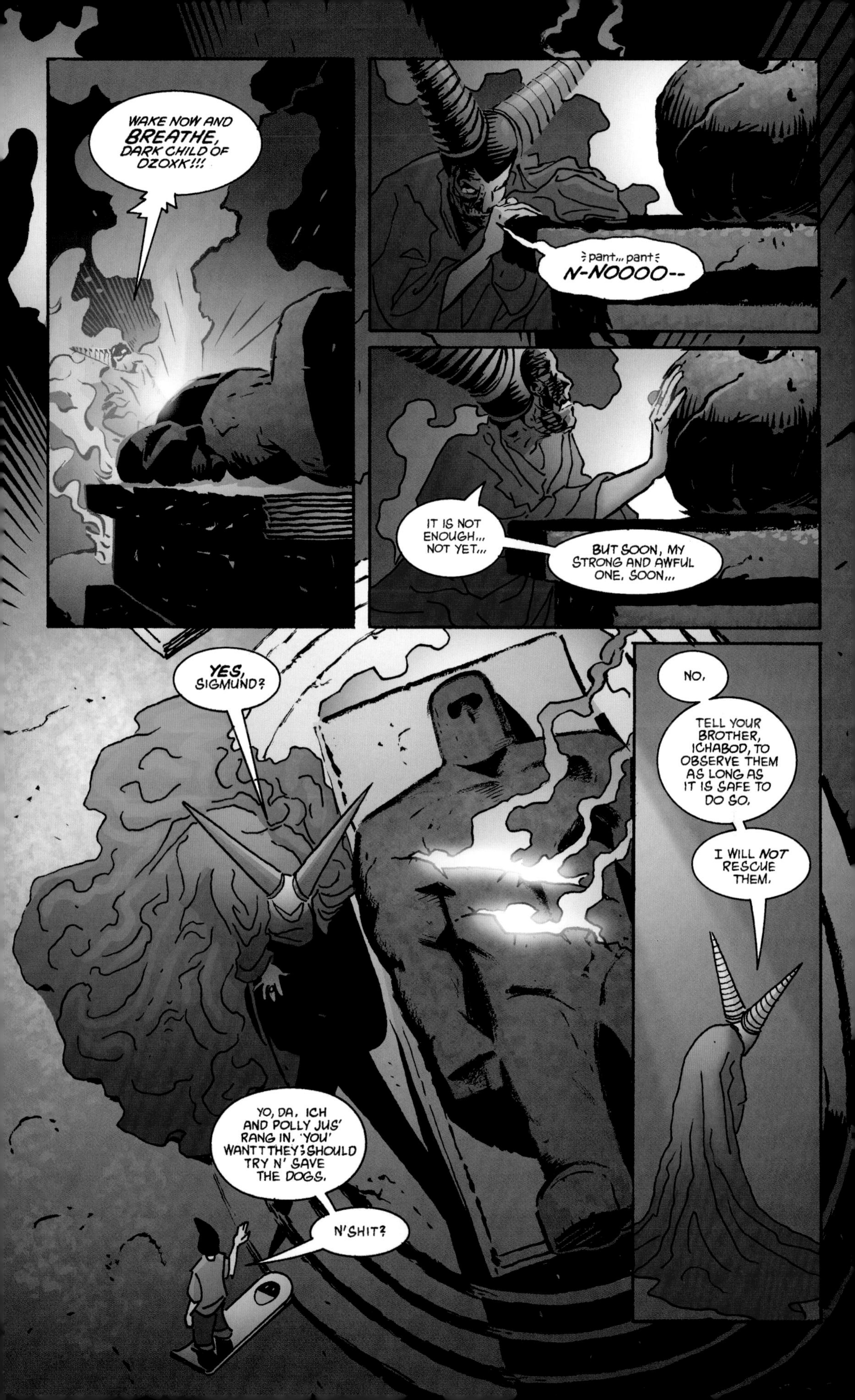
WAKE NOW AND BREATHE, DARK CHILD OF DZOXK!!!
pant... pant
N-NOOOO--
IT IS NOT ENOUGH... NOT YET...
BUT SOON, MY STRONG AND AWFUL ONE. SOON...
YES, SIGMUND?
YO, DA. ICH AND POLLY JUS' RANG IN. 'YOU' WANT T THEY; SHOULD TRY N' SAVE THE DOGS.
N'SHIT?
NO.
TELL YOUR BROTHER, ICHABOD, TO OBSERVE THEM AS LONG AS IT IS SAFE TO DO SO.
I WILL NOT RESCUE THEM.

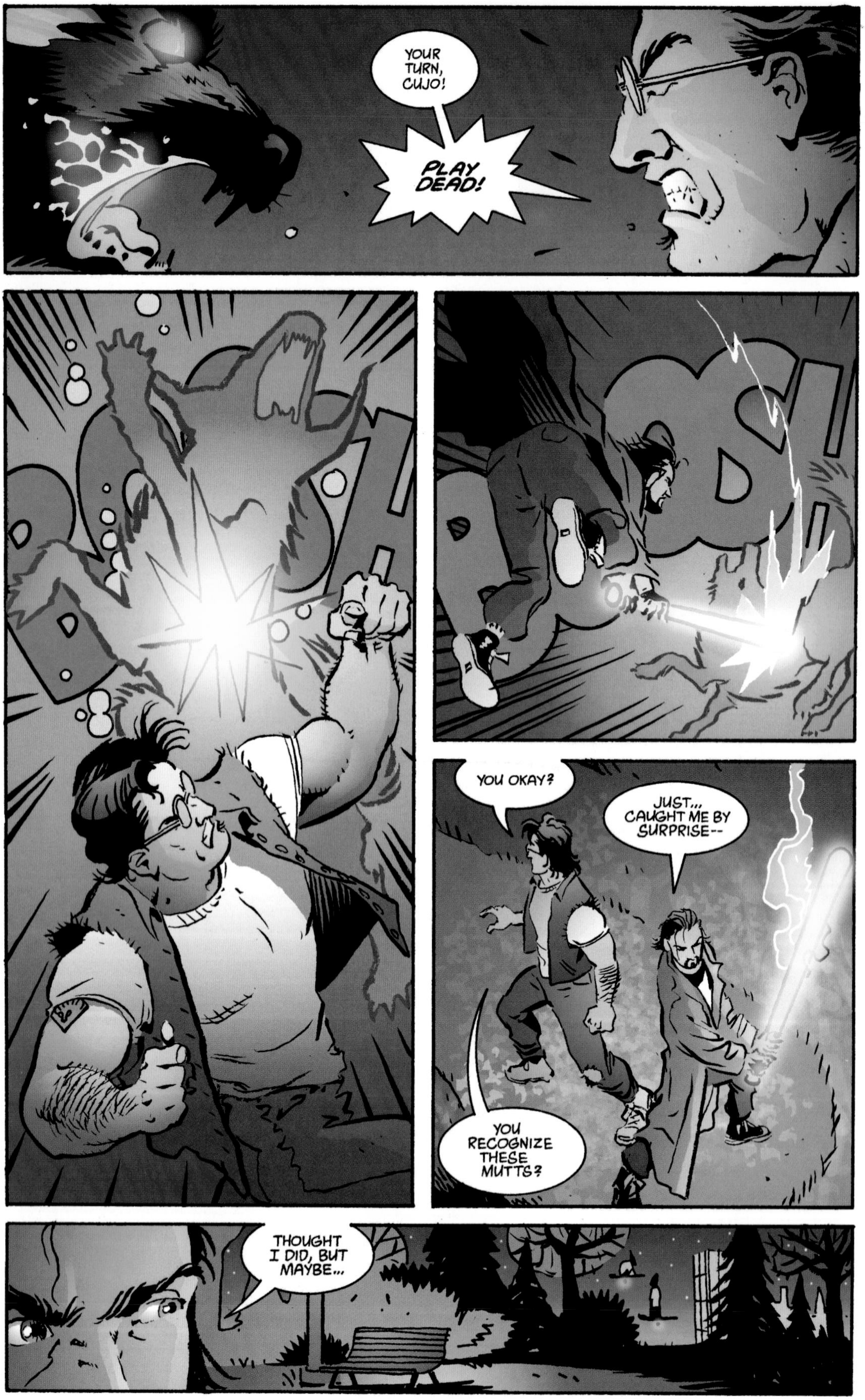
YOUR TURN, CUJO!
PLAY DEAD!
YOU OKAY?
JUST... CAUGHT ME BY SURPRISE--
YOU RECOGNIZE THESE MUTTS?
THOUGHT I DID, BUT MAYBE...

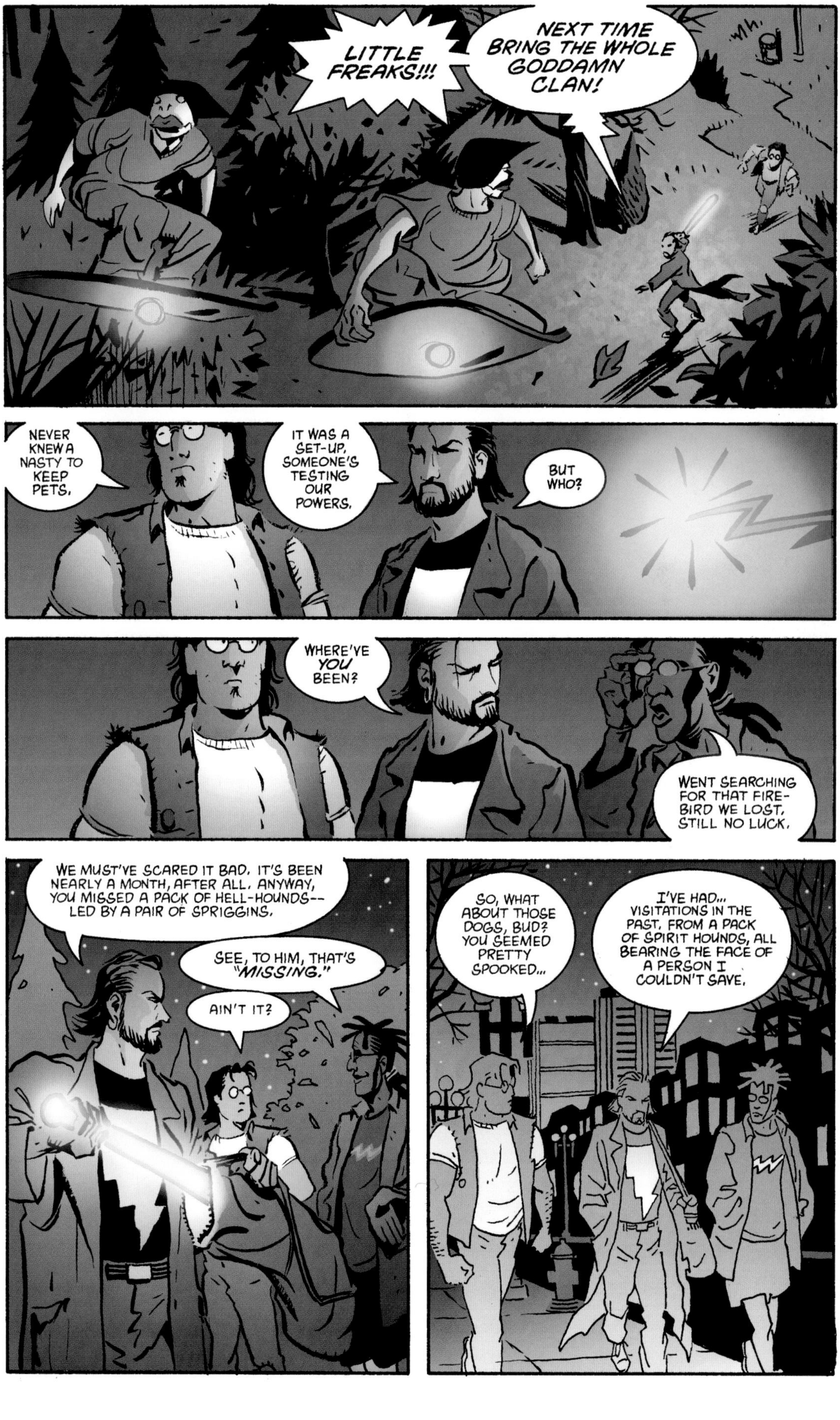
LITTLE FREAKS!!!
NEXT TIME BRING THE WHOLE GODDAMN CLAN!
NEVER KNEW A NASTY TO KEEP PETS.
IT WAS A SET-UP. SOMEONE'S TESTING OUR POWERS.
BUT WHO?
WHERE'VE YOU BEEN?
WENT SEARCHING FOR THAT FIRE-BIRD WE LOST. STILL NO LUCK.
WE MUST'VE SCARED IT BAD. IT'S BEEN NEARLY A MONTH, AFTER ALL. ANYWAY, YOU MISSED A PACK OF HELL-HOUNDS-- LED BY A PAIR OF SPRIGGINS.
SEE, TO HIM, THAT'S "MISSING."
AIN'T IT?
SO, WHAT ABOUT THOSE DOGS, BUD? YOU SEEMED PRETTY SPOOKED...
I'VE HAD... VISITATIONS IN THE PAST. FROM A PACK OF SPIRIT HOUNDS, ALL BEARING THE FACE OF A PERSON I COULDN'T SAVE.

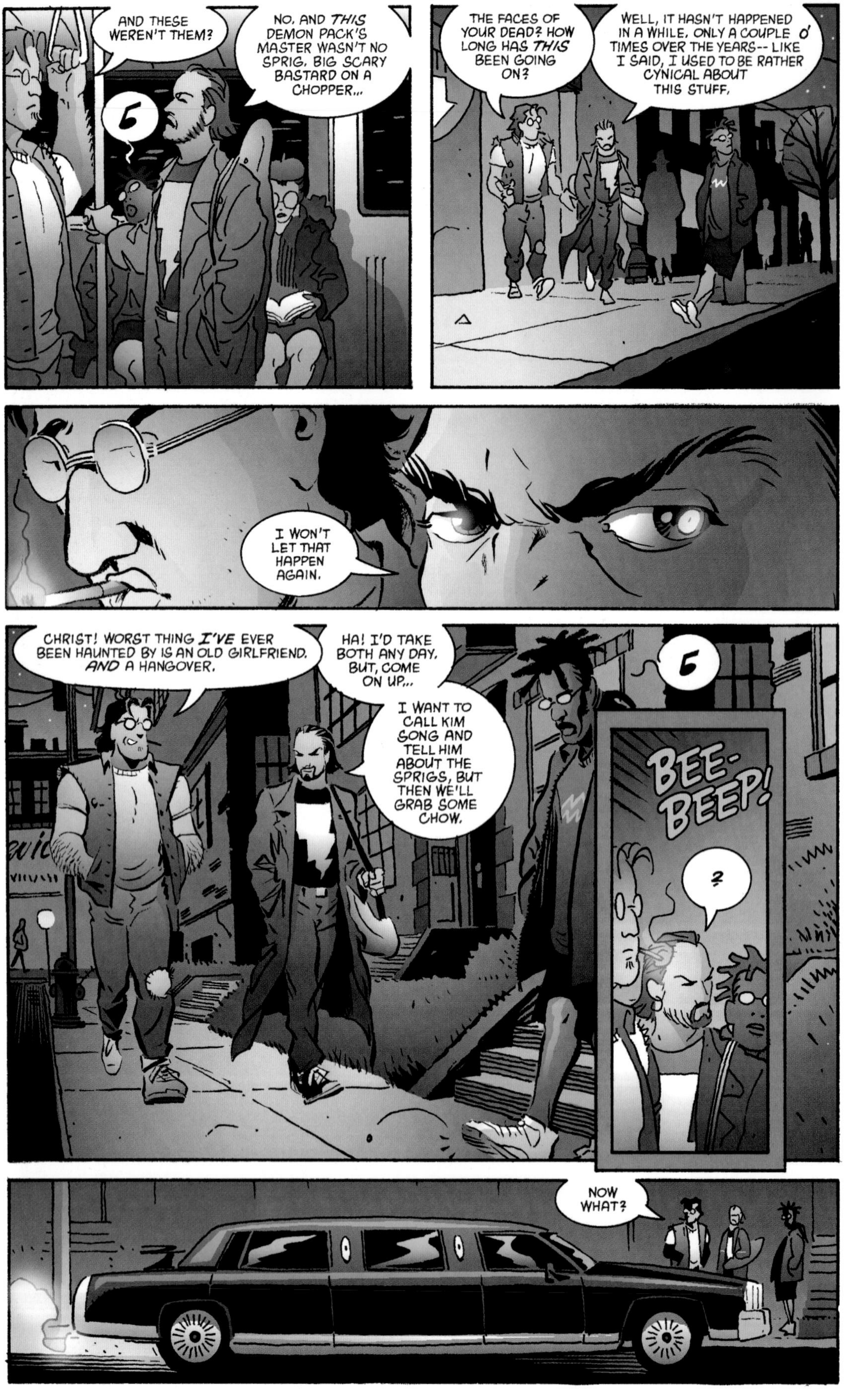
AND THESE WEREN'T THEM?
NO, AND THIS DEMON PACK'S MASTER WASN'T NO SPRIG. BIG SCARY BASTARD ON A CHOPPER...
THE FACES OF YOUR DEAD? HOW LONG HAS THIS BEEN GOING ON?
WELL, IT HASN'T HAPPENED IN A WHILE, ONLY A COUPLE O' TIMES OVER THE YEARS-- LIKE I SAID, I USED TO BE RATHER CYNICAL ABOUT THIS STUFF.
I WON'T LET THAT HAPPEN AGAIN.
CHRIST! WORST THING I'VE EVER BEEN HAUNTED BY IS AN OLD GIRLFRIEND. AND A HANGOVER.
HA! I'D TAKE BOTH ANY DAY. BUT, COME ON UP...
I WANT TO CALL KIM SONG AND TELL HIM ABOUT THE SPRIGS, BUT THEN WE'LL GRAB SOME CHOW.
BEE-BEEP!
?
NOW WHAT?

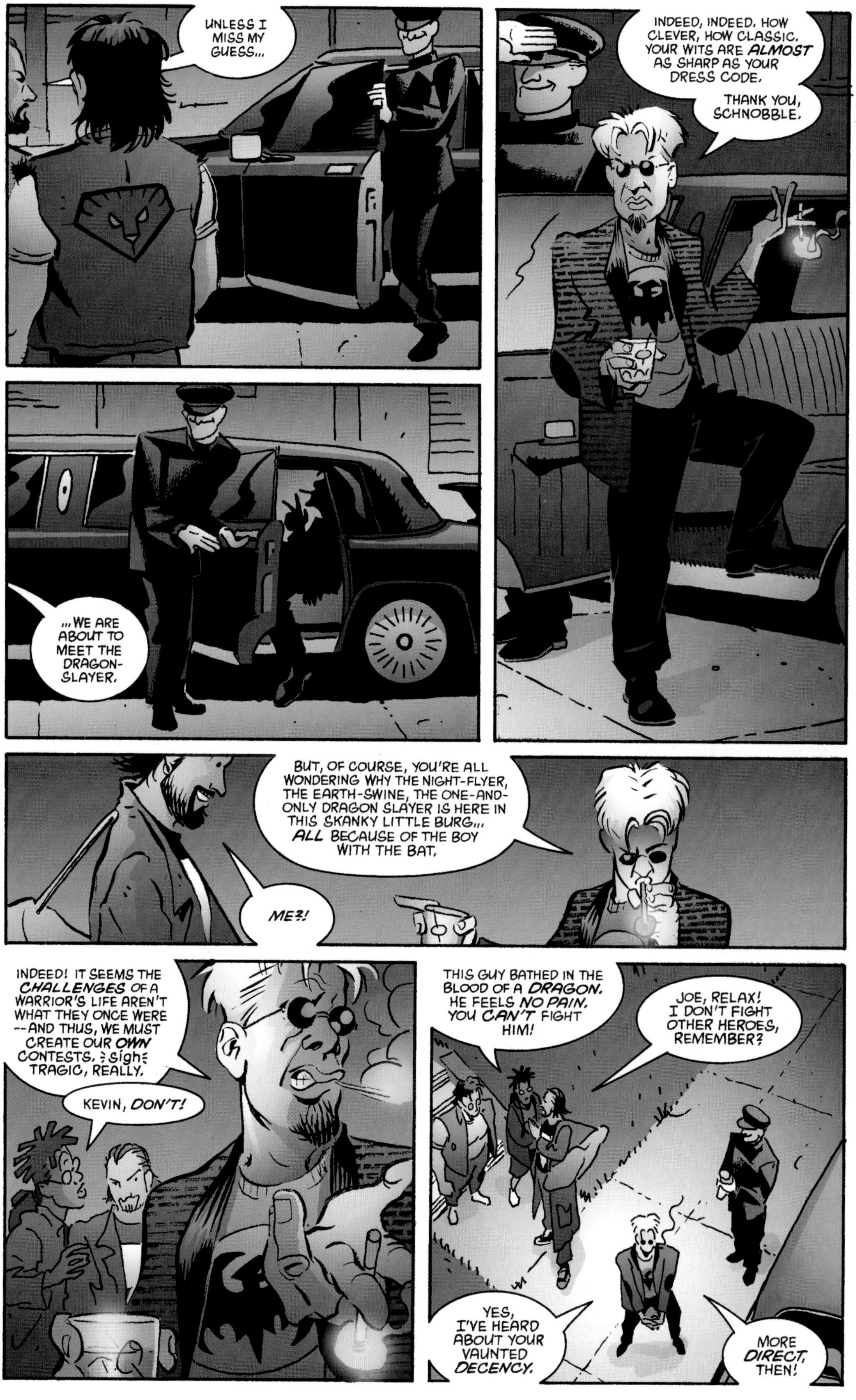
UNLESS I MISS MY GUESS...
INDEED, INDEED. HOW CLEVER, HOW CLASSIC. YOUR WITS ARE ALMOST AS SHARP AS YOUR DRESS CODE.
THANK YOU, SCHNOBBLE.
...WE ARE ABOUT TO MEET THE DRAGON-SLAYER.
BUT, OF COURSE, YOU'RE ALL WONDERING WHY THE NIGHT-FLYER, THE EARTH-SWINE, THE ONE-AND-ONLY DRAGON SLAYER IS HERE IN THIS SKANKY LITTLE BURG... ALL BECAUSE OF THE BOY WITH THE BAT.
ME?!
INDEED! IT SEEMS THE CHALLENGES OF A WARRIOR'S LIFE AREN'T WHAT THEY ONCE WERE --AND THUS, WE MUST CREATE OUR OWN CONTESTS. sigh TRAGIC, REALLY.
KEVIN, DON'T!
THIS GUY BATHED IN THE BLOOD OF A DRAGON. HE FEELS NO PAIN. YOU CAN'T FIGHT HIM!
JOE, RELAX! I DON'T FIGHT OTHER HEROES, REMEMBER?
YES, I'VE HEARD ABOUT YOUR VAUNTED DECENCY.
MORE DIRECT, THEN!

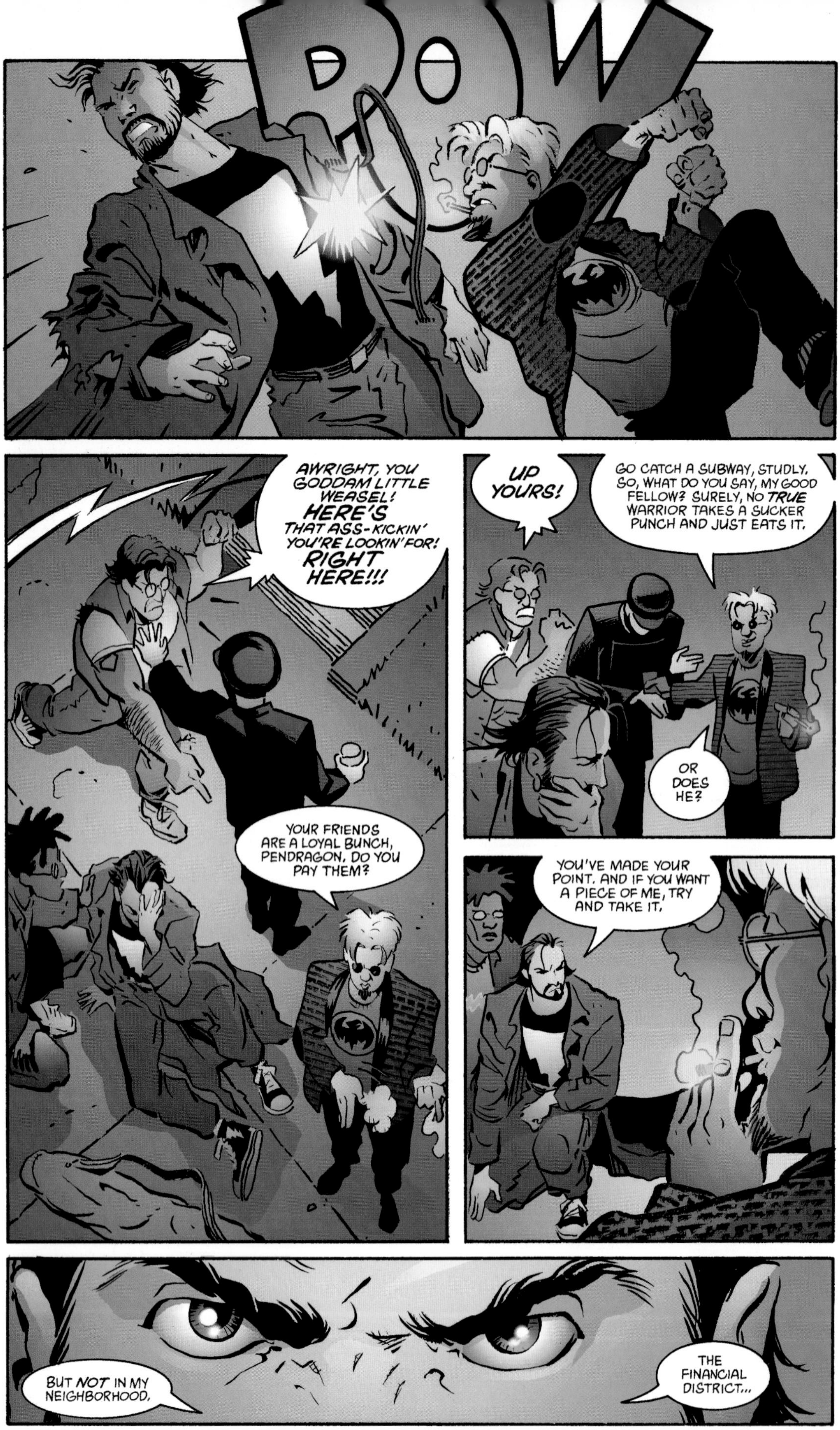
POW
AWRIGHT, YOU GODDAM LITTLE WEASEL! HERE'S THAT ASS-KICKIN' YOU'RE LOOKIN' FOR! RIGHT HERE!!!
YOUR FRIENDS ARE A LOYAL BUNCH, PENDRAGON. DO YOU PAY THEM?
UP YOURS!
GO CATCH A SUBWAY, STUDLY. SO, WHAT DO YOU SAY, MY GOOD FELLOW? SURELY, NO TRUE WARRIOR TAKES A SUCKER PUNCH AND JUST EATS IT.
OR DOES HE?
YOU'VE MADE YOUR POINT. AND IF YOU WANT A PIECE OF ME, TRY AND TAKE IT.
BUT NOT IN MY NEIGHBORHOOD.
THE FINANCIAL DISTRICT...

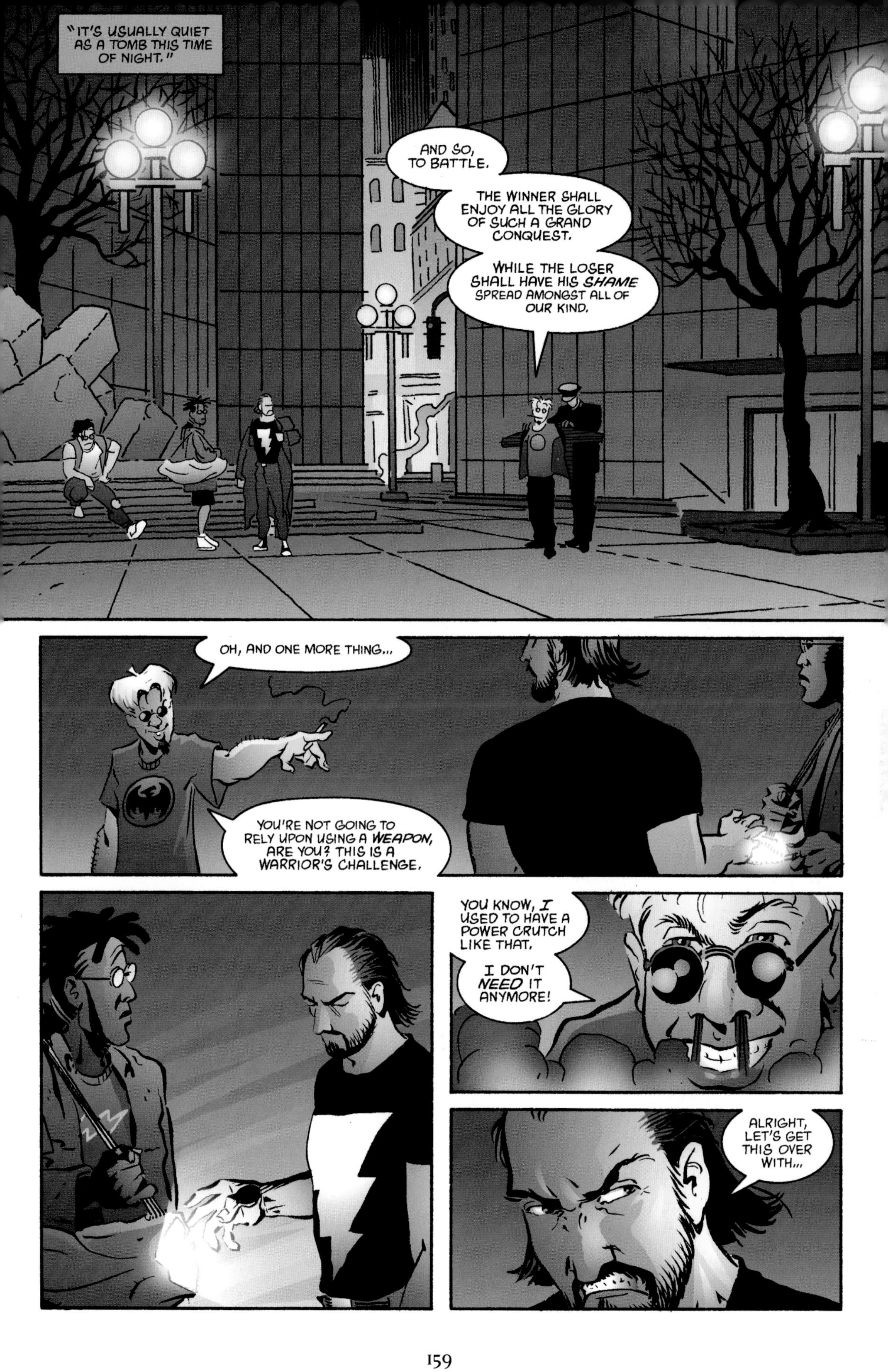
"IT'S USUALLY QUIET AS A TOMB THIS TIME OF NIGHT."
AND SO, TO BATTLE.
THE WINNER SHALL ENJOY ALL THE GLORY OF SUCH A GRAND CONQUEST.
WHILE THE LOSER SHALL HAVE HIS *SHAME* SPREAD AMONGST ALL OF OUR KIND.
OH, AND ONE MORE THING...
YOU'RE NOT GOING TO RELY UPON USING A *WEAPON*, ARE YOU? THIS IS A WARRIOR'S CHALLENGE.
YOU KNOW, *I* USED TO HAVE A POWER CRUTCH LIKE THAT.
I DON'T *NEED* IT ANYMORE!
ALRIGHT, LET'S GET THIS OVER WITH...

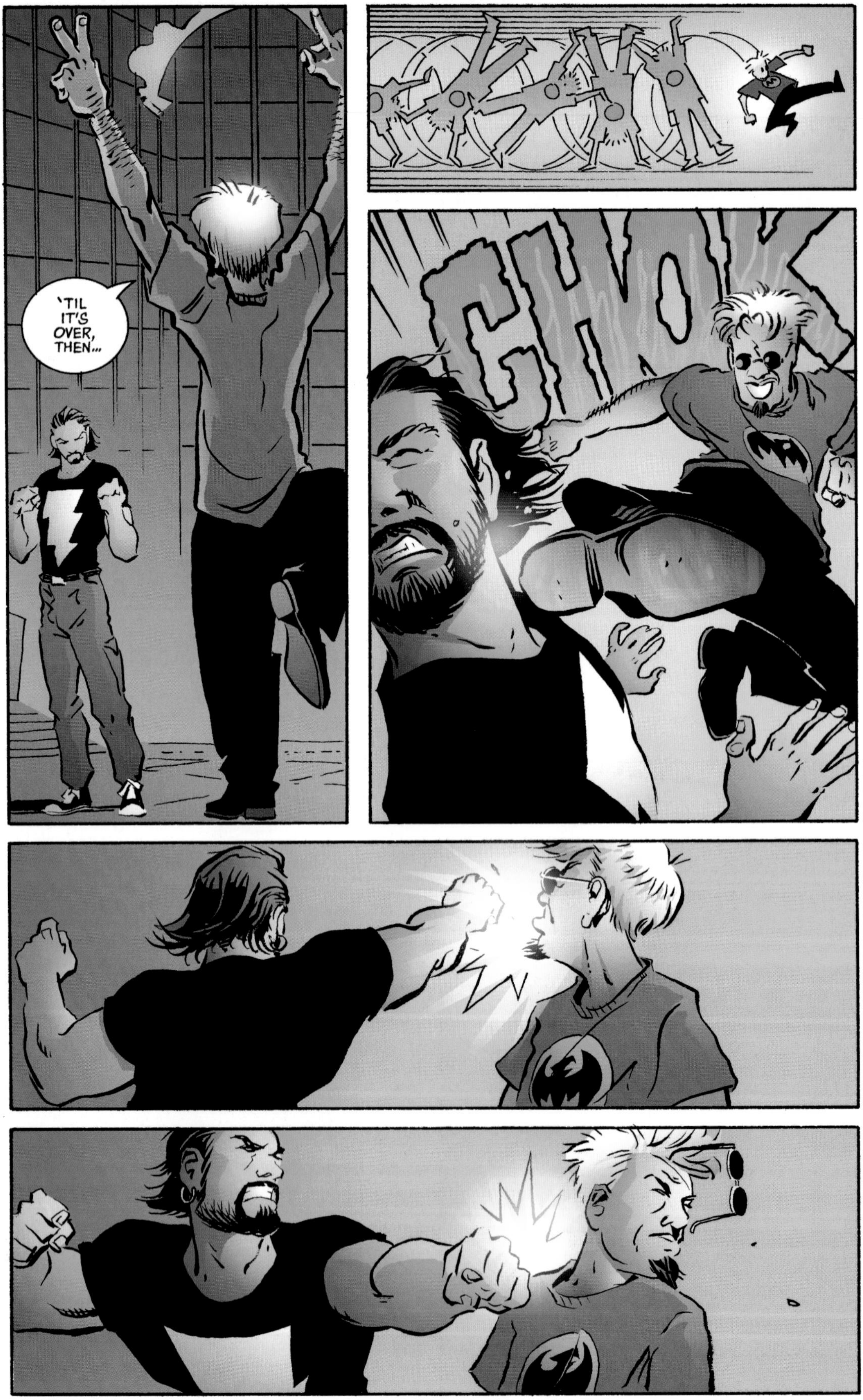
'TIL IT'S OVER, THEN...
CHOK

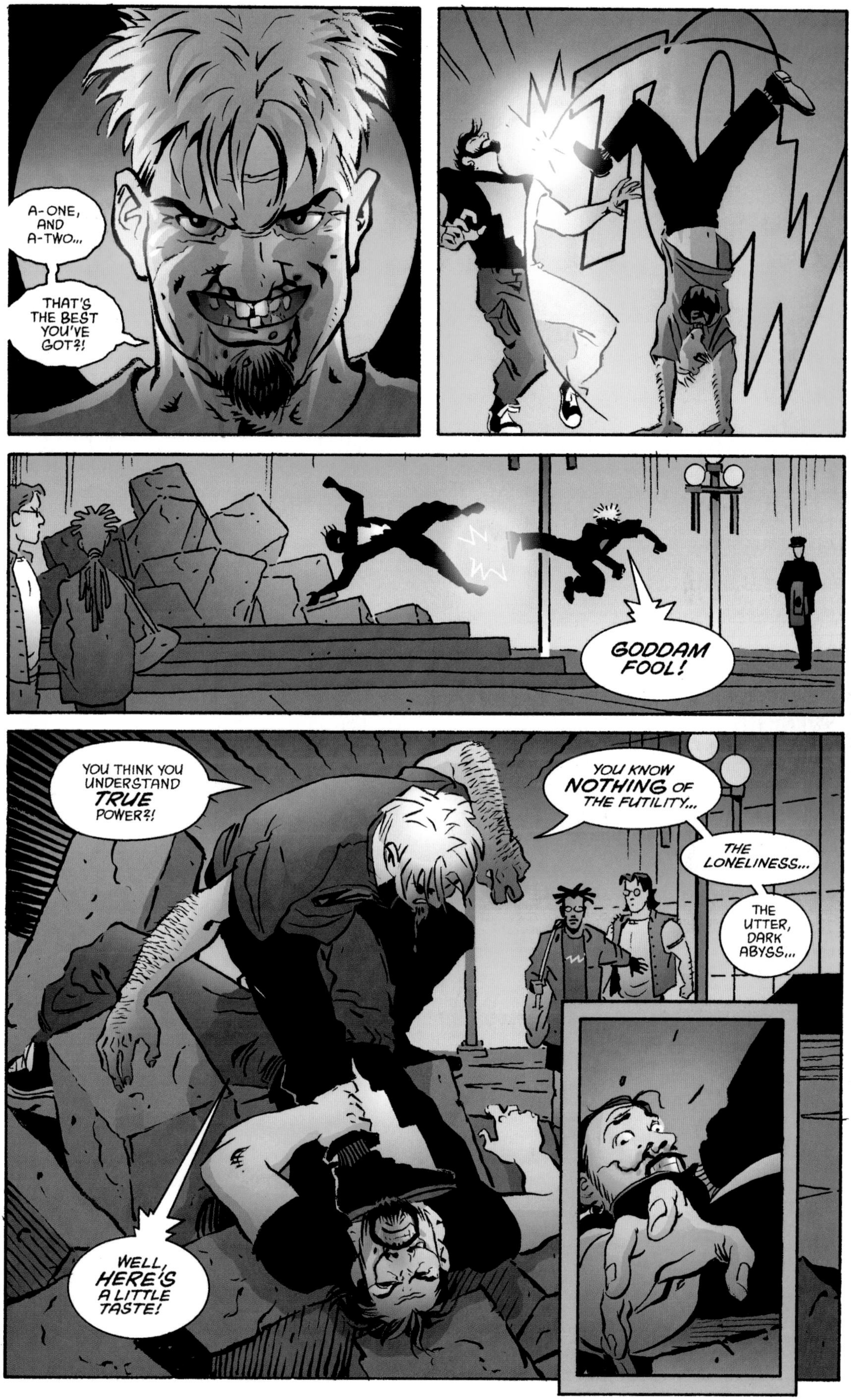
A-ONE, AND A-TWO...
THAT'S THE BEST YOU'VE GOT?!
GODDAM FOOL!
YOU THINK YOU UNDERSTAND TRUE POWER?!
YOU KNOW NOTHING OF THE FUTILITY...
THE LONELINESS...
THE UTTER, DARK ABYSS...
WELL, HERE'S A LITTLE TASTE!

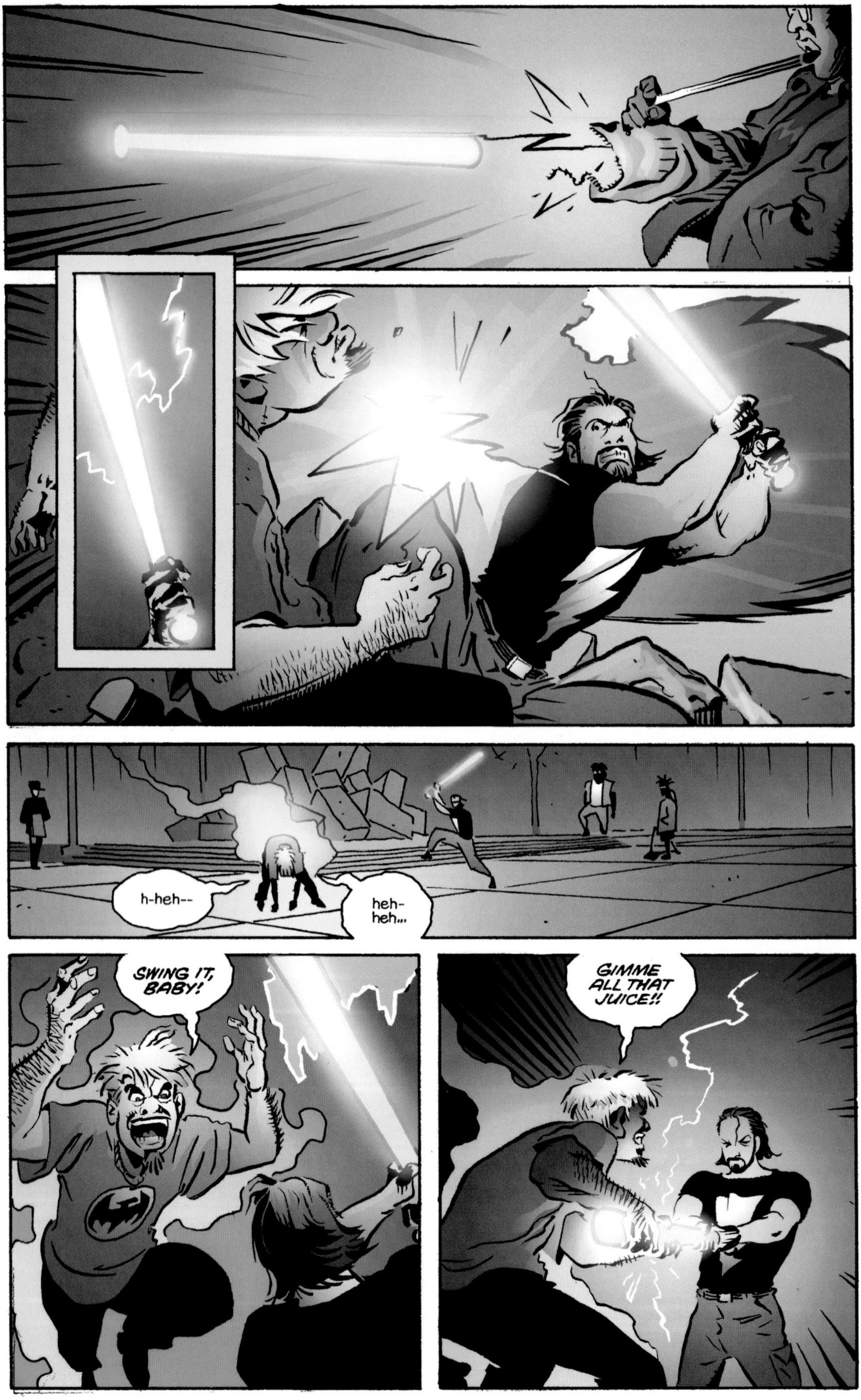
h-heh--
heh-heh...
SWING IT, BABY!
GIMME ALL THAT JUICE!!

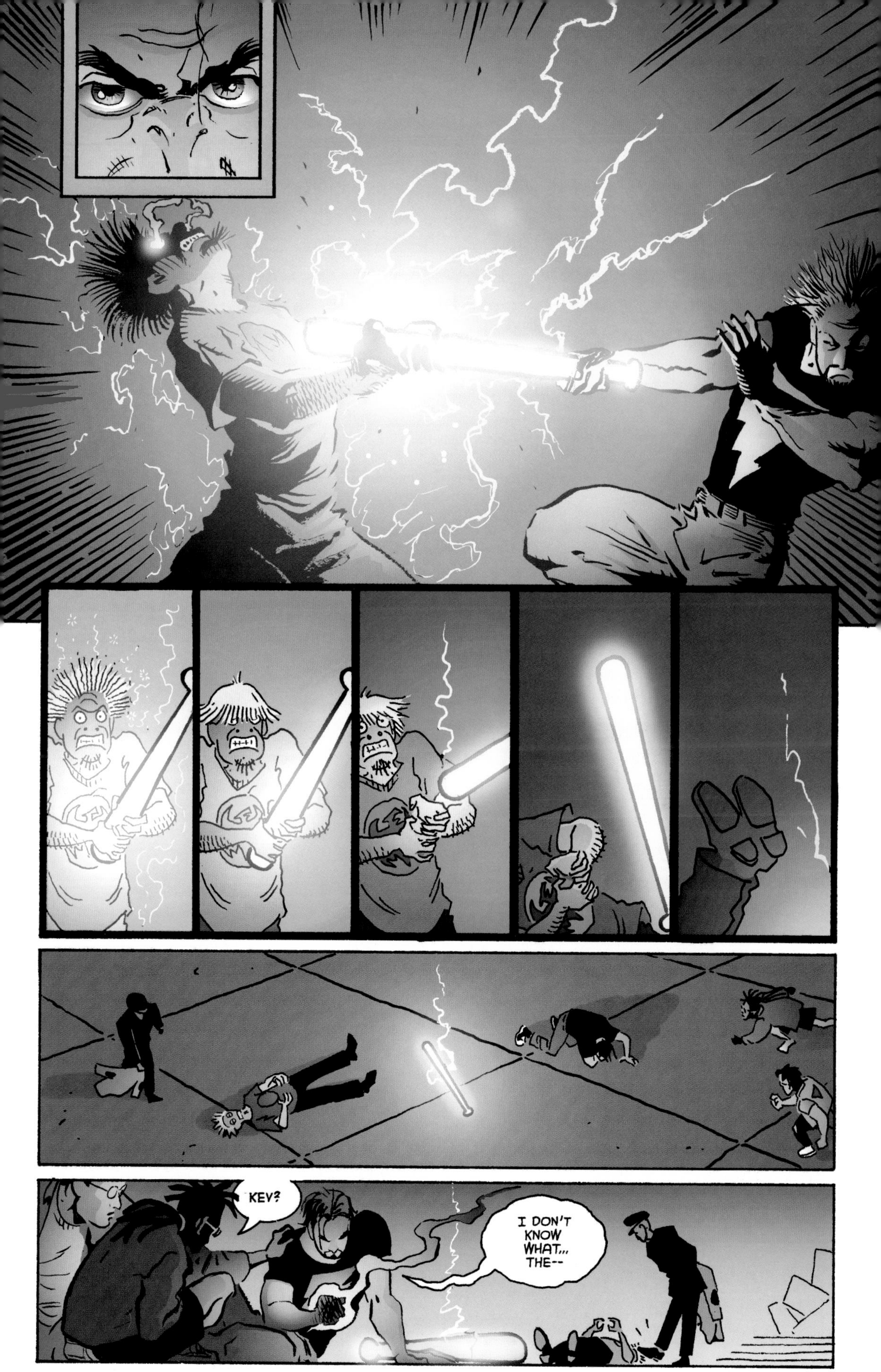
KEV?
I DON'T KNOW WHAT... THE--

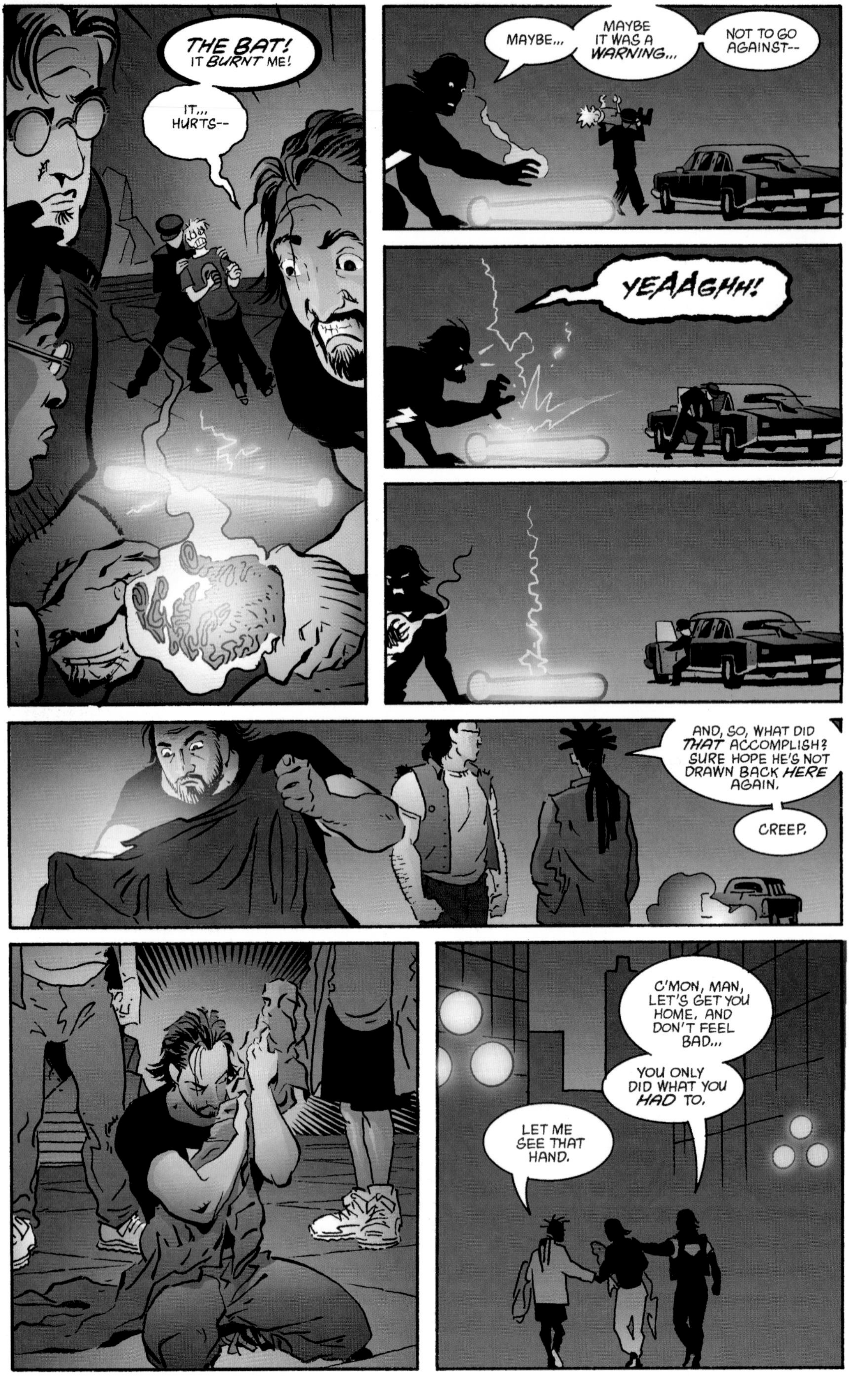
THE BAT! IT BURNT ME!
IT... HURTS--
MAYBE...
MAYBE IT WAS A WARNING...
NOT TO GO AGAINST--
YEAAGHH!
AND, SO, WHAT DID THAT ACCOMPLISH? SURE HOPE HE'S NOT DRAWN BACK HERE AGAIN.
CREEP.
C'MON, MAN, LET'S GET YOU HOME, AND DON'T FEEL BAD...
YOU ONLY DID WHAT YOU HAD TO.
LET ME SEE THAT HAND.

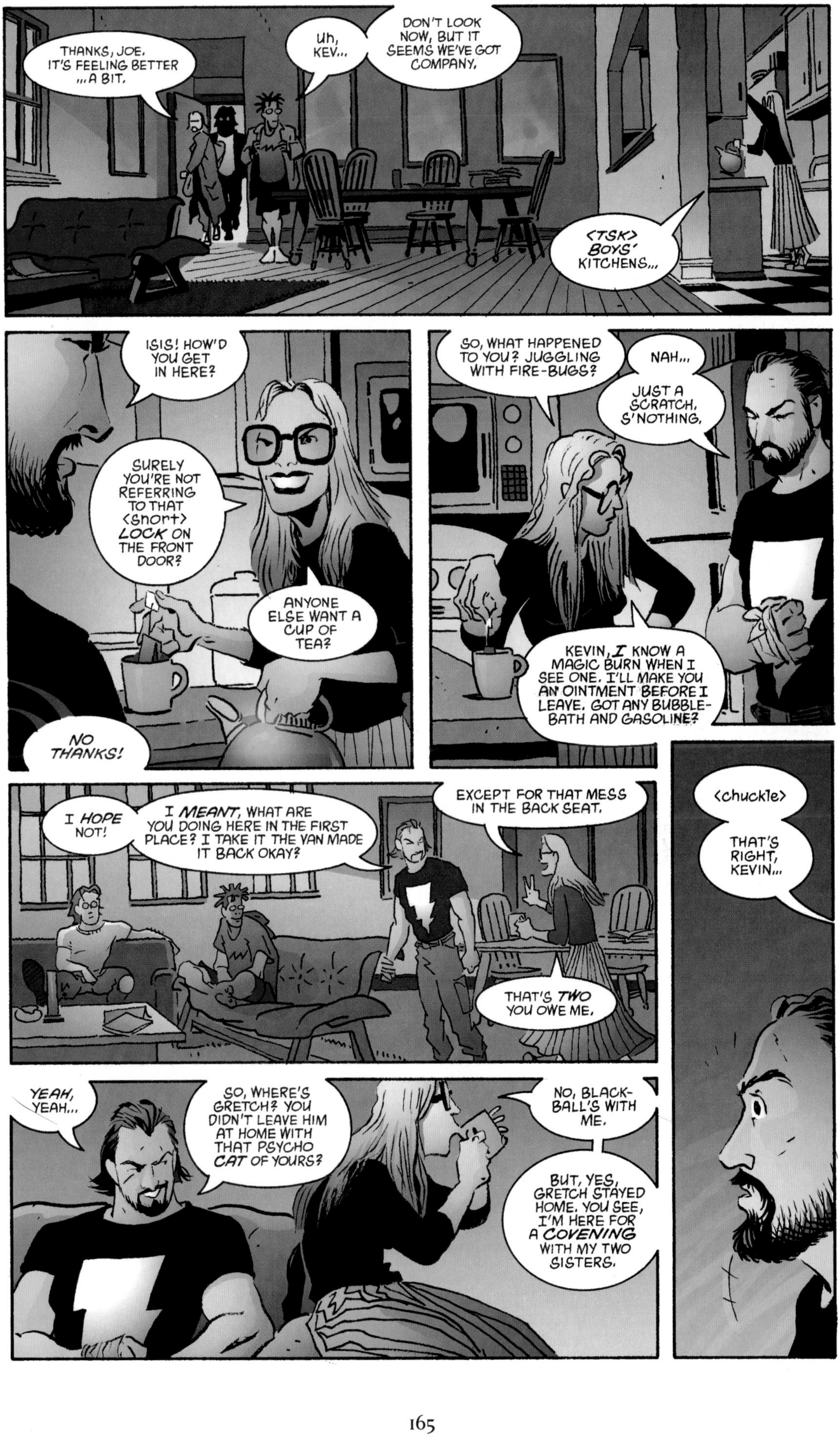
THANKS, JOE. IT'S FEELING BETTER ...A BIT.
Uh, KEV...
DON'T LOOK NOW, BUT IT SEEMS WE'VE GOT COMPANY.
<TSK> BOYS' KITCHENS...
ISIS! HOW'D YOU GET IN HERE?
SURELY YOU'RE NOT REFERRING TO THAT <snort> LOCK ON THE FRONT DOOR?
ANYONE ELSE WANT A CUP OF TEA?
NO THANKS!
SO, WHAT HAPPENED TO YOU? JUGGLING WITH FIRE-BUGS?
NAH... JUST A SCRATCH. S'NOTHING.
KEVIN, I KNOW A MAGIC BURN WHEN I SEE ONE. I'LL MAKE YOU AN OINTMENT BEFORE I LEAVE. GOT ANY BUBBLE-BATH AND GASOLINE?
I HOPE NOT!
I MEANT, WHAT ARE YOU DOING HERE IN THE FIRST PLACE? I TAKE IT THE VAN MADE IT BACK OKAY?
EXCEPT FOR THAT MESS IN THE BACK SEAT.
THAT'S TWO YOU OWE ME.
YEAH, YEAH...
SO, WHERE'S GRETCH? YOU DIDN'T LEAVE HIM AT HOME WITH THAT PSYCHO CAT OF YOURS?
NO, BLACK-BALL'S WITH ME.
BUT, YES, GRETCH STAYED HOME. YOU SEE, I'M HERE FOR A COVENING WITH MY TWO SISTERS.
<chuckle>
THAT'S RIGHT, KEVIN...

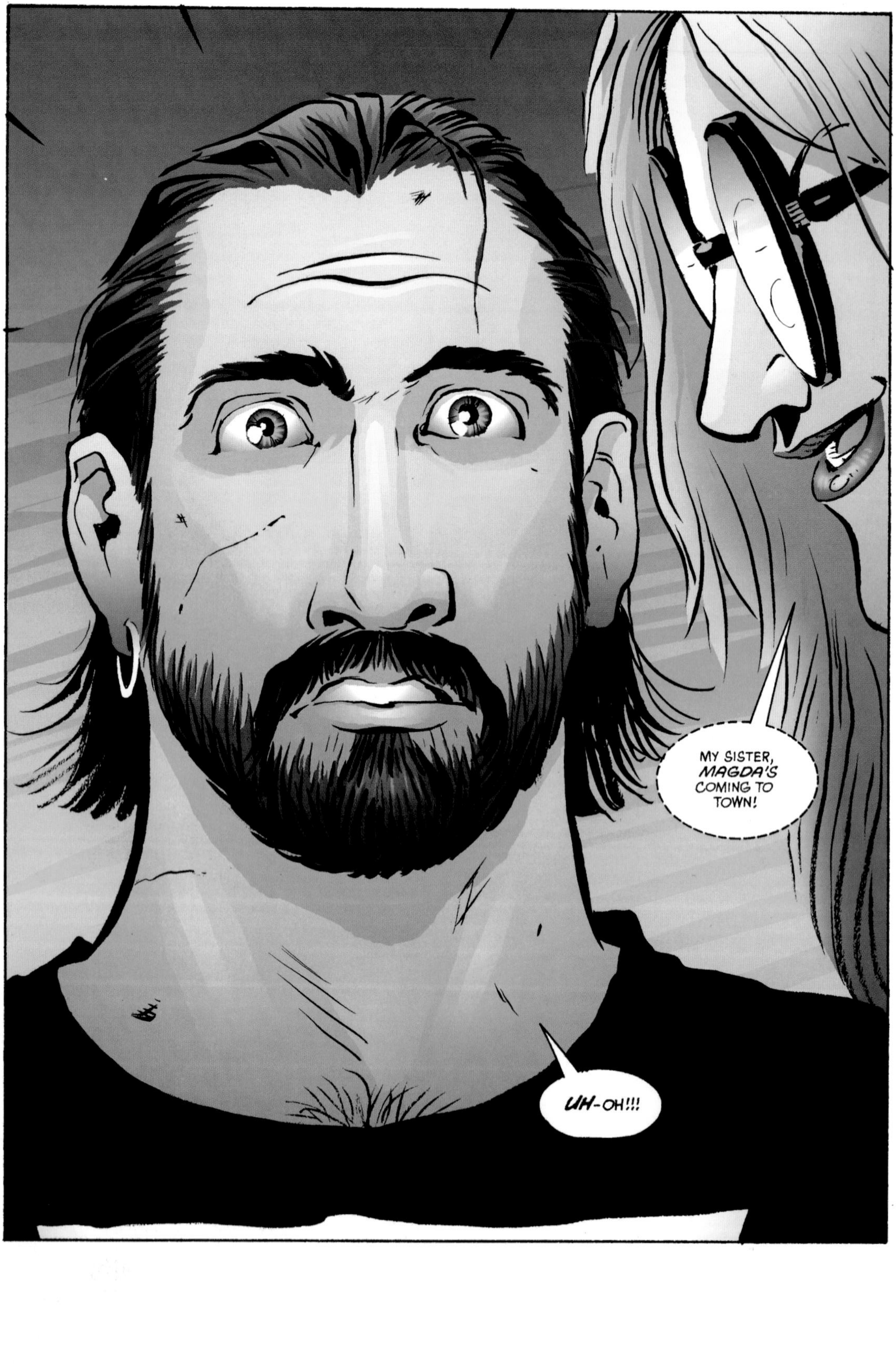
MY SISTER, MAGDA'S COMING TO TOWN!
UH-OH!!!

THE HERO DEFINED

MAGE®

chapter

7

"Infirm of Purpose"

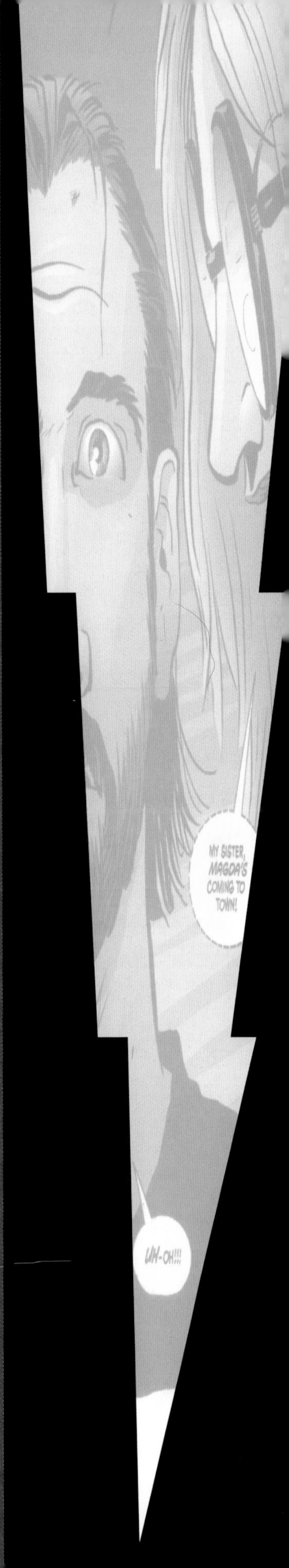
MY SISTER, MAGDA'S COMING TO TOWN!
UH-OH!!!

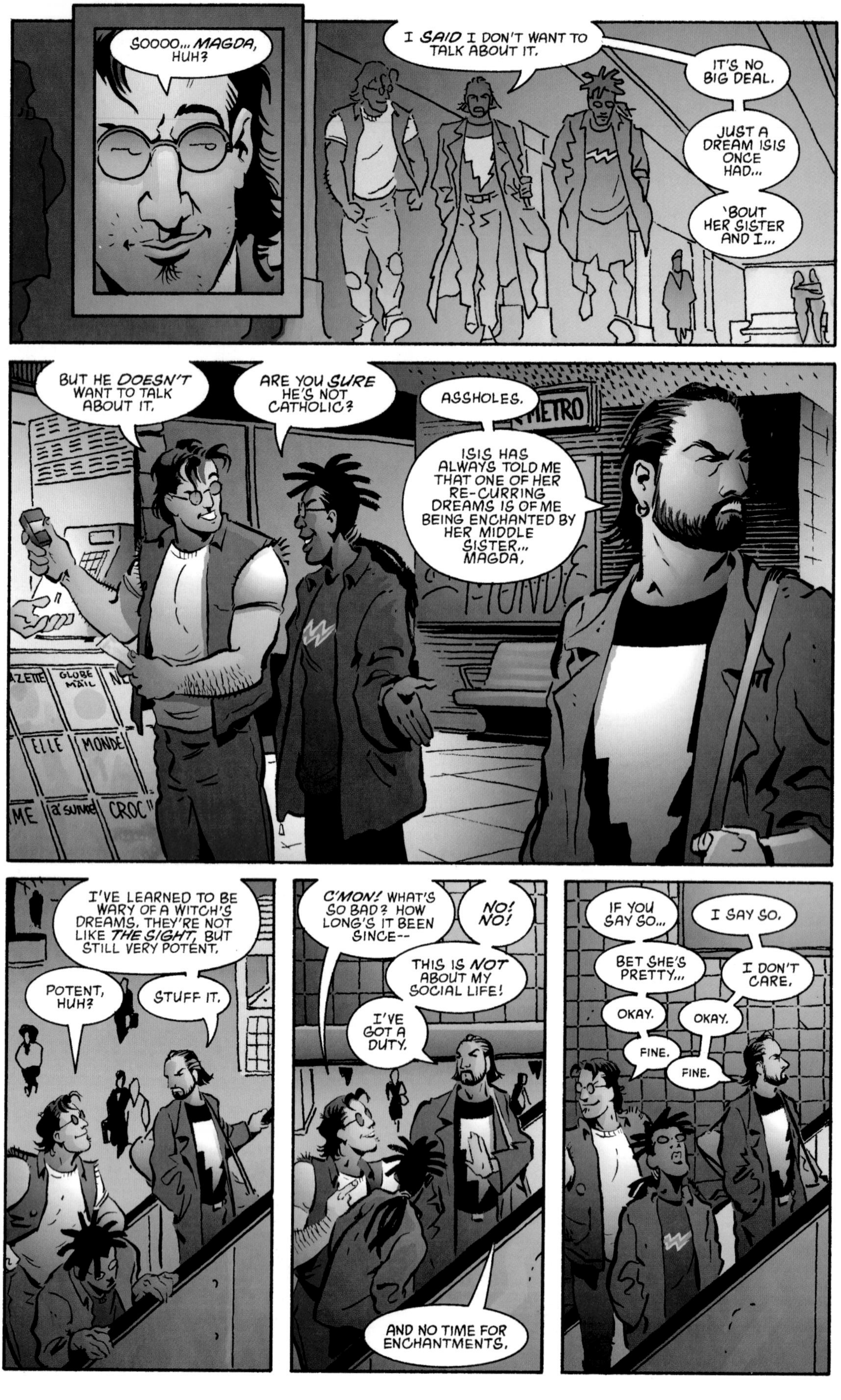
SOOOO... MAGDA, HUH?
I SAID I DON'T WANT TO TALK ABOUT IT.
IT'S NO BIG DEAL.
JUST A DREAM ISIS ONCE HAD...
'BOUT HER SISTER AND I...
BUT HE DOESN'T WANT TO TALK ABOUT IT.
ARE YOU SURE HE'S NOT CATHOLIC?
ASSHOLES.
ISIS HAS ALWAYS TOLD ME THAT ONE OF HER RE-CURRING DREAMS IS OF ME BEING ENCHANTED BY HER MIDDLE SISTER... MAGDA.
METRO
GLOBE MAIL
ELLE
MONDE
CROC
I'VE LEARNED TO BE WARY OF A WITCH'S DREAMS. THEY'RE NOT LIKE THE SIGHT, BUT STILL VERY POTENT.
POTENT, HUH?
STUFF IT.
C'MON! WHAT'S SO BAD? HOW LONG'S IT BEEN SINCE--
NO! NO!
THIS IS NOT ABOUT MY SOCIAL LIFE!
I'VE GOT A DUTY.
AND NO TIME FOR ENCHANTMENTS.
IF YOU SAY SO...
I SAY SO.
BET SHE'S PRETTY...
I DON'T CARE.
OKAY.
OKAY.
FINE.
FINE.

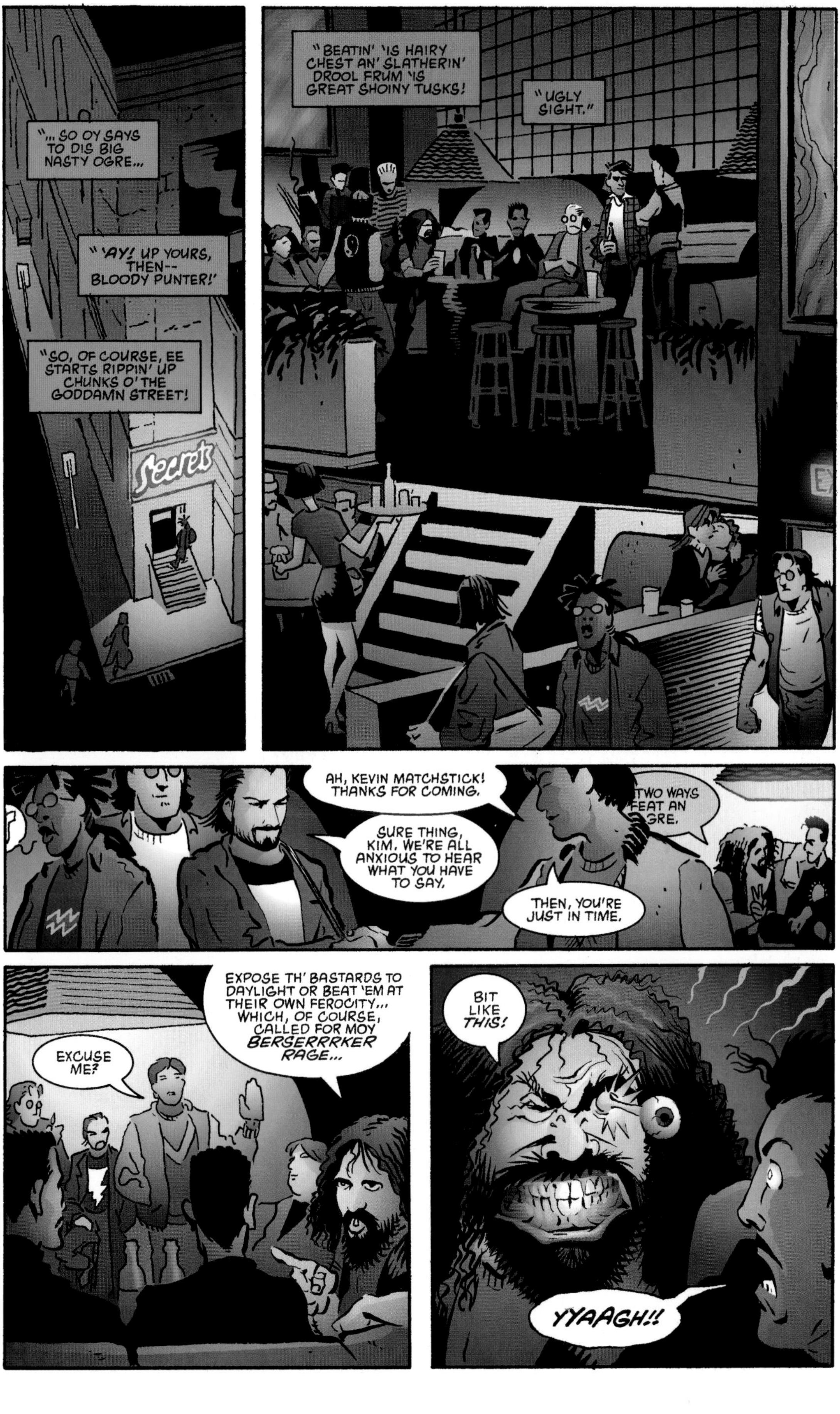
"...SO OY SAYS TO DIS BIG NASTY OGRE...
"'AY! UP YOURS, THEN-- BLOODY PUNTER!'
"SO, OF COURSE, EE STARTS RIPPIN' UP CHUNKS O' THE GODDAMN STREET!
Secrets
"BEATIN' 'IS HAIRY CHEST AN' SLATHERIN' DROOL FRUM 'IS GREAT SHOINY TUSKS!
"UGLY SIGHT."
AH, KEVIN MATCHSTICK! THANKS FOR COMING.
SURE THING, KIM. WE'RE ALL ANXIOUS TO HEAR WHAT YOU HAVE TO SAY.
TWO WAYS EAT AN GRE.
THEN, YOU'RE JUST IN TIME.
EXCUSE ME?
EXPOSE TH' BASTARDS TO DAYLIGHT OR BEAT 'EM AT THEIR OWN FEROCITY... WHICH, OF COURSE, CALLED FOR MOY BERSERRRKER RAGE...
BIT LIKE THIS!
YYAAGH!!

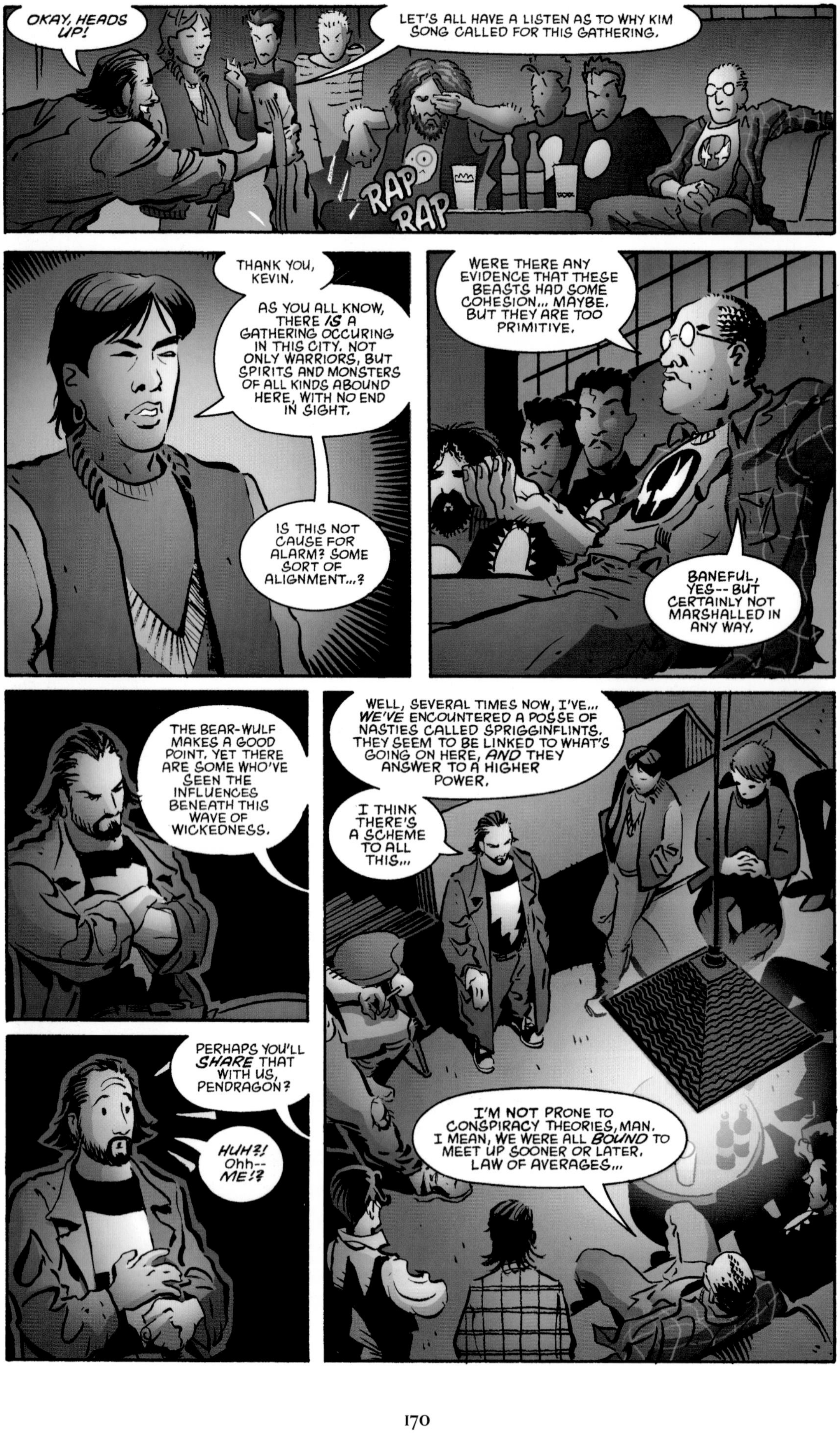
OKAY, HEADS UP!
LET'S ALL HAVE A LISTEN AS TO WHY KIM SONG CALLED FOR THIS GATHERING.
RAP RAP
THANK YOU, KEVIN.
AS YOU ALL KNOW, THERE IS A GATHERING OCCURING IN THIS CITY. NOT ONLY WARRIORS, BUT SPIRITS AND MONSTERS OF ALL KINDS ABOUND HERE, WITH NO END IN SIGHT.
IS THIS NOT CAUSE FOR ALARM? SOME SORT OF ALIGNMENT...?
WERE THERE ANY EVIDENCE THAT THESE BEASTS HAD SOME COHESION... MAYBE. BUT THEY ARE TOO PRIMITIVE.
BANEFUL, YES-- BUT CERTAINLY NOT MARSHALLED IN ANY WAY.
THE BEAR-WULF MAKES A GOOD POINT. YET THERE ARE SOME WHO'VE SEEN THE INFLUENCES BENEATH THIS WAVE OF WICKEDNESS.
PERHAPS YOU'LL SHARE THAT WITH US, PENDRAGON?
HUH?! Ohh-- ME!?
WELL, SEVERAL TIMES NOW, I'VE... WE'VE ENCOUNTERED A POSSE OF NASTIES CALLED SPRIGGINFLINTS. THEY SEEM TO BE LINKED TO WHAT'S GOING ON HERE, AND THEY ANSWER TO A HIGHER POWER.
I THINK THERE'S A SCHEME TO ALL THIS...
I'M NOT PRONE TO CONSPIRACY THEORIES, MAN. I MEAN, WE WERE ALL BOUND TO MEET UP SOONER OR LATER. LAW OF AVERAGES...

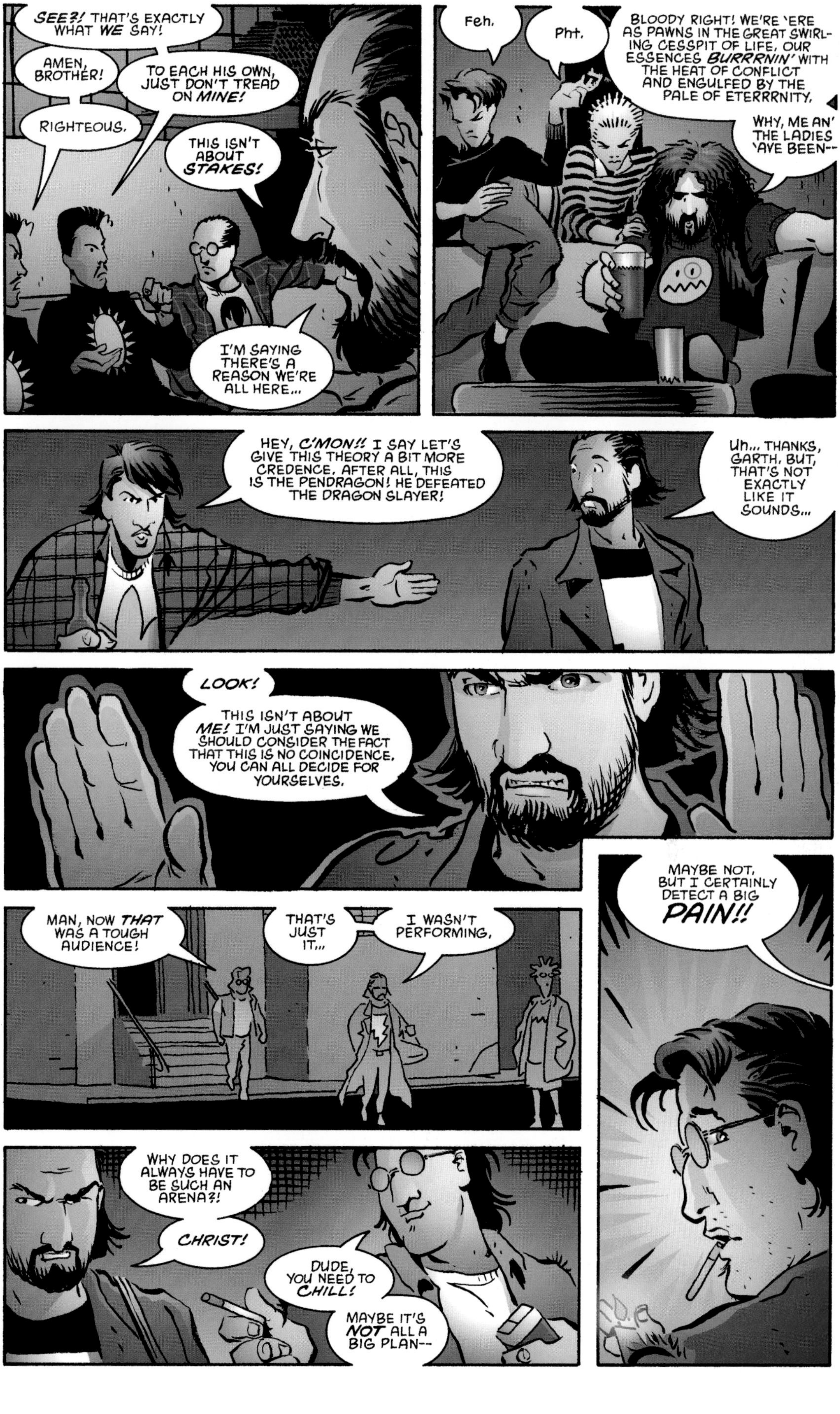
SEE?! THAT'S EXACTLY WHAT WE SAY!
AMEN, BROTHER!
TO EACH HIS OWN, JUST DON'T TREAD ON MINE!
RIGHTEOUS.
THIS ISN'T ABOUT STAKES!
I'M SAYING THERE'S A REASON WE'RE ALL HERE...
Feh.
Pht.
BLOODY RIGHT! WE'RE 'ERE AS PAWNS IN THE GREAT SWIRLING CESSPIT OF LIFE, OUR ESSENCES BURRRNIN' WITH THE HEAT OF CONFLICT AND ENGULFED BY THE PALE OF ETERRRNITY.
WHY, ME AN' THE LADIES 'AVE BEEN--
HEY, C'MON!! I SAY LET'S GIVE THIS THEORY A BIT MORE CREDENCE. AFTER ALL, THIS IS THE PENDRAGON! HE DEFEATED THE DRAGON SLAYER!
Uh... THANKS, GARTH, BUT, THAT'S NOT EXACTLY LIKE IT SOUNDS...
LOOK!
THIS ISN'T ABOUT ME! I'M JUST SAYING WE SHOULD CONSIDER THE FACT THAT THIS IS NO COINCIDENCE. YOU CAN ALL DECIDE FOR YOURSELVES.
MAN, NOW THAT WAS A TOUGH AUDIENCE!
THAT'S JUST IT...
I WASN'T PERFORMING.
WHY DOES IT ALWAYS HAVE TO BE SUCH AN ARENA?!
CHRIST!
DUDE, YOU NEED TO CHILL!
MAYBE IT'S NOT ALL A BIG PLAN--
MAYBE NOT, BUT I CERTAINLY DETECT A BIG PAIN!!

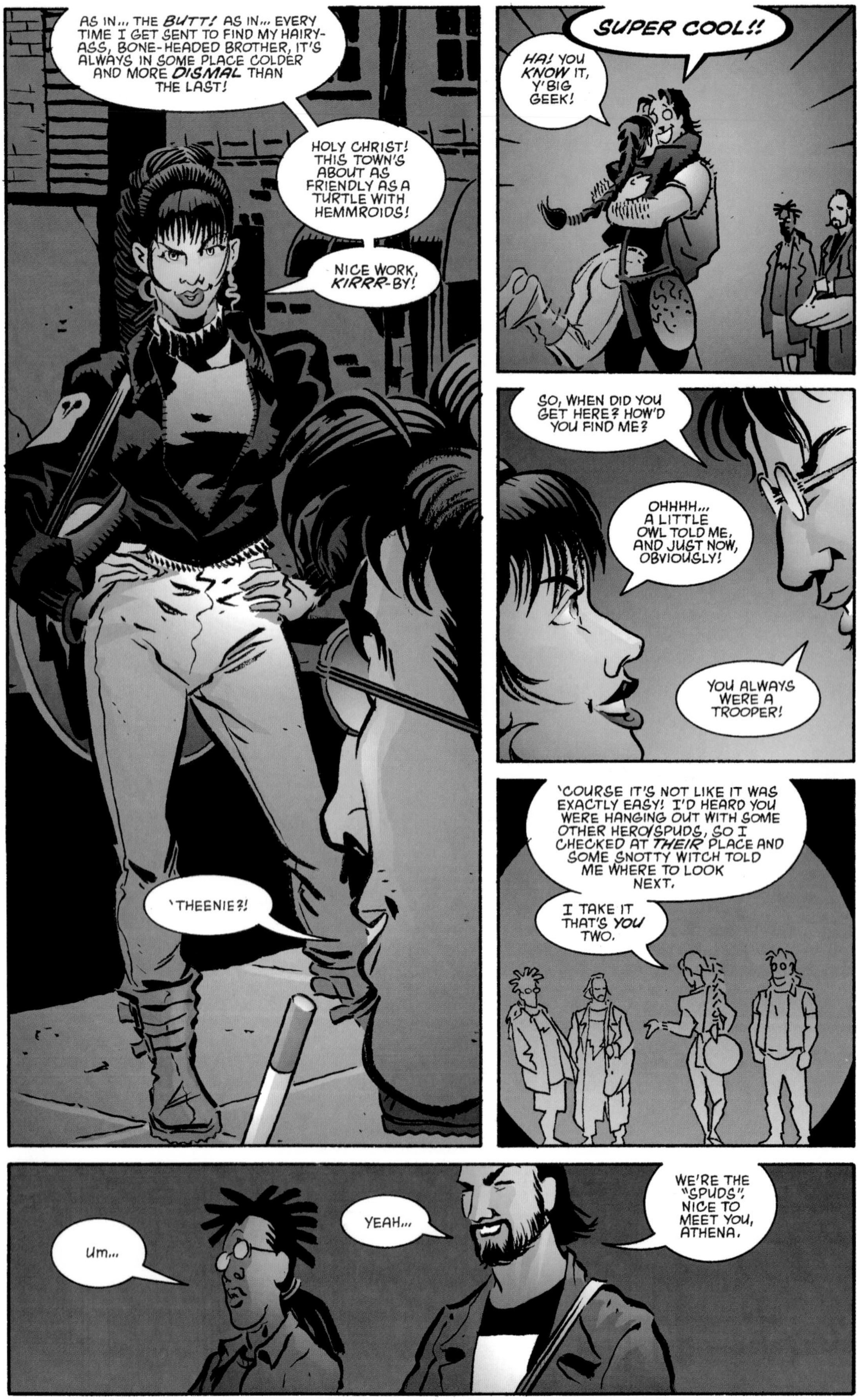
AS IN... THE BUTT! AS IN... EVERY TIME I GET SENT TO FIND MY HAIRY-ASS, BONE-HEADED BROTHER, IT'S ALWAYS IN SOME PLACE COLDER AND MORE DISMAL THAN THE LAST!
HOLY CHRIST! THIS TOWN'S ABOUT AS FRIENDLY AS A TURTLE WITH HEMMROIDS!
NICE WORK, KIRRR-BY!
'THEENIE?!
SUPER COOL!!
HA! YOU KNOW IT, Y'BIG GEEK!
SO, WHEN DID YOU GET HERE? HOW'D YOU FIND ME?
OHHHH... A LITTLE OWL TOLD ME, AND JUST NOW, OBVIOUSLY!
YOU ALWAYS WERE A TROOPER!
'COURSE IT'S NOT LIKE IT WAS EXACTLY EASY! I'D HEARD YOU WERE HANGING OUT WITH SOME OTHER HERO/SPUDS, SO I CHECKED AT THEIR PLACE AND SOME SNOTTY WITCH TOLD ME WHERE TO LOOK NEXT.
I TAKE IT THAT'S YOU TWO.
Um...
YEAH...
WE'RE THE "SPUDS". NICE TO MEET YOU, ATHENA.

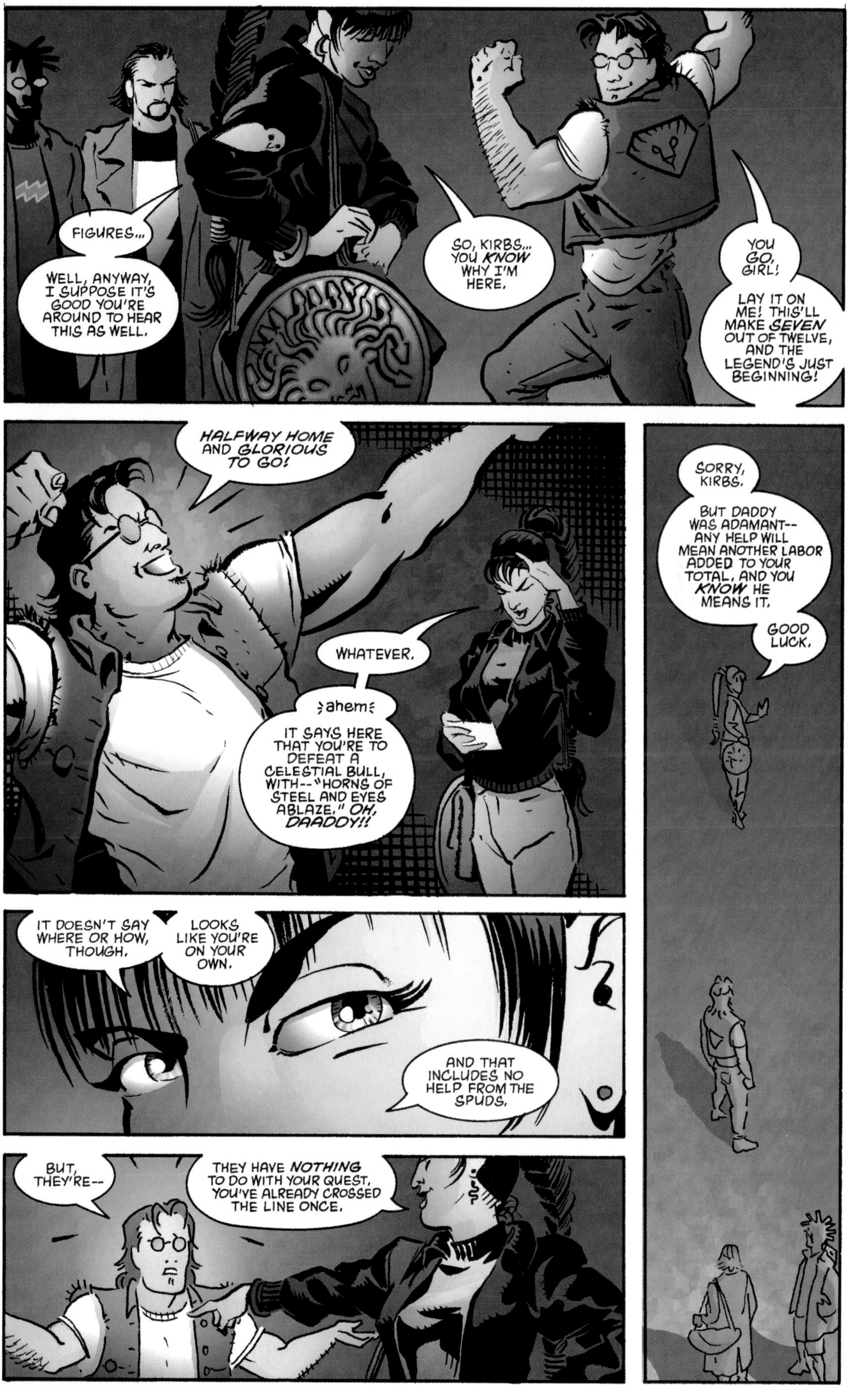
FIGURES...
WELL, ANYWAY, I SUPPOSE IT'S GOOD YOU'RE AROUND TO HEAR THIS AS WELL.
SO, KIRBS... YOU KNOW WHY I'M HERE.
YOU GO, GIRL!
LAY IT ON ME! THIS'LL MAKE SEVEN OUT OF TWELVE, AND THE LEGEND'S JUST BEGINNING!
HALFWAY HOME AND GLORIOUS TO GO!
WHATEVER.
ahem
IT SAYS HERE THAT YOU'RE TO DEFEAT A CELESTIAL BULL, WITH--"HORNS OF STEEL AND EYES ABLAZE." OH, DAADDY!!
IT DOESN'T SAY WHERE OR HOW, THOUGH.
LOOKS LIKE YOU'RE ON YOUR OWN.
AND THAT INCLUDES NO HELP FROM THE SPUDS.
BUT, THEY'RE--
THEY HAVE NOTHING TO DO WITH YOUR QUEST. YOU'VE ALREADY CROSSED THE LINE ONCE.
SORRY, KIRBS.
BUT DADDY WAS ADAMANT-- ANY HELP WILL MEAN ANOTHER LABOR ADDED TO YOUR TOTAL, AND YOU KNOW HE MEANS IT.
GOOD LUCK.

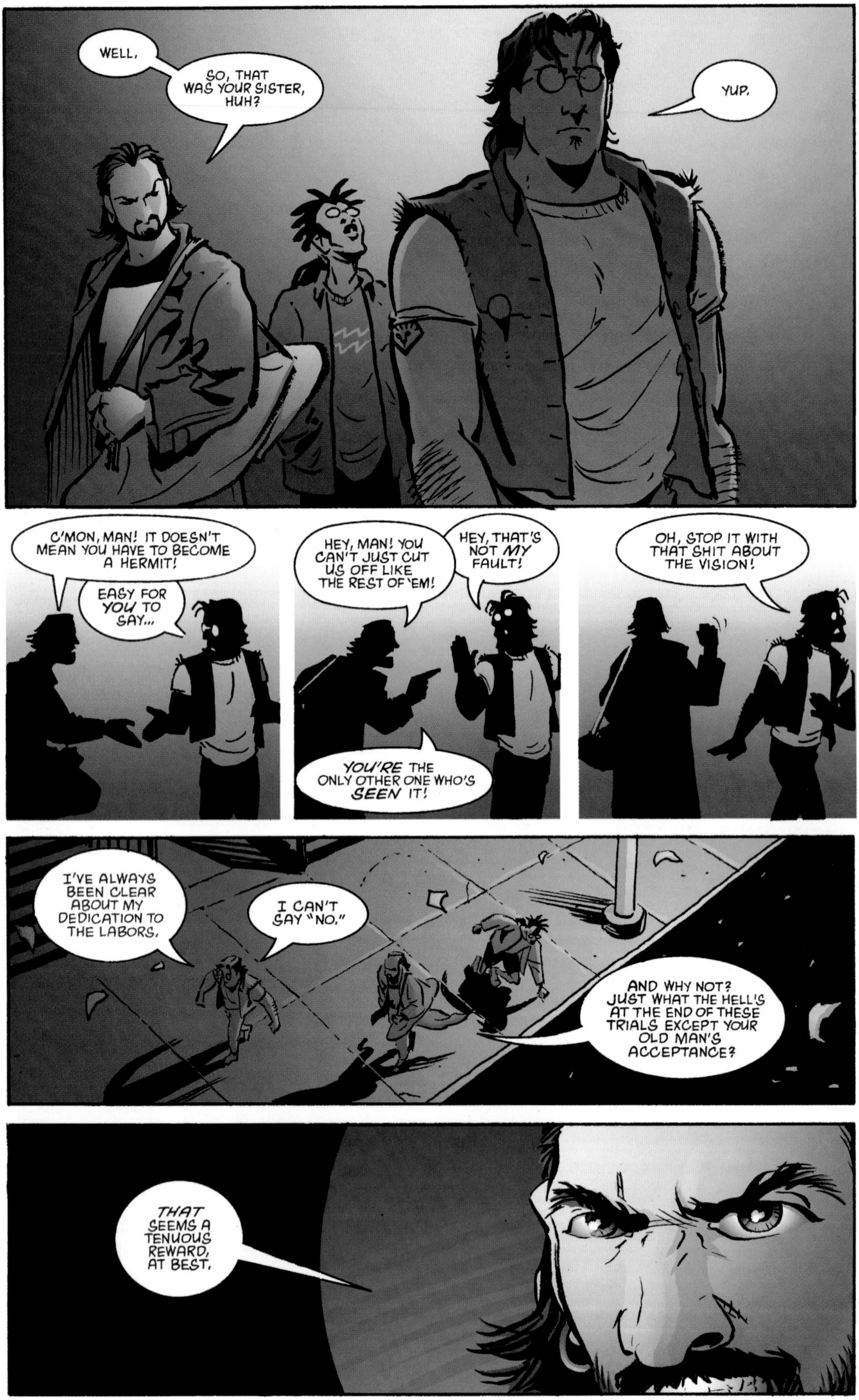
WELL,
SO, THAT WAS YOUR SISTER, HUH?
YUP.
C'MON, MAN! IT DOESN'T MEAN YOU HAVE TO BECOME A HERMIT!
EASY FOR YOU TO SAY...
HEY, MAN! YOU CAN'T JUST CUT US OFF LIKE THE REST OF 'EM!
HEY, THAT'S NOT MY FAULT!
YOU'RE THE ONLY OTHER ONE WHO'S SEEN IT!
OH, STOP IT WITH THAT SHIT ABOUT THE VISION!
I'VE ALWAYS BEEN CLEAR ABOUT MY DEDICATION TO THE LABORS.
I CAN'T SAY "NO."
AND WHY NOT? JUST WHAT THE HELL'S AT THE END OF THESE TRIALS EXCEPT YOUR OLD MAN'S ACCEPTANCE?
THAT SEEMS A TENUOUS REWARD, AT BEST.

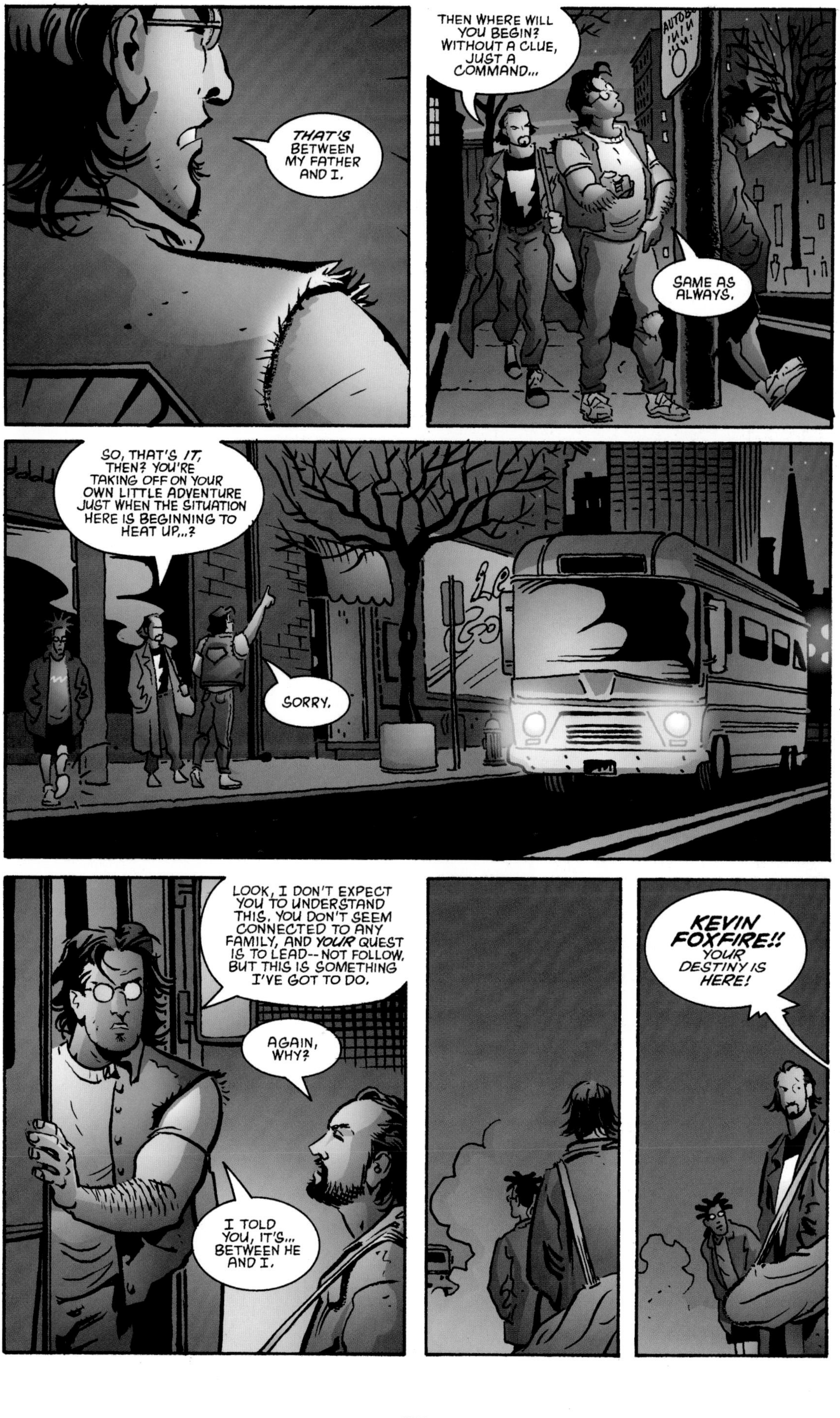
THAT'S BETWEEN MY FATHER AND I.
THEN WHERE WILL YOU BEGIN? WITHOUT A CLUE, JUST A COMMAND...
SAME AS ALWAYS.
SO, THAT'S IT, THEN? YOU'RE TAKING OFF ON YOUR OWN LITTLE ADVENTURE JUST WHEN THE SITUATION HERE IS BEGINNING TO HEAT UP...?
SORRY.
LOOK, I DON'T EXPECT YOU TO UNDERSTAND THIS. YOU DON'T SEEM CONNECTED TO ANY FAMILY, AND YOUR QUEST IS TO LEAD--NOT FOLLOW. BUT THIS IS SOMETHING I'VE GOT TO DO.
AGAIN, WHY?
I TOLD YOU, IT'S... BETWEEN HE AND I.
KEVIN FOXFIRE!! YOUR DESTINY IS HERE!

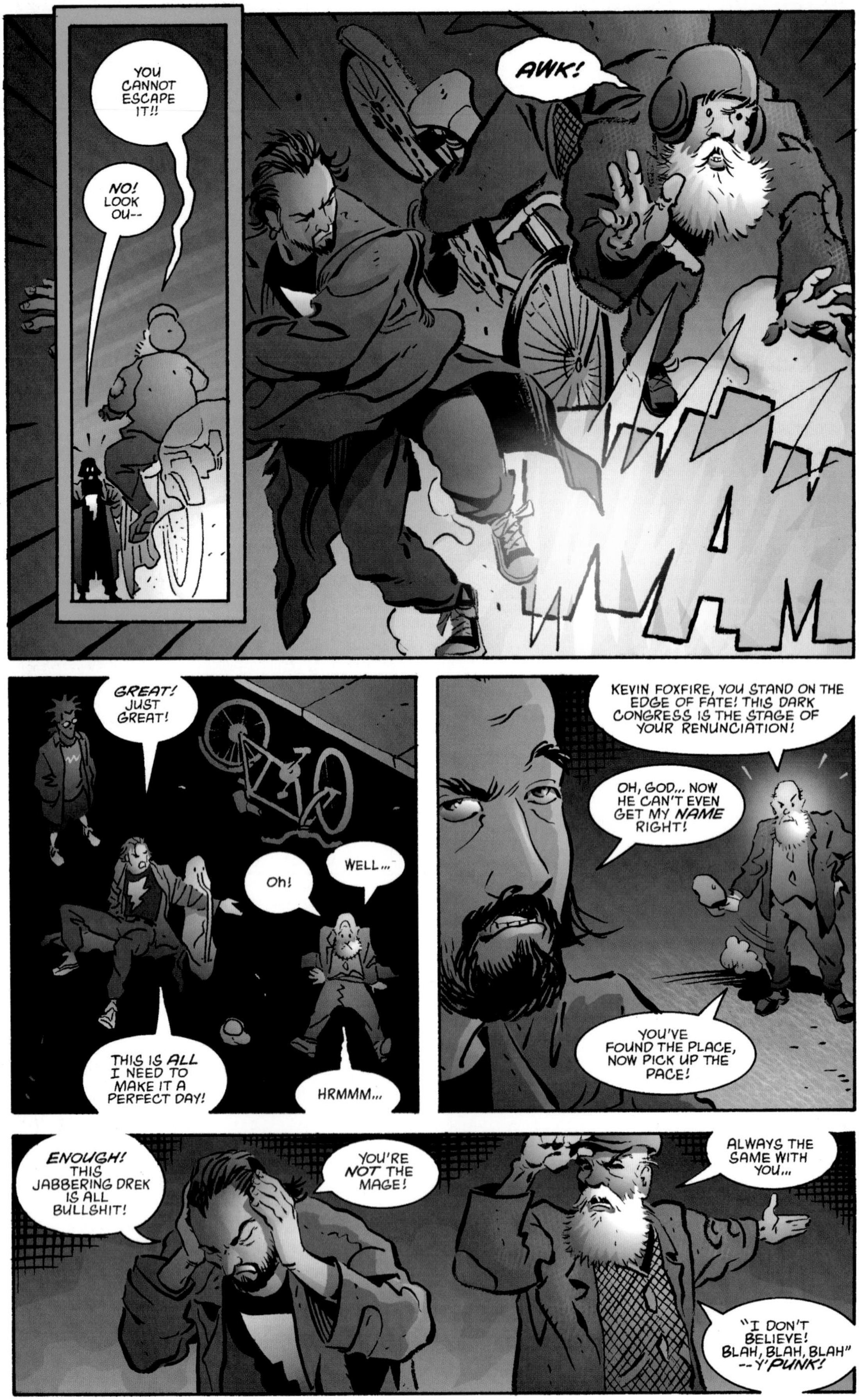
YOU CANNOT ESCAPE IT!!
NO! LOOK OU--
AWK!
WAM
GREAT! JUST GREAT!
THIS IS ALL I NEED TO MAKE IT A PERFECT DAY!
Oh!
WELL...
HRMMM...
KEVIN FOXFIRE, YOU STAND ON THE EDGE OF FATE! THIS DARK CONGRESS IS THE STAGE OF YOUR RENUNCIATION!
OH, GOD... NOW HE CAN'T EVEN GET MY NAME RIGHT!
YOU'VE FOUND THE PLACE, NOW PICK UP THE PACE!
ENOUGH! THIS JABBERING DREK IS ALL BULLSHIT!
YOU'RE NOT THE MAGE!
ALWAYS THE SAME WITH YOU...
"I DON'T BELIEVE! BLAH, BLAH, BLAH" --Y'PUNK!

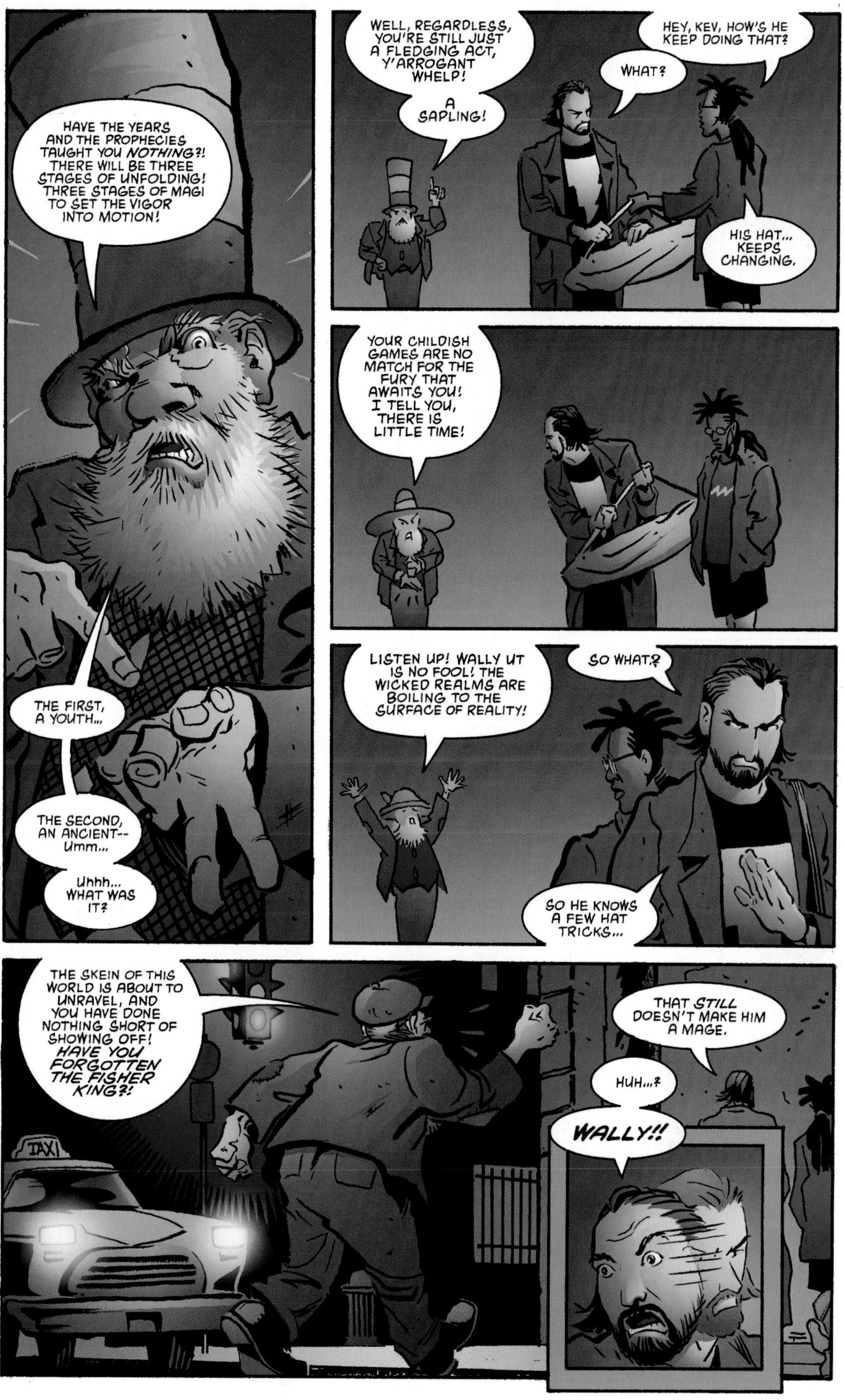
HAVE THE YEARS AND THE PROPHECIES TAUGHT YOU NOTHING?! THERE WILL BE THREE STAGES OF UNFOLDING! THREE STAGES OF MAGI TO SET THE VIGOR INTO MOTION!
THE FIRST, A YOUTH...
THE SECOND, AN ANCIENT-- Umm...
Uhhh... WHAT WAS IT?
WELL, REGARDLESS, YOU'RE STILL JUST A FLEDGING ACT, Y'ARROGANT WHELP!
A SAPLING!
WHAT?
HEY, KEV, HOW'S HE KEEP DOING THAT?
HIS HAT... KEEPS CHANGING.
YOUR CHILDISH GAMES ARE NO MATCH FOR THE FURY THAT AWAITS YOU! I TELL YOU, THERE IS LITTLE TIME!
LISTEN UP! WALLY UT IS NO FOOL! THE WICKED REALMS ARE BOILING TO THE SURFACE OF REALITY!
SO WHAT?
SO HE KNOWS A FEW HAT TRICKS...
THE SKEIN OF THIS WORLD IS ABOUT TO UNRAVEL, AND YOU HAVE DONE NOTHING SHORT OF SHOWING OFF! HAVE YOU FORGOTTEN THE FISHER KING?!
THAT STILL DOESN'T MAKE HIM A MAGE.
HUH...?
WALLY!!
TAXI

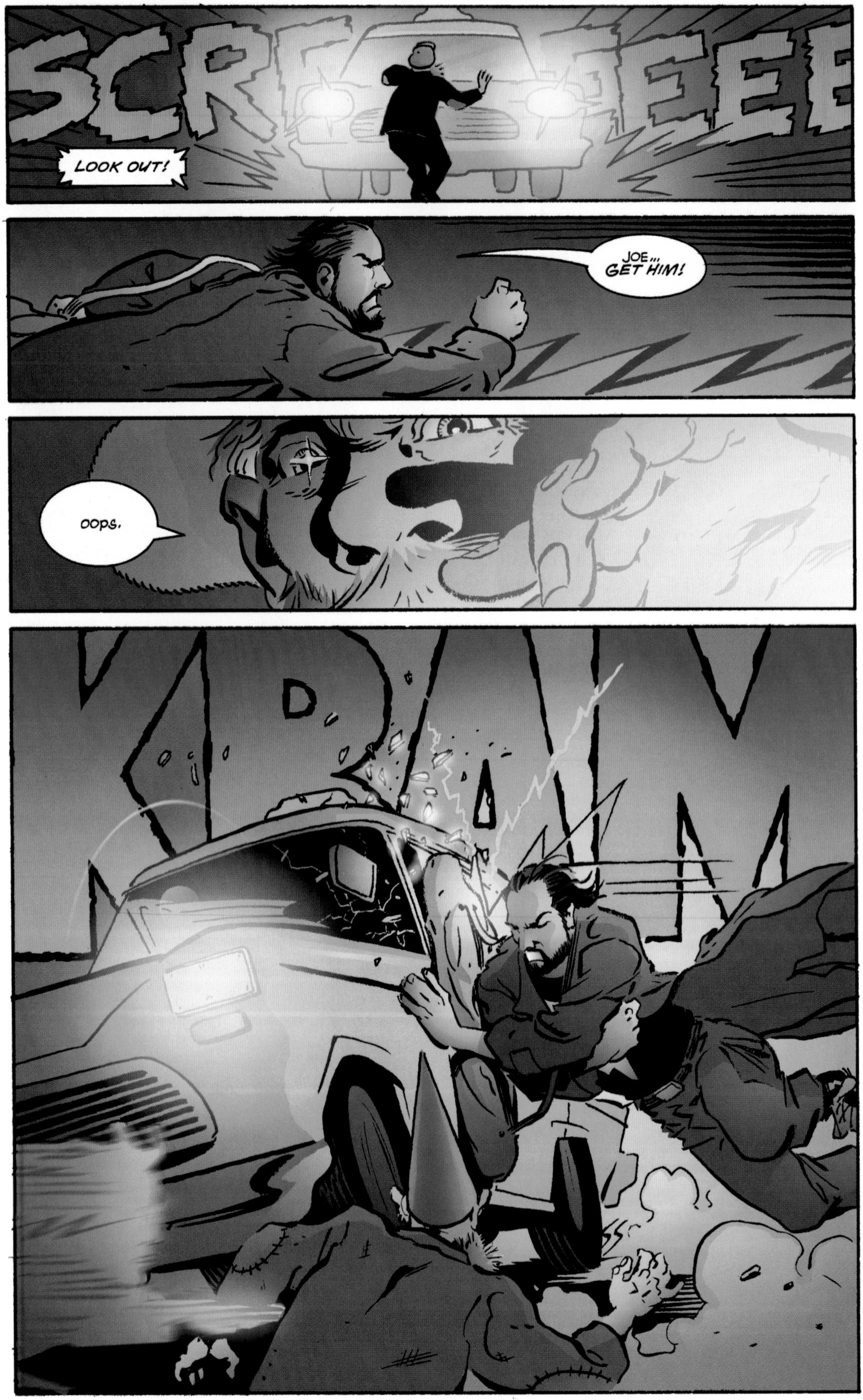
SCREEEE
LOOK OUT!
JOE... GET HIM!
OOPS.
KRAM

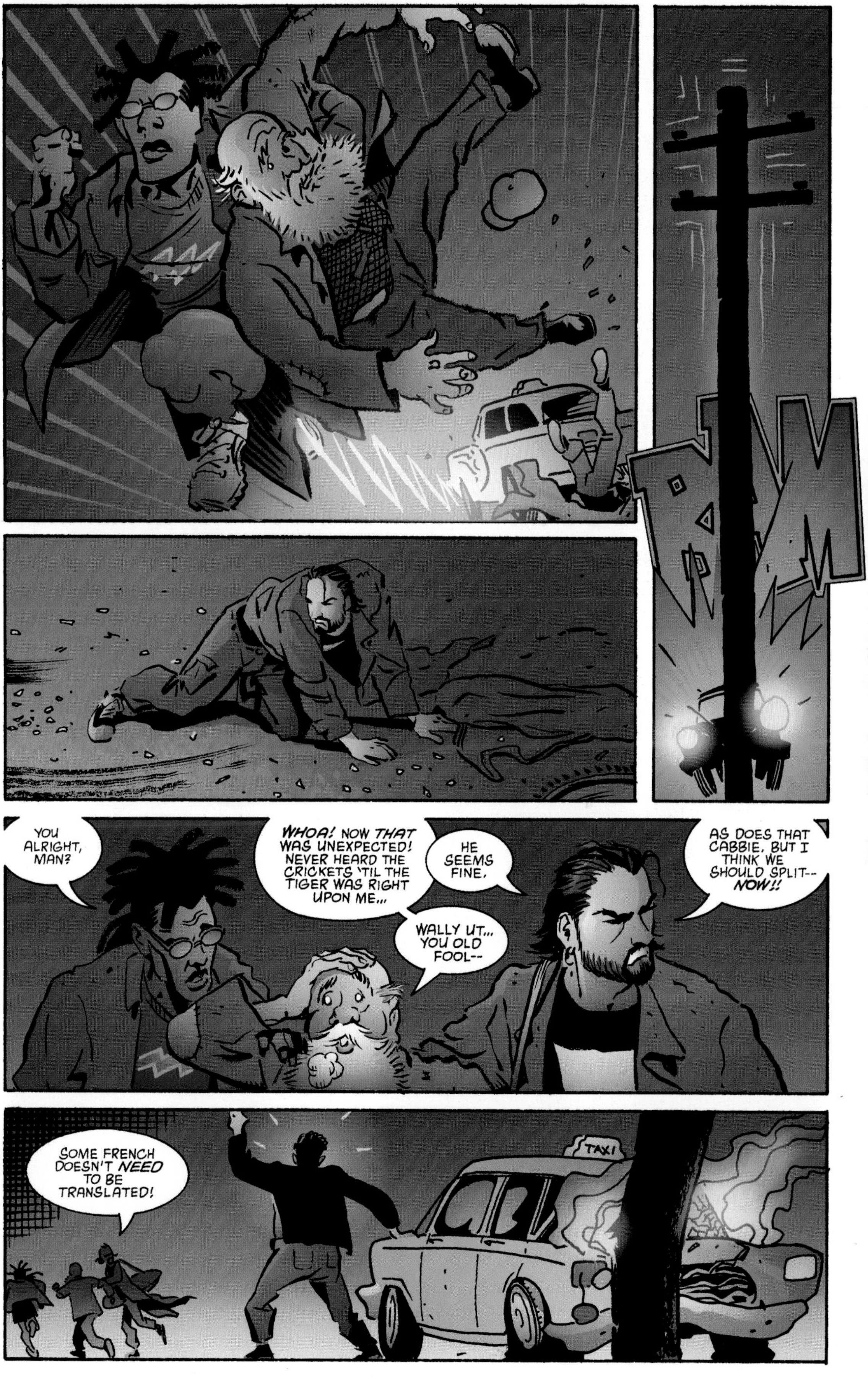
BAM
YOU ALRIGHT, MAN?
WHOA! NOW THAT WAS UNEXPECTED! NEVER HEARD THE CRICKETS 'TIL THE TIGER WAS RIGHT UPON ME...
HE SEEMS FINE.
WALLY UT... YOU OLD FOOL--
AS DOES THAT CABBIE, BUT I THINK WE SHOULD SPLIT-- NOW!!
SOME FRENCH DOESN'T NEED TO BE TRANSLATED!
TAXI

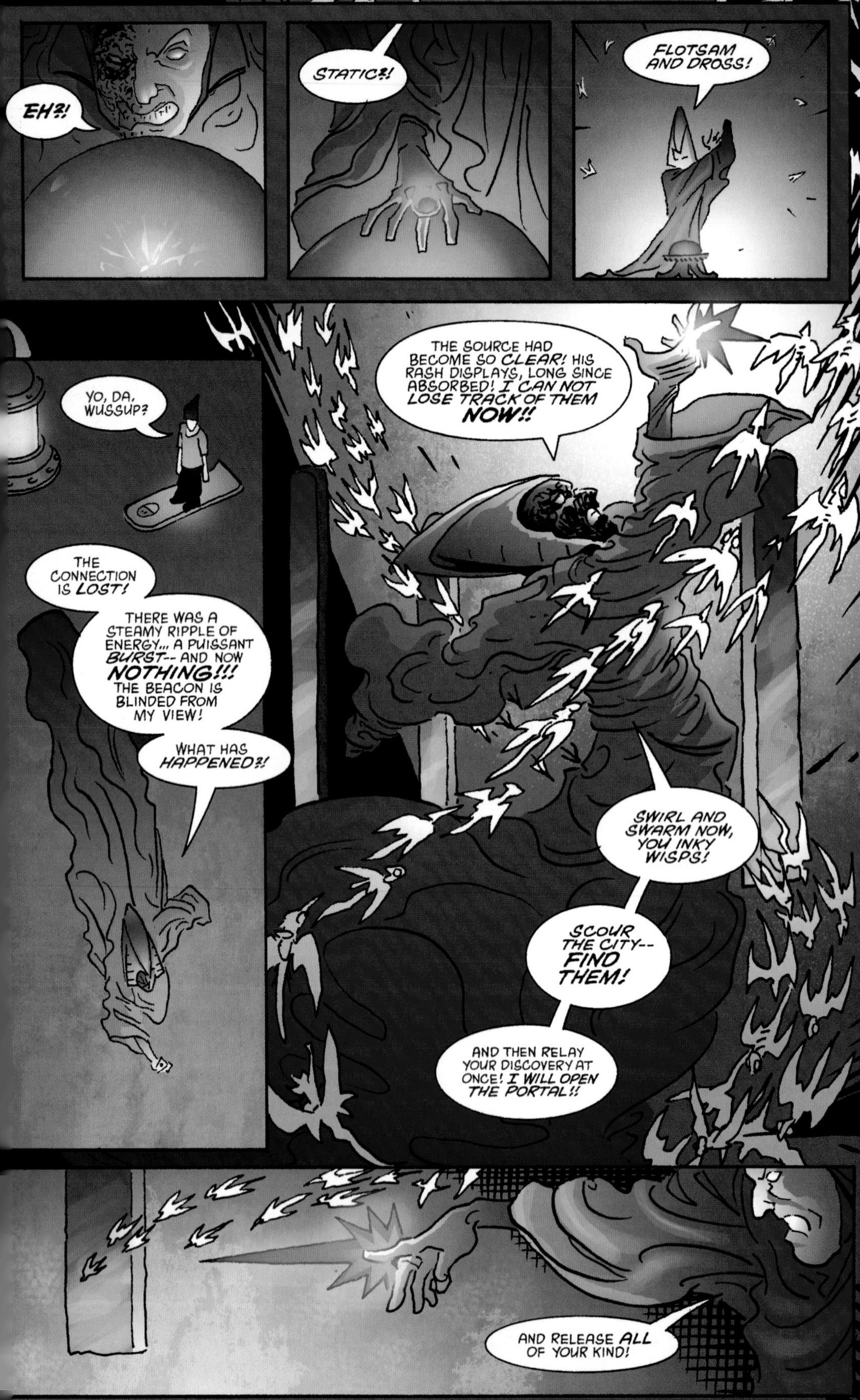
EH?!
STATIC?!
FLOTSAM AND DROSS!
YO, DA, WUSSUP?
THE CONNECTION IS LOST!
THERE WAS A STEAMY RIPPLE OF ENERGY... A PUISSANT BURST-- AND NOW NOTHING!!! THE BEACON IS BLINDED FROM MY VIEW!
WHAT HAS HAPPENED?!
THE SOURCE HAD BECOME SO CLEAR! HIS RASH DISPLAYS, LONG SINCE ABSORBED! I CAN NOT LOSE TRACK OF THEM NOW!!
SWIRL AND SWARM NOW, YOU INKY WISPS!
SCOUR THE CITY-- FIND THEM!
AND THEN RELAY YOUR DISCOVERY AT ONCE! I WILL OPEN THE PORTAL!!
AND RELEASE ALL OF YOUR KIND!

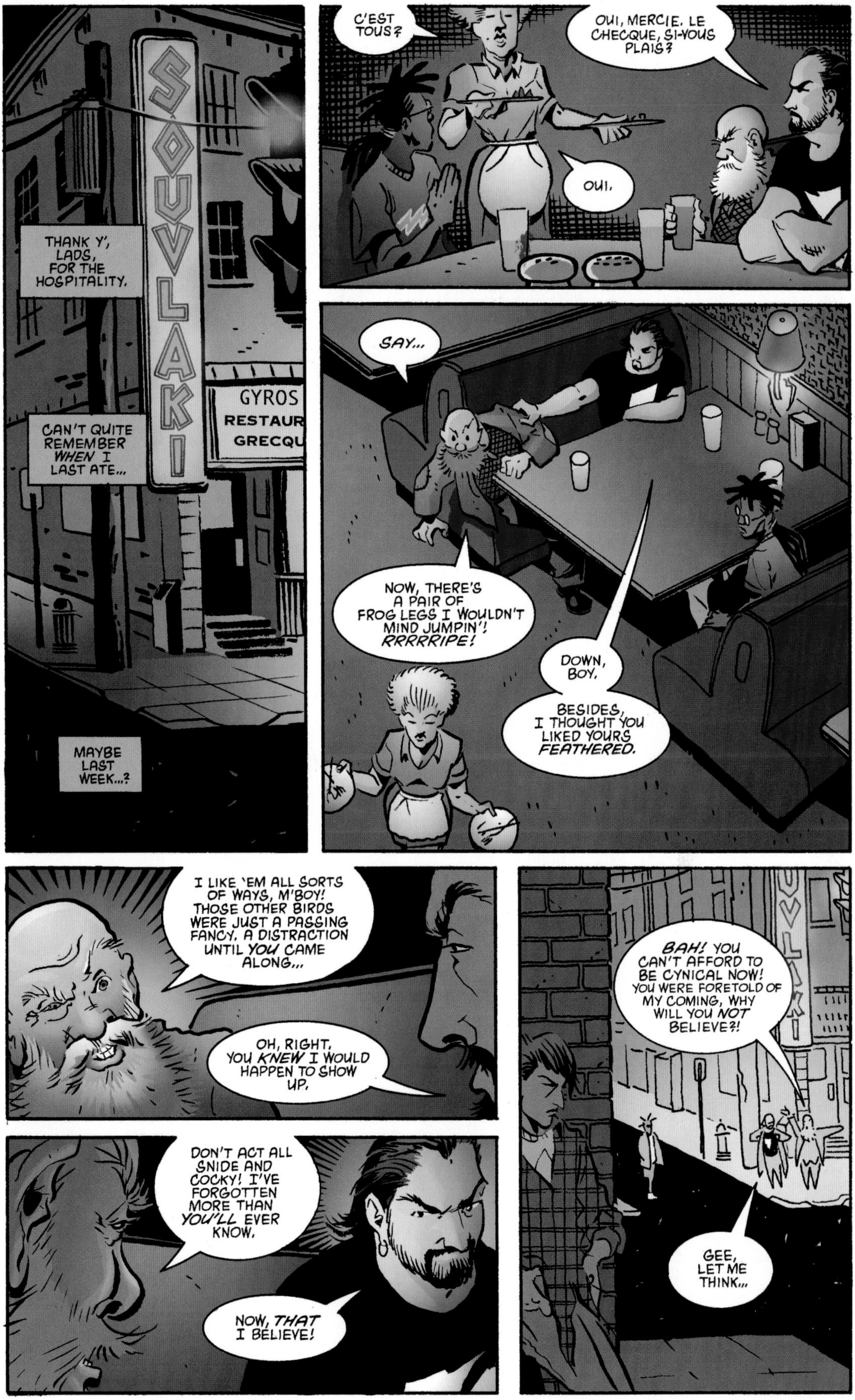
SOUVLAKI
GYROS
RESTAUR
GRECQU
THANK Y', LADS, FOR THE HOSPITALITY.
CAN'T QUITE REMEMBER WHEN I LAST ATE...
MAYBE LAST WEEK...?
C'EST TOUS?
OUI, MERCIE. LE CHECQUE, SI-VOUS PLAIS?
OUI.
SAY...
NOW, THERE'S A PAIR OF FROG LEGS I WOULDN'T MIND JUMPIN'! RRRRRIPE!
DOWN, BOY.
BESIDES, I THOUGHT YOU LIKED YOURS FEATHERED.
I LIKE 'EM ALL SORTS OF WAYS, M'BOY! THOSE OTHER BIRDS WERE JUST A PASSING FANCY. A DISTRACTION UNTIL YOU CAME ALONG...
OH, RIGHT. YOU KNEW I WOULD HAPPEN TO SHOW UP.
DON'T ACT ALL SNIDE AND COCKY! I'VE FORGOTTEN MORE THAN YOU'LL EVER KNOW.
NOW, THAT I BELIEVE!
BAH! YOU CAN'T AFFORD TO BE CYNICAL NOW! YOU WERE FORETOLD OF MY COMING, WHY WILL YOU NOT BELIEVE?!
GEE, LET ME THINK...

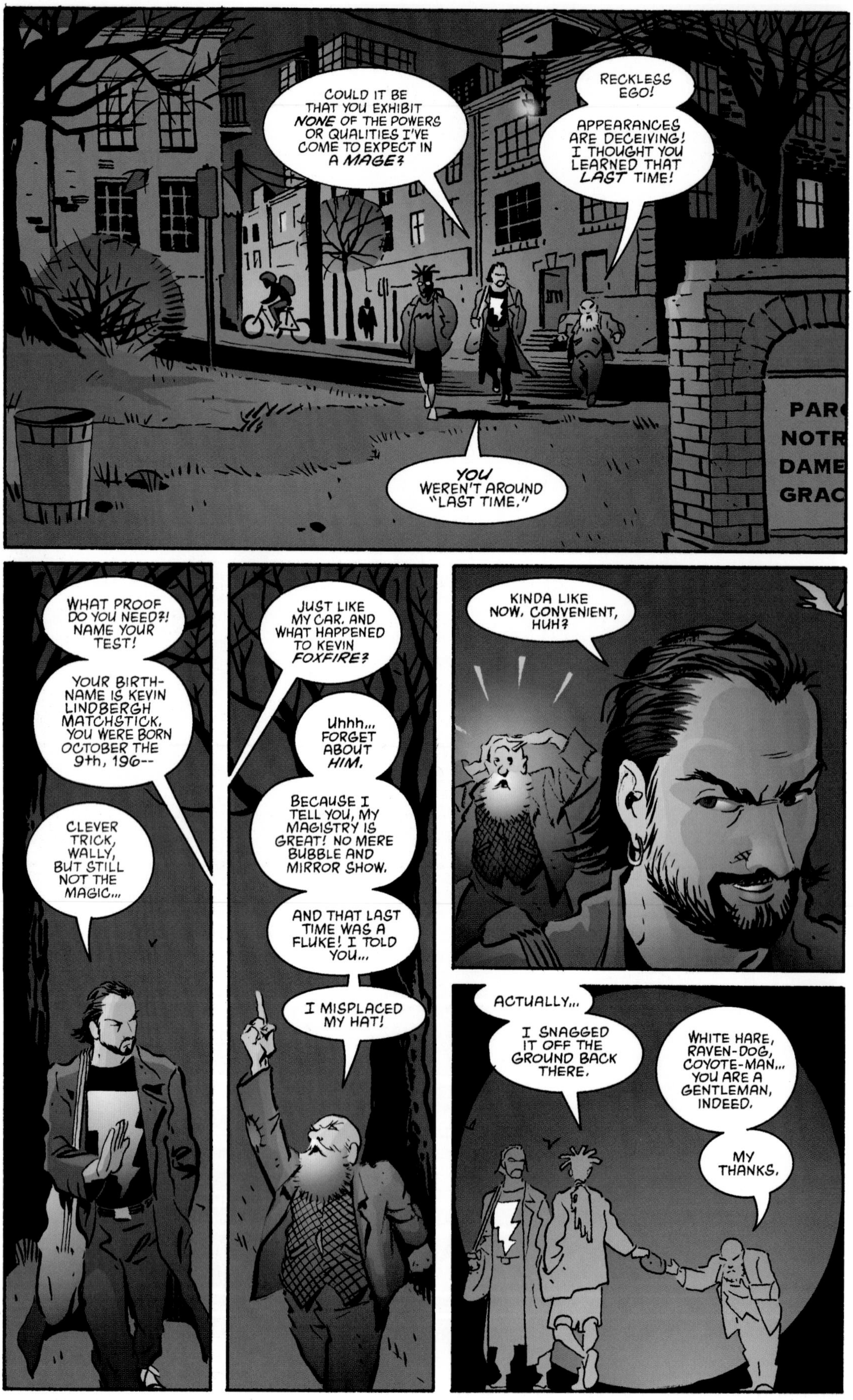
COULD IT BE THAT YOU EXHIBIT NONE OF THE POWERS OR QUALITIES I'VE COME TO EXPECT IN A MAGE?
RECKLESS EGO!
APPEARANCES ARE DECEIVING! I THOUGHT YOU LEARNED THAT LAST TIME!
PARC NOTR DAME GRAC
YOU WEREN'T AROUND "LAST TIME."
WHAT PROOF DO YOU NEED?! NAME YOUR TEST!
YOUR BIRTH-NAME IS KEVIN LINDBERGH MATCHSTICK. YOU WERE BORN OCTOBER THE 9th, 196--
CLEVER TRICK, WALLY, BUT STILL NOT THE MAGIC...
JUST LIKE MY CAR. AND WHAT HAPPENED TO KEVIN FOXFIRE?
Uhhh... FORGET ABOUT HIM.
BECAUSE I TELL YOU, MY MAGISTRY IS GREAT! NO MERE BUBBLE AND MIRROR SHOW.
AND THAT LAST TIME WAS A FLUKE! I TOLD YOU...
I MISPLACED MY HAT!
KINDA LIKE NOW, CONVENIENT, HUH?
ACTUALLY...
I SNAGGED IT OFF THE GROUND BACK THERE.
WHITE HARE, RAVEN-DOG, COYOTE-MAN... YOU ARE A GENTLEMAN, INDEED.
MY THANKS.

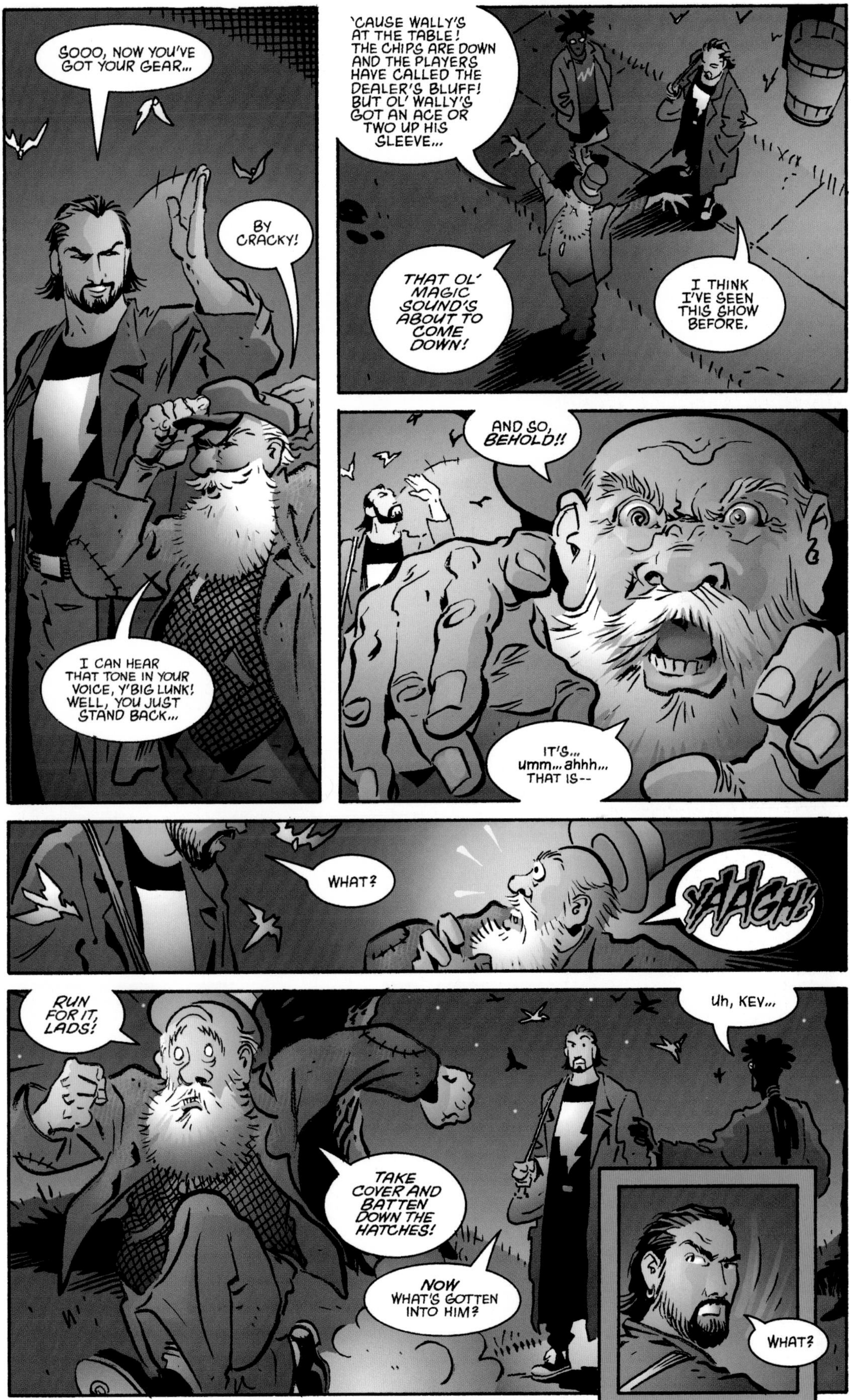
SOOO, NOW YOU'VE GOT YOUR GEAR...
BY CRACKY!
I CAN HEAR THAT TONE IN YOUR VOICE, Y'BIG LUNK! WELL, YOU JUST STAND BACK...
'CAUSE WALLY'S AT THE TABLE! THE CHIPS ARE DOWN AND THE PLAYERS HAVE CALLED THE DEALER'S BLUFF! BUT OL' WALLY'S GOT AN ACE OR TWO UP HIS SLEEVE...
THAT OL' MAGIC SOUND'S ABOUT TO COME DOWN!
I THINK I'VE SEEN THIS SHOW BEFORE.
AND SO, BEHOLD!!
IT'S... umm... ahhh... THAT IS--
WHAT?
YAAGH!
RUN FOR IT, LADS!
TAKE COVER AND BATTEN DOWN THE HATCHES!
NOW WHAT'S GOTTEN INTO HIM?
Uh, KEY...
WHAT?

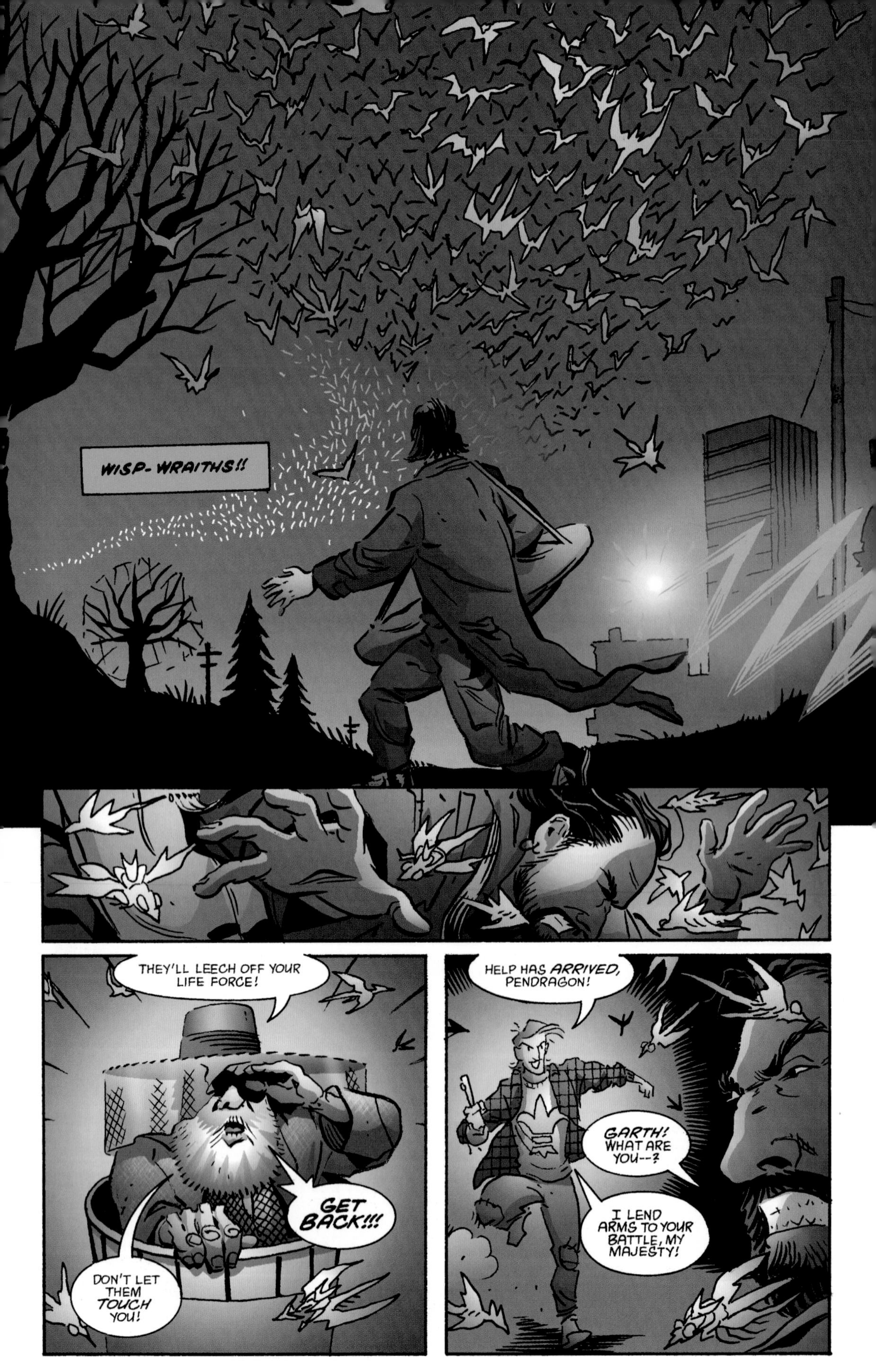
WISP-WRAITHS!!
THEY'LL LEECH OFF YOUR LIFE FORCE!
GET BACK!!!
DON'T LET THEM TOUCH YOU!
HELP HAS ARRIVED, PENDRAGON!
GARTH! WHAT ARE YOU--?
I LEND ARMS TO YOUR BATTLE, MY MAJESTY!

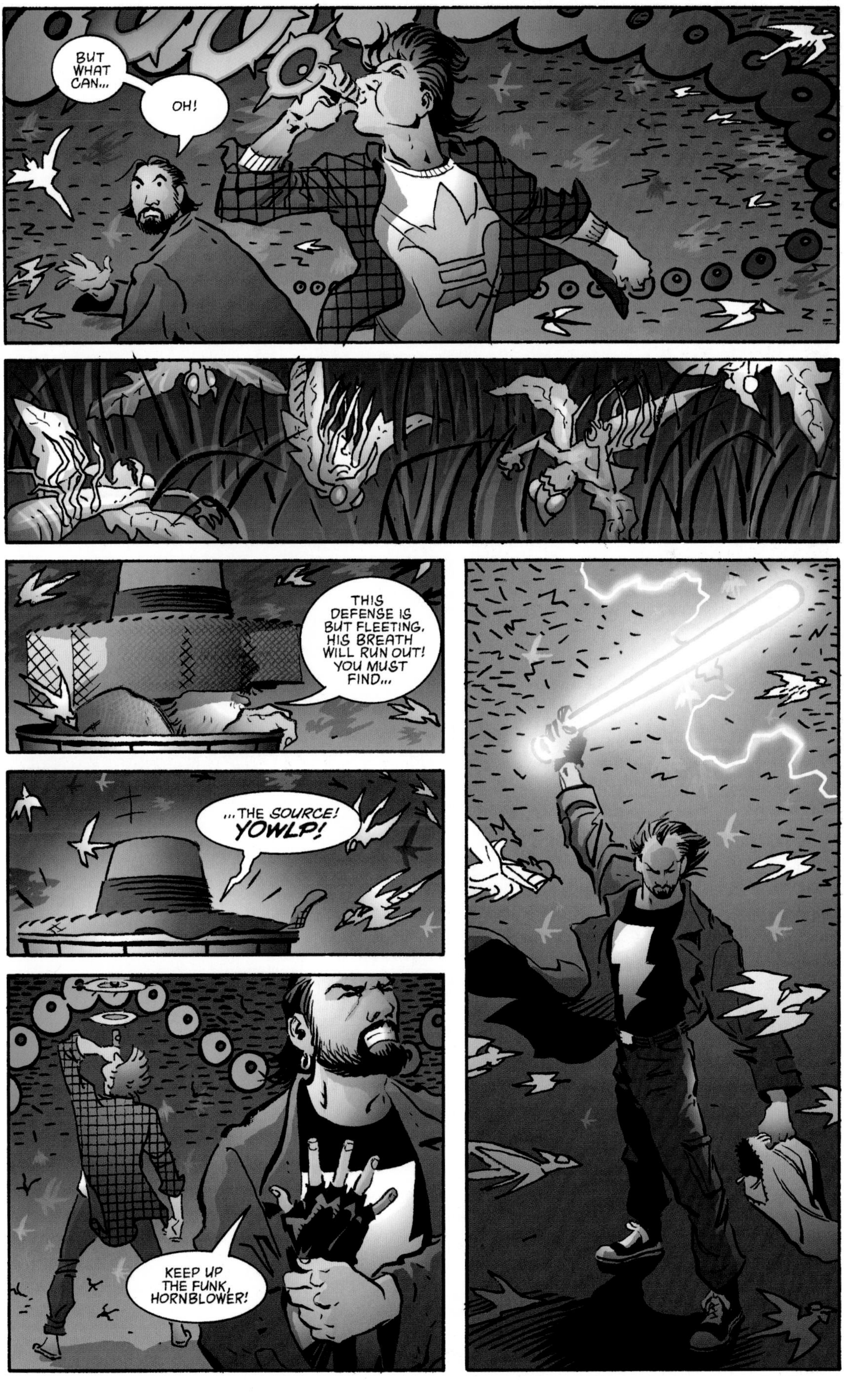
BUT WHAT CAN...
OH!
THIS DEFENSE IS BUT FLEETING, HIS BREATH WILL RUN OUT! YOU MUST FIND...
...THE SOURCE! YOWLP!
KEEP UP THE FUNK, HORNBLOWER!

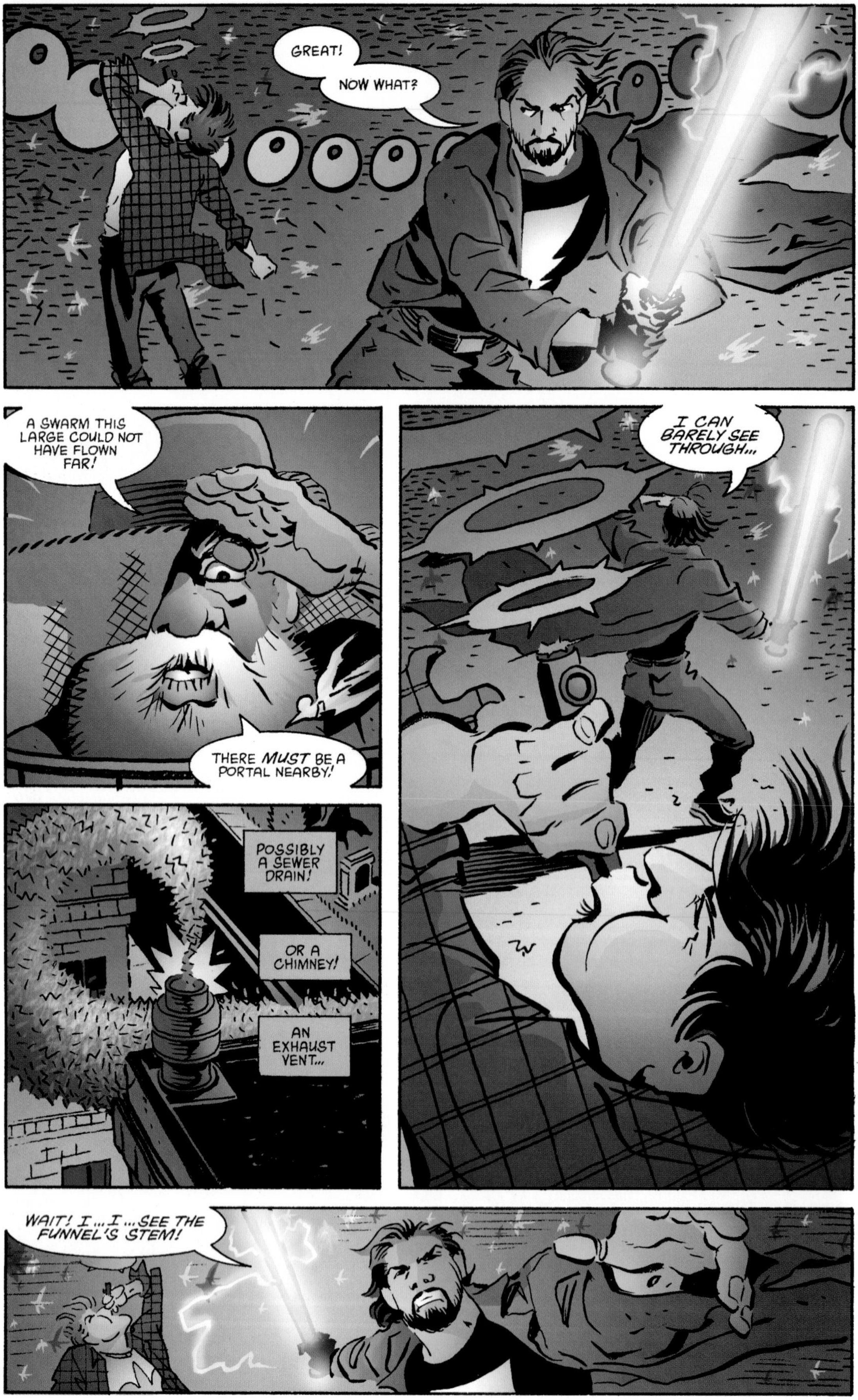
GREAT!
NOW WHAT?
A SWARM THIS LARGE COULD NOT HAVE FLOWN FAR!
THERE MUST BE A PORTAL NEARBY!
I CAN BARELY SEE THROUGH...
POSSIBLY A SEWER DRAIN!
OR A CHIMNEY!
AN EXHAUST VENT...
WAIT! I... I... SEE THE FUNNEL'S STEM!

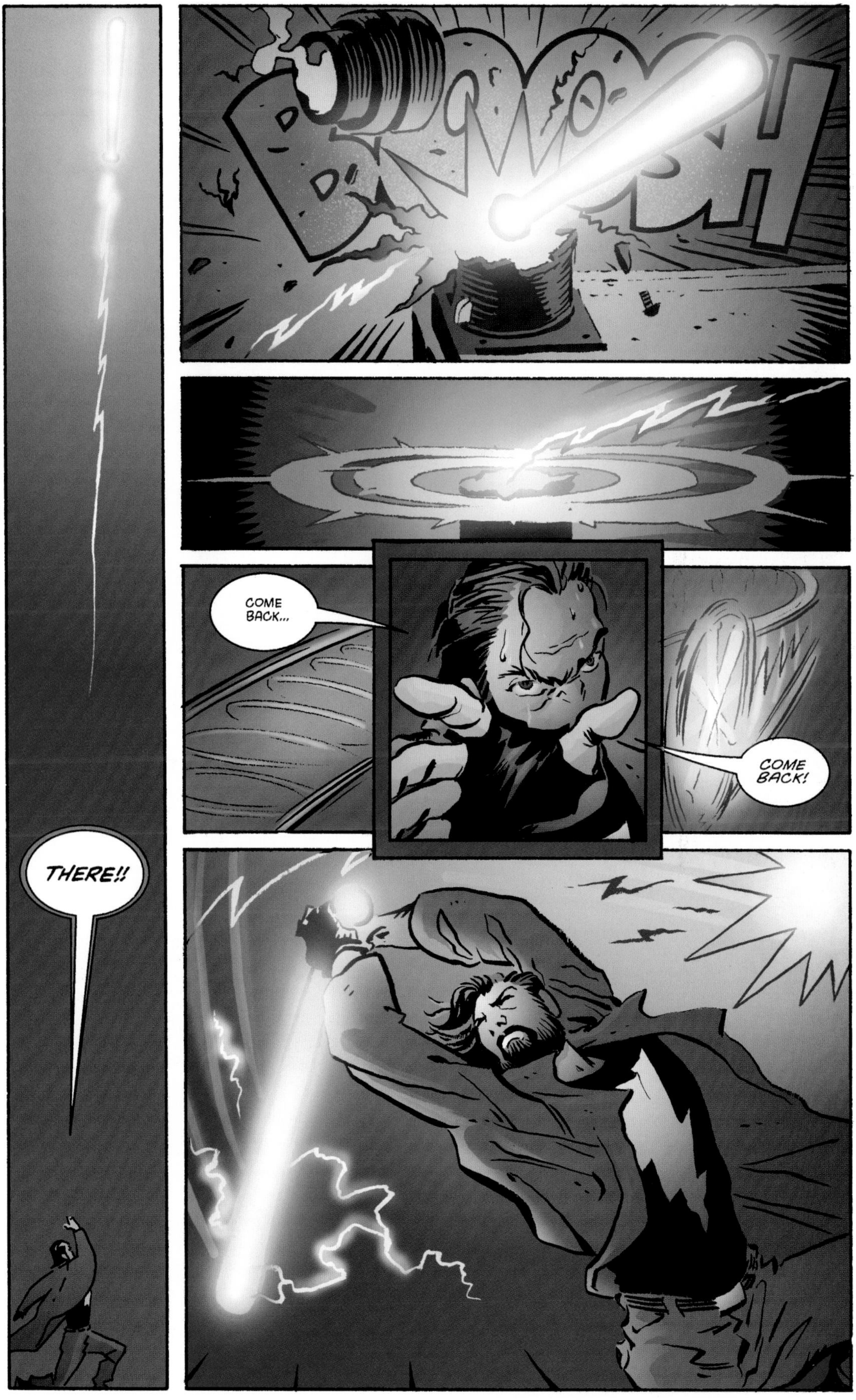
THERE!!
COME BACK...
COME BACK!

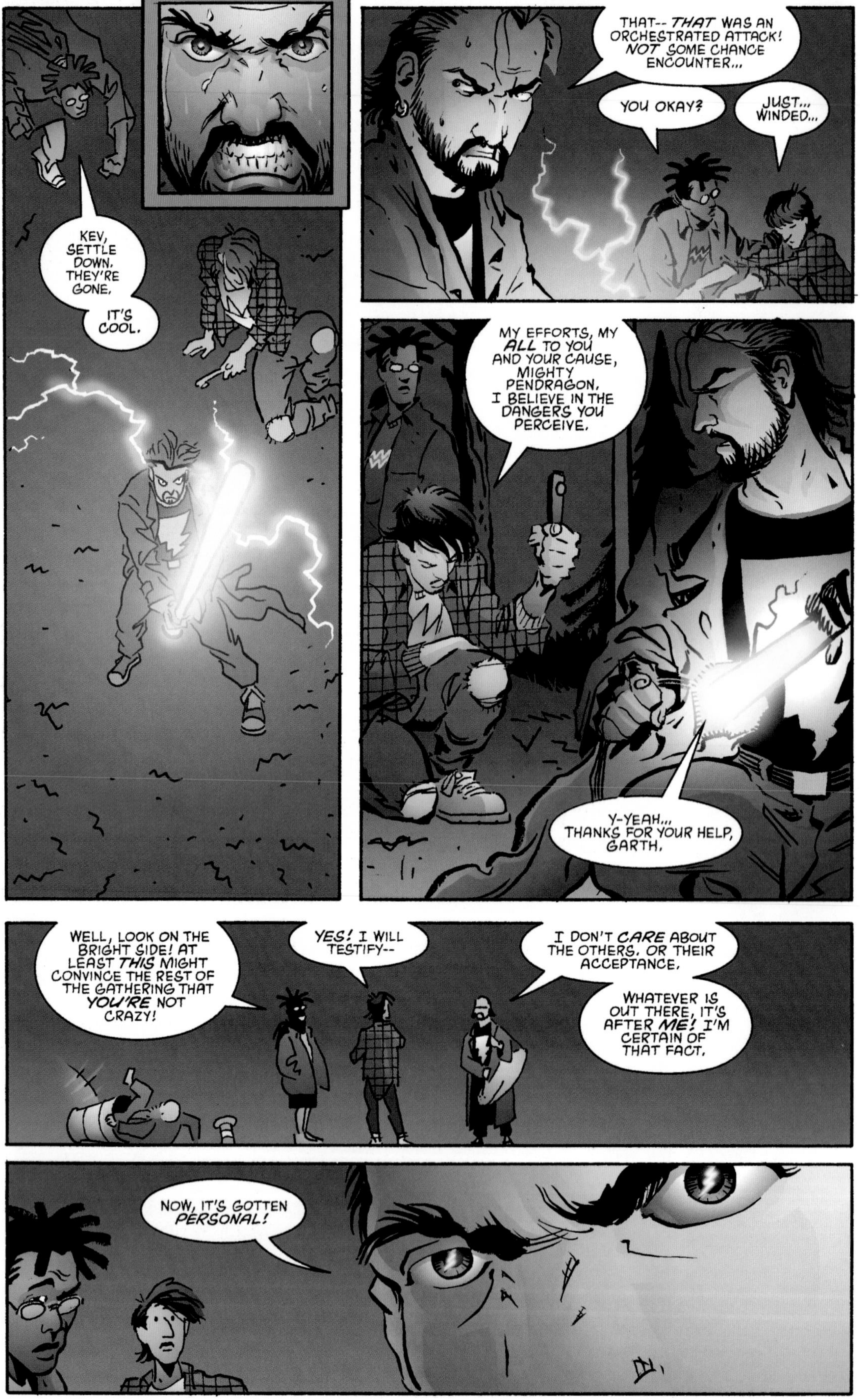
KEV, SETTLE DOWN. THEY'RE GONE.
IT'S COOL.
THAT-- THAT WAS AN ORCHESTRATED ATTACK! NOT SOME CHANCE ENCOUNTER...
YOU OKAY?
JUST... WINDED...
MY EFFORTS, MY ALL TO YOU AND YOUR CAUSE, MIGHTY PENDRAGON. I BELIEVE IN THE DANGERS YOU PERCEIVE.
Y-YEAH... THANKS FOR YOUR HELP, GARTH.
WELL, LOOK ON THE BRIGHT SIDE! AT LEAST THIS MIGHT CONVINCE THE REST OF THE GATHERING THAT YOU'RE NOT CRAZY!
YES! I WILL TESTIFY--
I DON'T CARE ABOUT THE OTHERS. OR THEIR ACCEPTANCE.
WHATEVER IS OUT THERE, IT'S AFTER ME! I'M CERTAIN OF THAT FACT.
NOW, IT'S GOTTEN PERSONAL!

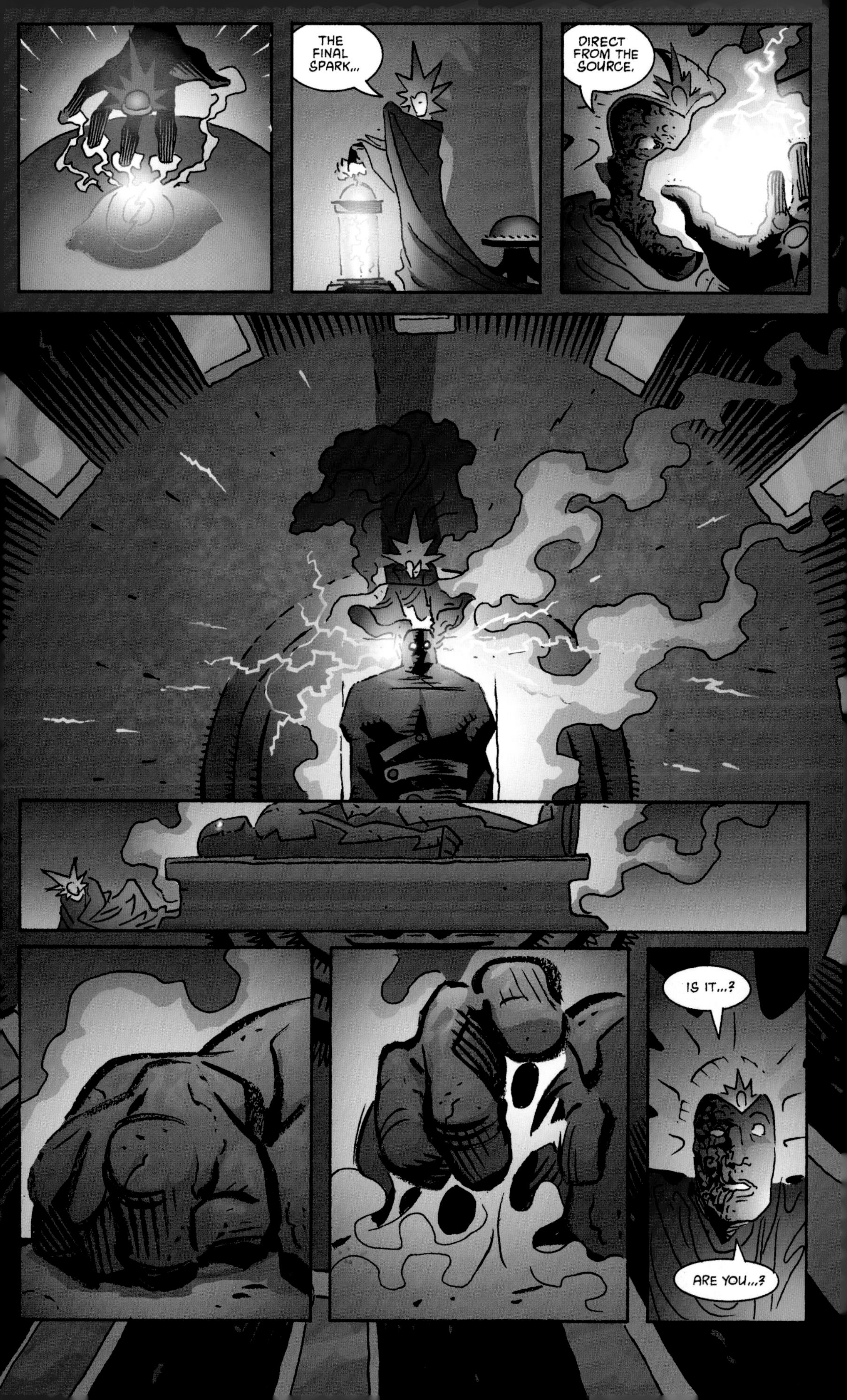
THE FINAL SPARK...
DIRECT FROM THE SOURCE.
IS IT...?
ARE YOU...?

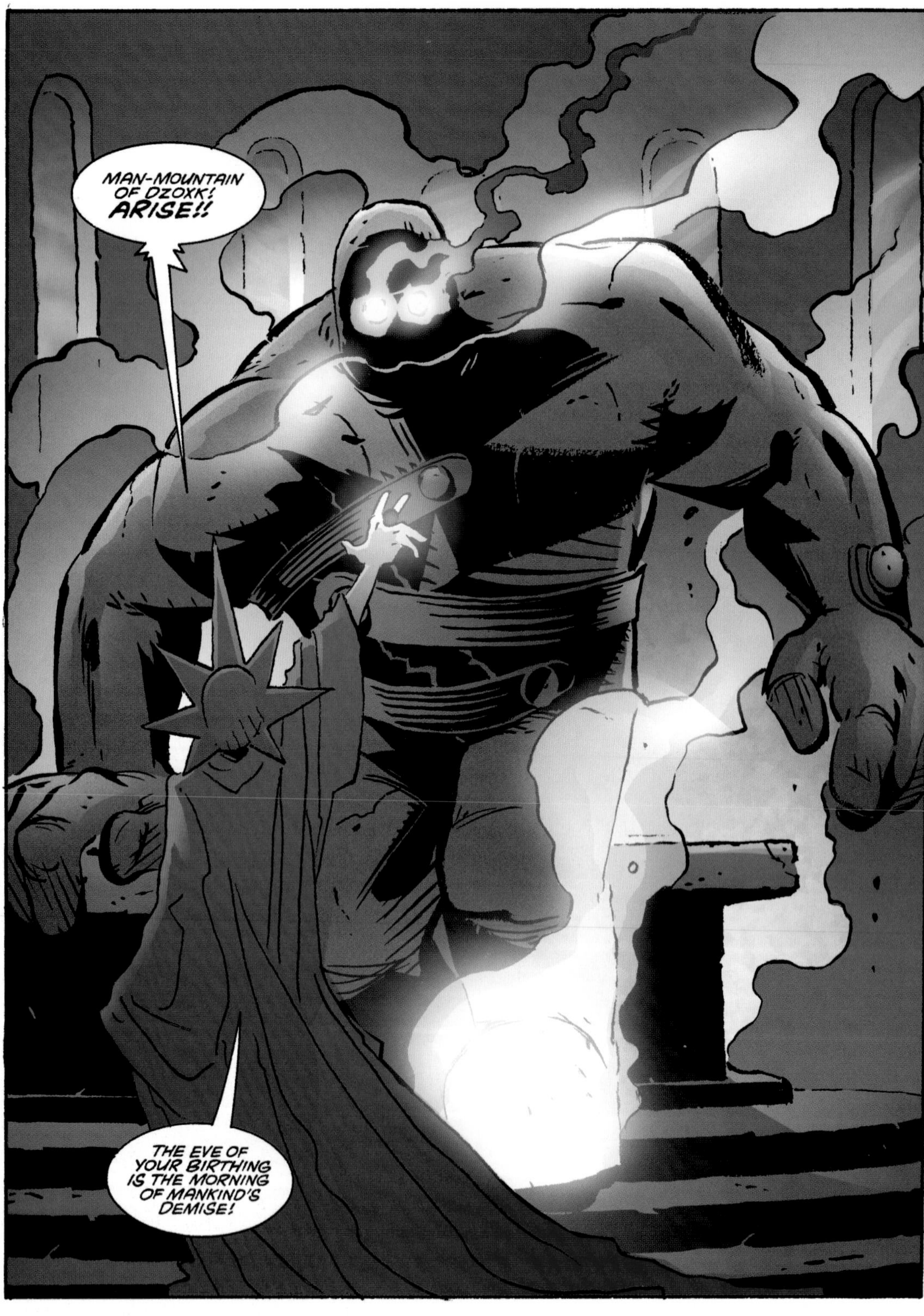
MAN-MOUNTAIN OF DZOXK! ARISE!!
THE EVE OF YOUR BIRTHING IS THE MORNING OF MANKIND'S DEMISE!

THE HERO DEFINED

MAGE®

chapter 8

"So Weary with Disasters"

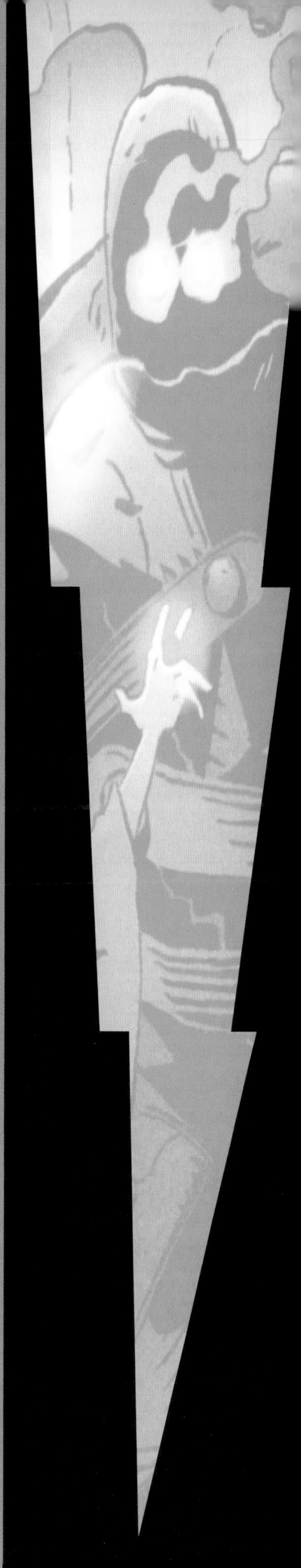

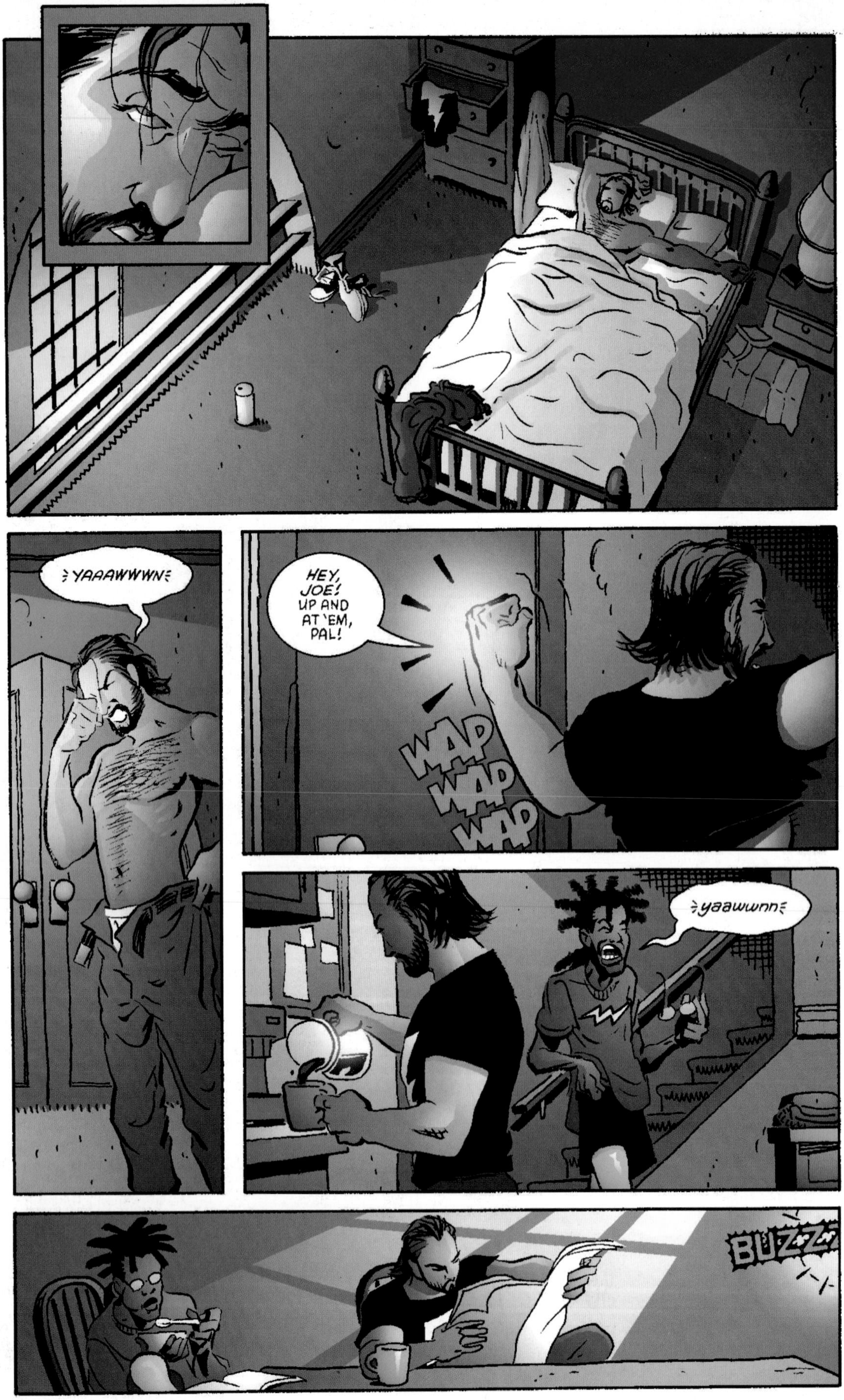

YAAAWWWN
HEY, JOE! UP AND AT 'EM, PAL!
WAP WAP WAP
yaawwnn
BUZZ

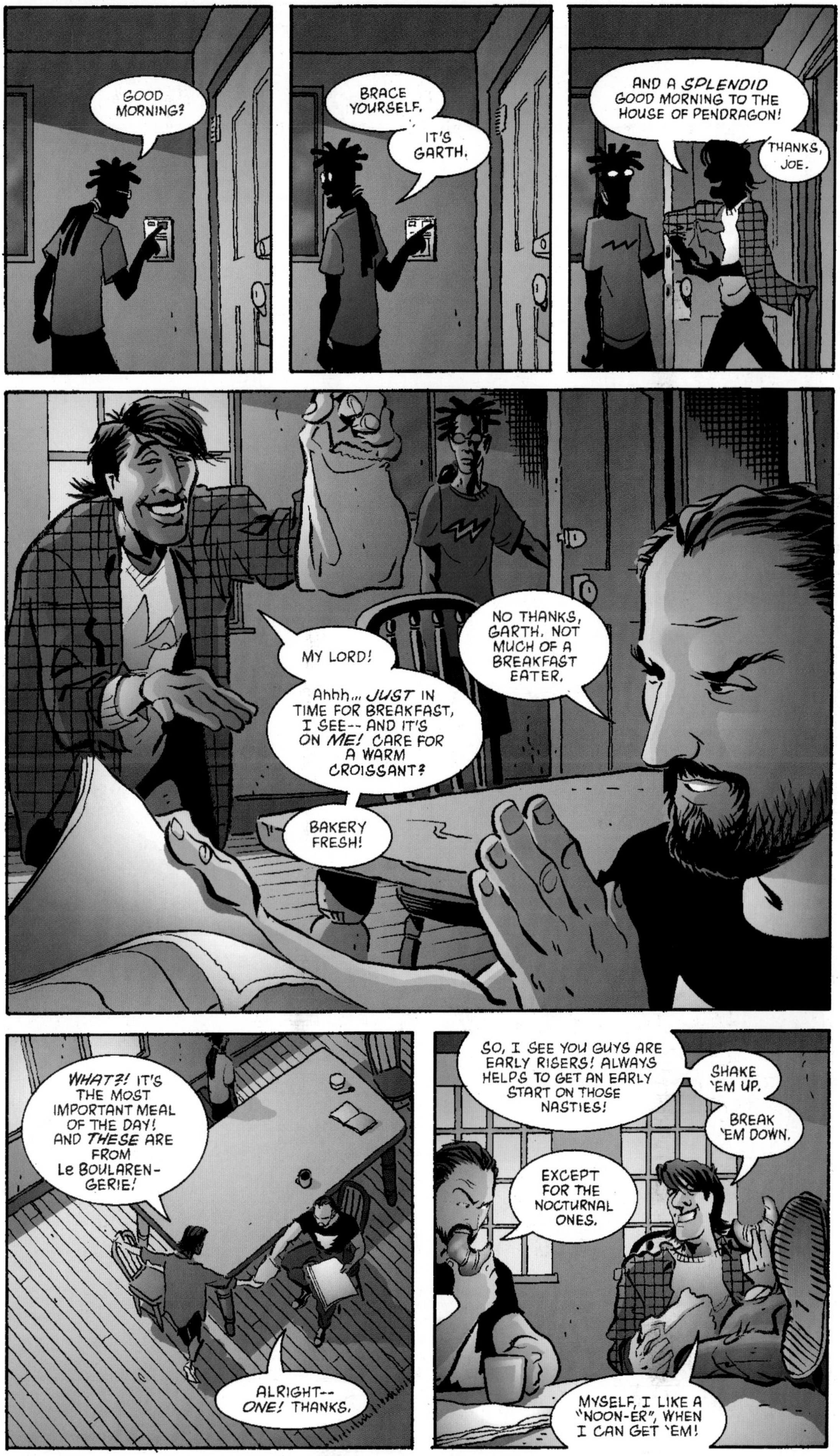
GOOD MORNING?
BRACE YOURSELF.
IT'S GARTH.
AND A *SPLENDID* GOOD MORNING TO THE HOUSE OF PENDRAGON!
THANKS, JOE.
MY LORD!
Ahhh... *JUST* IN TIME FOR BREAKFAST, I SEE-- AND IT'S ON *ME!* CARE FOR A WARM CROISSANT?
BAKERY FRESH!
NO THANKS, GARTH. NOT MUCH OF A BREAKFAST EATER.
WHAT?! IT'S THE MOST IMPORTANT MEAL OF THE DAY! AND *THESE* ARE FROM Le BOULAREN-GERIE!
ALRIGHT-- *ONE!* THANKS.
SO, I SEE YOU GUYS ARE EARLY RISERS! ALWAYS HELPS TO GET AN EARLY START ON THOSE NASTIES!
SHAKE 'EM UP.
BREAK 'EM DOWN.
EXCEPT FOR THE NOCTURNAL ONES.
MYSELF, I LIKE A "NOON-ER", WHEN I CAN GET 'EM!

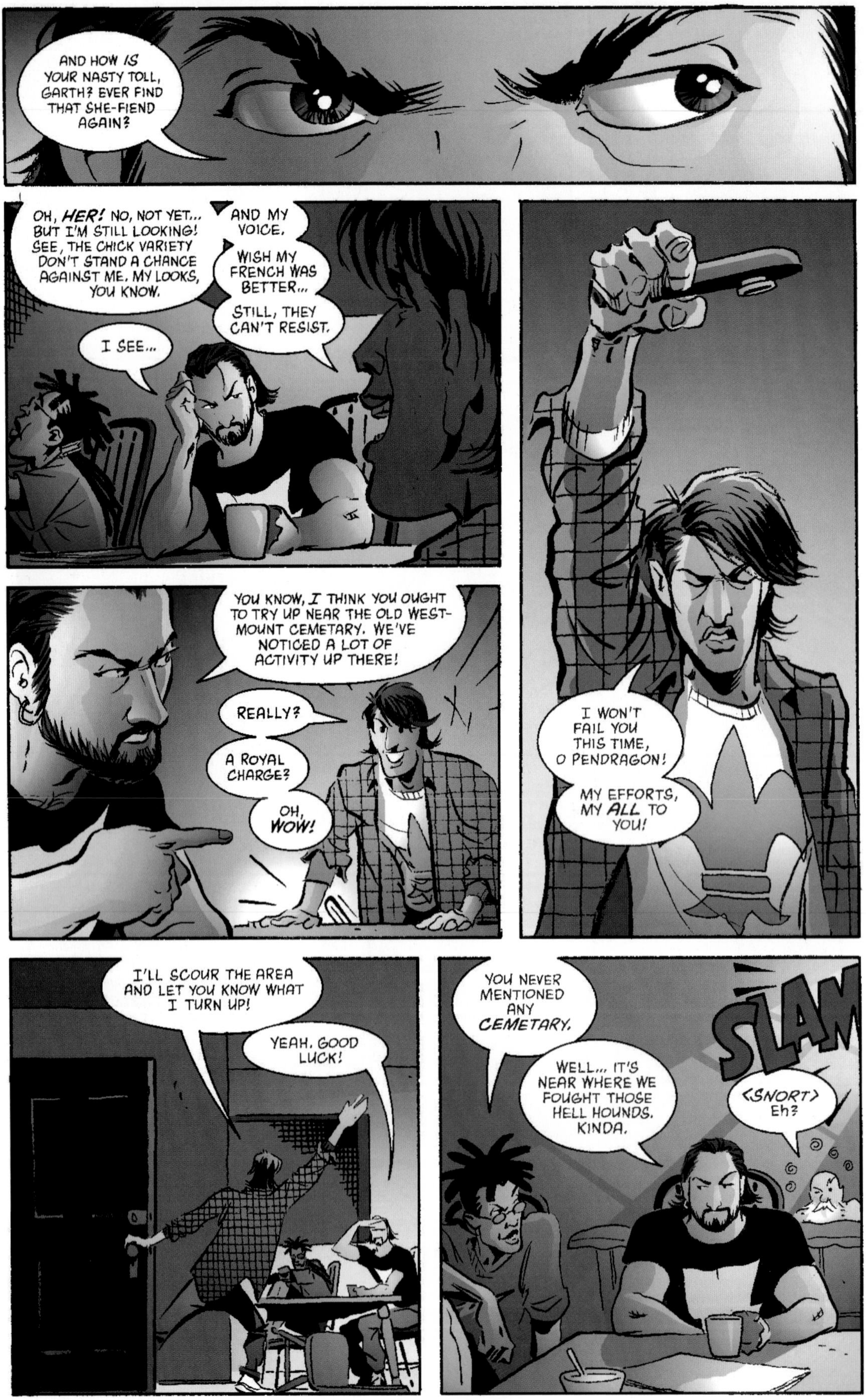
AND HOW IS YOUR NASTY TOLL, GARTH? EVER FIND THAT SHE-FIEND AGAIN?
OH, HER! NO, NOT YET... BUT I'M STILL LOOKING! SEE, THE CHICK VARIETY DON'T STAND A CHANCE AGAINST ME. MY LOOKS, YOU KNOW.
AND MY VOICE.
WISH MY FRENCH WAS BETTER...
STILL, THEY CAN'T RESIST.
I SEE...
I WON'T FAIL YOU THIS TIME, O PENDRAGON!
MY EFFORTS, MY ALL TO YOU!
YOU KNOW, I THINK YOU OUGHT TO TRY UP NEAR THE OLD WEST-MOUNT CEMETARY. WE'VE NOTICED A LOT OF ACTIVITY UP THERE!
REALLY?
A ROYAL CHARGE?
OH, WOW!
I'LL SCOUR THE AREA AND LET YOU KNOW WHAT I TURN UP!
YEAH, GOOD LUCK!
YOU NEVER MENTIONED ANY CEMETARY.
SLAM
WELL... IT'S NEAR WHERE WE FOUGHT THOSE HELL HOUNDS. KINDA.
<SNORT> Eh?

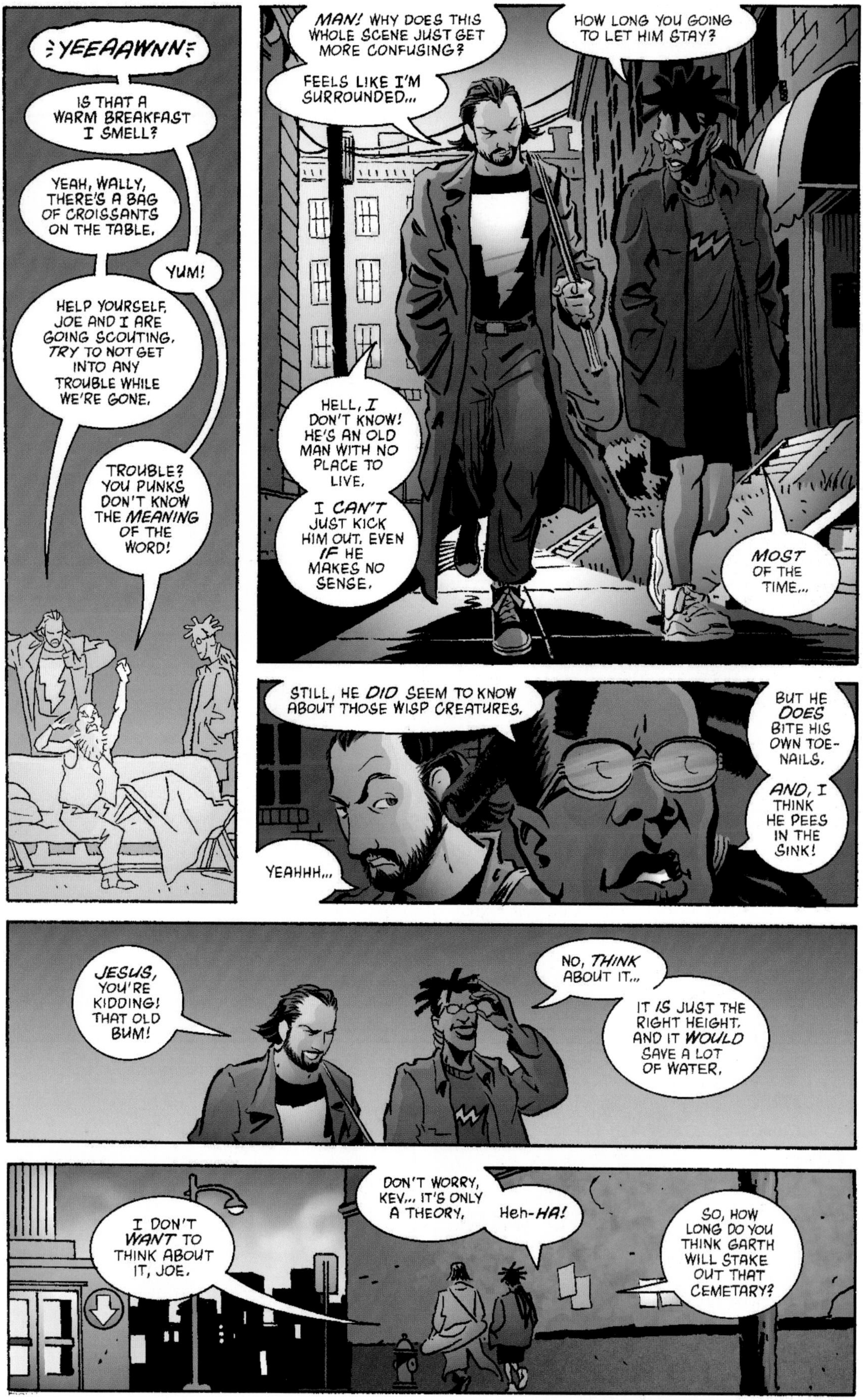
YEEAAWNN
IS THAT A WARM BREAKFAST I SMELL?
YEAH, WALLY, THERE'S A BAG OF CROISSANTS ON THE TABLE.
YUM!
HELP YOURSELF. JOE AND I ARE GOING SCOUTING. TRY TO NOT GET INTO ANY TROUBLE WHILE WE'RE GONE.
TROUBLE? YOU PUNKS DON'T KNOW THE MEANING OF THE WORD!
MAN! WHY DOES THIS WHOLE SCENE JUST GET MORE CONFUSING?
FEELS LIKE I'M SURROUNDED...
HOW LONG YOU GOING TO LET HIM STAY?
HELL, I DON'T KNOW! HE'S AN OLD MAN WITH NO PLACE TO LIVE.
I CAN'T JUST KICK HIM OUT. EVEN IF HE MAKES NO SENSE.
MOST OF THE TIME...
STILL, HE DID SEEM TO KNOW ABOUT THOSE WISP CREATURES.
YEAHHH...
BUT HE DOES BITE HIS OWN TOE-NAILS.
AND, I THINK HE PEES IN THE SINK!
JESUS, YOU'RE KIDDING! THAT OLD BUM!
NO, THINK ABOUT IT...
IT IS JUST THE RIGHT HEIGHT. AND IT WOULD SAVE A LOT OF WATER.
I DON'T WANT TO THINK ABOUT IT, JOE.
DON'T WORRY, KEV... IT'S ONLY A THEORY.
Heh-HA!
SO, HOW LONG DO YOU THINK GARTH WILL STAKE OUT THAT CEMETARY?

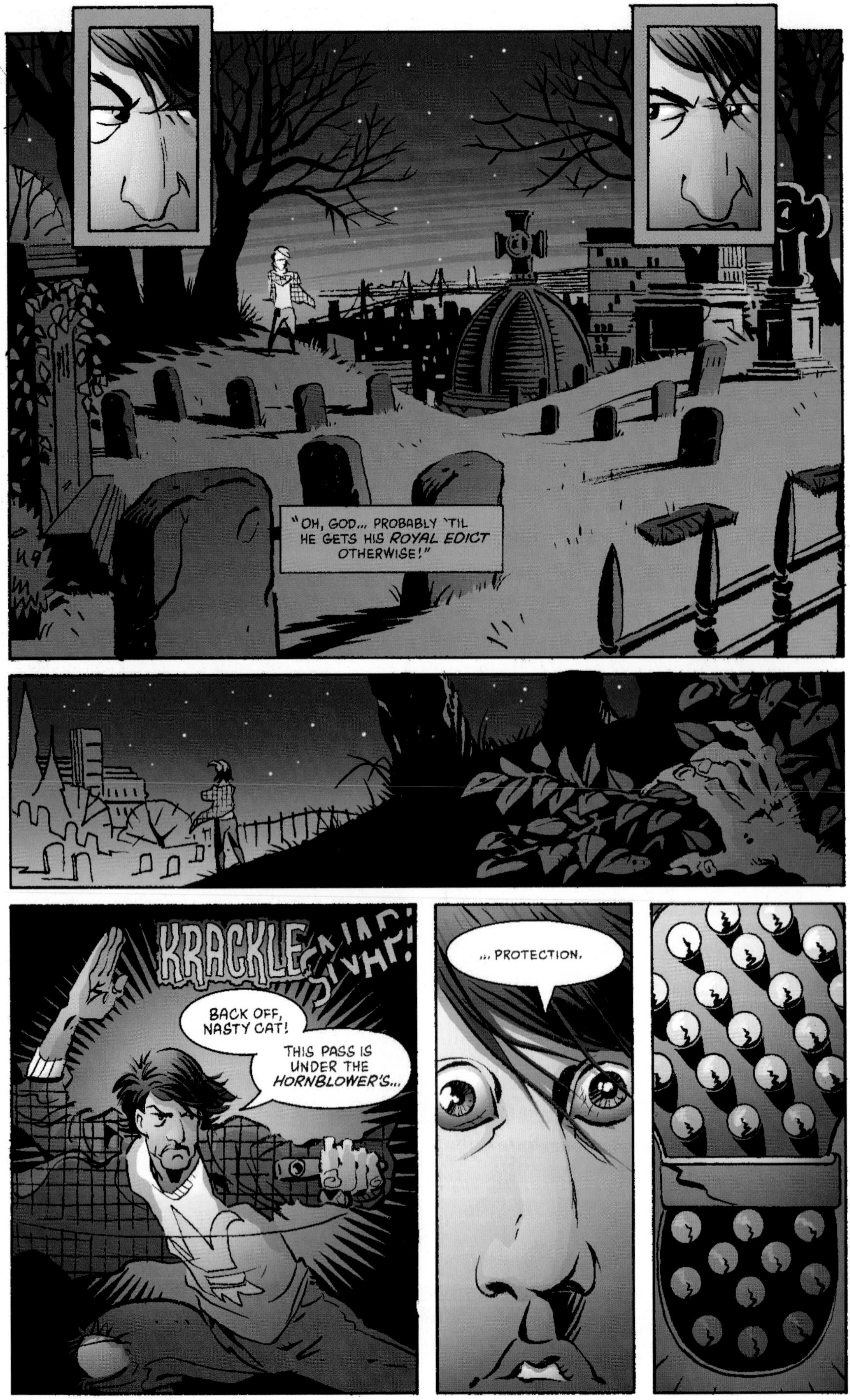
"OH, GOD... PROBABLY 'TIL HE GETS HIS ROYAL EDICT OTHERWISE!"
KRACKLE SNAP!
BACK OFF, NASTY CAT!
THIS PASS IS UNDER THE HORNBLOWER'S...
... PROTECTION.

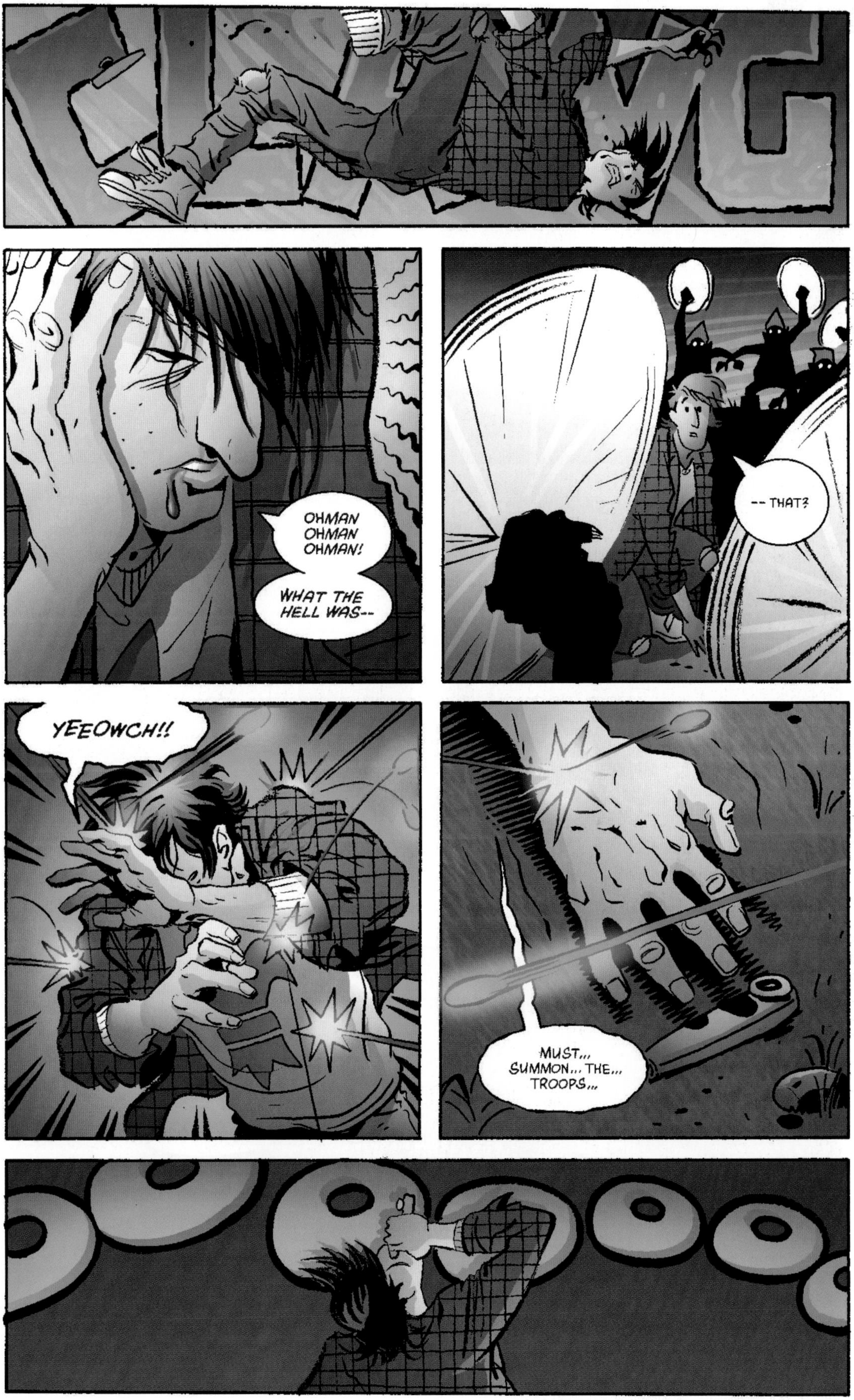
OHMAN
OHMAN
OHMAN!
WHAT THE HELL WAS--
-- THAT?
YEEOWCH!!
MUST... SUMMON... THE... TROOPS...

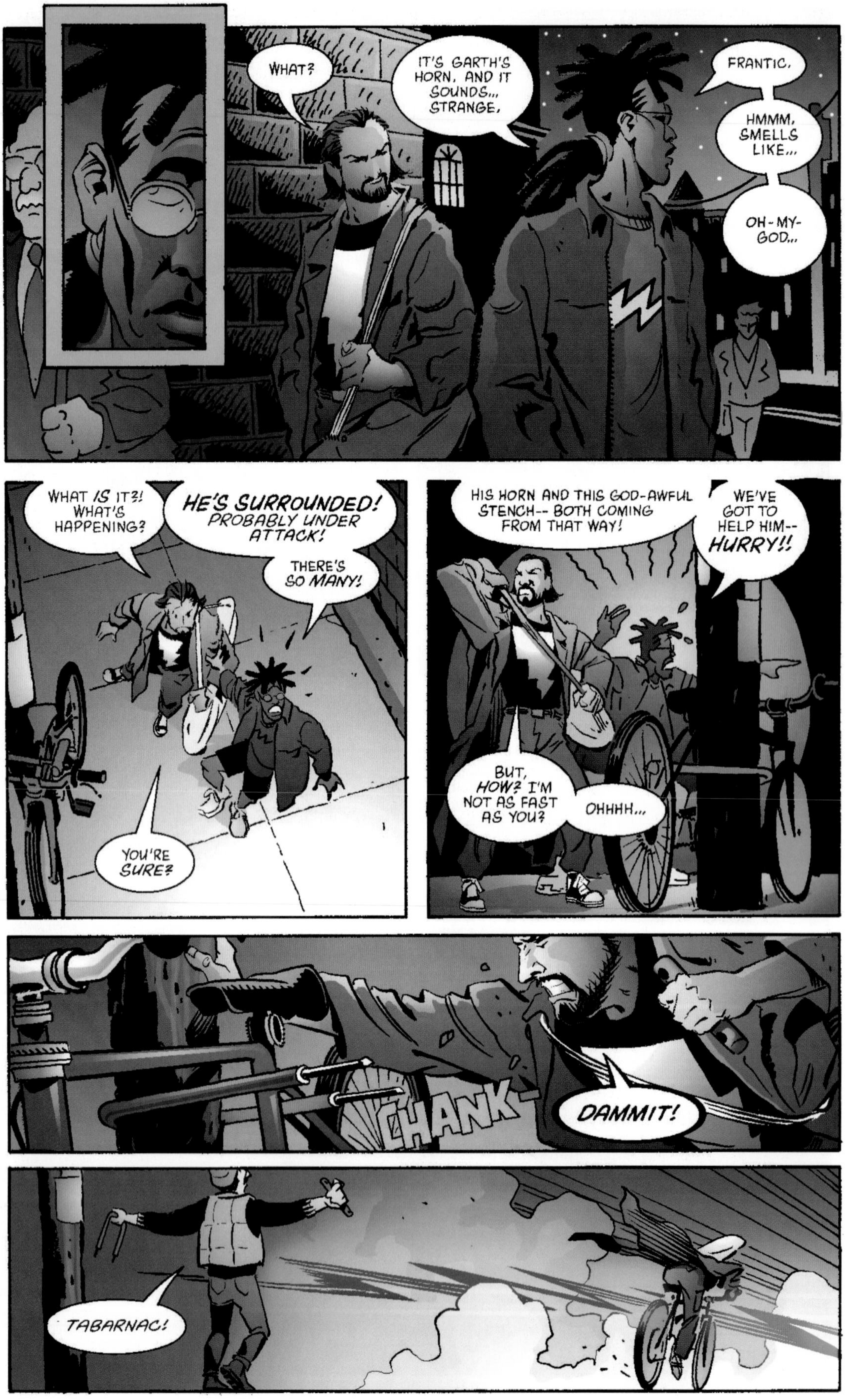
WHAT?
IT'S GARTH'S HORN, AND IT SOUNDS... STRANGE.
FRANTIC.
HMMM, SMELLS LIKE...
OH-MY-GOD...
WHAT *IS* IT?! WHAT'S HAPPENING?
HE'S SURROUNDED! PROBABLY UNDER ATTACK!
THERE'S SO *MANY!*
YOU'RE *SURE?*
HIS HORN AND THIS GOD-AWFUL STENCH-- BOTH COMING FROM THAT WAY!
WE'VE GOT TO HELP HIM-- ***HURRY!!***
BUT, *HOW?* I'M NOT AS FAST AS YOU?
OHHHH...
CHANK-
DAMMIT!
TABARNAC!

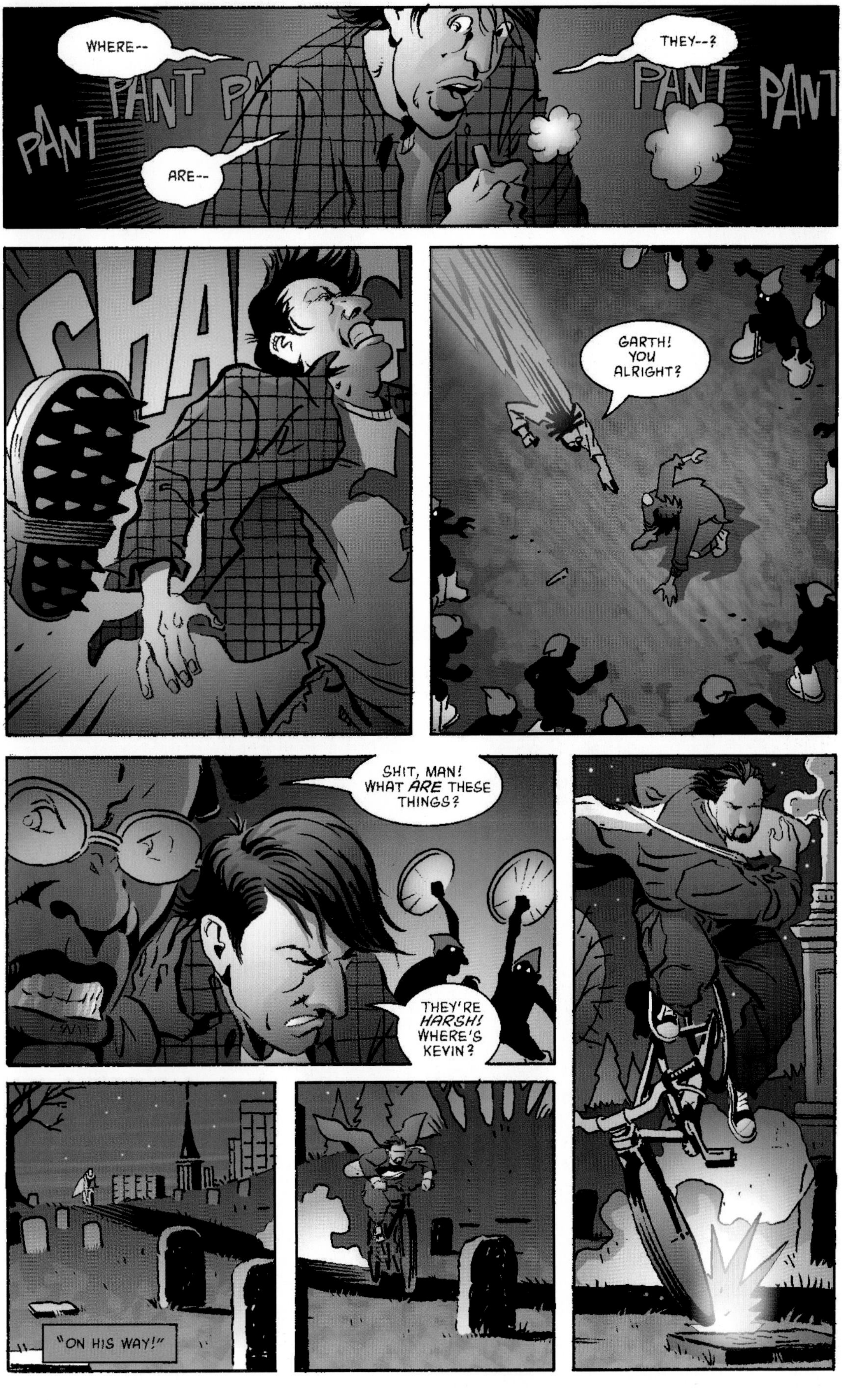
WHERE--
PANT PANT PA
ARE--
THEY--?
PANT PANT
CHA
GARTH! YOU ALRIGHT?
SHIT, MAN! WHAT ARE THESE THINGS?
THEY'RE HARSH! WHERE'S KEVIN?
"ON HIS WAY!"

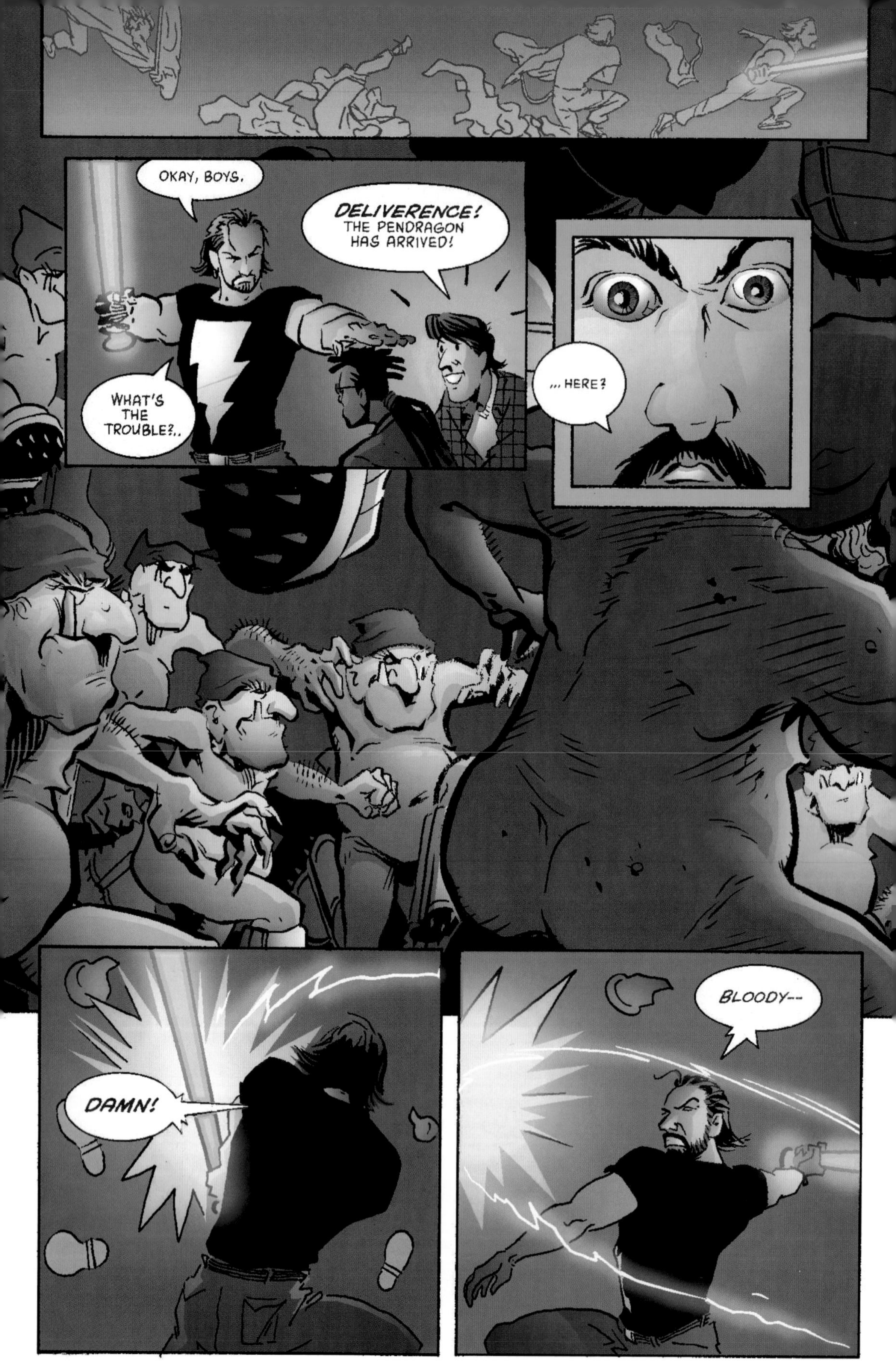
OKAY, BOYS.
WHAT'S THE TROUBLE?..
DELIVERENCE! THE PENDRAGON HAS ARRIVED!
...HERE?
DAMN!
BLOODY--

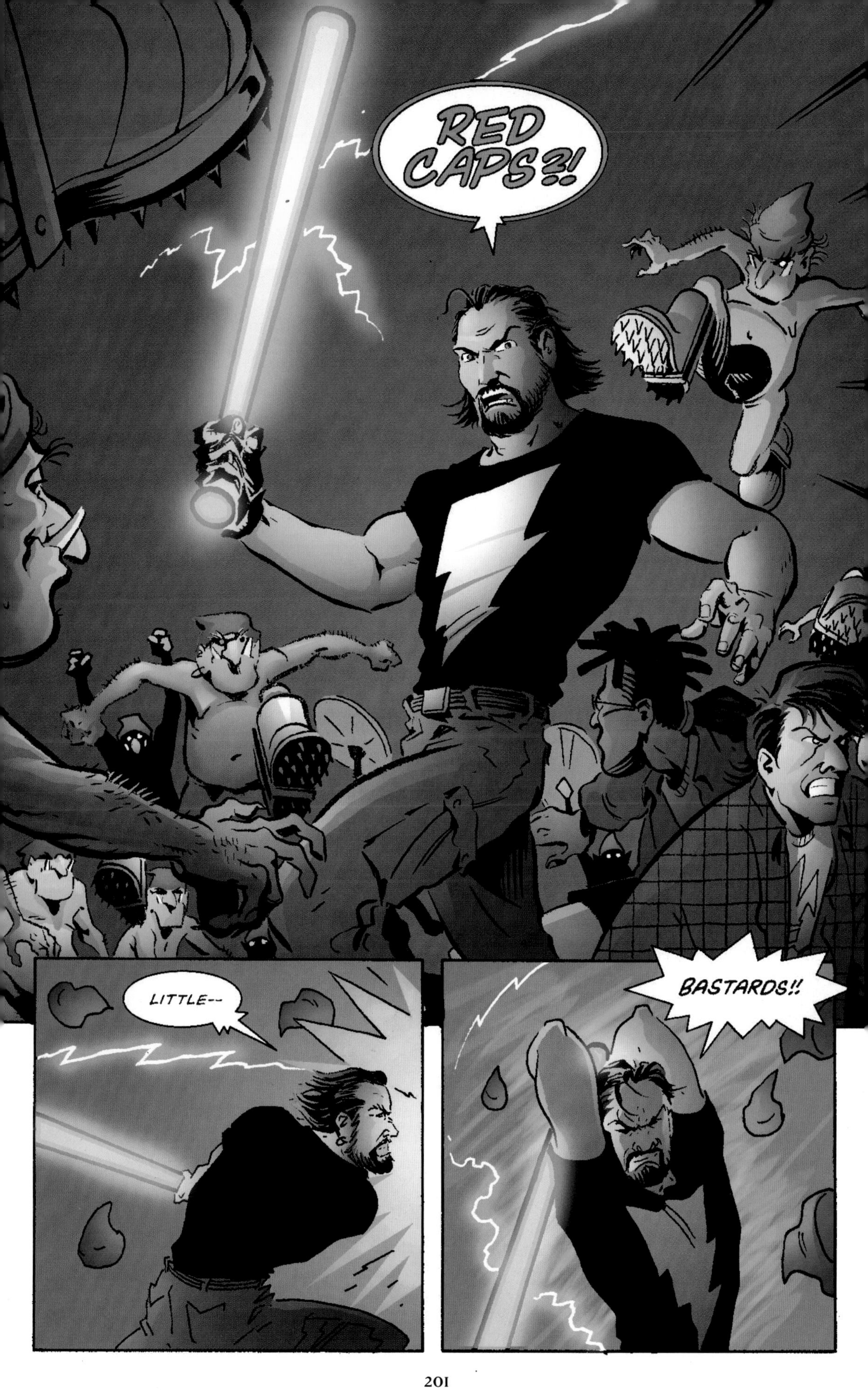
RED CAPS?!
LITTLE--
BASTARDS!!

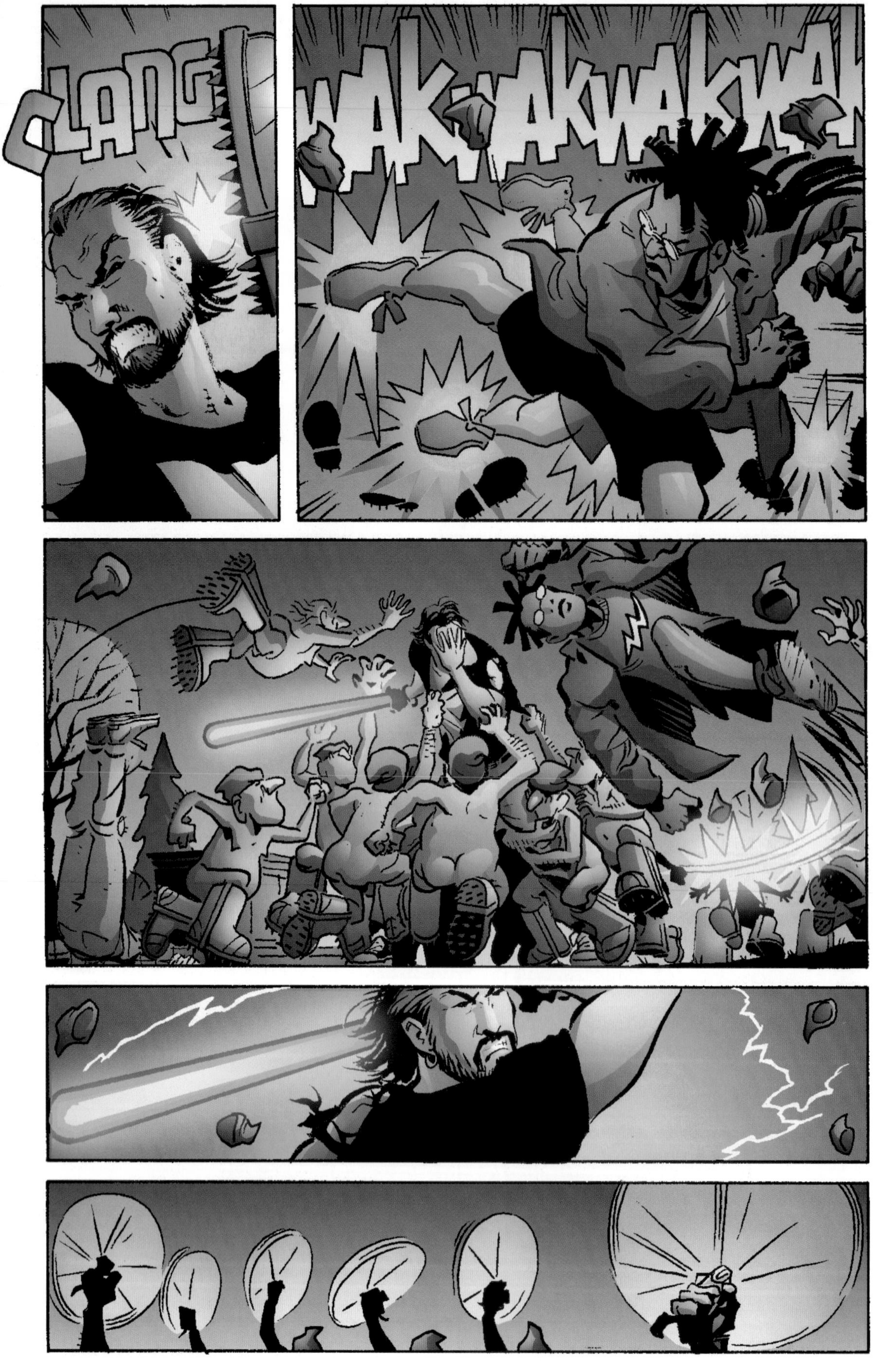
CLANG!
WAKWAKWAKWA

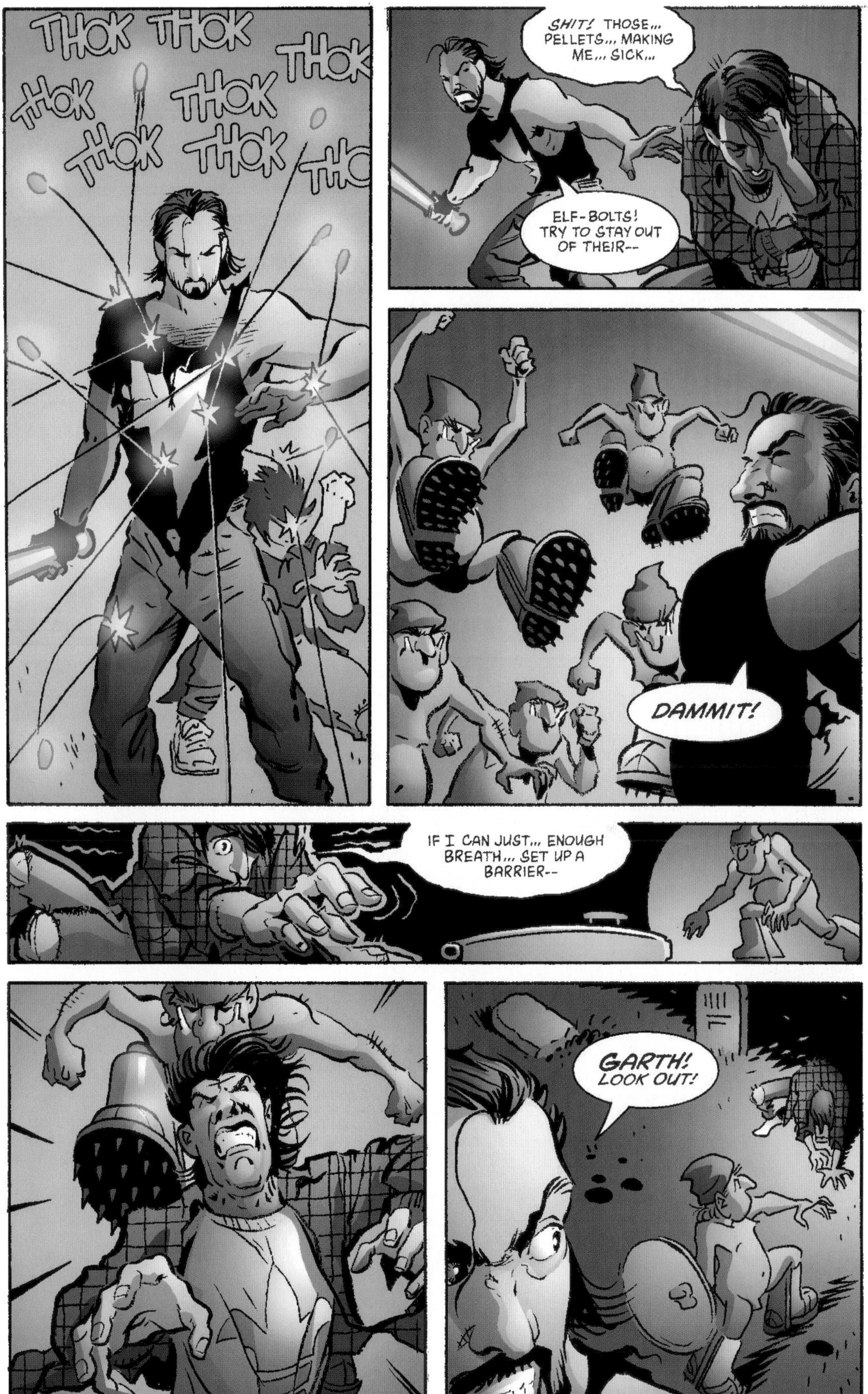
THOK THOK
THOK THOK
THOK
THOK THOK
THO
SHIT! THOSE... PELLETS... MAKING ME... SICK...
ELF-BOLTS! TRY TO STAY OUT OF THEIR--
DAMMIT!
IF I CAN JUST... ENOUGH BREATH... SET UP A BARRIER--
GARTH! LOOK OUT!

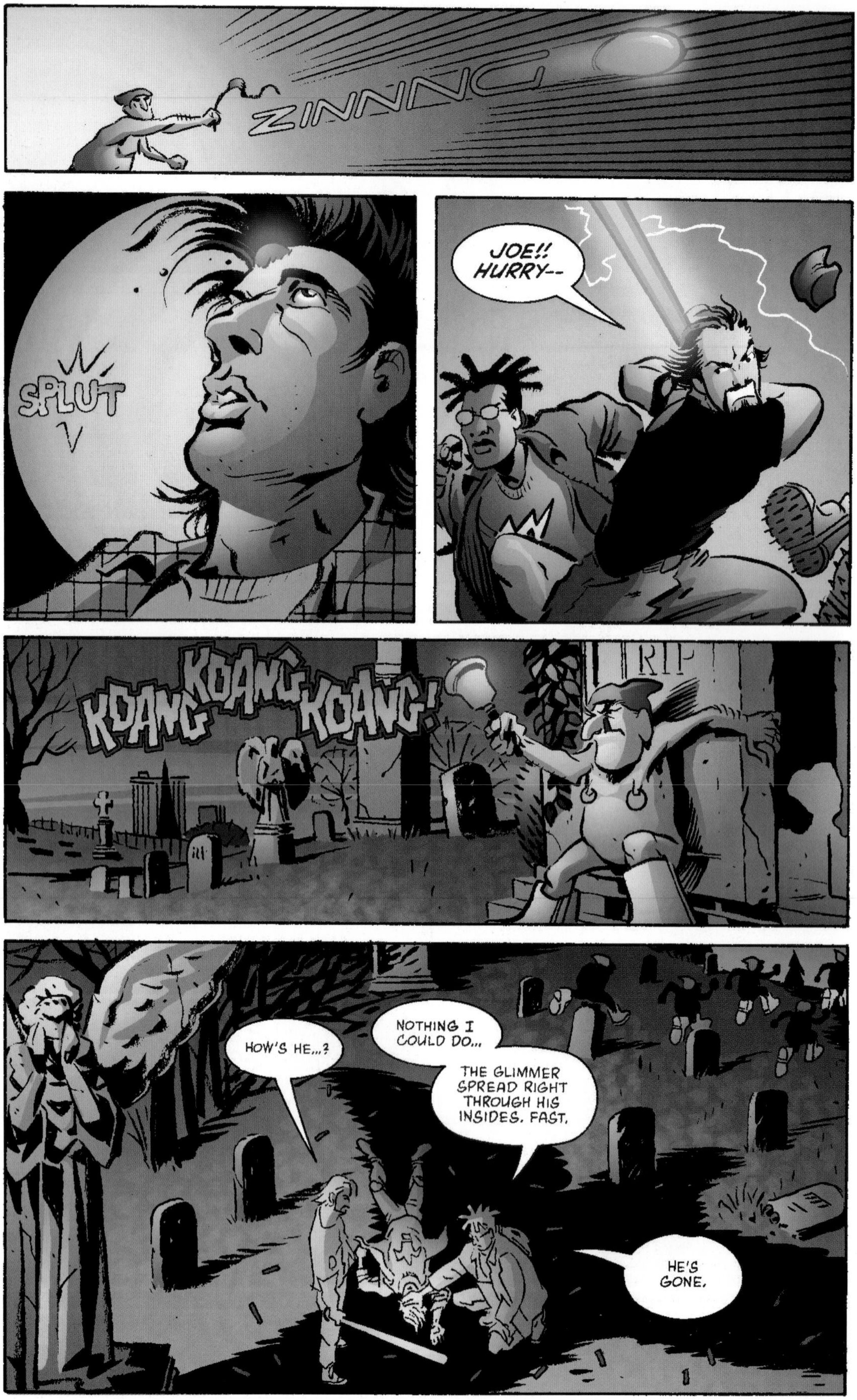
ZINNNG
SPLUT
JOE!! HURRY--
KOANG KOANG KOANG!
RIP
HOW'S HE...?
NOTHING I COULD DO...
THE GLIMMER SPREAD RIGHT THROUGH HIS INSIDES. FAST.
HE'S GONE.

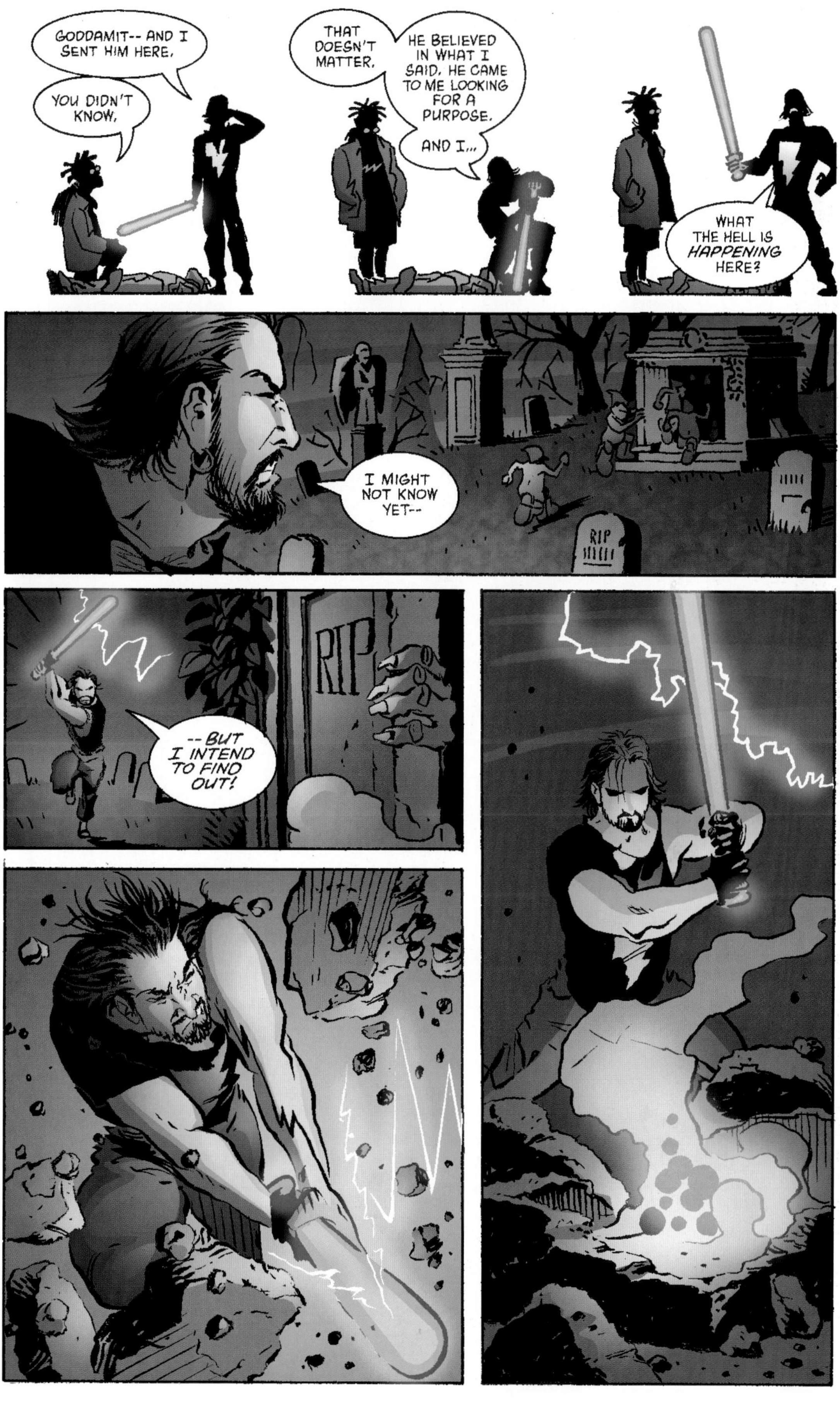
GODDAMIT-- AND I SENT HIM HERE.
YOU DIDN'T KNOW.
THAT DOESN'T MATTER.
HE BELIEVED IN WHAT I SAID. HE CAME TO ME LOOKING FOR A PURPOSE.
AND I...
WHAT THE HELL IS *HAPPENING* HERE?
I MIGHT NOT KNOW YET--
RIP
RIP
--*BUT I INTEND TO FIND OUT!*

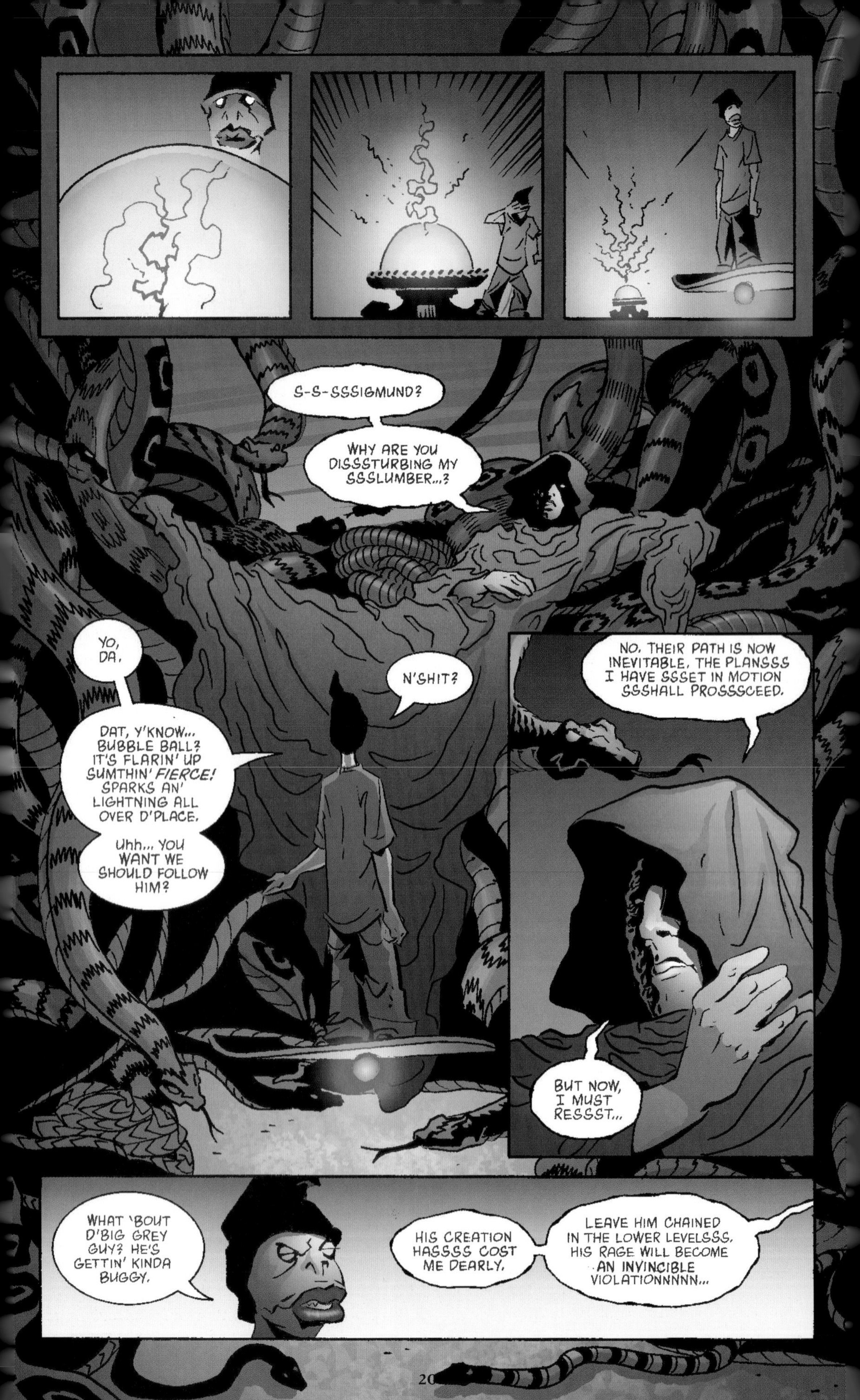
S-S-SSSIGMUND?
WHY ARE YOU DISSSTURBING MY SSSLUMBER...?
YO, DA.
N'SHIT?
DAT, Y'KNOW... BUBBLE BALL? IT'S FLARIN' UP SUMTHIN' *FIERCE!* SPARKS AN' LIGHTNING ALL OVER D'PLACE.
Uhh... YOU WANT WE SHOULD FOLLOW HIM?
NO. THEIR PATH IS NOW INEVITABLE. THE PLANSSS I HAVE SSSET IN MOTION SSSHALL PROSSSCEED.
BUT NOW, I MUST RESSST...
WHAT 'BOUT D'BIG GREY GUY? HE'S GETTIN' KINDA BUGGY.
HIS CREATION HASSSS COST ME DEARLY.
LEAVE HIM CHAINED IN THE LOWER LEVELSSS. HIS RAGE WILL BECOME AN INVINCIBLE VIOLATIONNNNN...

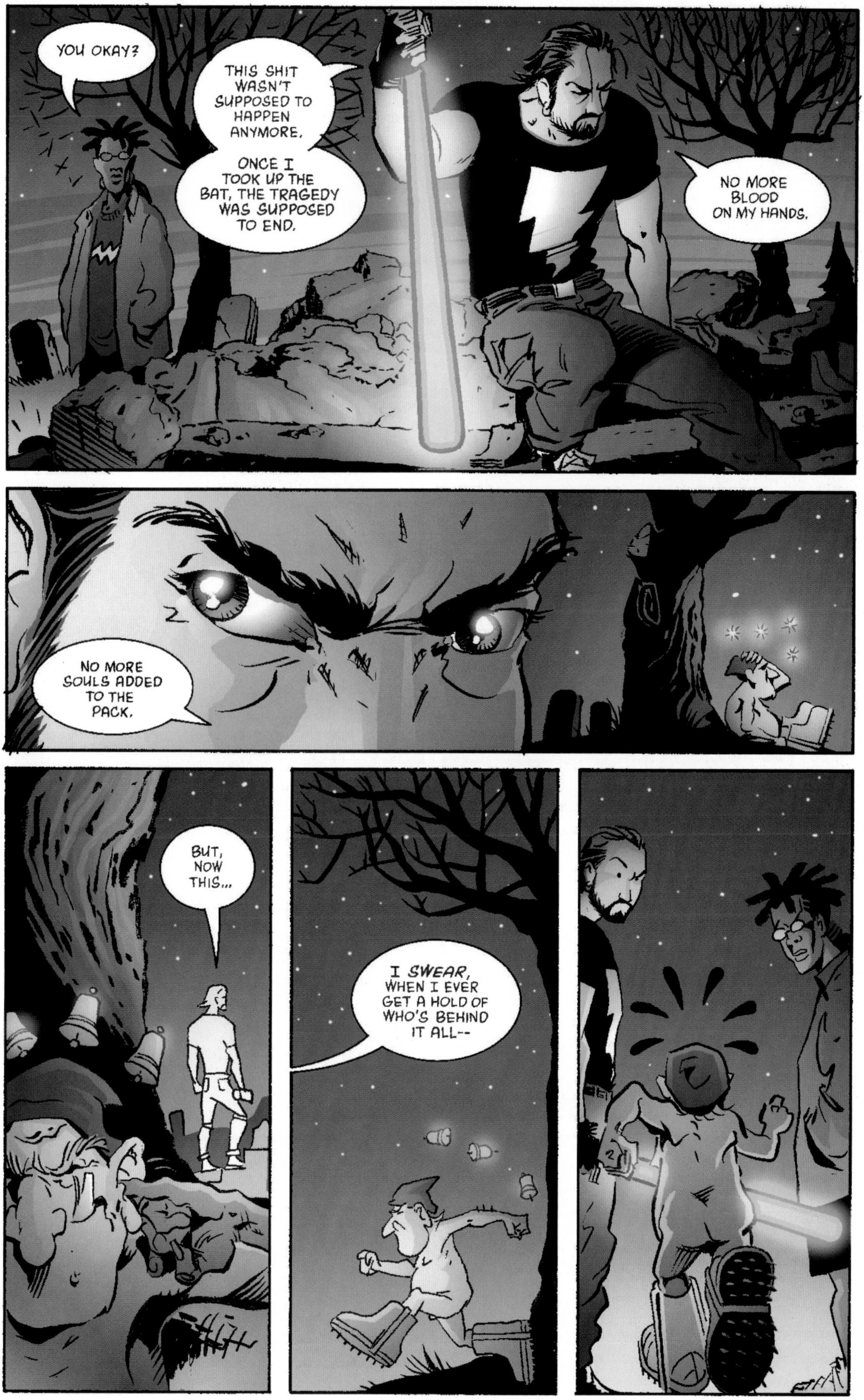
YOU OKAY?
THIS SHIT WASN'T SUPPOSED TO HAPPEN ANYMORE.
ONCE I TOOK UP THE BAT, THE TRAGEDY WAS SUPPOSED TO END.
NO MORE BLOOD ON MY HANDS.
NO MORE SOULS ADDED TO THE PACK.
BUT, NOW THIS...
I SWEAR, WHEN I EVER GET A HOLD OF WHO'S BEHIND IT ALL--

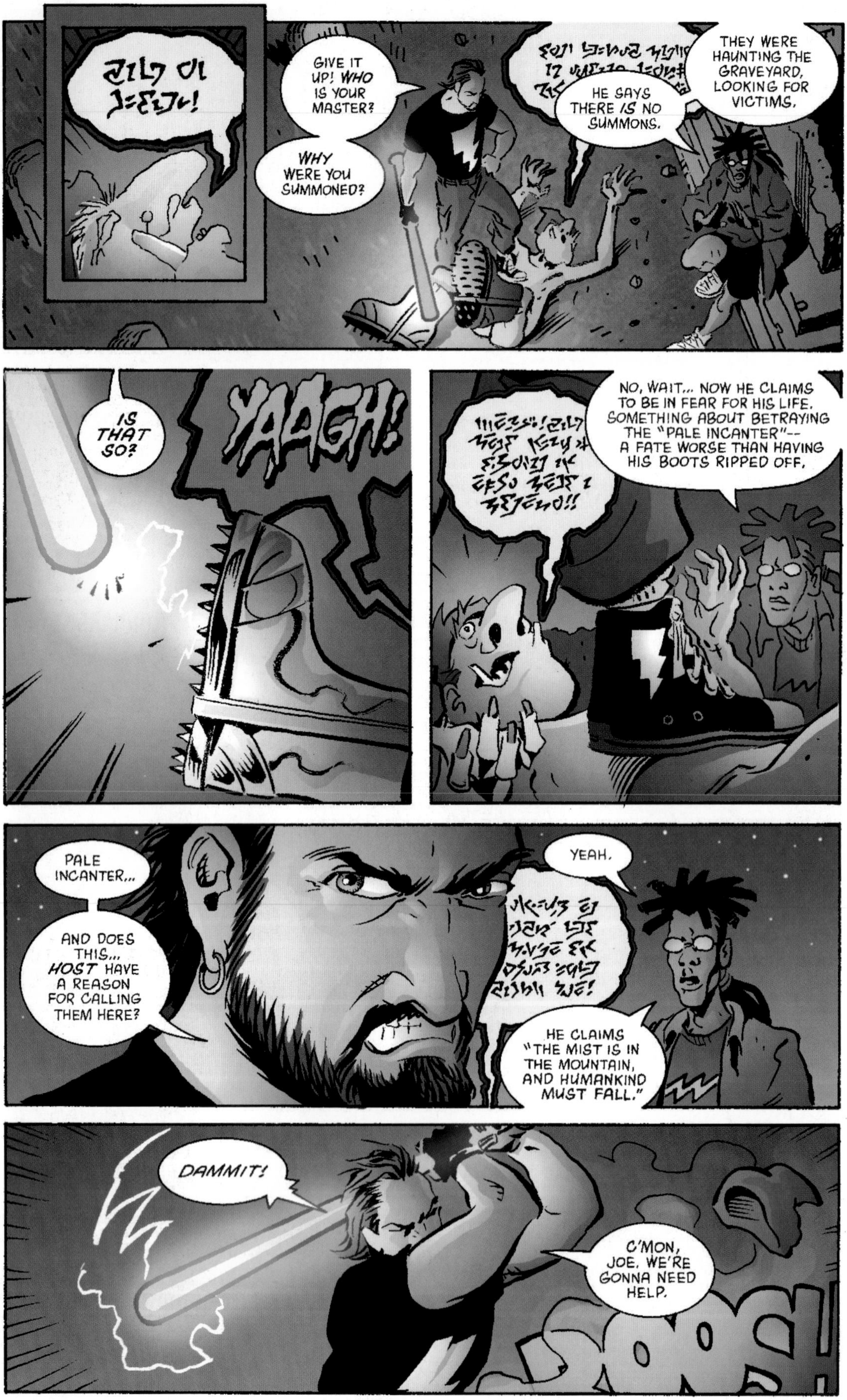
GIVE IT UP! WHO IS YOUR MASTER?
WHY WERE YOU SUMMONED?
HE SAYS THERE IS NO SUMMONS.
THEY WERE HAUNTING THE GRAVEYARD, LOOKING FOR VICTIMS.
IS THAT SO?
YAAGH!
NO, WAIT... NOW HE CLAIMS TO BE IN FEAR FOR HIS LIFE. SOMETHING ABOUT BETRAYING THE "PALE INCANTER"-- A FATE WORSE THAN HAVING HIS BOOTS RIPPED OFF.
PALE INCANTER...
AND DOES THIS... HOST HAVE A REASON FOR CALLING THEM HERE?
YEAH.
HE CLAIMS "THE MIST IS IN THE MOUNTAIN, AND HUMANKIND MUST FALL."
DAMMIT!
C'MON, JOE. WE'RE GONNA NEED HELP.

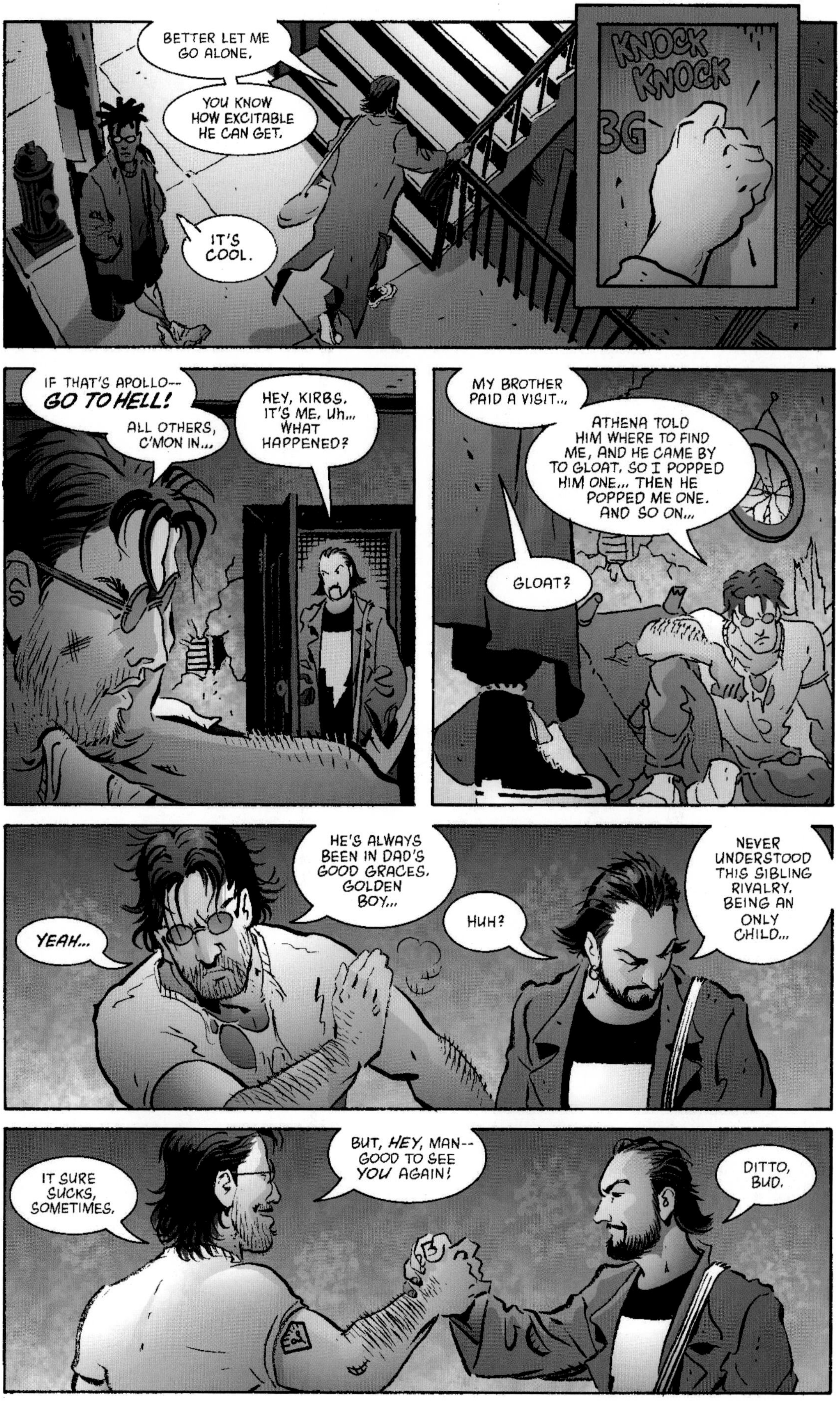
BETTER LET ME GO ALONE.
YOU KNOW HOW EXCITABLE HE CAN GET.
IT'S COOL.
KNOCK KNOCK
3G
IF THAT'S APOLLO-- GO TO HELL!
ALL OTHERS, C'MON IN...
HEY, KIRBS. IT'S ME. Uh... WHAT HAPPENED?
MY BROTHER PAID A VISIT...
ATHENA TOLD HIM WHERE TO FIND ME, AND HE CAME BY TO GLOAT. SO I POPPED HIM ONE... THEN HE POPPED ME ONE. AND SO ON...
GLOAT?
YEAH...
HE'S ALWAYS BEEN IN DAD'S GOOD GRACES. GOLDEN BOY...
HUH?
NEVER UNDERSTOOD THIS SIBLING RIVALRY. BEING AN ONLY CHILD...
IT SURE SUCKS, SOMETIMES.
BUT, HEY, MAN-- GOOD TO SEE YOU AGAIN!
DITTO, BUD.

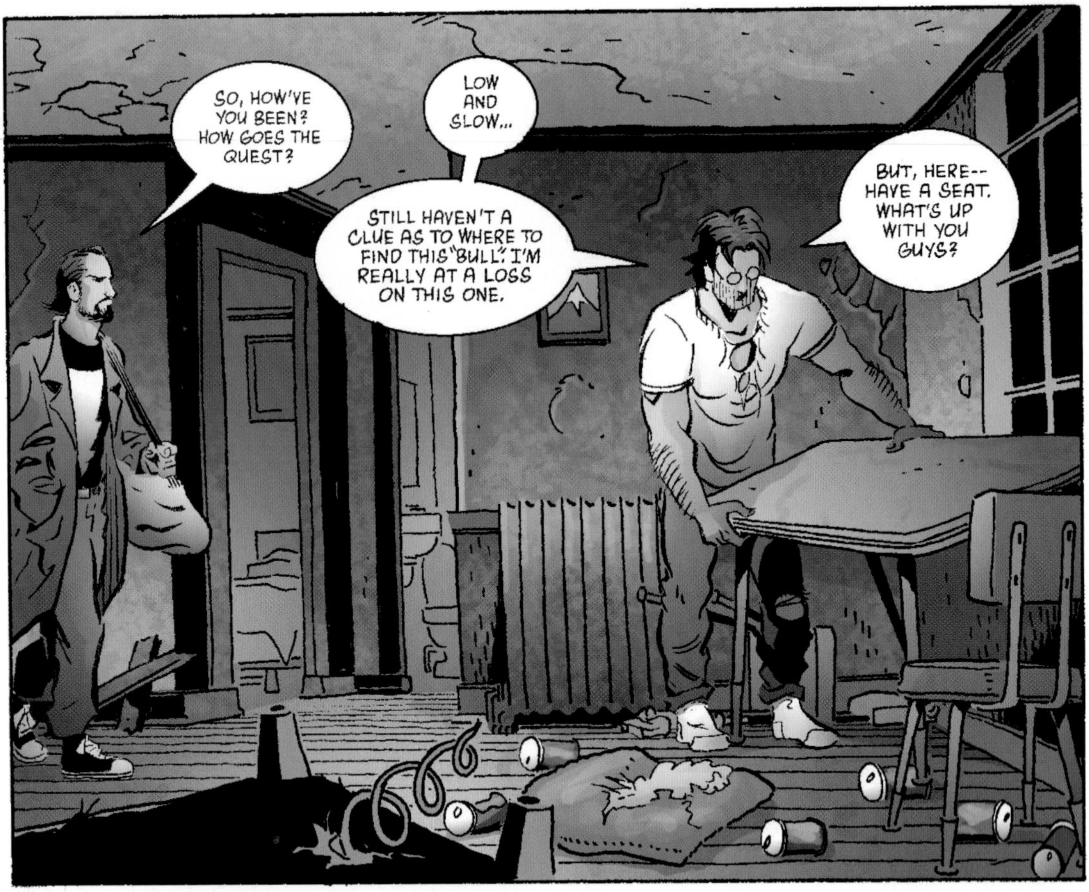
SO, HOW'VE YOU BEEN? HOW GOES THE QUEST?
LOW AND SLOW...
STILL HAVEN'T A CLUE AS TO WHERE TO FIND THIS "BULL." I'M REALLY AT A LOSS ON THIS ONE.
BUT, HERE-- HAVE A SEAT. WHAT'S UP WITH YOU GUYS?
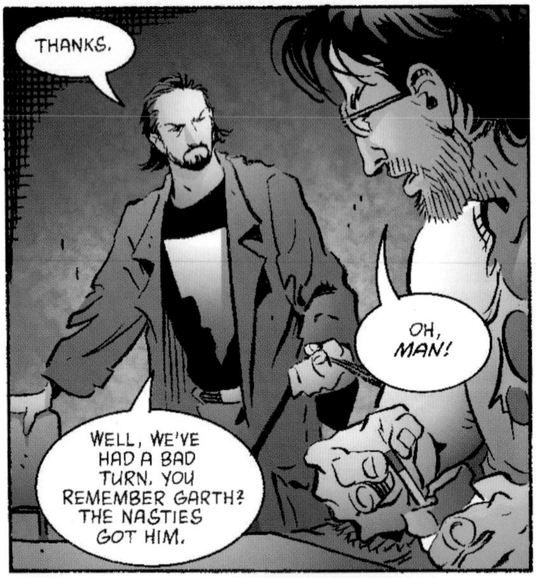
THANKS.
OH, MAN!
WELL, WE'VE HAD A BAD TURN. YOU REMEMBER GARTH? THE NASTIES GOT HIM.
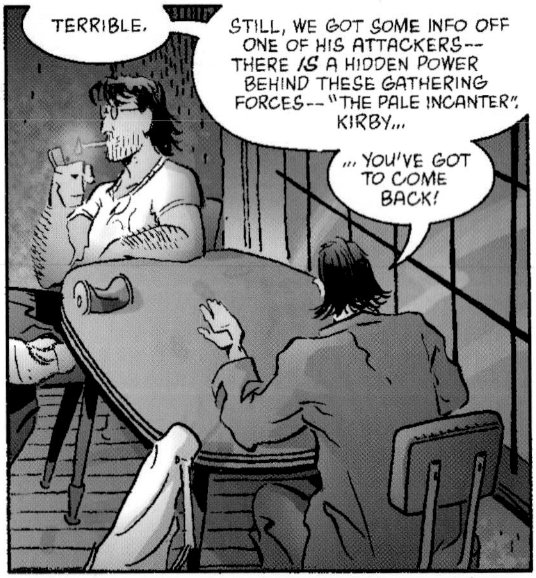
TERRIBLE.
STILL, WE GOT SOME INFO OFF ONE OF HIS ATTACKERS-- THERE *IS* A HIDDEN POWER BEHIND THESE GATHERING FORCES-- "THE PALE INCANTER". KIRBY...
... YOU'VE GOT TO COME BACK!
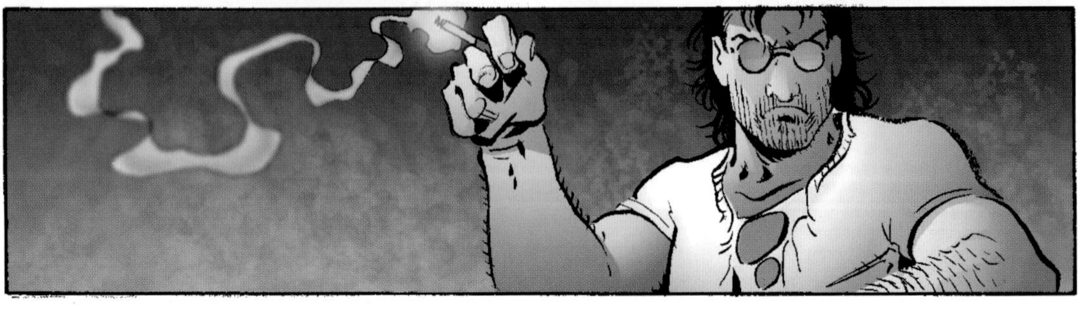

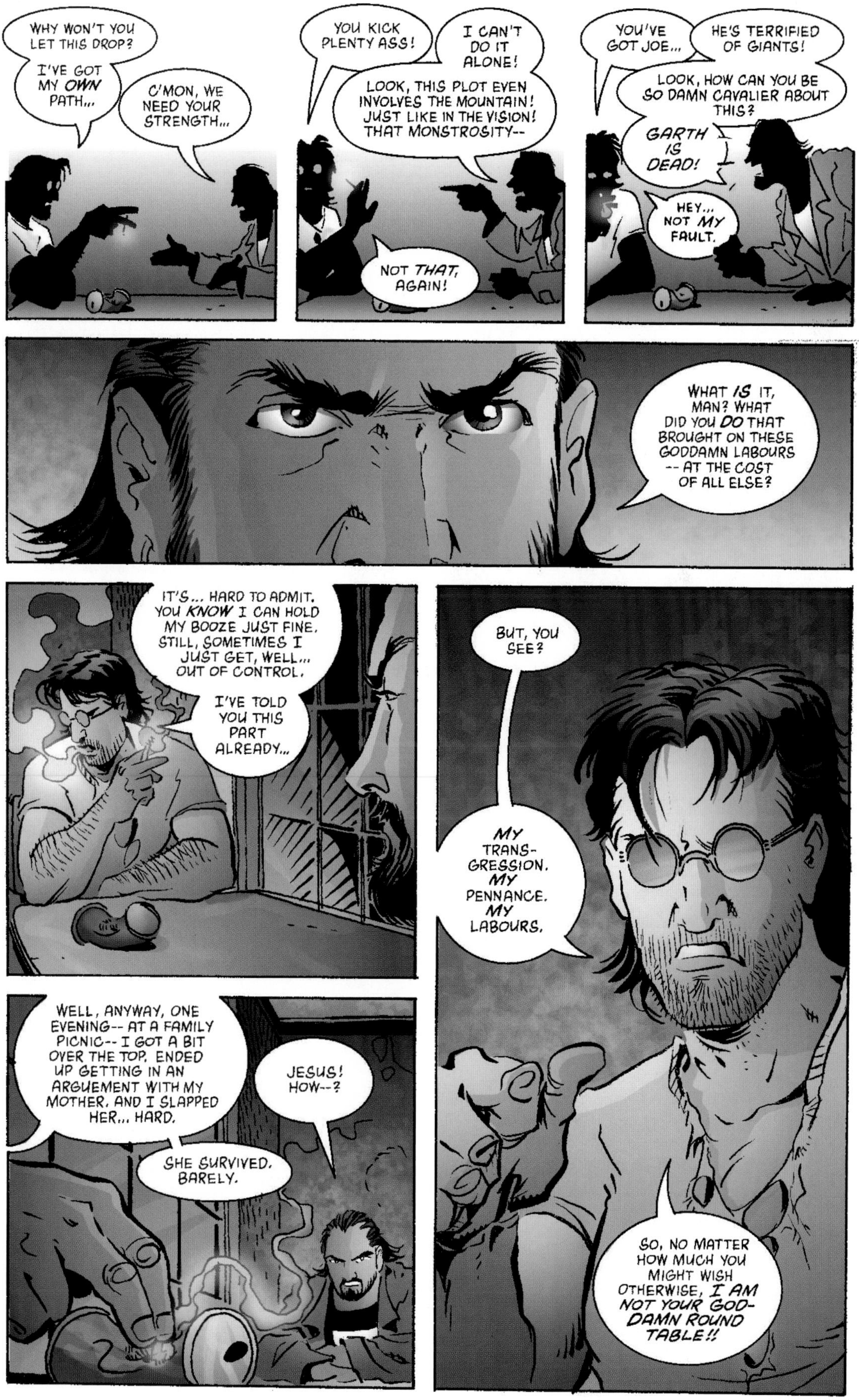
WHY WON'T YOU LET THIS DROP?
I'VE GOT MY OWN PATH...
C'MON, WE NEED YOUR STRENGTH...
YOU KICK PLENTY ASS!
I CAN'T DO IT ALONE!
LOOK, THIS PLOT EVEN INVOLVES THE MOUNTAIN! JUST LIKE IN THE VISION! THAT MONSTROSITY--
NOT THAT, AGAIN!
YOU'VE GOT JOE...
HE'S TERRIFIED OF GIANTS!
LOOK, HOW CAN YOU BE SO DAMN CAVALIER ABOUT THIS?
GARTH IS DEAD!
HEY... NOT MY FAULT.
WHAT IS IT, MAN? WHAT DID YOU DO THAT BROUGHT ON THESE GODDAMN LABOURS -- AT THE COST OF ALL ELSE?
IT'S... HARD TO ADMIT. YOU KNOW I CAN HOLD MY BOOZE JUST FINE. STILL, SOMETIMES I JUST GET, WELL... OUT OF CONTROL.
I'VE TOLD YOU THIS PART ALREADY...
WELL, ANYWAY, ONE EVENING-- AT A FAMILY PICNIC-- I GOT A BIT OVER THE TOP, ENDED UP GETTING IN AN ARGUEMENT WITH MY MOTHER, AND I SLAPPED HER... HARD.
JESUS! HOW--?
SHE SURVIVED. BARELY.
BUT, YOU SEE?
MY TRANSGRESSION. MY PENNANCE. MY LABOURS.
SO, NO MATTER HOW MUCH YOU MIGHT WISH OTHERWISE, I AM NOT YOUR GOD-DAMN ROUND TABLE!!

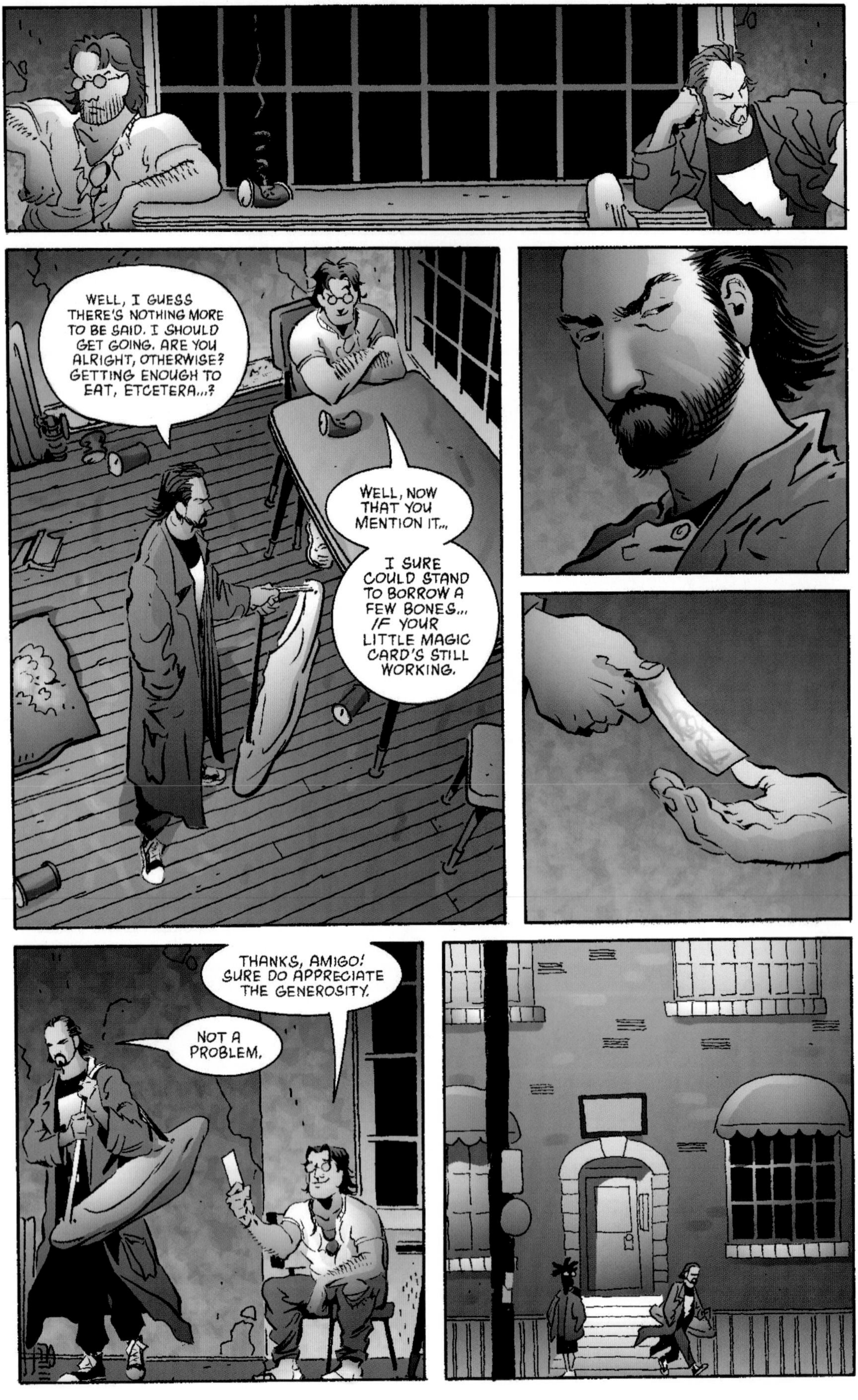
WELL, I GUESS THERE'S NOTHING MORE TO BE SAID. I SHOULD GET GOING. ARE YOU ALRIGHT, OTHERWISE? GETTING ENOUGH TO EAT, ETCETERA...?
WELL, NOW THAT YOU MENTION IT...
I SURE COULD STAND TO BORROW A FEW BONES... *IF* YOUR LITTLE MAGIC CARD'S STILL WORKING.
THANKS, AMIGO! SURE DO APPRECIATE THE GENEROSITY.
NOT A PROBLEM.

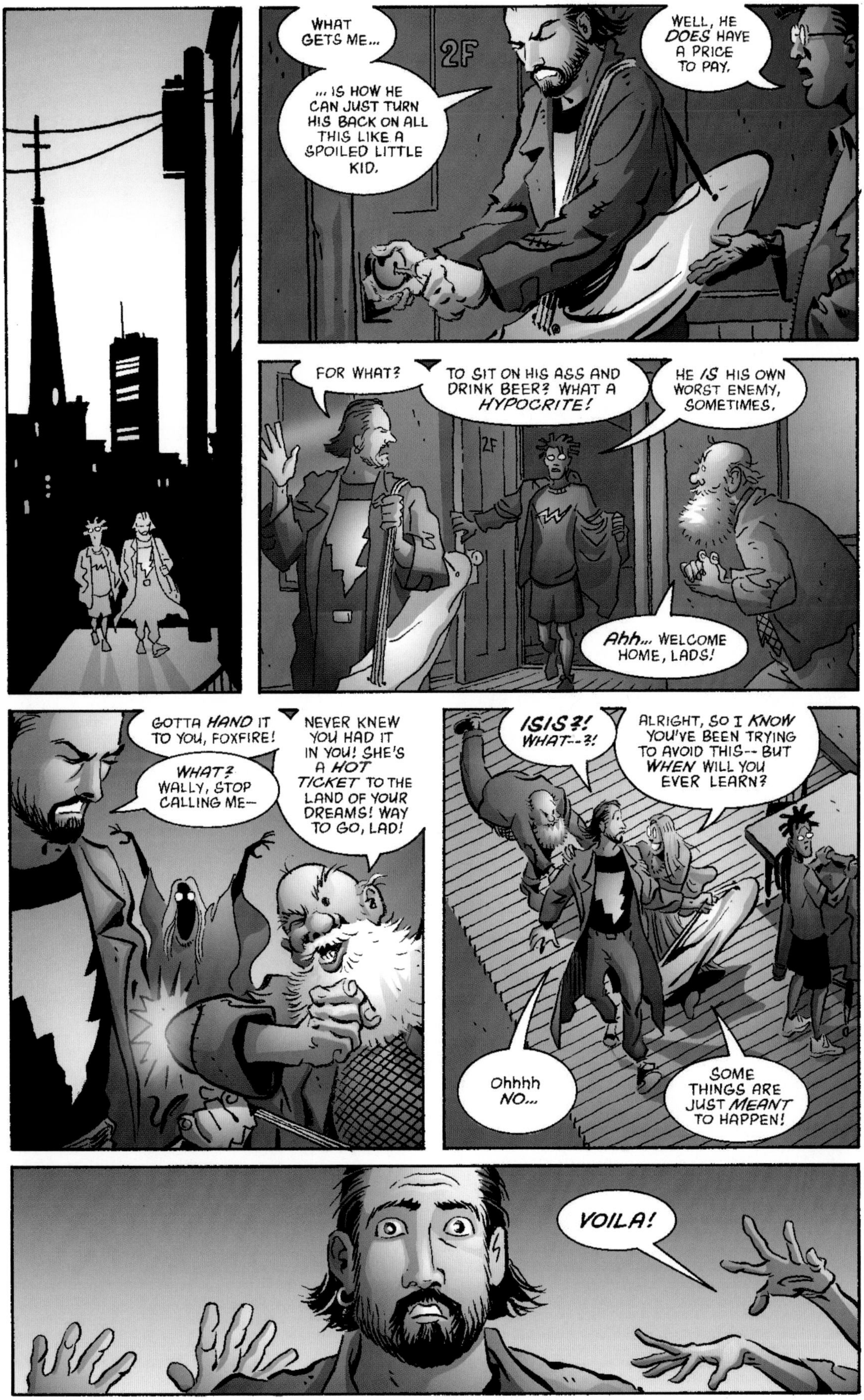
WHAT GETS ME...
...IS HOW HE CAN JUST TURN HIS BACK ON ALL THIS LIKE A SPOILED LITTLE KID.
WELL, HE DOES HAVE A PRICE TO PAY.
2F
FOR WHAT?
TO SIT ON HIS ASS AND DRINK BEER? WHAT A HYPOCRITE!
HE IS HIS OWN WORST ENEMY, SOMETIMES.
2F
Ahh... WELCOME HOME, LADS!
GOTTA HAND IT TO YOU, FOXFIRE!
WHAT? WALLY, STOP CALLING ME—
NEVER KNEW YOU HAD IT IN YOU! SHE'S A HOT TICKET TO THE LAND OF YOUR DREAMS! WAY TO GO, LAD!
ISIS?! WHAT--?!
ALRIGHT, SO I KNOW YOU'VE BEEN TRYING TO AVOID THIS-- BUT WHEN WILL YOU EVER LEARN?
Ohhhh NO...
SOME THINGS ARE JUST MEANT TO HAPPEN!
VOILA!

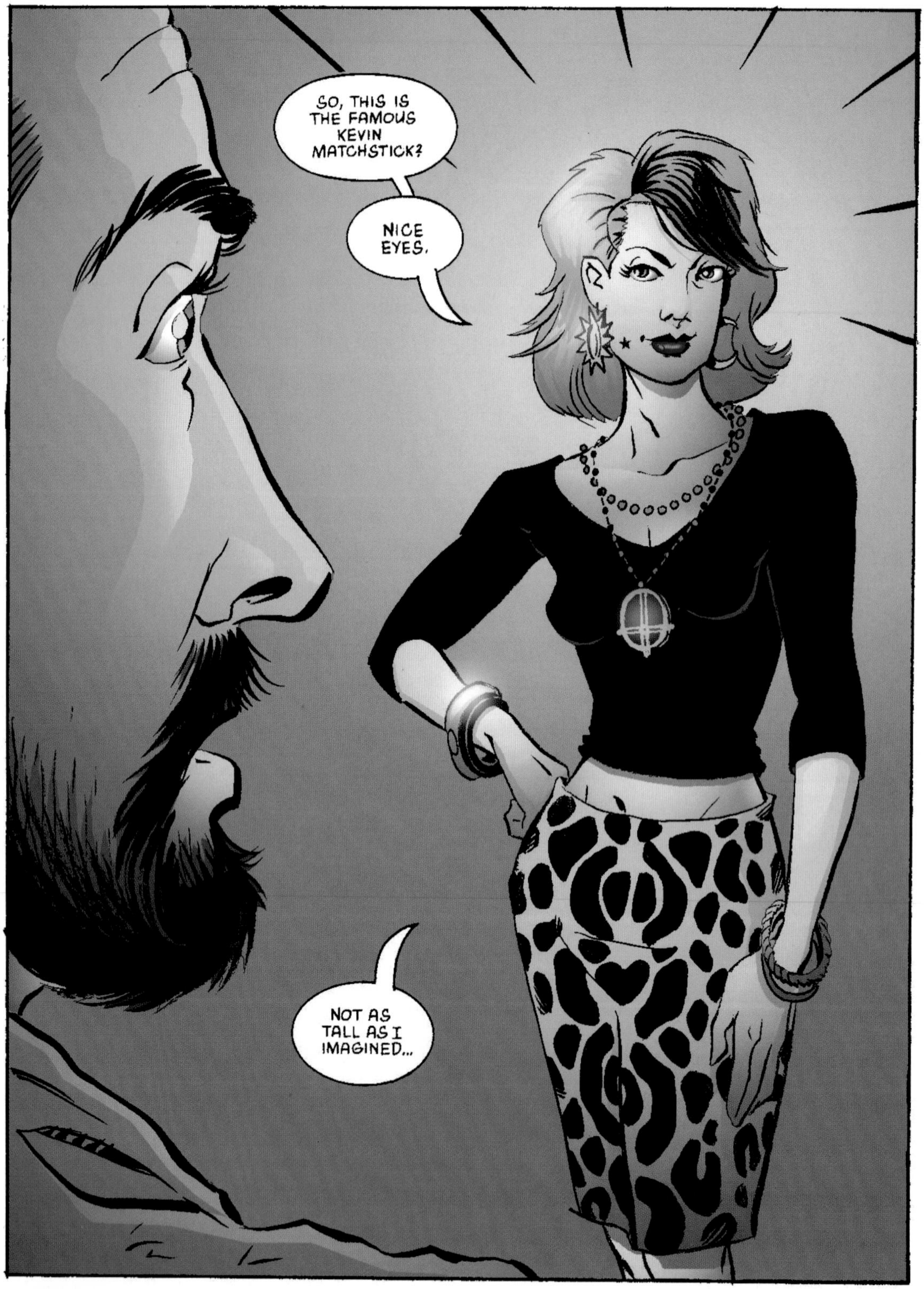
SO, THIS IS THE FAMOUS KEVIN MATCHSTICK?
NICE EYES.
NOT AS TALL AS I IMAGINED...

THE HERO DEFINED
MAGE

chapter
9

"The Weird
Sisters"

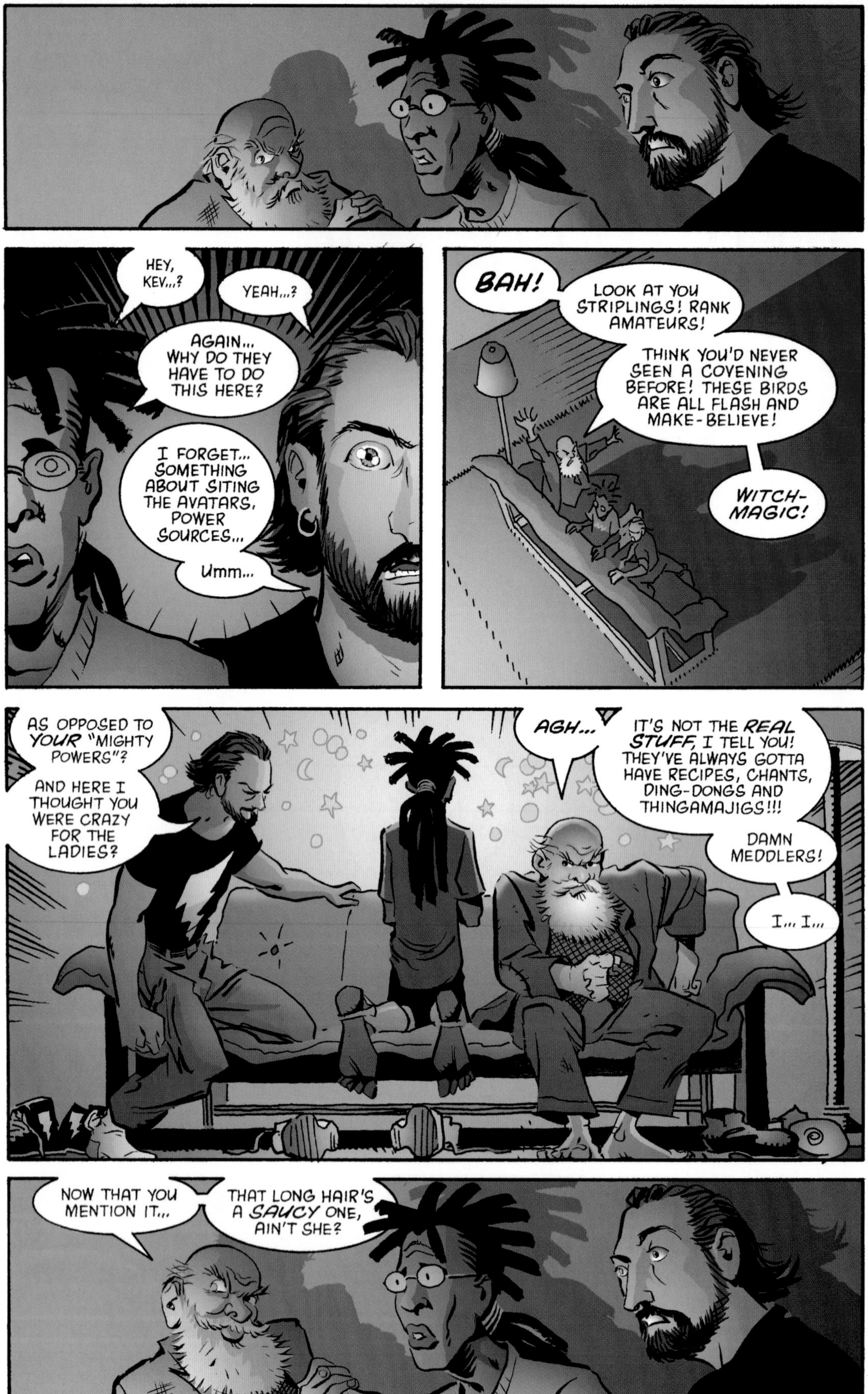
HEY, KEV...?
YEAH...?
AGAIN... WHY DO THEY HAVE TO DO THIS HERE?
I FORGET... SOMETHING ABOUT SITING THE AVATARS, POWER SOURCES...
Umm...
BAH!
LOOK AT YOU STRIPLINGS! RANK AMATEURS!
THINK YOU'D NEVER SEEN A COVENING BEFORE! THESE BIRDS ARE ALL FLASH AND MAKE-BELIEVE!
WITCH-MAGIC!
AS OPPOSED TO YOUR "MIGHTY POWERS"?
AND HERE I THOUGHT YOU WERE CRAZY FOR THE LADIES?
AGH...
IT'S NOT THE REAL STUFF, I TELL YOU! THEY'VE ALWAYS GOTTA HAVE RECIPES, CHANTS, DING-DONGS AND THINGAMAJIGS!!!
DAMN MEDDLERS!
I... I...
NOW THAT YOU MENTION IT...
THAT LONG HAIR'S A SAUCY ONE, AIN'T SHE?

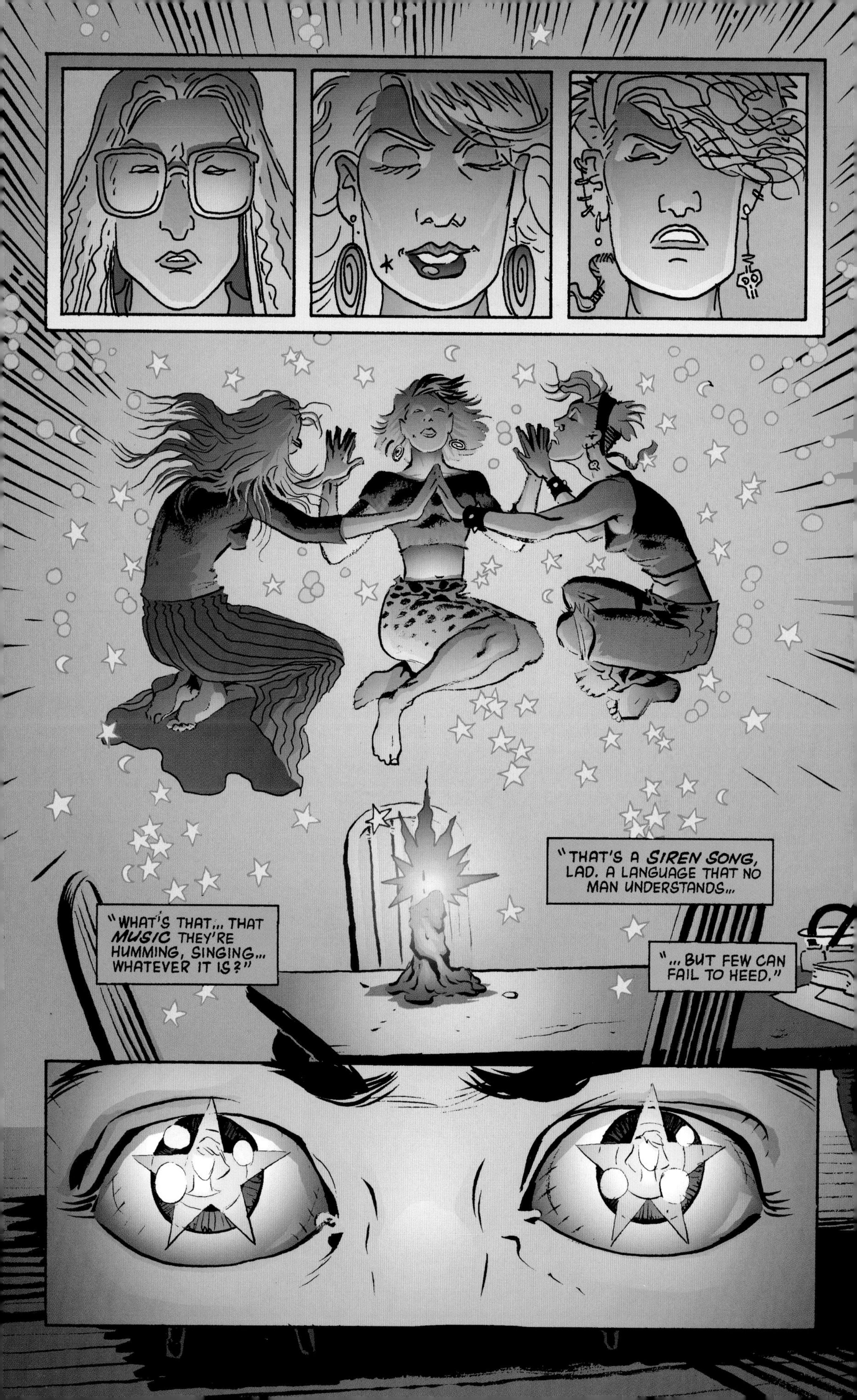
"WHAT'S THAT... THAT MUSIC THEY'RE HUMMING, SINGING... WHATEVER IT IS?"
"THAT'S A SIREN SONG, LAD. A LANGUAGE THAT NO MAN UNDERSTANDS...
"...BUT FEW CAN FAIL TO HEED."

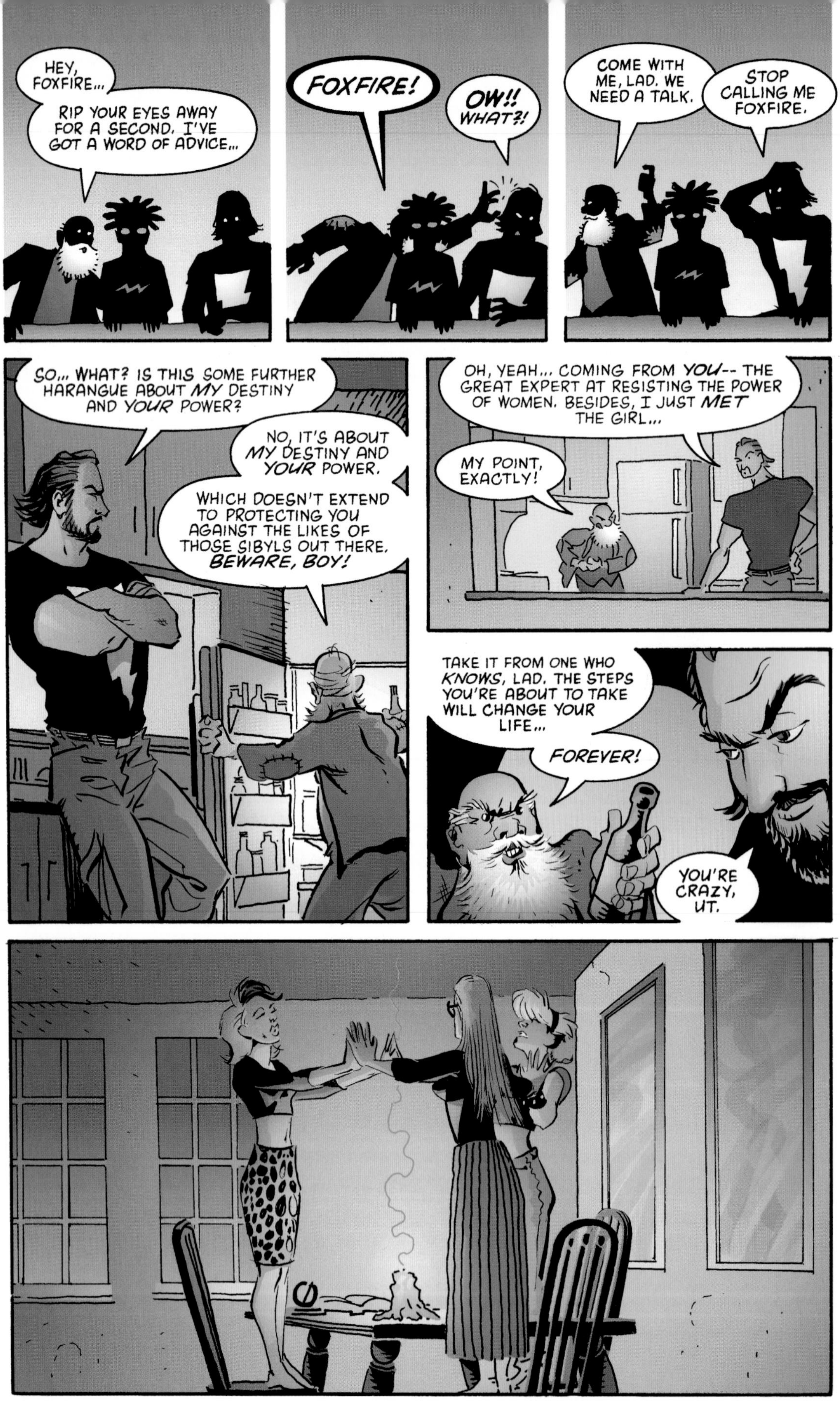
HEY, FOXFIRE...
RIP YOUR EYES AWAY FOR A SECOND. I'VE GOT A WORD OF ADVICE...
FOXFIRE!
OW!! WHAT?!
COME WITH ME, LAD. WE NEED A TALK.
STOP CALLING ME FOXFIRE.
SO... WHAT? IS THIS SOME FURTHER HARANGUE ABOUT MY DESTINY AND YOUR POWER?
NO, IT'S ABOUT MY DESTINY AND YOUR POWER.
WHICH DOESN'T EXTEND TO PROTECTING YOU AGAINST THE LIKES OF THOSE SIBYLS OUT THERE. BEWARE, BOY!
OH, YEAH... COMING FROM YOU-- THE GREAT EXPERT AT RESISTING THE POWER OF WOMEN. BESIDES, I JUST MET THE GIRL...
MY POINT, EXACTLY!
TAKE IT FROM ONE WHO KNOWS, LAD. THE STEPS YOU'RE ABOUT TO TAKE WILL CHANGE YOUR LIFE...
FOREVER!
YOU'RE CRAZY, UT.

WELL, THAT'S ONE DOWN, TOMORROW NIGHT, WE'LL CLEAR THE SECOND POINT.

Ooohhh...

I JUST LOVE THAT AFTER-GLIMMER, DON'T YOU, ISH?

SOMETIMES, YES, OTHER TIMES...

FEELS LIKE MY SKIN'S GONNA COME OFF-- *yaaawwwn!*

THANKS FOR LETTING US USE YOUR PLACE, KEVIN. THE DARK AGENTS ARE IN THEIR FINAL PHASING.

MEANING WHAT?

THAT WHAT-EVER'S CREATING THIS ARCANE VORTEX IS NEARING ITS OBJECTIVE.

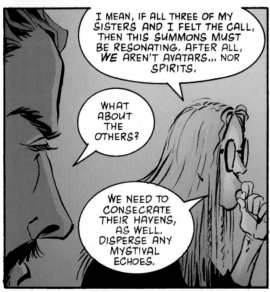

I MEAN, IF ALL THREE OF MY SISTERS AND I FELT THE CALL, THEN THIS SUMMONS MUST BE RESONATING. AFTER ALL, *WE* AREN'T AVATARS... NOR SPIRITS.

WHAT ABOUT THE OTHERS?

WE NEED TO CONSECRATE THEIR HAVENS, AS WELL. DISPERSE ANY MYSTIVAL ECHOES.

SEE?! THIS IS THE PALE INCANTER AT WORK!

NEVER DOUBTED YOU FOR A SECOND, KEV!

I TOLD YOU SO!

KEVIN?

Y-Y-Y-ES?

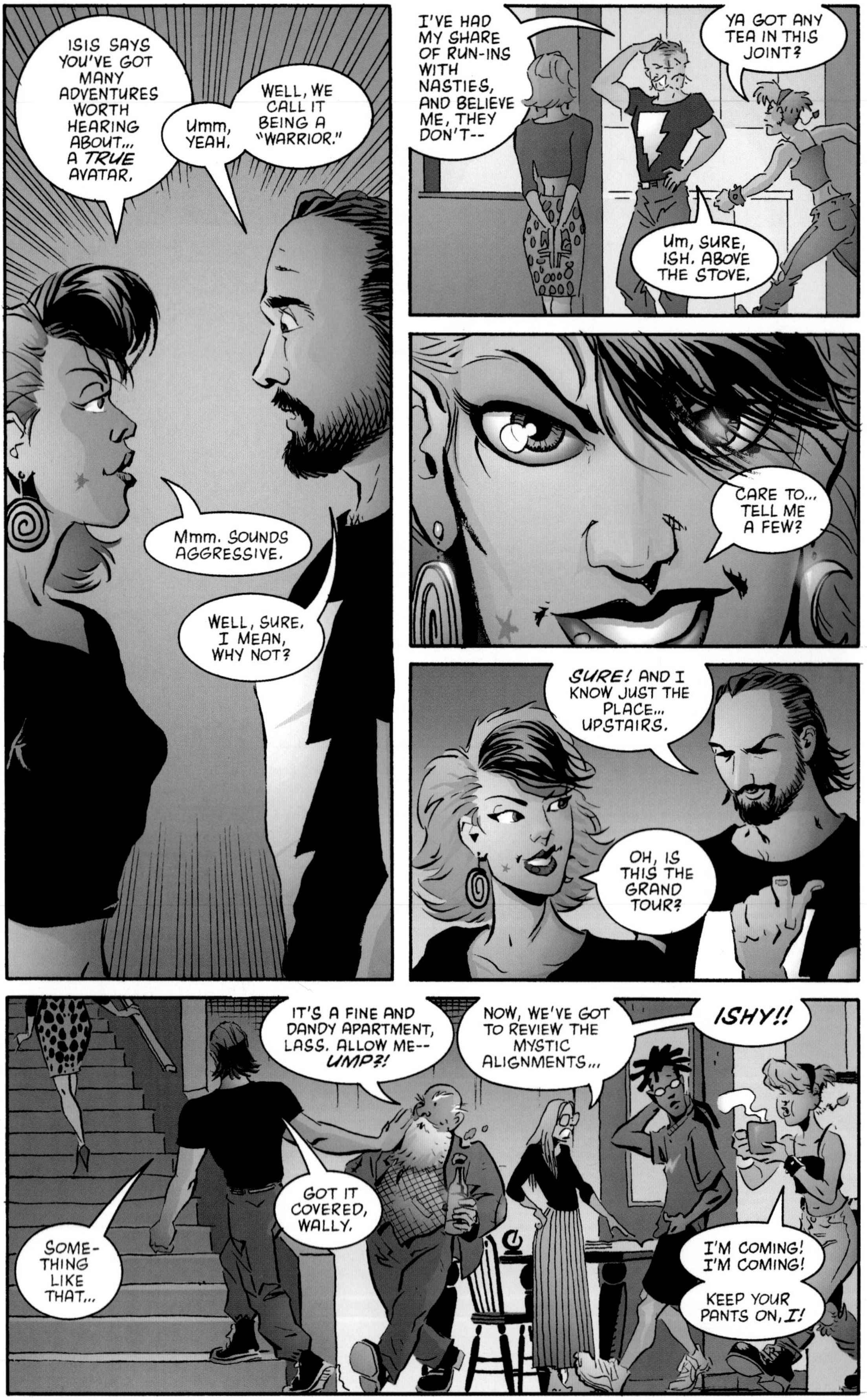
ISIS SAYS YOU'VE GOT MANY ADVENTURES WORTH HEARING ABOUT... A *TRUE* AVATAR.
Umm, YEAH.
WELL, WE CALL IT BEING A "WARRIOR."
Mmm. SOUNDS AGGRESSIVE.
WELL, SURE, I MEAN, WHY NOT?
I'VE HAD MY SHARE OF RUN-INS WITH NASTIES, AND BELIEVE ME, THEY DON'T--
YA GOT ANY TEA IN THIS JOINT?
Um, SURE, ISH. ABOVE THE STOVE.
CARE TO... TELL ME A FEW?
SURE! AND I KNOW JUST THE PLACE... UPSTAIRS.
OH, IS THIS THE GRAND TOUR?
SOME-THING LIKE THAT...
IT'S A FINE AND DANDY APARTMENT, LASS. ALLOW ME-- *UMP?!*
GOT IT COVERED, WALLY.
NOW, WE'VE GOT TO REVIEW THE MYSTIC ALIGNMENTS...
ISHY!!
I'M COMING! I'M COMING!
KEEP YOUR PANTS ON, *I!*

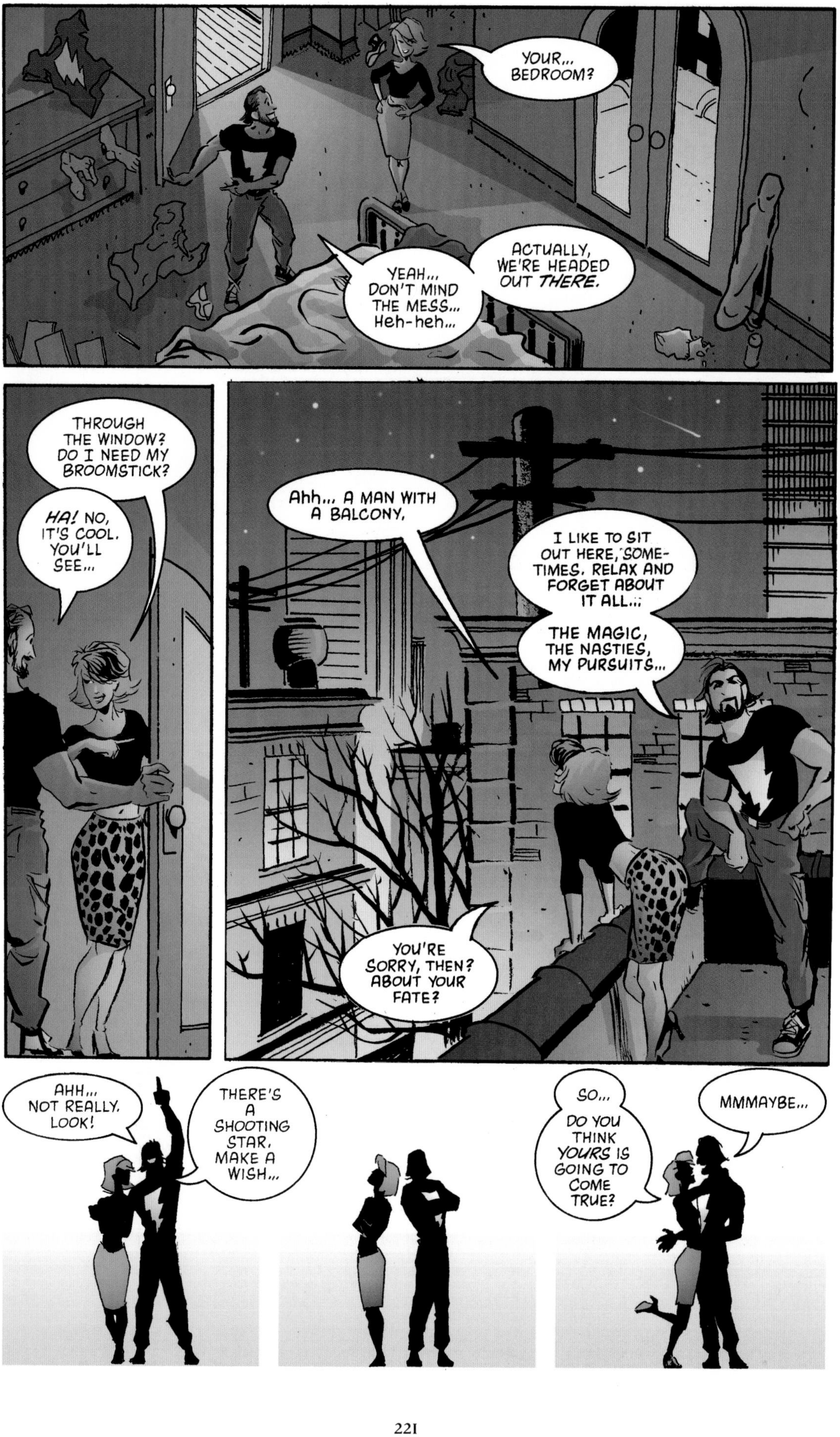
YOUR... BEDROOM?
YEAH... DON'T MIND THE MESS... Heh-heh...
ACTUALLY, WE'RE HEADED OUT *THERE.*
THROUGH THE WINDOW? DO I NEED MY BROOMSTICK?
HA! NO, IT'S COOL. YOU'LL SEE...
Ahh... A MAN WITH A BALCONY.
I LIKE TO SIT OUT HERE, SOME-TIMES. RELAX AND FORGET ABOUT IT ALL...
THE MAGIC, THE NASTIES, MY PURSUITS...
YOU'RE SORRY, THEN? ABOUT YOUR FATE?
AHH... NOT REALLY. LOOK!
THERE'S A SHOOTING STAR. MAKE A WISH...
SO... DO YOU THINK *YOURS* IS GOING TO COME TRUE?
MMMAYBE...

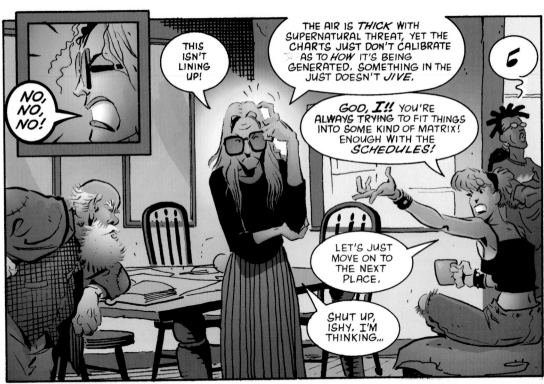

NO, NO, NO!

THIS ISN'T LINING UP!

THE AIR IS *THICK* WITH SUPERNATURAL THREAT, YET THE CHARTS JUST DON'T CALIBRATE AS TO *HOW* IT'S BEING GENERATED. SOMETHING IN THE JUST DOESN'T *JIVE.*

6

GOD, *I!!* YOU'RE ALWAYS TRYING TO FIT THINGS INTO SOME KIND OF MATRIX! ENOUGH WITH THE *SCHEDULES!*

LET'S JUST MOVE ON TO THE NEXT PLACE.

SHUT UP, ISHY. I'M THINKING...

SO, ISH...

WHAT'S IT LIKE, BEING PART OF A COVEN? ANY FUNNY "SPELLS-GONE-BAD" STORIES?

Heh-*HA!*

Mmm...?

I'LL GIVE YOU A "SPELL-GONE-BAD"! THERE WAS THIS GUY WHO CAME TO ME LOOKING FOR A LOVE POTION. TOLD ME IT WAS FOR HIM AND HIS WIFE... THAT THEY JUST WEREN'T *INTO* THEIR MARRIAGE ANYMORE.

TURNS OUT, HE USED IT TO *STEAL* HIS *BROTHER'S* WIFE!

I FIXED *HIS* ASS! SLIPPED ANOTHER POTION INTO HIS COFFEE THAT MADE HIM FALL IN LOVE WITH A GOAT!

SERVES HIM RIGHT.

DICKHEAD!

AND BEING IN A COVEN'S FINE, SISTERS ARE SISTERS.

YOUR NAME'S JOE, RIGHT?

MISS HUNTER! I'D LIKE A WORD WITH YOU, IF I MAY, IT'S ABOUT YOUR TERRIBLY *ERRONEOUS* CHARTS!

Eh?

KEEP AWAY FROM ME, YOU OLD QUACK! I'M BUSY.

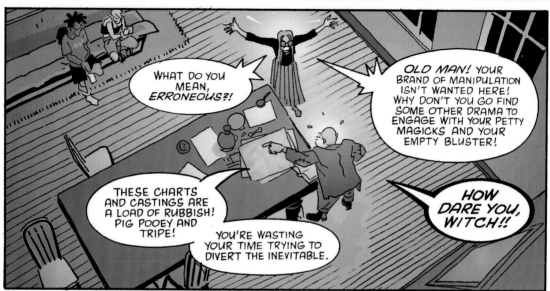

WHAT DO YOU MEAN, *ERRONEOUS?!*

OLD MAN! YOUR BRAND OF MANIPULATION ISN'T WANTED HERE! WHY DON'T YOU GO FIND SOME OTHER DRAMA TO ENGAGE WITH YOUR PETTY MAGICKS AND YOUR EMPTY BLUSTER!

THESE CHARTS AND CASTINGS ARE A LOAD OF RUBBISH! PIG POOEY AND TRIPE!

YOU'RE WASTING YOUR TIME TRYING TO DIVERT THE INEVITABLE.

HOW *DARE YOU,* WITCH!!

MY POWER IS UNTOLD! MY MASTERY IS SUPREME!! I OUGHTTA--

YER'A FRAUD, YOU STUPID OLD GIT! I'VE HALF A MIND TO--

≥Sigh≤

WHY AM I ARGUING WITH *YOU?* THERE'S TOO DAMN MUCH TO DO...

MARK MY WORDS, HAG! THIS IS NO MERE SCHEDULE OF ILLUSIONS!

A CONFRONTATION IS COMING THAT WILL TEST THE FOXFIRE'S METTLE--

SPEAKING OF WHICH...

WHERE *ARE* THOSE TWO?

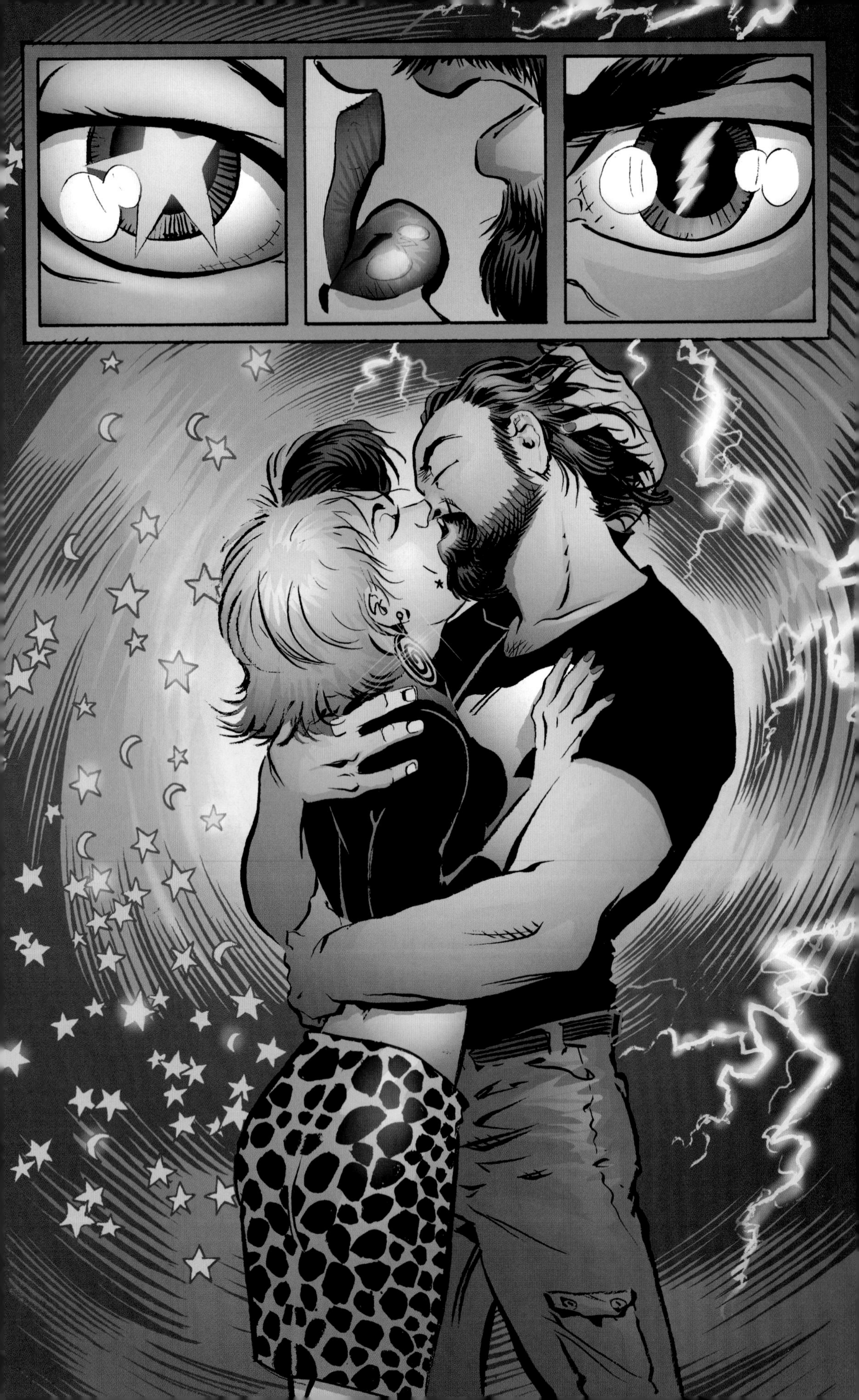

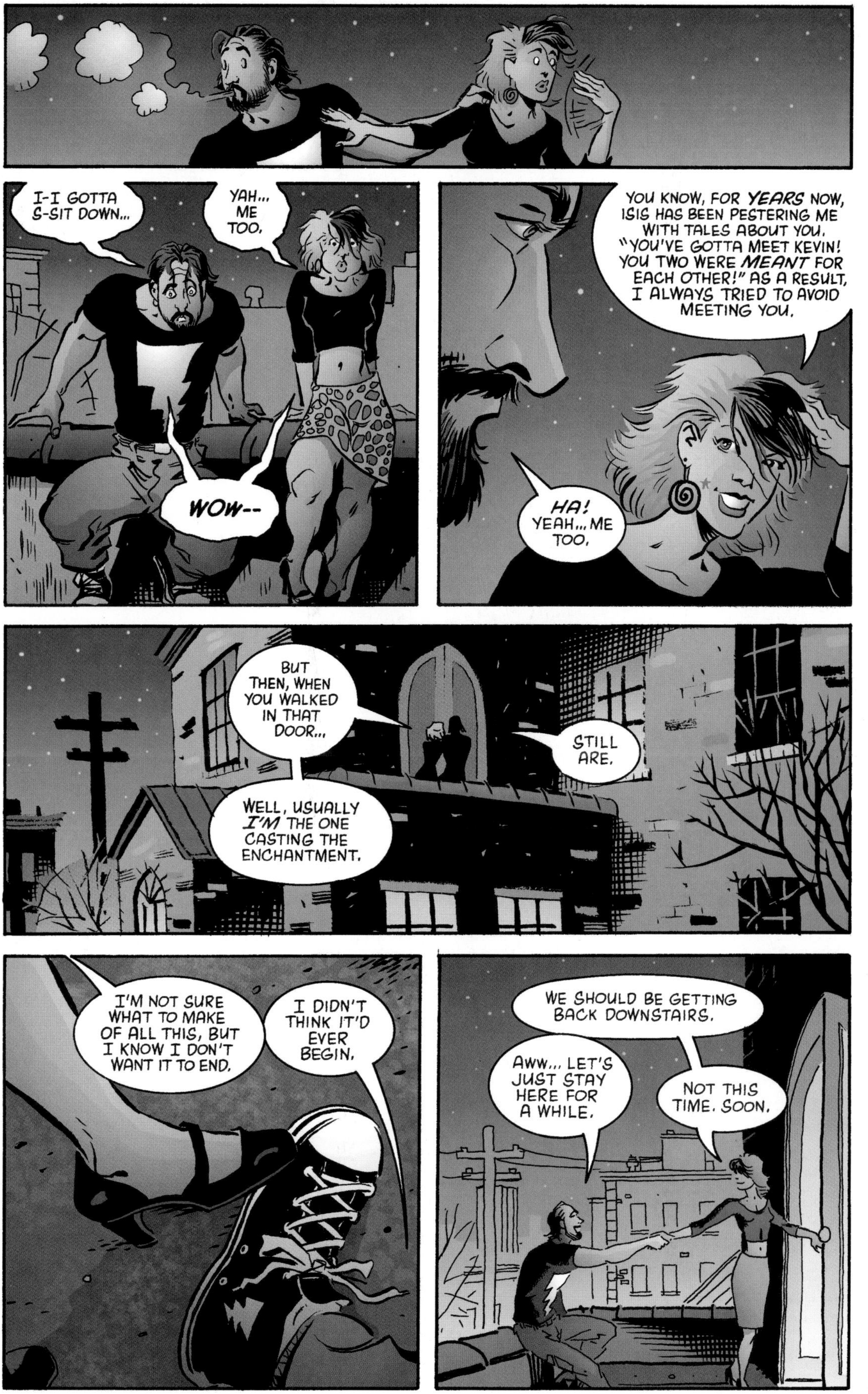
I-I GOTTA S-SIT DOWN...
YAH... ME TOO.
WOW--
YOU KNOW, FOR YEARS NOW, ISIS HAS BEEN PESTERING ME WITH TALES ABOUT YOU. "YOU'VE GOTTA MEET KEVIN! YOU TWO WERE MEANT FOR EACH OTHER!" AS A RESULT, I ALWAYS TRIED TO AVOID MEETING YOU.
HA! YEAH... ME TOO.
BUT THEN, WHEN YOU WALKED IN THAT DOOR...
WELL, USUALLY I'M THE ONE CASTING THE ENCHANTMENT.
STILL ARE.
I'M NOT SURE WHAT TO MAKE OF ALL THIS, BUT I KNOW I DON'T WANT IT TO END.
I DIDN'T THINK IT'D EVER BEGIN.
WE SHOULD BE GETTING BACK DOWNSTAIRS.
AWW... LET'S JUST STAY HERE FOR A WHILE.
NOT THIS TIME. SOON.

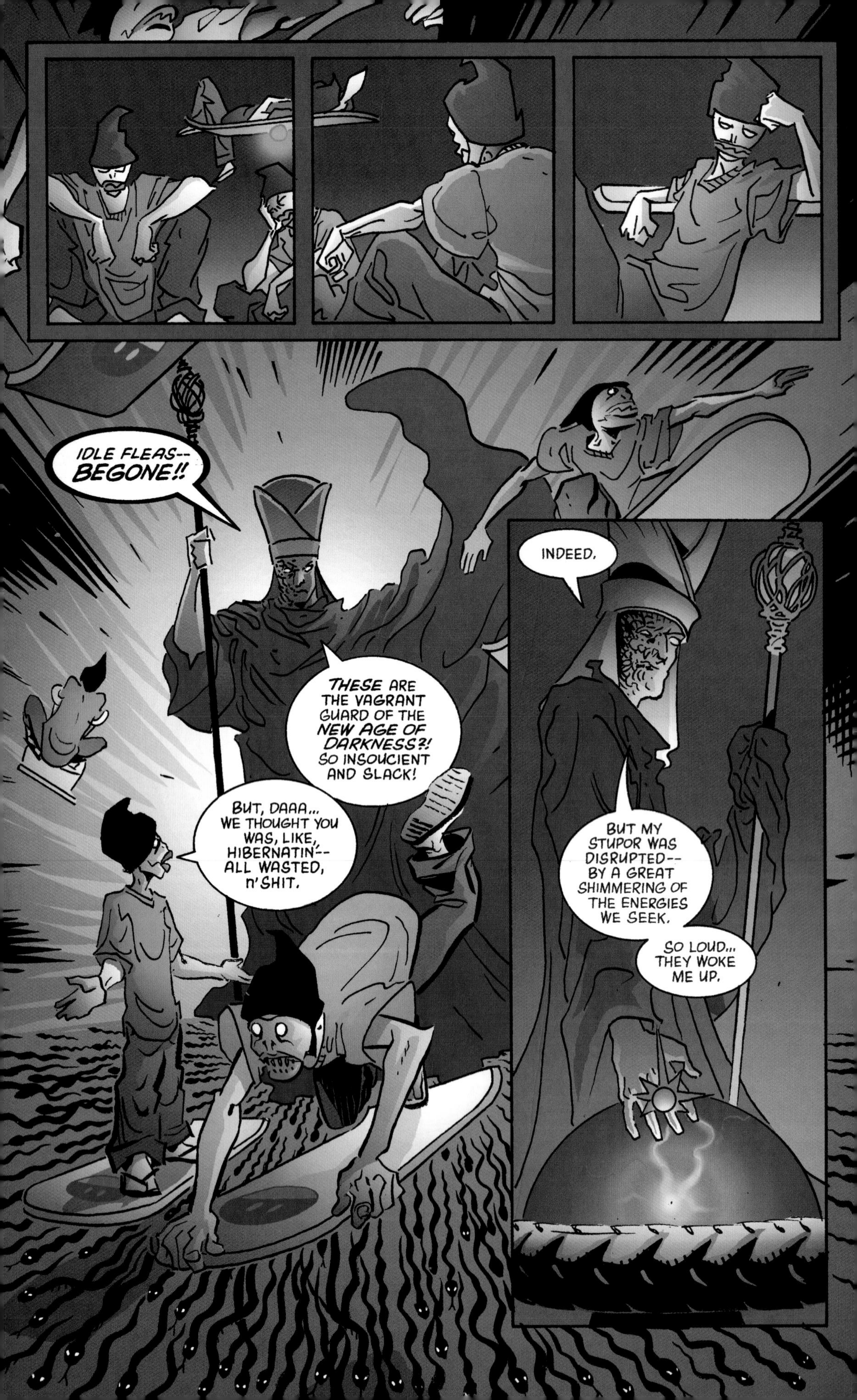
IDLE FLEAS-- BEGONE!!
THESE ARE THE VAGRANT GUARD OF THE NEW AGE OF DARKNESS?! SO INSOUCIENT AND SLACK!
BUT, DAAA... WE THOUGHT YOU WAS, LIKE, HIBERNATIN'-- ALL WASTED, N'SHIT.
INDEED.
BUT MY STUPOR WAS DISRUPTED-- BY A GREAT SHIMMERING OF THE ENERGIES WE SEEK.
SO LOUD... THEY WOKE ME UP.

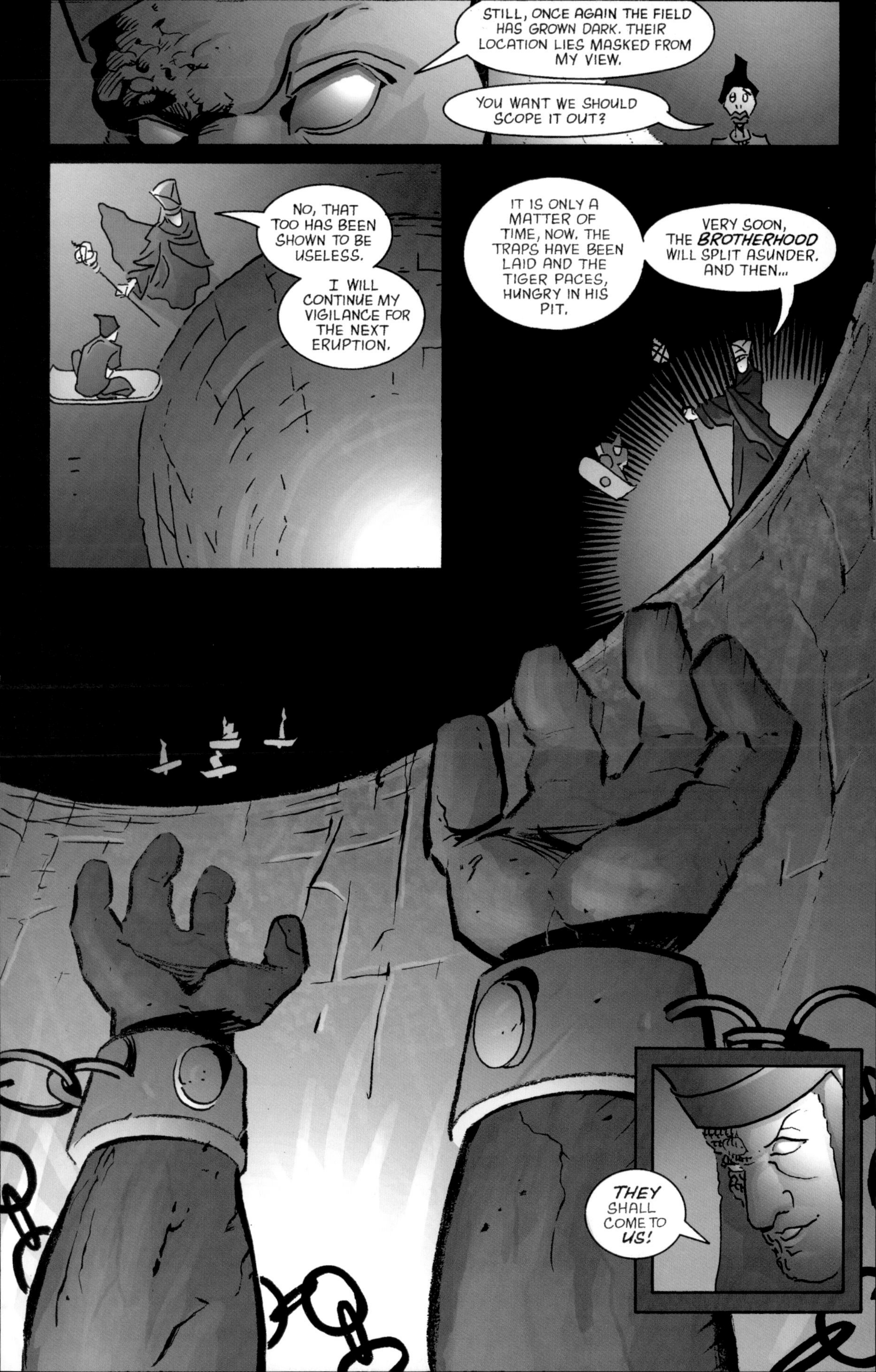
STILL, ONCE AGAIN THE FIELD HAS GROWN DARK. THEIR LOCATION LIES MASKED FROM MY VIEW.
YOU WANT WE SHOULD SCOPE IT OUT?
NO, THAT TOO HAS BEEN SHOWN TO BE USELESS.
I WILL CONTINUE MY VIGILANCE FOR THE NEXT ERUPTION.
IT IS ONLY A MATTER OF TIME, NOW. THE TRAPS HAVE BEEN LAID AND THE TIGER PACES, HUNGRY IN HIS PIT.
VERY SOON, THE BROTHERHOOD WILL SPLIT ASUNDER. AND THEN...
THEY SHALL COME TO US!

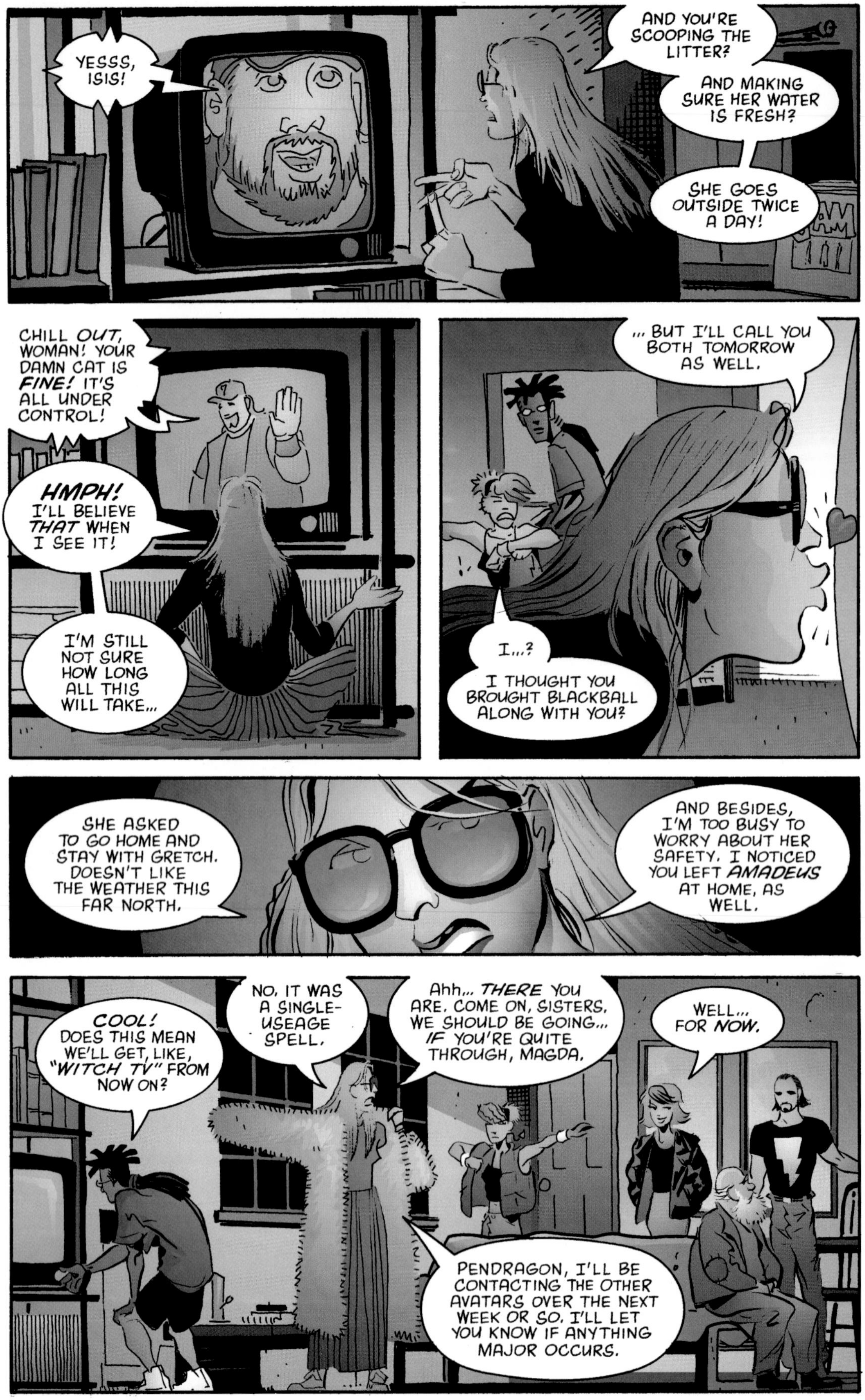
YESSS, ISIS!
AND YOU'RE SCOOPING THE LITTER?
AND MAKING SURE HER WATER IS FRESH?
SHE GOES OUTSIDE TWICE A DAY!
CHILL OUT, WOMAN! YOUR DAMN CAT IS FINE! IT'S ALL UNDER CONTROL!
HMPH! I'LL BELIEVE THAT WHEN I SEE IT!
I'M STILL NOT SURE HOW LONG ALL THIS WILL TAKE...
... BUT I'LL CALL YOU BOTH TOMORROW AS WELL.
I...?
I THOUGHT YOU BROUGHT BLACKBALL ALONG WITH YOU?
SHE ASKED TO GO HOME AND STAY WITH GRETCH. DOESN'T LIKE THE WEATHER THIS FAR NORTH.
AND BESIDES, I'M TOO BUSY TO WORRY ABOUT HER SAFETY. I NOTICED YOU LEFT AMADEUS AT HOME, AS WELL.
COOL! DOES THIS MEAN WE'LL GET, LIKE, "WITCH TV" FROM NOW ON?
NO, IT WAS A SINGLE-USEAGE SPELL.
Ahh... THERE YOU ARE. COME ON, SISTERS, WE SHOULD BE GOING... IF YOU'RE QUITE THROUGH, MAGDA.
WELL... FOR NOW.
PENDRAGON, I'LL BE CONTACTING THE OTHER AVATARS OVER THE NEXT WEEK OR SO. I'LL LET YOU KNOW IF ANYTHING MAJOR OCCURS.

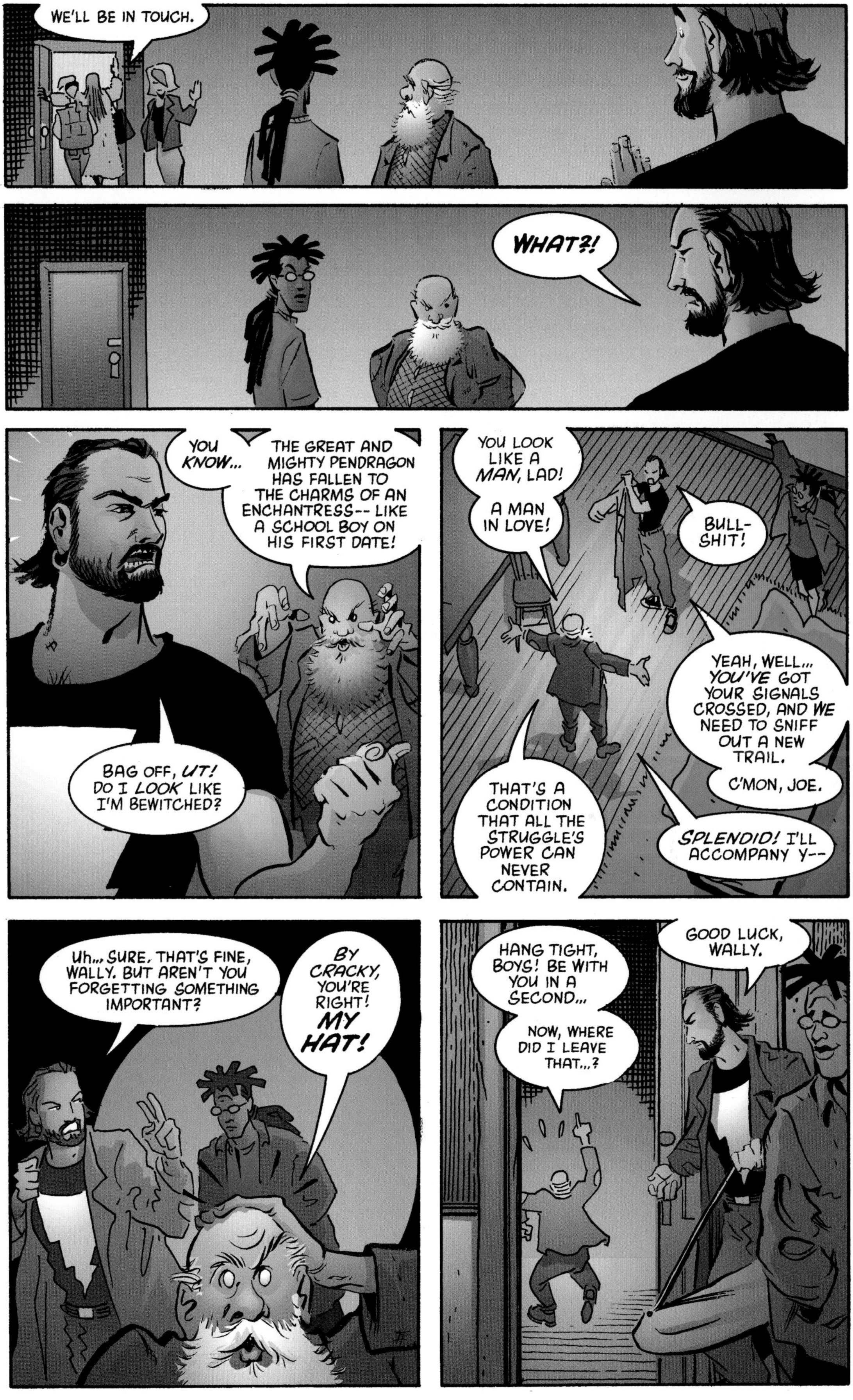
WE'LL BE IN TOUCH.
WHAT?!
YOU KNOW...
THE GREAT AND MIGHTY PENDRAGON HAS FALLEN TO THE CHARMS OF AN ENCHANTRESS-- LIKE A SCHOOL BOY ON HIS FIRST DATE!
BAG OFF, UT! DO I LOOK LIKE I'M BEWITCHED?
YOU LOOK LIKE A MAN, LAD!
A MAN IN LOVE!
BULL-SHIT!
YEAH, WELL... YOU'VE GOT YOUR SIGNALS CROSSED, AND WE NEED TO SNIFF OUT A NEW TRAIL.
C'MON, JOE.
THAT'S A CONDITION THAT ALL THE STRUGGLE'S POWER CAN NEVER CONTAIN.
SPLENDID! I'LL ACCOMPANY Y--
Uh... SURE. THAT'S FINE, WALLY. BUT AREN'T YOU FORGETTING SOMETHING IMPORTANT?
BY CRACKY, YOU'RE RIGHT! MY HAT!
HANG TIGHT, BOYS! BE WITH YOU IN A SECOND...
NOW, WHERE DID I LEAVE THAT...?
GOOD LUCK, WALLY.

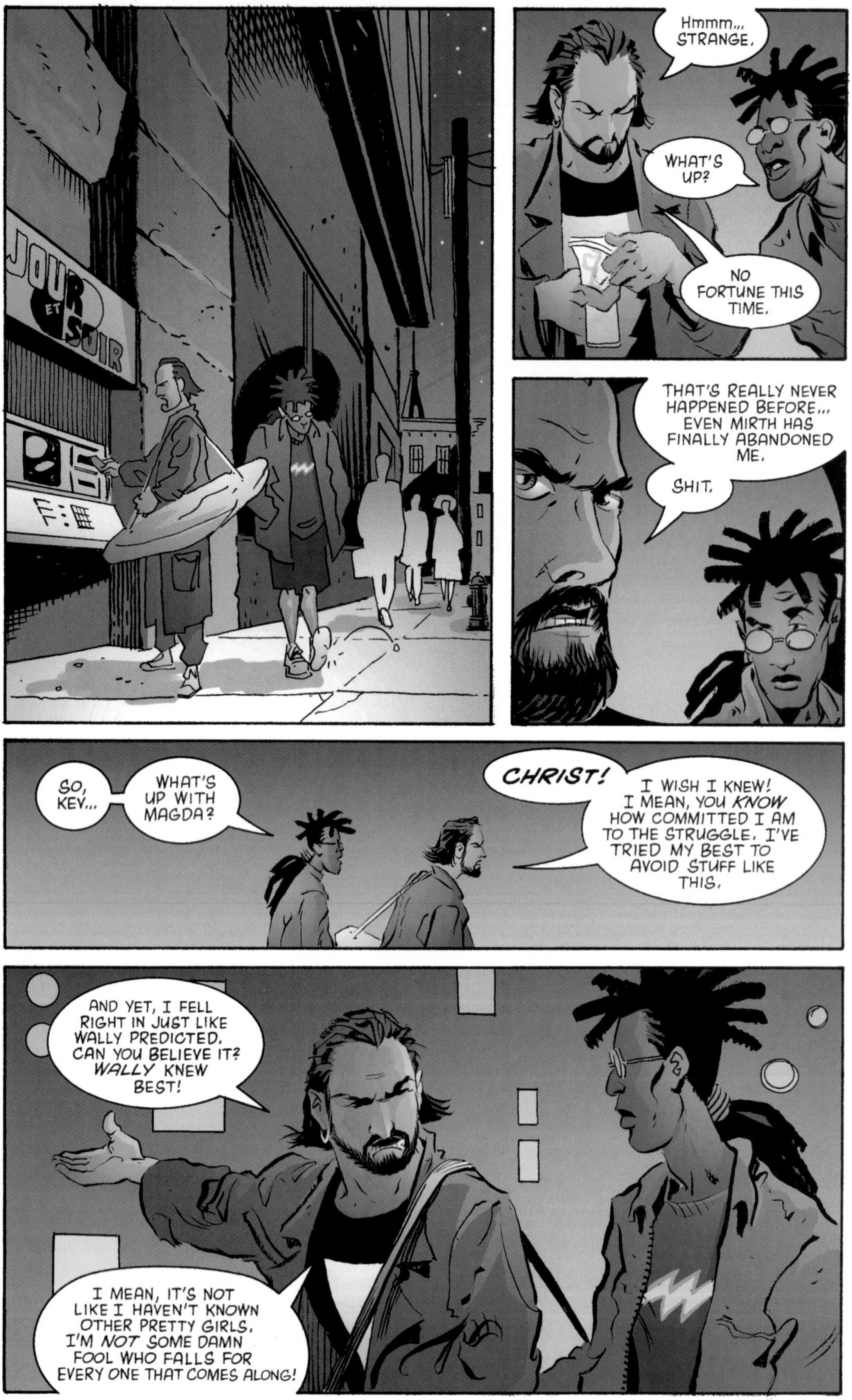
JOUR ET SOIR
Hmmm... STRANGE.
WHAT'S UP?
NO FORTUNE THIS TIME.
THAT'S REALLY NEVER HAPPENED BEFORE... EVEN MIRTH HAS FINALLY ABANDONED ME.
SHIT.
SO, KEV...
WHAT'S UP WITH MAGDA?
CHRIST!
I WISH I KNEW! I MEAN, YOU *KNOW* HOW COMMITTED I AM TO THE STRUGGLE. I'VE TRIED MY BEST TO AVOID STUFF LIKE THIS.
AND YET, I FELL RIGHT IN JUST LIKE WALLY PREDICTED. CAN YOU BELIEVE IT? *WALLY* KNEW BEST!
I MEAN, IT'S NOT LIKE I HAVEN'T KNOWN OTHER PRETTY GIRLS. I'M *NOT* SOME DAMN FOOL WHO FALLS FOR EVERY ONE THAT COMES ALONG!

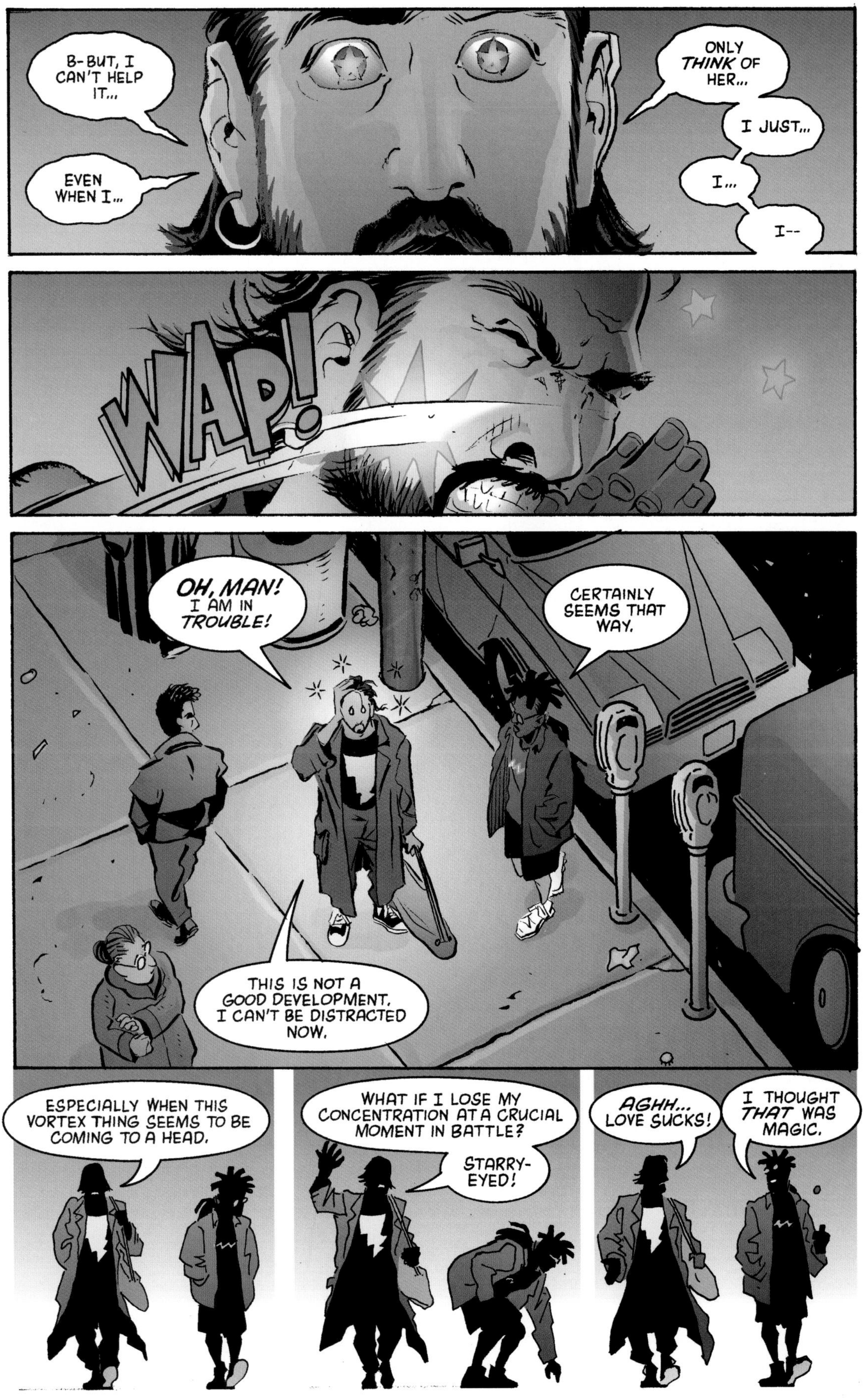
B-BUT, I CAN'T HELP IT...
EVEN WHEN I...
ONLY *THINK* OF HER...
I JUST...
I...
I--
WAP!
OH, MAN! I AM IN *TROUBLE!*
CERTAINLY SEEMS THAT WAY.
THIS IS NOT A GOOD DEVELOPMENT. I CAN'T BE DISTRACTED NOW.
ESPECIALLY WHEN THIS VORTEX THING SEEMS TO BE COMING TO A HEAD.
WHAT IF I LOSE MY CONCENTRATION AT A CRUCIAL MOMENT IN BATTLE?
STARRY-EYED!
AGHH... LOVE SUCKS!
I THOUGHT *THAT* WAS MAGIC.

ALRIGHT, LET'S GET BACK TO THE "REAL" WORLD.

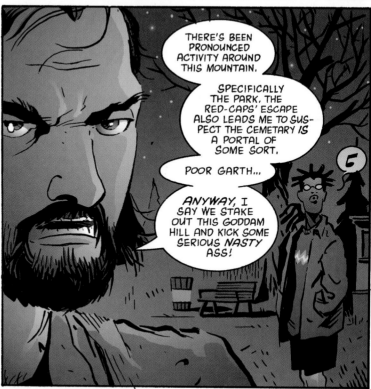

THERE'S BEEN PRONOUNCED ACTIVITY AROUND THIS MOUNTAIN.

SPECIFICALLY THE PARK, THE RED-CAPS' ESCAPE ALSO LEADS ME TO SUS-PECT THE CEMETARY *IS* A PORTAL OF SOME SORT.

POOR GARTH...

ANYWAY, I SAY WE STAKE OUT THIS GODDAM HILL AND KICK SOME SERIOUS *NASTY ASS!*

MAN, I *NEED* THIS!

232

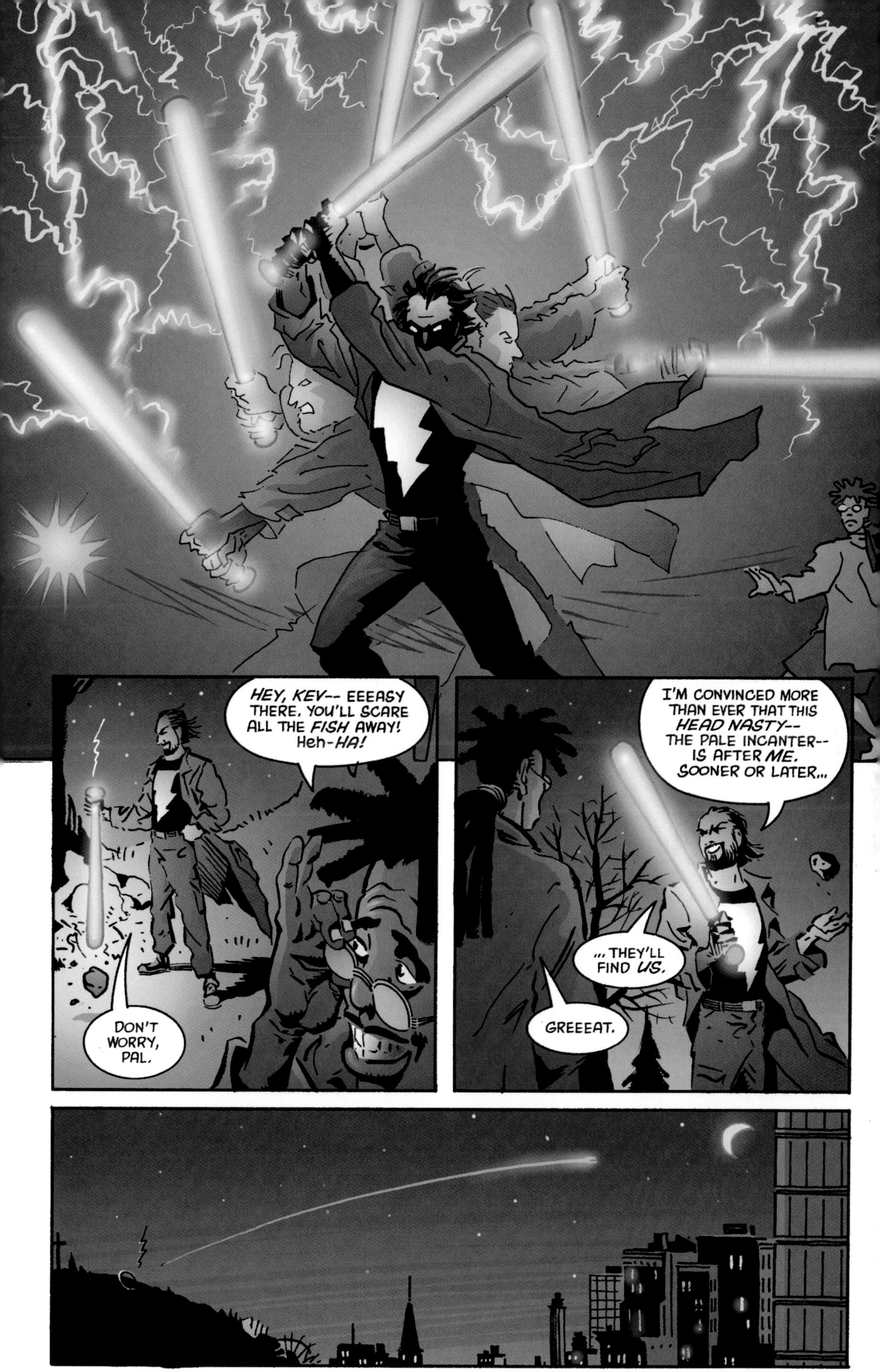
HEY, KEV-- EEEASY THERE. YOU'LL SCARE ALL THE FISH AWAY! Heh-HA!
DON'T WORRY, PAL.
I'M CONVINCED MORE THAN EVER THAT THIS HEAD NASTY-- THE PALE INCANTER-- IS AFTER ME. SOONER OR LATER...
...THEY'LL FIND US.
GREEEAT.

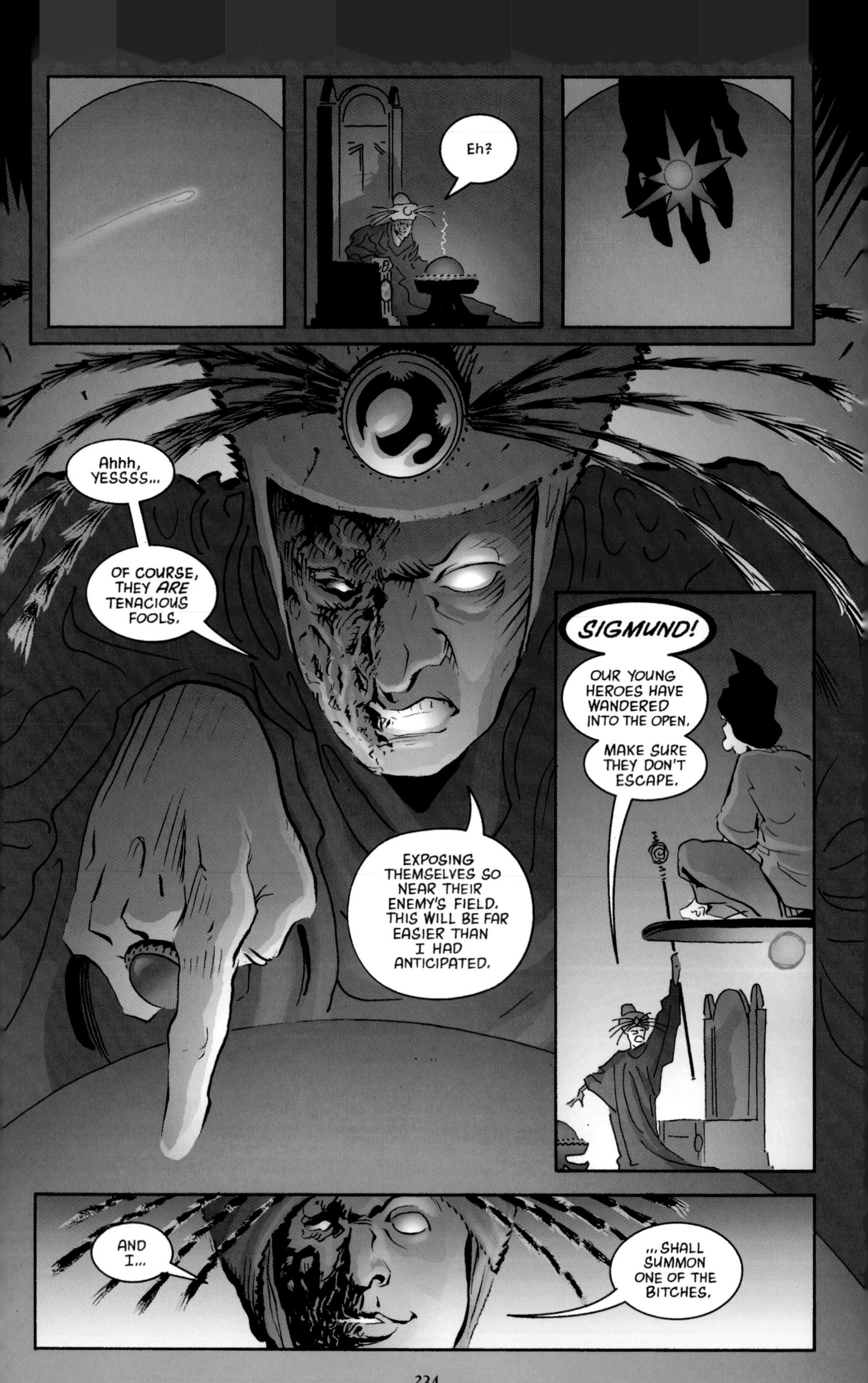
Eh?
Ahhh, YESSSS...
OF COURSE, THEY ARE TENACIOUS FOOLS.
EXPOSING THEMSELVES SO NEAR THEIR ENEMY'S FIELD. THIS WILL BE FAR EASIER THAN I HAD ANTICIPATED.
SIGMUND!
OUR YOUNG HEROES HAVE WANDERED INTO THE OPEN.
MAKE SURE THEY DON'T ESCAPE.
AND I...
...SHALL SUMMON ONE OF THE BITCHES.

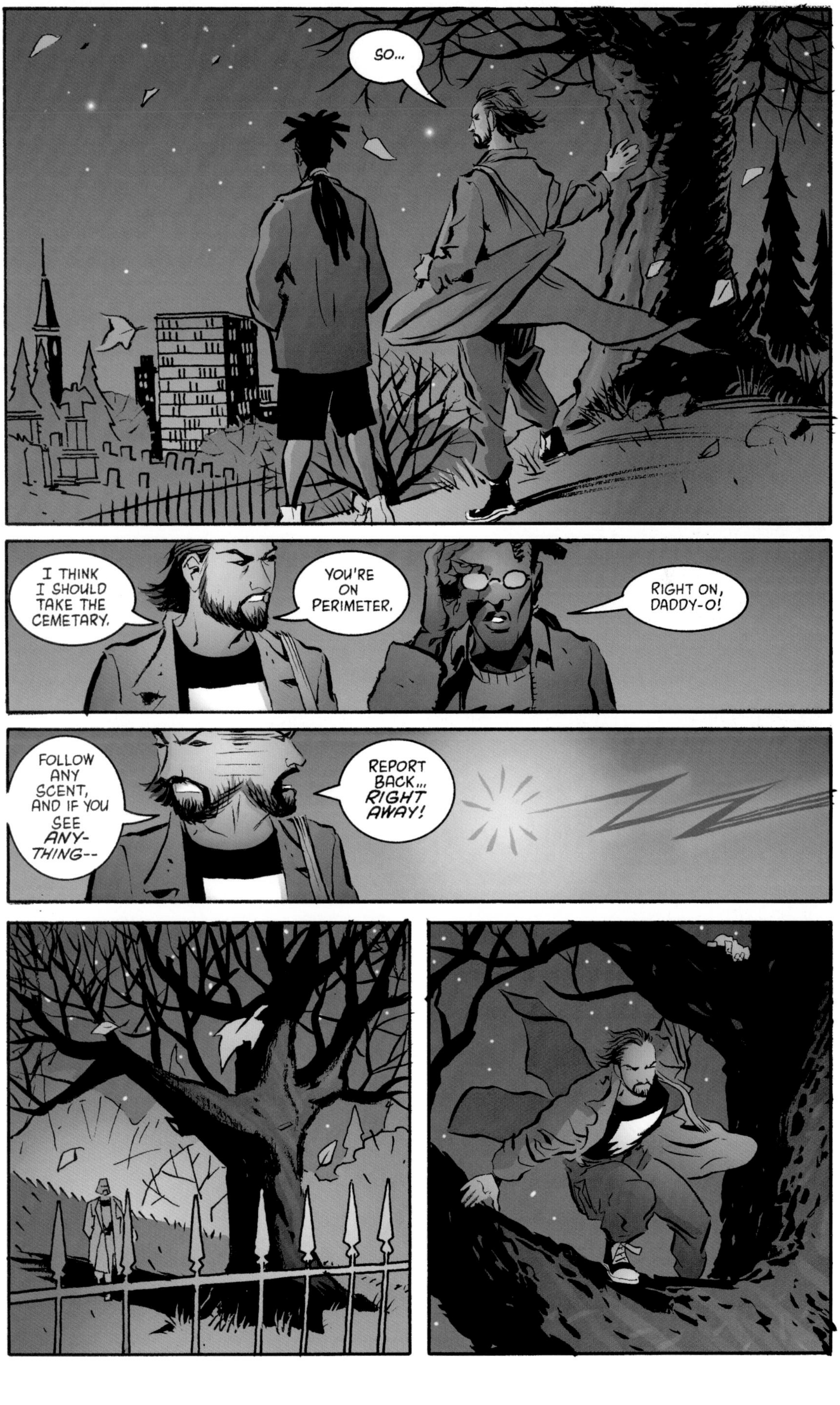
SO...
I THINK I SHOULD TAKE THE CEMETARY.
YOU'RE ON PERIMETER.
RIGHT ON, DADDY-O!
FOLLOW ANY SCENT, AND IF YOU SEE *ANY-THING--*
REPORT BACK... *RIGHT AWAY!*

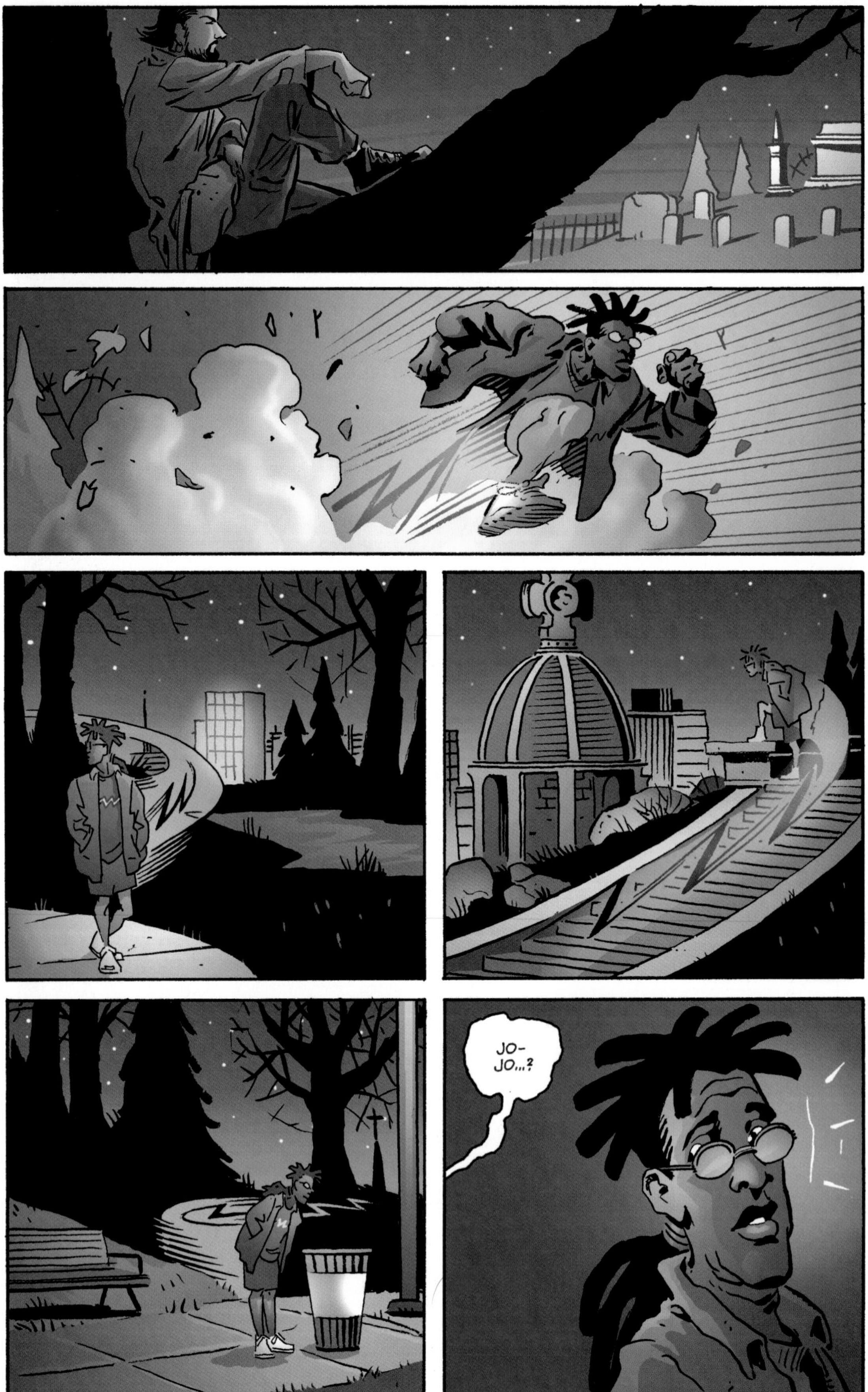
JO-
JO...?

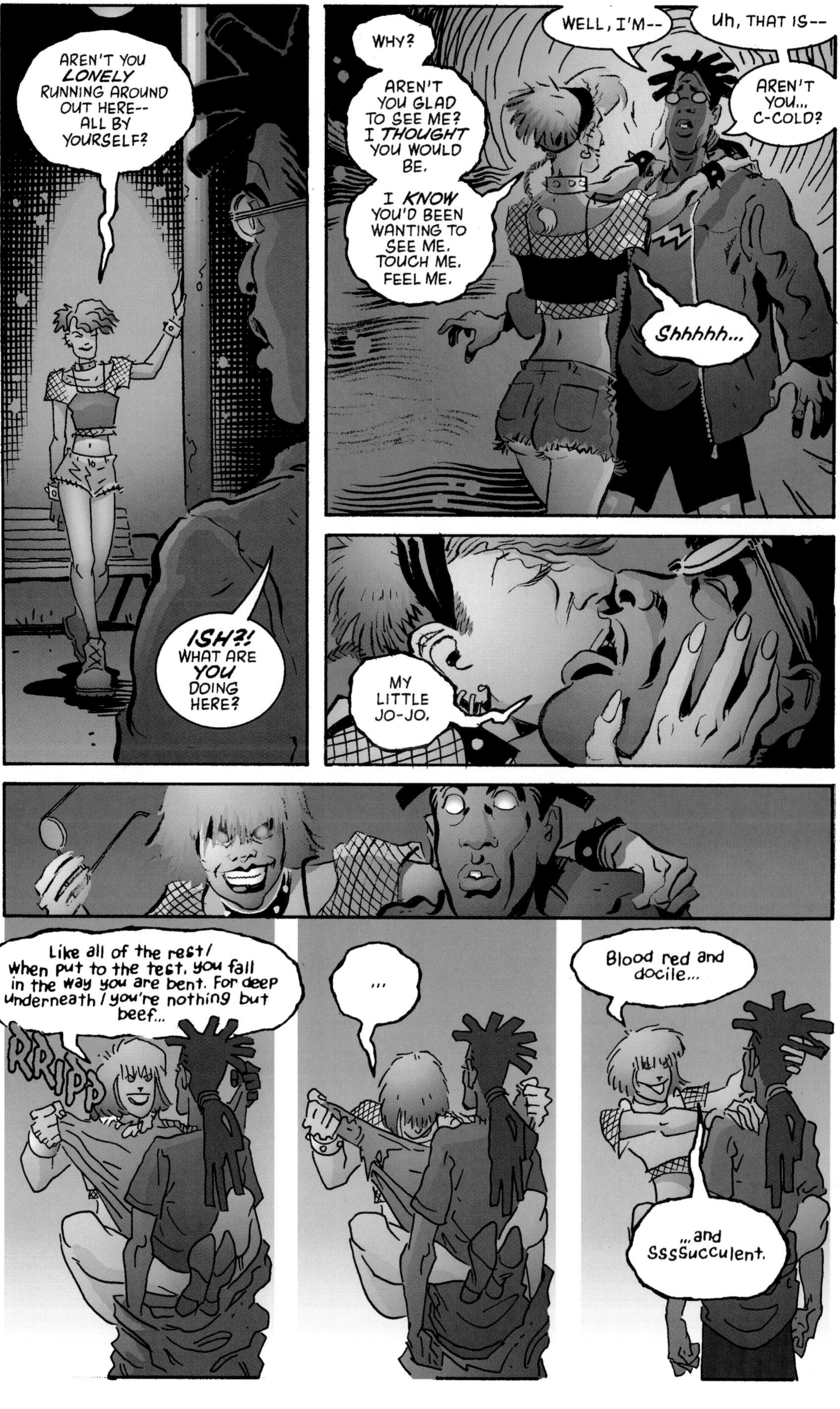

AREN'T YOU LONELY RUNNING AROUND OUT HERE-- ALL BY YOURSELF?
ISH?! WHAT ARE YOU DOING HERE?
WHY?
AREN'T YOU GLAD TO SEE ME? I THOUGHT YOU WOULD BE.
I KNOW YOU'D BEEN WANTING TO SEE ME. TOUCH ME. FEEL ME.
WELL, I'M--
Uh, THAT IS--
AREN'T YOU... C-COLD?
Shhhhh...
MY LITTLE JO-JO.
Like all of the rest/ when put to the test, you fall in the way you are bent. For deep underneath / you're nothing but beef...
RRIPP
...
Blood red and docile...
...and SssSucculent.

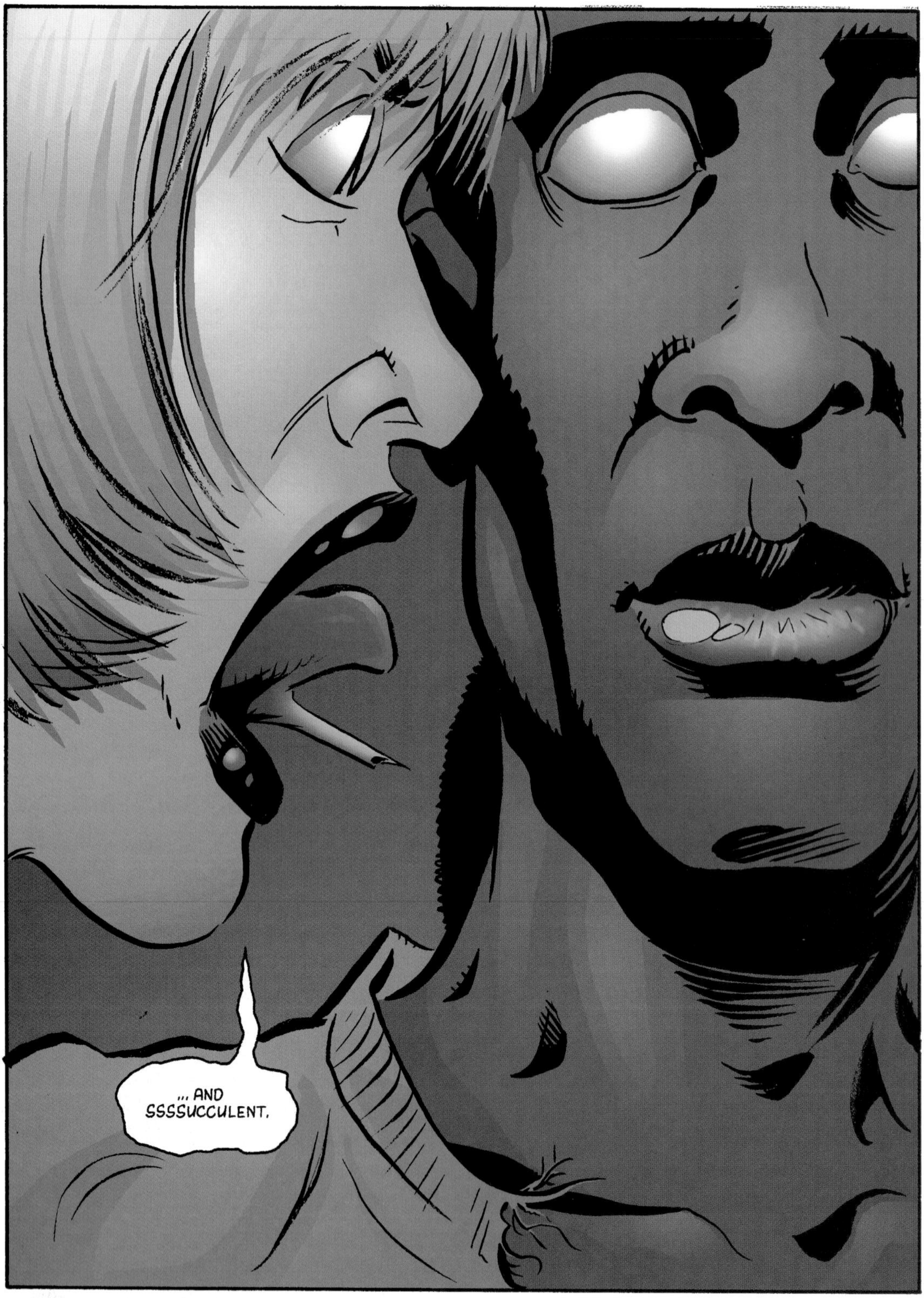
... AND SSSSUCCULENT.

THE HERO DEFINED

MAGE®

chapter 10

"Foul is Fair"

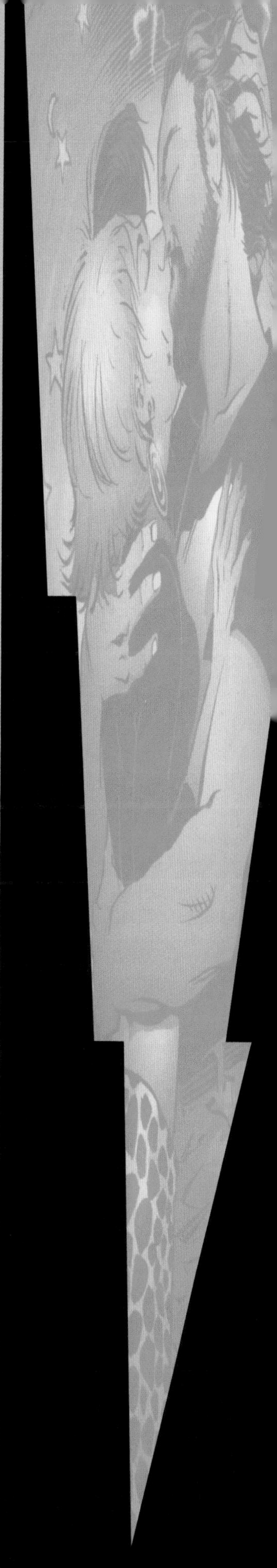

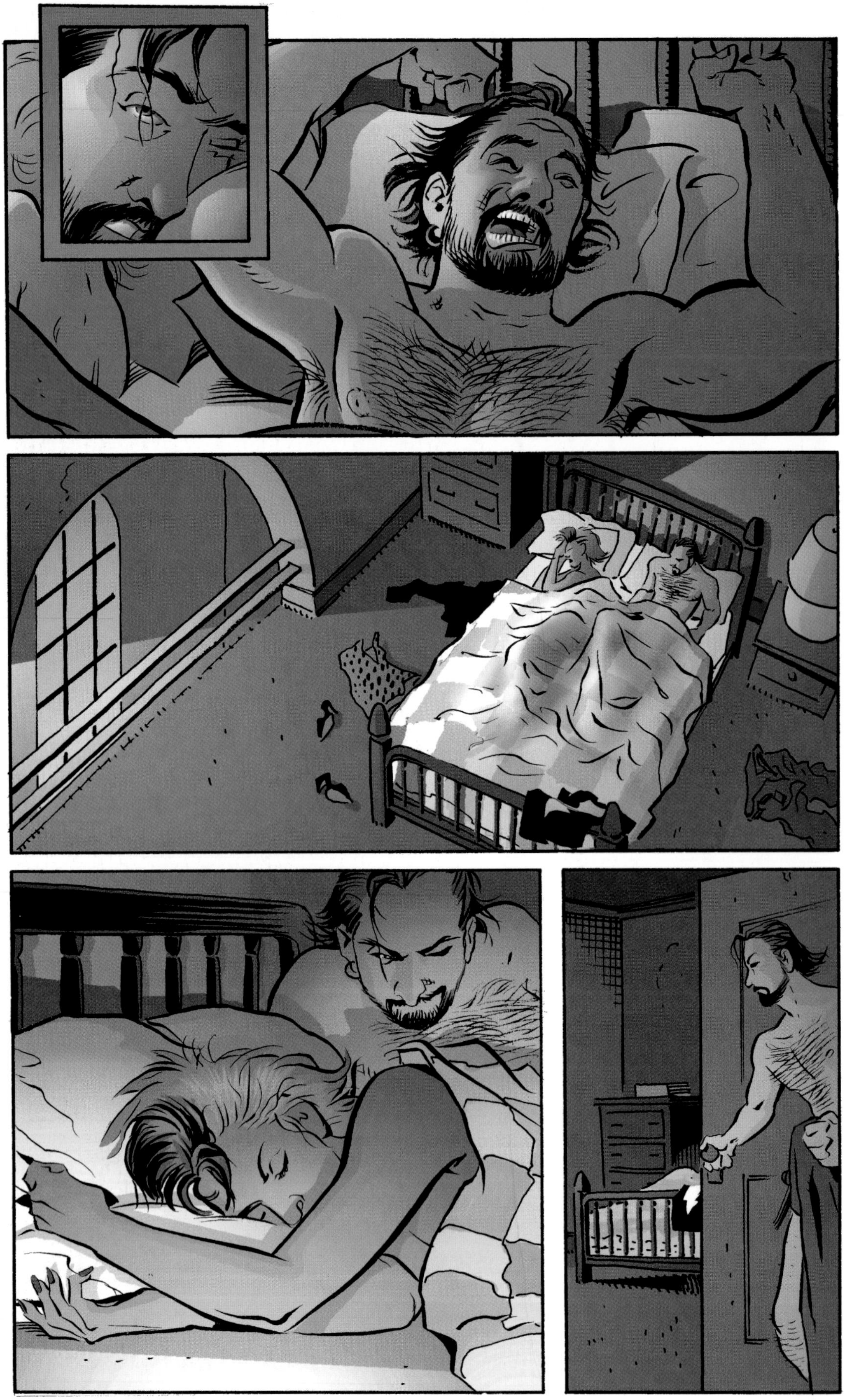

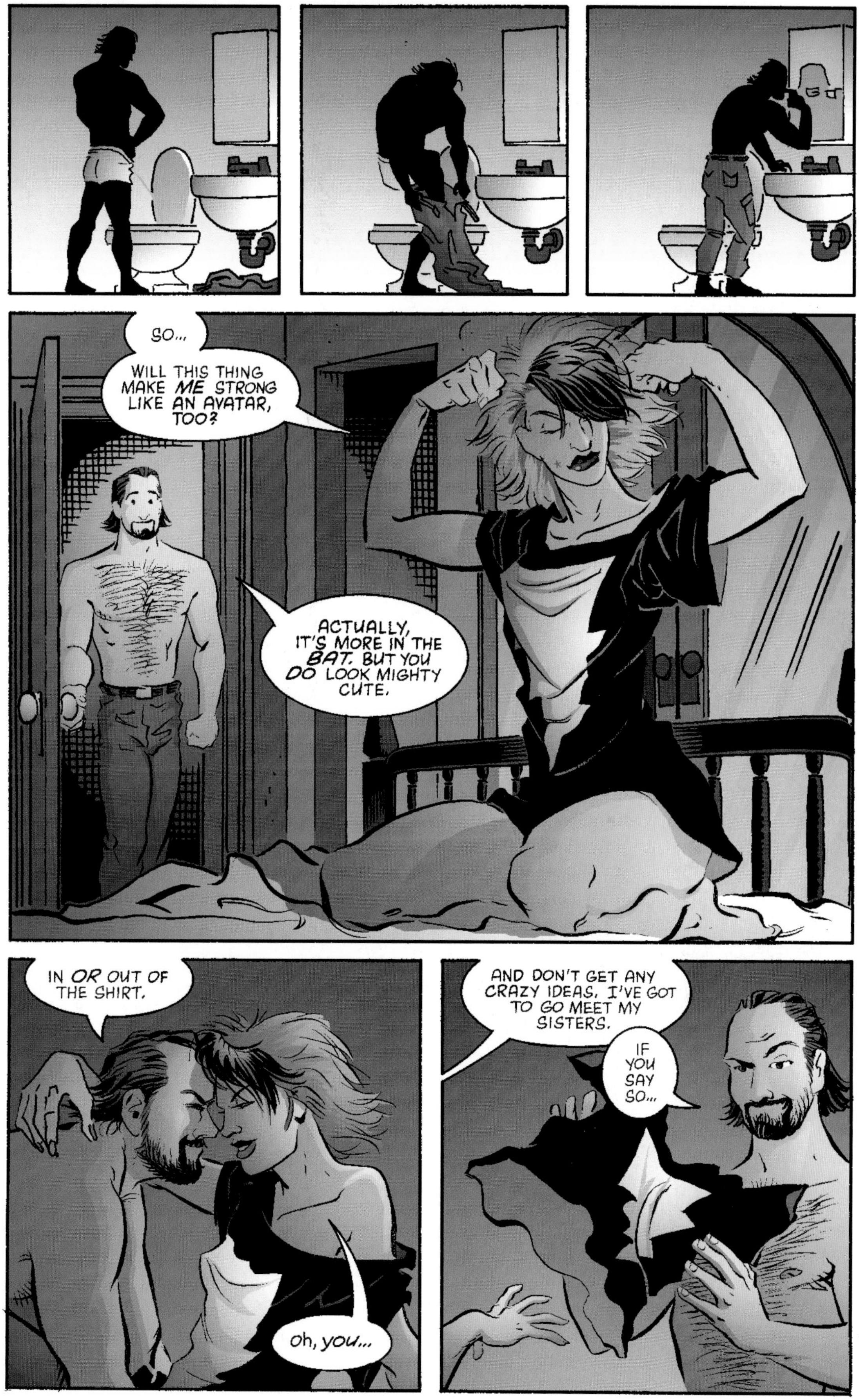
SO...
WILL THIS THING MAKE ME STRONG LIKE AN AVATAR, TOO?
ACTUALLY, IT'S MORE IN THE BAT. BUT YOU DO LOOK MIGHTY CUTE.
IN OR OUT OF THE SHIRT.
oh, you...
AND DON'T GET ANY CRAZY IDEAS. I'VE GOT TO GO MEET MY SISTERS.
IF YOU SAY SO...

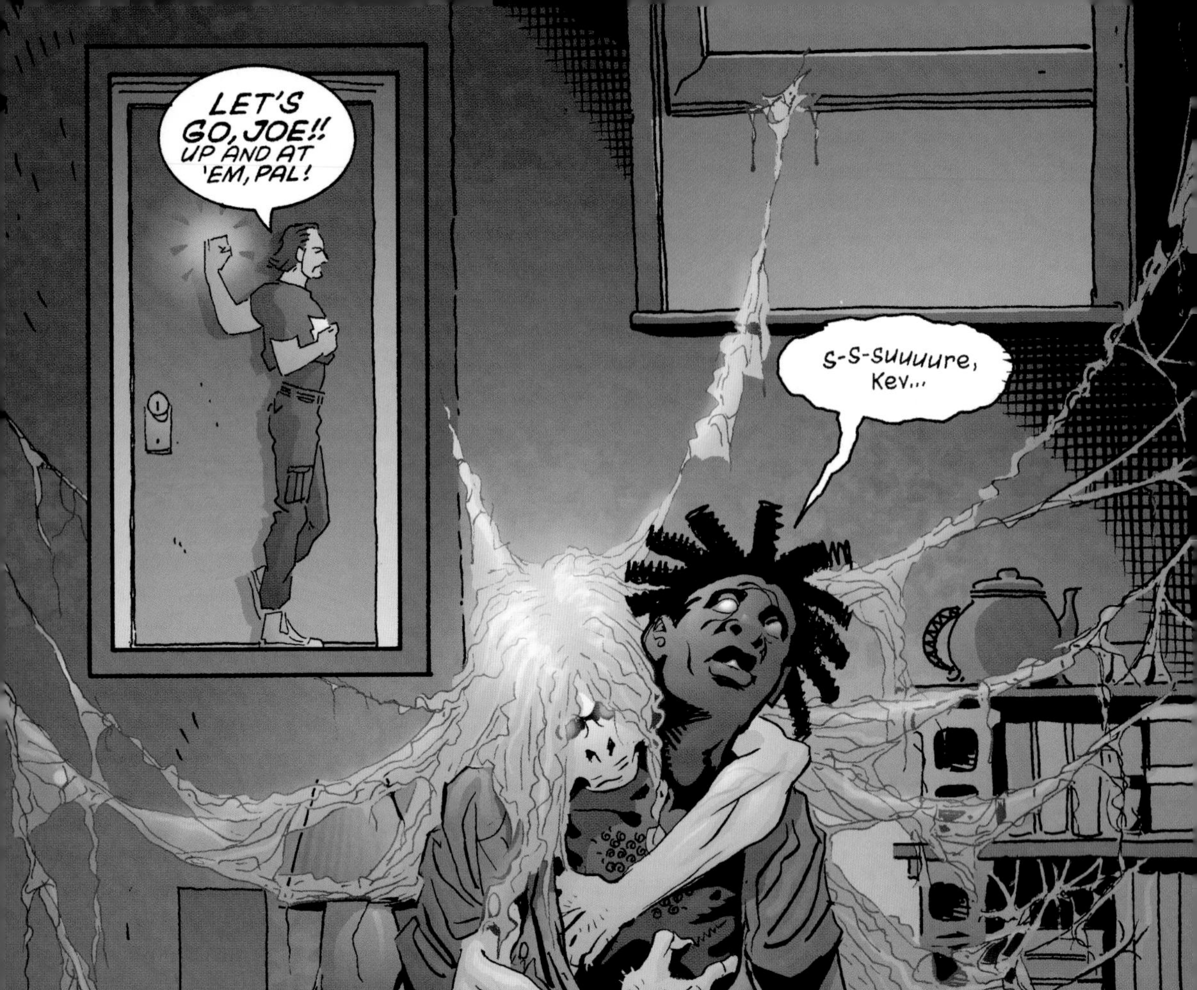
LET'S GO, JOE!! UP AND AT 'EM, PAL!
S-S-SUUUURE, KEV...
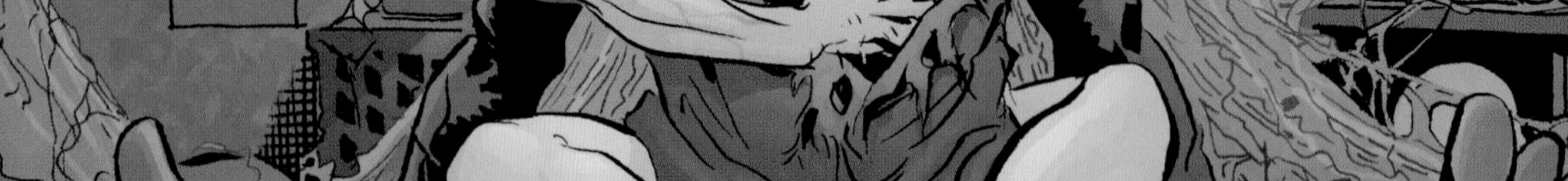
Whatever you saayyyyyyy...

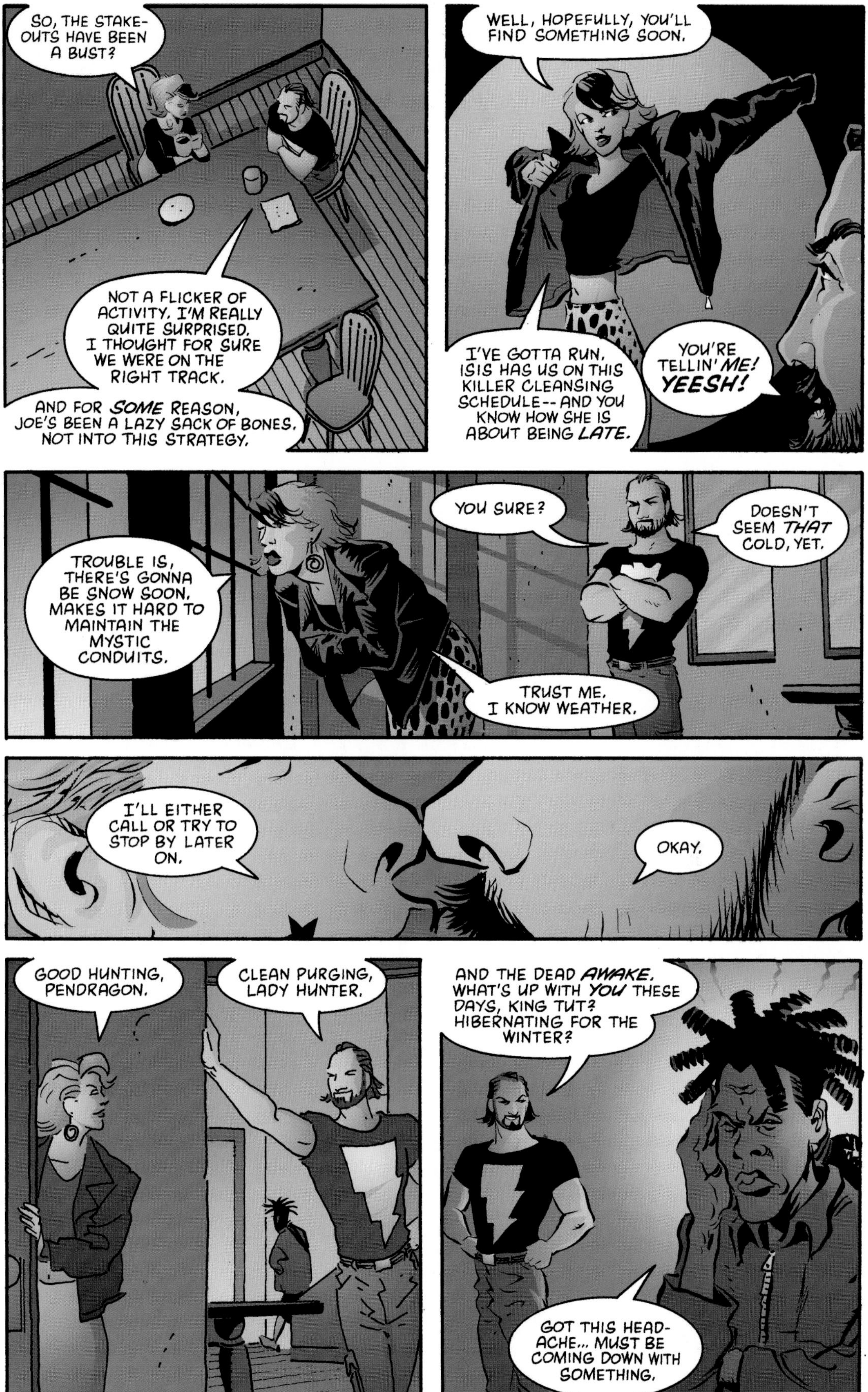
SO, THE STAKE-OUTS HAVE BEEN A BUST?
NOT A FLICKER OF ACTIVITY. I'M REALLY QUITE SURPRISED. I THOUGHT FOR SURE WE WERE ON THE RIGHT TRACK.
AND FOR SOME REASON, JOE'S BEEN A LAZY SACK OF BONES. NOT INTO THIS STRATEGY.
WELL, HOPEFULLY, YOU'LL FIND SOMETHING SOON.
I'VE GOTTA RUN. ISIS HAS US ON THIS KILLER CLEANSING SCHEDULE-- AND YOU KNOW HOW SHE IS ABOUT BEING LATE.
YOU'RE TELLIN' ME! YEESH!
TROUBLE IS, THERE'S GONNA BE SNOW SOON. MAKES IT HARD TO MAINTAIN THE MYSTIC CONDUITS.
YOU SURE?
DOESN'T SEEM THAT COLD, YET.
TRUST ME. I KNOW WEATHER.
I'LL EITHER CALL OR TRY TO STOP BY LATER ON.
OKAY.
GOOD HUNTING, PENDRAGON.
CLEAN PURGING, LADY HUNTER.
AND THE DEAD AWAKE. WHAT'S UP WITH YOU THESE DAYS, KING TUT? HIBERNATING FOR THE WINTER?
GOT THIS HEAD-ACHE... MUST BE COMING DOWN WITH SOMETHING.

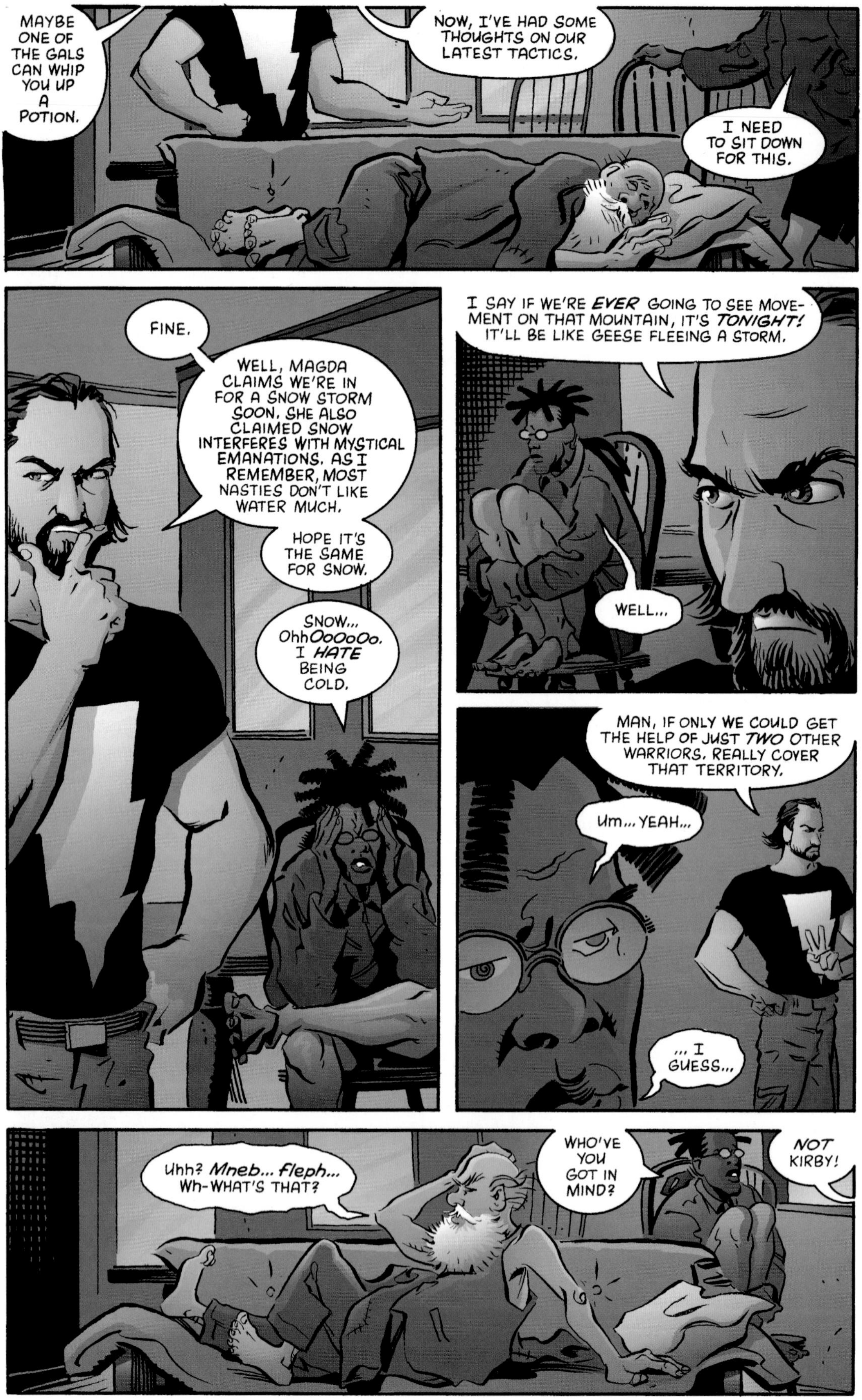
MAYBE ONE OF THE GALS CAN WHIP YOU UP A POTION.
NOW, I'VE HAD SOME THOUGHTS ON OUR LATEST TACTICS.
I NEED TO SIT DOWN FOR THIS.
FINE.
WELL, MAGDA CLAIMS WE'RE IN FOR A SNOW STORM SOON. SHE ALSO CLAIMED SNOW INTERFERES WITH MYSTICAL EMANATIONS. AS I REMEMBER, MOST NASTIES DON'T LIKE WATER MUCH.
HOPE IT'S THE SAME FOR SNOW.
SNOW... OhhOOoOOo. I HATE BEING COLD.
I SAY IF WE'RE EVER GOING TO SEE MOVEMENT ON THAT MOUNTAIN, IT'S TONIGHT! IT'LL BE LIKE GEESE FLEEING A STORM.
WELL...
MAN, IF ONLY WE COULD GET THE HELP OF JUST TWO OTHER WARRIORS. REALLY COVER THAT TERRITORY.
Um... YEAH...
... I GUESS...
Uhh? Mneb... Fleph... Wh-WHAT'S THAT?
WHO'VE YOU GOT IN MIND?
NOT KIRBY!

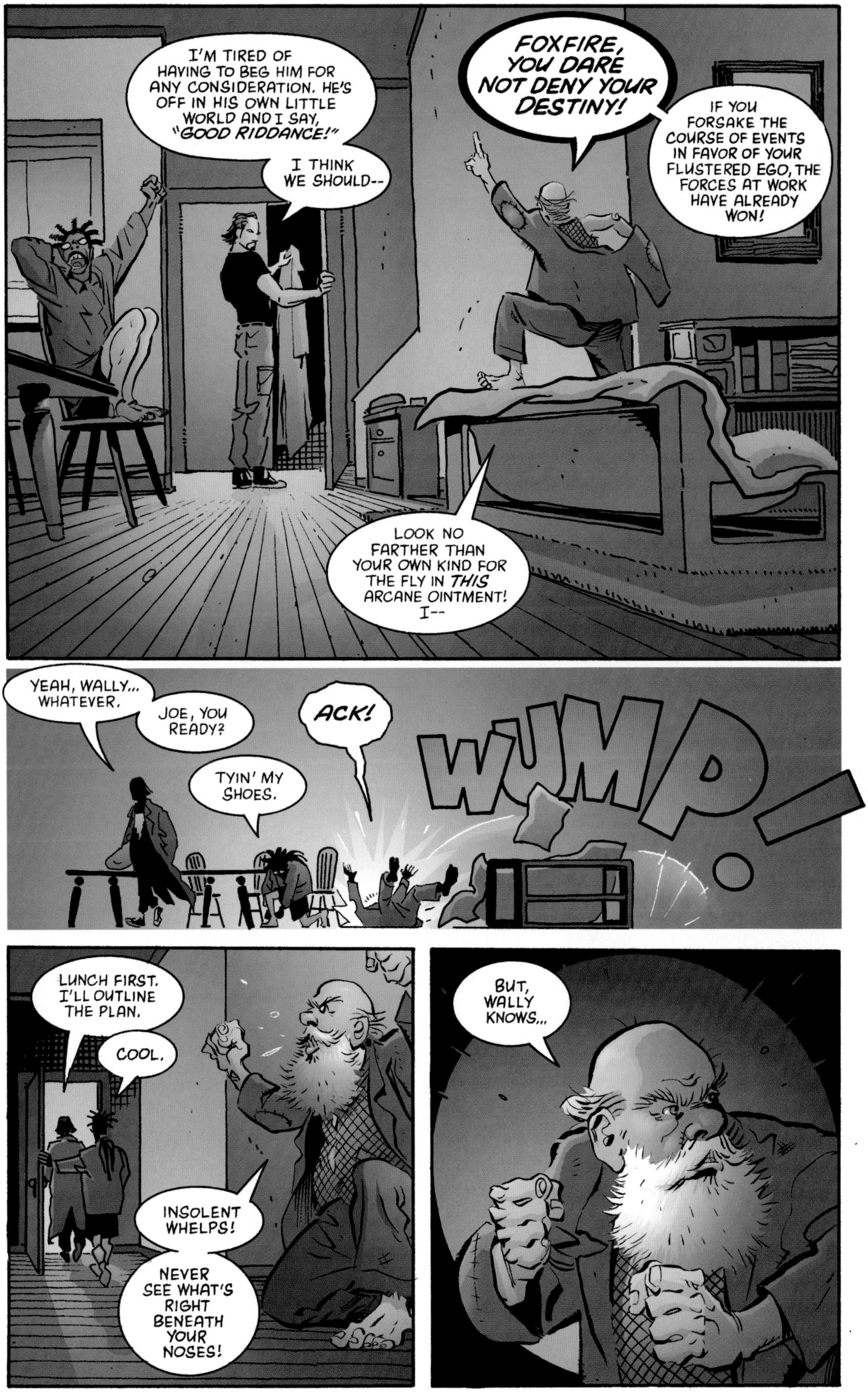
I'M TIRED OF HAVING TO BEG HIM FOR ANY CONSIDERATION. HE'S OFF IN HIS OWN LITTLE WORLD AND I SAY, "GOOD RIDDANCE!"
I THINK WE SHOULD--
FOXFIRE, YOU DARE NOT DENY YOUR DESTINY!
IF YOU FORSAKE THE COURSE OF EVENTS IN FAVOR OF YOUR FLUSTERED EGO, THE FORCES AT WORK HAVE ALREADY WON!
LOOK NO FARTHER THAN YOUR OWN KIND FOR THE FLY IN THIS ARCANE OINTMENT! I--
YEAH, WALLY... WHATEVER.
JOE, YOU READY?
TYIN' MY SHOES.
ACK!
WUMP!
LUNCH FIRST. I'LL OUTLINE THE PLAN.
COOL.
INSOLENT WHELPS!
NEVER SEE WHAT'S RIGHT BENEATH YOUR NOSES!
BUT, WALLY KNOWS...

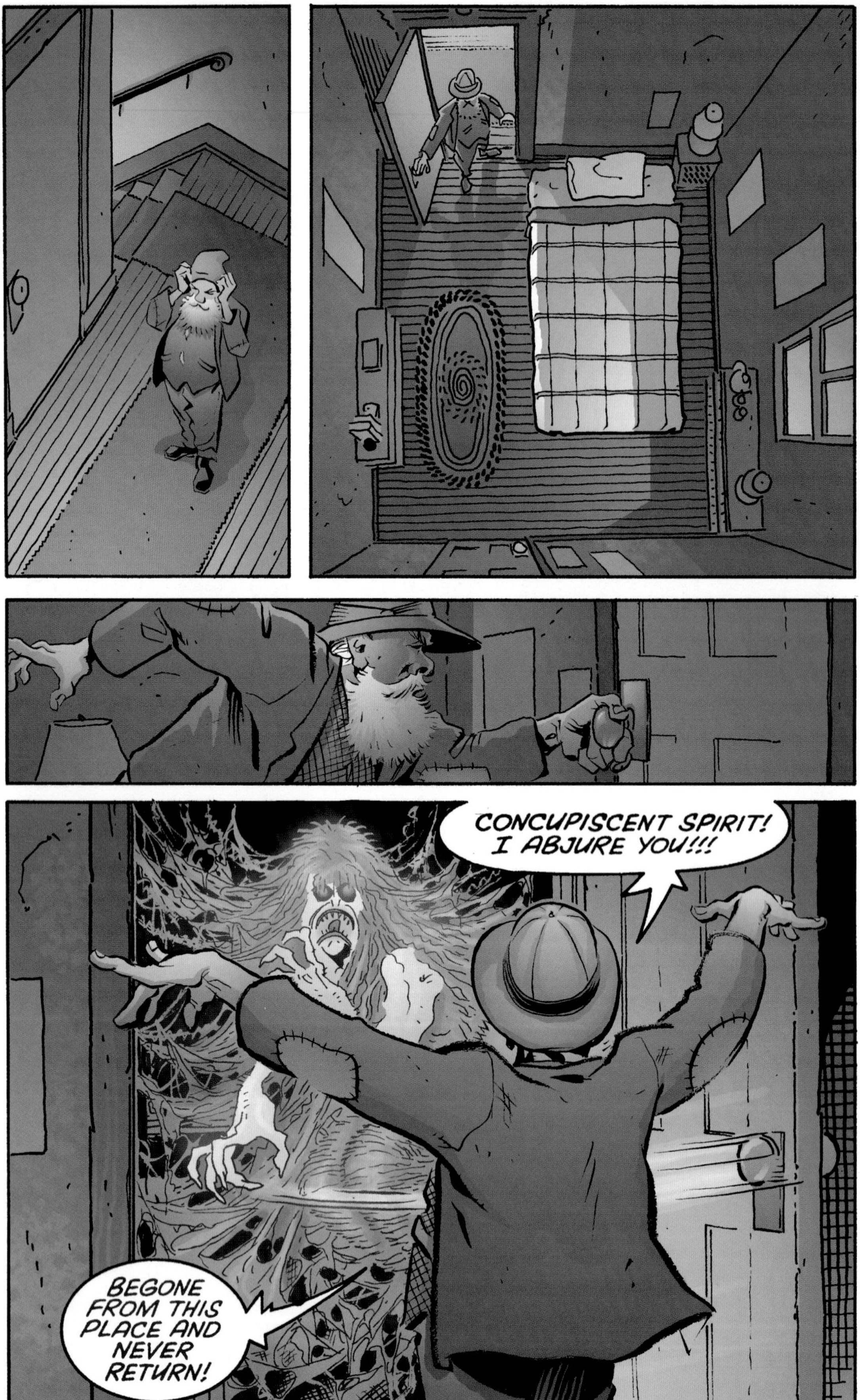
CONCUPISCENT SPIRIT! I ABJURE YOU!!!
BEGONE FROM THIS PLACE AND NEVER RETURN!

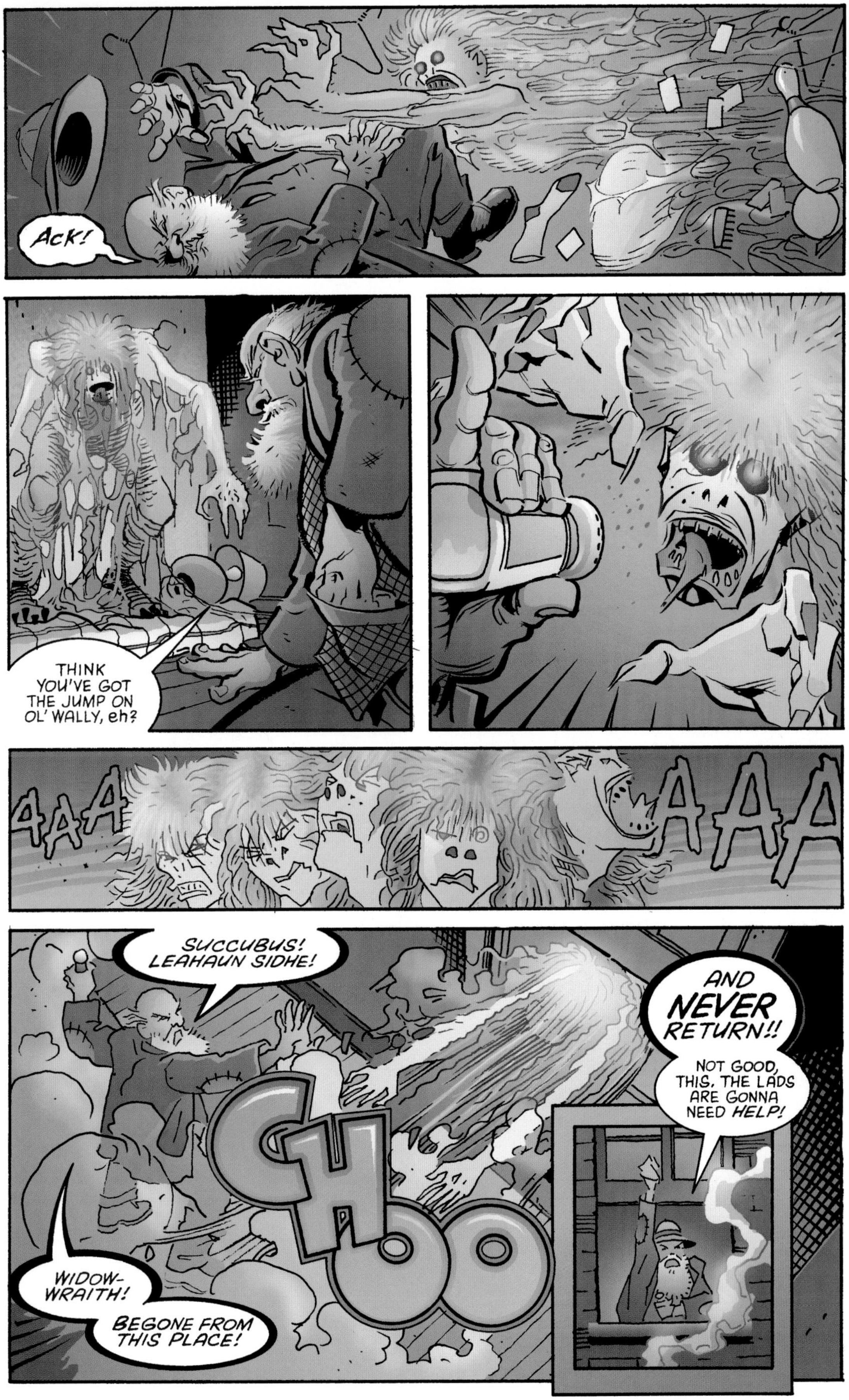
ACK!
THINK YOU'VE GOT THE JUMP ON OL' WALLY, eh?
AAAAAA
SUCCUBUS! LEAHAUN SIDHE!
AND NEVER RETURN!!
CHOO
WIDOW-WRAITH!
BEGONE FROM THIS PLACE!
NOT GOOD, THIS. THE LADS ARE GONNA NEED HELP!

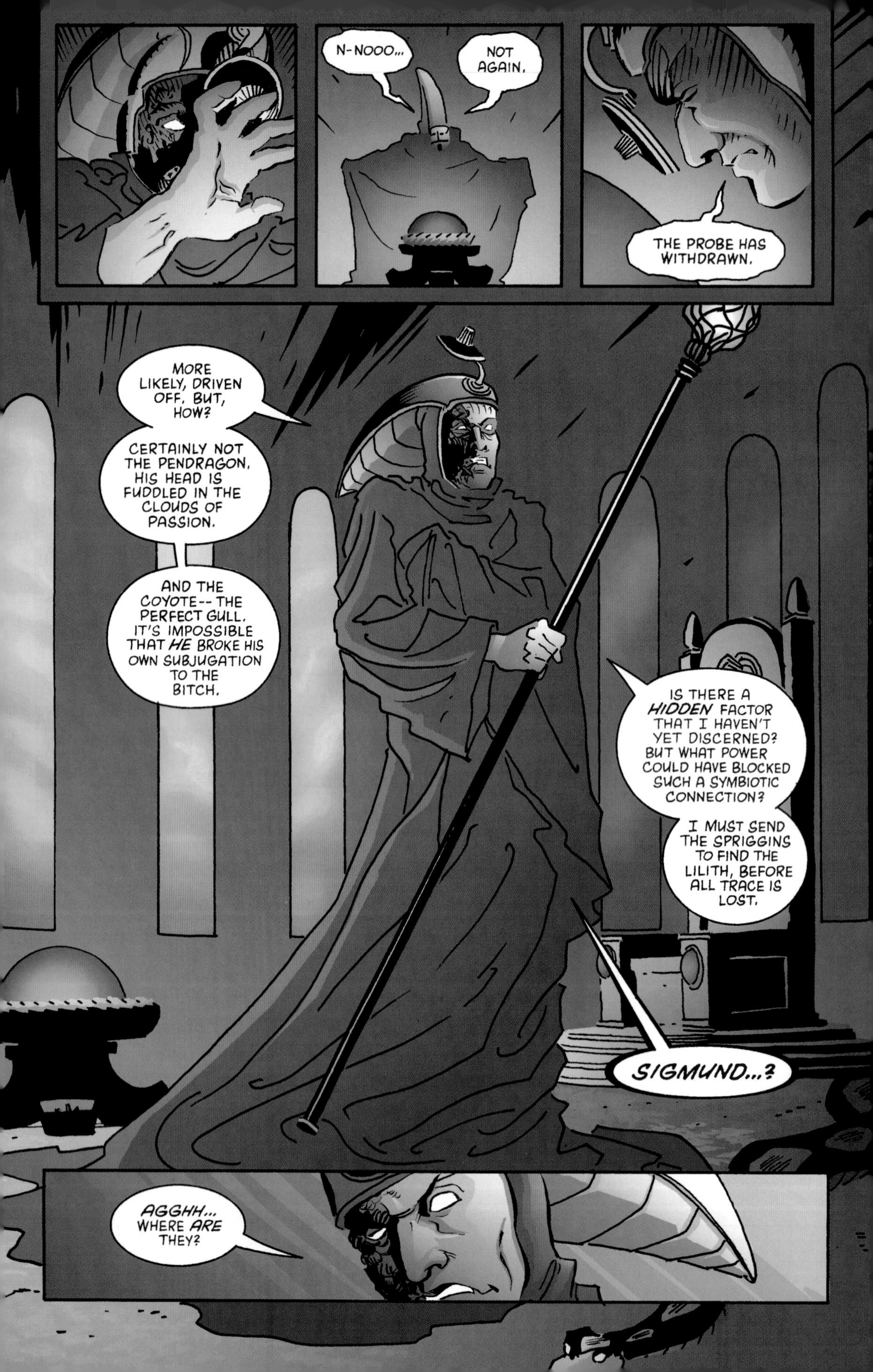
N-NOOO...
NOT AGAIN.
THE PROBE HAS WITHDRAWN.
MORE LIKELY, DRIVEN OFF. BUT, HOW?
CERTAINLY NOT THE PENDRAGON. HIS HEAD IS FUDDLED IN THE CLOUDS OF PASSION.
AND THE COYOTE-- THE PERFECT GULL. IT'S IMPOSSIBLE THAT HE BROKE HIS OWN SUBJUGATION TO THE BITCH.
IS THERE A HIDDEN FACTOR THAT I HAVEN'T YET DISCERNED? BUT WHAT POWER COULD HAVE BLOCKED SUCH A SYMBIOTIC CONNECTION?
I MUST SEND THE SPRIGGINS TO FIND THE LILITH, BEFORE ALL TRACE IS LOST.
SIGMUND...?
AGGHH... WHERE ARE THEY?

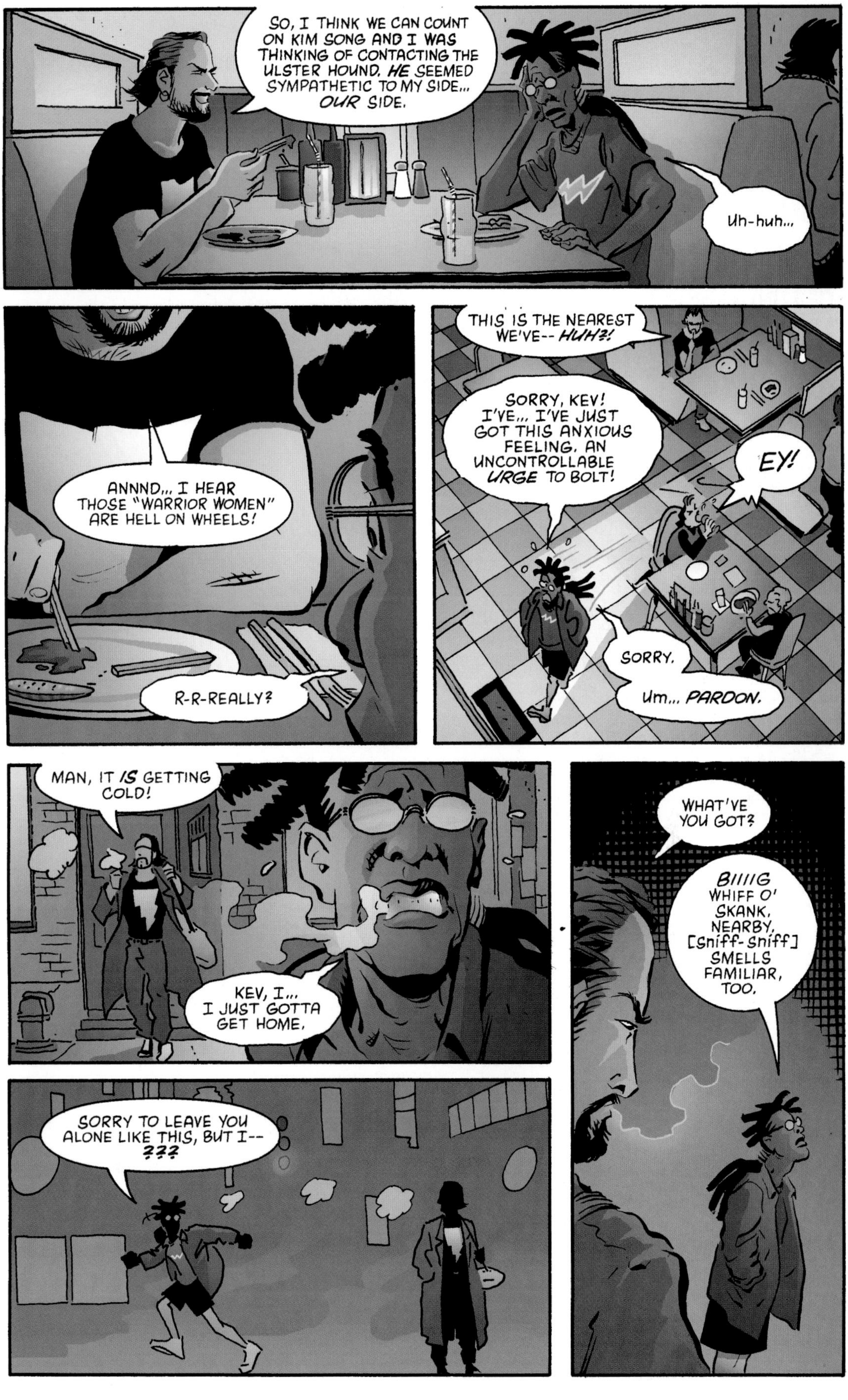
SO, I THINK WE CAN COUNT ON KIM SONG AND I WAS THINKING OF CONTACTING THE ULSTER HOUND. HE SEEMED SYMPATHETIC TO MY SIDE... OUR SIDE.
Uh-huh...
ANNND... I HEAR THOSE "WARRIOR WOMEN" ARE HELL ON WHEELS!
R-R-REALLY?
THIS IS THE NEAREST WE'VE-- HUH?!
SORRY, KEV! I'VE... I'VE JUST GOT THIS ANXIOUS FEELING. AN UNCONTROLLABLE URGE TO BOLT!
EY!
SORRY.
Um... PARDON.
MAN, IT IS GETTING COLD!
KEV, I... I JUST GOTTA GET HOME.
WHAT'VE YOU GOT?
BIIIIG WHIFF O' SKANK, NEARBY. [sniff-sniff] SMELLS FAMILIAR, TOO.
SORRY TO LEAVE YOU ALONE LIKE THIS, BUT I-- ???

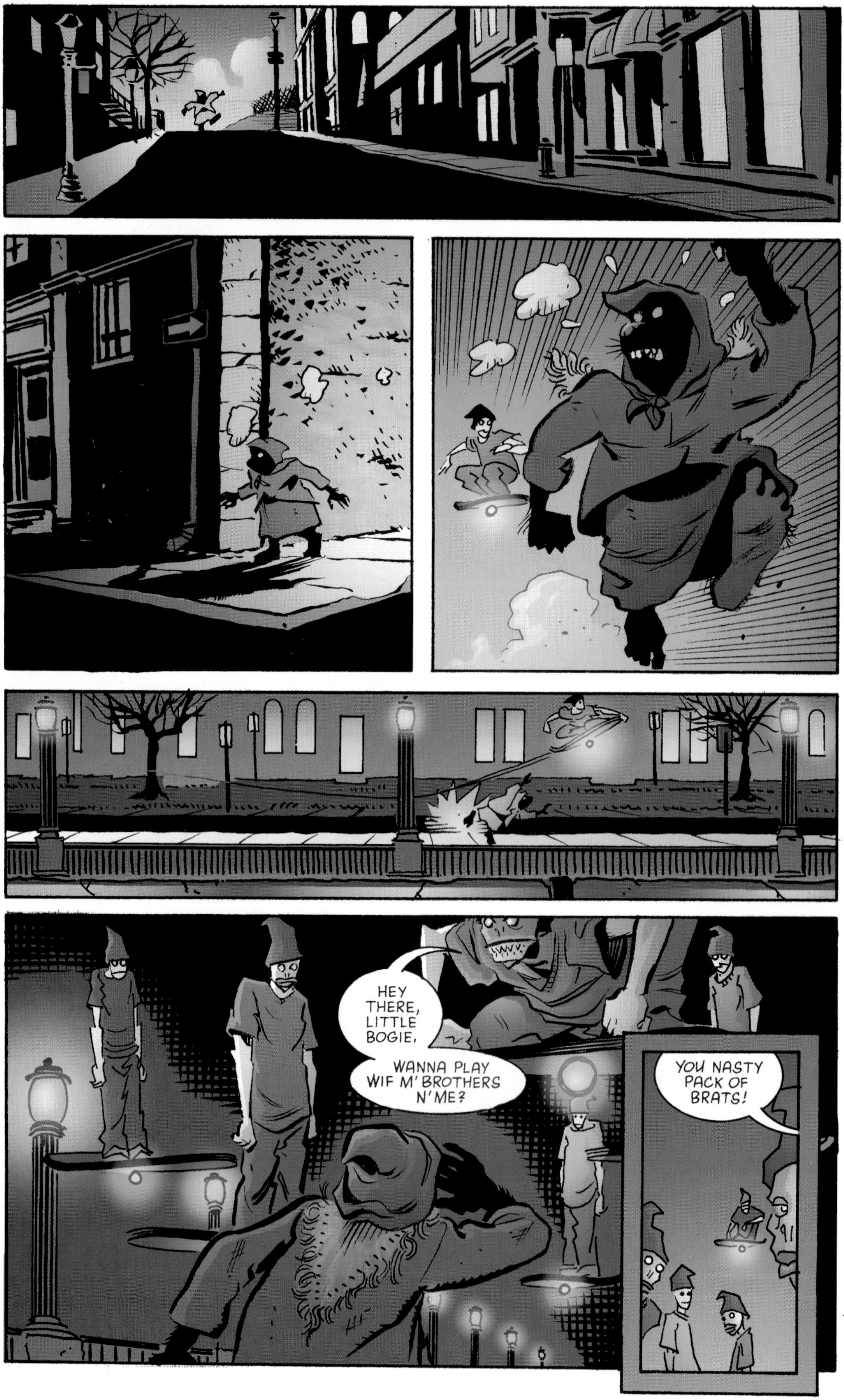
HEY THERE, LITTLE BOGIE.
WANNA PLAY WIF M' BROTHERS N' ME?
YOU NASTY PACK OF BRATS!

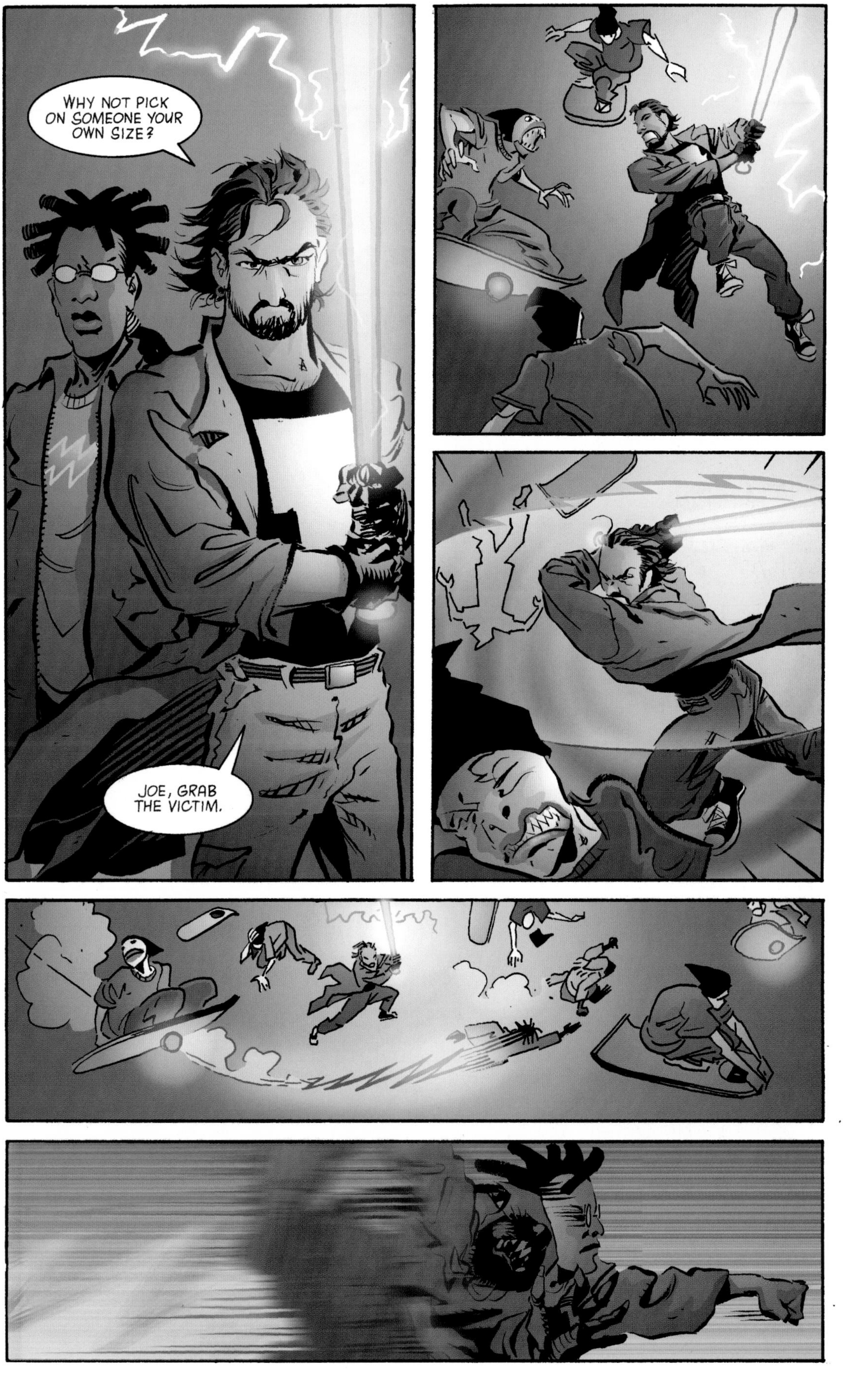
WHY NOT PICK ON SOMEONE YOUR OWN SIZE?
JOE, GRAB THE VICTIM.

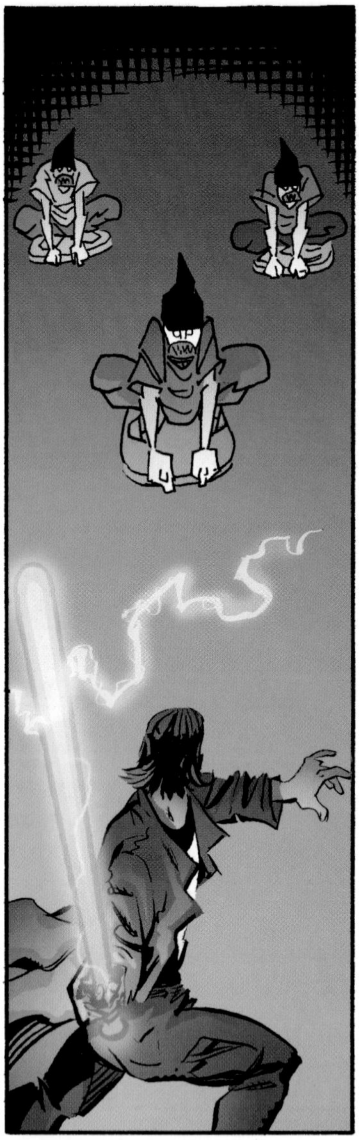

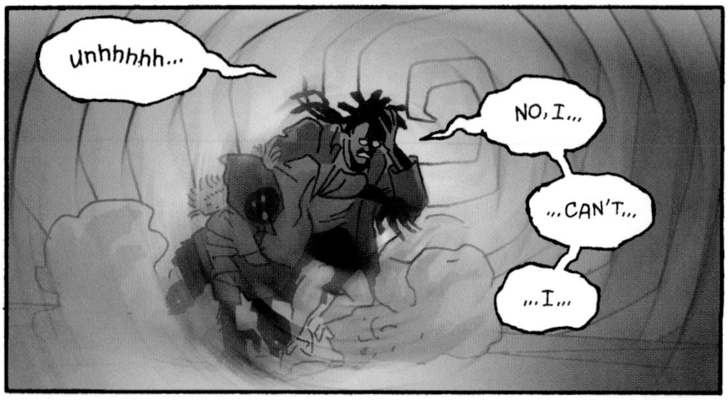
Unhhhhh...
NO, I...
...CAN'T...
...I...

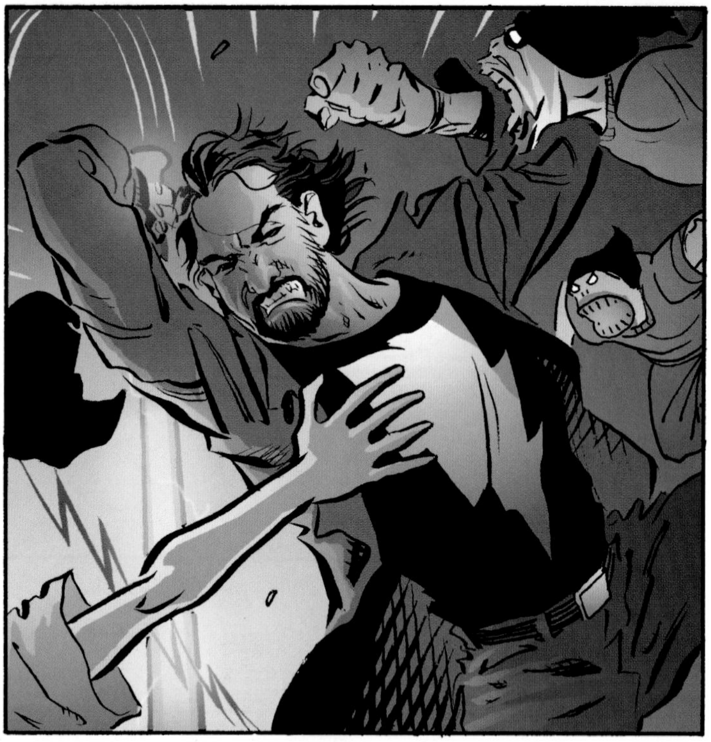

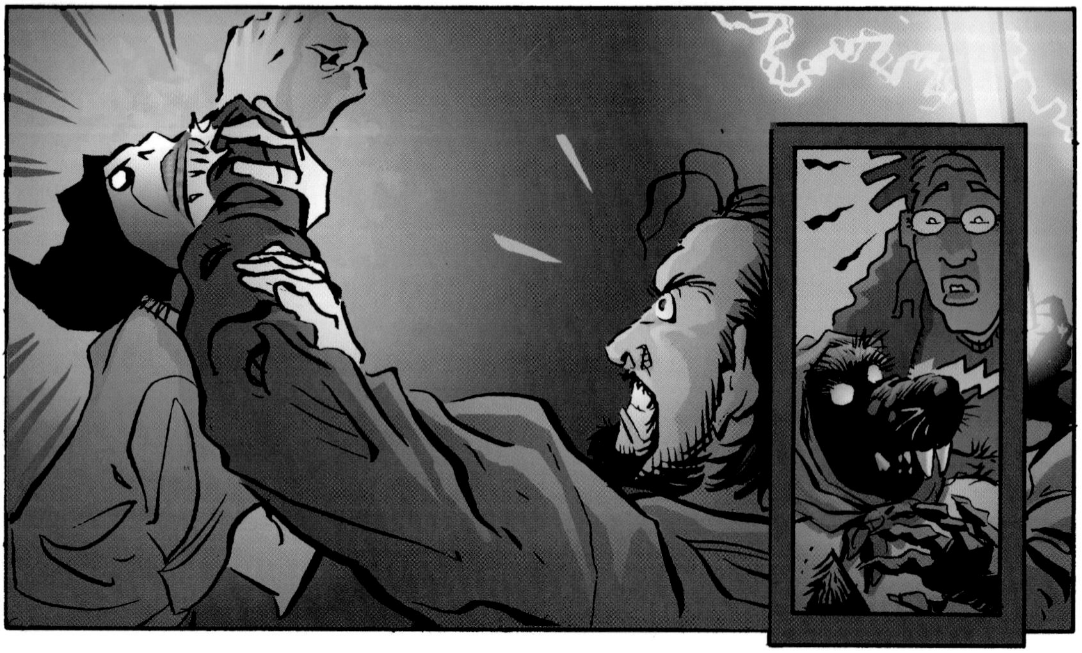

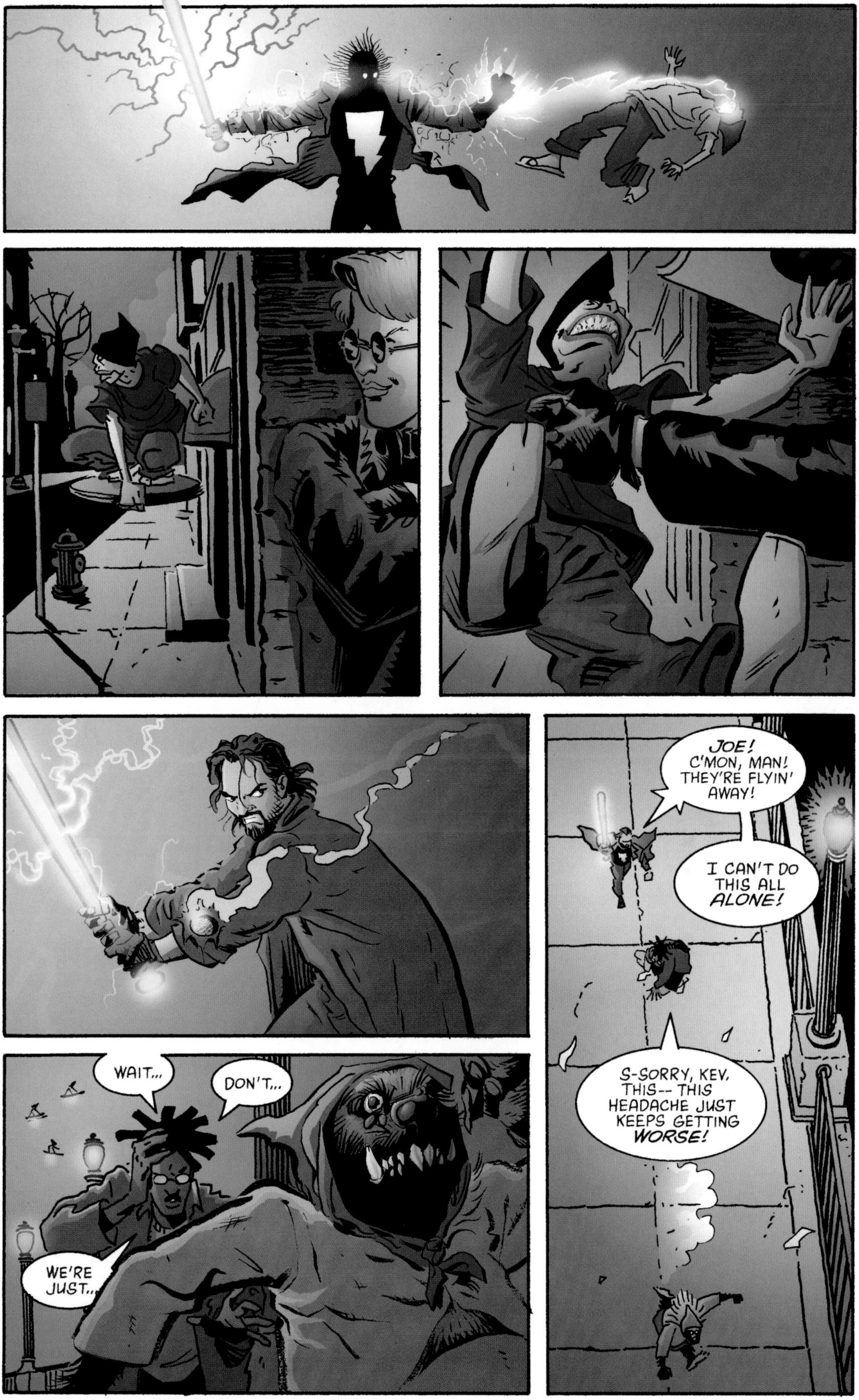
WAIT...
DON'T...
WE'RE JUST...
JOE! C'MON, MAN! THEY'RE FLYIN' AWAY!
I CAN'T DO THIS ALL *ALONE!*
S-SORRY, KEV. THIS-- THIS HEADACHE JUST KEEPS GETTING *WORSE!*

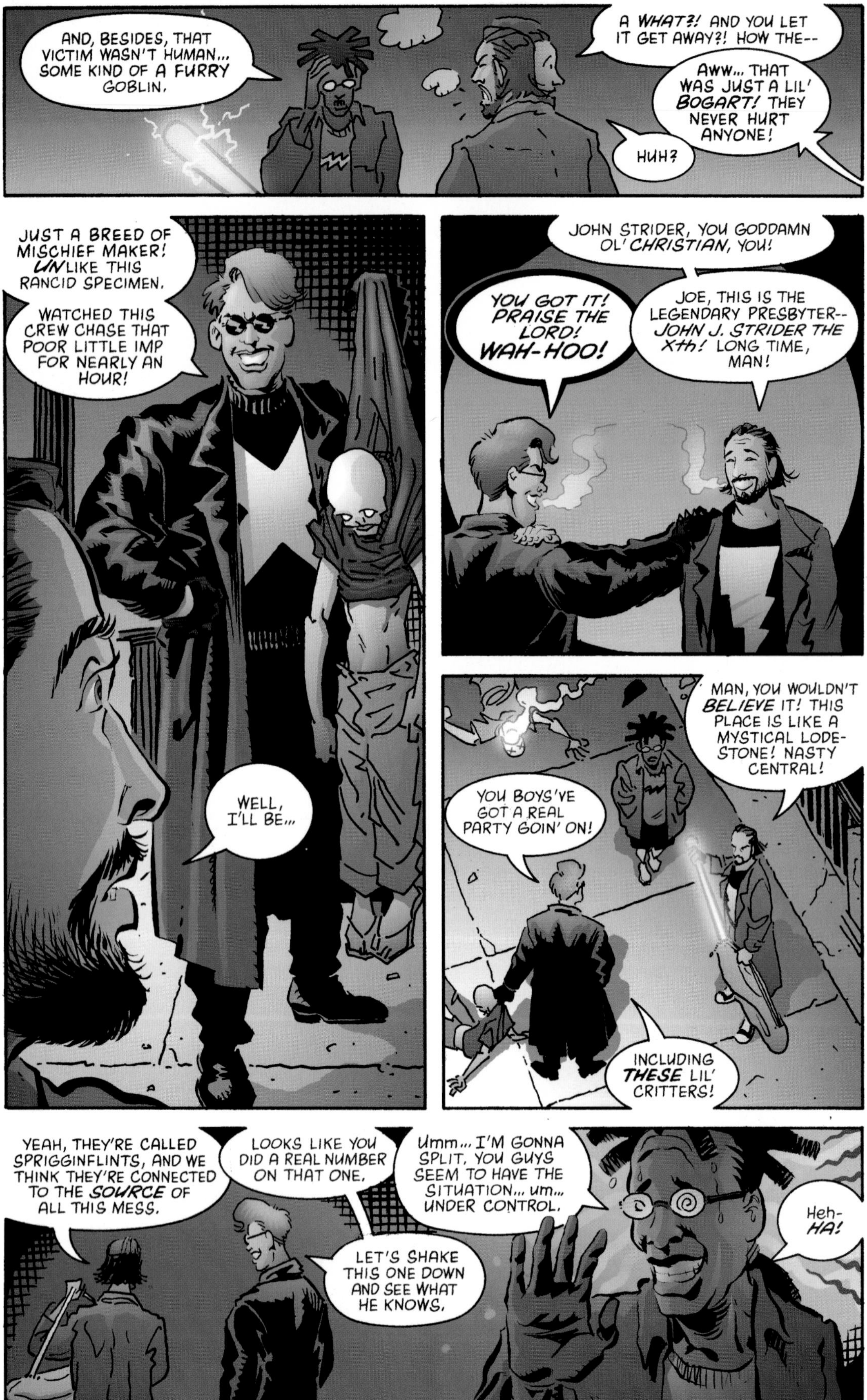
AND, BESIDES, THAT VICTIM WASN'T HUMAN... SOME KIND OF A FURRY GOBLIN.
A WHAT?! AND YOU LET IT GET AWAY?! HOW THE--
AWW... THAT WAS JUST A LIL' BOGART! THEY NEVER HURT ANYONE!
HUH?
JUST A BREED OF MISCHIEF MAKER! UNLIKE THIS RANCID SPECIMEN.
WATCHED THIS CREW CHASE THAT POOR LITTLE IMP FOR NEARLY AN HOUR!
WELL, I'LL BE...
JOHN STRIDER, YOU GODDAMN OL' CHRISTIAN, YOU!
YOU GOT IT! PRAISE THE LORD! WAH-HOO!
JOE, THIS IS THE LEGENDARY PRESBYTER-- JOHN J. STRIDER THE Xth! LONG TIME, MAN!
MAN, YOU WOULDN'T BELIEVE IT! THIS PLACE IS LIKE A MYSTICAL LODE-STONE! NASTY CENTRAL!
YOU BOYS'VE GOT A REAL PARTY GOIN' ON!
INCLUDING THESE LIL' CRITTERS!
YEAH, THEY'RE CALLED SPRIGGINFLINTS, AND WE THINK THEY'RE CONNECTED TO THE SOURCE OF ALL THIS MESS.
LOOKS LIKE YOU DID A REAL NUMBER ON THAT ONE.
LET'S SHAKE THIS ONE DOWN AND SEE WHAT HE KNOWS.
Umm... I'M GONNA SPLIT. YOU GUYS SEEM TO HAVE THE SITUATION... um... UNDER CONTROL.
Heh-HA!

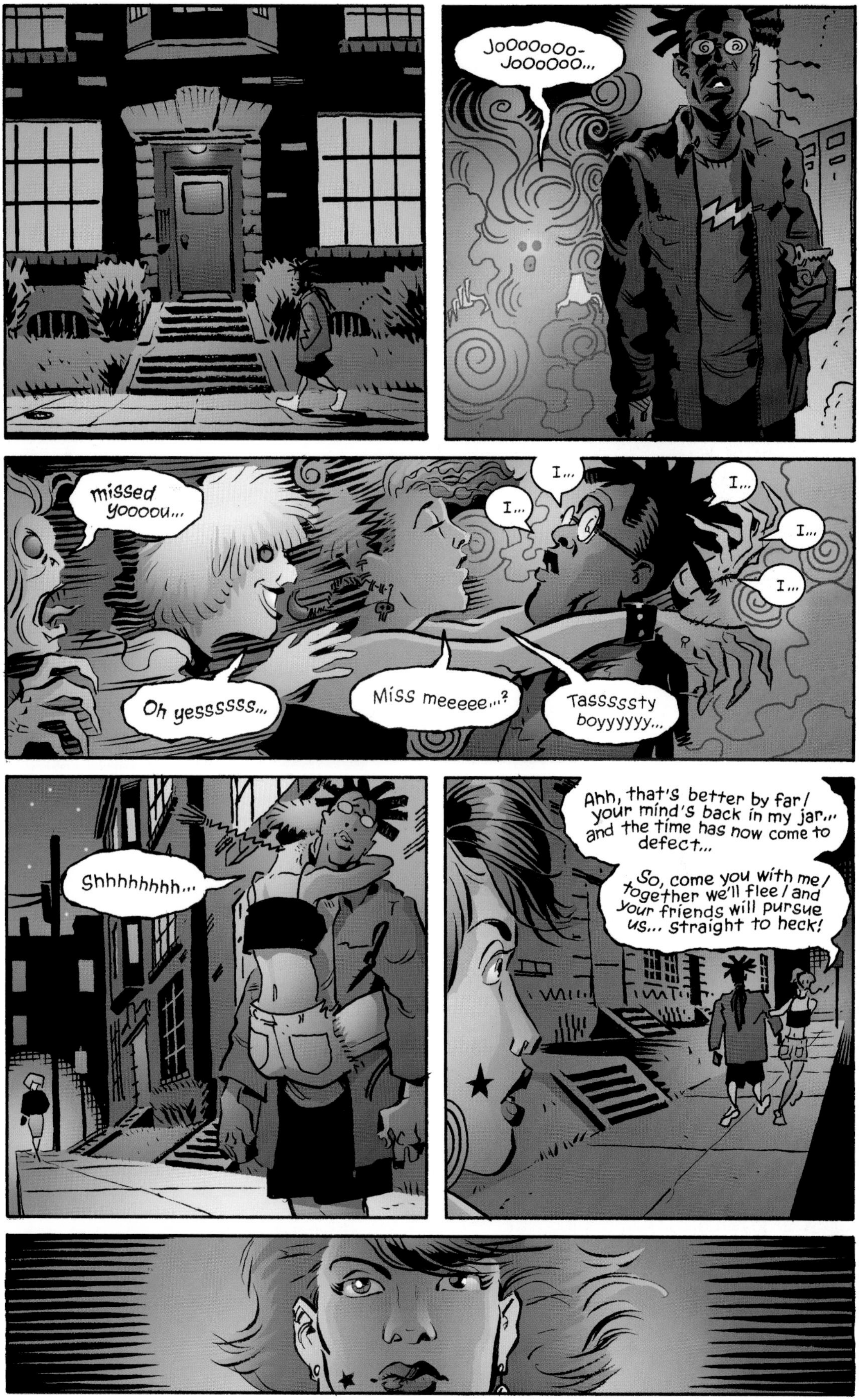
JOOOOOOO-
JOOOOOO...
missed yooooU...
I...
I...
I...
I...
I...
Oh yesssssss...
Miss meeeee...?
Tasssssty boyyyyyy...
Shhhhhhhh...
Ahh, that's better by far / your mind's back in my jar... and the time has now come to defect...
So, come you with me / together we'll flee / and your friends will pursue us... straight to heck!

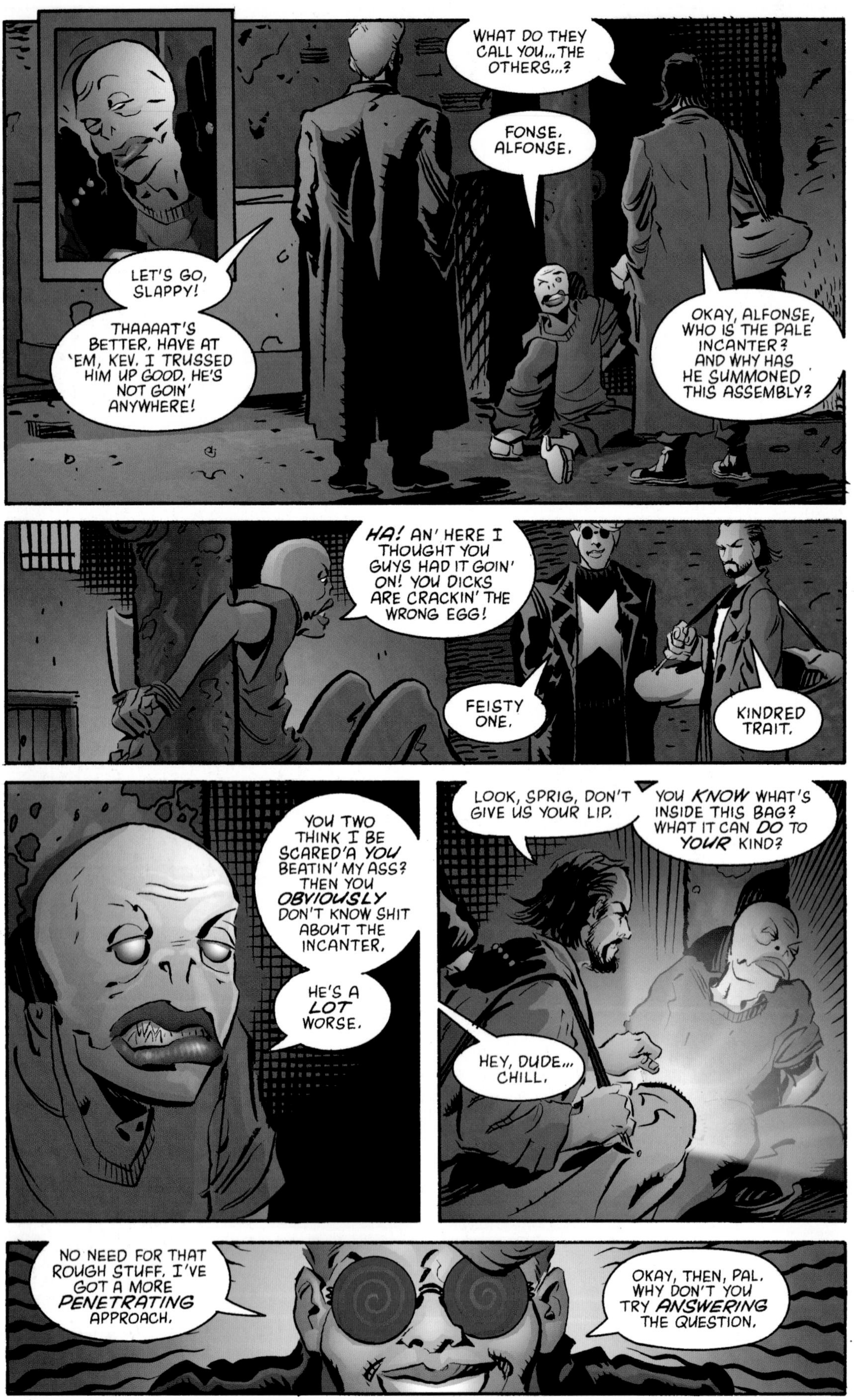
WHAT DO THEY CALL YOU... THE OTHERS...?
FONSE. ALFONSE.
LET'S GO, SLAPPY!
THAAAAT'S BETTER. HAVE AT 'EM, KEV. I TRUSSED HIM UP GOOD. HE'S NOT GOIN' ANYWHERE!
OKAY, ALFONSE, WHO IS THE PALE INCANTER? AND WHY HAS HE SUMMONED THIS ASSEMBLY?
HA! AN' HERE I THOUGHT YOU GUYS HAD IT GOIN' ON! YOU DICKS ARE CRACKIN' THE WRONG EGG!
FEISTY ONE.
KINDRED TRAIT.
YOU TWO THINK I BE SCARED'A YOU BEATIN' MY ASS? THEN YOU OBVIOUSLY DON'T KNOW SHIT ABOUT THE INCANTER.
HE'S A LOT WORSE.
LOOK, SPRIG, DON'T GIVE US YOUR LIP.
YOU KNOW WHAT'S INSIDE THIS BAG? WHAT IT CAN DO TO YOUR KIND?
HEY, DUDE... CHILL.
NO NEED FOR THAT ROUGH STUFF. I'VE GOT A MORE PENETRATING APPROACH.
OKAY, THEN, PAL. WHY DON'T YOU TRY ANSWERING THE QUESTION.

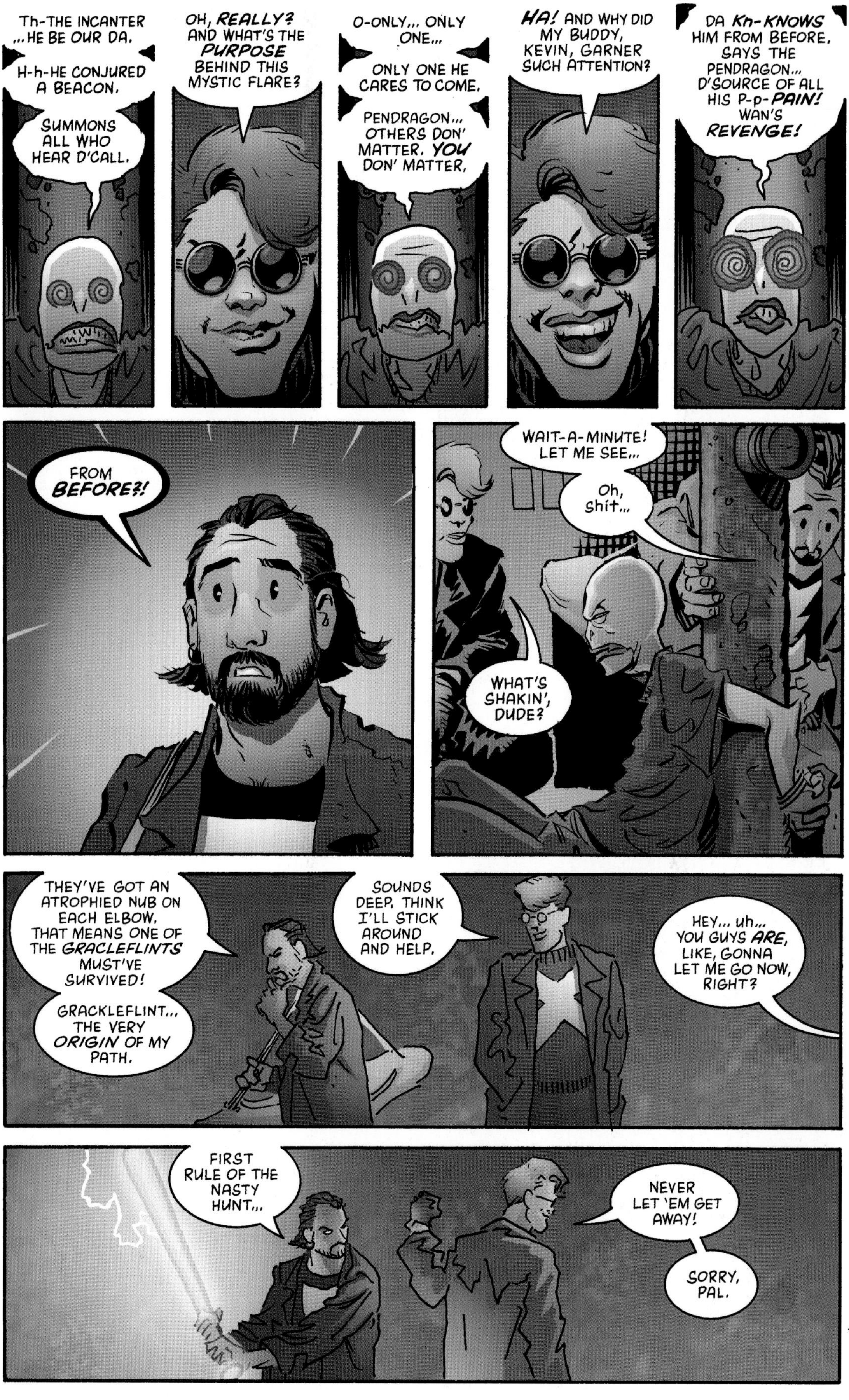
Th-THE INCANTER ...HE BE OUR DA.
H-h-HE CONJURED A BEACON.
SUMMONS ALL WHO HEAR D'CALL.
OH, REALLY? AND WHAT'S THE PURPOSE BEHIND THIS MYSTIC FLARE?
O-ONLY... ONLY ONE...
ONLY ONE HE CARES TO COME.
PENDRAGON... OTHERS DON' MATTER. YOU DON' MATTER.
HA! AND WHY DID MY BUDDY, KEVIN, GARNER SUCH ATTENTION?
DA Kn-KNOWS HIM FROM BEFORE, SAYS THE PENDRAGON... D'SOURCE OF ALL HIS P-p-PAIN! WAN'S REVENGE!
FROM BEFORE?!
WAIT-A-MINUTE! LET ME SEE...
Oh, shit...
WHAT'S SHAKIN', DUDE?
THEY'VE GOT AN ATROPHIED NUB ON EACH ELBOW. THAT MEANS ONE OF THE GRACLEFLINTS MUST'VE SURVIVED!
GRACKLEFLINT... THE VERY ORIGIN OF MY PATH.
SOUNDS DEEP. THINK I'LL STICK AROUND AND HELP.
HEY... uh... YOU GUYS ARE, LIKE, GONNA LET ME GO NOW, RIGHT?
FIRST RULE OF THE NASTY HUNT...
NEVER LET 'EM GET AWAY!
SORRY, PAL.

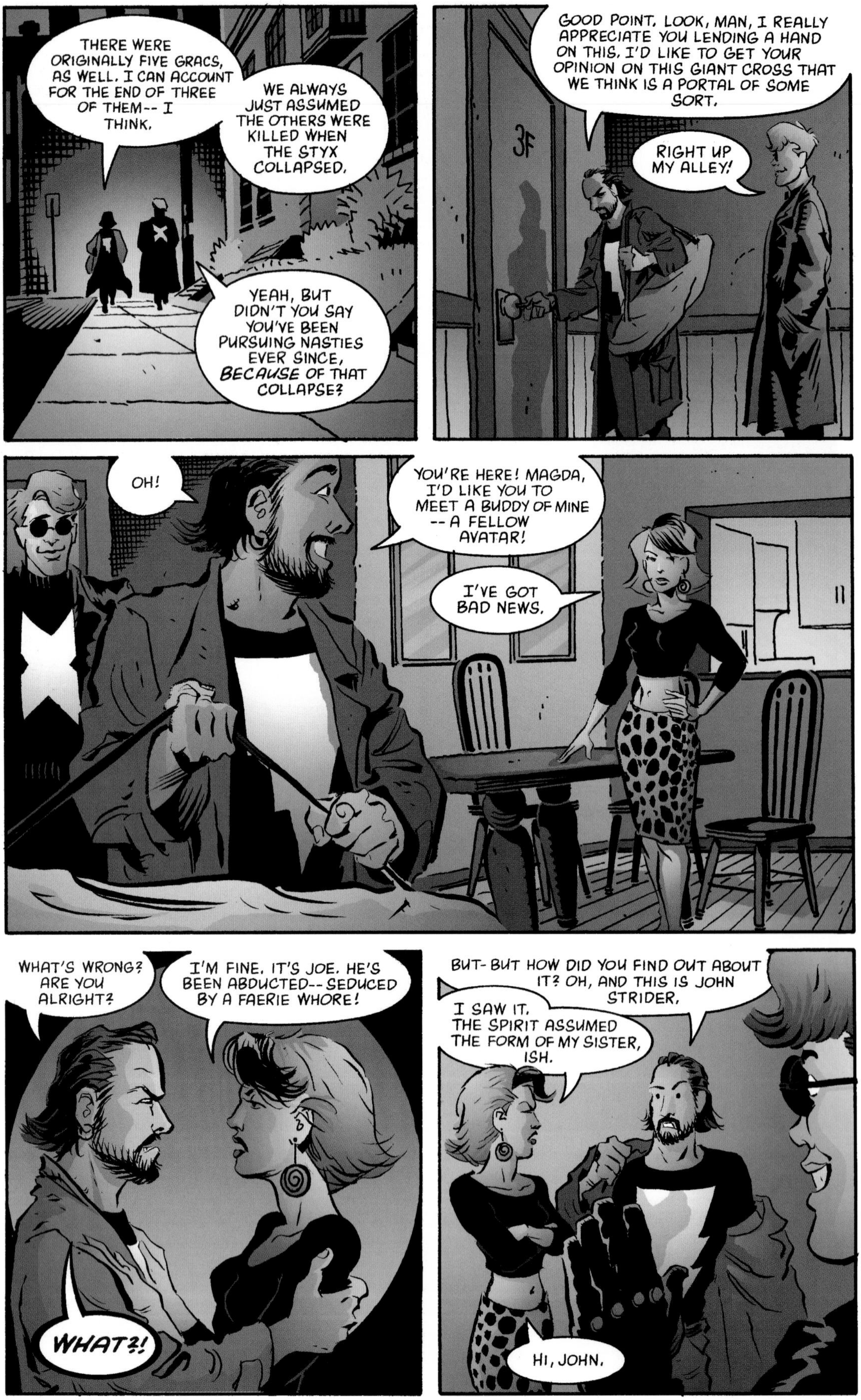
THERE WERE ORIGINALLY FIVE GRACS, AS WELL. I CAN ACCOUNT FOR THE END OF THREE OF THEM-- I THINK.
WE ALWAYS JUST ASSUMED THE OTHERS WERE KILLED WHEN THE STYX COLLAPSED.
YEAH, BUT DIDN'T YOU SAY YOU'VE BEEN PURSUING NASTIES EVER SINCE, *BECAUSE* OF THAT COLLAPSE?
GOOD POINT. LOOK, MAN, I REALLY APPRECIATE YOU LENDING A HAND ON THIS. I'D LIKE TO GET YOUR OPINION ON THIS GIANT CROSS THAT WE THINK IS A PORTAL OF SOME SORT.
3F
RIGHT UP MY ALLEY!
OH!
YOU'RE HERE! MAGDA, I'D LIKE YOU TO MEET A BUDDY OF MINE -- A FELLOW AVATAR!
I'VE GOT BAD NEWS.
WHAT'S WRONG? ARE YOU ALRIGHT?
I'M FINE. IT'S JOE. HE'S BEEN ABDUCTED-- SEDUCED BY A FAERIE WHORE!
WHAT?!
BUT- BUT HOW DID YOU FIND OUT ABOUT IT? OH, AND THIS IS JOHN STRIDER.
I SAW IT. THE SPIRIT ASSUMED THE FORM OF MY SISTER, ISH.
HI, JOHN.

HEY THERE! SO... YOU'RE SURE IT WASN'T HER?

I *KNOW* MY SISTER.

THE THING HAD HIM TOTALLY UNDER ITS THRALL, TOO MUCH FOR ME, SO I DECIDED TO SEE WHAT I COULD FIND HERE. C'MON, I'LL SHOW YOU...

DON'T TELL ME HIS DOOR'S LOCKED. I MEAN, YOU GOT INTO THE APARTMENT...

IT'S GOT A WARDING ON IT.

I'VE TRIED TO UNRAVEL IT, BUT THE MAGIC'S TOO STRONG. I'D NEED SEVERAL HOURS AND MY CAT TO GET THROUGH.

IT'S DEFINITELY NOT FAERIE, THOUGH. SOMETHING DIFFERENT...

≥*SIGH*≤ IT'S NO USE.

HERE.

LET *ME* TRY.

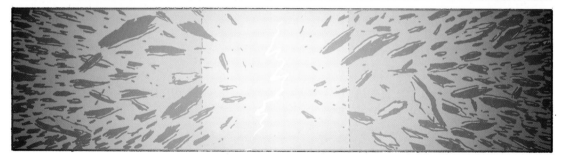

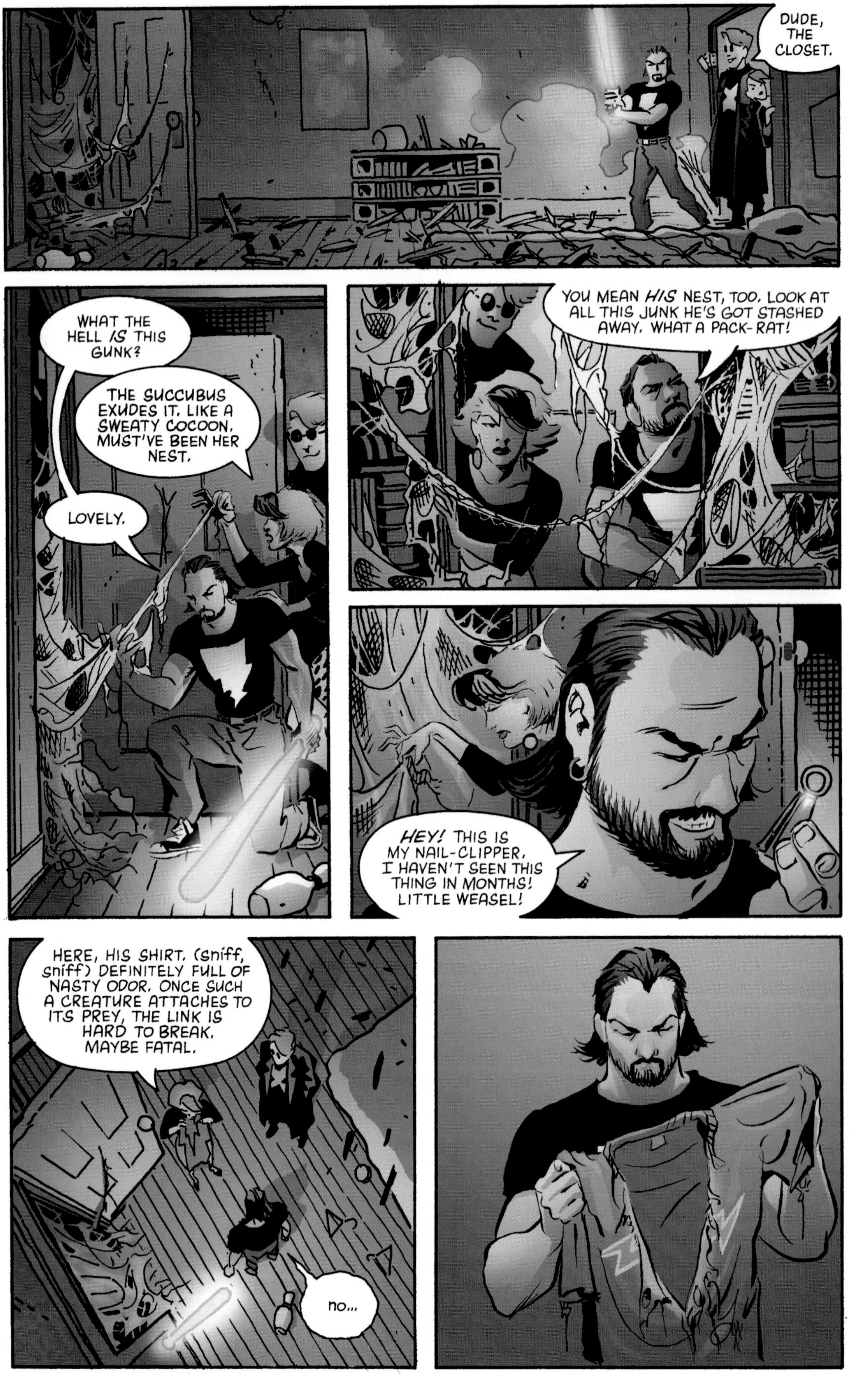
DUDE, THE CLOSET.
WHAT THE HELL IS THIS GUNK?
THE SUCCUBUS EXUDES IT. LIKE A SWEATY COCOON. MUST'VE BEEN HER NEST.
LOVELY.
YOU MEAN HIS NEST, TOO. LOOK AT ALL THIS JUNK HE'S GOT STASHED AWAY. WHAT A PACK-RAT!
HEY! THIS IS MY NAIL-CLIPPER. I HAVEN'T SEEN THIS THING IN MONTHS! LITTLE WEASEL!
HERE, HIS SHIRT. (sniff, sniff) DEFINITELY FULL OF NASTY ODOR. ONCE SUCH A CREATURE ATTACHES TO ITS PREY, THE LINK IS HARD TO BREAK. MAYBE FATAL.
no...

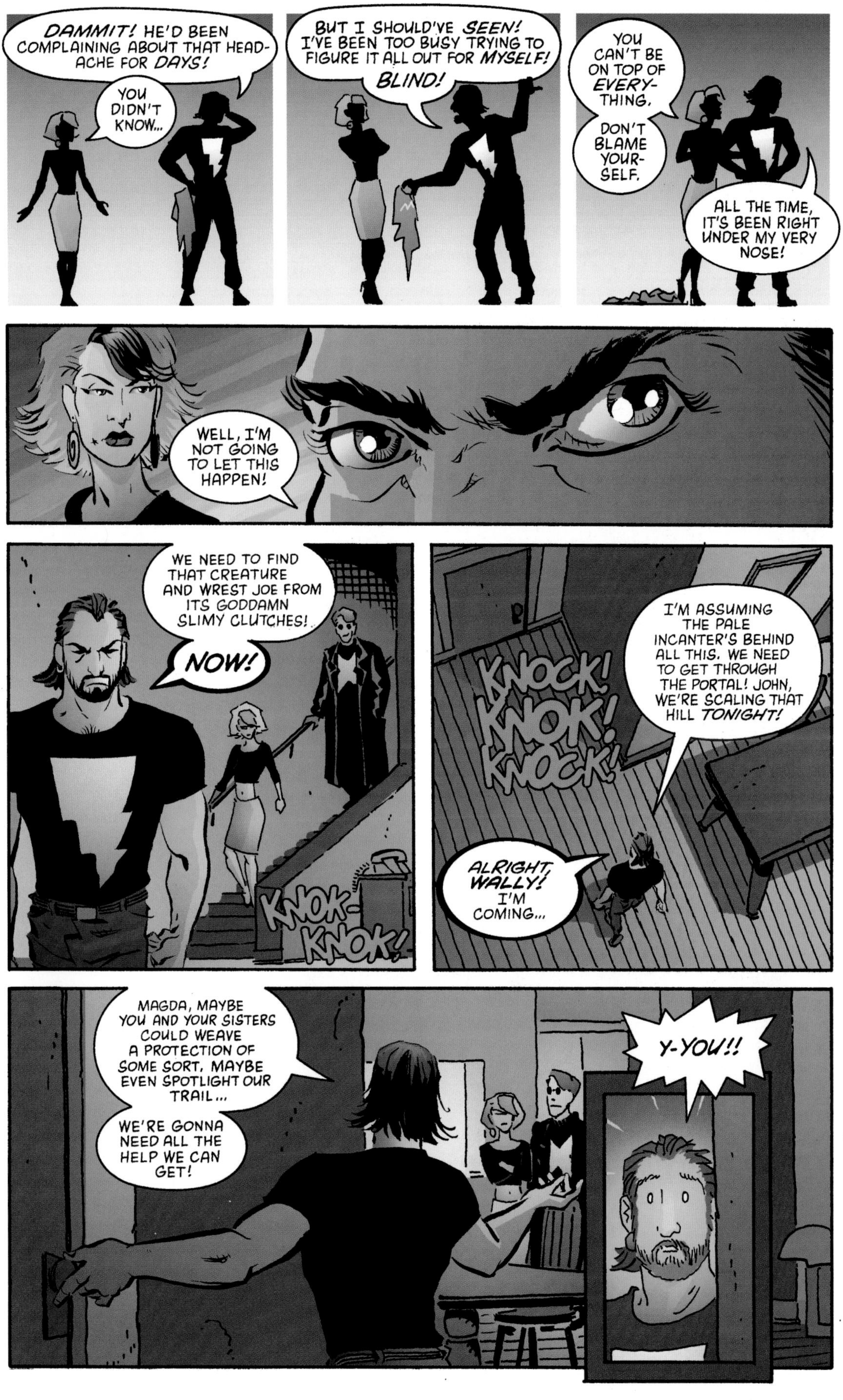
DAMMIT! HE'D BEEN COMPLAINING ABOUT THAT HEAD-ACHE FOR DAYS!
YOU DIDN'T KNOW...
BUT I SHOULD'VE SEEN! I'VE BEEN TOO BUSY TRYING TO FIGURE IT ALL OUT FOR MYSELF!
BLIND!
YOU CAN'T BE ON TOP OF EVERY-THING.
DON'T BLAME YOUR-SELF.
ALL THE TIME, IT'S BEEN RIGHT UNDER MY VERY NOSE!
WELL, I'M NOT GOING TO LET THIS HAPPEN!
WE NEED TO FIND THAT CREATURE AND WREST JOE FROM ITS GODDAMN SLIMY CLUTCHES!
NOW!
KNOK-KNOK!
KNOCK! KNOK! KNOCK!
I'M ASSUMING THE PALE INCANTER'S BEHIND ALL THIS. WE NEED TO GET THROUGH THE PORTAL! JOHN, WE'RE SCALING THAT HILL TONIGHT!
ALRIGHT, WALLY! I'M COMING...
MAGDA, MAYBE YOU AND YOUR SISTERS COULD WEAVE A PROTECTION OF SOME SORT, MAYBE EVEN SPOTLIGHT OUR TRAIL...
WE'RE GONNA NEED ALL THE HELP WE CAN GET!
Y-YOU!!

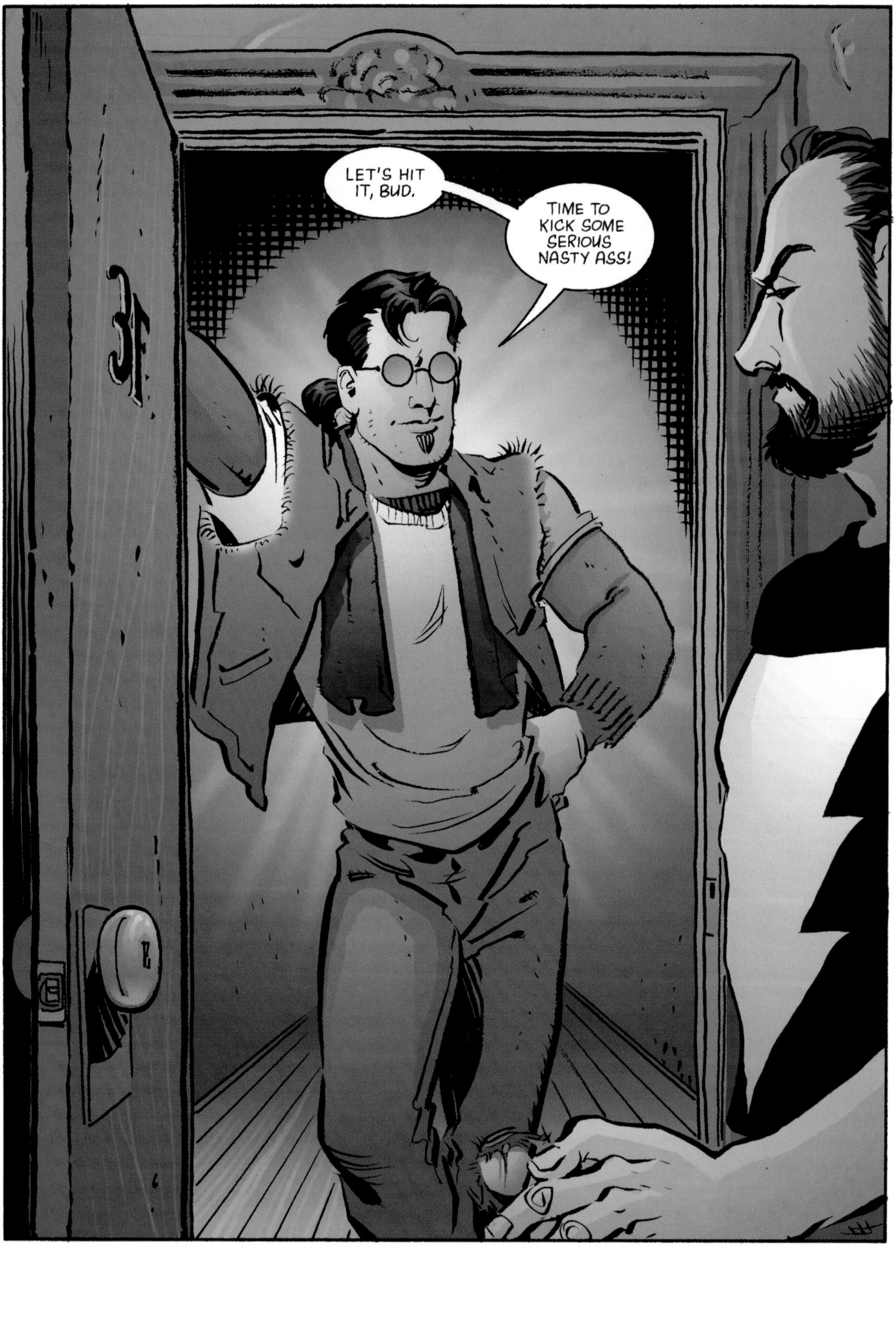

LET'S HIT IT, BUD.
TIME TO KICK SOME SERIOUS NASTY ASS!

THE HERO DEFINED

MAGE®

LET'S HIT IT, BUD.
TIME TO KICK SOM SERIOUS NASTY AS

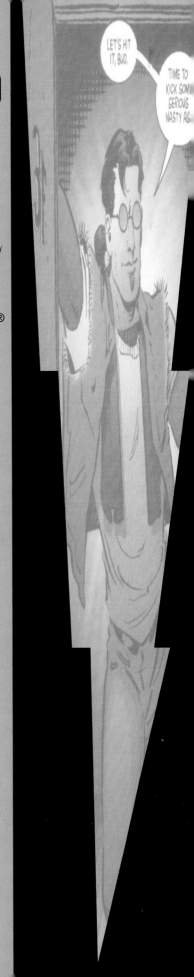

chapter 11

"Dwindle, Peak and Pine"

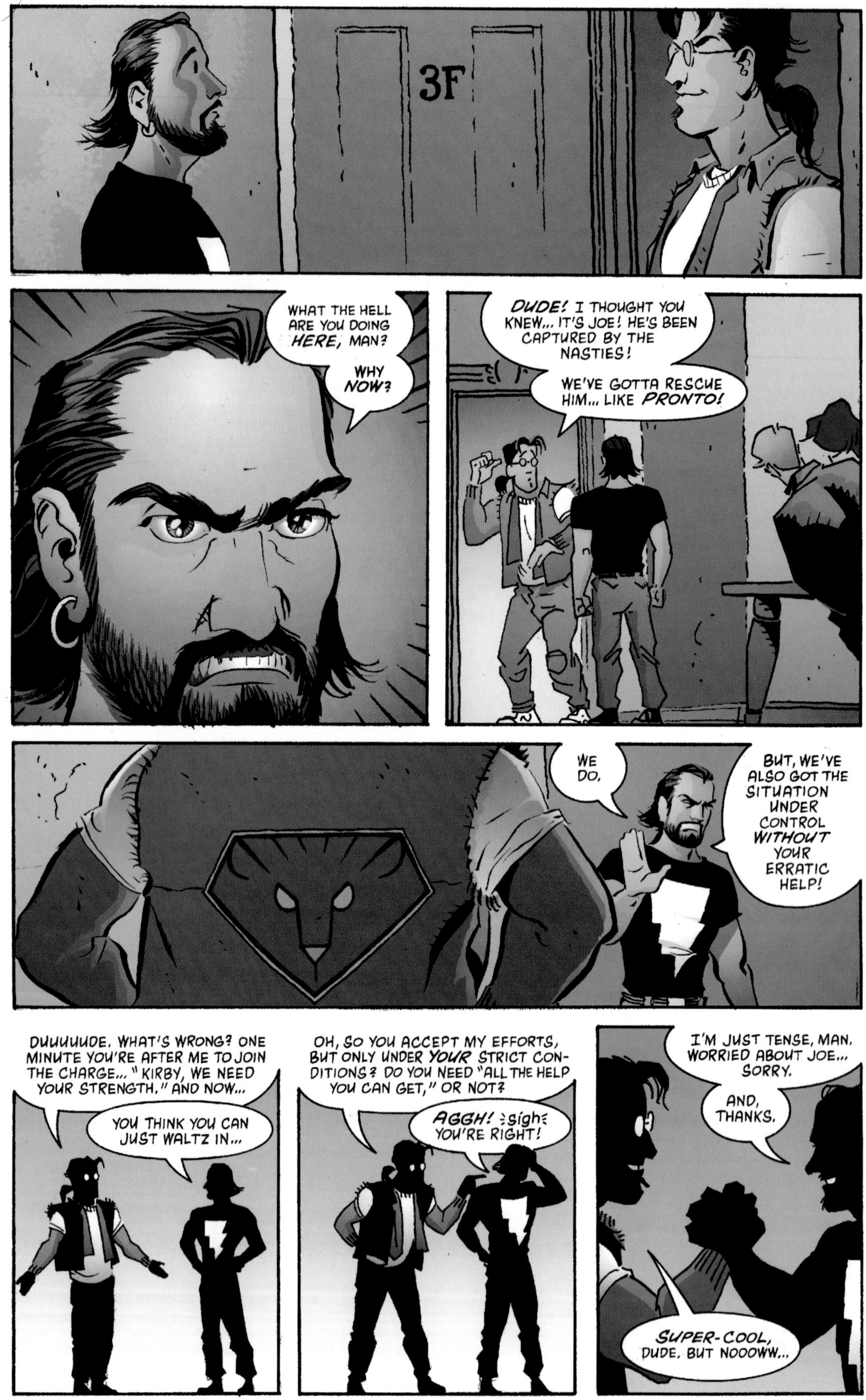
3F
WHAT THE HELL ARE YOU DOING HERE, MAN?
WHY NOW?
DUDE! I THOUGHT YOU KNEW... IT'S JOE! HE'S BEEN CAPTURED BY THE NASTIES!
WE'VE GOTTA RESCUE HIM... LIKE PRONTO!
WE DO.
BUT, WE'VE ALSO GOT THE SITUATION UNDER CONTROL WITHOUT YOUR ERRATIC HELP!
DUUUUUDE. WHAT'S WRONG? ONE MINUTE YOU'RE AFTER ME TO JOIN THE CHARGE... "KIRBY, WE NEED YOUR STRENGTH," AND NOW...
YOU THINK YOU CAN JUST WALTZ IN...
OH, SO YOU ACCEPT MY EFFORTS, BUT ONLY UNDER YOUR STRICT CONDITIONS? DO YOU NEED "ALL THE HELP YOU CAN GET," OR NOT?
AGGH! sigh YOU'RE RIGHT!
I'M JUST TENSE, MAN. WORRIED ABOUT JOE... SORRY.
AND, THANKS.
SUPER-COOL, DUDE, BUT NOOOWW...

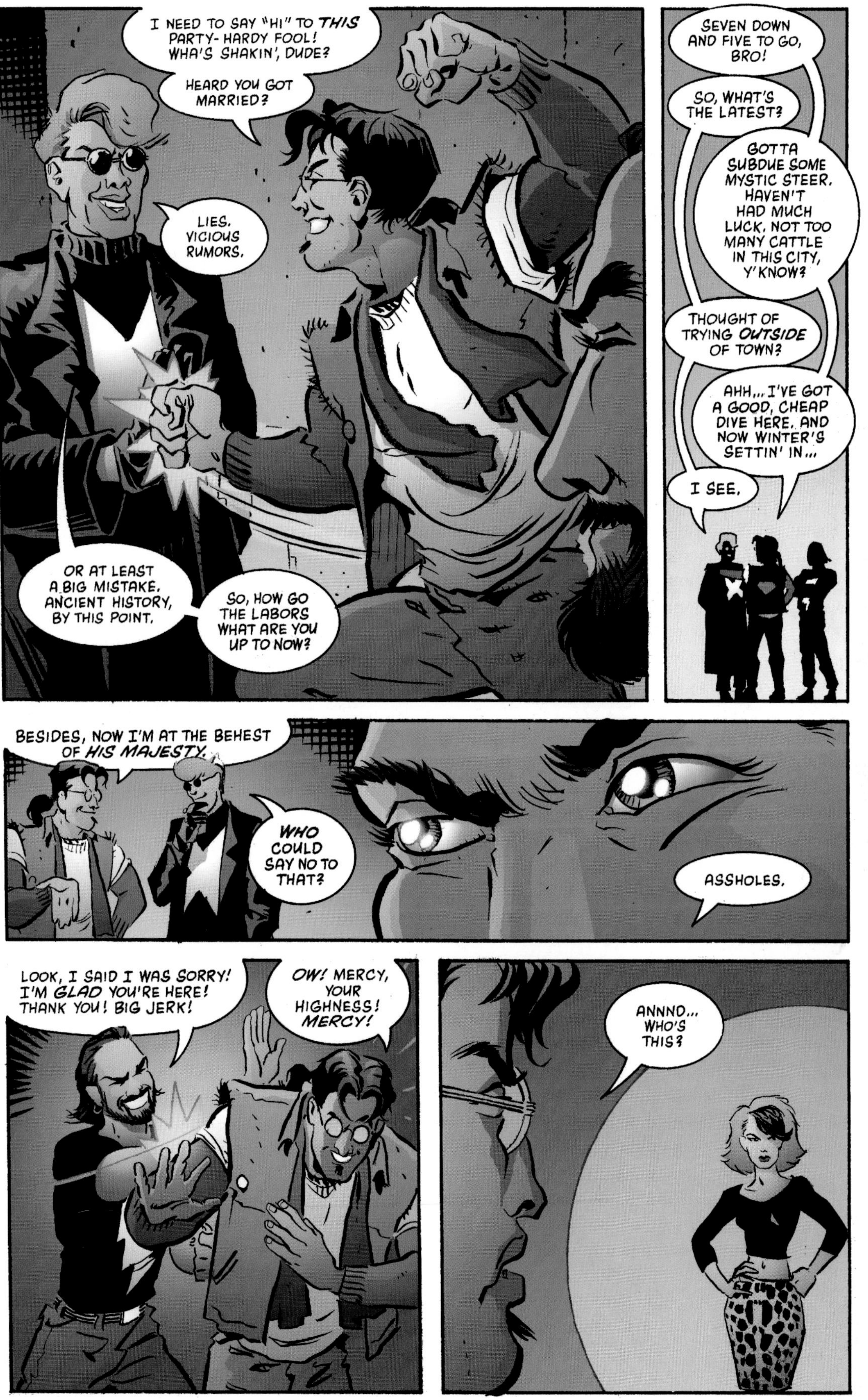

I NEED TO SAY "HI" TO *THIS* PARTY- HARDY FOOL! WHA'S SHAKIN', DUDE?
HEARD YOU GOT MARRIED?
LIES. VICIOUS RUMORS.
OR AT LEAST A BIG MISTAKE. ANCIENT HISTORY, BY THIS POINT.
SO, HOW GO THE LABORS WHAT ARE YOU UP TO NOW?
SEVEN DOWN AND FIVE TO GO, BRO!
SO, WHAT'S THE LATEST?
GOTTA SUBDUE SOME MYSTIC STEER. HAVEN'T HAD MUCH LUCK. NOT TOO MANY CATTLE IN THIS CITY, Y'KNOW?
THOUGHT OF TRYING *OUTSIDE* OF TOWN?
AHH... I'VE GOT A *GOOD*, CHEAP DIVE HERE. AND NOW WINTER'S SETTIN' IN...
I SEE.
BESIDES, NOW I'M AT THE BEHEST OF *HIS MAJESTY*.
WHO COULD SAY NO TO THAT?
ASSHOLES.
LOOK, I SAID I WAS SORRY! I'M *GLAD* YOU'RE HERE! THANK YOU! BIG JERK!
OW! MERCY, YOUR HIGHNESS! *MERCY!*
ANNND... WHO'S THIS?

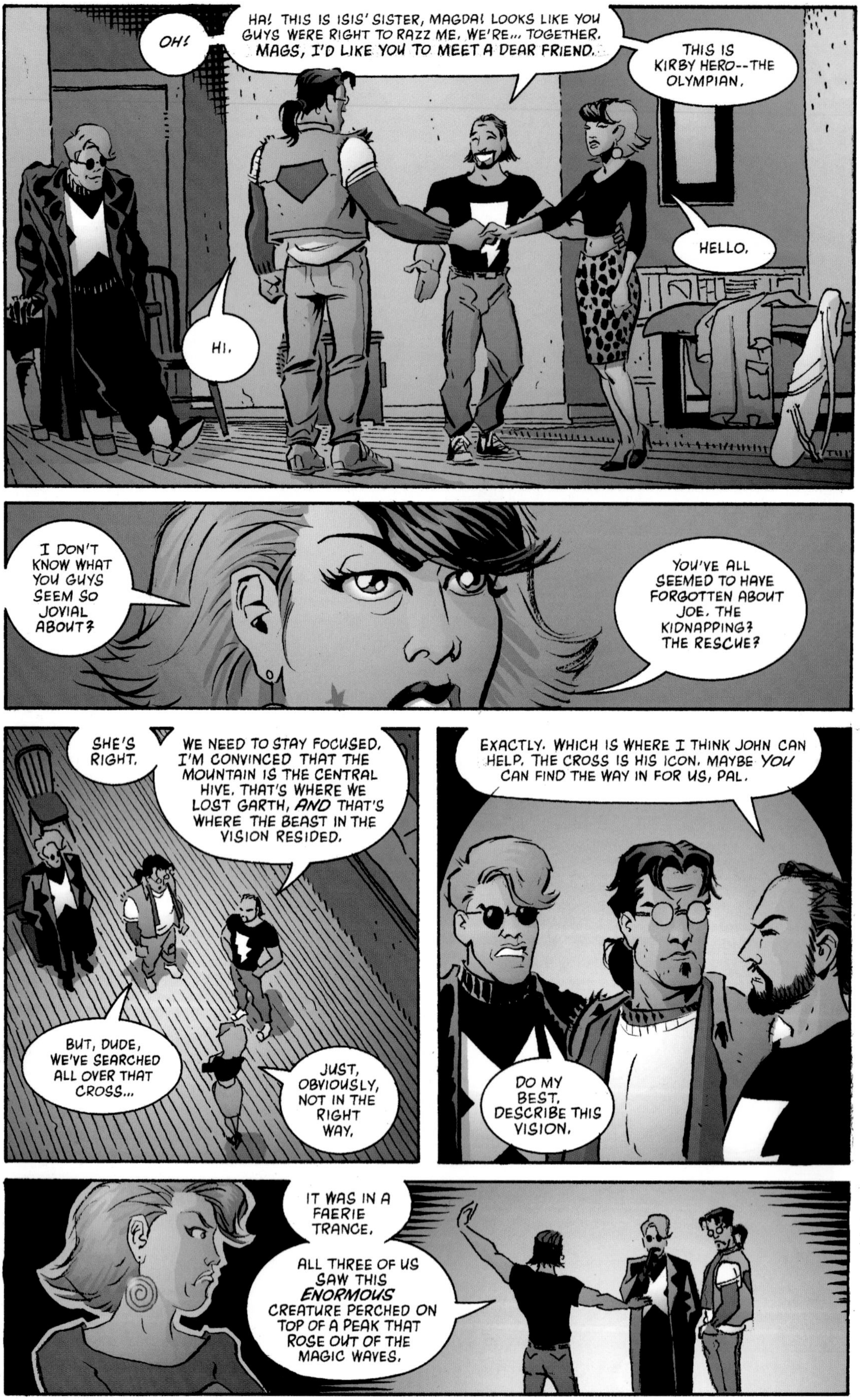
OH!
HA! THIS IS ISIS' SISTER, MAGDA! LOOKS LIKE YOU GUYS WERE RIGHT TO RAZZ ME. WE'RE... TOGETHER. MAGS, I'D LIKE YOU TO MEET A DEAR FRIEND.
THIS IS KIRBY HERO--THE OLYMPIAN.
HI.
HELLO.
I DON'T KNOW WHAT YOU GUYS SEEM SO JOVIAL ABOUT?
YOU'VE ALL SEEMED TO HAVE FORGOTTEN ABOUT JOE. THE KIDNAPPING? THE RESCUE?
SHE'S RIGHT.
WE NEED TO STAY FOCUSED. I'M CONVINCED THAT THE MOUNTAIN IS THE CENTRAL HIVE. THAT'S WHERE WE LOST GARTH, AND THAT'S WHERE THE BEAST IN THE VISION RESIDED.
BUT, DUDE, WE'VE SEARCHED ALL OVER THAT CROSS...
JUST, OBVIOUSLY, NOT IN THE RIGHT WAY.
EXACTLY. WHICH IS WHERE I THINK JOHN CAN HELP. THE CROSS IS HIS ICON. MAYBE YOU CAN FIND THE WAY IN FOR US, PAL.
DO MY BEST. DESCRIBE THIS VISION.
IT WAS IN A FAERIE TRANCE.
ALL THREE OF US SAW THIS ENORMOUS CREATURE PERCHED ON TOP OF A PEAK THAT ROSE OUT OF THE MAGIC WAVES.

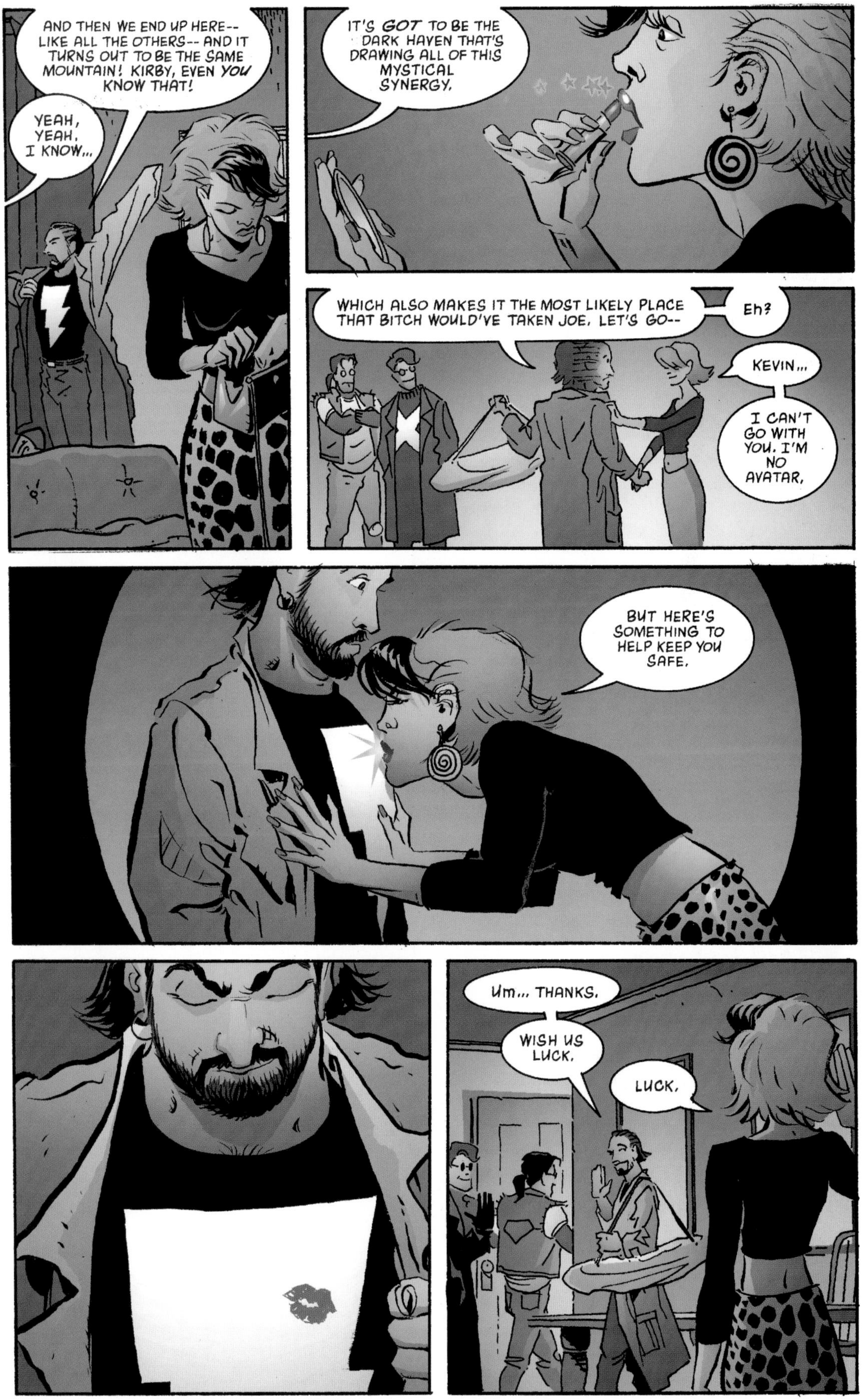
AND THEN WE END UP HERE-- LIKE ALL THE OTHERS-- AND IT TURNS OUT TO BE THE SAME MOUNTAIN! KIRBY, EVEN YOU KNOW THAT!
YEAH, YEAH. I KNOW...
IT'S GOT TO BE THE DARK HAVEN THAT'S DRAWING ALL OF THIS MYSTICAL SYNERGY.
WHICH ALSO MAKES IT THE MOST LIKELY PLACE THAT BITCH WOULD'VE TAKEN JOE. LET'S GO--
Eh?
KEVIN...
I CAN'T GO WITH YOU. I'M NO AVATAR.
BUT HERE'S SOMETHING TO HELP KEEP YOU SAFE.
Um... THANKS.
WISH US LUCK.
LUCK.

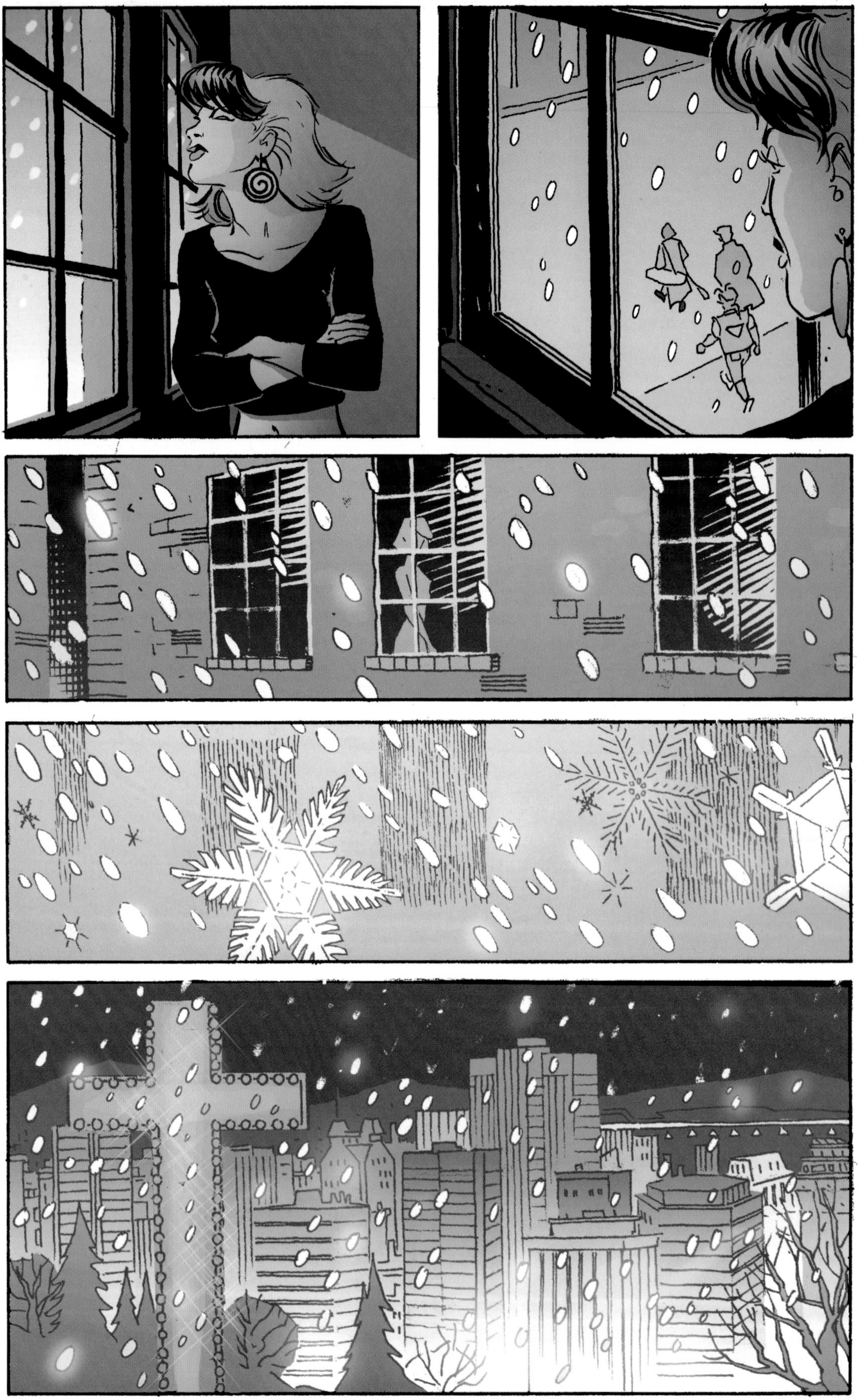

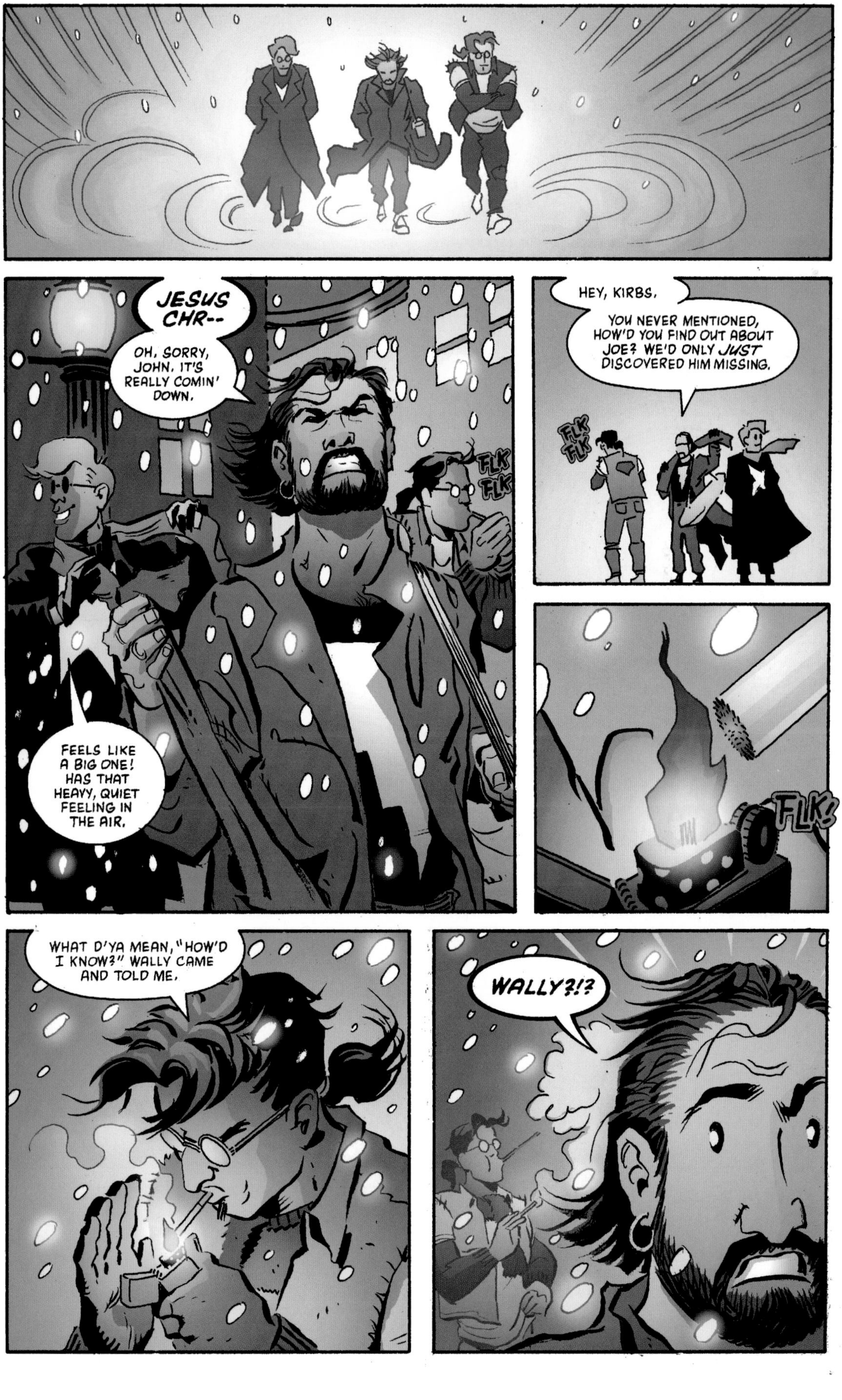
JESUS CHR--
OH, SORRY, JOHN. IT'S REALLY COMIN' DOWN.
FLK FLK
FEELS LIKE A BIG ONE! HAS THAT HEAVY, QUIET FEELING IN THE AIR.
HEY, KIRBS.
YOU NEVER MENTIONED, HOW'D YOU FIND OUT ABOUT JOE? WE'D ONLY JUST DISCOVERED HIM MISSING.
FLK FLK
FLK!
WHAT D'YA MEAN, "HOW'D I KNOW?" WALLY CAME AND TOLD ME.
WALLY?!?

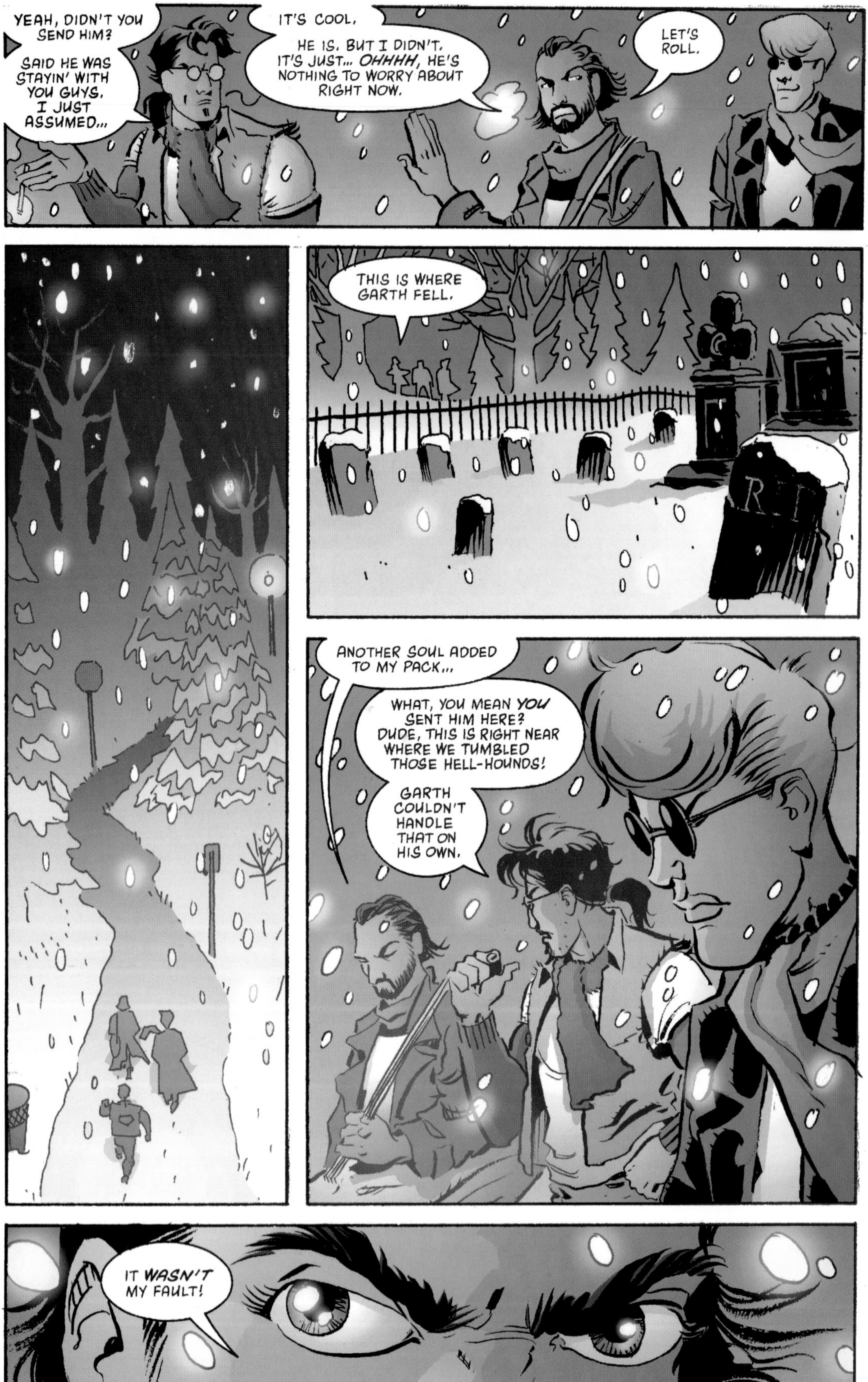
YEAH, DIDN'T YOU SEND HIM?
SAID HE WAS STAYIN' WITH YOU GUYS, I JUST ASSUMED...
IT'S COOL.
HE IS. BUT I DIDN'T. IT'S JUST... OHHHH, HE'S NOTHING TO WORRY ABOUT RIGHT NOW.
LET'S ROLL.
THIS IS WHERE GARTH FELL.
ANOTHER SOUL ADDED TO MY PACK...
WHAT, YOU MEAN YOU SENT HIM HERE? DUDE, THIS IS RIGHT NEAR WHERE WE TUMBLED THOSE HELL-HOUNDS!
GARTH COULDN'T HANDLE THAT ON HIS OWN.
IT WASN'T MY FAULT!

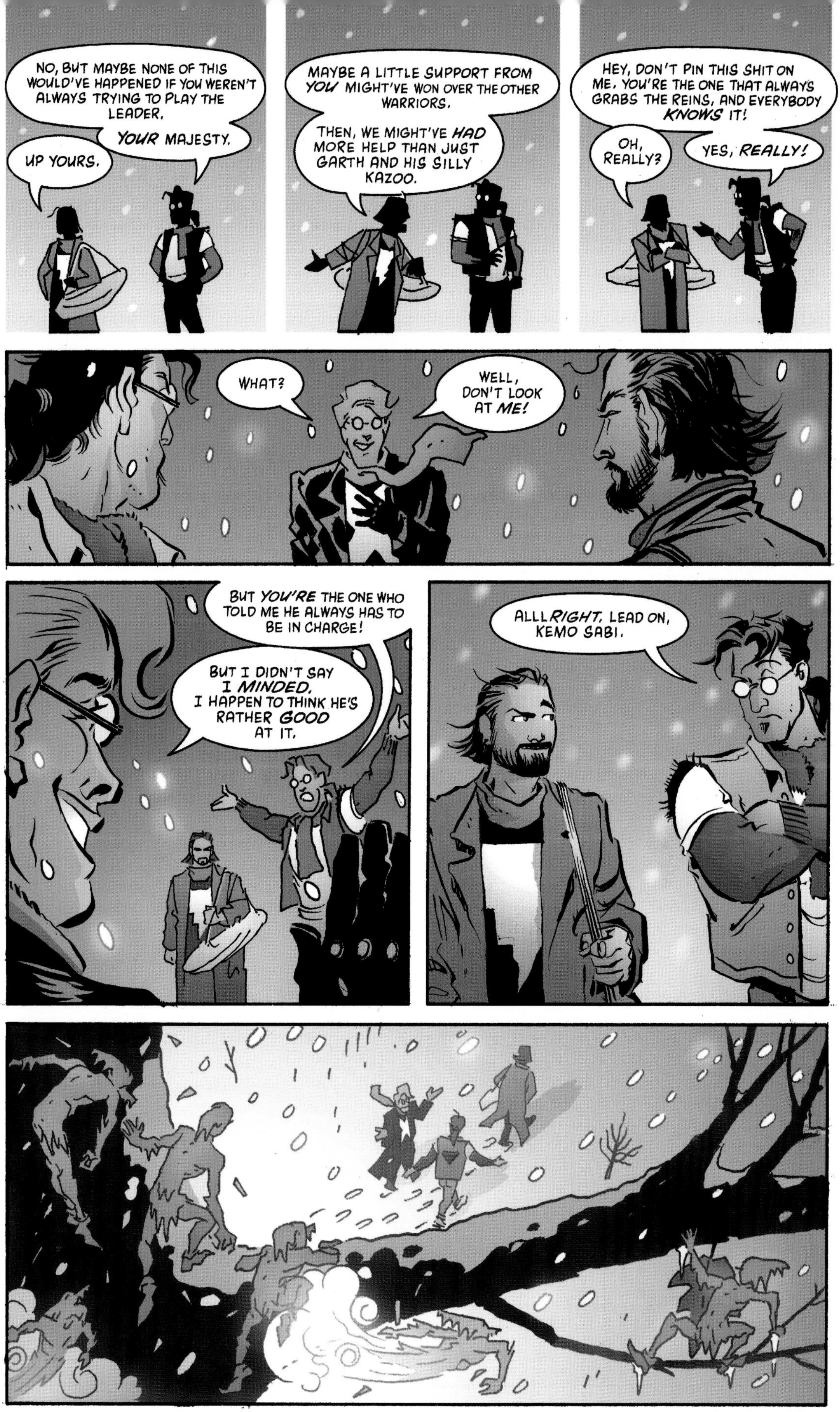
NO, BUT MAYBE NONE OF THIS WOULD'VE HAPPENED IF YOU WEREN'T ALWAYS TRYING TO PLAY THE LEADER.
YOUR MAJESTY.
UP YOURS.
MAYBE A LITTLE SUPPORT FROM YOU MIGHT'VE WON OVER THE OTHER WARRIORS.
THEN, WE MIGHT'VE HAD MORE HELP THAN JUST GARTH AND HIS SILLY KAZOO.
HEY, DON'T PIN THIS SHIT ON ME. YOU'RE THE ONE THAT ALWAYS GRABS THE REINS, AND EVERYBODY KNOWS IT!
OH, REALLY?
YES, REALLY!
WHAT?
WELL, DON'T LOOK AT ME!
BUT YOU'RE THE ONE WHO TOLD ME HE ALWAYS HAS TO BE IN CHARGE!
BUT I DIDN'T SAY I MINDED. I HAPPEN TO THINK HE'S RATHER GOOD AT IT.
ALLLRIGHT. LEAD ON, KEMO SABI.

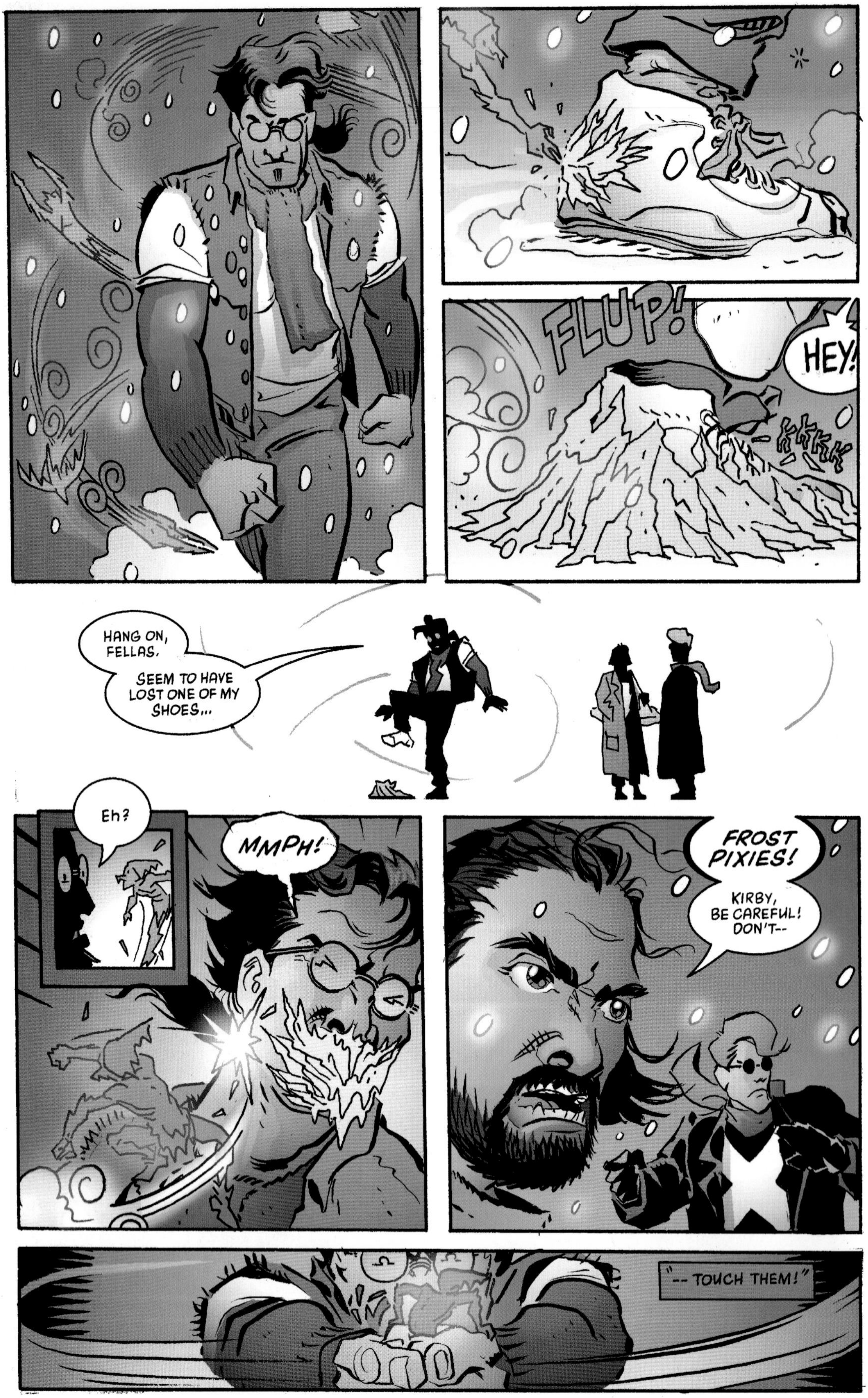
FLUP!
HEY!
KKKK
HANG ON, FELLAS.
SEEM TO HAVE LOST ONE OF MY SHOES...
Eh?
MMPH!
FROST PIXIES!
KIRBY, BE CAREFUL! DON'T--
"-- TOUCH THEM!"

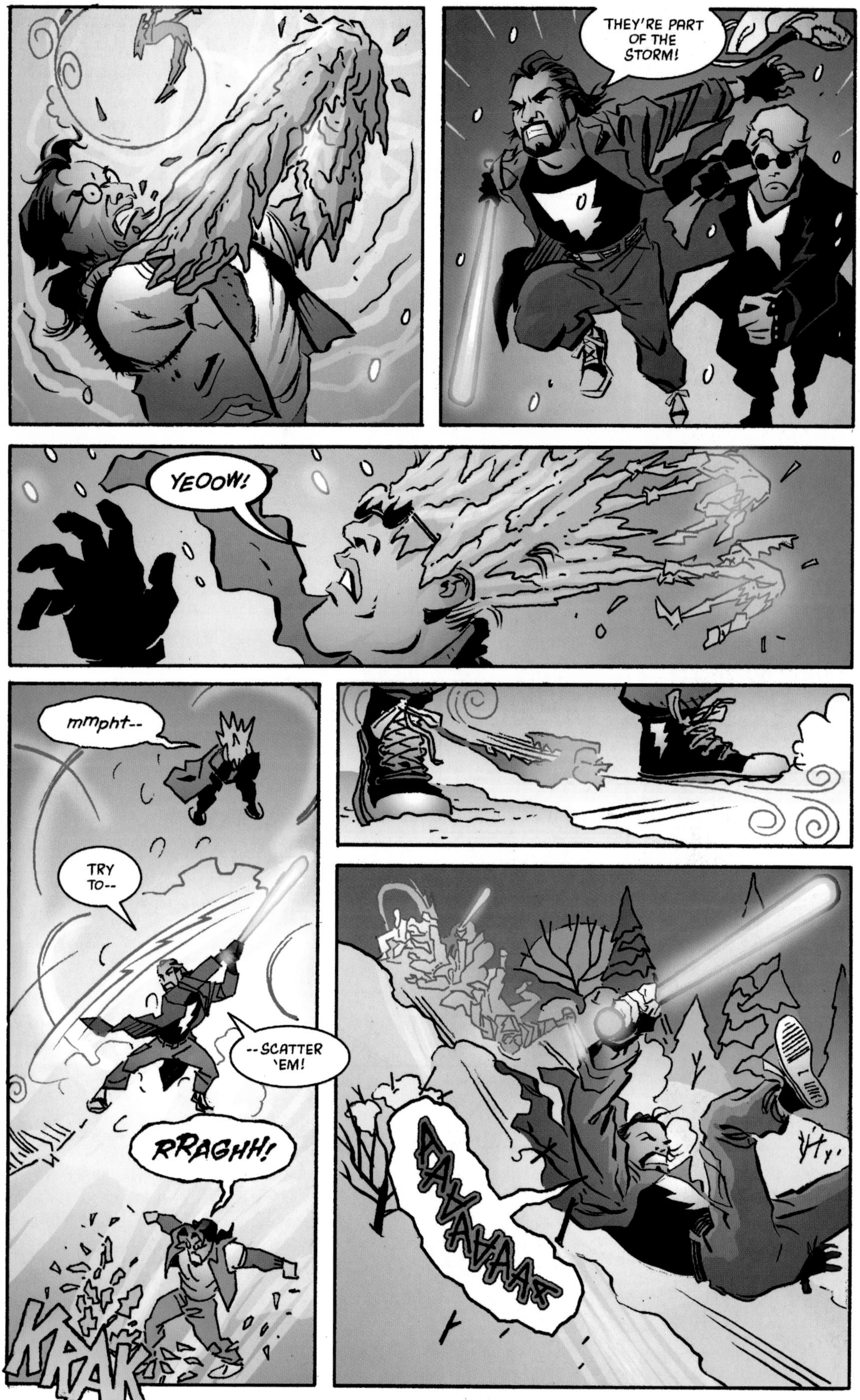
THEY'RE PART OF THE STORM!
YEOOW!
mmpht--
TRY TO--
--SCATTER 'EM!
RRAGHH!
KRAK

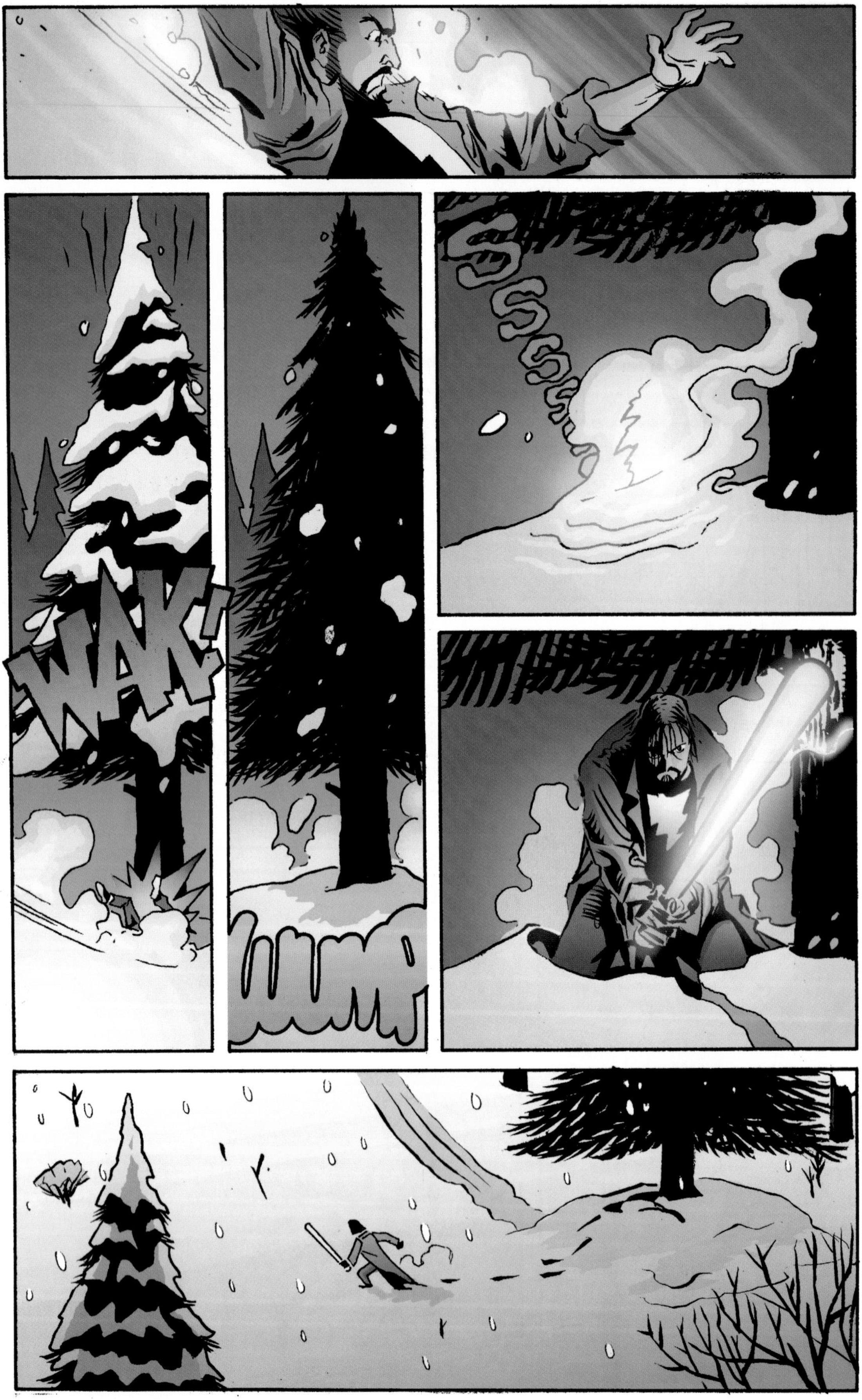
WAK!
WUMP
SSSS

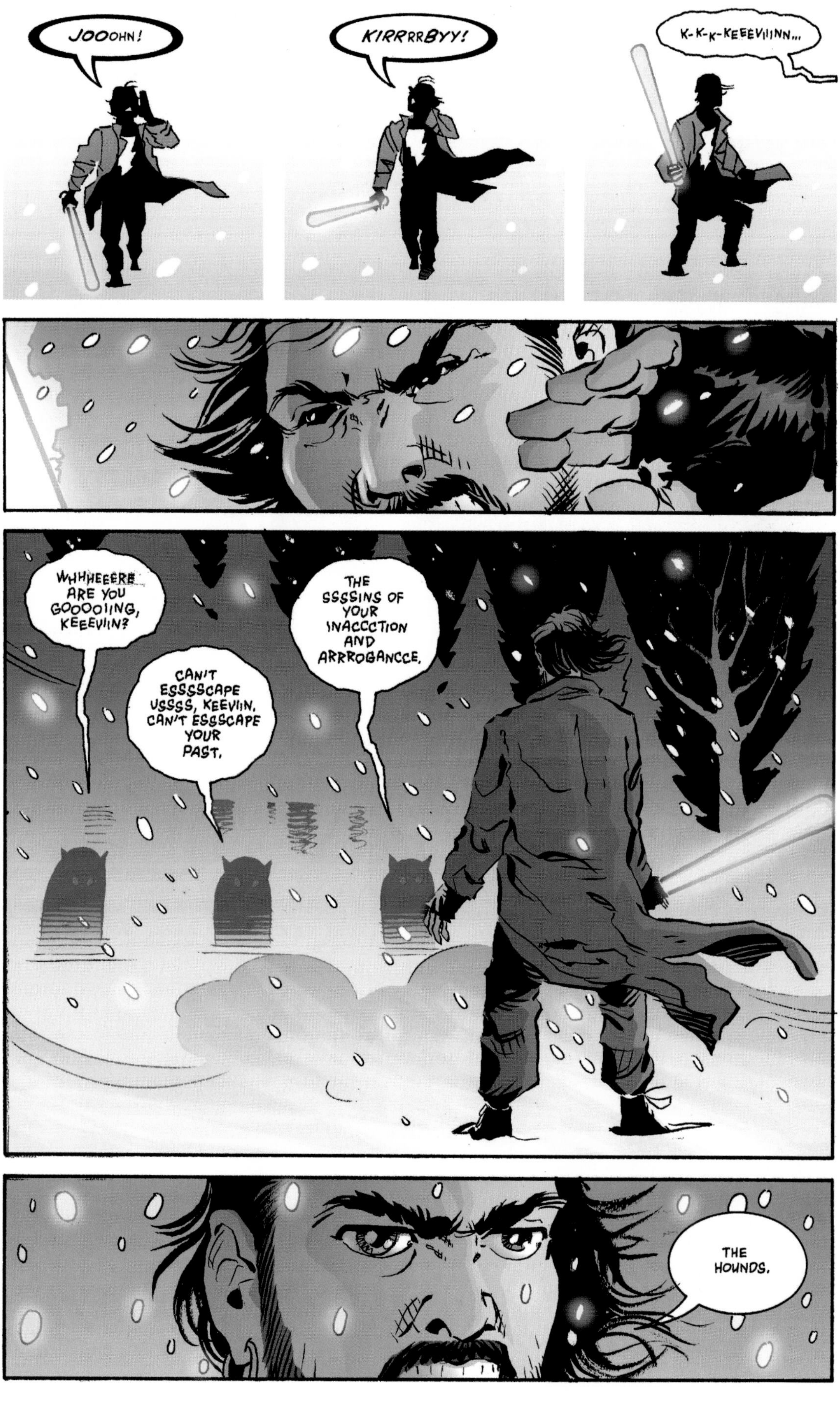
JOOOHN!
KIRRRRBYY!
K-K-K-KEEEVIIINN...
WHHHEEERE ARE YOU GOOOOIING, KEEEVIIN?
CAN'T ESSSSCAPE USSSS, KEEVIIN. CAN'T ESSSCAPE YOUR PAST.
THE SSSSINS OF YOUR INACCCTION AND ARRROGANCCE.
THE HOUNDS.

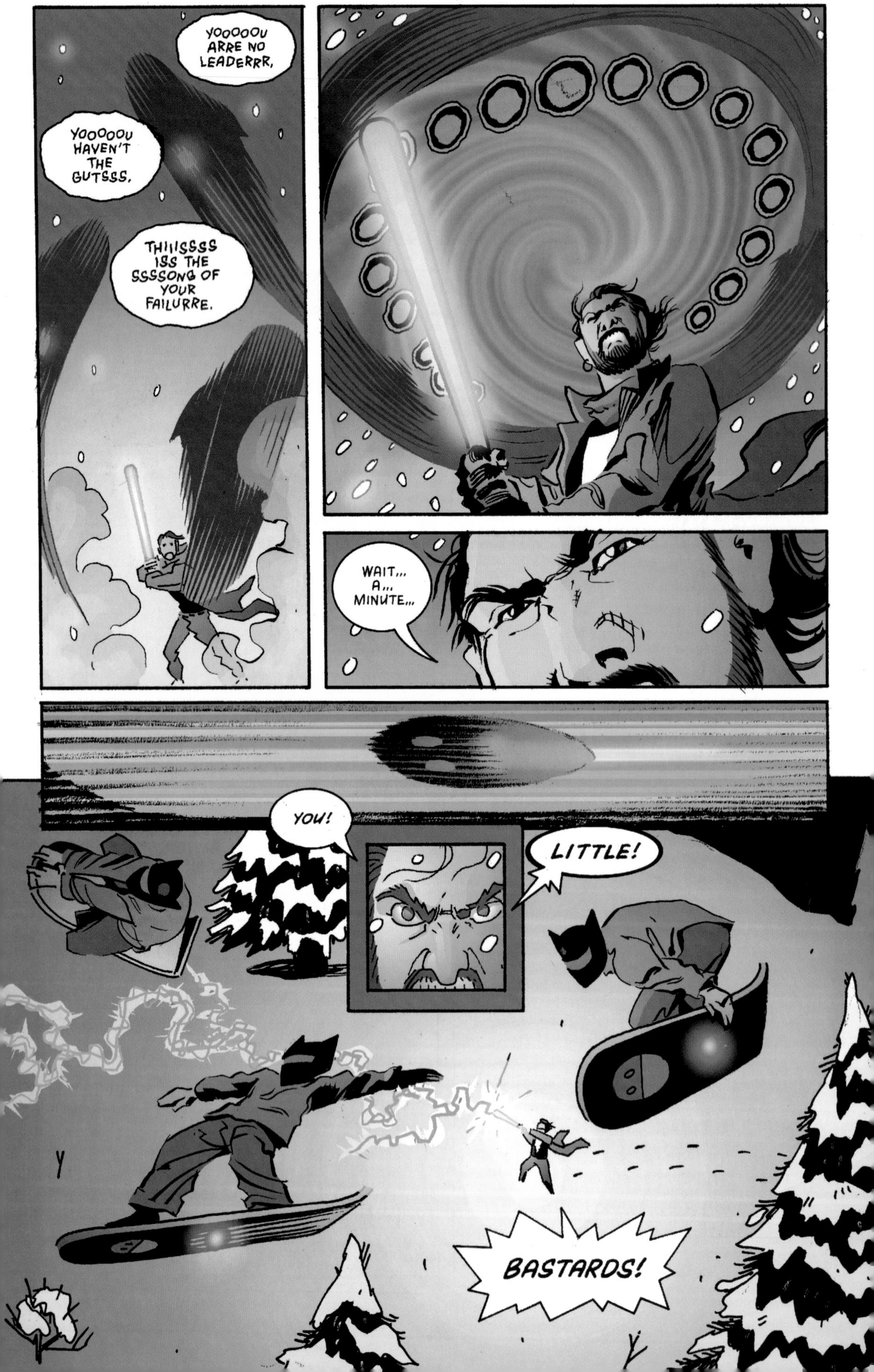
YOOOOOU ARRE NO LEADERRR,
YOOOOOU HAVEN'T THE GUTSSS,
THIIISSSS ISS THE SSSSONG OF YOUR FAILURRE.
WAIT... A... MINUTE...
YOU!
LITTLE!
BASTARDS!

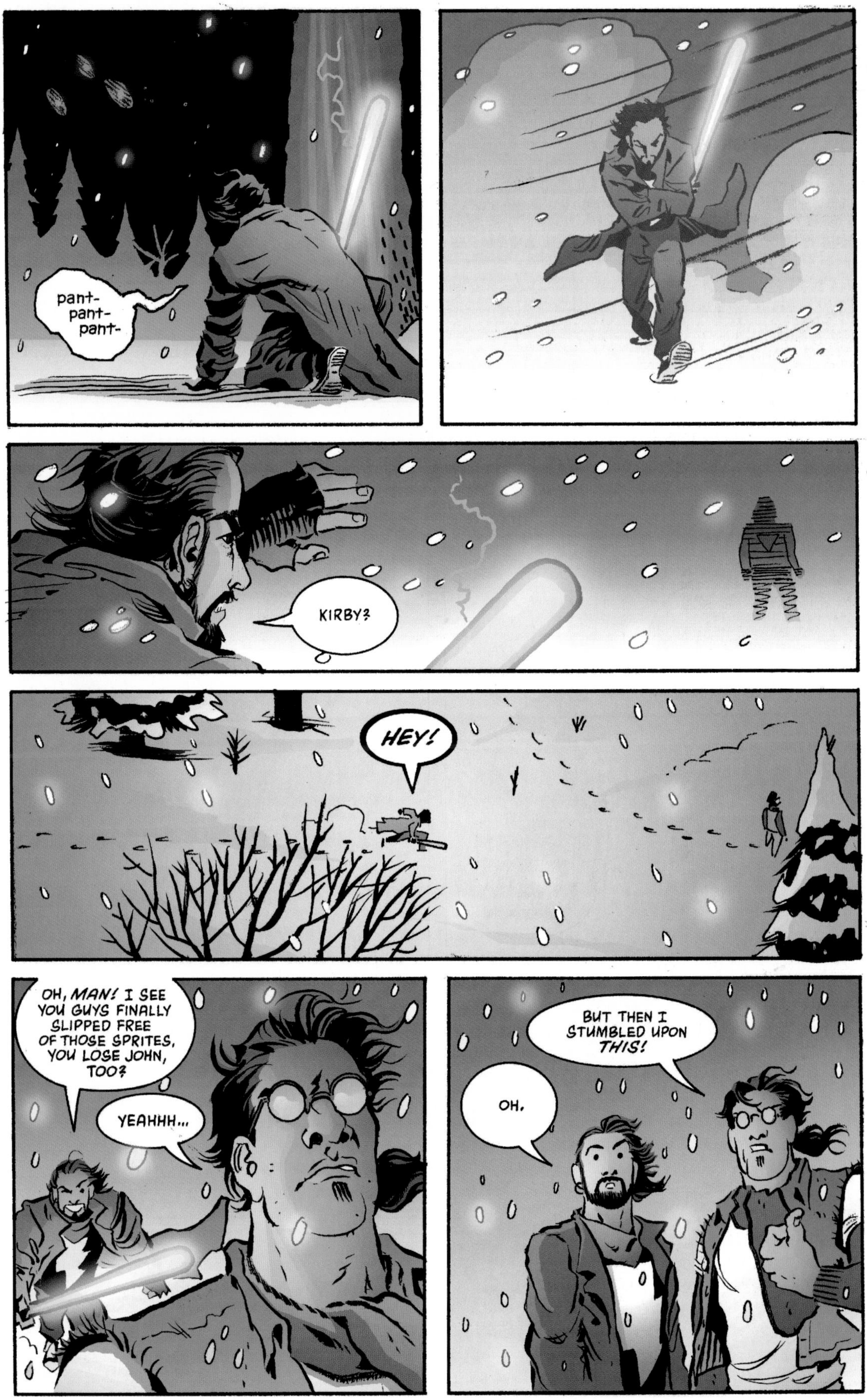
pant-
pant-
pant-
KIRBY?
HEY!
OH, MAN! I SEE YOU GUYS FINALLY SLIPPED FREE OF THOSE SPRITES, YOU LOSE JOHN, TOO?
YEAHHH...
BUT THEN I STUMBLED UPON THIS!
OH.

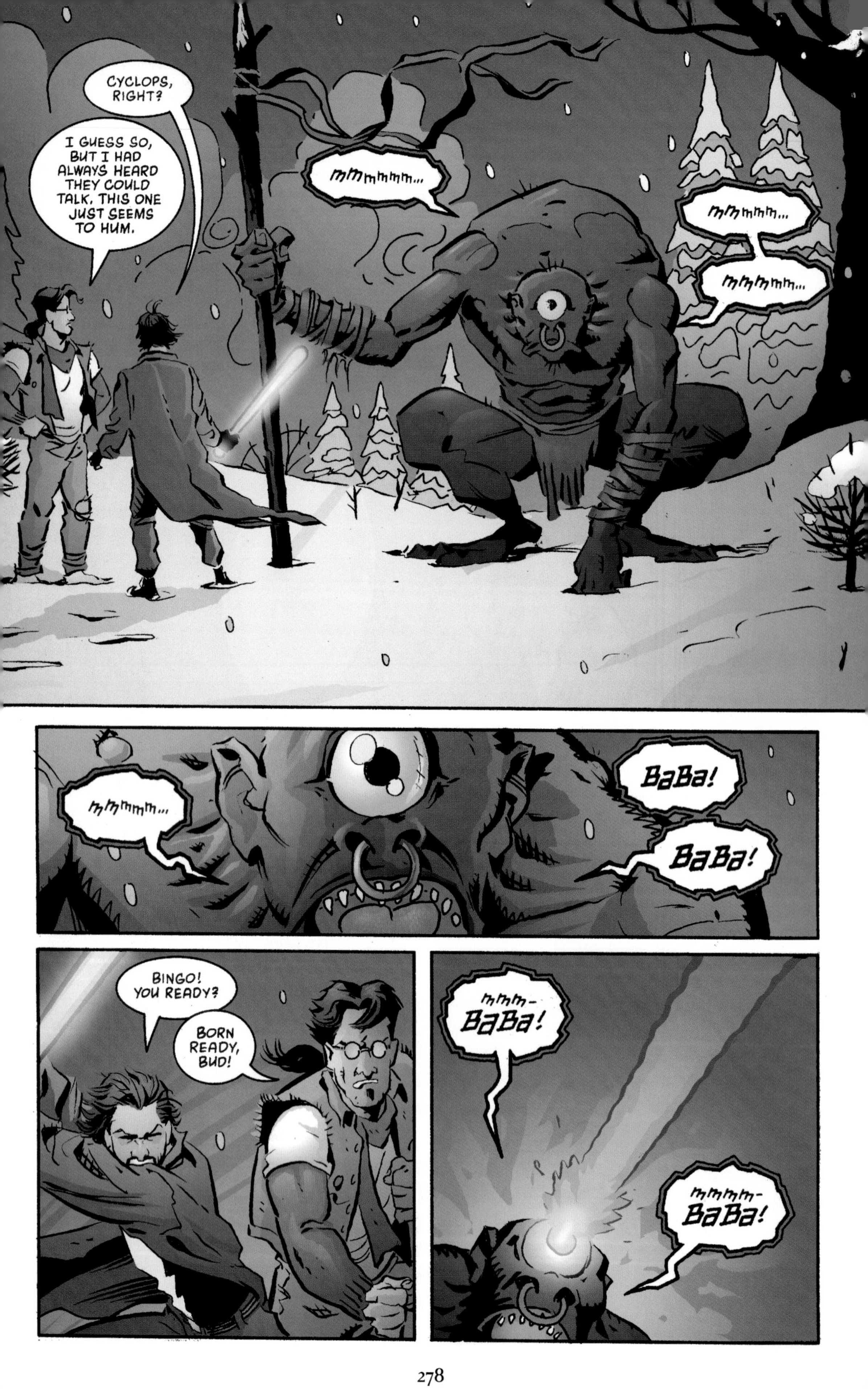
CYCLOPS, RIGHT?
I GUESS SO, BUT I HAD ALWAYS HEARD THEY COULD TALK. THIS ONE JUST SEEMS TO HUM.
mmmmmm...
mmmmm...
mmmmm...
mmmmm...
BaBa!
BaBa!
BINGO! YOU READY?
BORN READY, BUD!
mmm-BaBa!
mmmm-BaBa!

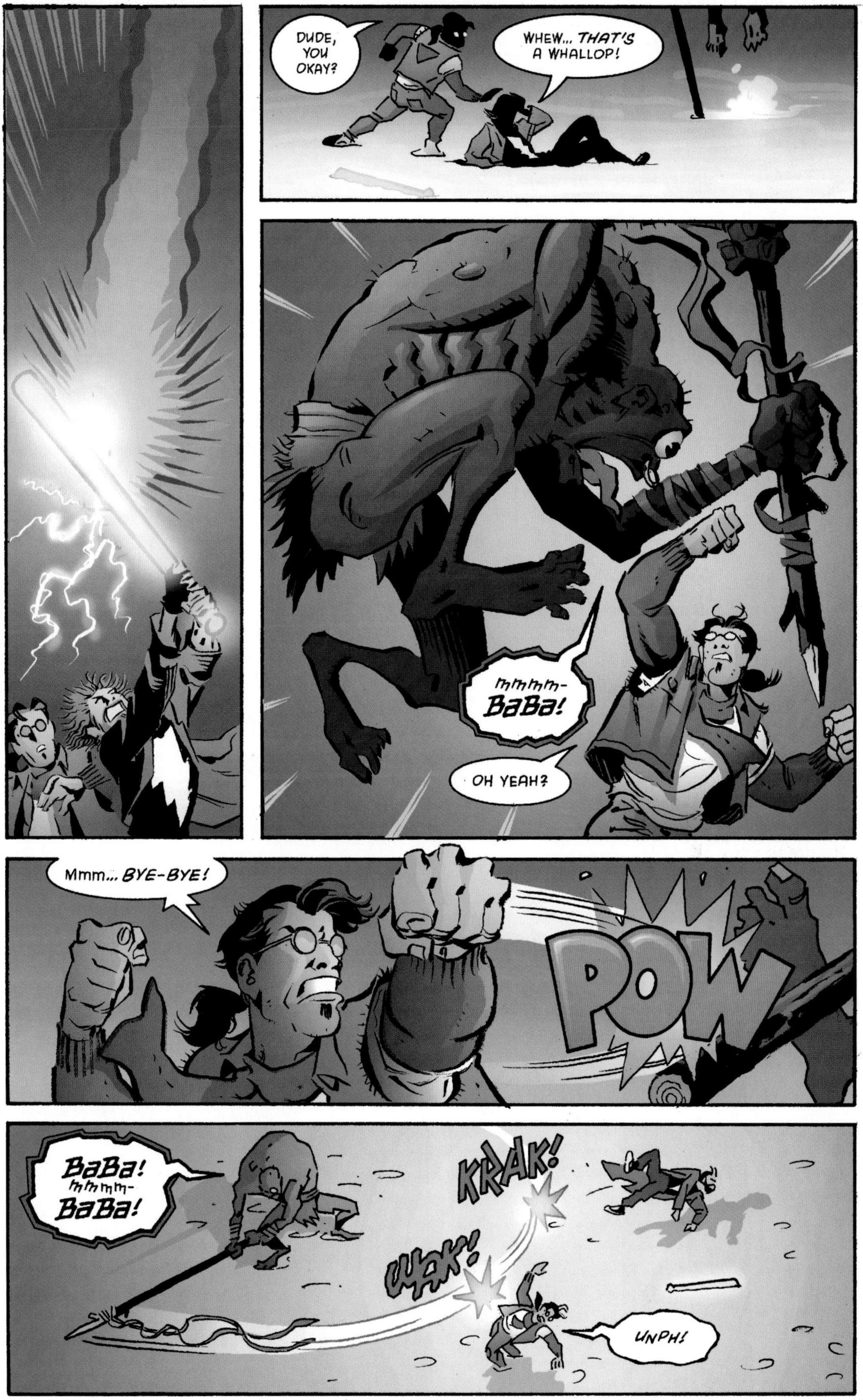
DUDE, YOU OKAY?
WHEW... THAT'S A WHALLOP!
mmmm-BaBa!
OH YEAH?
Mmm... BYE-BYE!
POW
BaBa! mmmm-BaBa!
KRAK!
WAK!
UNPH!

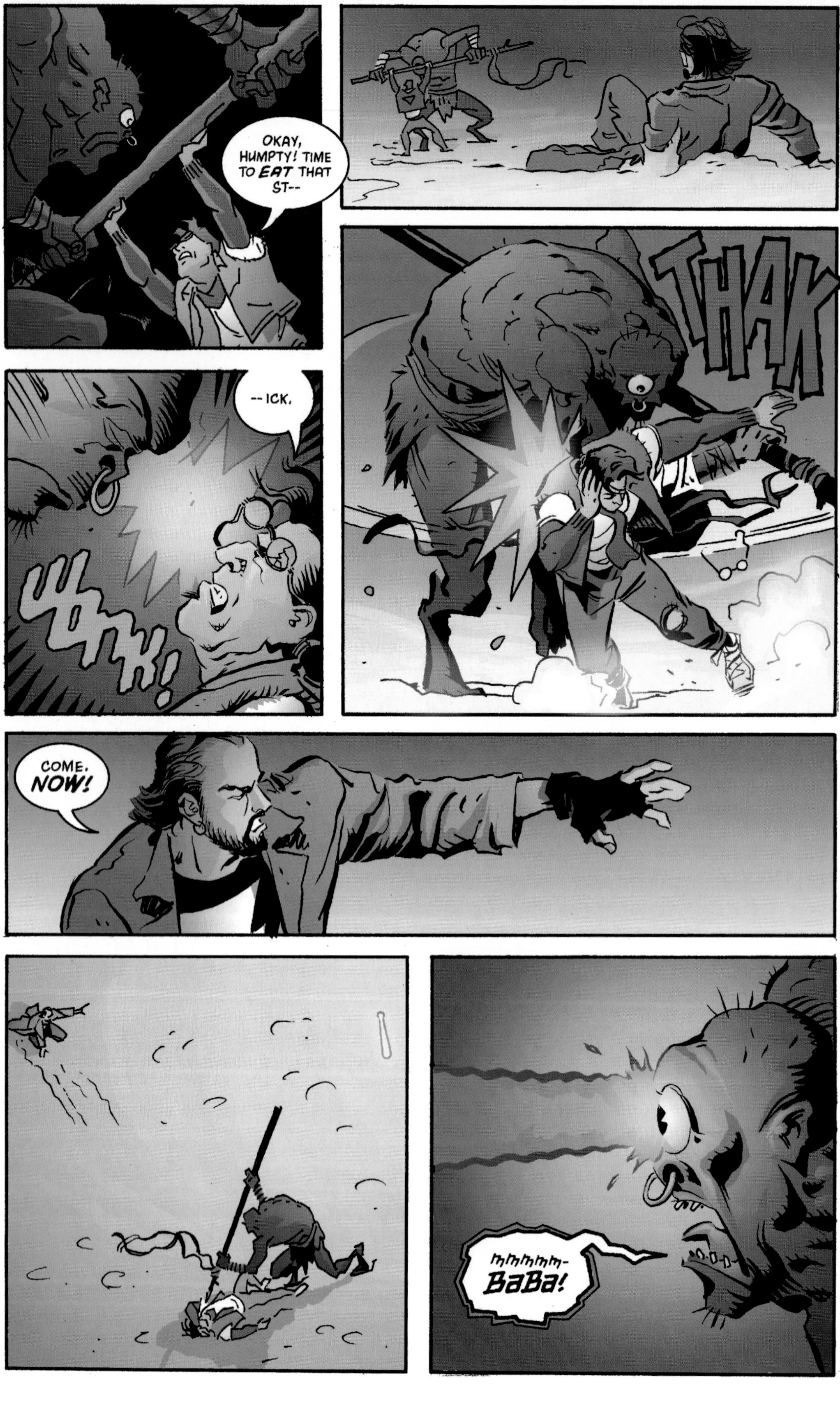
OKAY, HUMPTY! TIME TO EAT THAT ST--
THAK
--ICK.
YONK!
COME. NOW!
mmmmm-BaBa!

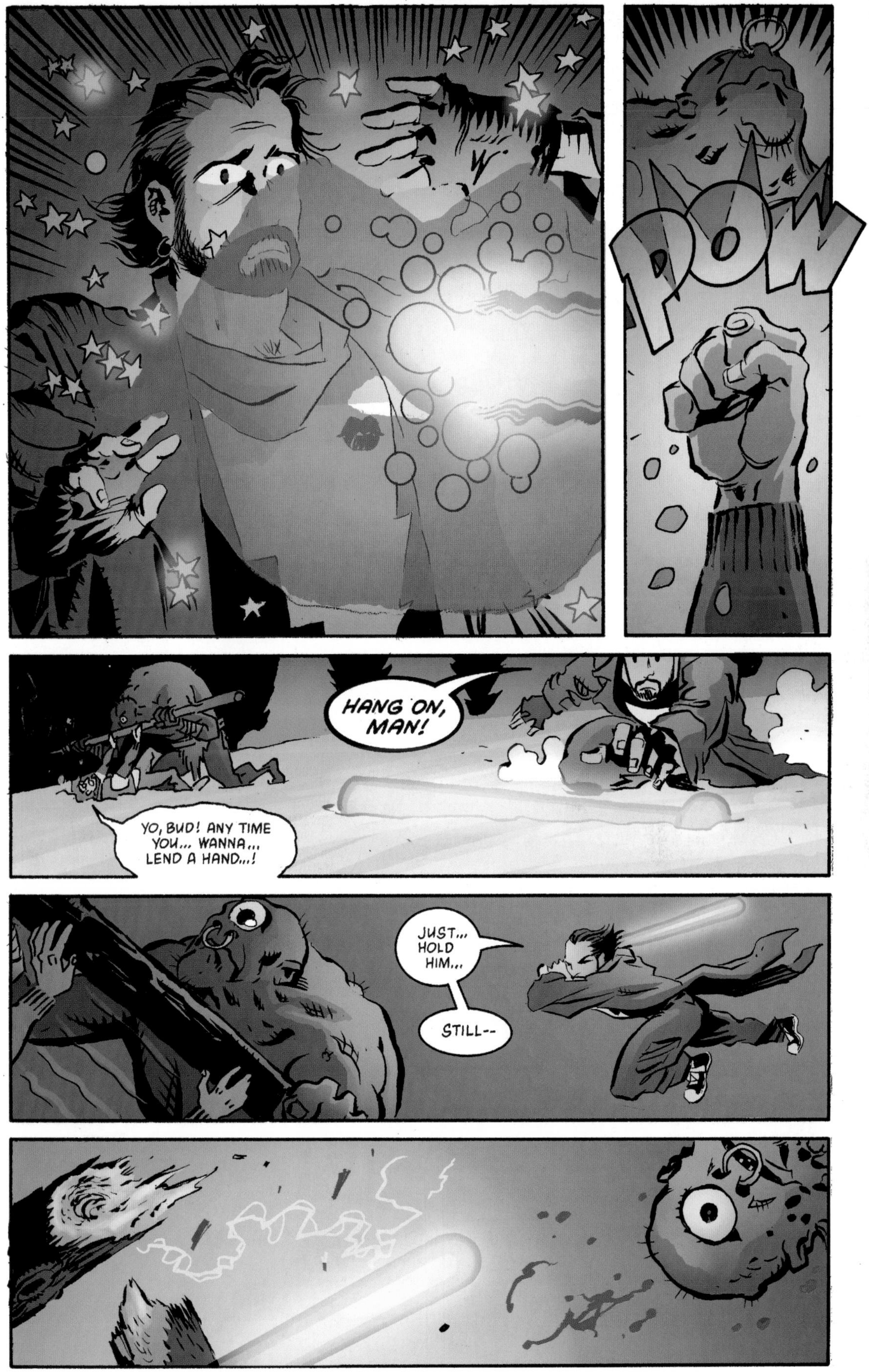
POW
YO, BUD! ANY TIME YOU... WANNA... LEND A HAND...!
HANG ON, MAN!
JUST... HOLD HIM...
STILL--

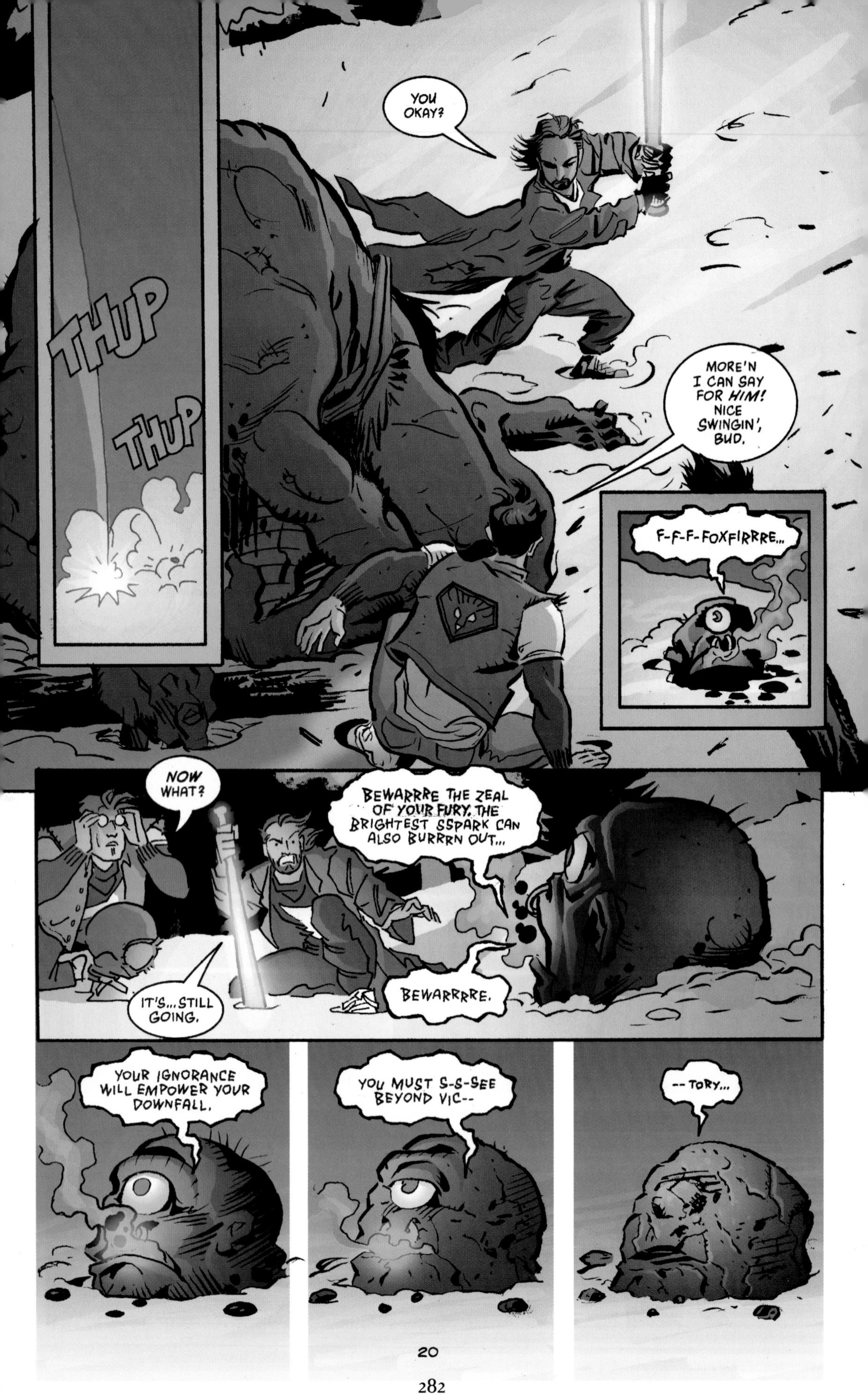
THUP
THUP
YOU OKAY?
MORE'N I CAN SAY FOR HIM! NICE SWINGIN', BUD.
F-F-F-FOXFIRRRE...
NOW WHAT?
BEWARRRE THE ZEAL OF YOUR FURY. THE BRIGHTEST SSPARK CAN ALSO BURRRN OUT...
IT'S...STILL GOING.
BEWARRRRE.
YOUR IGNORANCE WILL EMPOWER YOUR DOWNFALL.
YOU MUST S-S-SEE BEYOND VIC--
--TORY...
20

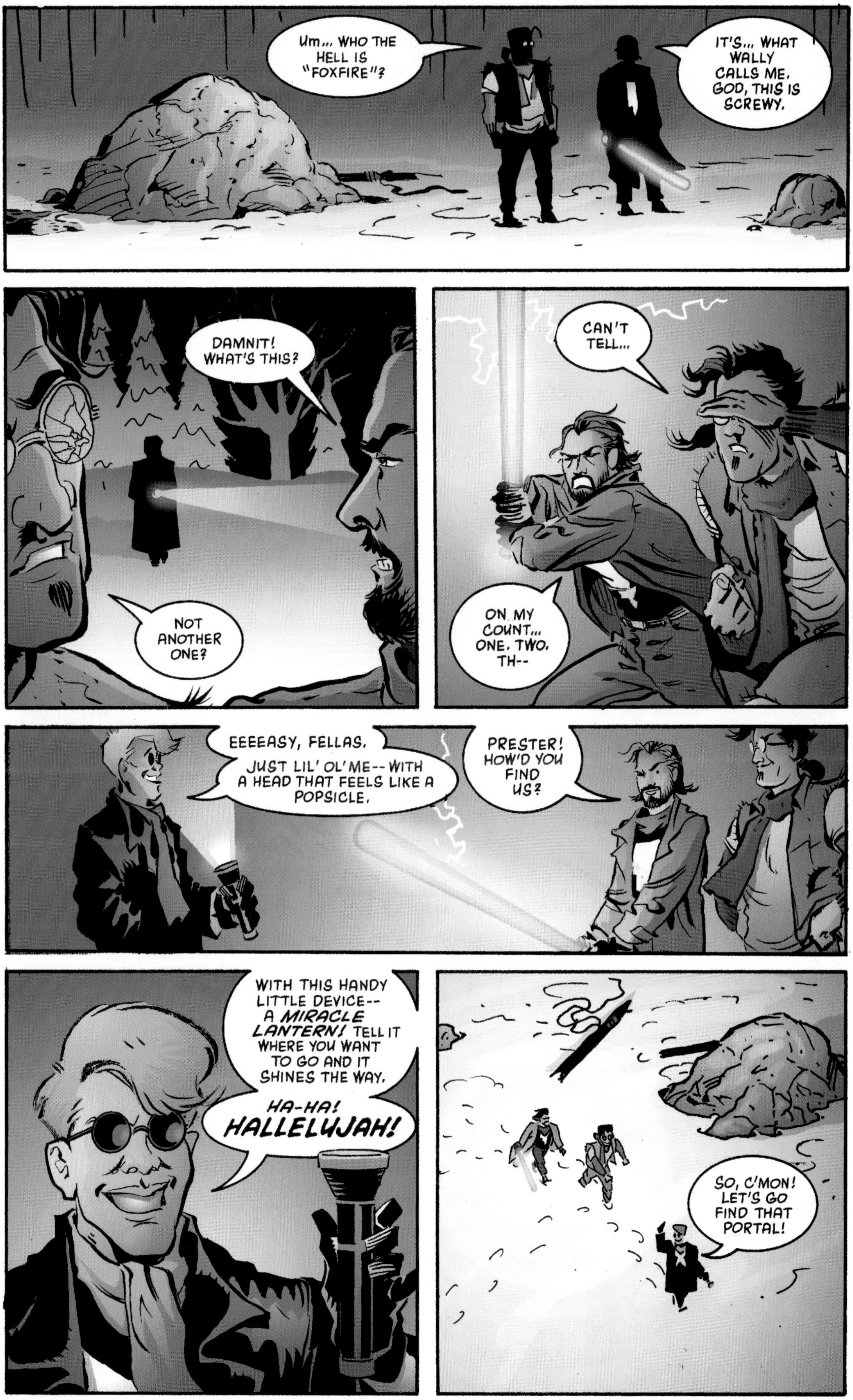
Um... WHO THE HELL IS "FOXFIRE"?
IT'S... WHAT WALLY CALLS ME. GOD, THIS IS SCREWY.
DAMNIT! WHAT'S THIS?
NOT ANOTHER ONE?
CAN'T TELL...
ON MY COUNT... ONE, TWO, TH--
EEEEASY, FELLAS.
JUST LIL' OL' ME-- WITH A HEAD THAT FEELS LIKE A POPSICLE.
PRESTER! HOW'D YOU FIND US?
WITH THIS HANDY LITTLE DEVICE-- A *MIRACLE LANTERN!* TELL IT WHERE YOU WANT TO GO AND IT SHINES THE WAY.
HA-HA! **HALLELUJAH!**
SO, C'MON! LET'S GO FIND THAT PORTAL!

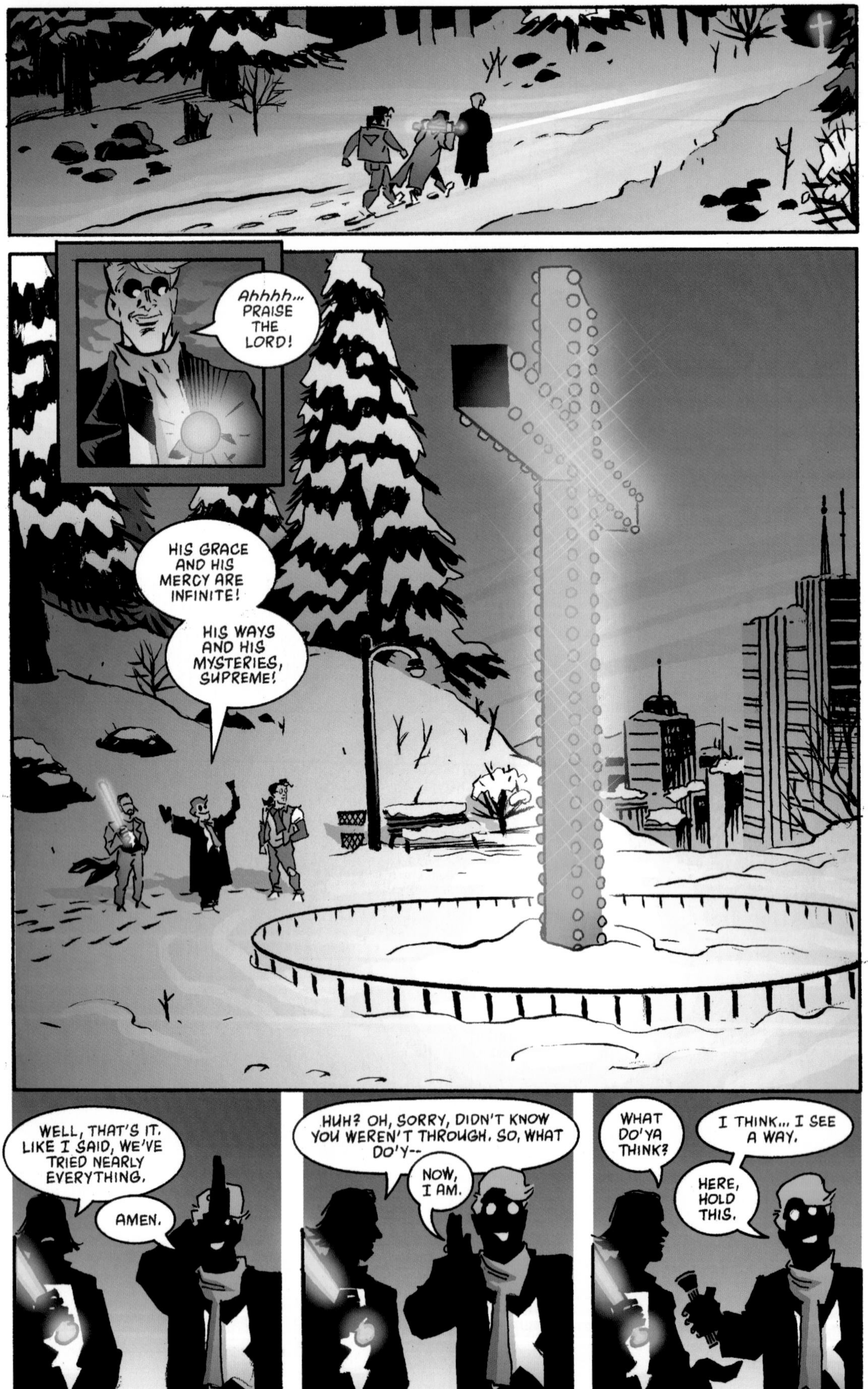
Ahhhh... PRAISE THE LORD!
HIS GRACE AND HIS MERCY ARE INFINITE!
HIS WAYS AND HIS MYSTERIES, SUPREME!
WELL, THAT'S IT. LIKE I SAID, WE'VE TRIED NEARLY EVERYTHING.
AMEN.
HUH? OH, SORRY, DIDN'T KNOW YOU WEREN'T THROUGH. SO, WHAT DO'Y--
NOW, I AM.
WHAT DO'YA THINK?
I THINK... I SEE A WAY.
HERE, HOLD THIS.

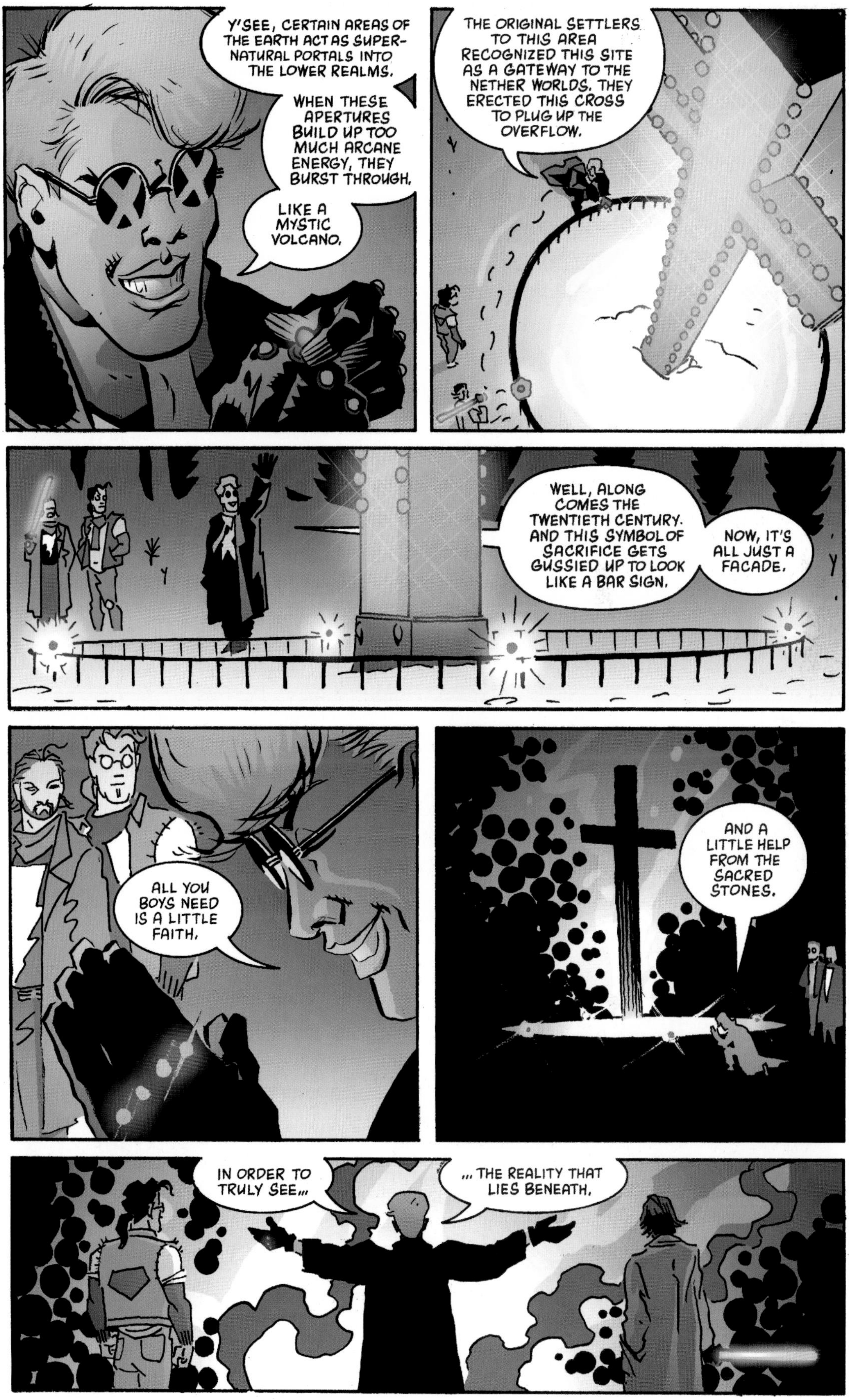
Y'SEE, CERTAIN AREAS OF THE EARTH ACT AS SUPER-NATURAL PORTALS INTO THE LOWER REALMS.
WHEN THESE APERTURES BUILD UP TOO MUCH ARCANE ENERGY, THEY BURST THROUGH.
LIKE A MYSTIC VOLCANO.
THE ORIGINAL SETTLERS TO THIS AREA RECOGNIZED THIS SITE AS A GATEWAY TO THE NETHER WORLDS. THEY ERECTED THIS CROSS TO PLUG UP THE OVERFLOW.
WELL, ALONG COMES THE TWENTIETH CENTURY. AND THIS SYMBOL OF SACRIFICE GETS GUSSIED UP TO LOOK LIKE A BAR SIGN.
NOW, IT'S ALL JUST A FACADE.
ALL YOU BOYS NEED IS A LITTLE FAITH.
AND A LITTLE HELP FROM THE SACRED STONES.
IN ORDER TO TRULY SEE...
...THE REALITY THAT LIES BENEATH.

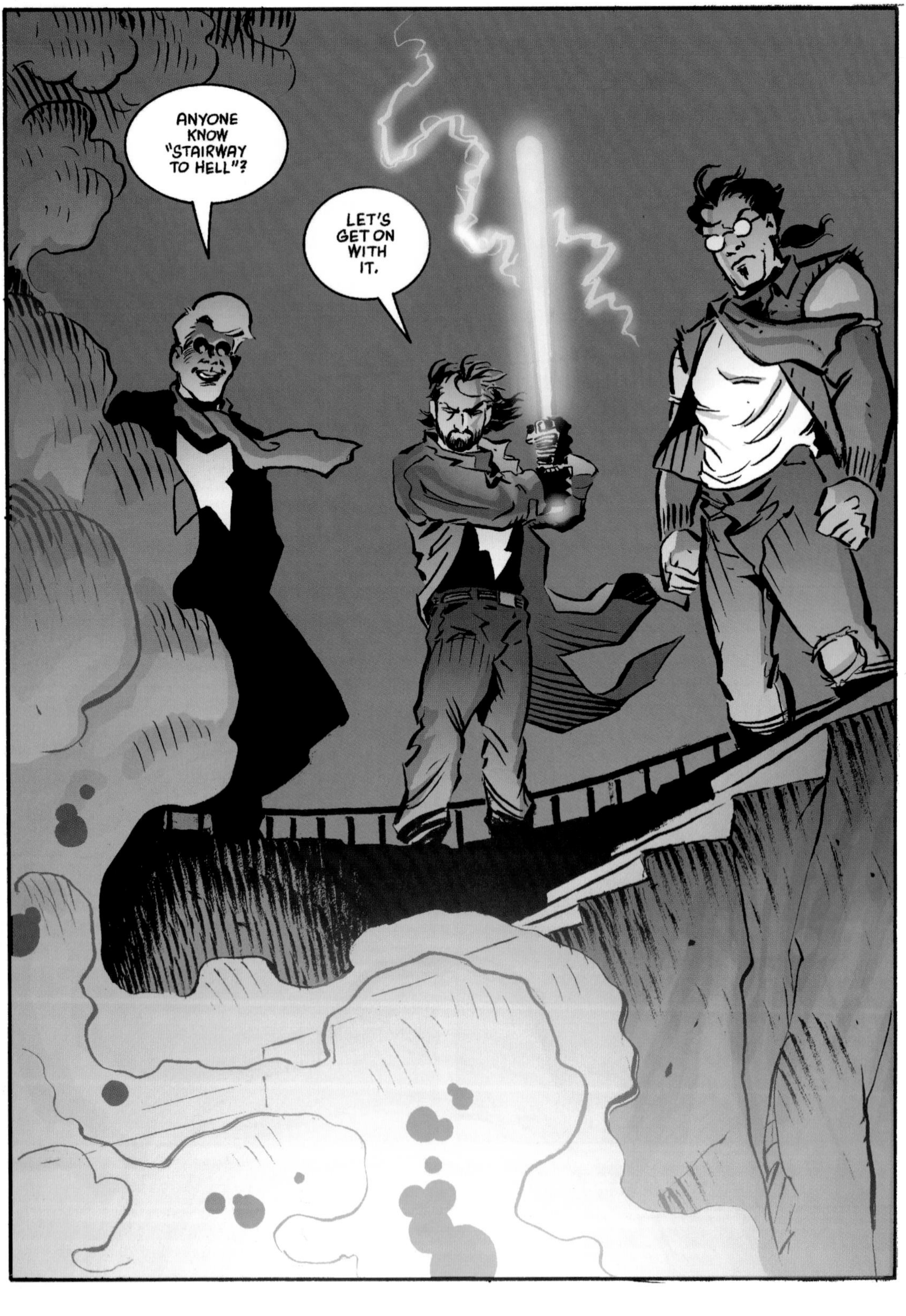
ANYONE KNOW "STAIRWAY TO HELL"?
LET'S GET ON WITH IT.

THE HERO DEFINED

MAGE®

chapter 12

"A Charmed Life"

LET'S GET ON WITH IT.

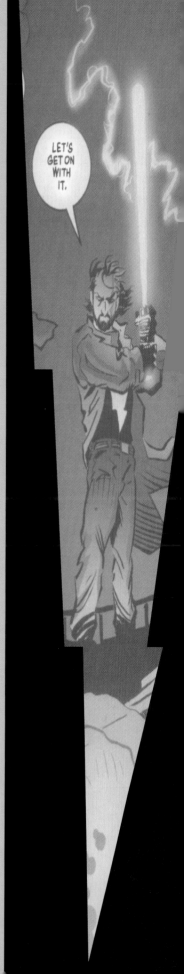

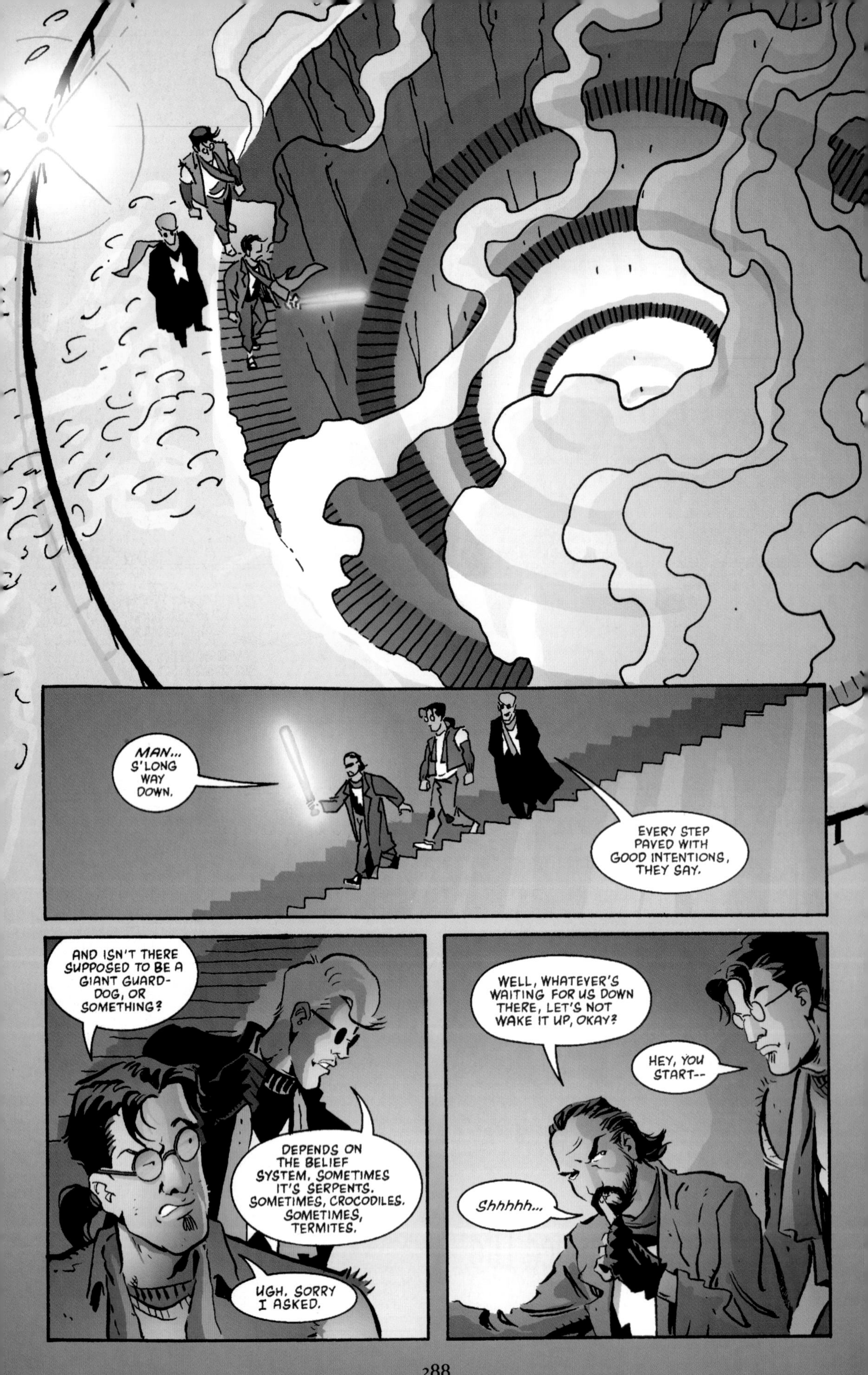
MAN... S'LONG WAY DOWN.
EVERY STEP PAVED WITH GOOD INTENTIONS, THEY SAY.
AND ISN'T THERE SUPPOSED TO BE A GIANT GUARD-DOG, OR SOMETHING?
DEPENDS ON THE BELIEF SYSTEM. SOMETIMES IT'S SERPENTS. SOMETIMES, CROCODILES. SOMETIMES, TERMITES.
UGH. SORRY I ASKED.
WELL, WHATEVER'S WAITING FOR US DOWN THERE, LET'S NOT WAKE IT UP, OKAY?
HEY, YOU START--
Shhhhh...

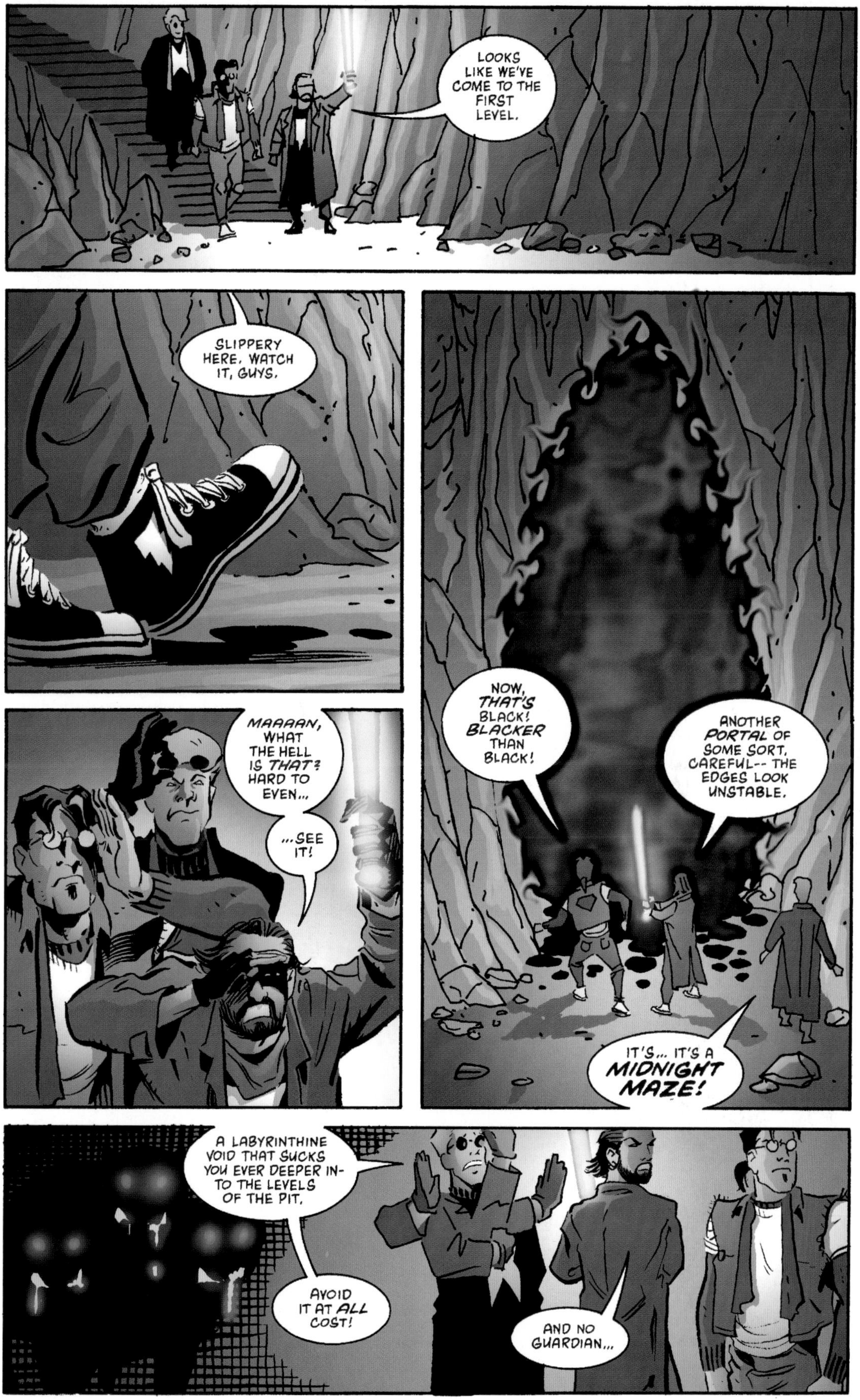
LOOKS LIKE WE'VE COME TO THE FIRST LEVEL.
SLIPPERY HERE. WATCH IT, GUYS.
MAAAAN, WHAT THE HELL IS THAT? HARD TO EVEN...
...SEE IT!
NOW, THAT'S BLACK! BLACKER THAN BLACK!
ANOTHER PORTAL OF SOME SORT, CAREFUL-- THE EDGES LOOK UNSTABLE.
IT'S... IT'S A MIDNIGHT MAZE!
A LABYRINTHINE VOID THAT SUCKS YOU EVER DEEPER IN-TO THE LEVELS OF THE PIT.
AVOID IT AT ALL COST!
AND NO GUARDIAN...

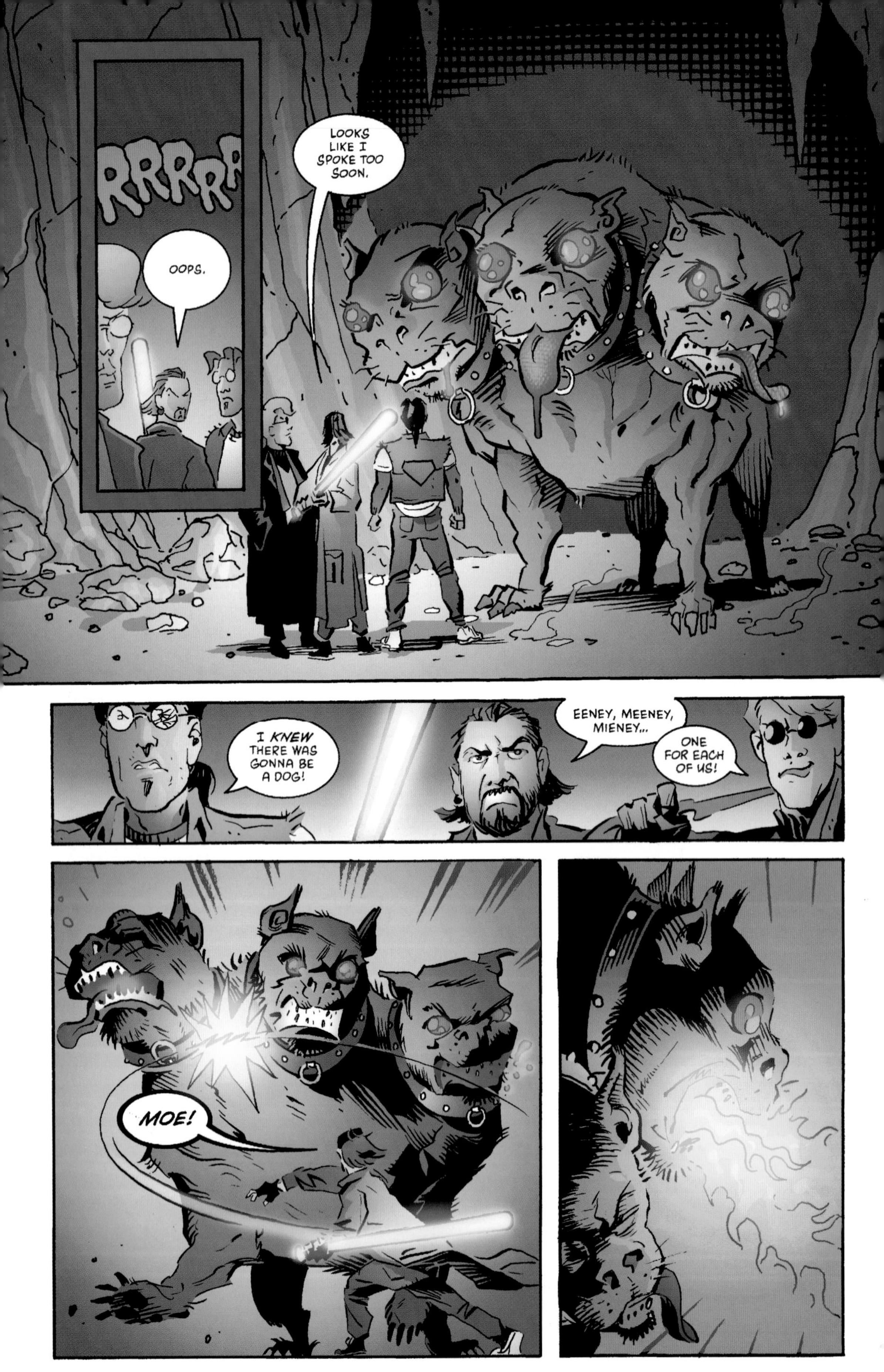
RRRRR
OOPS.
LOOKS LIKE I SPOKE TOO SOON.
I KNEW THERE WAS GONNA BE A DOG!
EENEY, MEENEY, MIENEY...
ONE FOR EACH OF US!
MOE!

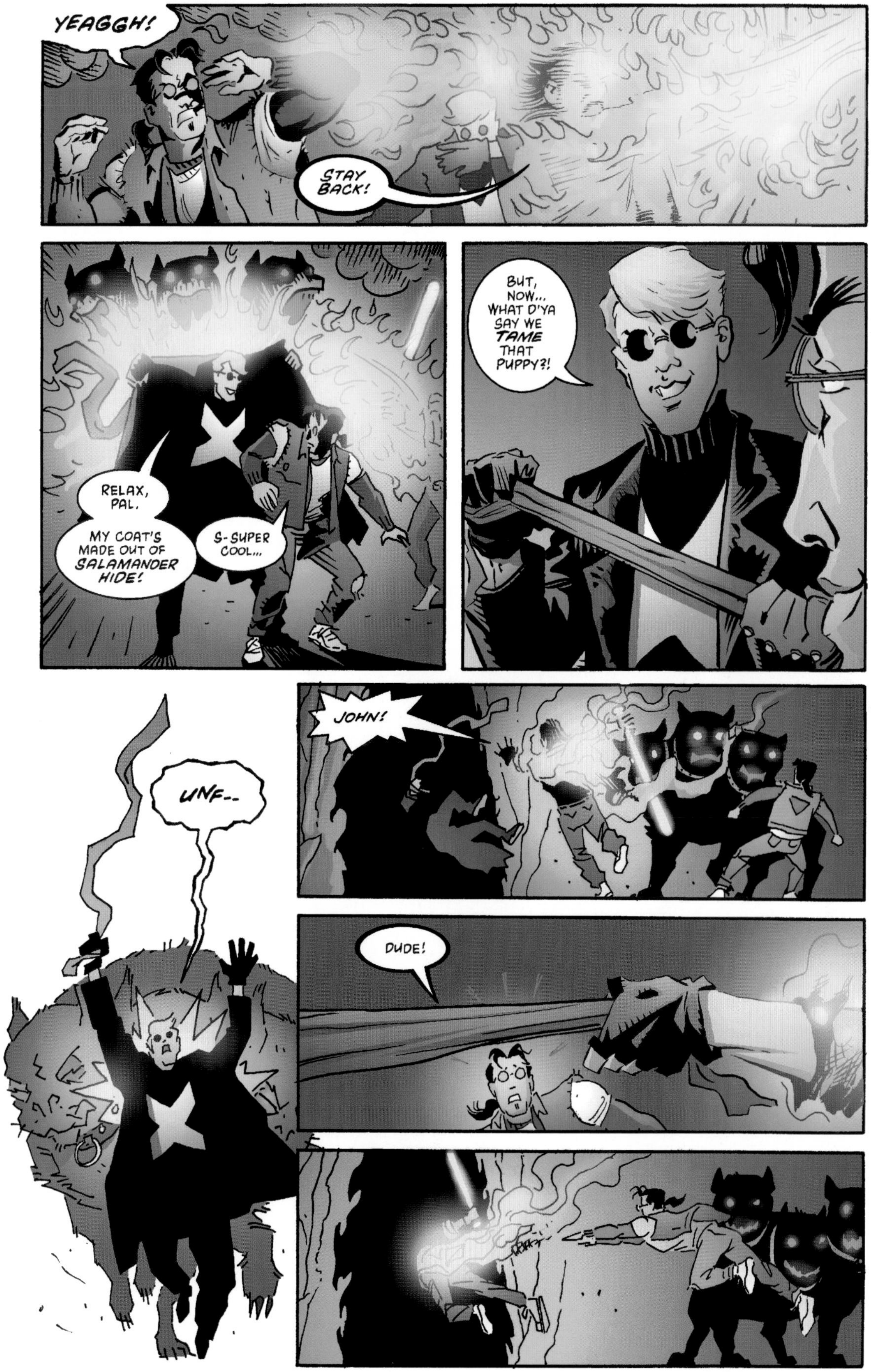
YEAGGH!
STAY BACK!
RELAX, PAL.
MY COAT'S MADE OUT OF SALAMANDER HIDE!
S-SUPER COOL...
BUT, NOW... WHAT D'YA SAY WE TAME THAT PUPPY?!
UNF--
JOHN!
DUDE!

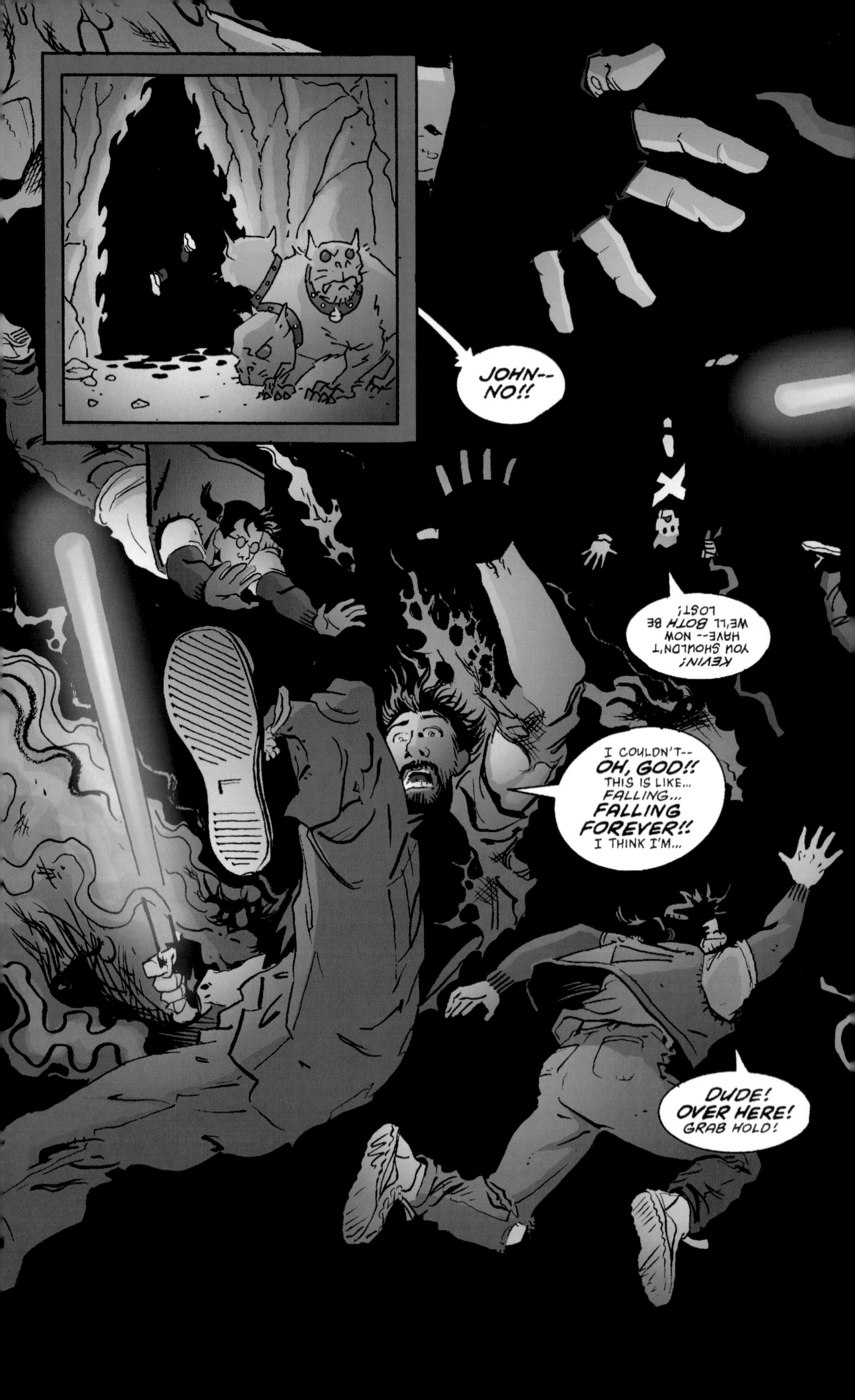
JOHN-- NO!!
KEVIN! YOU SHOULDN'T HAVE-- NOW WE'LL BOTH BE LOST!
I COULDN'T-- OH, GOD!! THIS IS LIKE... FALLING... FALLING FOREVER!! I THINK I'M...
DUDE! OVER HERE! GRAB HOLD!

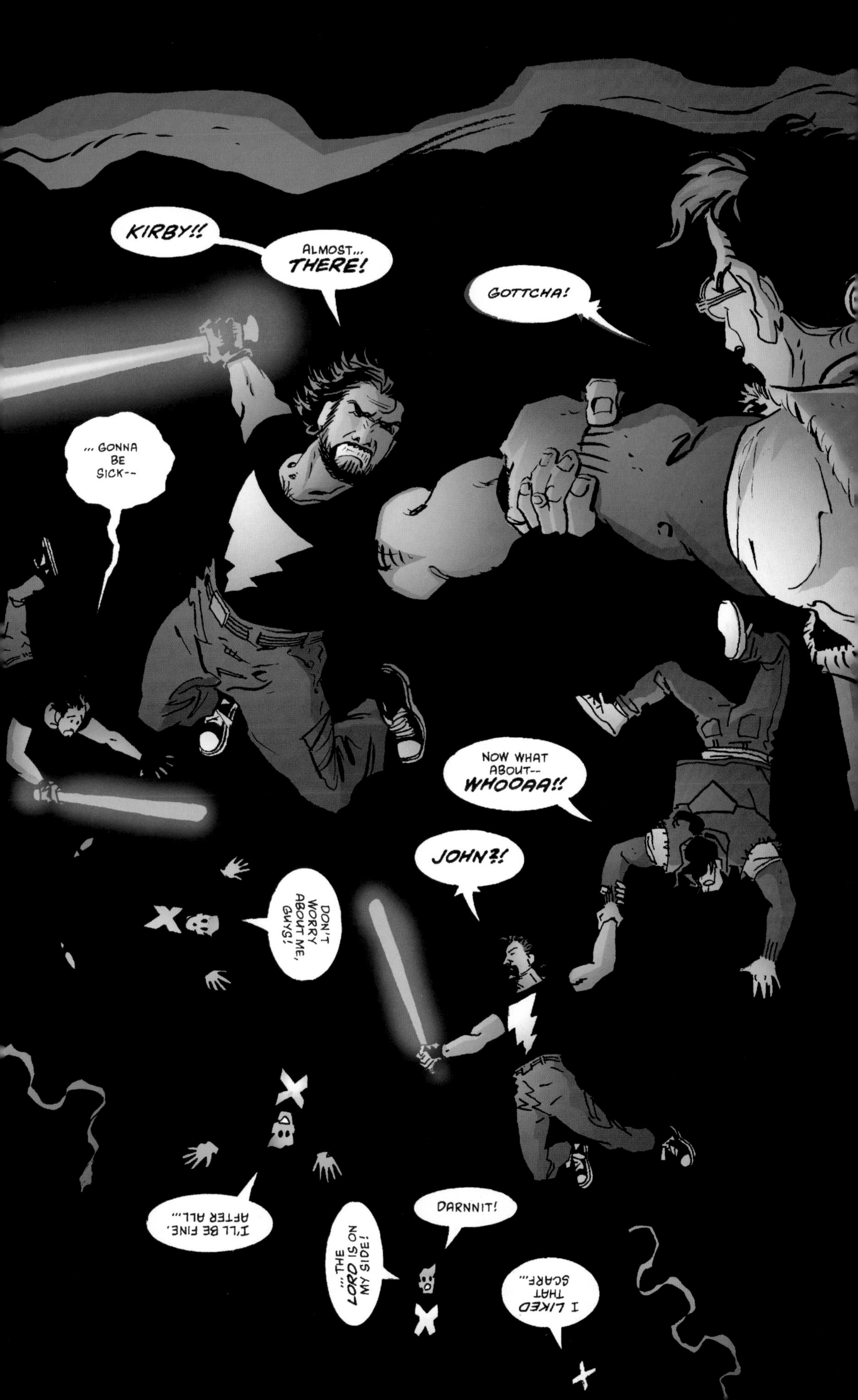
KIRBY!!
ALMOST... THERE!
GOTTCHA!
... GONNA BE SICK--
NOW WHAT ABOUT-- WHOOAA!!
JOHN?!
DON'T WORRY ABOUT ME, GUYS!
I'LL BE FINE, AFTER ALL...
... THE LORD IS ON MY SIDE!
DARNNIT!
I LIKED THAT SCARF...

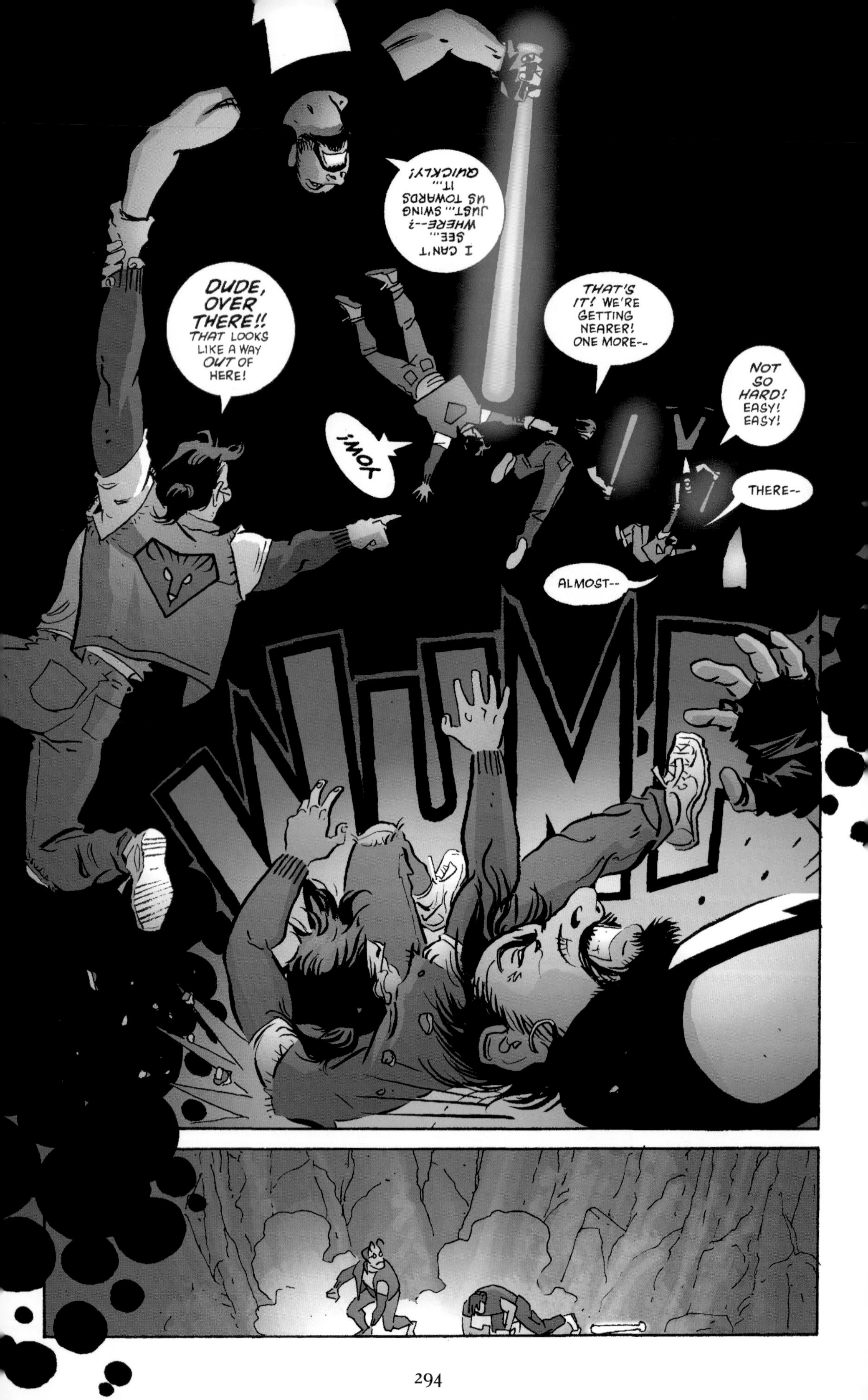
I CAN'T SEE... WHERE--? JUST... SWING US TOWARDS IT... QUICKLY!
DUDE, OVER THERE!! THAT LOOKS LIKE A WAY OUT OF HERE!
THAT'S IT! WE'RE GETTING NEARER! ONE MORE--
NOT SO HARD! EASY! EASY!
YOW!
THERE--
ALMOST--
WHUMP

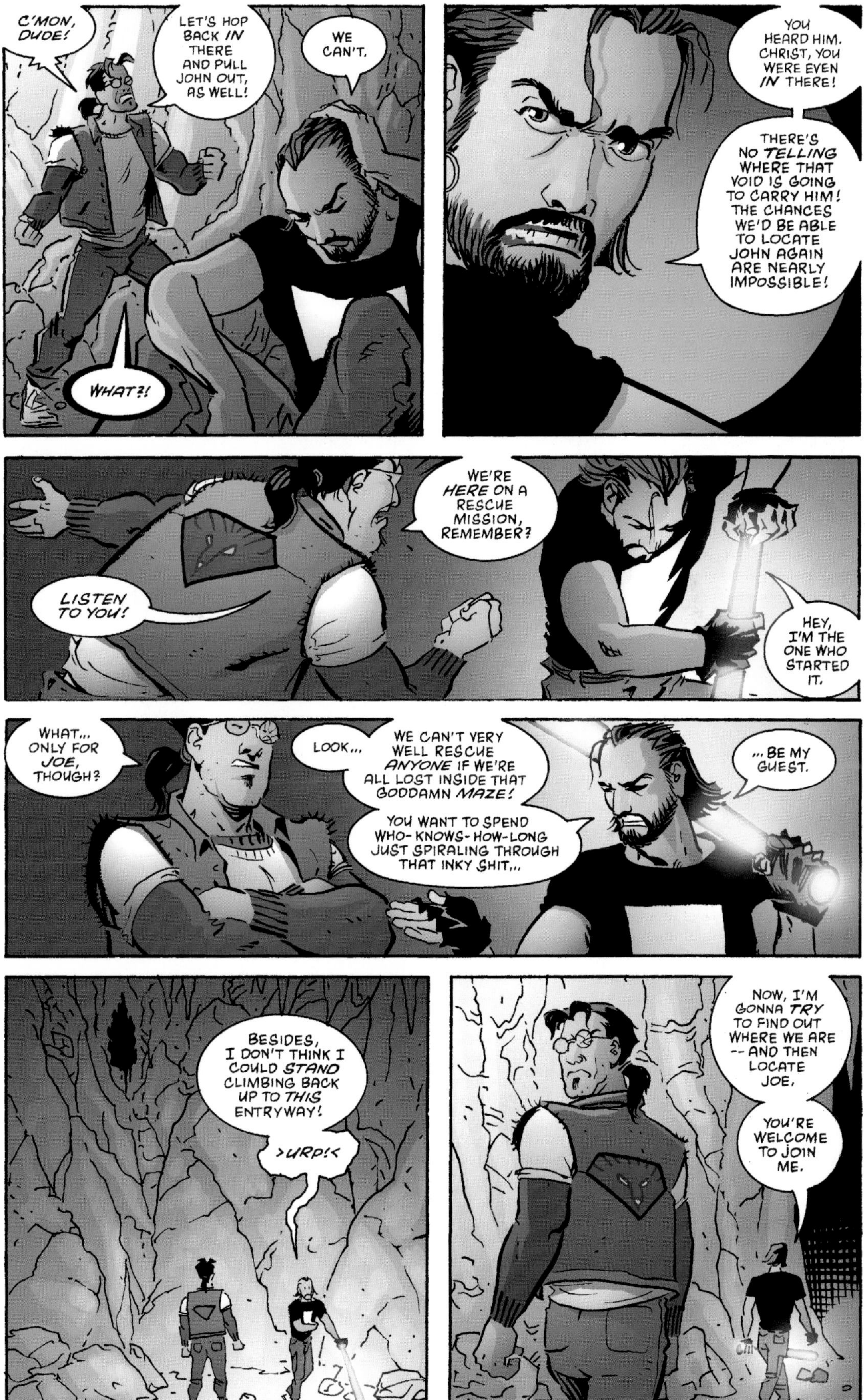
C'MON, DUDE!
LET'S HOP BACK IN THERE AND PULL JOHN OUT, AS WELL!
WE CAN'T.
WHAT?!
YOU HEARD HIM. CHRIST, YOU WERE EVEN IN THERE!
THERE'S NO TELLING WHERE THAT VOID IS GOING TO CARRY HIM! THE CHANCES WE'D BE ABLE TO LOCATE JOHN AGAIN ARE NEARLY IMPOSSIBLE!
LISTEN TO YOU!
WE'RE HERE ON A RESCUE MISSION, REMEMBER?
HEY, I'M THE ONE WHO STARTED IT.
WHAT... ONLY FOR JOE, THOUGH?
LOOK...
WE CAN'T VERY WELL RESCUE ANYONE IF WE'RE ALL LOST INSIDE THAT GODDAMN MAZE!
YOU WANT TO SPEND WHO-KNOWS-HOW-LONG JUST SPIRALING THROUGH THAT INKY SHIT...
...BE MY GUEST.
BESIDES, I DON'T THINK I COULD STAND CLIMBING BACK UP TO THIS ENTRYWAY!
>URP!<
NOW, I'M GONNA TRY TO FIND OUT WHERE WE ARE -- AND THEN LOCATE JOE.
YOU'RE WELCOME TO JOIN ME.

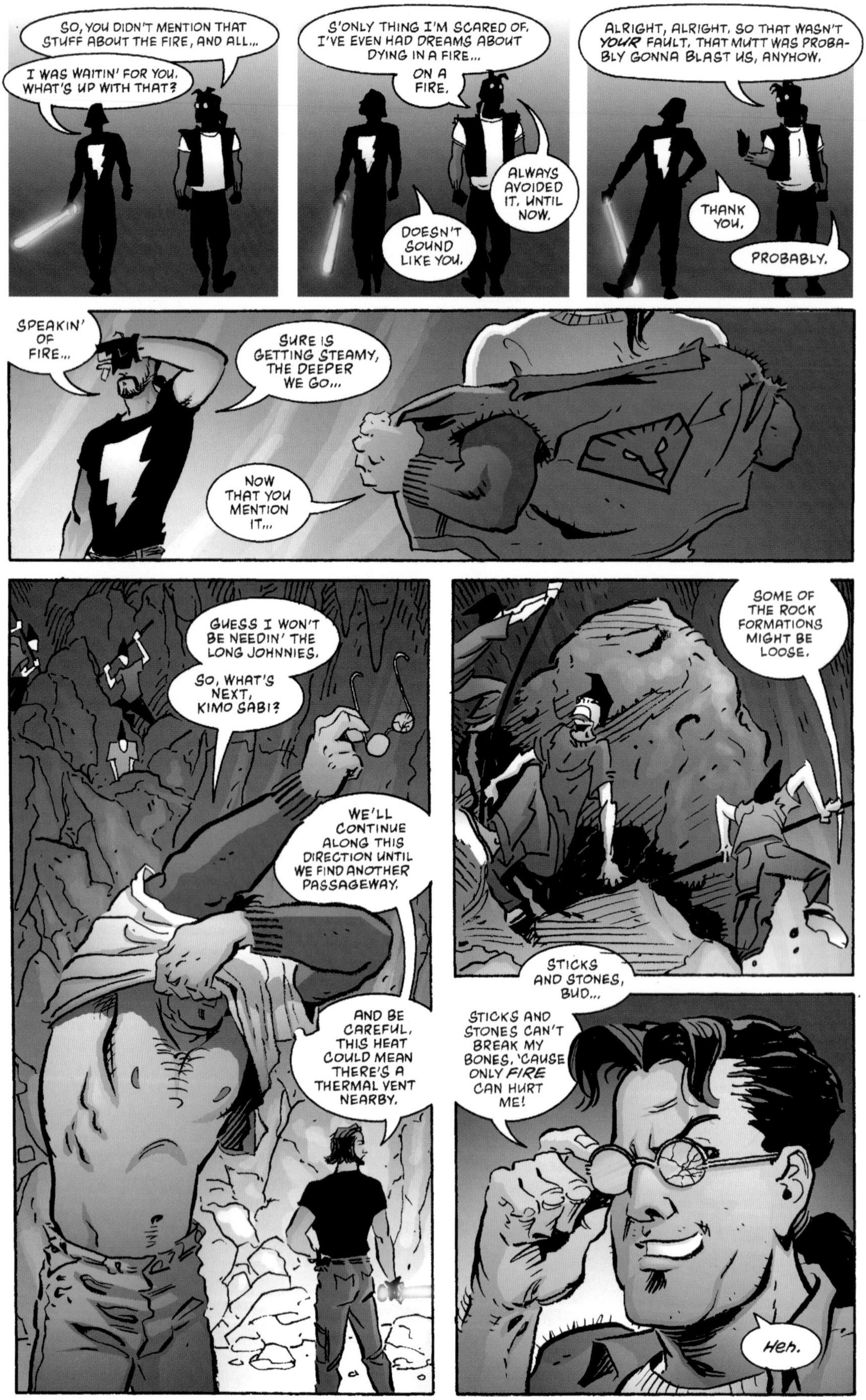

SO, YOU DIDN'T MENTION THAT STUFF ABOUT THE FIRE, AND ALL...
I WAS WAITIN' FOR YOU. WHAT'S UP WITH THAT?
S'ONLY THING I'M SCARED OF. I'VE EVEN HAD DREAMS ABOUT DYING IN A FIRE...
ON A FIRE.
ALWAYS AVOIDED IT. UNTIL NOW.
DOESN'T SOUND LIKE YOU.
ALRIGHT, ALRIGHT. SO THAT WASN'T *YOUR* FAULT. THAT MUTT WAS PROBABLY GONNA BLAST US, ANYHOW.
THANK YOU.
PROBABLY.
SPEAKIN' OF FIRE...
SURE IS GETTING STEAMY, THE DEEPER WE GO...
NOW THAT YOU MENTION IT...
GUESS I WON'T BE NEEDIN' THE LONG JOHNNIES.
SO, WHAT'S NEXT, KIMO SABI?
WE'LL CONTINUE ALONG THIS DIRECTION UNTIL WE FIND ANOTHER PASSAGEWAY.
AND BE CAREFUL. THIS HEAT COULD MEAN THERE'S A THERMAL VENT NEARBY.
SOME OF THE ROCK FORMATIONS MIGHT BE LOOSE.
STICKS AND STONES, BUD...
STICKS AND STONES CAN'T BREAK MY BONES, 'CAUSE ONLY *FIRE* CAN HURT ME!
Heh.

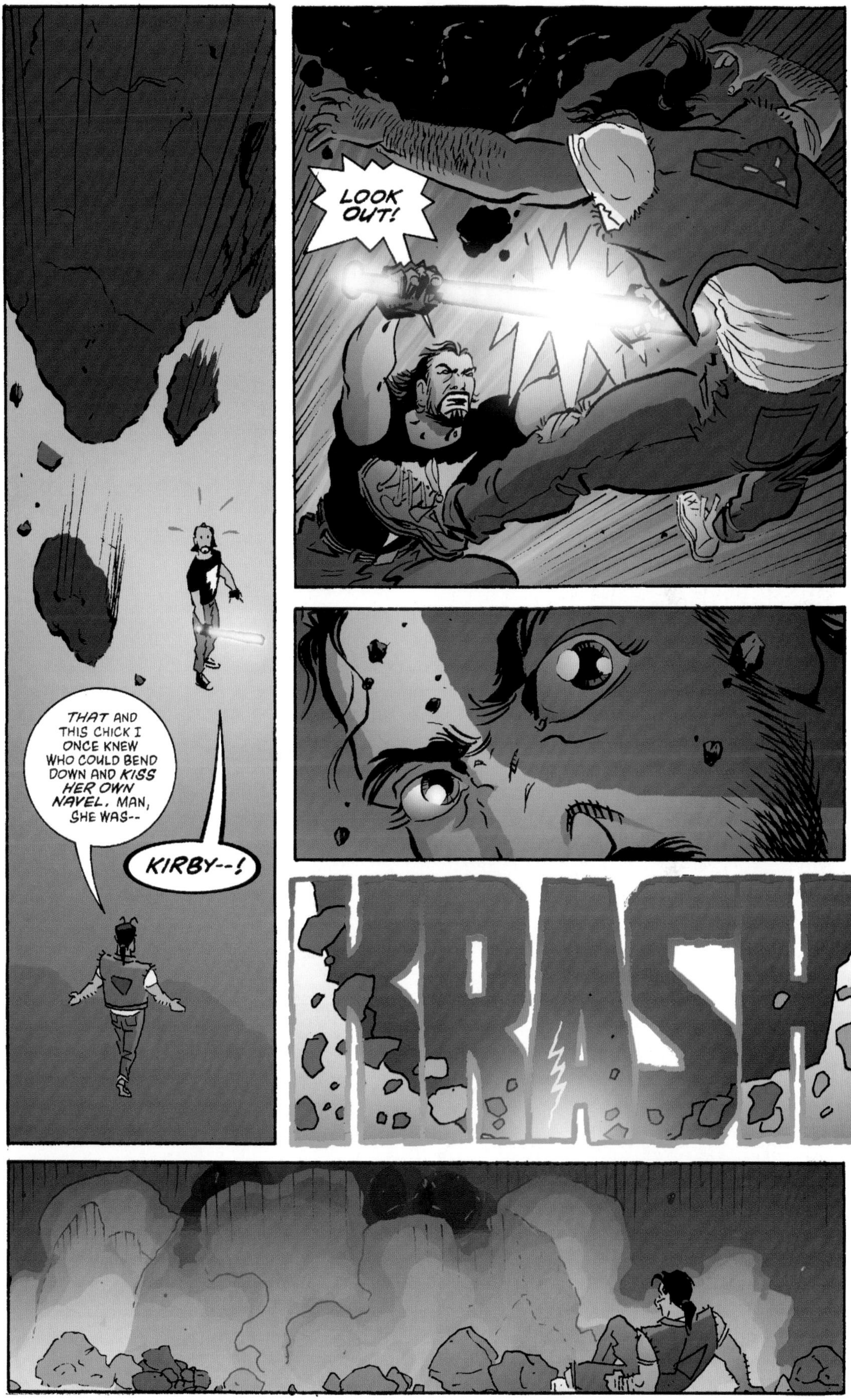
THAT AND THIS CHICK I ONCE KNEW WHO COULD BEND DOWN AND KISS HER OWN NAVEL. MAN, SHE WAS--
KIRBY--!
LOOK OUT!
KRASH

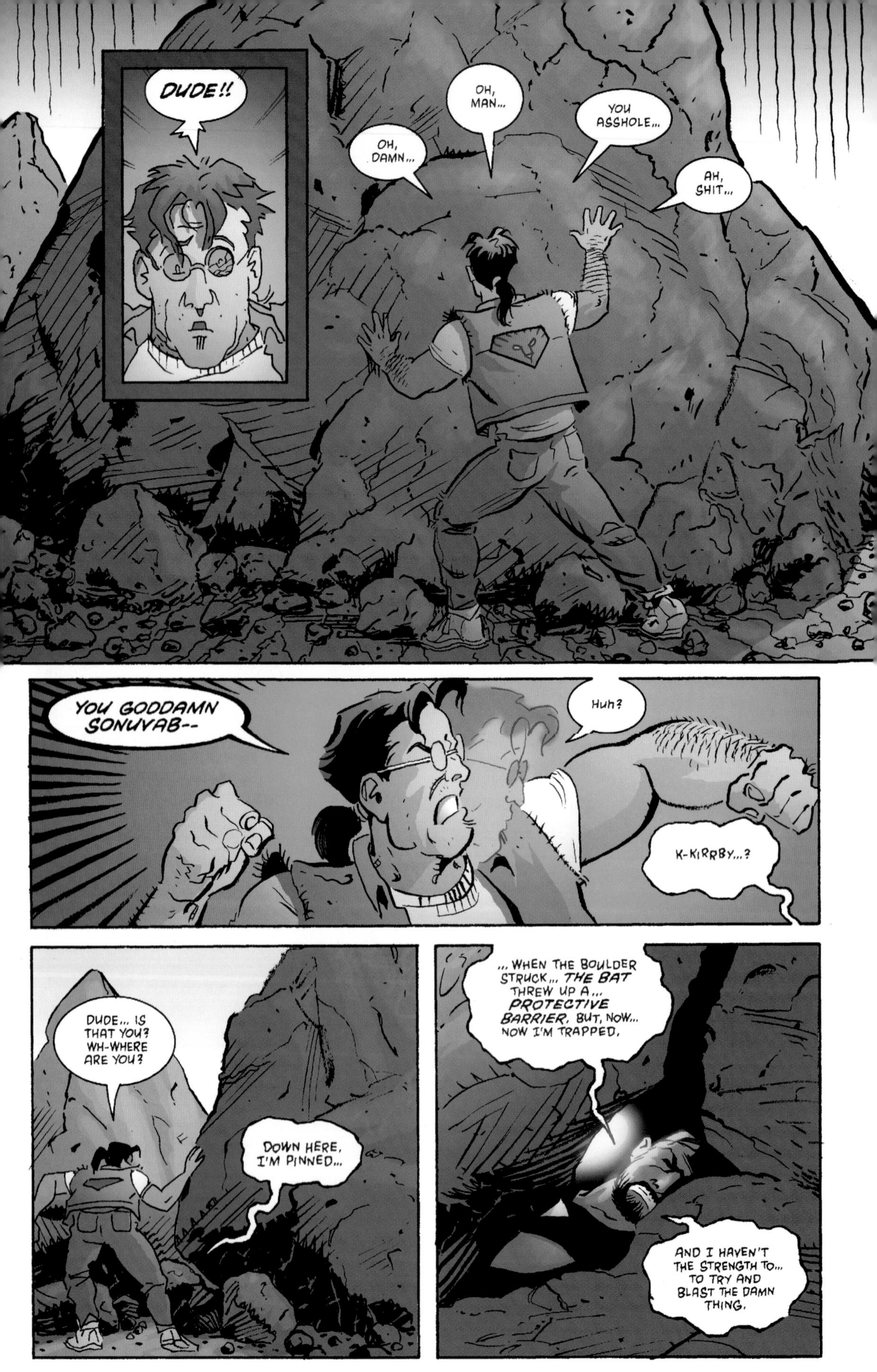
DUDE!!
OH, DAMN...
OH, MAN...
YOU ASSHOLE...
AH, SHIT...
YOU GODDAMN SONUVAB--
Huh?
K-KIRRBY...?
DUDE... IS THAT YOU? WH-WHERE ARE YOU?
DOWN HERE. I'M PINNED...
...WHEN THE BOULDER STRUCK... THE BAT THREW UP A... PROTECTIVE BARRIER. BUT, NOW... NOW I'M TRAPPED.
AND I HAVEN'T THE STRENGTH TO... TO TRY AND BLAST THE DAMN THING.

OKAY, HANG TIGHT! I'LL JUST ROLL THIS SUCKER OFF Y--

NO!

I CAN FEEL THE ROCK... TIGHT AGAINST MY LEGS.

IF YOU ROLL IT WRONG, YOU'LL CRUSH THEM. AND I THINK POUNDING IT TO BITS MIGHT DO THE SAME.

WHAT?!

YOU *KNOW* WHAT! *THIS THING* AND I WOULD'VE JUST *BOUNCED OFF* EACH OTHER! IF YOU HADN'T BEEN TRYING TO PLAY *BOSS*--

LOOK, YOU CAN LECTURE ME LATER!

RIGHT NOW, OUR OPTIONS *SUCK!*

WE'RE GOING TO HAVE TO THINK OF SOMETHING ELSE.

WAY AHEAD OF YOU, BUD...

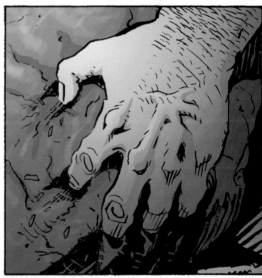

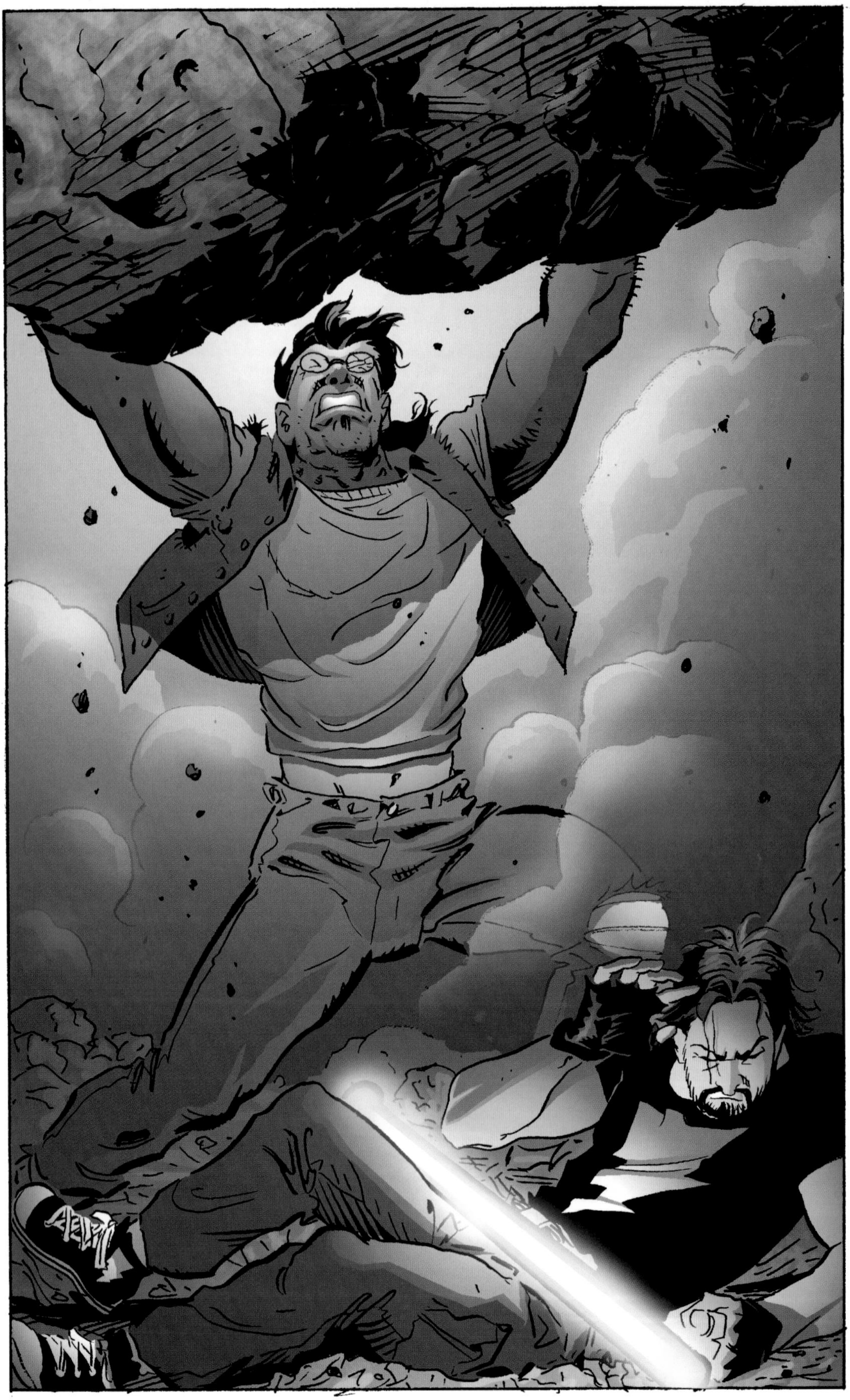

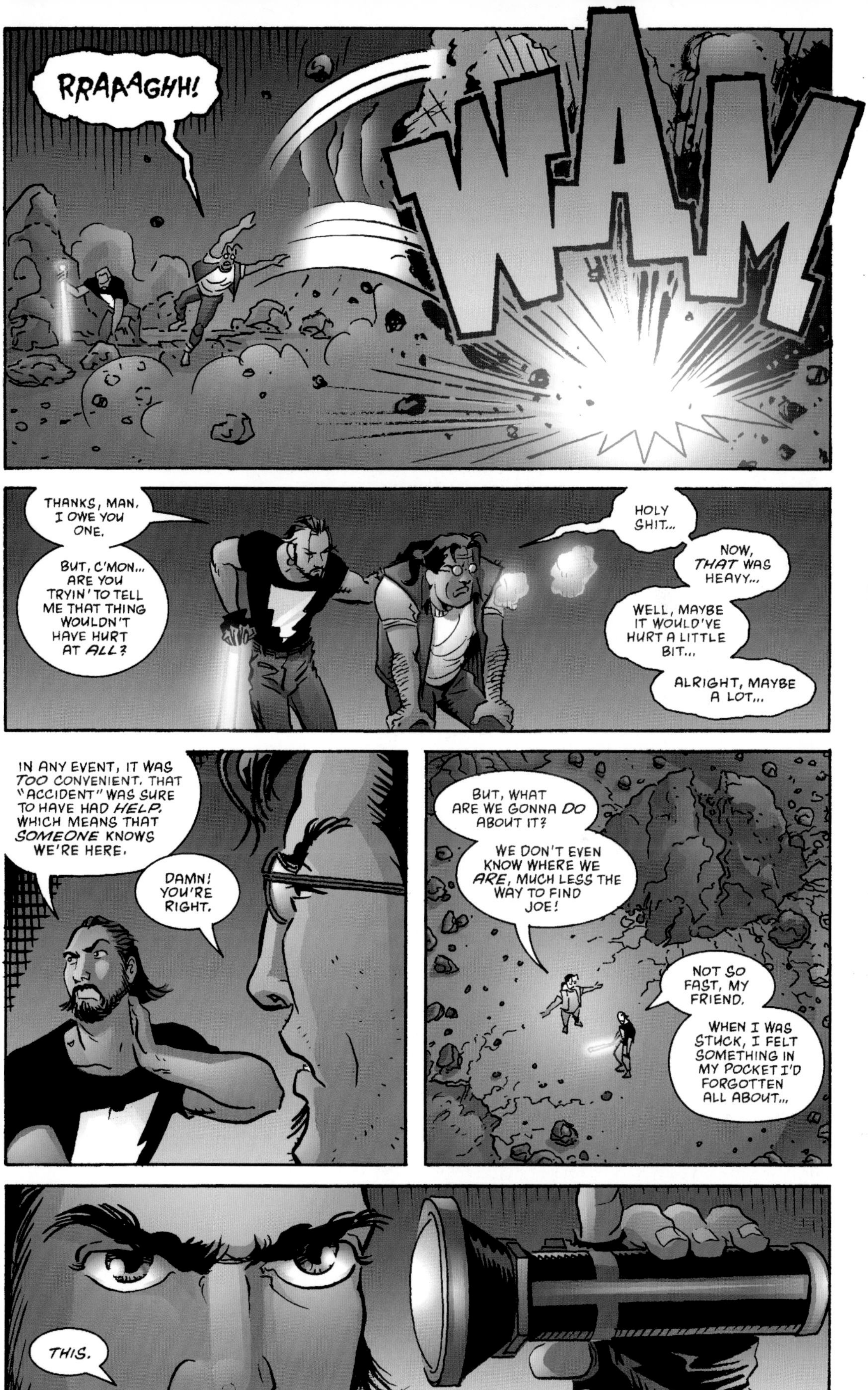
RRAAAGHH!
WAM
THANKS, MAN. I OWE YOU ONE.
BUT, C'MON... ARE YOU TRYIN' TO TELL ME THAT THING WOULDN'T HAVE HURT AT ALL?
HOLY SHIT...
NOW, THAT WAS HEAVY...
WELL, MAYBE IT WOULD'VE HURT A LITTLE BIT...
ALRIGHT, MAYBE A LOT...
IN ANY EVENT, IT WAS TOO CONVENIENT. THAT "ACCIDENT" WAS SURE TO HAVE HAD HELP. WHICH MEANS THAT SOMEONE KNOWS WE'RE HERE.
DAMN! YOU'RE RIGHT.
BUT, WHAT ARE WE GONNA DO ABOUT IT?
WE DON'T EVEN KNOW WHERE WE ARE, MUCH LESS THE WAY TO FIND JOE!
NOT SO FAST, MY FRIEND.
WHEN I WAS STUCK, I FELT SOMETHING IN MY POCKET I'D FORGOTTEN ALL ABOUT...
THIS.

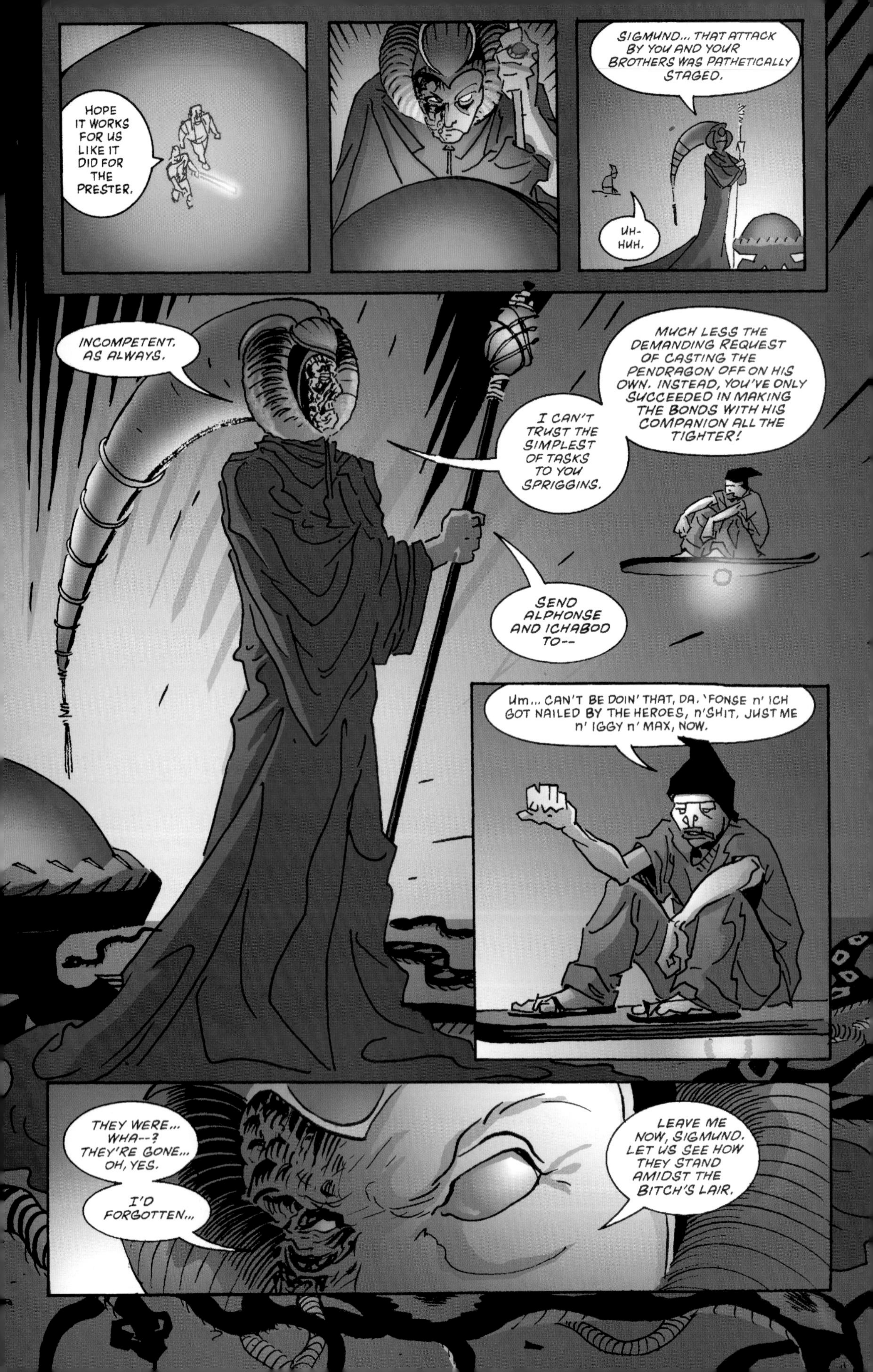
HOPE IT WORKS FOR US LIKE IT DID FOR THE PRESTER.
SIGMUND... THAT ATTACK BY YOU AND YOUR BROTHERS WAS PATHETICALLY STAGED.
UH-HUH.
INCOMPETENT, AS ALWAYS.
I CAN'T TRUST THE SIMPLEST OF TASKS TO YOU SPRIGGINS.
MUCH LESS THE DEMANDING REQUEST OF CASTING THE PENDRAGON OFF ON HIS OWN. INSTEAD, YOU'VE ONLY SUCCEEDED IN MAKING THE BONDS WITH HIS COMPANION ALL THE TIGHTER!
SEND ALPHONSE AND ICHABOD TO--
Um... CAN'T BE DOIN' THAT, DA. 'FONSE n' ICH GOT NAILED BY THE HEROES, n'SHIT. JUST ME n' IGGY n' MAX, NOW.
THEY WERE... WHA--? THEY'RE GONE... OH, YES.
I'D FORGOTTEN...
LEAVE ME NOW, SIGMUND. LET US SEE HOW THEY STAND AMIDST THE BITCH'S LAIR.

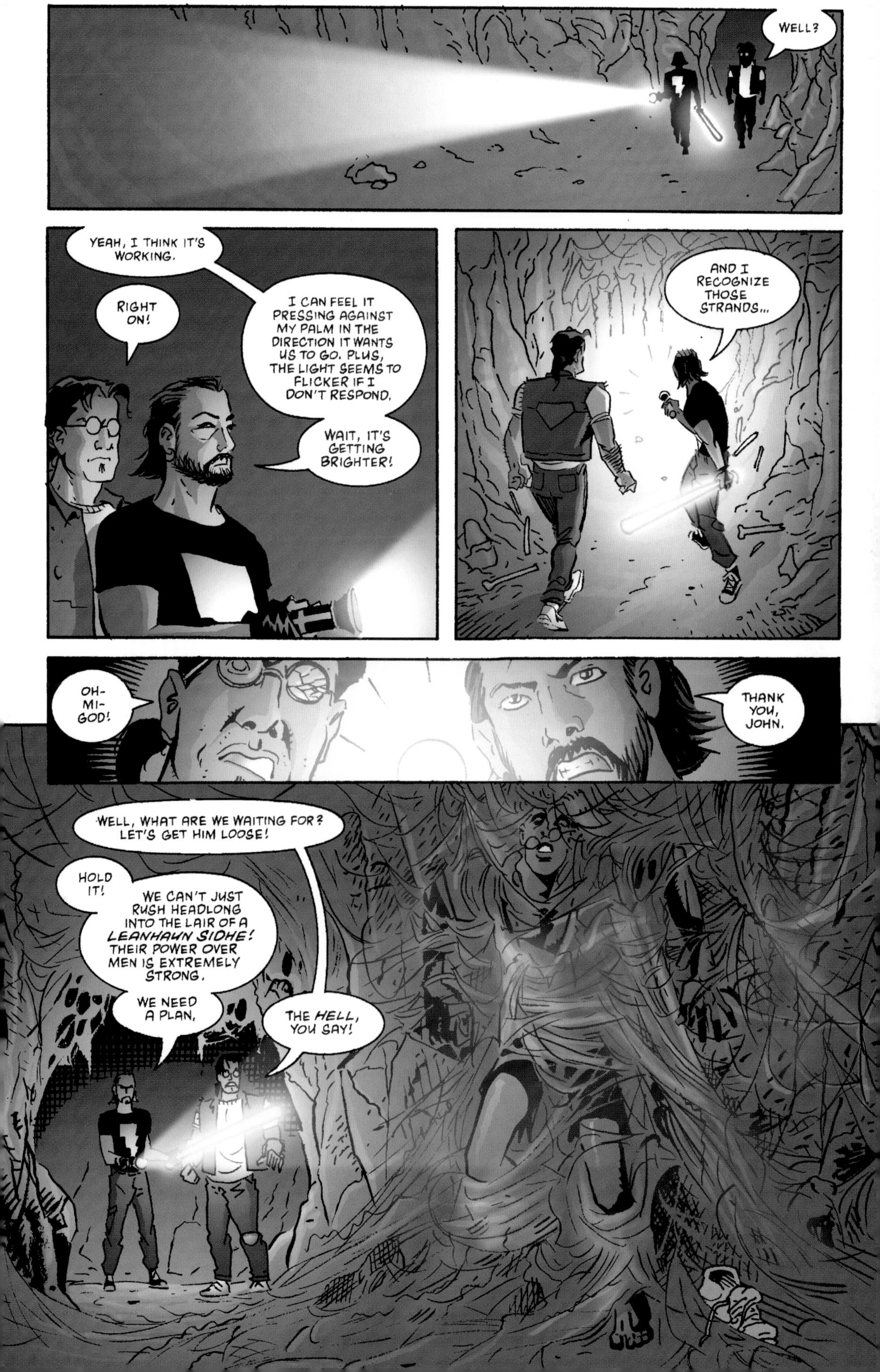

WELL?
YEAH, I THINK IT'S WORKING.
RIGHT ON!
I CAN FEEL IT PRESSING AGAINST MY PALM IN THE DIRECTION IT WANTS US TO GO. PLUS, THE LIGHT SEEMS TO FLICKER IF I DON'T RESPOND.
WAIT, IT'S GETTING BRIGHTER!
AND I RECOGNIZE THOSE STRANDS...
OH-MI-GOD!
THANK YOU, JOHN.
WELL, WHAT ARE WE WAITING FOR? LET'S GET HIM LOOSE!
HOLD IT!
WE CAN'T JUST RUSH HEADLONG INTO THE LAIR OF A LEANHAUN SIDHE! THEIR POWER OVER MEN IS EXTREMELY STRONG.
WE NEED A PLAN.
THE HELL, YOU SAY!

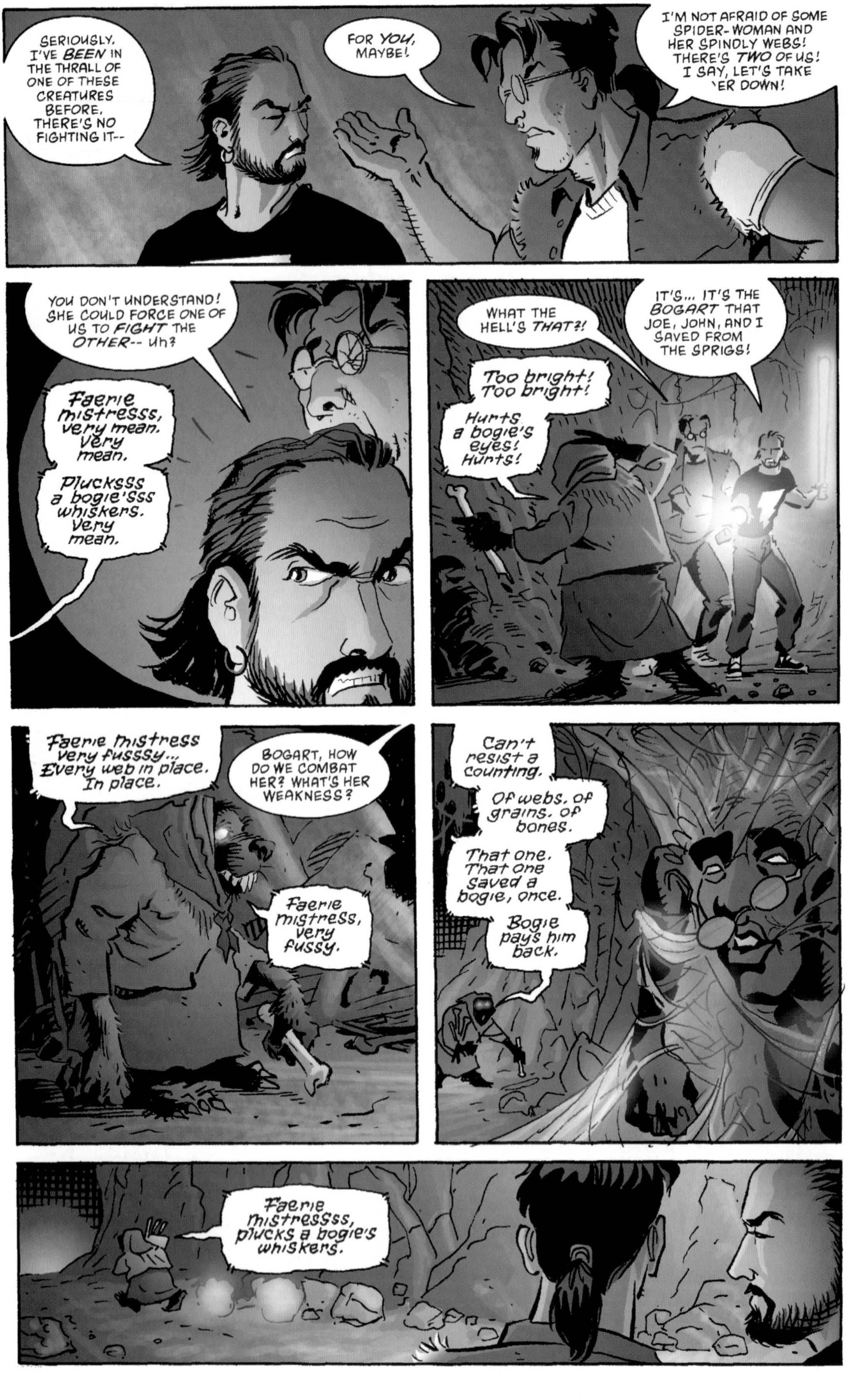
SERIOUSLY. I'VE BEEN IN THE THRALL OF ONE OF THESE CREATURES BEFORE. THERE'S NO FIGHTING IT--
FOR YOU, MAYBE!
I'M NOT AFRAID OF SOME SPIDER-WOMAN AND HER SPINDLY WEBS! THERE'S TWO OF US! I SAY, LET'S TAKE 'ER DOWN!
YOU DON'T UNDERSTAND! SHE COULD FORCE ONE OF US TO FIGHT THE OTHER-- uh?
Faerie mistresss, very mean. Very mean.
Pluckssss a bogie'sss whiskers. Very mean.
WHAT THE HELL'S THAT?!
IT'S... IT'S THE BOGART THAT JOE, JOHN, AND I SAVED FROM THE SPRIGS!
Too bright! Too bright!
Hurts a bogie's eyes! Hurts!
Faerie mistress very fusssy... Every web in place. In place.
BOGART, HOW DO WE COMBAT HER? WHAT'S HER WEAKNESS?
Faerie mistress, very fussy.
Can't resist a counting.
Of webs, of grains, of bones.
That one. That one saved a bogie, once.
Bogie pays him back.
Faerie mistressss, plucks a bogie's whiskers.

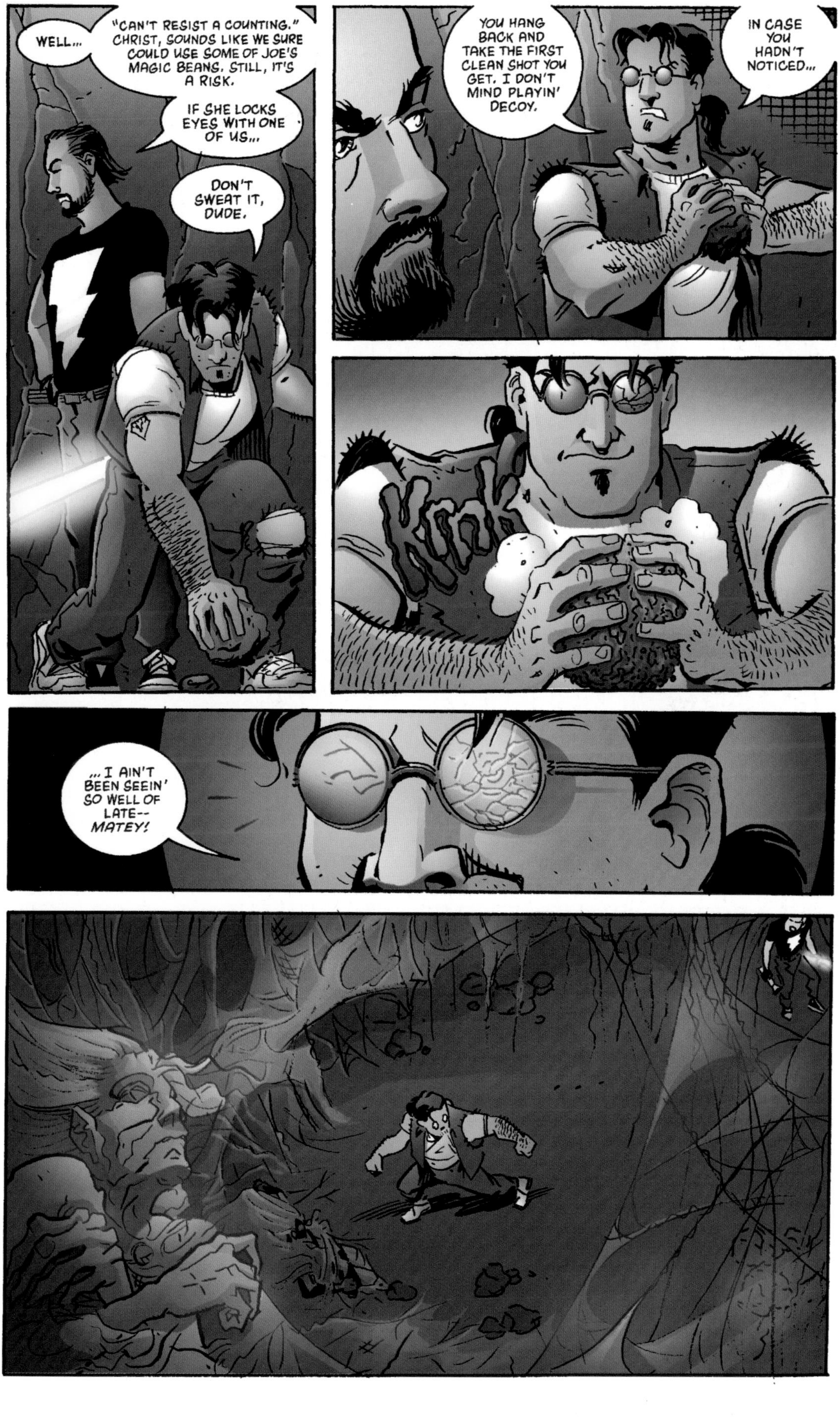
WELL...
"CAN'T RESIST A COUNTING." CHRIST, SOUNDS LIKE WE SURE COULD USE SOME OF JOE'S MAGIC BEANS. STILL, IT'S A RISK.
IF SHE LOCKS EYES WITH ONE OF US...
DON'T SWEAT IT, DUDE.
YOU HANG BACK AND TAKE THE FIRST CLEAN SHOT YOU GET. I DON'T MIND PLAYIN' DECOY.
IN CASE YOU HADN'T NOTICED...
Krak
...I AIN'T BEEN SEEIN' SO WELL OF LATE-- MATEY!

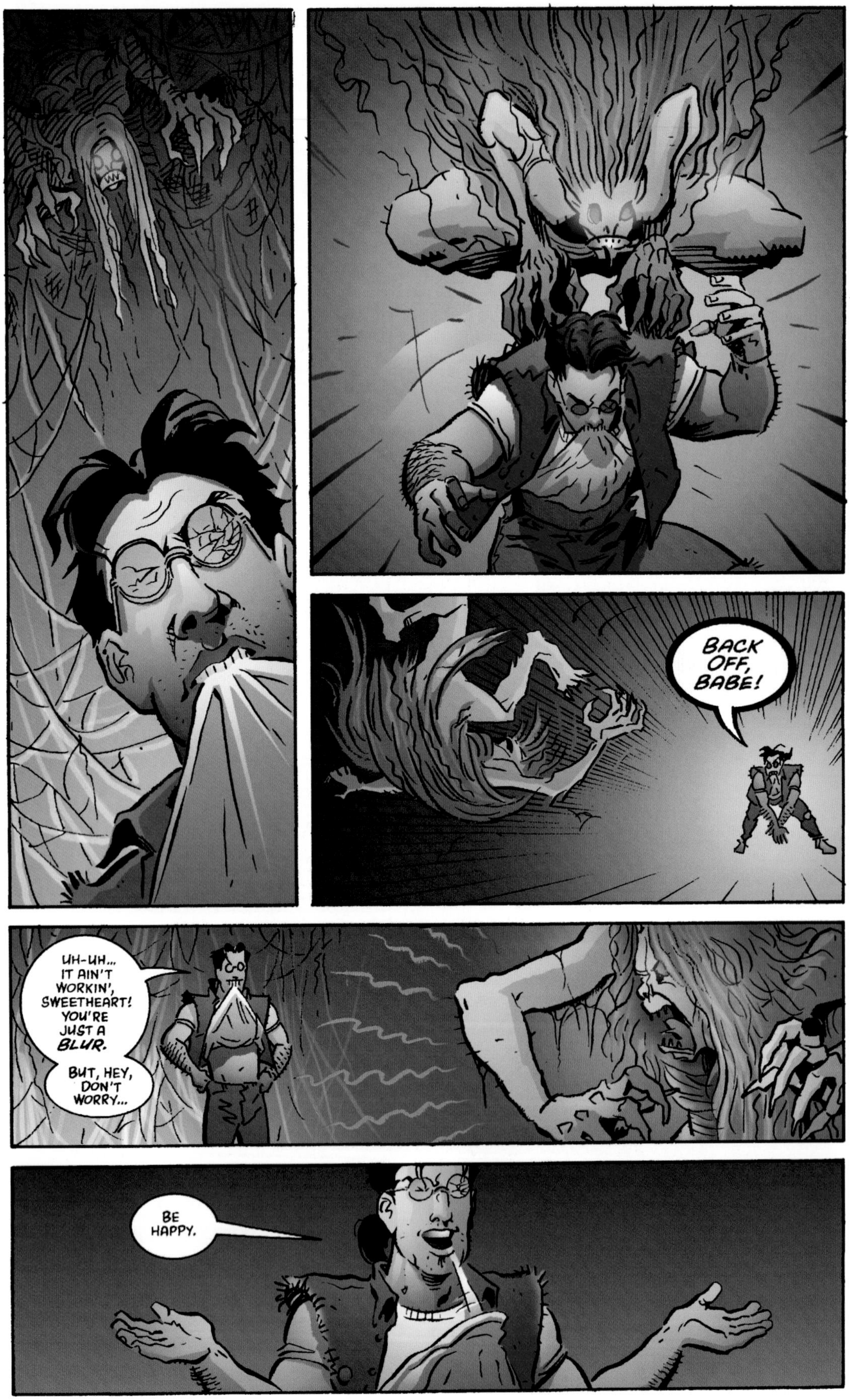
BACK OFF, BABE!
UH-UH... IT AIN'T WORKIN', SWEETHEART! YOU'RE JUST A BLUR.
BUT, HEY, DON'T WORRY...
BE HAPPY.

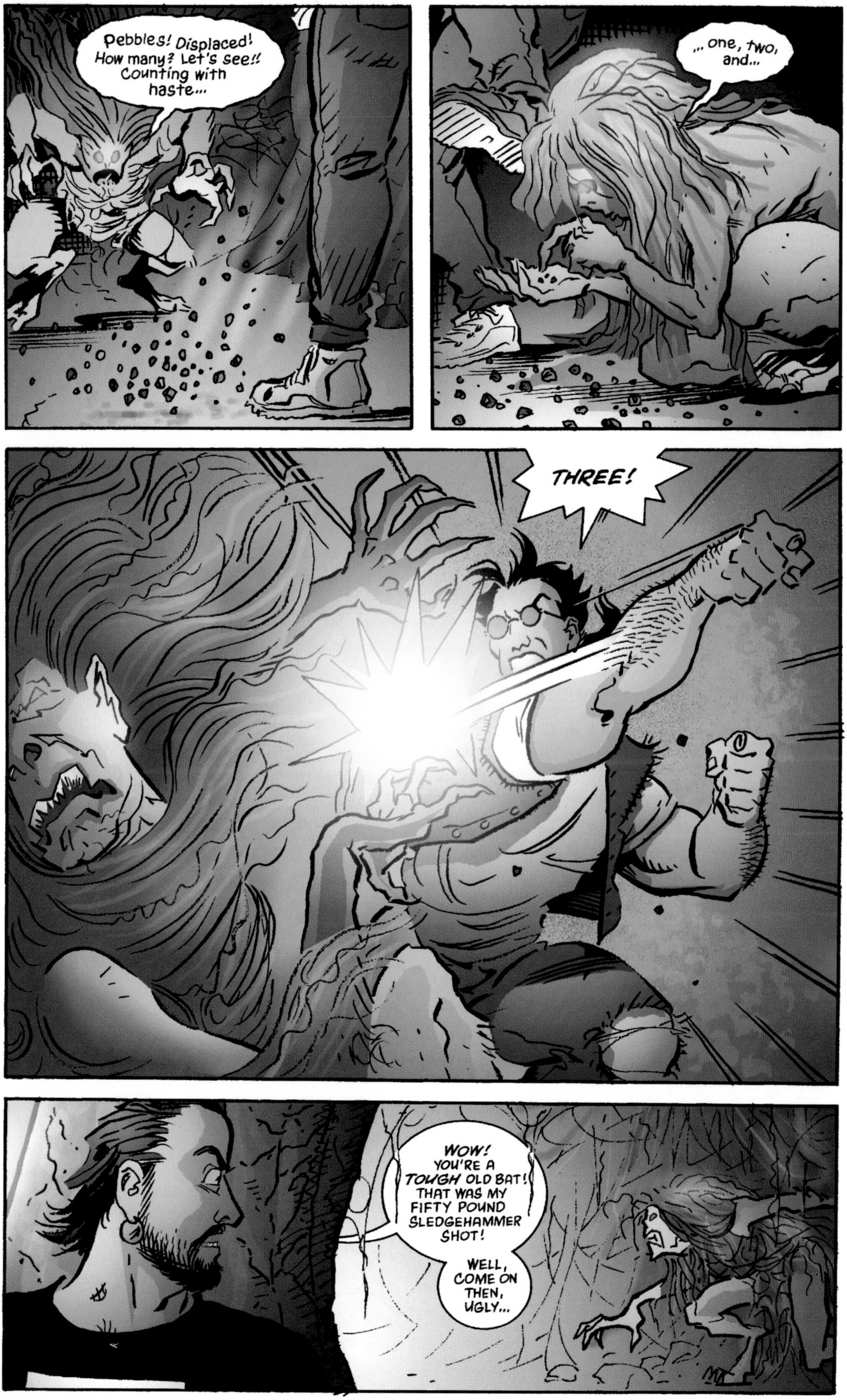
Pebbles! Displaced! How many? Let's see!! Counting with haste...
... one, two, and...
THREE!
WOW! YOU'RE A TOUGH OLD BAT! THAT WAS MY FIFTY POUND SLEDGEHAMMER SHOT!
WELL, COME ON THEN, UGLY...

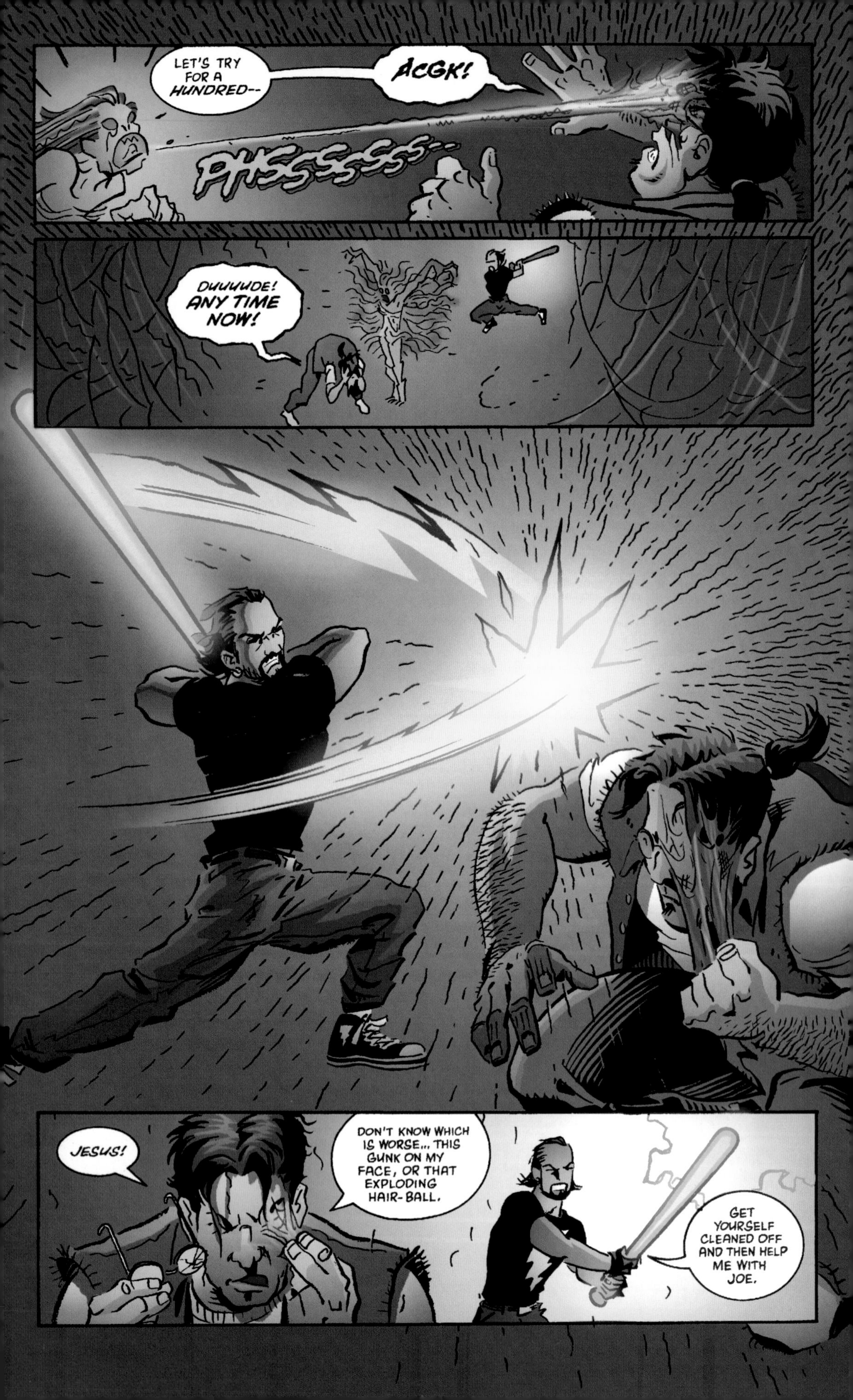
LET'S TRY FOR A HUNDRED--
ACGK!
PHSSSSSSS--
DUUUUDE! ANY TIME NOW!
JESUS!
DON'T KNOW WHICH IS WORSE... THIS GUNK ON MY FACE, OR THAT EXPLODING HAIR-BALL.
GET YOURSELF CLEANED OFF AND THEN HELP ME WITH JOE.

THIS STUFF IS **NATTY!**

AND HE STILL LOOKS PRETTY **ZONKED** OUT...

HOLD HIM **STEADY.** I'M GOING TO GIVE HIM A TINY JOLT WITH THE BAT.

DUDE, LOOK... HIS HAIR'S GONE **WHITE!**

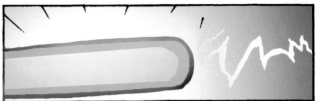

WAP

WAP

S-S-SORRY, FELLAS...

N-NEVER FELT A SURGE LIKE **THAT** BEFORE! FEELS LIKE I COULD RUN TO THE MOON! **TWICE!**

IT'S **COOL,** MAN. YOU OKAY?

HEH-**HA!**

I WILL BE.

BUT... WHERE **ARE** WE?

INSIDE THE MYSTIC MOUNTAIN. AND NOW THAT WE'VE GOT YOU BACK...

... IT'S **TIME** TO FIND OUR WAY OUT OF HERE!

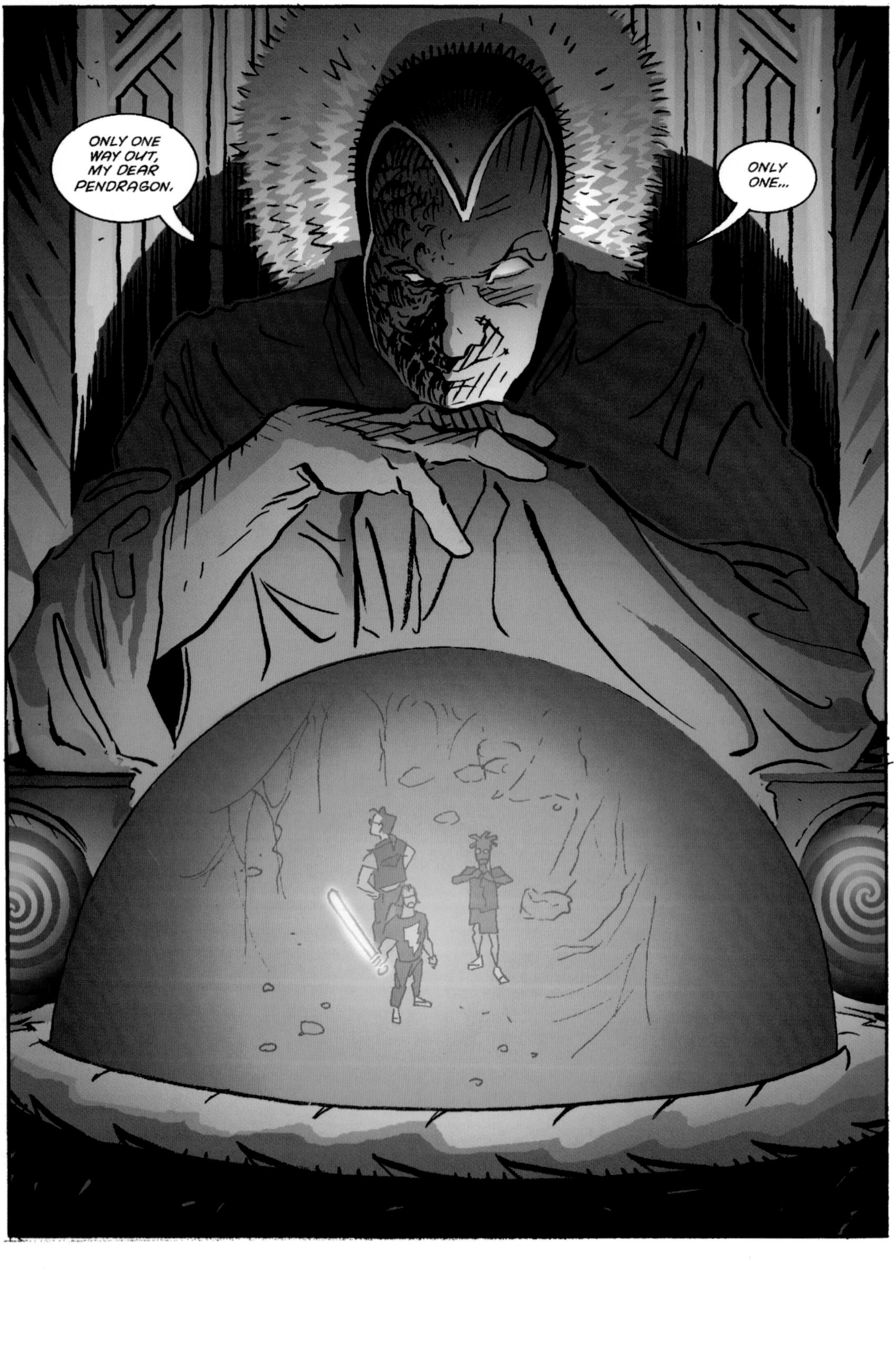
ONLY ONE WAY OUT, MY DEAR PENDRAGON.
ONLY ONE...

THE HERO DEFINED

MAGE®

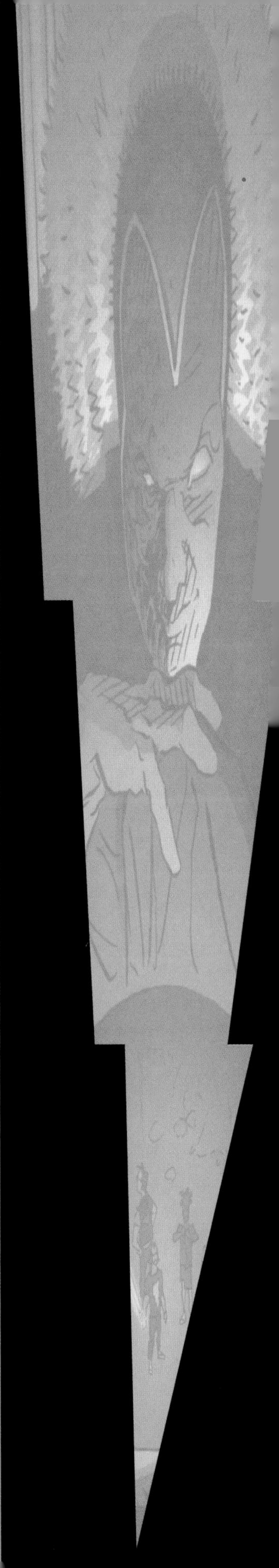

chapter 13

"Out Damned Spot!"

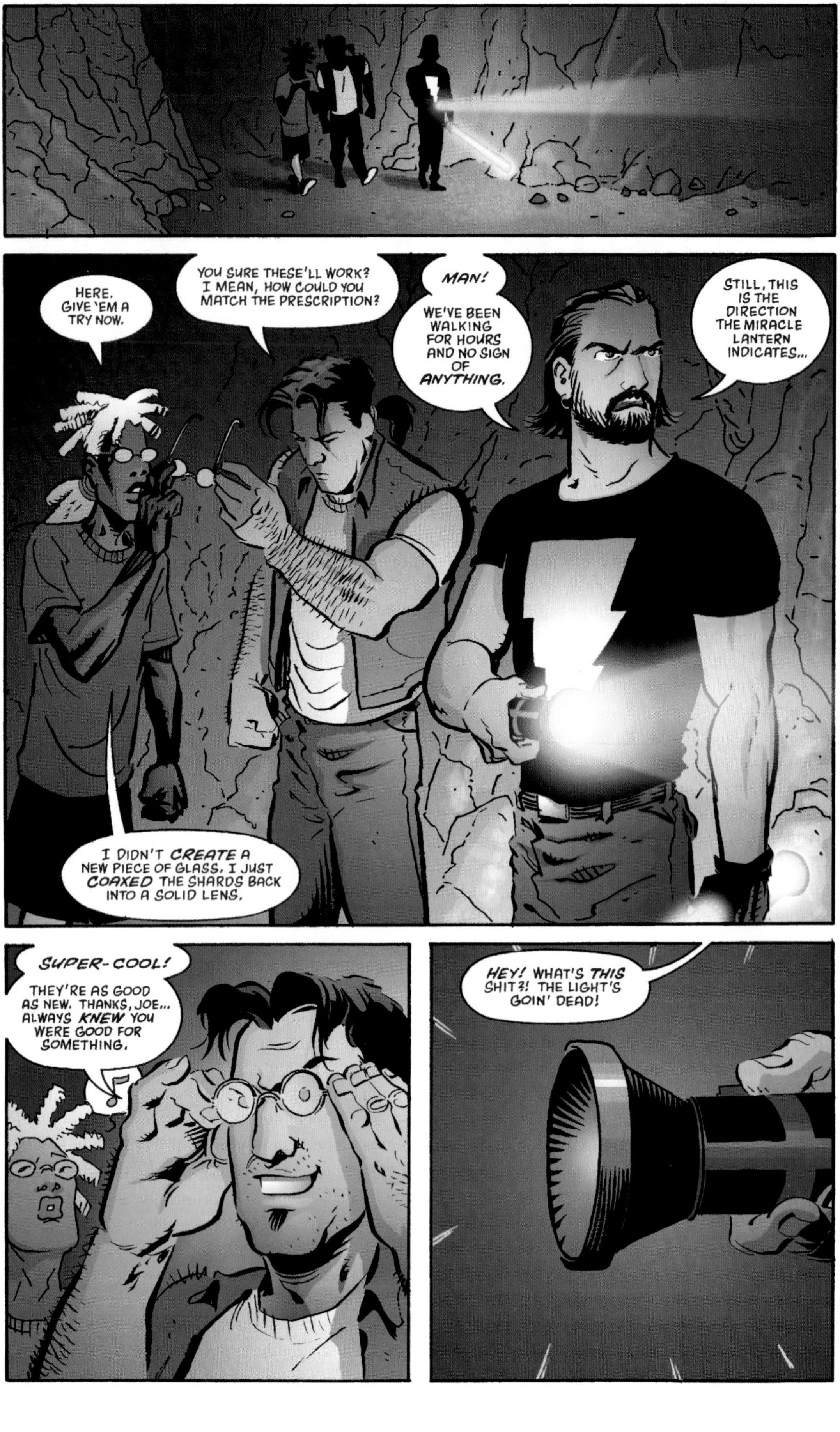
HERE. GIVE 'EM A TRY NOW.
YOU SURE THESE'LL WORK? I MEAN, HOW COULD YOU MATCH THE PRESCRIPTION?
MAN!
WE'VE BEEN WALKING FOR HOURS AND NO SIGN OF ANYTHING.
STILL, THIS IS THE DIRECTION THE MIRACLE LANTERN INDICATES...
I DIDN'T CREATE A NEW PIECE OF GLASS. I JUST COAXED THE SHARDS BACK INTO A SOLID LENS.
SUPER-COOL!
THEY'RE AS GOOD AS NEW. THANKS, JOE... ALWAYS KNEW YOU WERE GOOD FOR SOMETHING.
HEY! WHAT'S THIS SHIT?! THE LIGHT'S GOIN' DEAD!

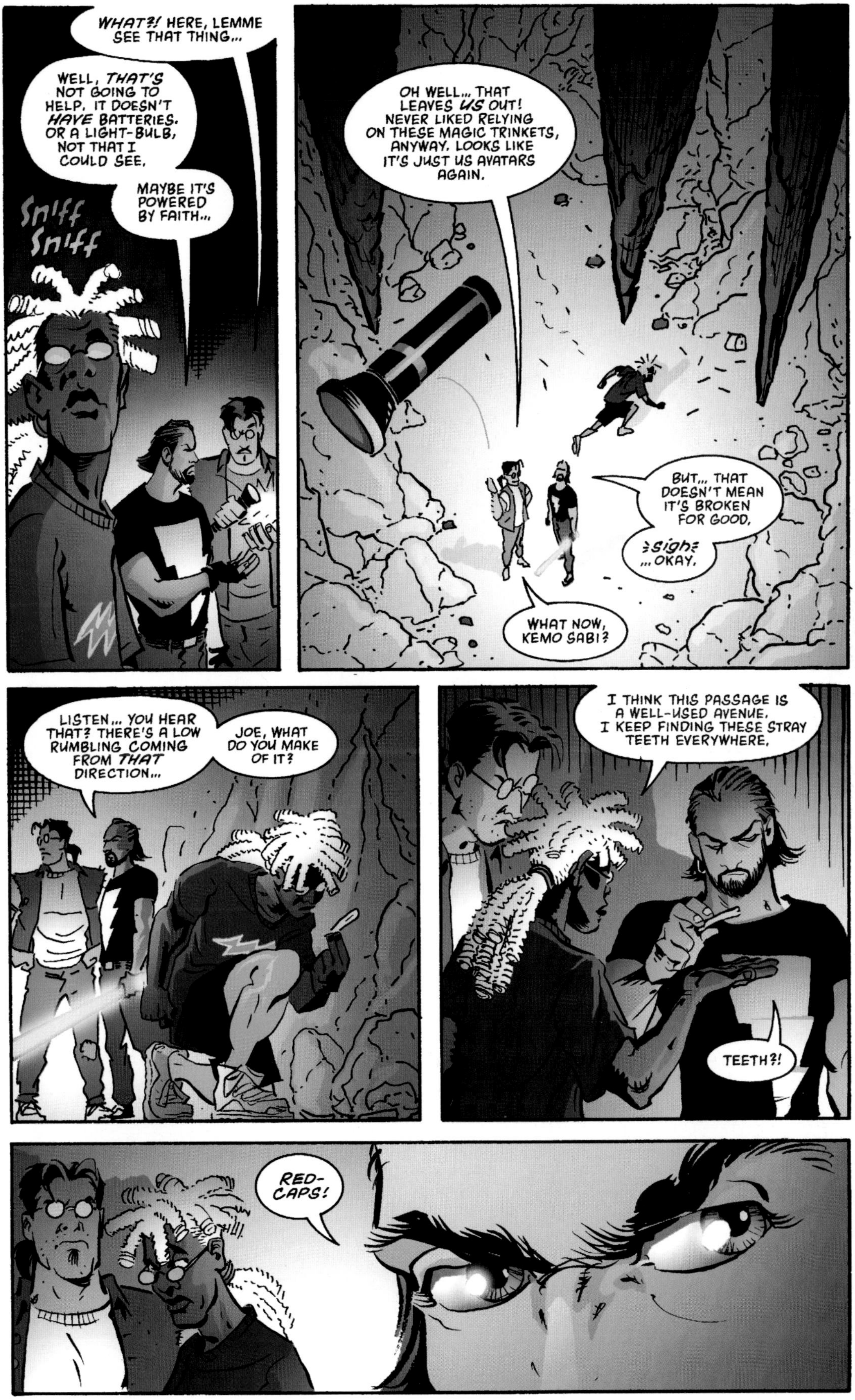
WHAT?! HERE, LEMME SEE THAT THING...
WELL, THAT'S NOT GOING TO HELP. IT DOESN'T HAVE BATTERIES. OR A LIGHT-BULB, NOT THAT I COULD SEE.
MAYBE IT'S POWERED BY FAITH...
Sniff Sniff
OH WELL... THAT LEAVES US OUT! NEVER LIKED RELYING ON THESE MAGIC TRINKETS, ANYWAY. LOOKS LIKE IT'S JUST US AVATARS AGAIN.
BUT... THAT DOESN'T MEAN IT'S BROKEN FOR GOOD.
sigh ...OKAY.
WHAT NOW, KEMO SABI?
LISTEN... YOU HEAR THAT? THERE'S A LOW RUMBLING COMING FROM THAT DIRECTION...
JOE, WHAT DO YOU MAKE OF IT?
I THINK THIS PASSAGE IS A WELL-USED AVENUE. I KEEP FINDING THESE STRAY TEETH EVERYWHERE.
TEETH?!
RED-CAPS!

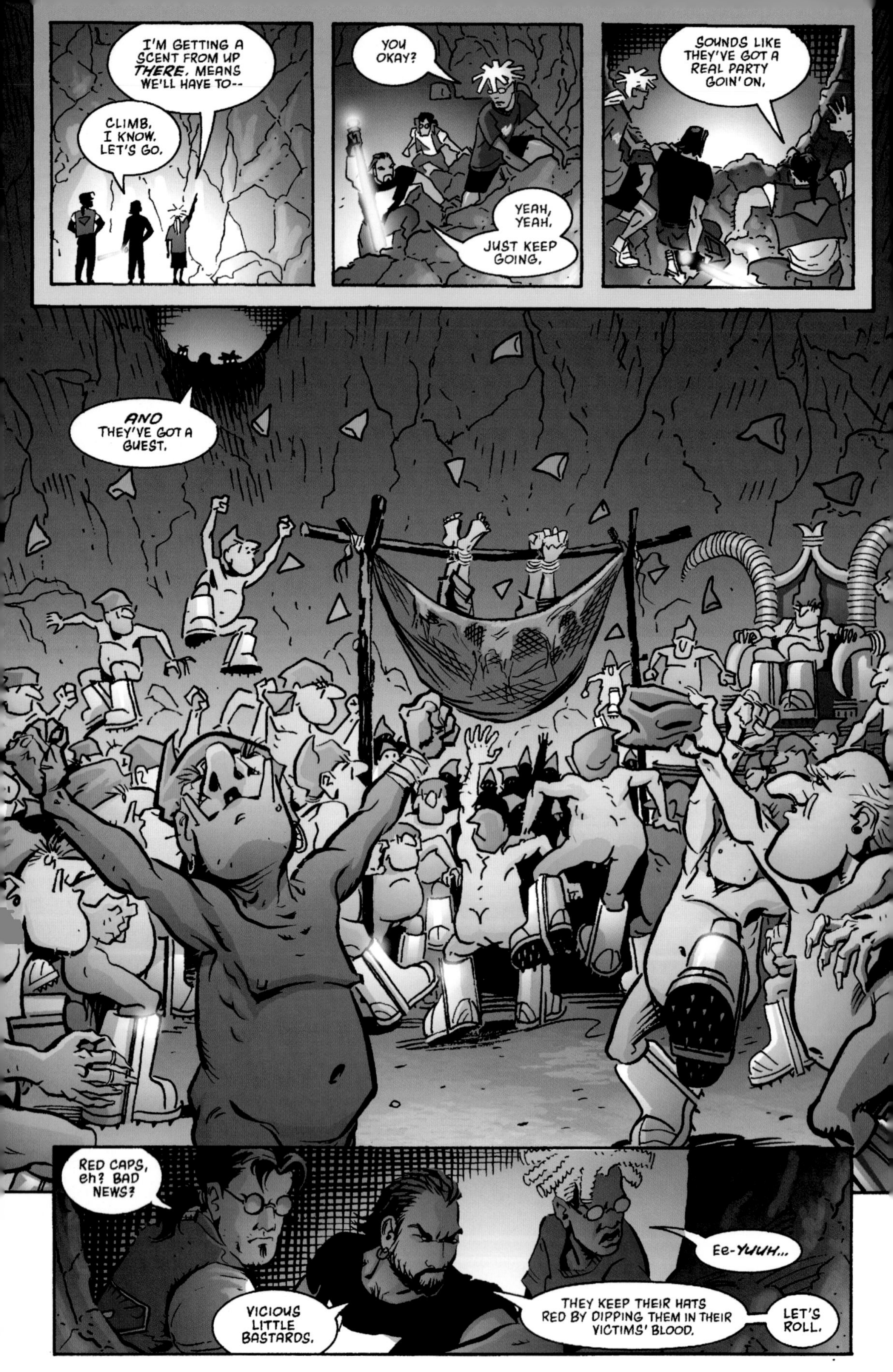
I'M GETTING A SCENT FROM UP THERE. MEANS WE'LL HAVE TO--
CLIMB, I KNOW. LET'S GO.
YOU OKAY?
YEAH, YEAH, JUST KEEP GOING.
SOUNDS LIKE THEY'VE GOT A REAL PARTY GOIN' ON.
AND THEY'VE GOT A GUEST.
RED CAPS, eh? BAD NEWS?
VICIOUS LITTLE BASTARDS.
Ee-YUUH...
THEY KEEP THEIR HATS RED BY DIPPING THEM IN THEIR VICTIMS' BLOOD.
LET'S ROLL.

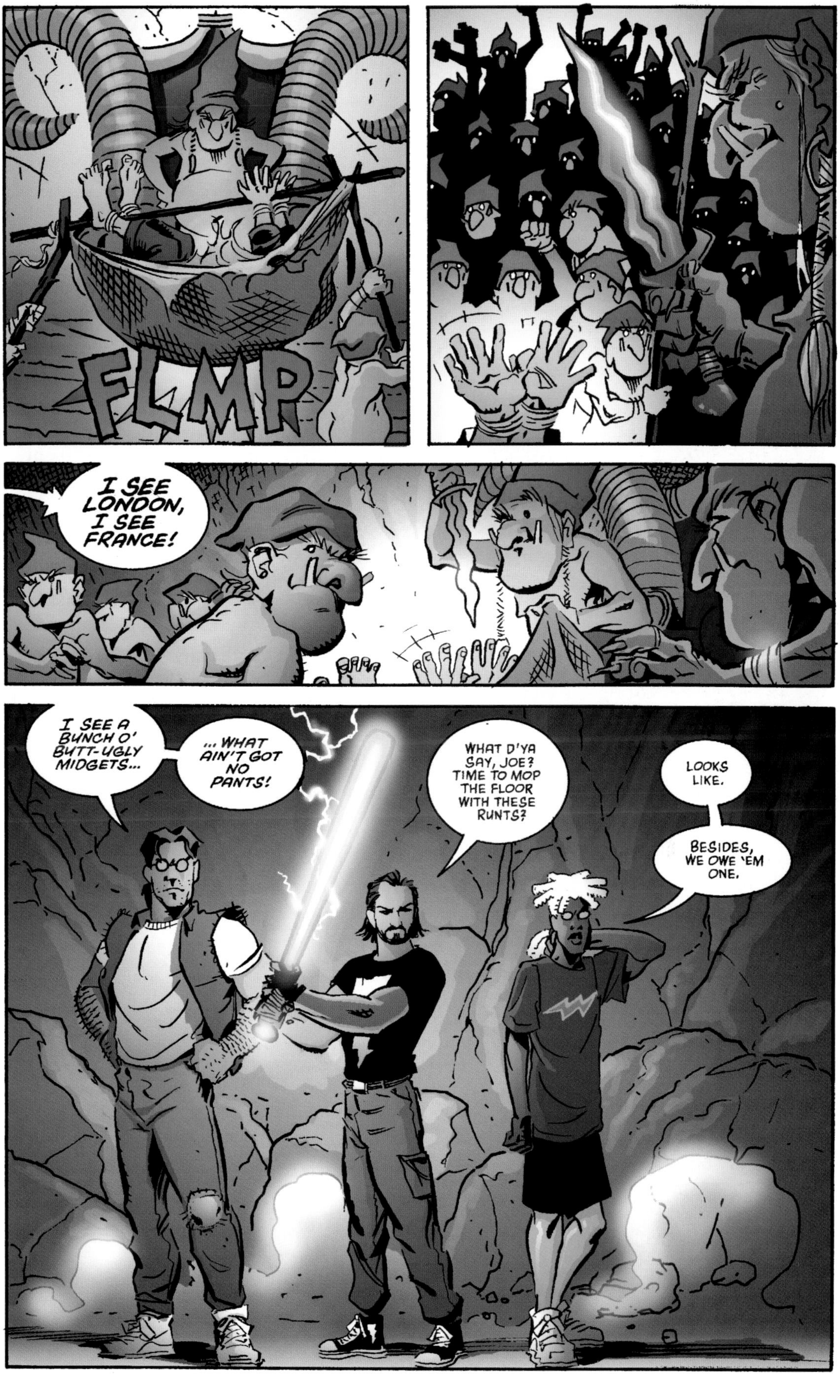
FLMP
I SEE LONDON, I SEE FRANCE!
I SEE A BUNCH O' BUTT-UGLY MIDGETS...
...WHAT AIN'T GOT NO PANTS!
WHAT D'YA SAY, JOE? TIME TO MOP THE FLOOR WITH THESE RUNTS?
LOOKS LIKE.
BESIDES, WE OWE 'EM ONE.

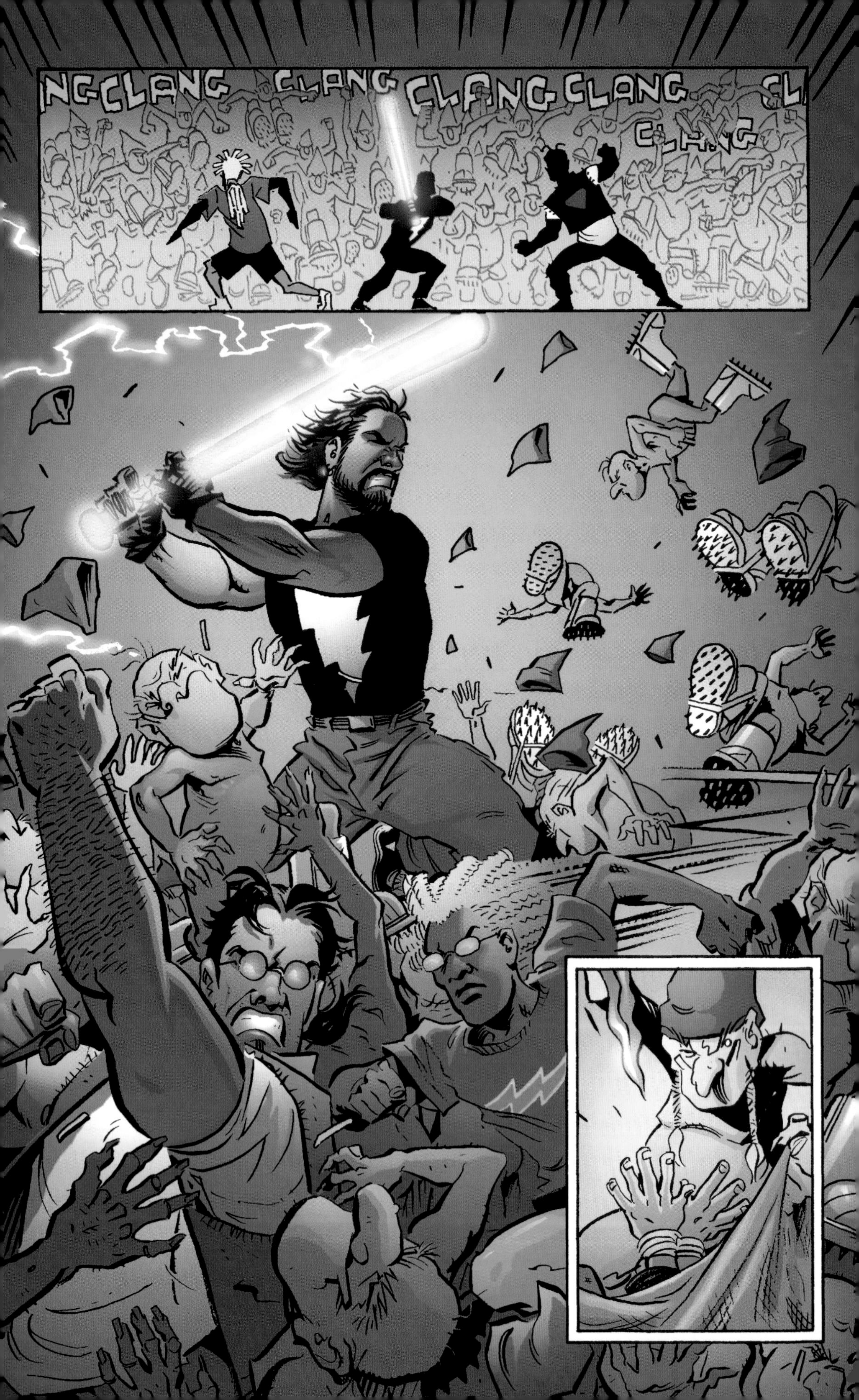

NGCLANG
CLANG
CLANG CLANG
CLANG
CL
CLANG

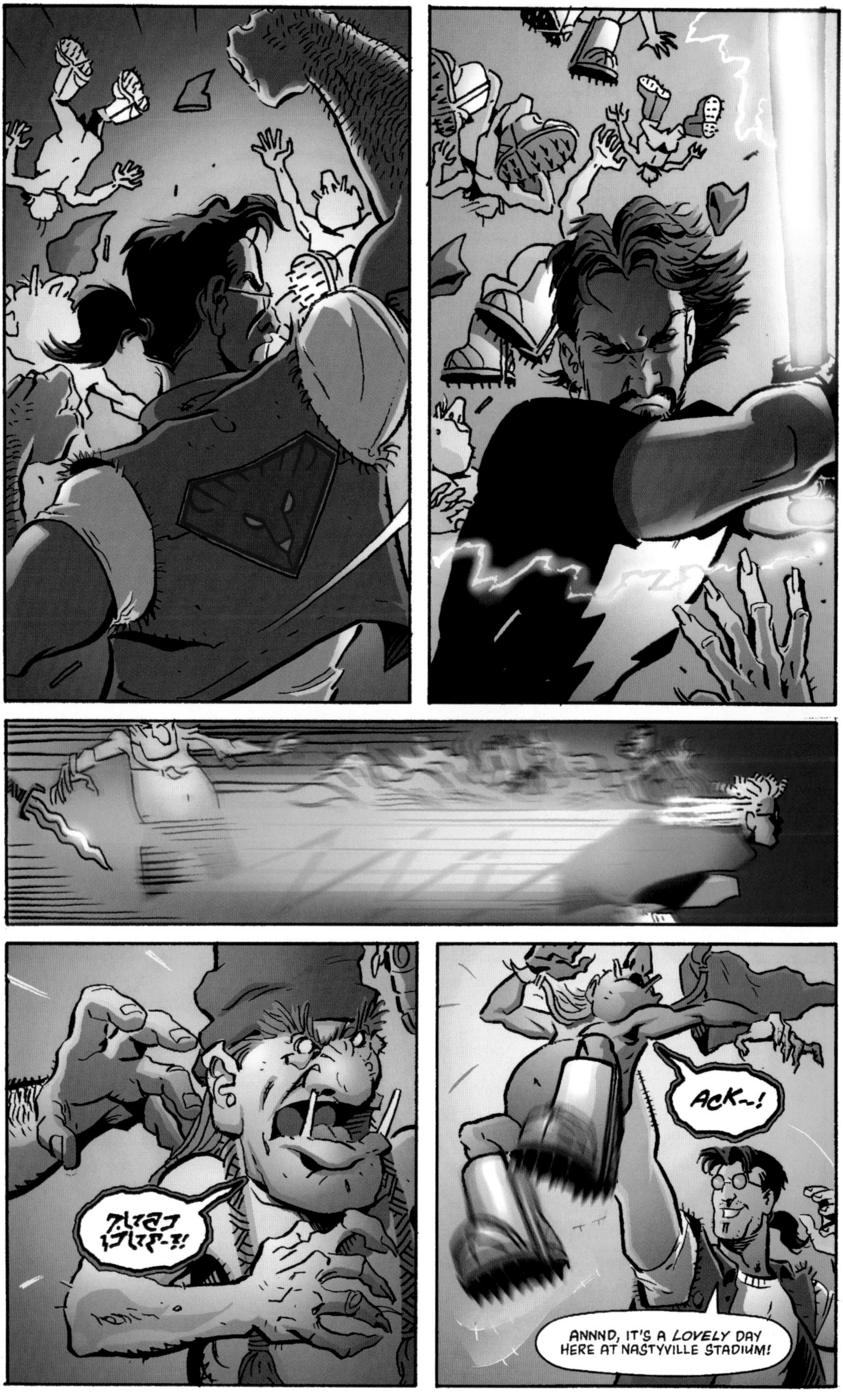
ACK--!
ANNND, IT'S A LOVELY DAY HERE AT NASTYVILLE STADIUM!

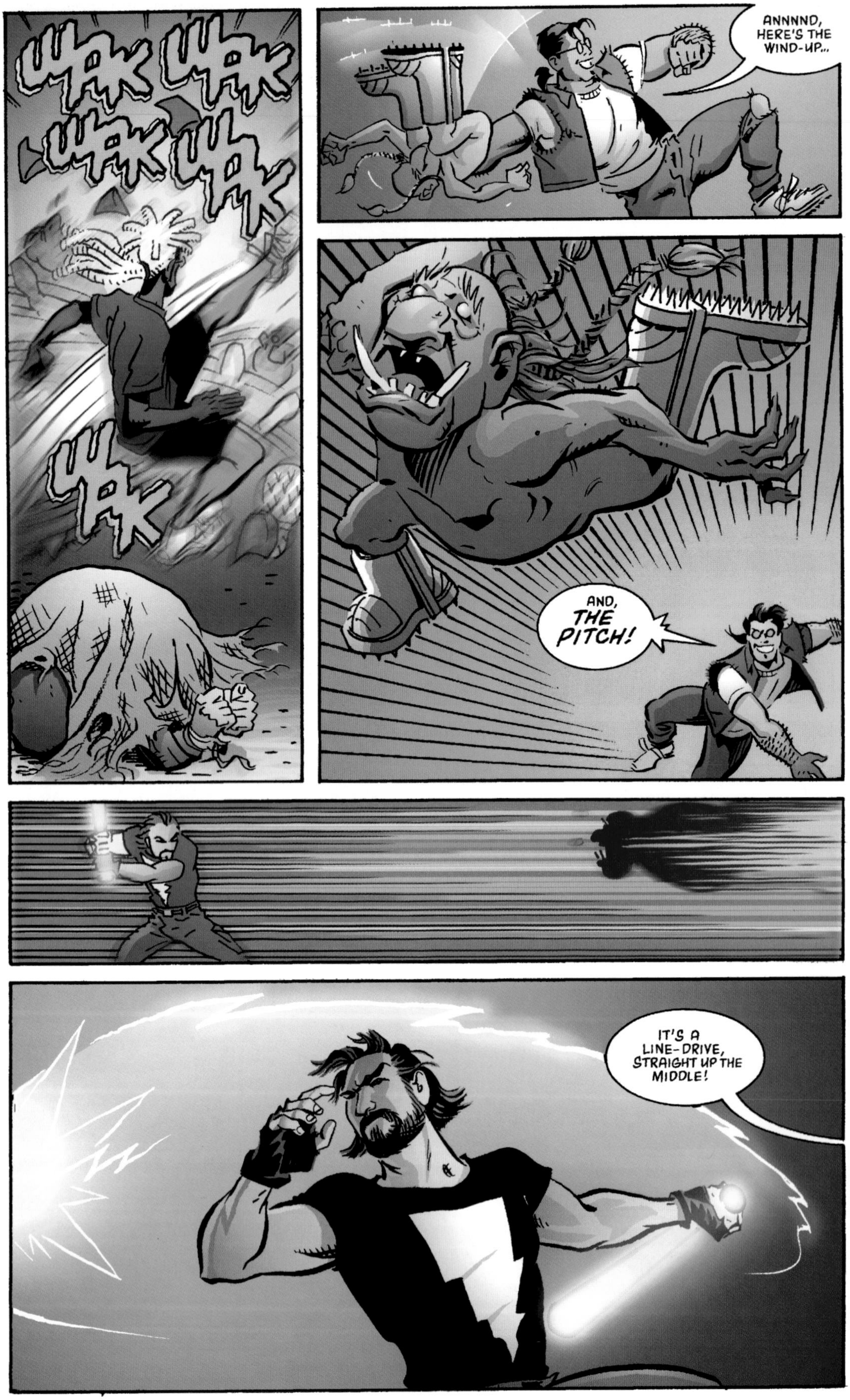
WAK WAK
WAK WAK
WAK
ANNNND, HERE'S THE WIND-UP...
AND, *THE PITCH!*
IT'S A LINE-DRIVE, STRAIGHT UP THE MIDDLE!

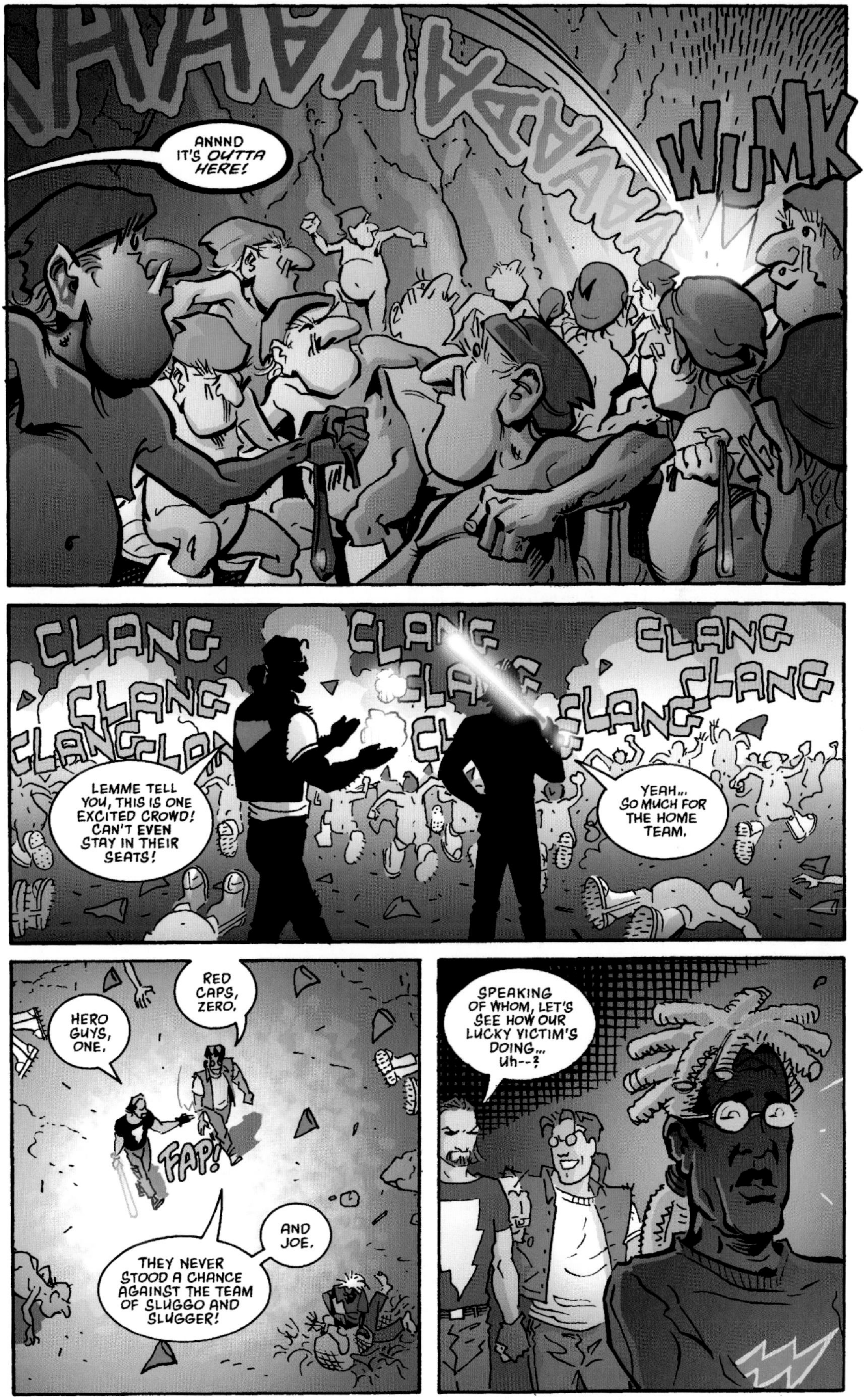
VAVAVAVAVAVAVAVAVA
ANNND IT'S *OUTTA HERE!*
WUMK
CLANG CLANG CLANG CLANG
LEMME TELL YOU, THIS IS ONE EXCITED CROWD! CAN'T EVEN STAY IN THEIR SEATS!
CLANG CLANG CLANG CLANG CLANG CLANG
YEAH... SO MUCH FOR THE HOME TEAM.
HERO GUYS, ONE.
RED CAPS, ZERO.
FAP!
THEY NEVER STOOD A CHANCE AGAINST THE TEAM OF SLUGGO AND SLUGGER!
AND JOE.
SPEAKING OF WHOM, LET'S SEE HOW OUR LUCKY VICTIM'S DOING... Uh--?

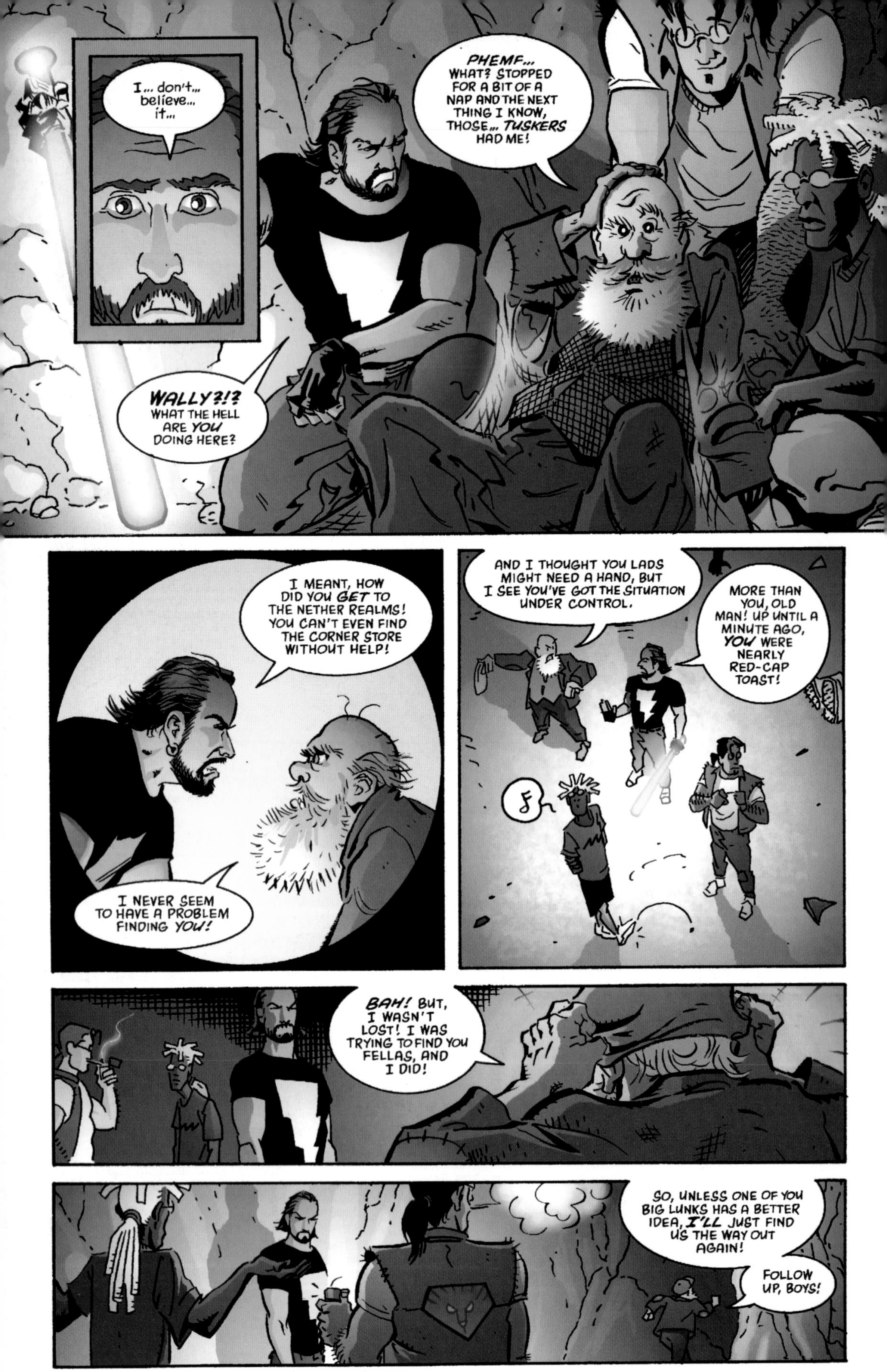
I... don't... believe... it...
PHEMF... WHAT? STOPPED FOR A BIT OF A NAP AND THE NEXT THING I KNOW, THOSE... TUSKERS HAD ME!
WALLY?!? WHAT THE HELL ARE YOU DOING HERE?
I MEANT, HOW DID YOU GET TO THE NETHER REALMS! YOU CAN'T EVEN FIND THE CORNER STORE WITHOUT HELP!
I NEVER SEEM TO HAVE A PROBLEM FINDING YOU!
AND I THOUGHT YOU LADS MIGHT NEED A HAND, BUT I SEE YOU'VE GOT THE SITUATION UNDER CONTROL.
MORE THAN YOU, OLD MAN! UP UNTIL A MINUTE AGO, YOU WERE NEARLY RED-CAP TOAST!
BAH! BUT, I WASN'T LOST! I WAS TRYING TO FIND YOU FELLAS, AND I DID!
SO, UNLESS ONE OF YOU BIG LUNKS HAS A BETTER IDEA, I'LL JUST FIND US THE WAY OUT AGAIN!
FOLLOW UP, BOYS!

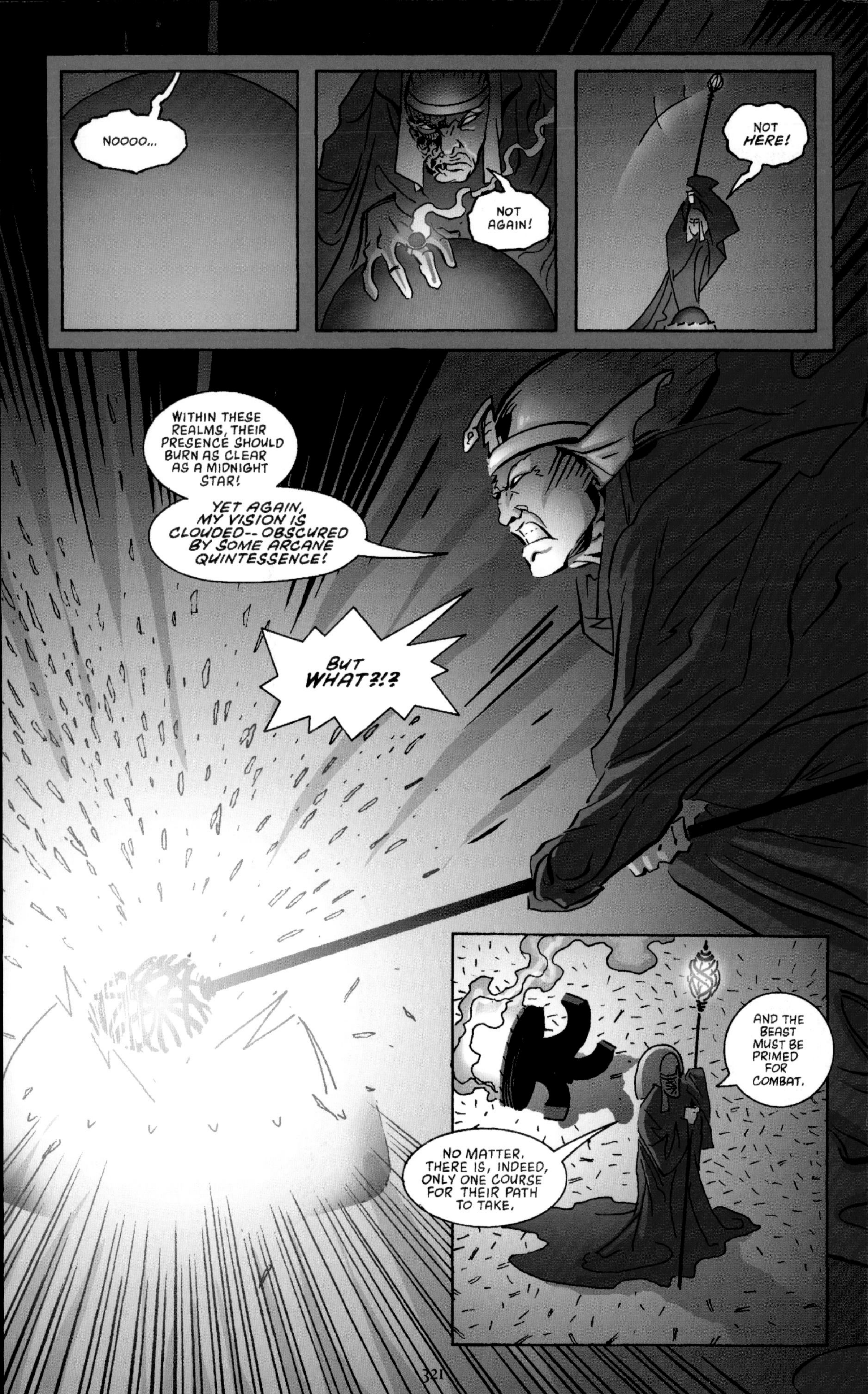
NOOOO...
NOT AGAIN!
NOT HERE!
WITHIN THESE REALMS, THEIR PRESENCE SHOULD BURN AS CLEAR AS A MIDNIGHT STAR!
YET AGAIN, MY VISION IS CLOUDED-- OBSCURED BY SOME ARCANE QUINTESSENCE!
BUT WHAT?!?
AND THE BEAST MUST BE PRIMED FOR COMBAT.
NO MATTER. THERE IS, INDEED, ONLY ONE COURSE FOR THEIR PATH TO TAKE.

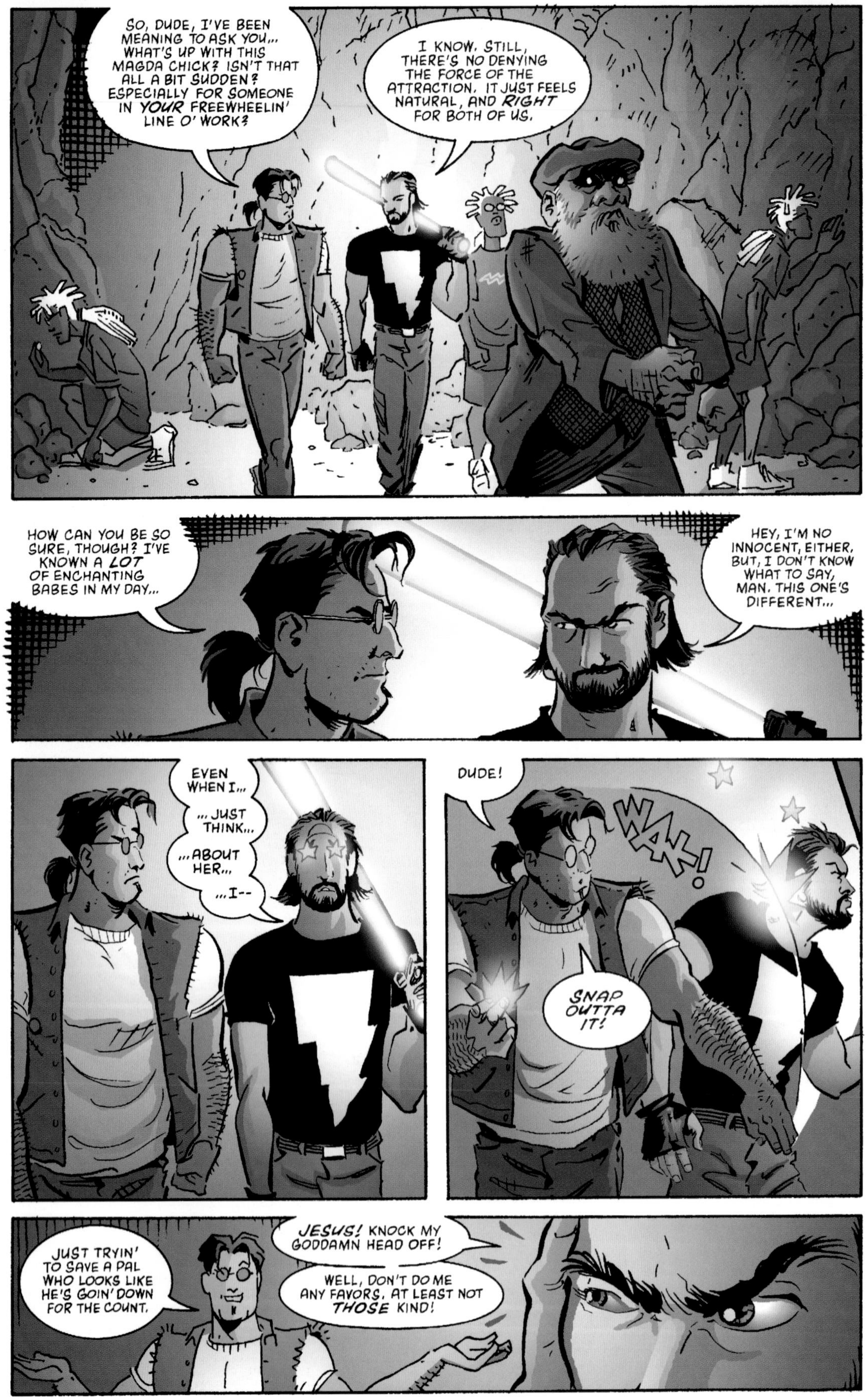
SO, DUDE, I'VE BEEN MEANING TO ASK YOU... WHAT'S UP WITH THIS MAGDA CHICK? ISN'T THAT ALL A BIT SUDDEN? ESPECIALLY FOR SOMEONE IN YOUR FREEWHEELIN' LINE O' WORK?
I KNOW. STILL, THERE'S NO DENYING THE FORCE OF THE ATTRACTION. IT JUST FEELS NATURAL, AND RIGHT FOR BOTH OF US.
HOW CAN YOU BE SO SURE, THOUGH? I'VE KNOWN A LOT OF ENCHANTING BABES IN MY DAY...
HEY, I'M NO INNOCENT, EITHER, BUT, I DON'T KNOW WHAT TO SAY, MAN. THIS ONE'S DIFFERENT...
EVEN WHEN I...
...JUST THINK...
...ABOUT HER...
...I--
DUDE!
WAK!
SNAP OUTTA IT!
JUST TRYIN' TO SAVE A PAL WHO LOOKS LIKE HE'S GOIN' DOWN FOR THE COUNT.
JESUS! KNOCK MY GODDAMN HEAD OFF!
WELL, DON'T DO ME ANY FAVORS. AT LEAST NOT THOSE KIND!

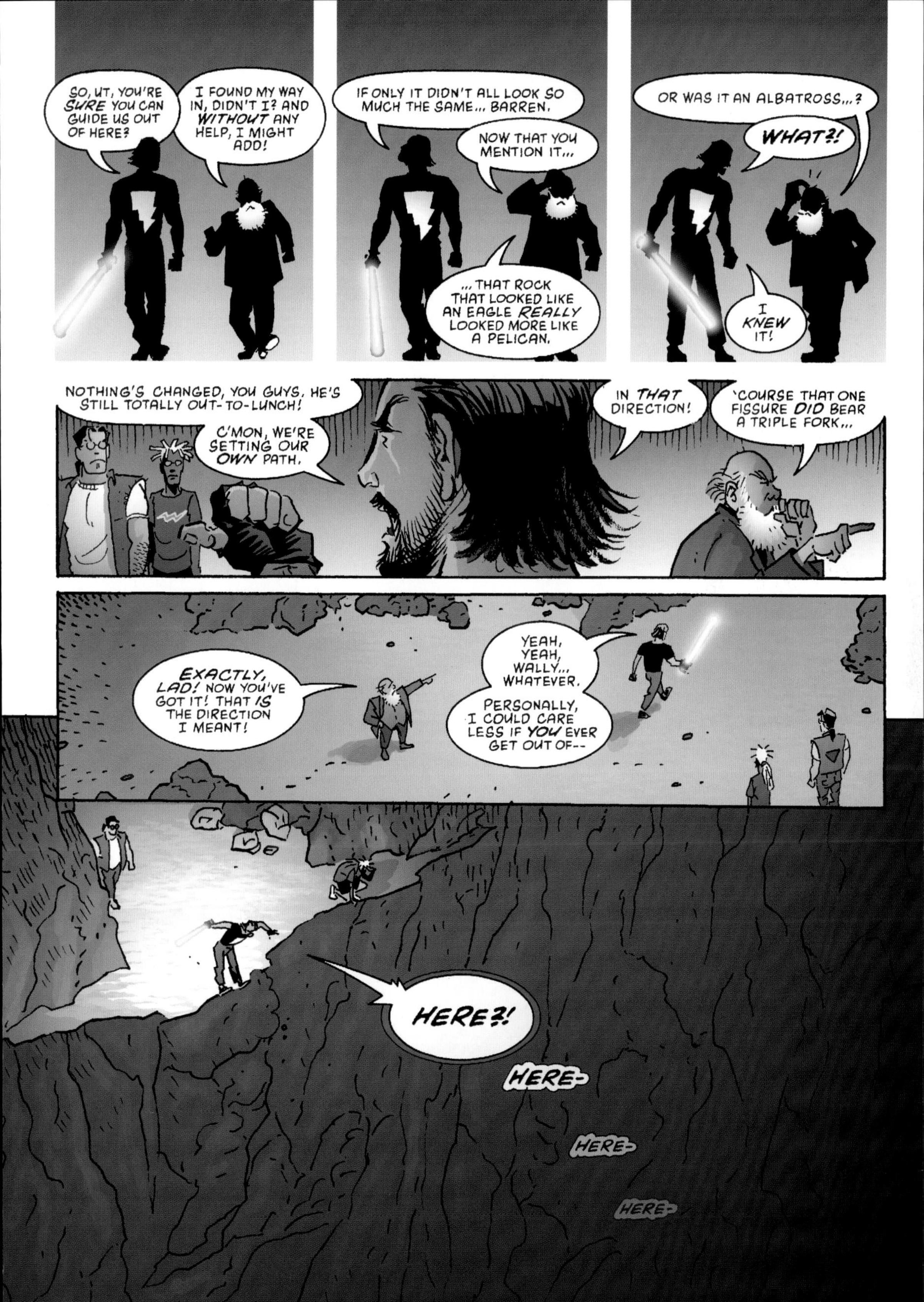
SO, UT, YOU'RE SURE YOU CAN GUIDE US OUT OF HERE?
I FOUND MY WAY IN, DIDN'T I? AND WITHOUT ANY HELP, I MIGHT ADD!
IF ONLY IT DIDN'T ALL LOOK SO MUCH THE SAME... BARREN.
NOW THAT YOU MENTION IT...
...THAT ROCK THAT LOOKED LIKE AN EAGLE REALLY LOOKED MORE LIKE A PELICAN.
OR WAS IT AN ALBATROSS...?
WHAT?!
I KNEW IT!
NOTHING'S CHANGED, YOU GUYS, HE'S STILL TOTALLY OUT-TO-LUNCH!
C'MON, WE'RE SETTING OUR OWN PATH.
IN THAT DIRECTION!
'COURSE THAT ONE FISSURE DID BEAR A TRIPLE FORK...
EXACTLY, LAD! NOW YOU'VE GOT IT! THAT IS THE DIRECTION I MEANT!
YEAH, YEAH, WALLY... WHATEVER.
PERSONALLY, I COULD CARE LESS IF YOU EVER GET OUT OF--
HERE?!
HERE-
HERE-
HERE-

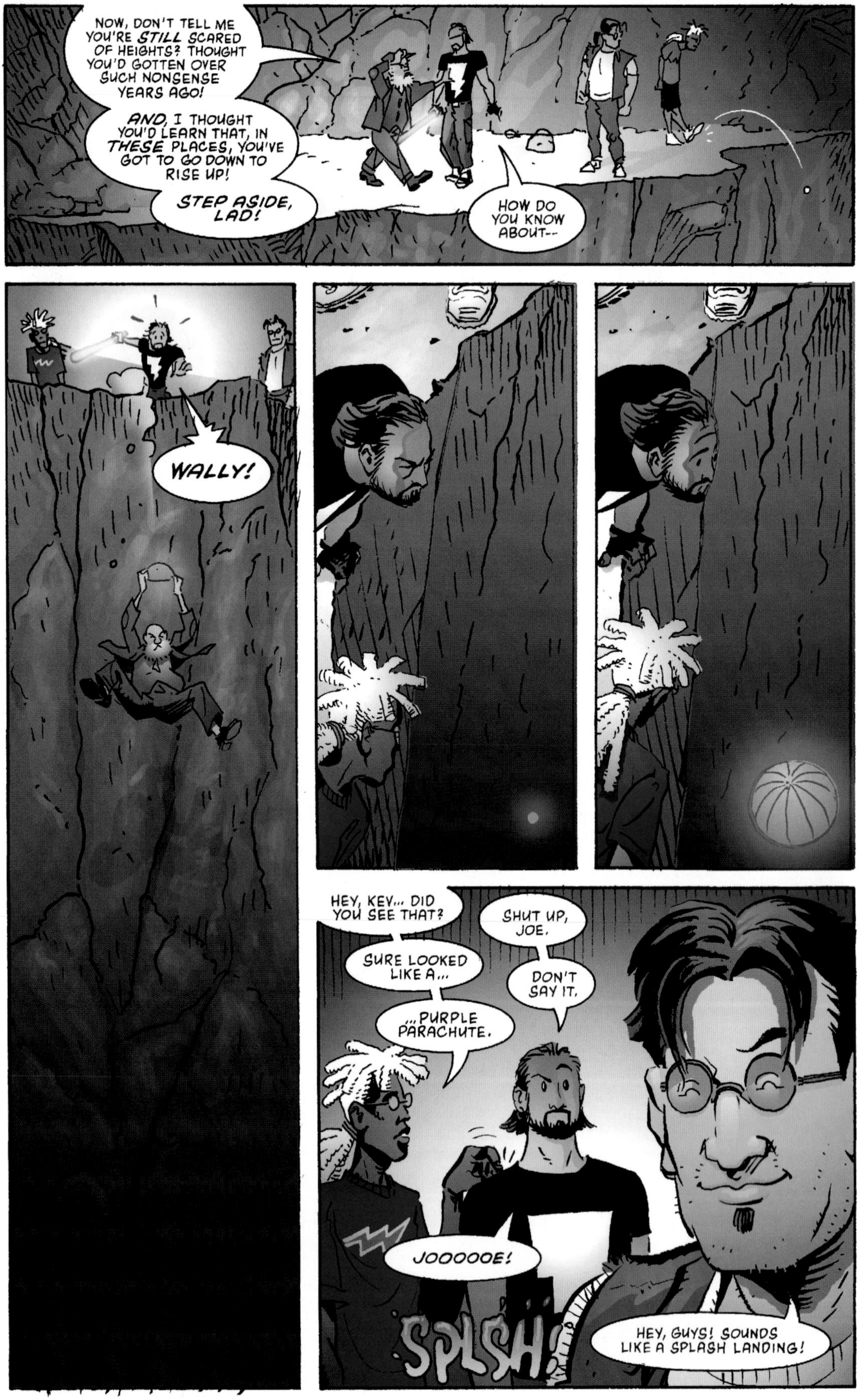
NOW, DON'T TELL ME YOU'RE STILL SCARED OF HEIGHTS? THOUGHT YOU'D GOTTEN OVER SUCH NONSENSE YEARS AGO!
AND, I THOUGHT YOU'D LEARN THAT, IN THESE PLACES, YOU'VE GOT TO GO DOWN TO RISE UP!
STEP ASIDE, LAD!
HOW DO YOU KNOW ABOUT--
WALLY!
HEY, KEV... DID YOU SEE THAT?
SHUT UP, JOE.
SURE LOOKED LIKE A...
DON'T SAY IT.
...PURPLE PARACHUTE.
JOOOOOE!
SPLSH!
HEY, GUYS! SOUNDS LIKE A SPLASH LANDING!

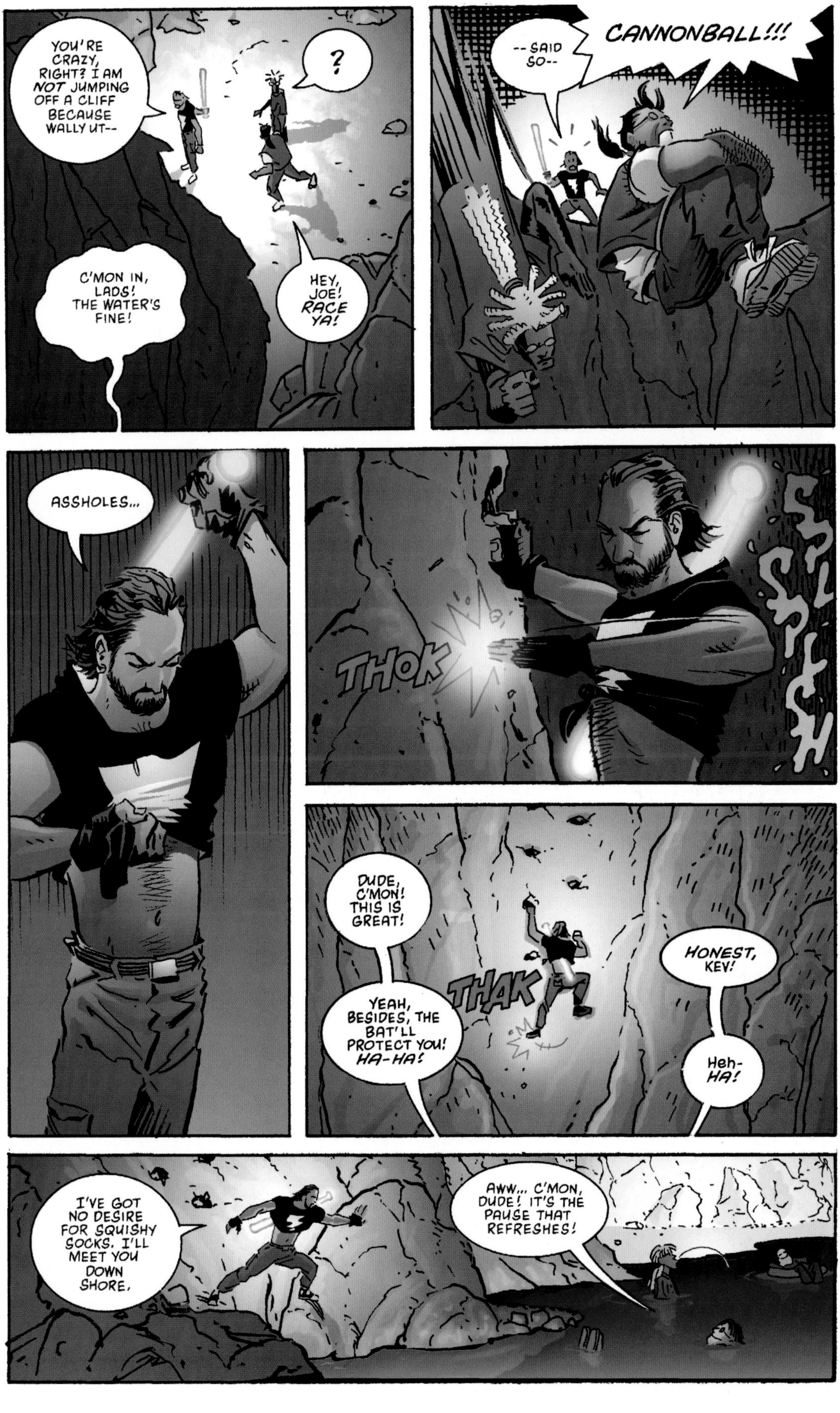

YOU'RE CRAZY, RIGHT? I AM NOT JUMPING OFF A CLIFF BECAUSE WALLY UT--
?
C'MON IN, LADS! THE WATER'S FINE!
HEY, JOE! RACE YA!
--SAID SO--
CANNONBALL!!!
ASSHOLES...
THOK
SPLASH
DUDE, C'MON! THIS IS GREAT!
YEAH, BESIDES, THE BAT'LL PROTECT YOU! HA-HA!
THAK
HONEST, KEV!
Heh-HA!
I'VE GOT NO DESIRE FOR SQUISHY SOCKS. I'LL MEET YOU DOWN SHORE.
AWW... C'MON, DUDE! IT'S THE PAUSE THAT REFRESHES!

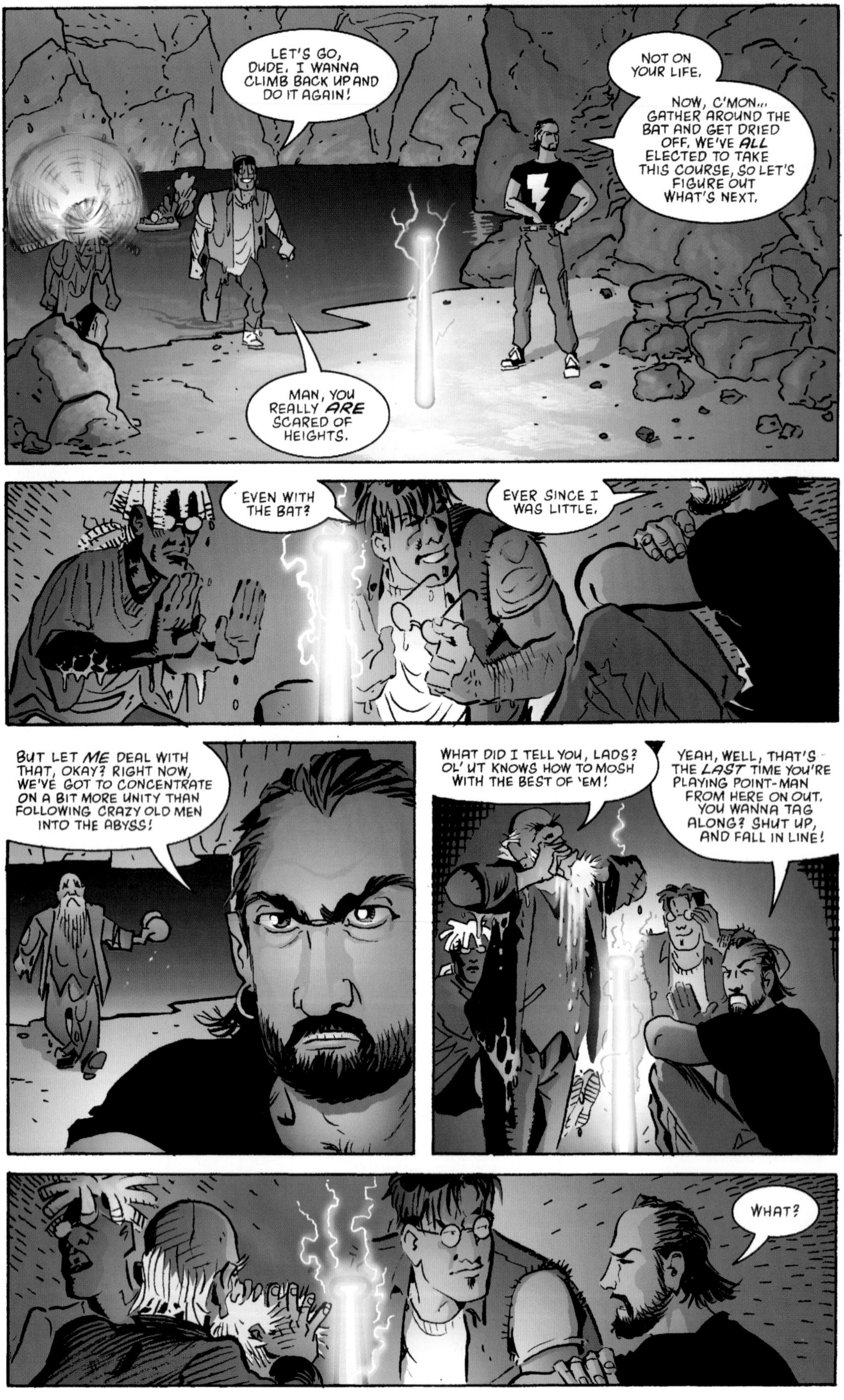
LET'S GO, DUDE. I WANNA CLIMB BACK UP AND DO IT AGAIN!
NOT ON YOUR LIFE.
NOW, C'MON... GATHER AROUND THE BAT AND GET DRIED OFF. WE'VE ALL ELECTED TO TAKE THIS COURSE, SO LET'S FIGURE OUT WHAT'S NEXT.
MAN, YOU REALLY ARE SCARED OF HEIGHTS.
EVEN WITH THE BAT?
EVER SINCE I WAS LITTLE.
BUT LET ME DEAL WITH THAT, OKAY? RIGHT NOW, WE'VE GOT TO CONCENTRATE ON A BIT MORE UNITY THAN FOLLOWING CRAZY OLD MEN INTO THE ABYSS!
WHAT DID I TELL YOU, LADS? OL' UT KNOWS HOW TO MOSH WITH THE BEST OF 'EM!
YEAH, WELL, THAT'S THE LAST TIME YOU'RE PLAYING POINT-MAN FROM HERE ON OUT. YOU WANNA TAG ALONG? SHUT UP, AND FALL IN LINE!
WHAT?

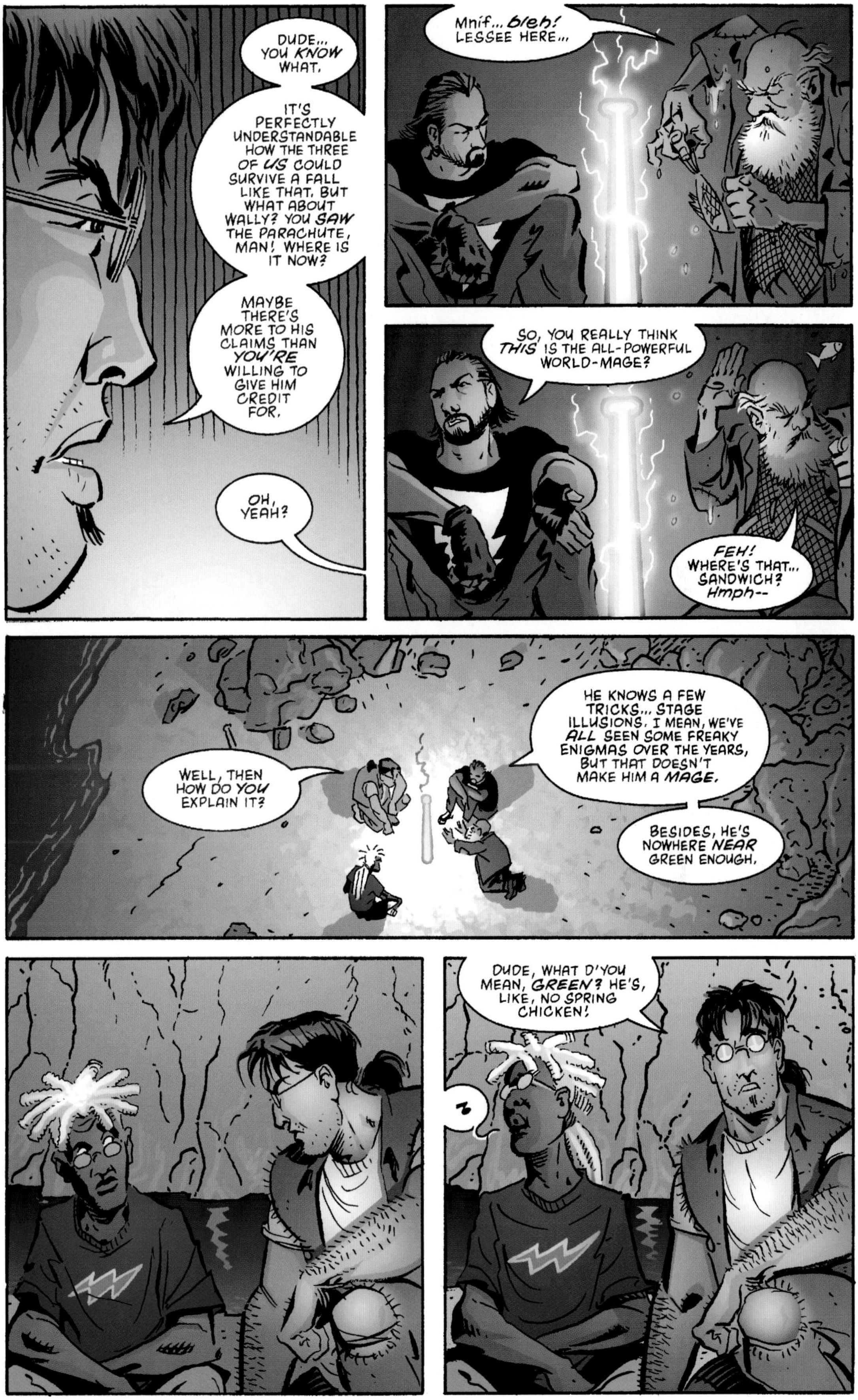
DUDE... YOU KNOW WHAT.
IT'S PERFECTLY UNDERSTANDABLE HOW THE THREE OF US COULD SURVIVE A FALL LIKE THAT. BUT WHAT ABOUT WALLY? YOU SAW THE PARACHUTE, MAN! WHERE IS IT NOW?
MAYBE THERE'S MORE TO HIS CLAIMS THAN YOU'RE WILLING TO GIVE HIM CREDIT FOR.
OH, YEAH?
Mnif... bleh! LESSEE HERE...
SO, YOU REALLY THINK THIS IS THE ALL-POWERFUL WORLD-MAGE?
FEH! WHERE'S THAT... SANDWICH? Hmph--
WELL, THEN HOW DO YOU EXPLAIN IT?
HE KNOWS A FEW TRICKS... STAGE ILLUSIONS. I MEAN, WE'VE ALL SEEN SOME FREAKY ENIGMAS OVER THE YEARS, BUT THAT DOESN'T MAKE HIM A MAGE.
BESIDES, HE'S NOWHERE NEAR GREEN ENOUGH.
DUDE, WHAT D'YOU MEAN, GREEN? HE'S, LIKE, NO SPRING CHICKEN!
?

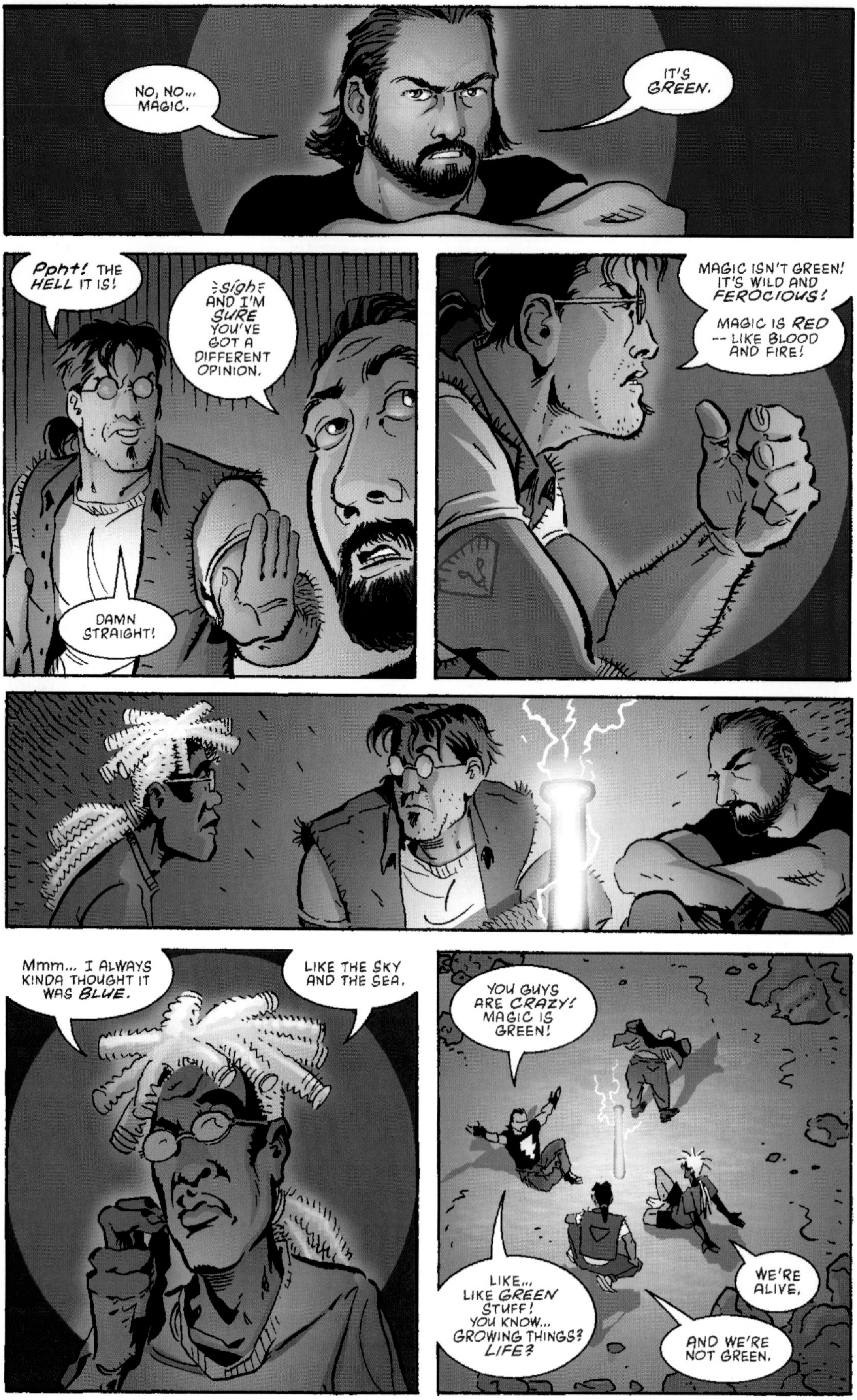
NO, NO... MAGIC.
IT'S GREEN.
Ppht! THE HELL IT IS!
sigh AND I'M SURE YOU'VE GOT A DIFFERENT OPINION.
DAMN STRAIGHT!
MAGIC ISN'T GREEN! IT'S WILD AND FEROCIOUS!
MAGIC IS RED -- LIKE BLOOD AND FIRE!
Mmm... I ALWAYS KINDA THOUGHT IT WAS BLUE.
LIKE THE SKY AND THE SEA.
YOU GUYS ARE CRAZY! MAGIC IS GREEN!
LIKE... LIKE GREEN STUFF! YOU KNOW... GROWING THINGS? LIFE?
WE'RE ALIVE.
AND WE'RE NOT GREEN.

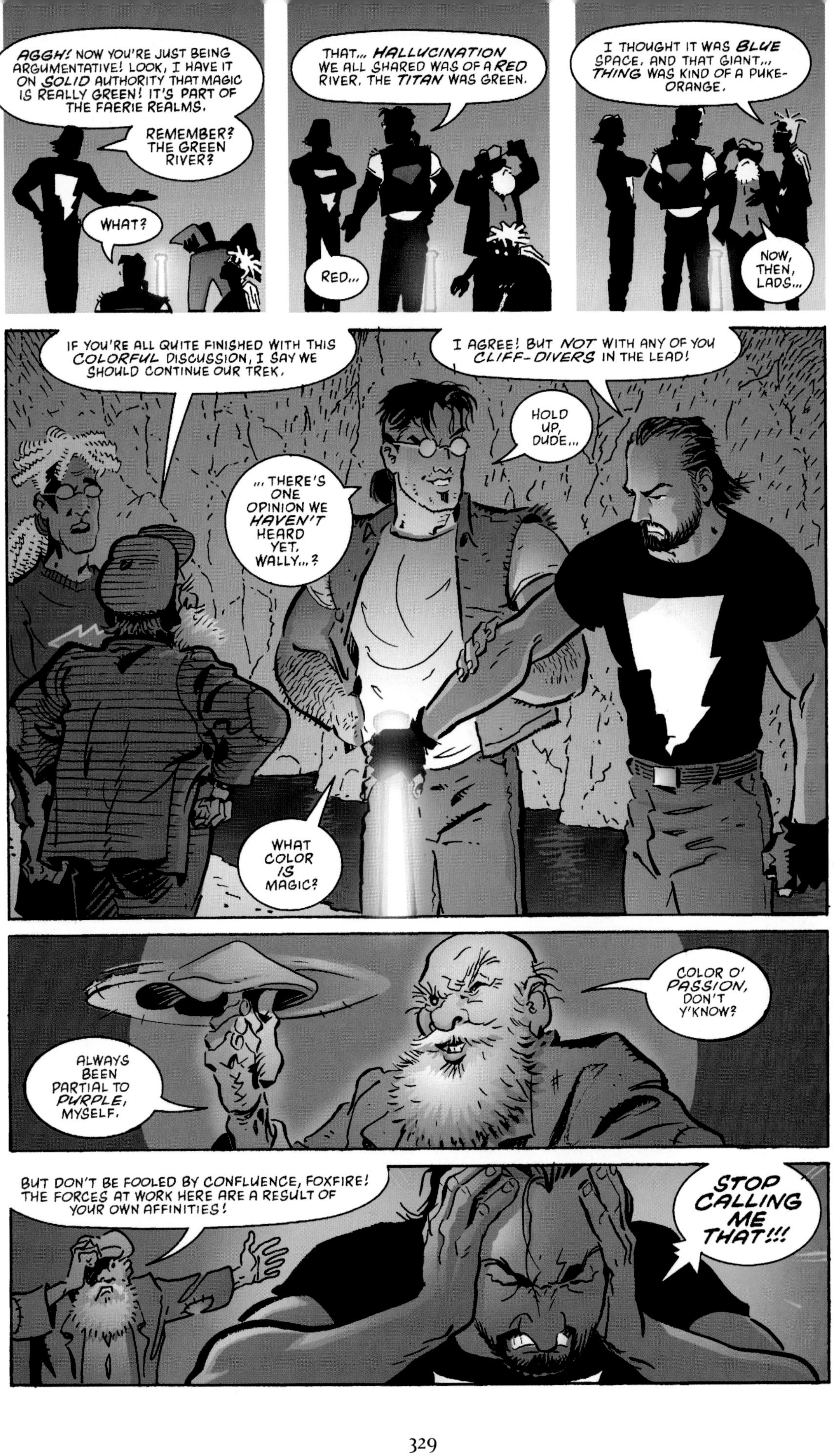

AGGH! NOW YOU'RE JUST BEING ARGUMENTATIVE! LOOK, I HAVE IT ON SOLID AUTHORITY THAT MAGIC IS REALLY GREEN! IT'S PART OF THE FAERIE REALMS.
REMEMBER? THE GREEN RIVER?
WHAT?
THAT... HALLUCINATION WE ALL SHARED WAS OF A RED RIVER. THE TITAN WAS GREEN.
RED...
I THOUGHT IT WAS BLUE SPACE, AND THAT GIANT... THING WAS KIND OF A PUKE-ORANGE.
NOW, THEN, LADS...
IF YOU'RE ALL QUITE FINISHED WITH THIS COLORFUL DISCUSSION, I SAY WE SHOULD CONTINUE OUR TREK.
I AGREE! BUT NOT WITH ANY OF YOU CLIFF-DIVERS IN THE LEAD!
HOLD UP, DUDE...
...THERE'S ONE OPINION WE HAVEN'T HEARD YET, WALLY...?
WHAT COLOR IS MAGIC?
ALWAYS BEEN PARTIAL TO PURPLE, MYSELF.
COLOR O' PASSION, DON'T Y'KNOW?
BUT DON'T BE FOOLED BY CONFLUENCE, FOXFIRE! THE FORCES AT WORK HERE ARE A RESULT OF YOUR OWN AFFINITIES!
STOP CALLING ME THAT!!!

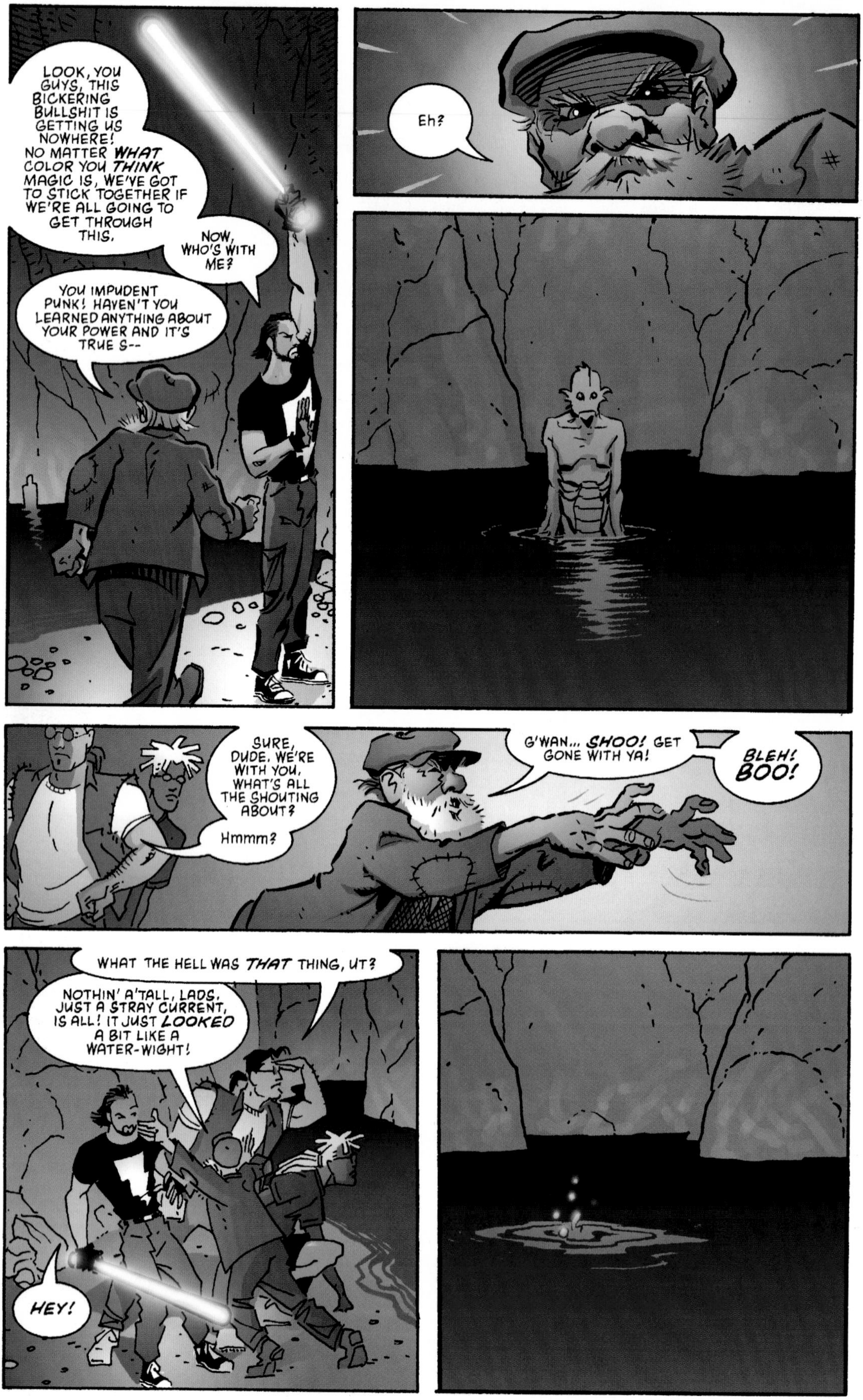
LOOK, YOU GUYS, THIS BICKERING BULLSHIT IS GETTING US NOWHERE! NO MATTER WHAT COLOR YOU THINK MAGIC IS, WE'VE GOT TO STICK TOGETHER IF WE'RE ALL GOING TO GET THROUGH THIS.
NOW, WHO'S WITH ME?
YOU IMPUDENT PUNK! HAVEN'T YOU LEARNED ANYTHING ABOUT YOUR POWER AND IT'S TRUE S--
Eh?
SURE, DUDE. WE'RE WITH YOU. WHAT'S ALL THE SHOUTING ABOUT?
Hmmm?
G'WAN... SHOO! GET GONE WITH YA!
BLEH! BOO!
WHAT THE HELL WAS THAT THING, UT?
NOTHIN' A'TALL, LADS. JUST A STRAY CURRENT, IS ALL! IT JUST LOOKED A BIT LIKE A WATER-WIGHT!
HEY!

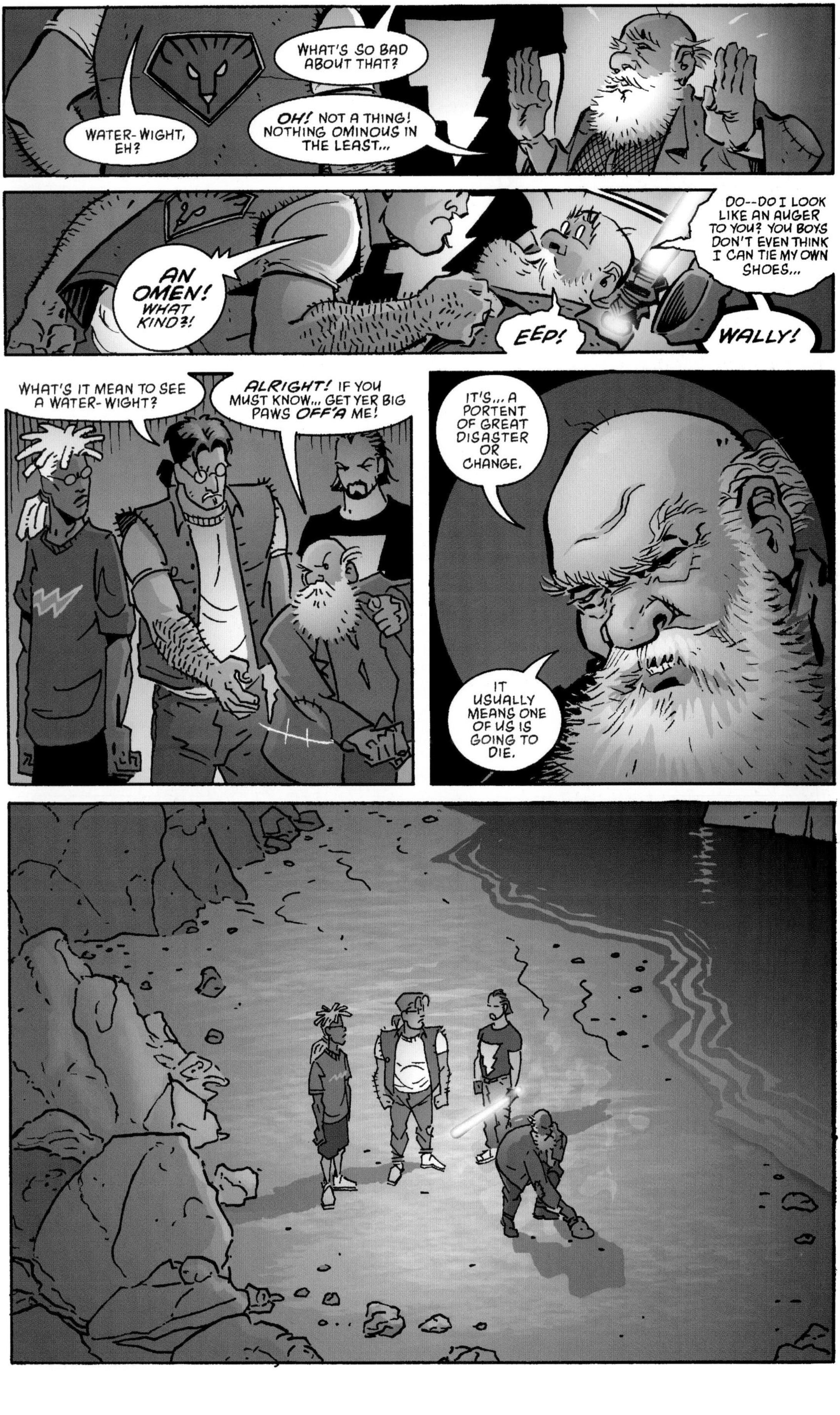
WATER-WIGHT, EH?
WHAT'S SO BAD ABOUT THAT?
OH! NOT A THING! NOTHING OMINOUS IN THE LEAST...
AN OMEN! WHAT KIND?!
EEP!
DO--DO I LOOK LIKE AN AUGER TO YOU? YOU BOYS DON'T EVEN THINK I CAN TIE MY OWN SHOES...
WALLY!
WHAT'S IT MEAN TO SEE A WATER-WIGHT?
ALRIGHT! IF YOU MUST KNOW... GET YER BIG PAWS OFF'A ME!
IT'S... A PORTENT OF GREAT DISASTER OR CHANGE.
IT USUALLY MEANS ONE OF US IS GOING TO DIE.

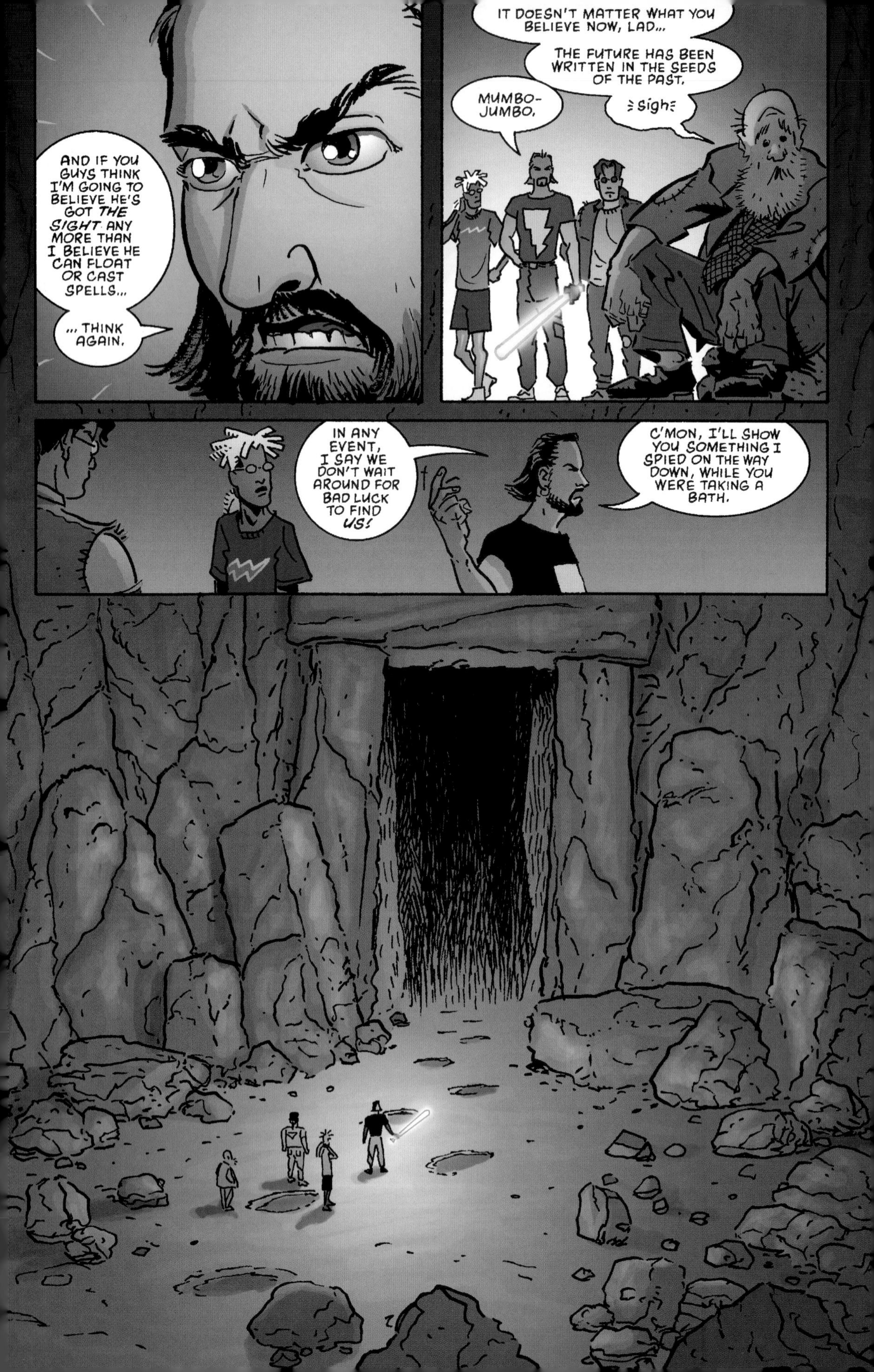
AND IF YOU GUYS THINK I'M GOING TO BELIEVE HE'S GOT THE SIGHT ANY MORE THAN I BELIEVE HE CAN FLOAT OR CAST SPELLS...
...THINK AGAIN.
IT DOESN'T MATTER WHAT YOU BELIEVE NOW, LAD...
THE FUTURE HAS BEEN WRITTEN IN THE SEEDS OF THE PAST.
MUMBO-JUMBO.
sigh
IN ANY EVENT, I SAY WE DON'T WAIT AROUND FOR BAD LUCK TO FIND US!
C'MON, I'LL SHOW YOU SOMETHING I SPIED ON THE WAY DOWN, WHILE YOU WERE TAKING A BATH.

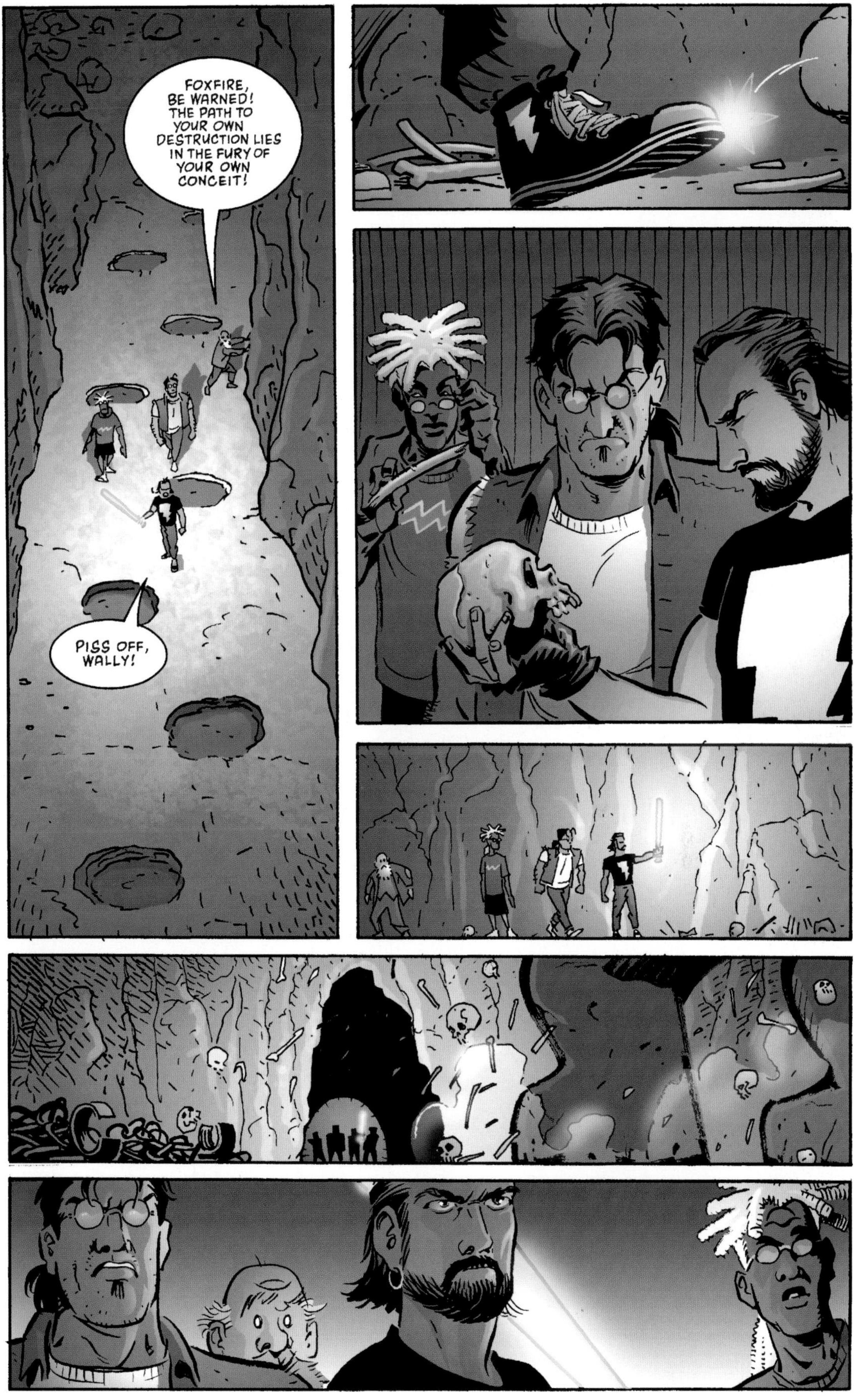
FOXFIRE, BE WARNED! THE PATH TO YOUR OWN DESTRUCTION LIES IN THE FURY OF YOUR OWN CONCEIT!
PISS OFF, WALLY!

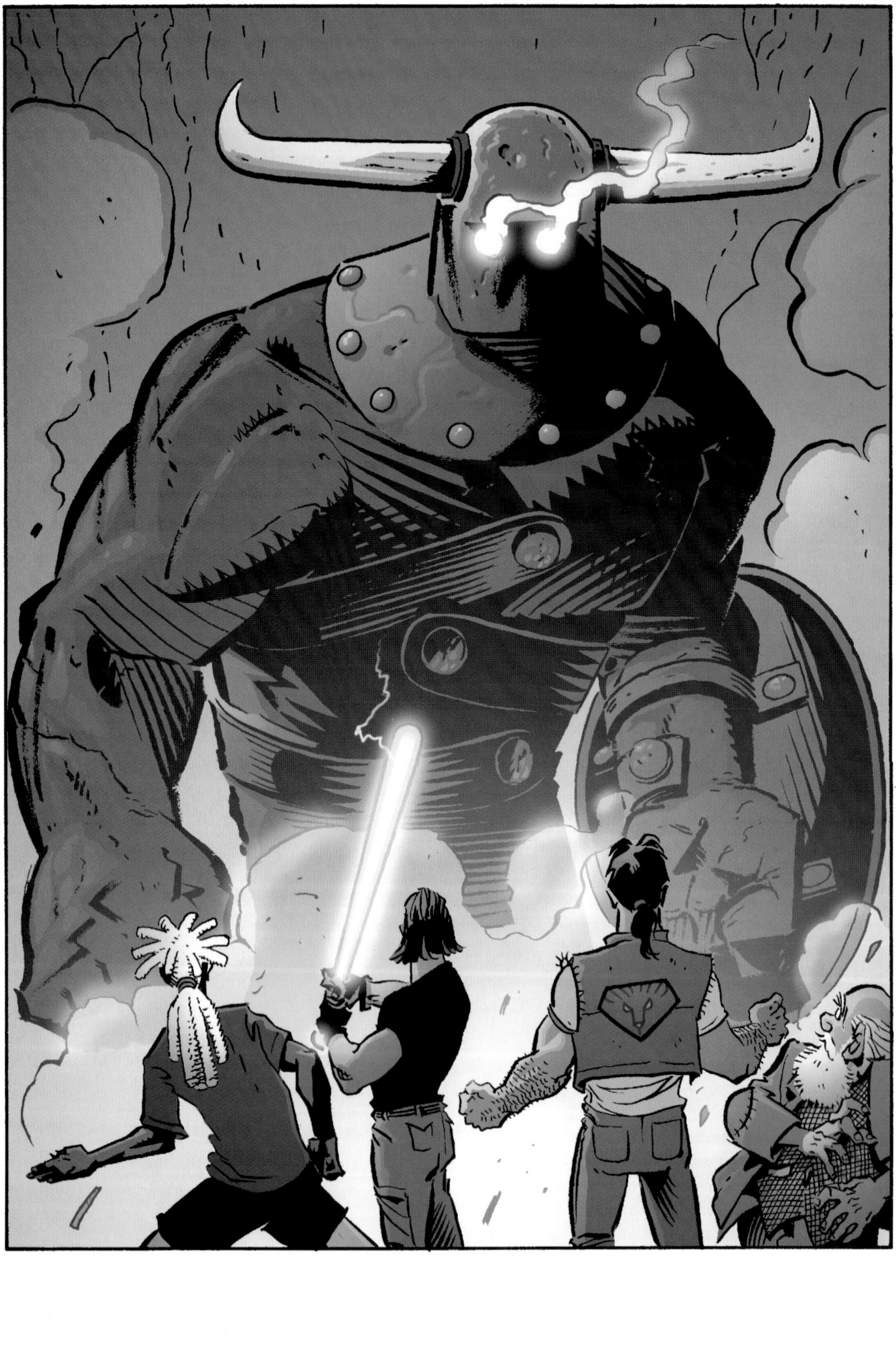

THE HERO DEFINED

MAGE®

chapter

14

"When the Battle's Lost and Won"

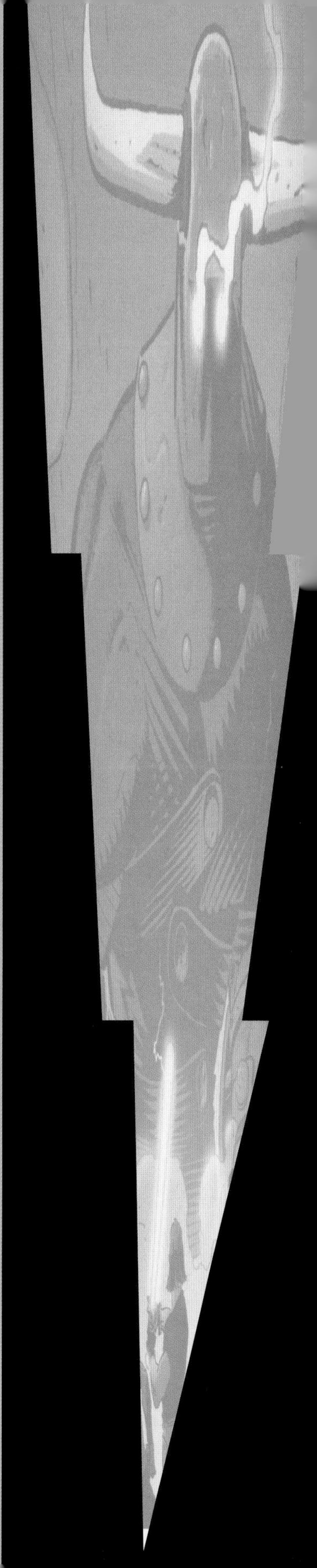

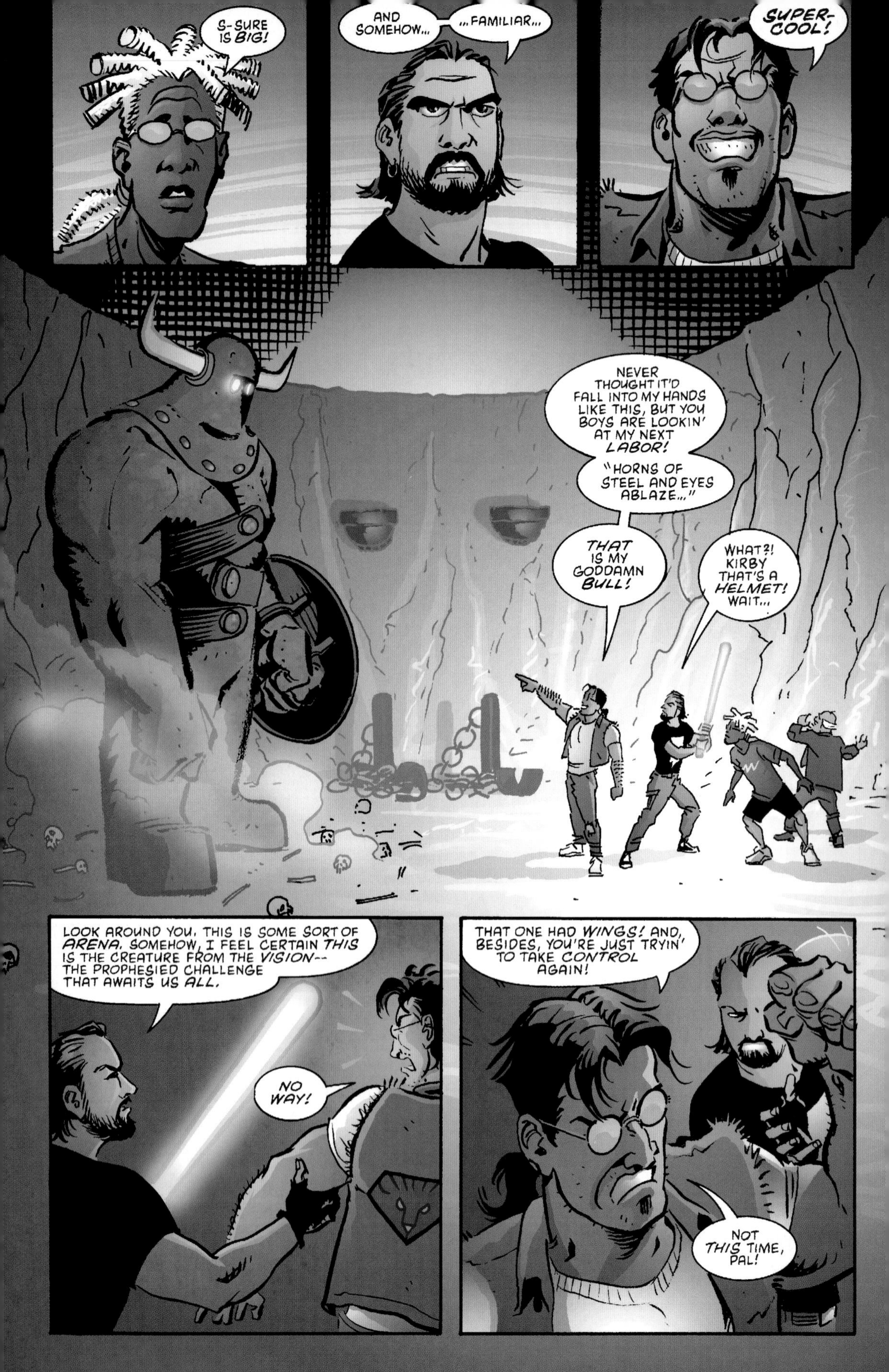

S-SURE IS BIG!
AND SOMEHOW...
...FAMILIAR...
SUPER-COOL!
NEVER THOUGHT IT'D FALL INTO MY HANDS LIKE THIS, BUT YOU BOYS ARE LOOKIN' AT MY NEXT LABOR!
"HORNS OF STEEL AND EYES ABLAZE..."
THAT IS MY GODDAMN BULL!
WHAT?! KIRBY THAT'S A HELMET! WAIT...
LOOK AROUND YOU. THIS IS SOME SORT OF ARENA. SOMEHOW, I FEEL CERTAIN THIS IS THE CREATURE FROM THE VISION-- THE PROPHESIED CHALLENGE THAT AWAITS US ALL.
NO WAY!
THAT ONE HAD WINGS! AND, BESIDES, YOU'RE JUST TRYIN' TO TAKE CONTROL AGAIN!
NOT THIS TIME, PAL!

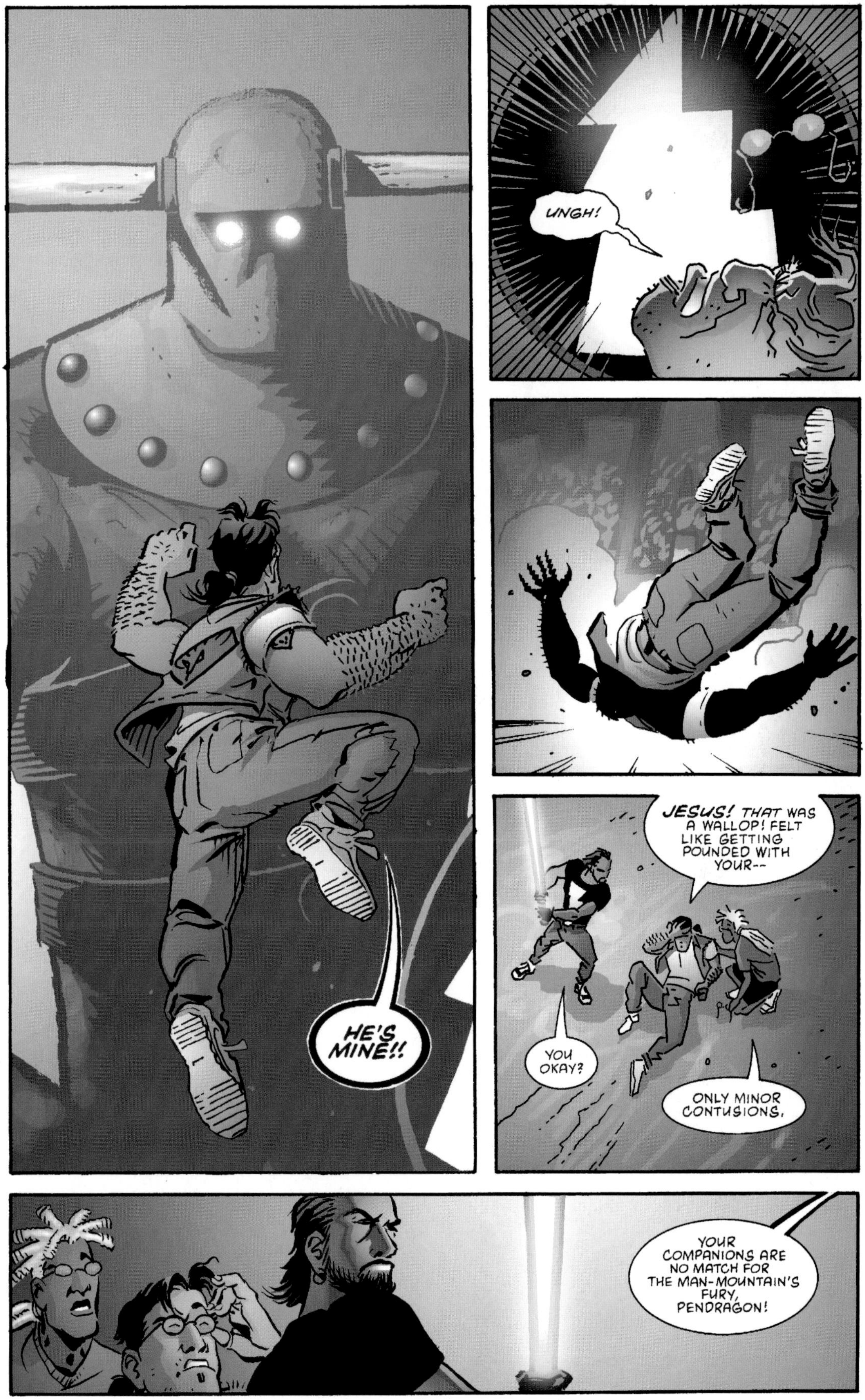
HE'S MINE!!
UNGH!
JESUS! THAT WAS A WALLOP! FELT LIKE GETTING POUNDED WITH YOUR--
YOU OKAY?
ONLY MINOR CONTUSIONS.
YOUR COMPANIONS ARE NO MATCH FOR THE MAN-MOUNTAIN'S FURY, PENDRAGON!

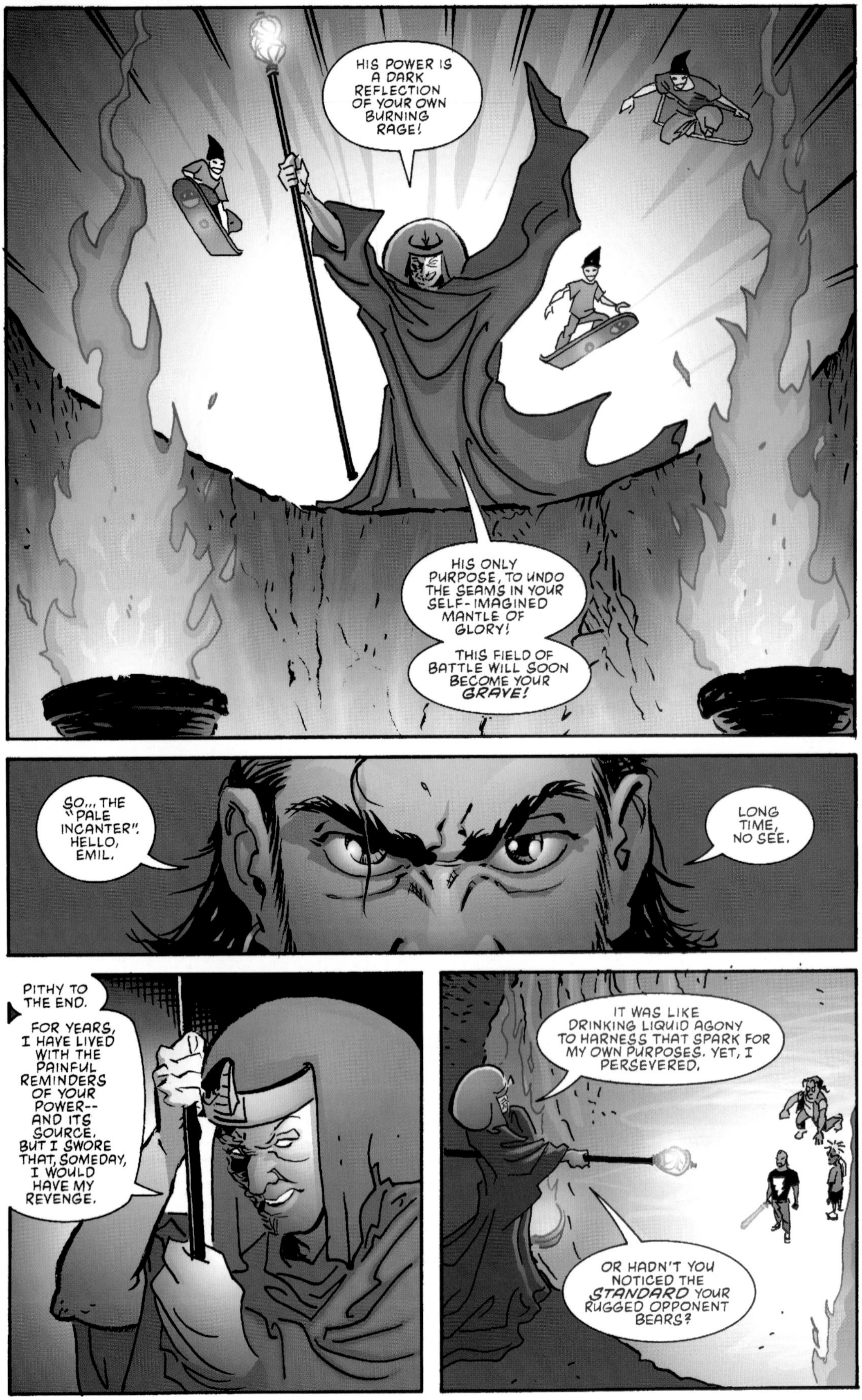
HIS POWER IS A DARK REFLECTION OF YOUR OWN BURNING RAGE!
HIS ONLY PURPOSE, TO UNDO THE SEAMS IN YOUR SELF-IMAGINED MANTLE OF GLORY!
THIS FIELD OF BATTLE WILL SOON BECOME YOUR GRAVE!
SO... THE "PALE INCANTER". HELLO, EMIL.
LONG TIME, NO SEE.
PITHY TO THE END.
FOR YEARS, I HAVE LIVED WITH THE PAINFUL REMINDERS OF YOUR POWER-- AND ITS SOURCE. BUT I SWORE THAT, SOMEDAY, I WOULD HAVE MY REVENGE.
IT WAS LIKE DRINKING LIQUID AGONY TO HARNESS THAT SPARK FOR MY OWN PURPOSES. YET, I PERSEVERED.
OR HADN'T YOU NOTICED THE STANDARD YOUR RUGGED OPPONENT BEARS?

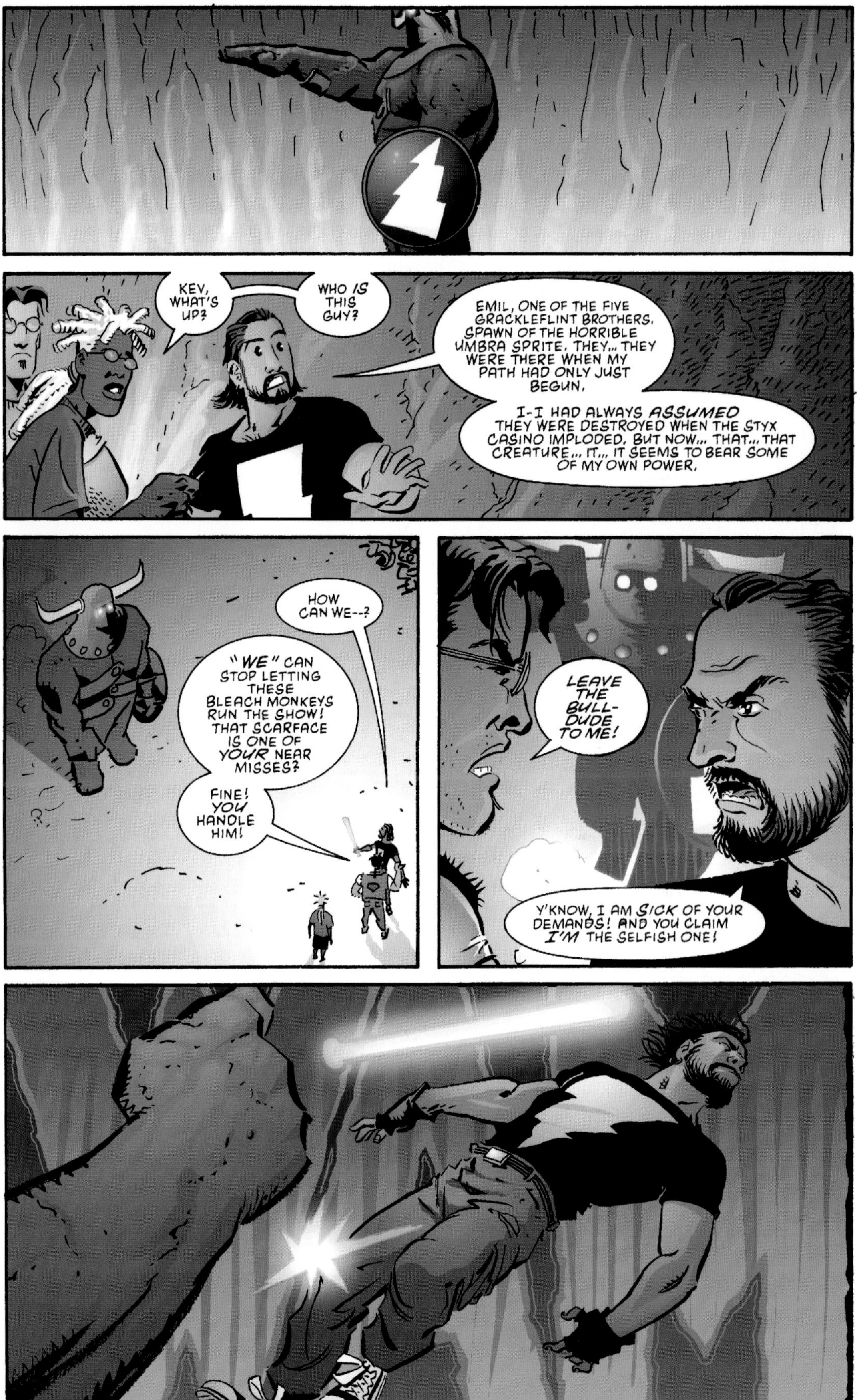
KEV, WHAT'S UP?
WHO IS THIS GUY?
EMIL, ONE OF THE FIVE GRACKLEFLINT BROTHERS, SPAWN OF THE HORRIBLE UMBRA SPRITE. THEY... THEY WERE THERE WHEN MY PATH HAD ONLY JUST BEGUN.
I-I HAD ALWAYS ASSUMED THEY WERE DESTROYED WHEN THE STYX CASINO IMPLODED. BUT NOW... THAT... THAT CREATURE... IT... IT SEEMS TO BEAR SOME OF MY OWN POWER.
HOW CAN WE--?
"WE" CAN STOP LETTING THESE BLEACH MONKEYS RUN THE SHOW! THAT SCARFACE IS ONE OF YOUR NEAR MISSES?
FINE! YOU HANDLE HIM!
LEAVE THE BULL-DUDE TO ME!
Y'KNOW, I AM SICK OF YOUR DEMANDS! AND YOU CLAIM I'M THE SELFISH ONE!

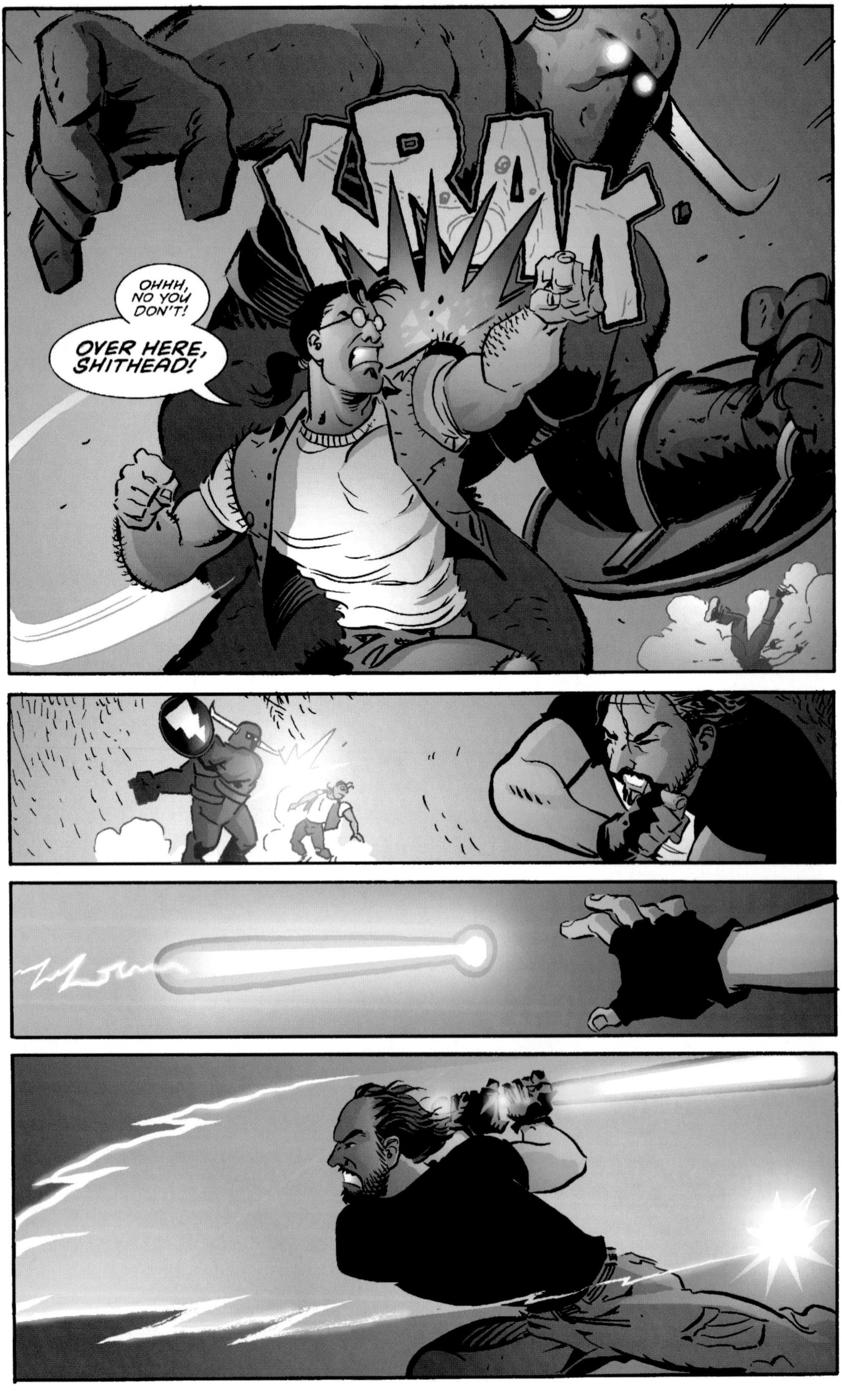
KRAK
OHHH, NO YOU DON'T!
OVER HERE, SHITHEAD!

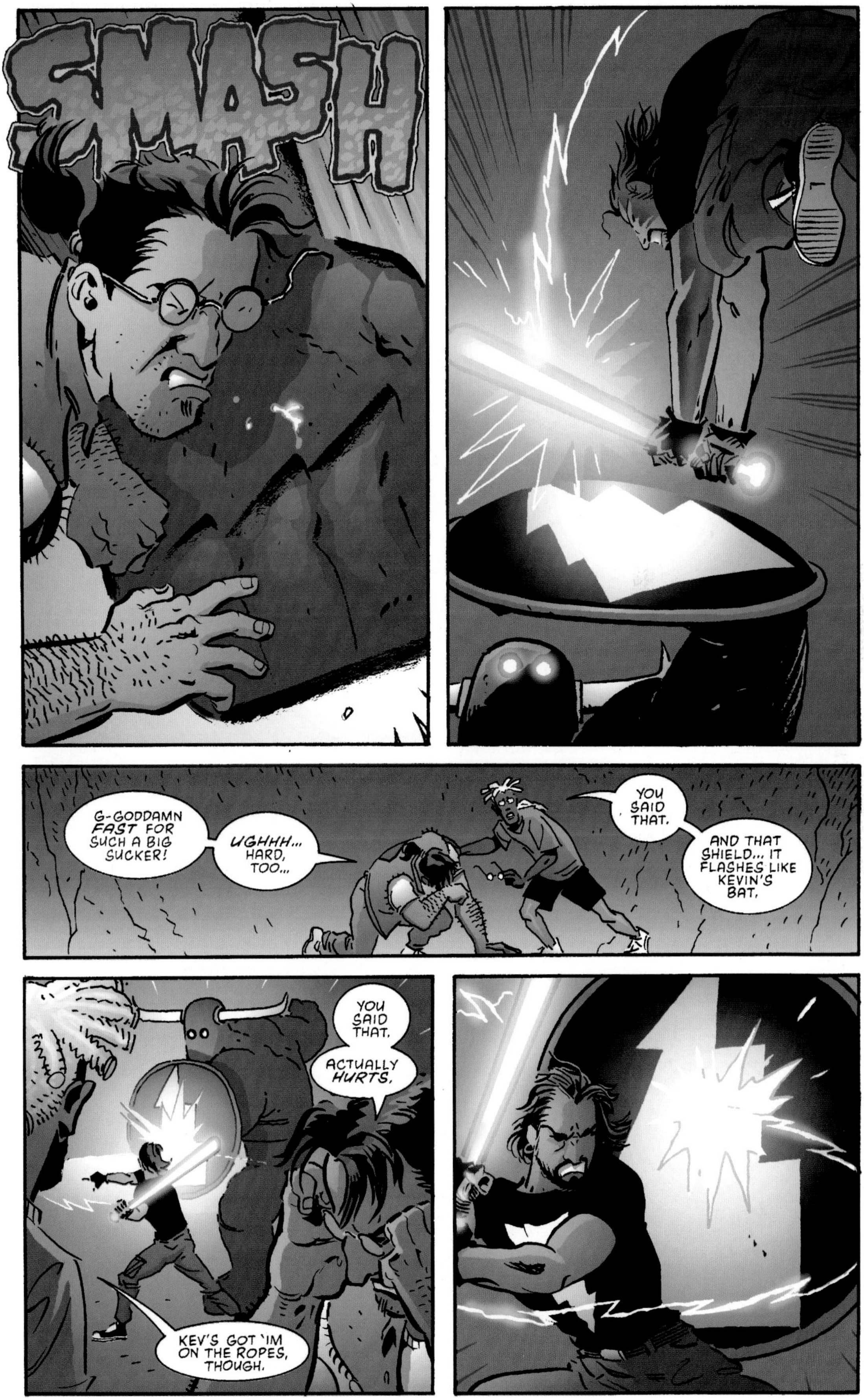
SMASH
G-GODDAMN FAST FOR SUCH A BIG SUCKER!
UGHHH... HARD, TOO...
YOU SAID THAT.
AND THAT SHIELD... IT FLASHES LIKE KEVIN'S BAT.
YOU SAID THAT.
ACTUALLY HURTS.
KEV'S GOT 'IM ON THE ROPES, THOUGH.

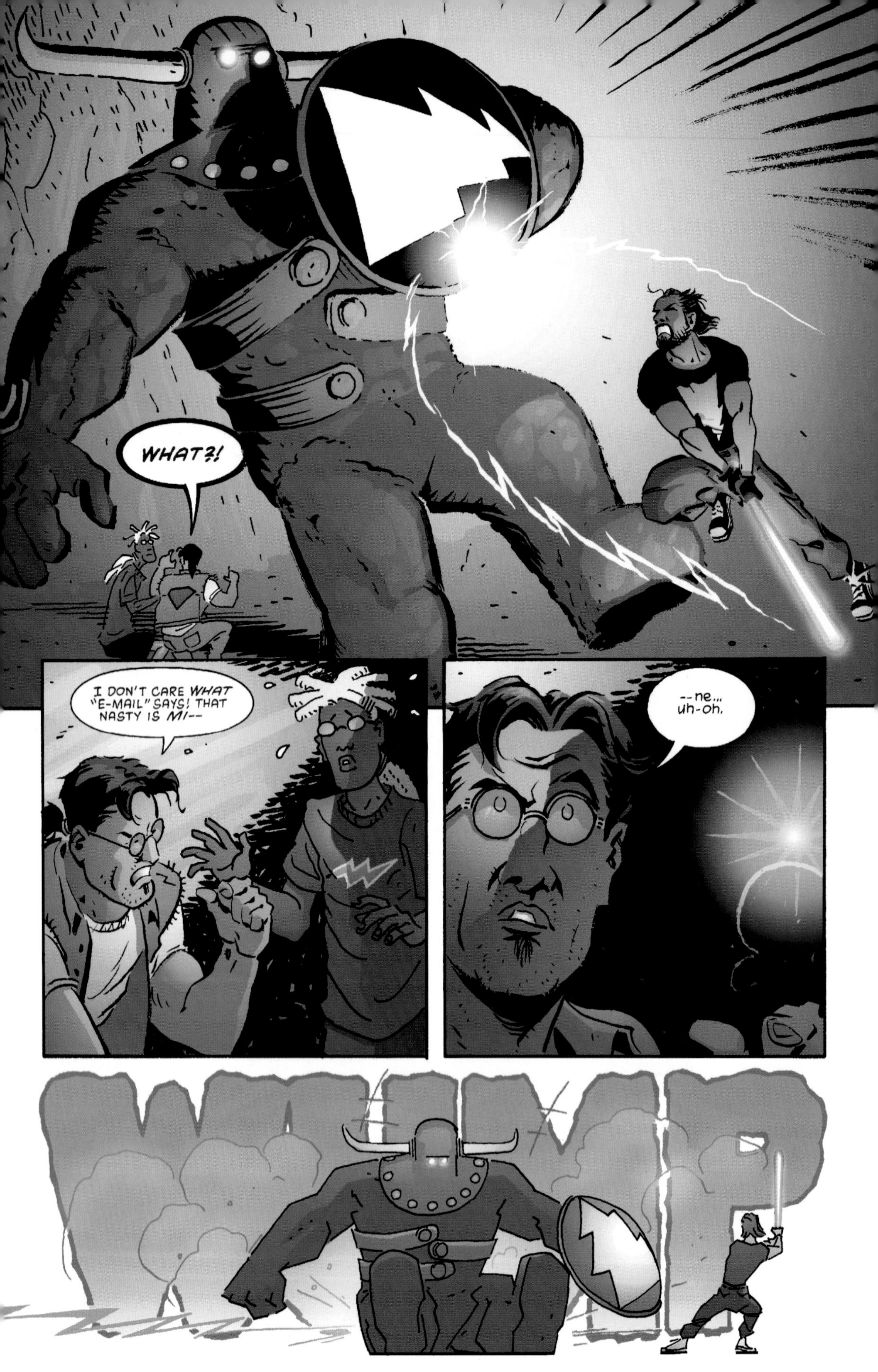
WHAT?!
I DON'T CARE WHAT "E-MAIL" SAYS! THAT NASTY IS MI--
--ne... uh-oh.

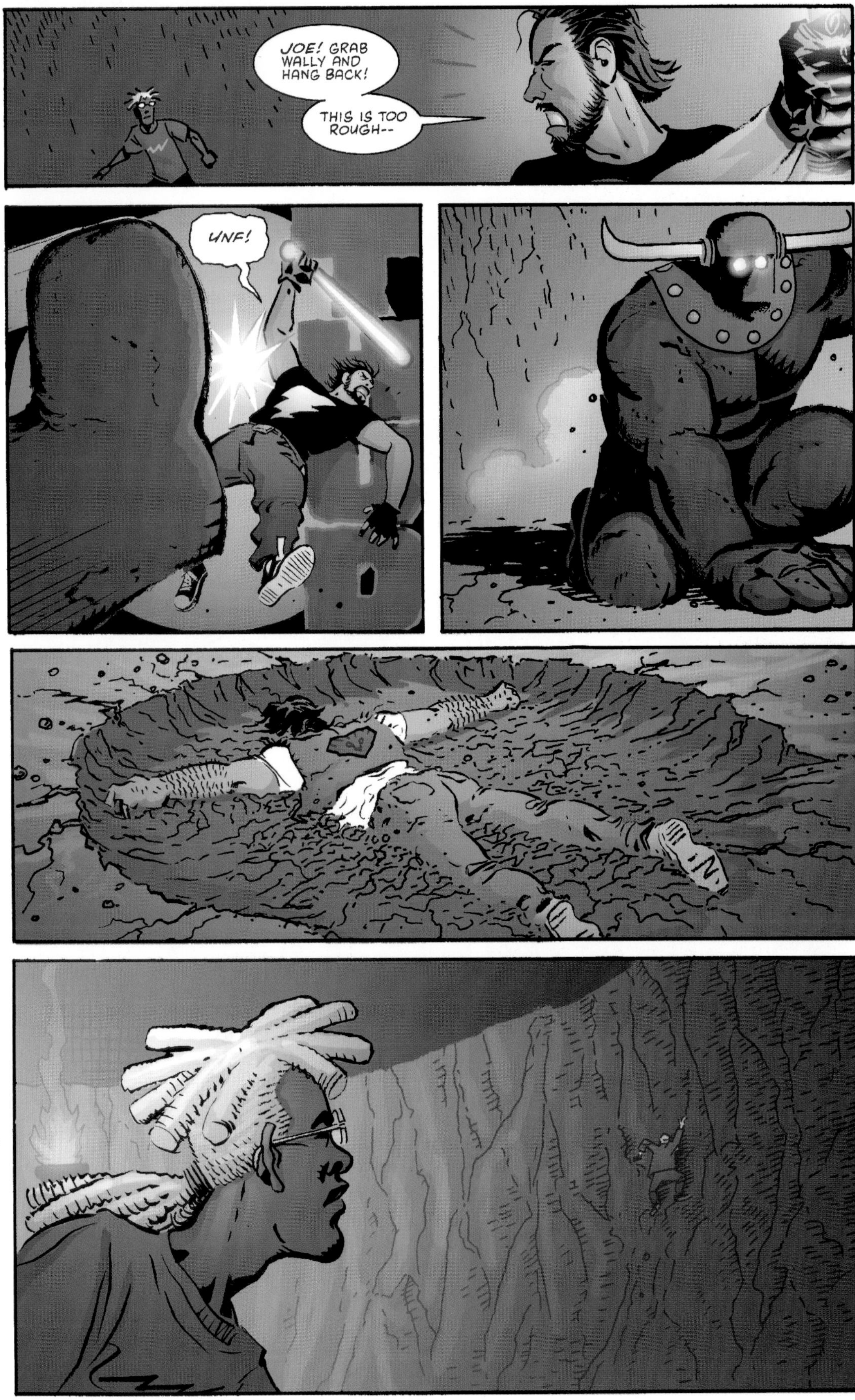
JOE! GRAB WALLY AND HANG BACK!
THIS IS TOO ROUGH--
UNF!

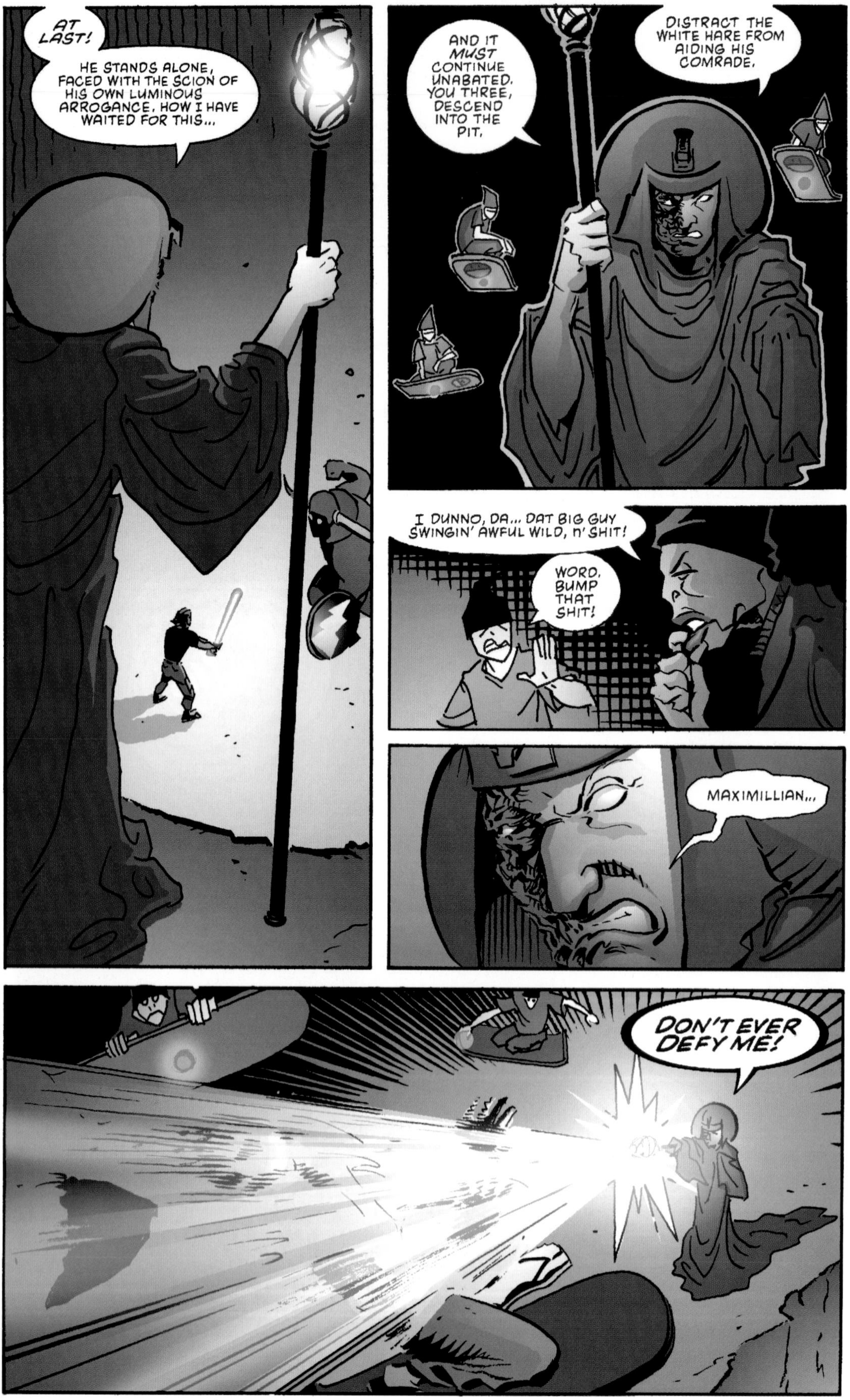
AT LAST!
HE STANDS ALONE, FACED WITH THE SCION OF HIS OWN LUMINOUS ARROGANCE. HOW I HAVE WAITED FOR THIS...
AND IT MUST CONTINUE UNABATED. YOU THREE, DESCEND INTO THE PIT.
DISTRACT THE WHITE HARE FROM AIDING HIS COMRADE.
I DUNNO, DA... DAT BIG GUY SWINGIN' AWFUL WILD, N' SHIT!
WORD. BUMP THAT SHIT!
MAXIMILLIAN...
DON'T EVER DEFY ME!

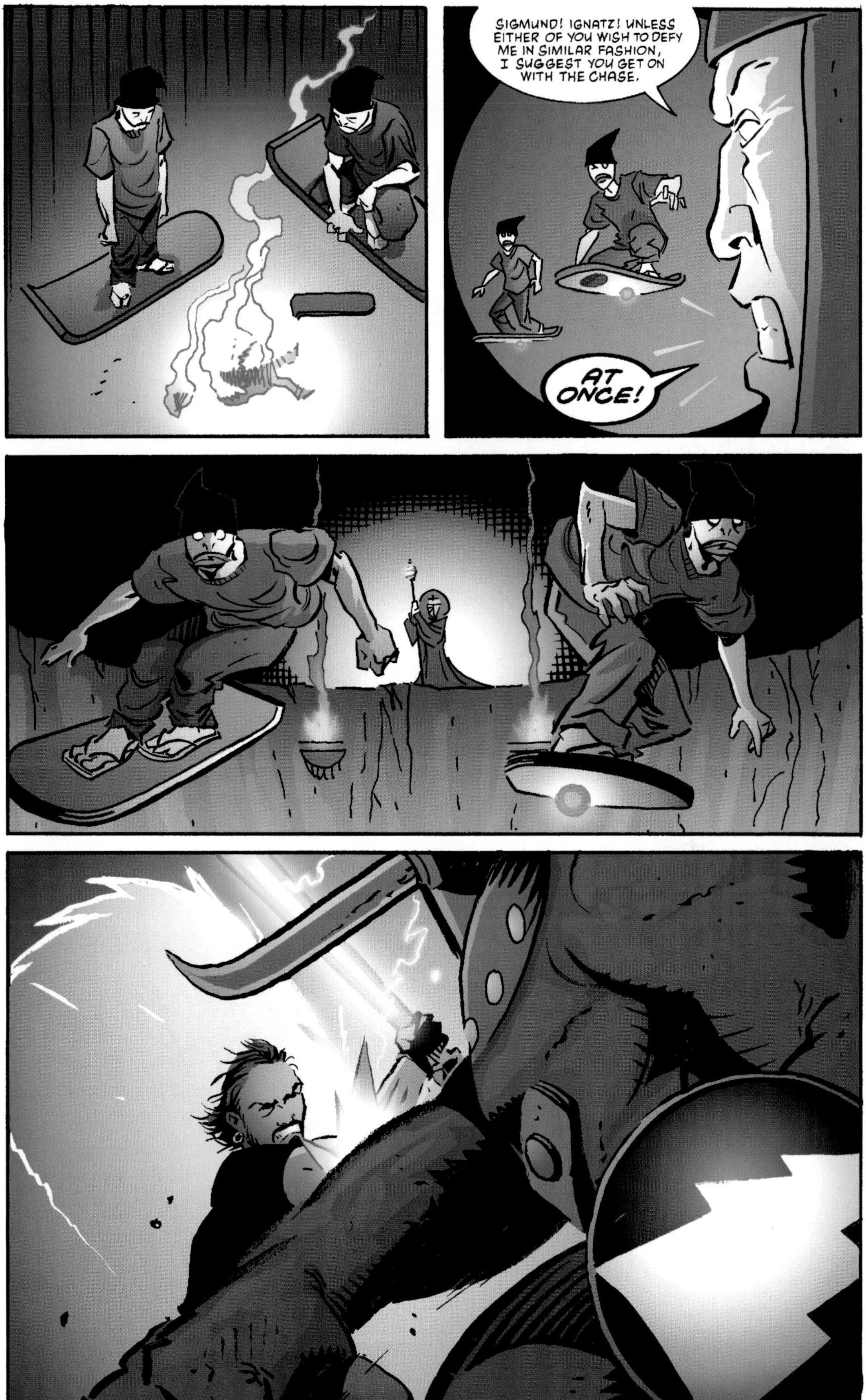
SIGMUND! IGNATZ! UNLESS EITHER OF YOU WISH TO DEFY ME IN SIMILAR FASHION, I SUGGEST YOU GET ON WITH THE CHASE.
AT ONCE!

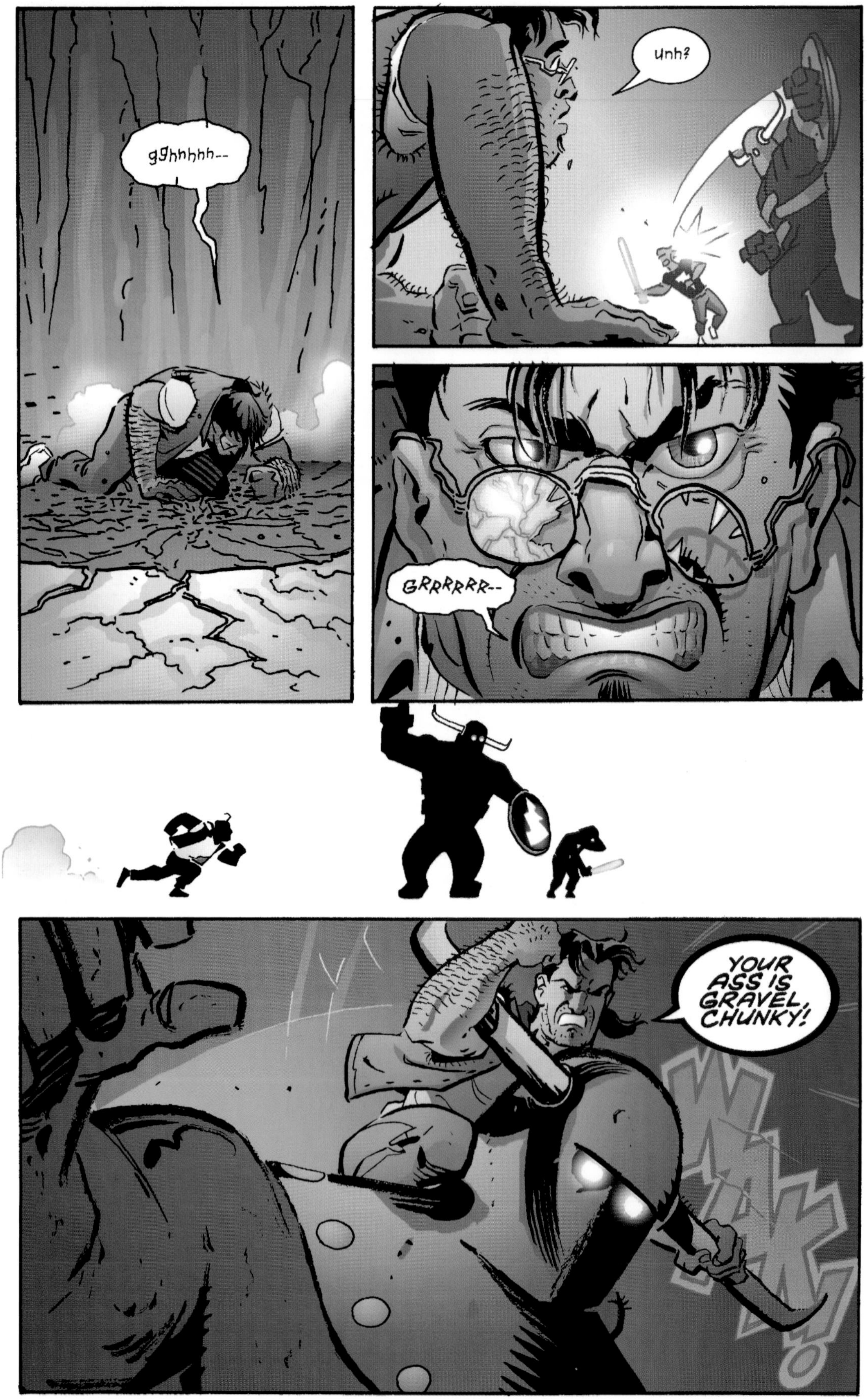
gghhhhh--
unh?
GRRRRRR--
YOUR ASS IS GRAVEL, CHUNKY!

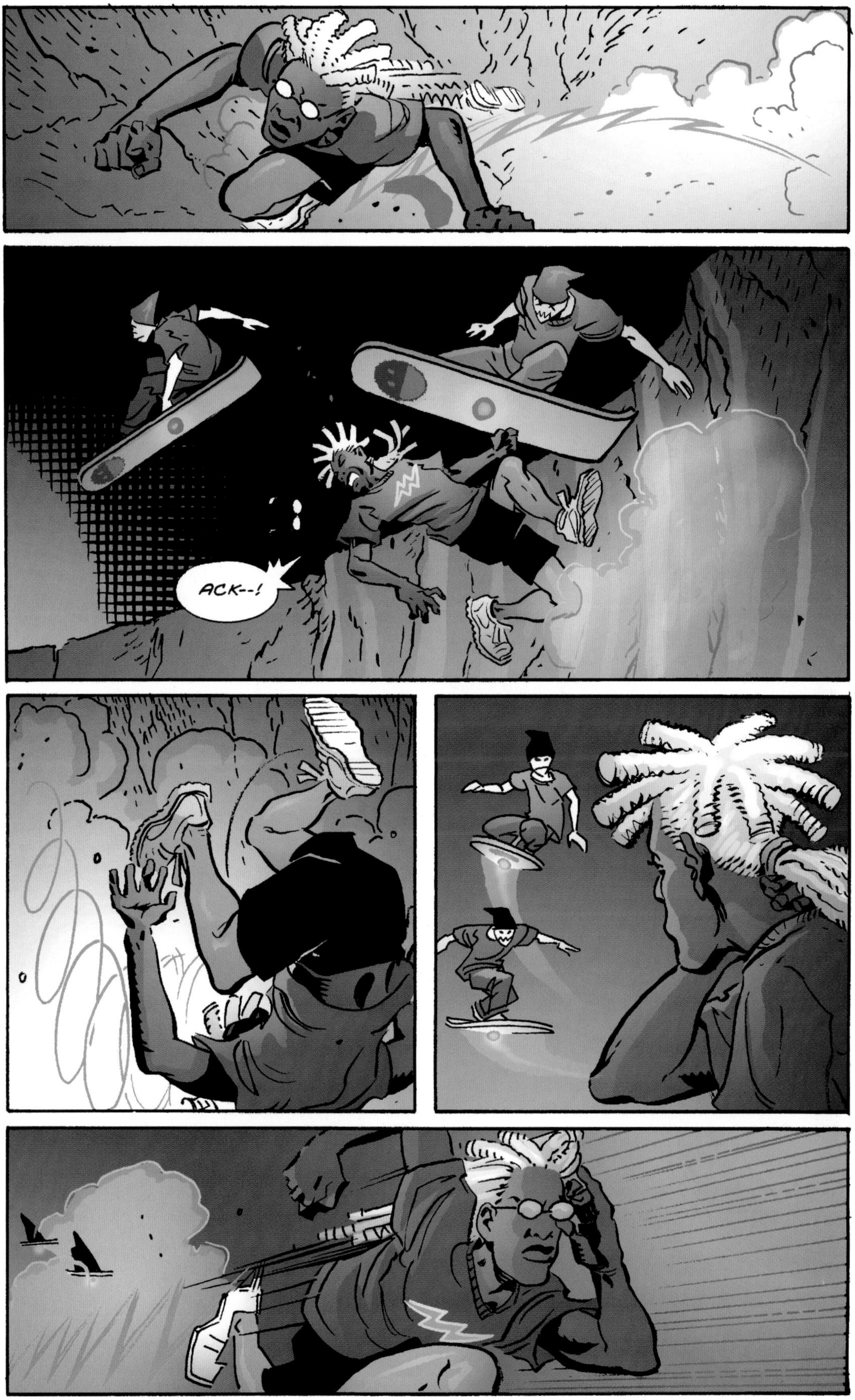
ACK--!

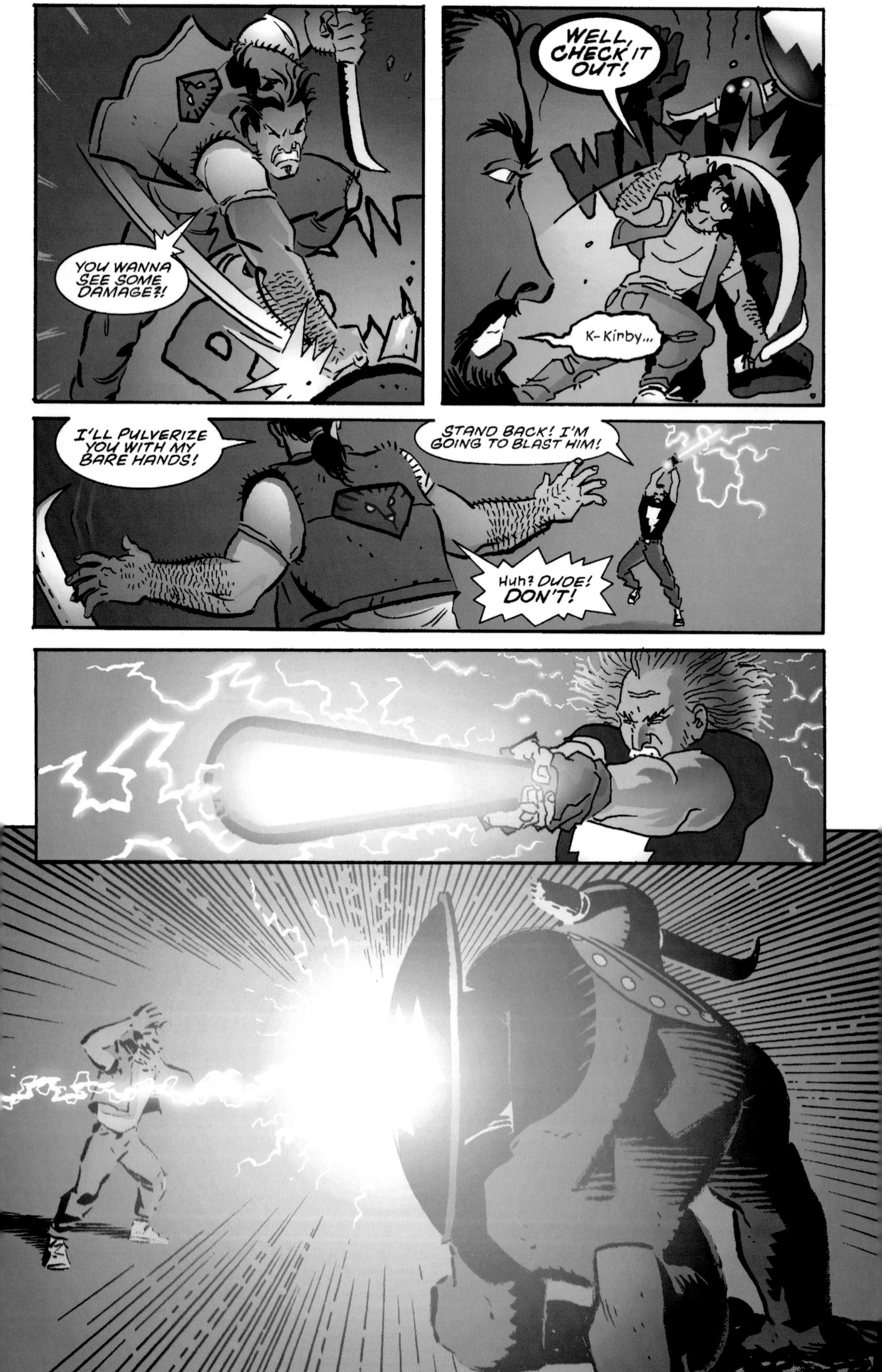
YOU WANNA SEE SOME DAMAGE?!
WELL, CHECK IT OUT!
K-Kirby...
I'LL PULVERIZE YOU WITH MY BARE HANDS!
STAND BACK! I'M GOING TO BLAST HIM!
Huh? DUDE! DON'T!

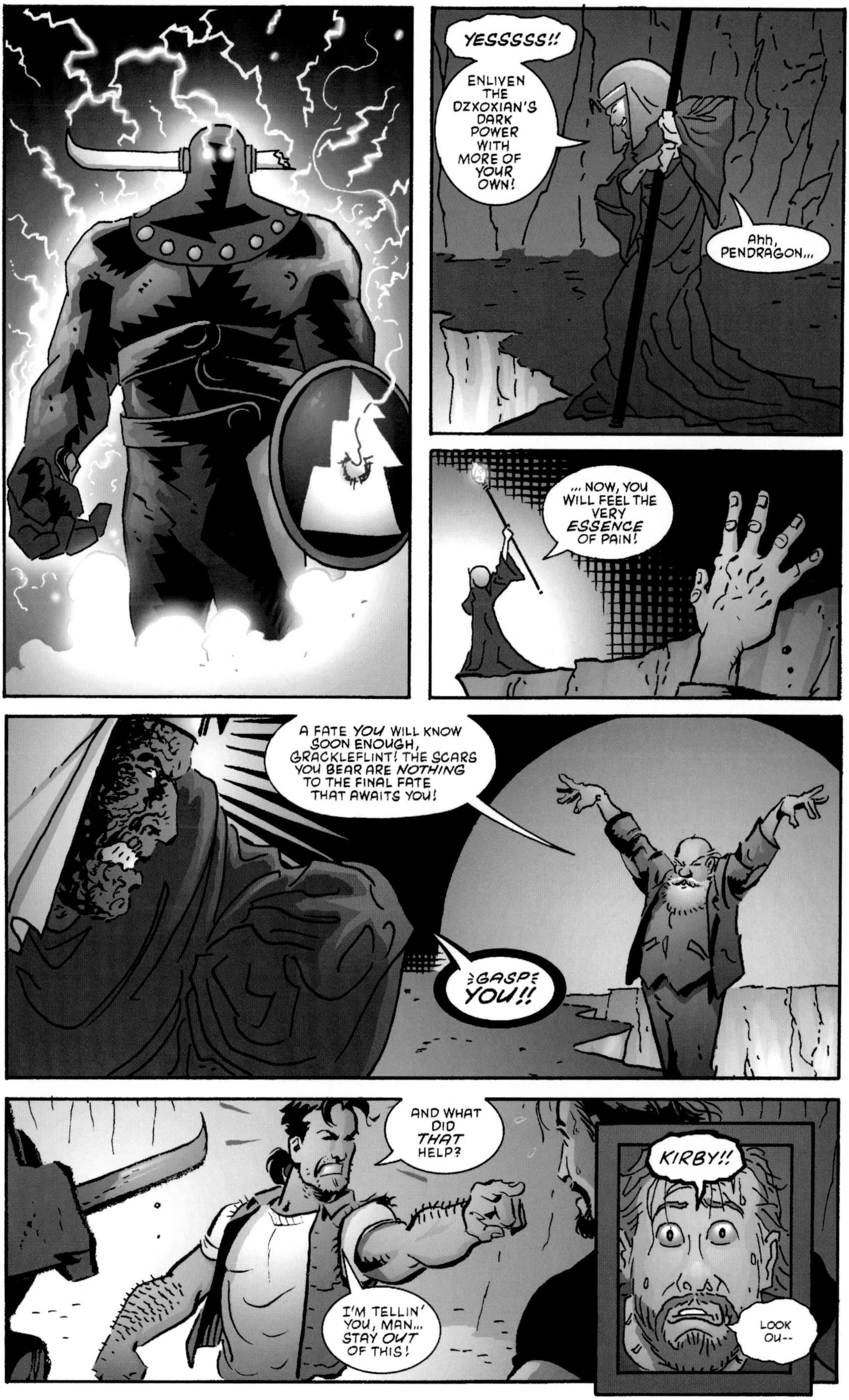
YESSSSS!!
ENLIVEN THE DZXOXIAN'S DARK POWER WITH MORE OF YOUR OWN!
Ahh, PENDRAGON...
... NOW, YOU WILL FEEL THE VERY ESSENCE OF PAIN!
A FATE YOU WILL KNOW SOON ENOUGH, GRACKLEFLINT! THE SCARS YOU BEAR ARE NOTHING TO THE FINAL FATE THAT AWAITS YOU!
GASP YOU!!
AND WHAT DID THAT HELP?
I'M TELLIN' YOU, MAN... STAY OUT OF THIS!
KIRBY!!
LOOK OU--

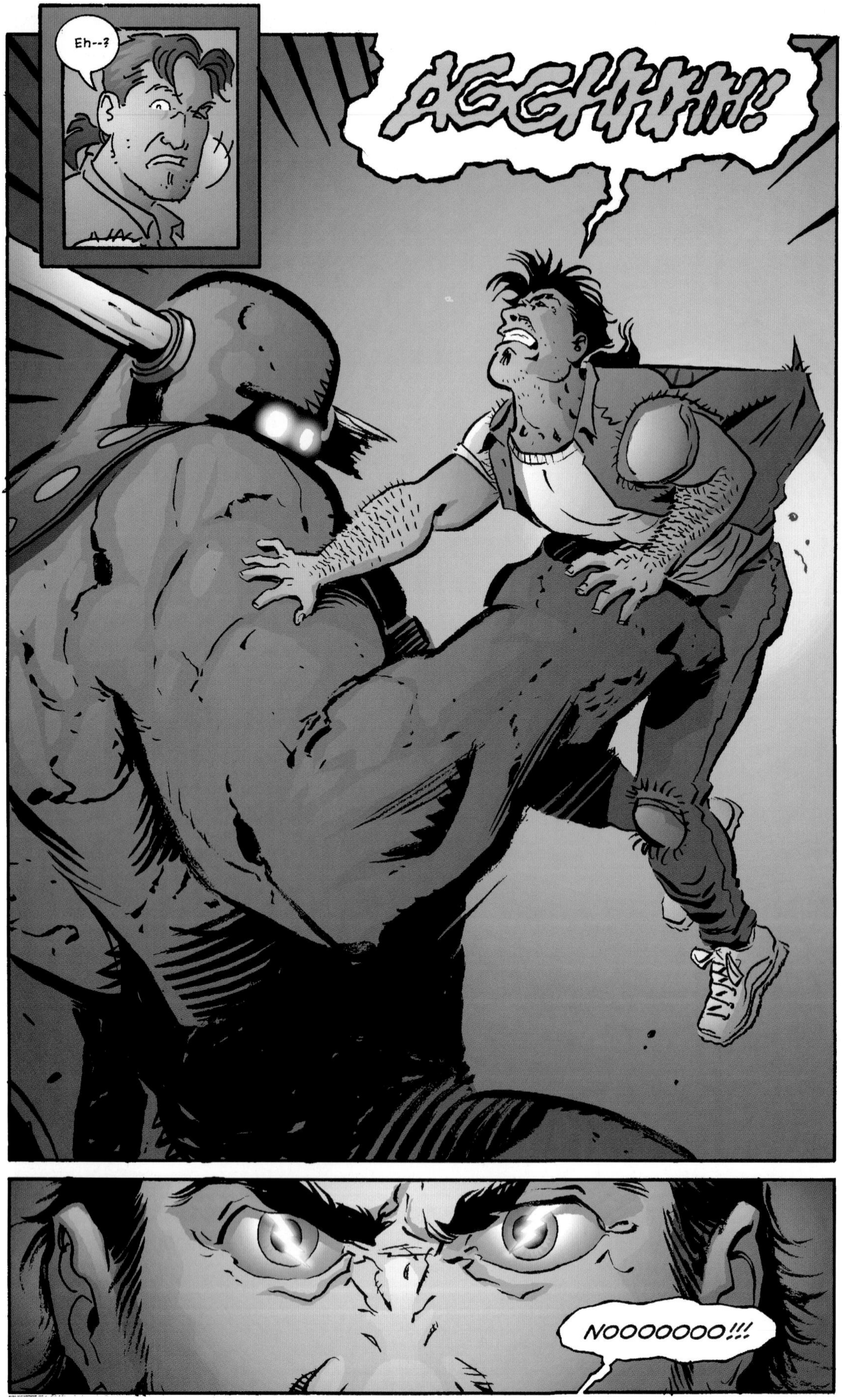
Eh--?
AGGHHHH!
NOOOOOOO!!!

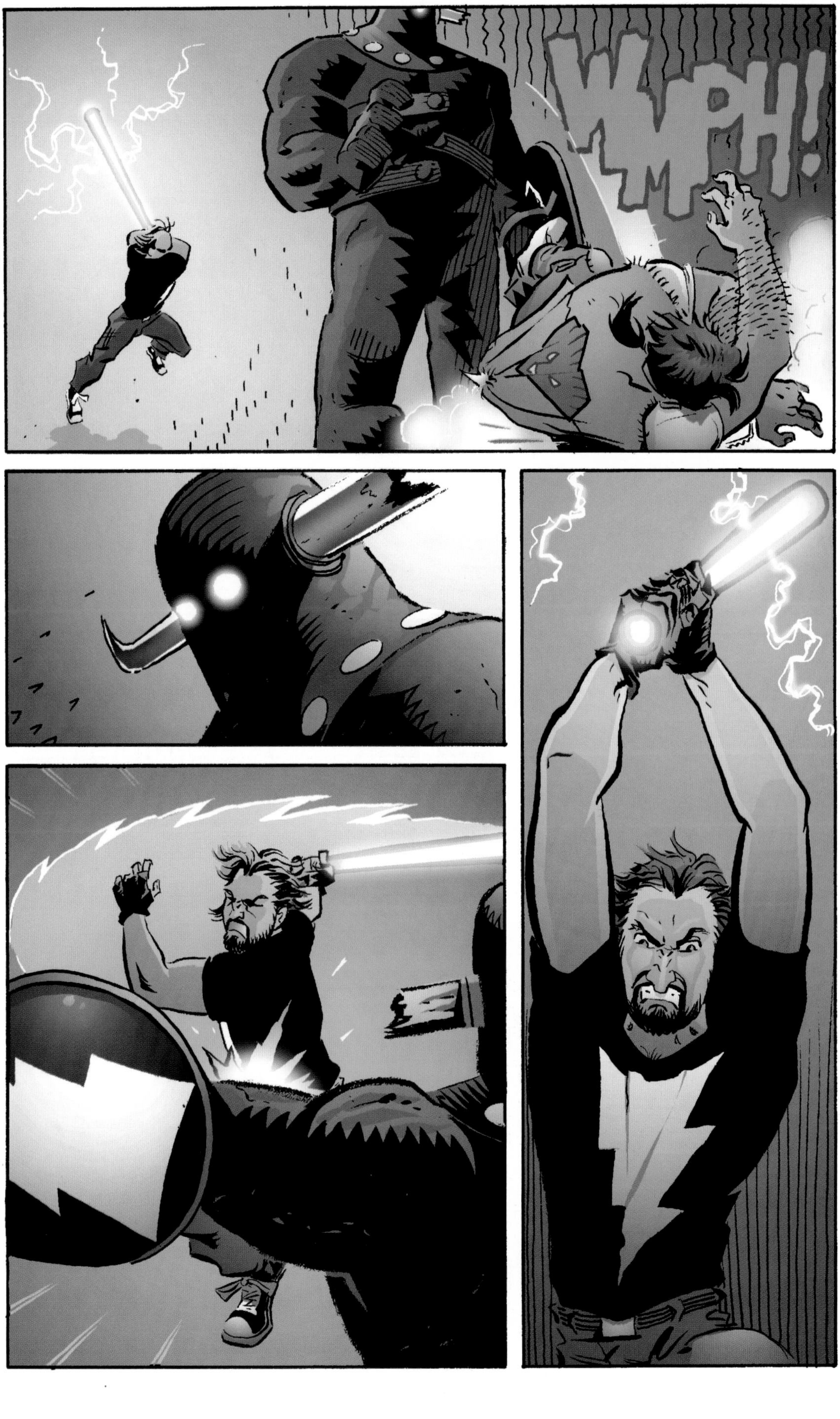
WMPH!

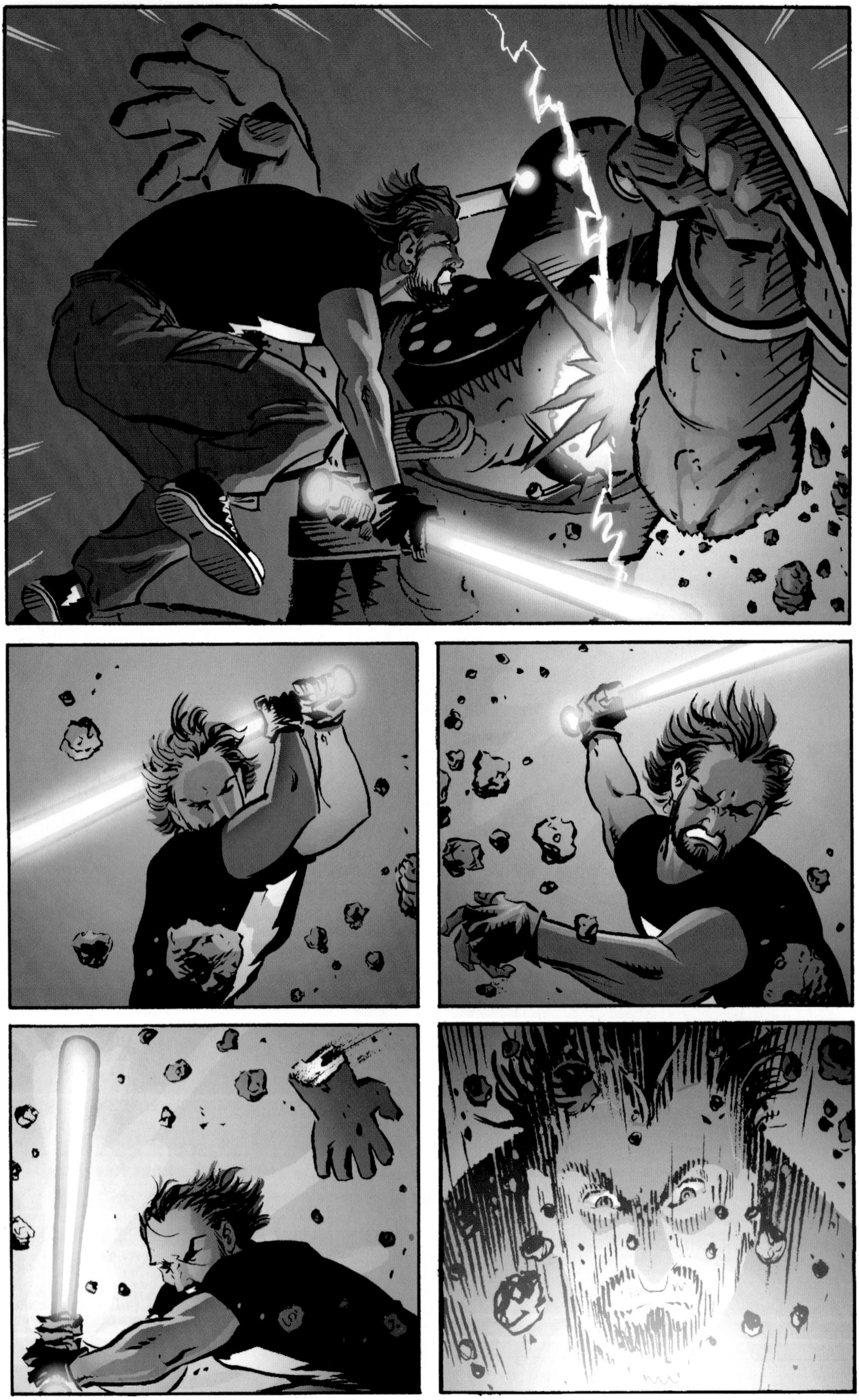

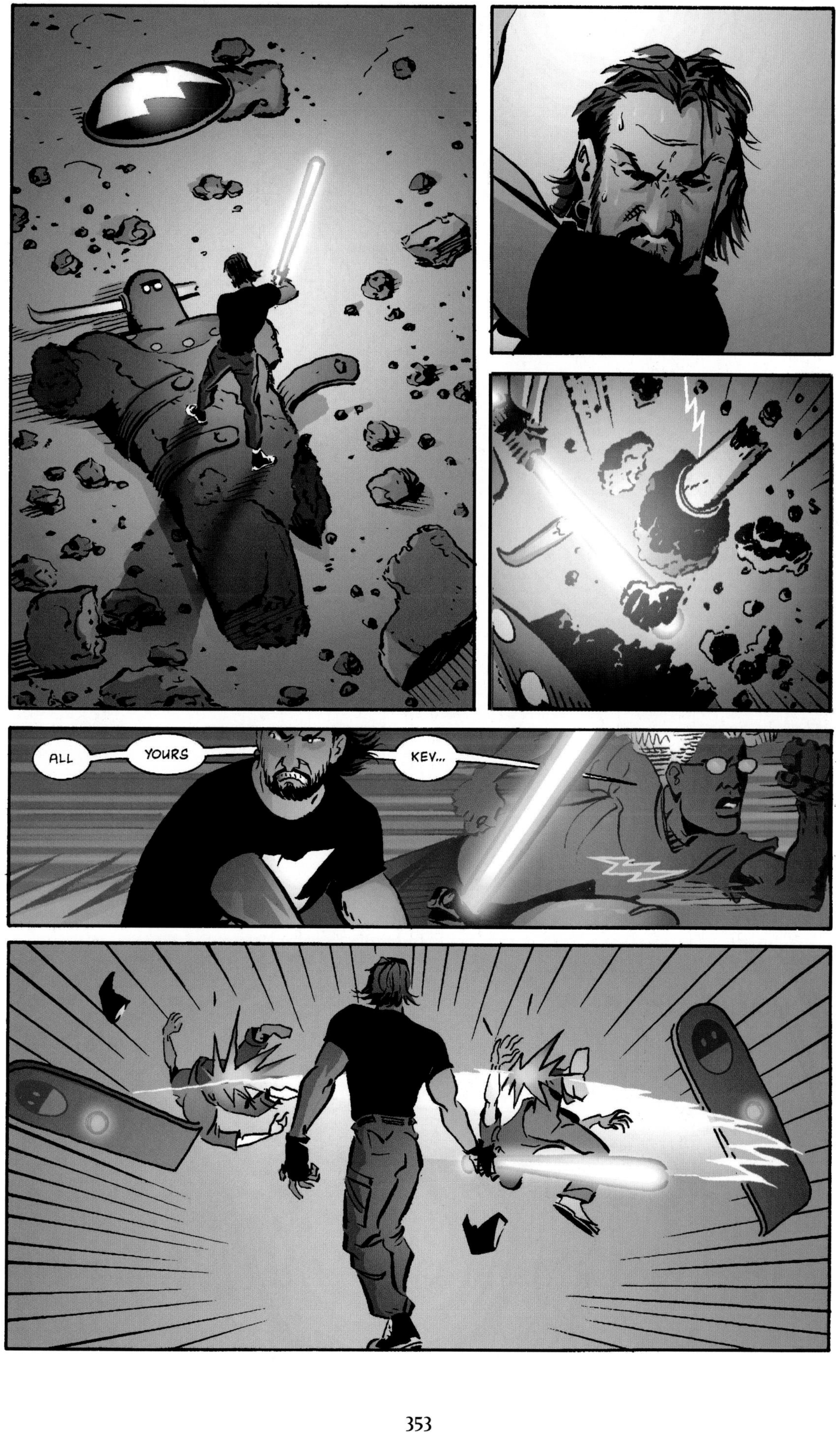
ALL
YOURS
KEV...

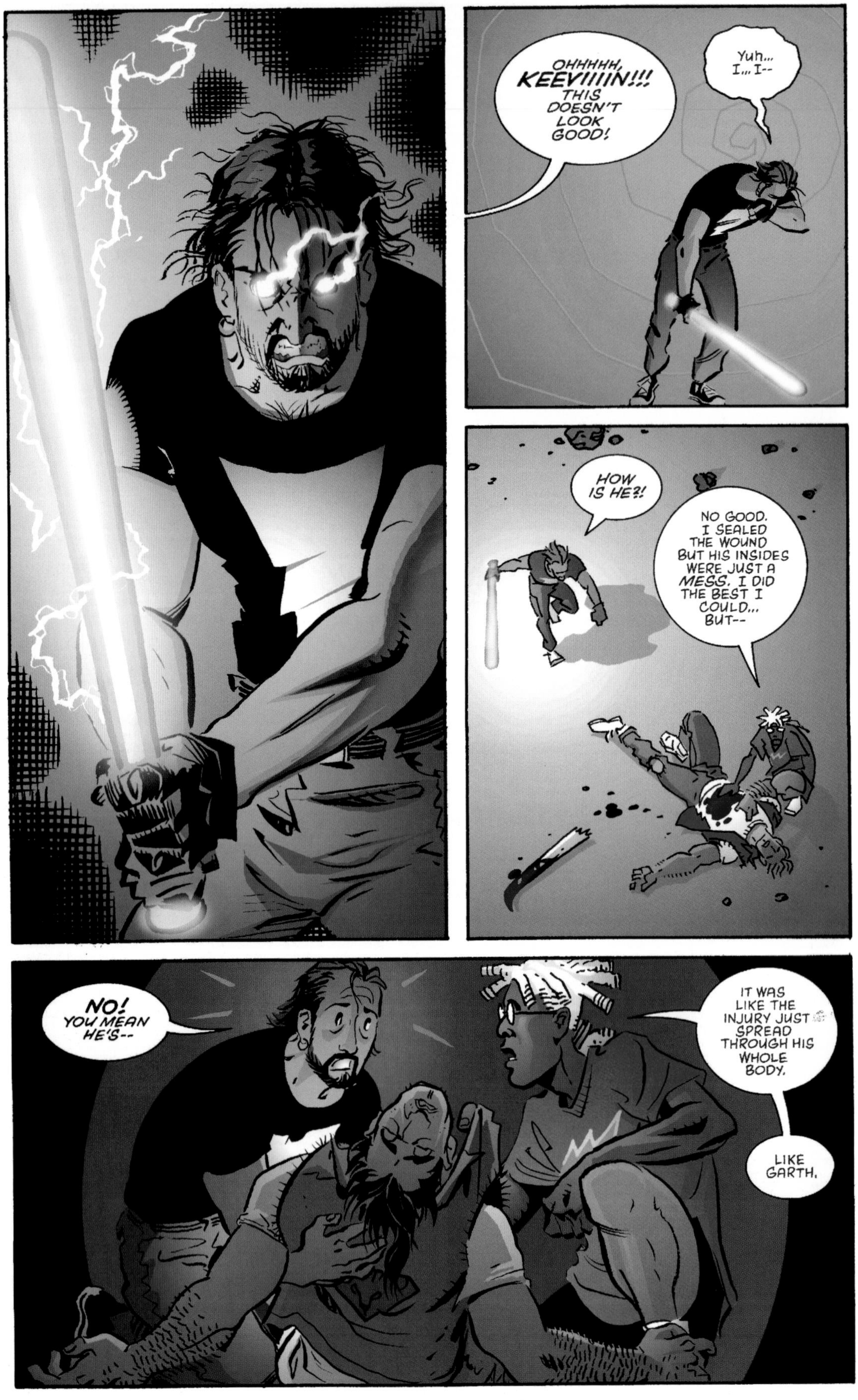
OHHHHH, KEEVIIIIN!!! THIS DOESN'T LOOK GOOD!
Yuh... I... I--
HOW IS HE?!
NO GOOD. I SEALED THE WOUND BUT HIS INSIDES WERE JUST A MESS. I DID THE BEST I COULD... BUT--
NO! YOU MEAN HE'S--
IT WAS LIKE THE INJURY JUST SPREAD THROUGH HIS WHOLE BODY.
LIKE GARTH.

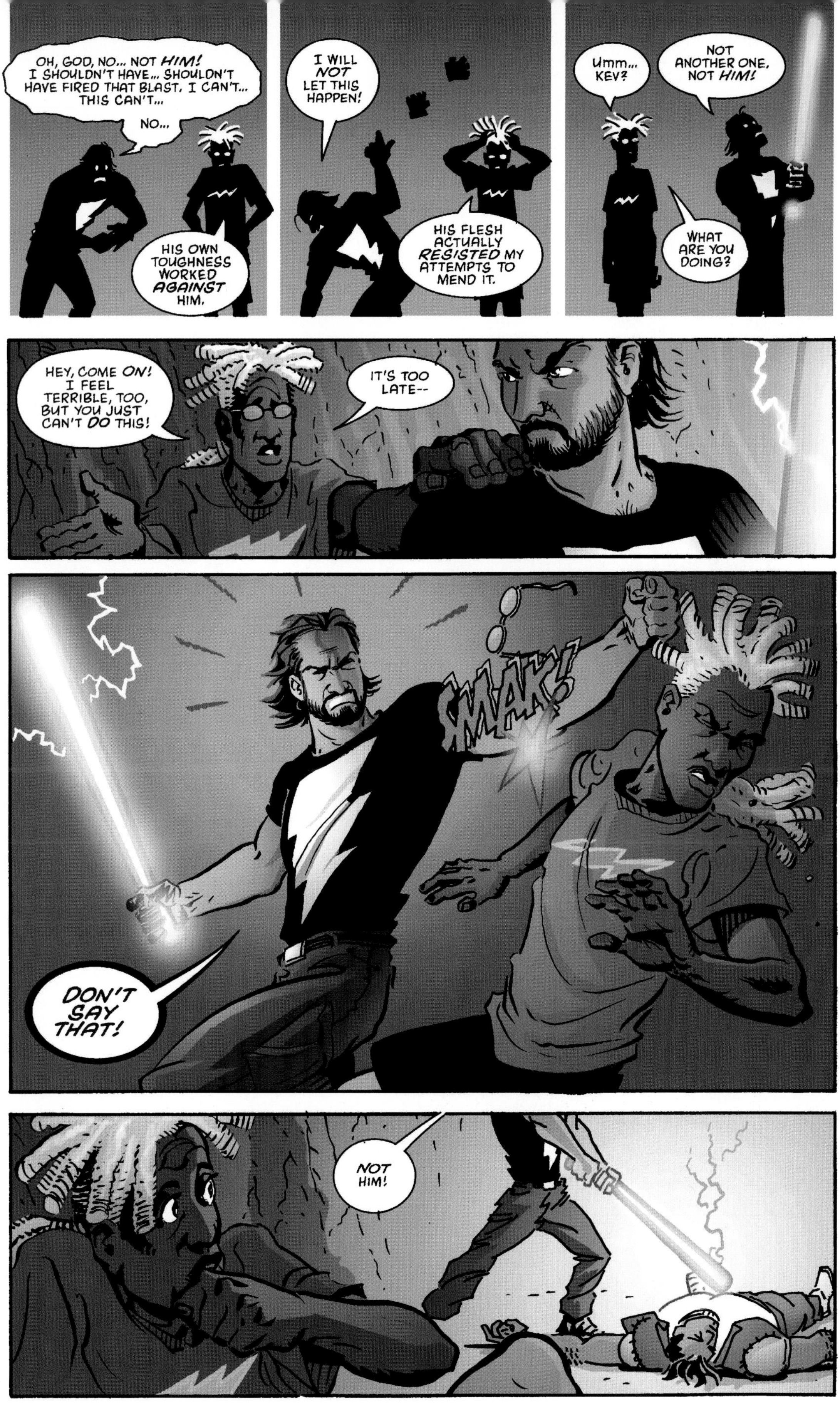
OH, GOD, NO... NOT HIM! I SHOULDN'T HAVE... SHOULDN'T HAVE FIRED THAT BLAST. I CAN'T... THIS CAN'T...
NO...
HIS OWN TOUGHNESS WORKED AGAINST HIM.
I WILL NOT LET THIS HAPPEN!
HIS FLESH ACTUALLY RESISTED MY ATTEMPTS TO MEND IT.
UMM... KEV?
NOT ANOTHER ONE, NOT HIM!
WHAT ARE YOU DOING?
HEY, COME ON! I FEEL TERRIBLE, TOO, BUT YOU JUST CAN'T DO THIS!
IT'S TOO LATE--
SMAK!
DON'T SAY THAT!
NOT HIM!

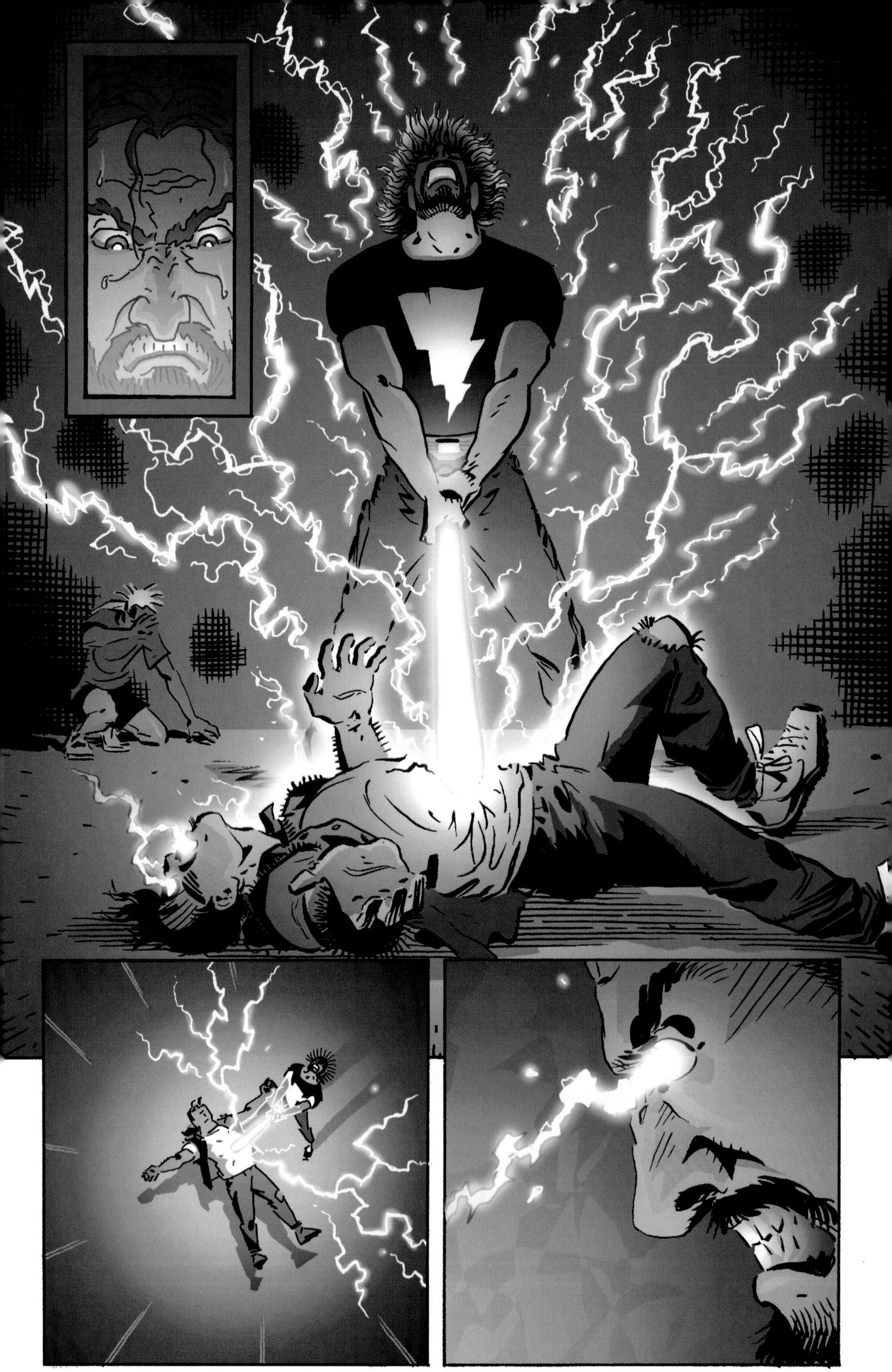

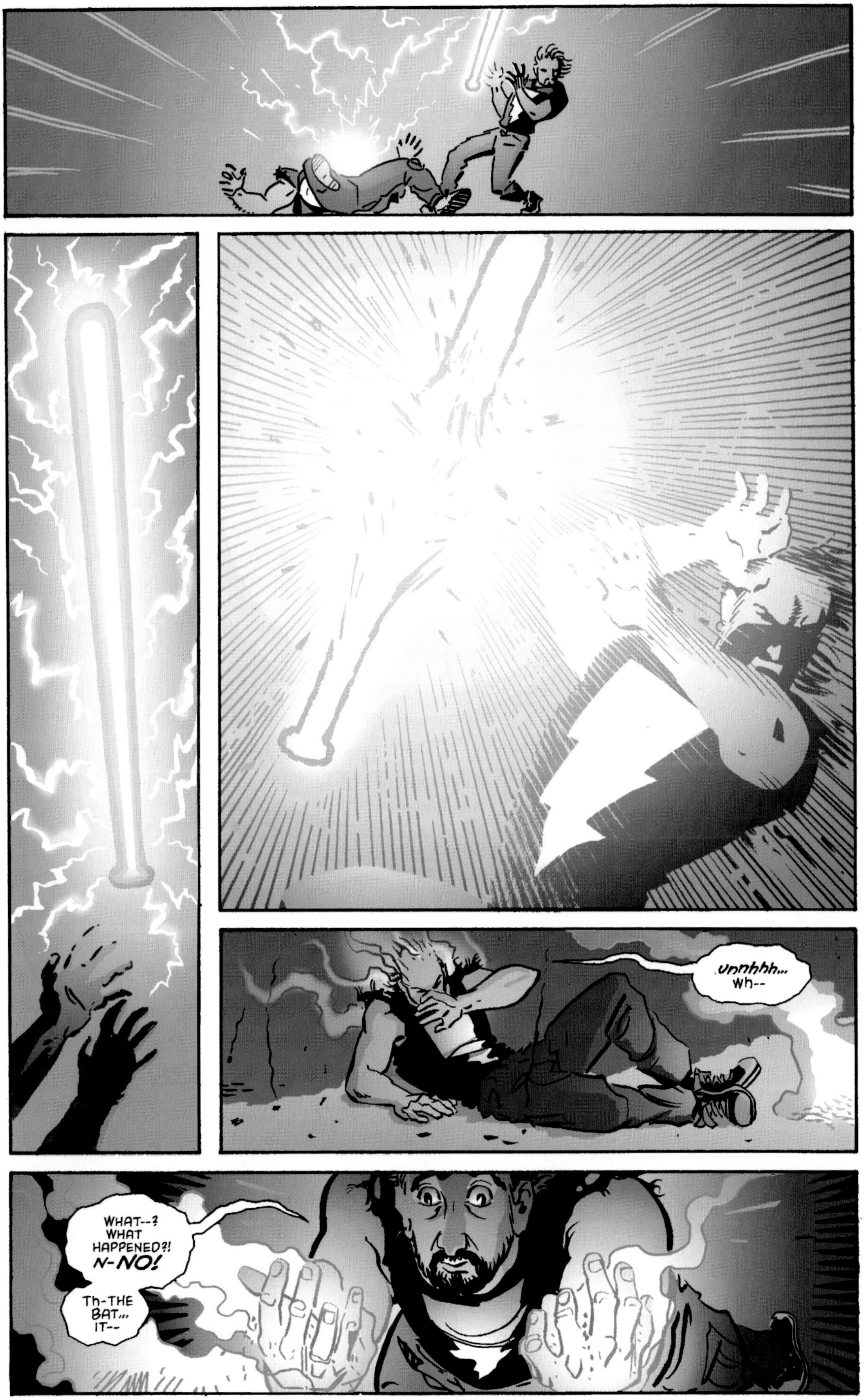
unnhhh... Wh--
WHAT--? WHAT HAPPENED?! N-NO!
Th-THE BAT... IT--

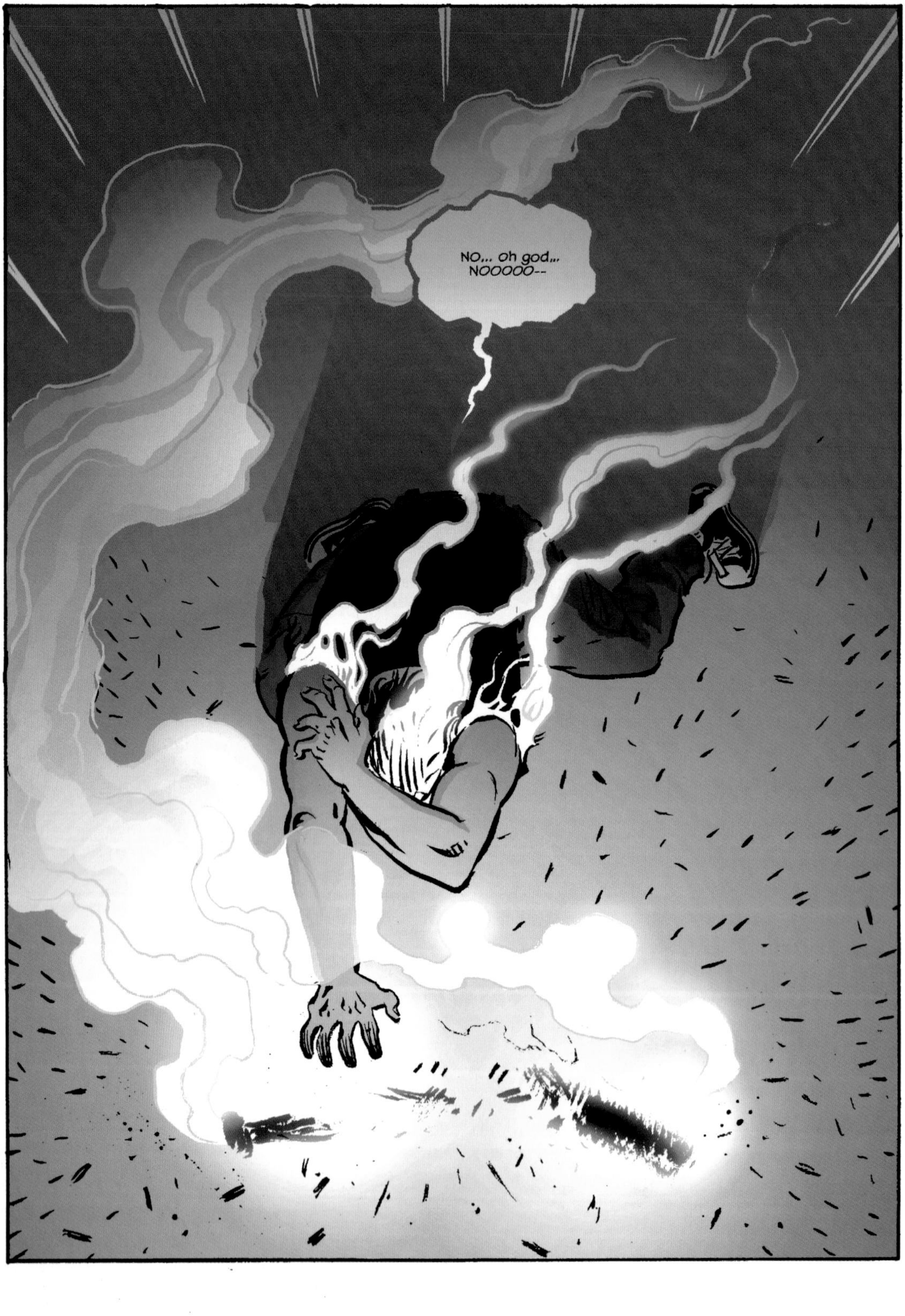
NO... oh god... NOOOOO--

THE HERO DEFINED

MAGE®

chapter 15

"All That May Become a Man"

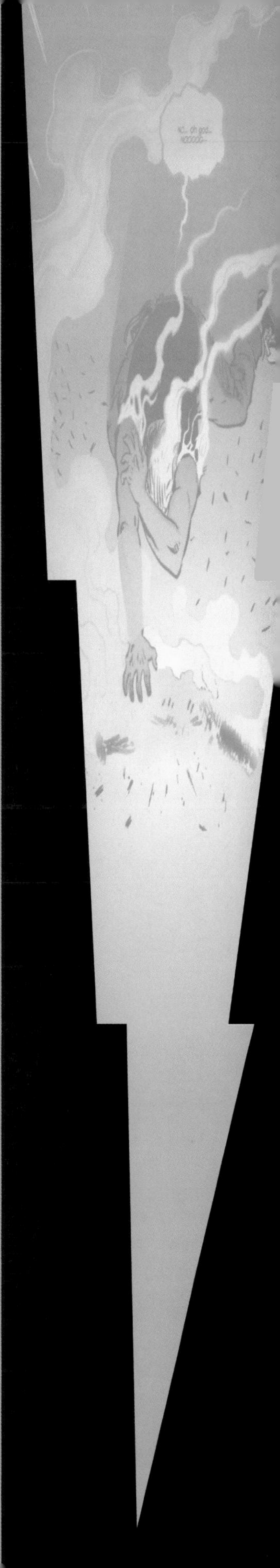

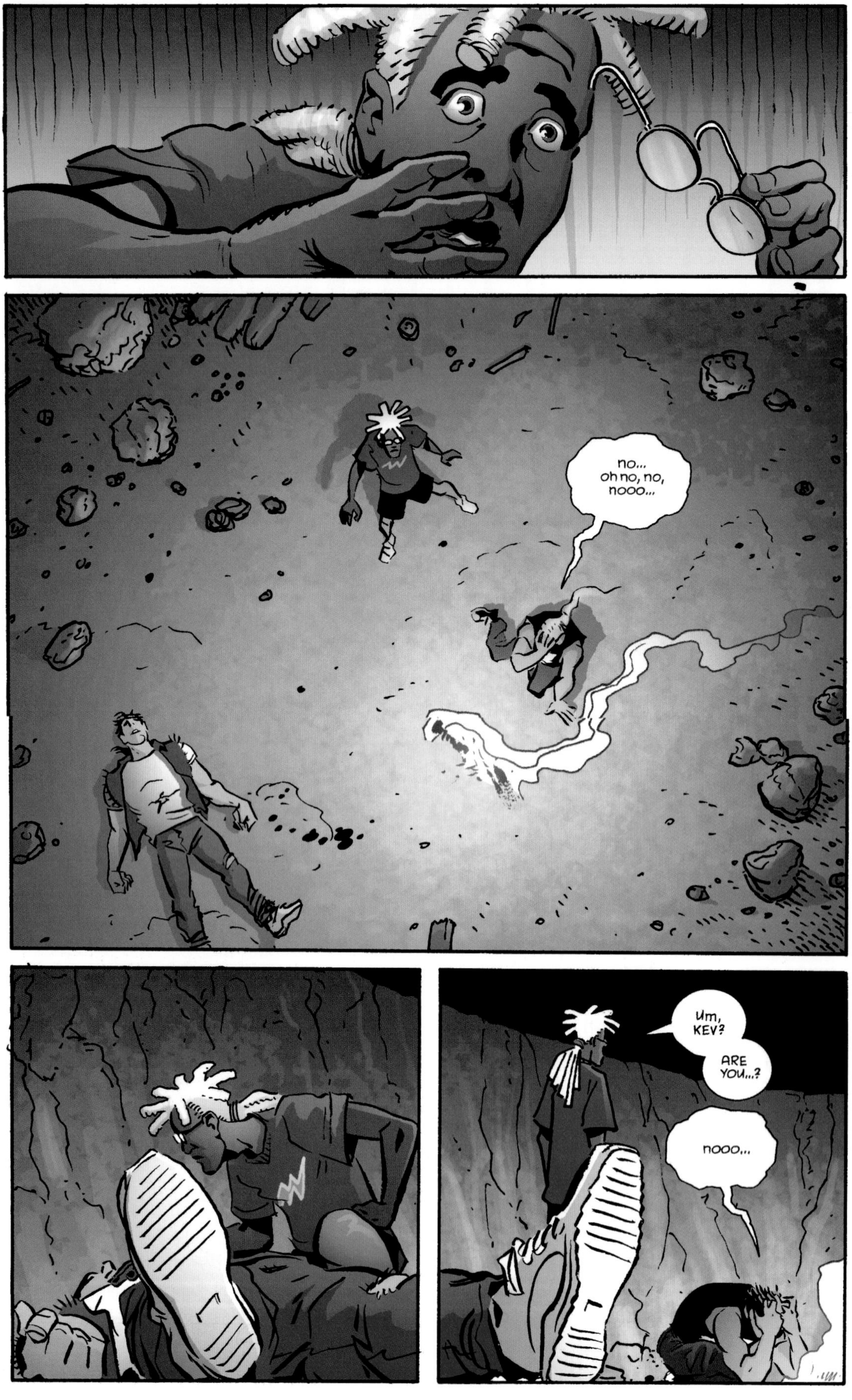
no... oh no, no, nooo...
Um, KEV?
ARE YOU...?
nooo...

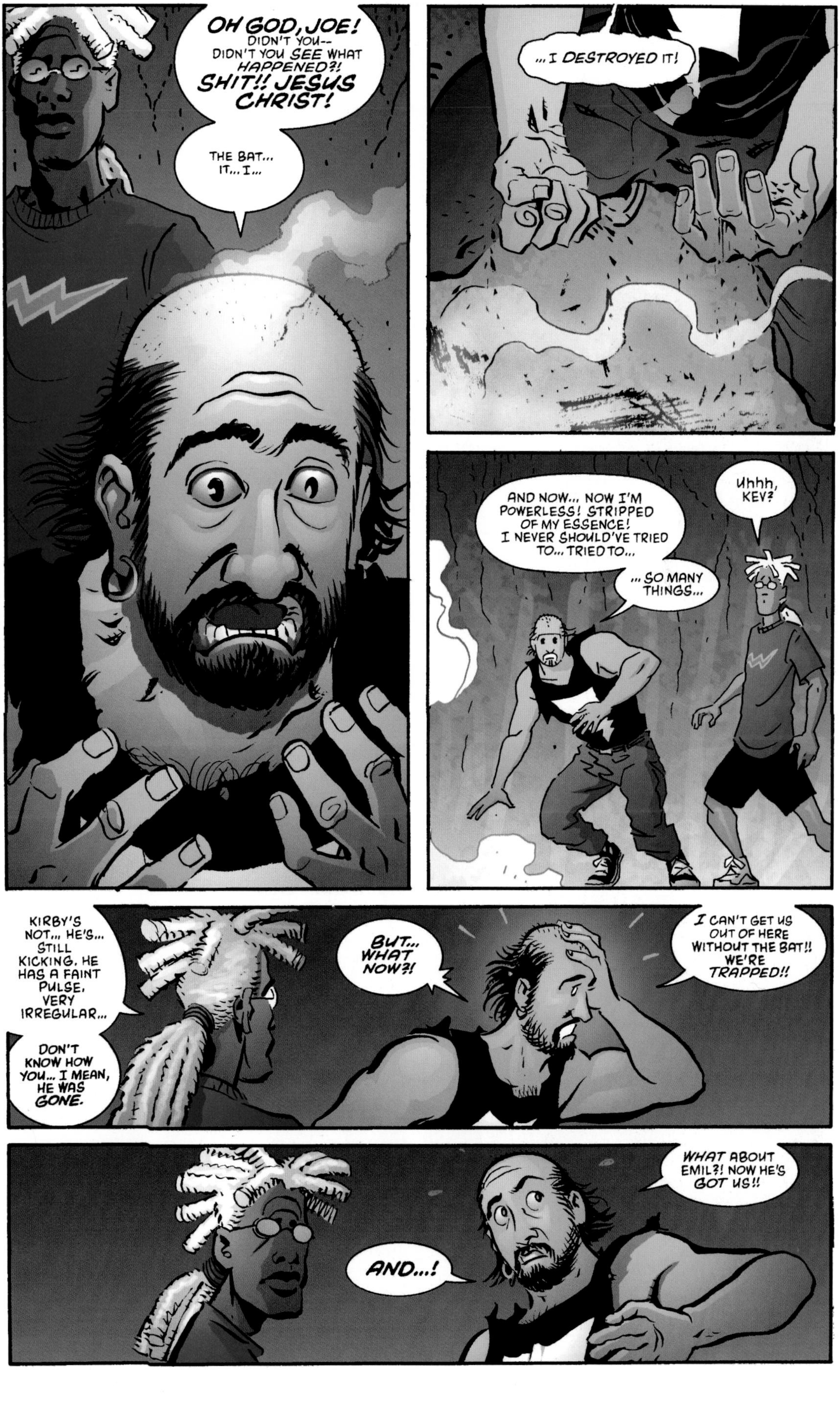
OH GOD, JOE! DIDN'T YOU-- DIDN'T YOU SEE WHAT HAPPENED?! SHIT!! JESUS CHRIST!
THE BAT... IT... I...
...I DESTROYED IT!
AND NOW... NOW I'M POWERLESS! STRIPPED OF MY ESSENCE! I NEVER SHOULD'VE TRIED TO... TRIED TO...
...SO MANY THINGS...
Uhhh, KEV?
KIRBY'S NOT... HE'S... STILL KICKING. HE HAS A FAINT PULSE. VERY IRREGULAR...
DON'T KNOW HOW YOU... I MEAN, HE WAS GONE.
BUT... WHAT NOW?!
I CAN'T GET US OUT OF HERE WITHOUT THE BAT!! WE'RE TRAPPED!!
WHAT ABOUT EMIL?! NOW HE'S GOT US!!
AND...!

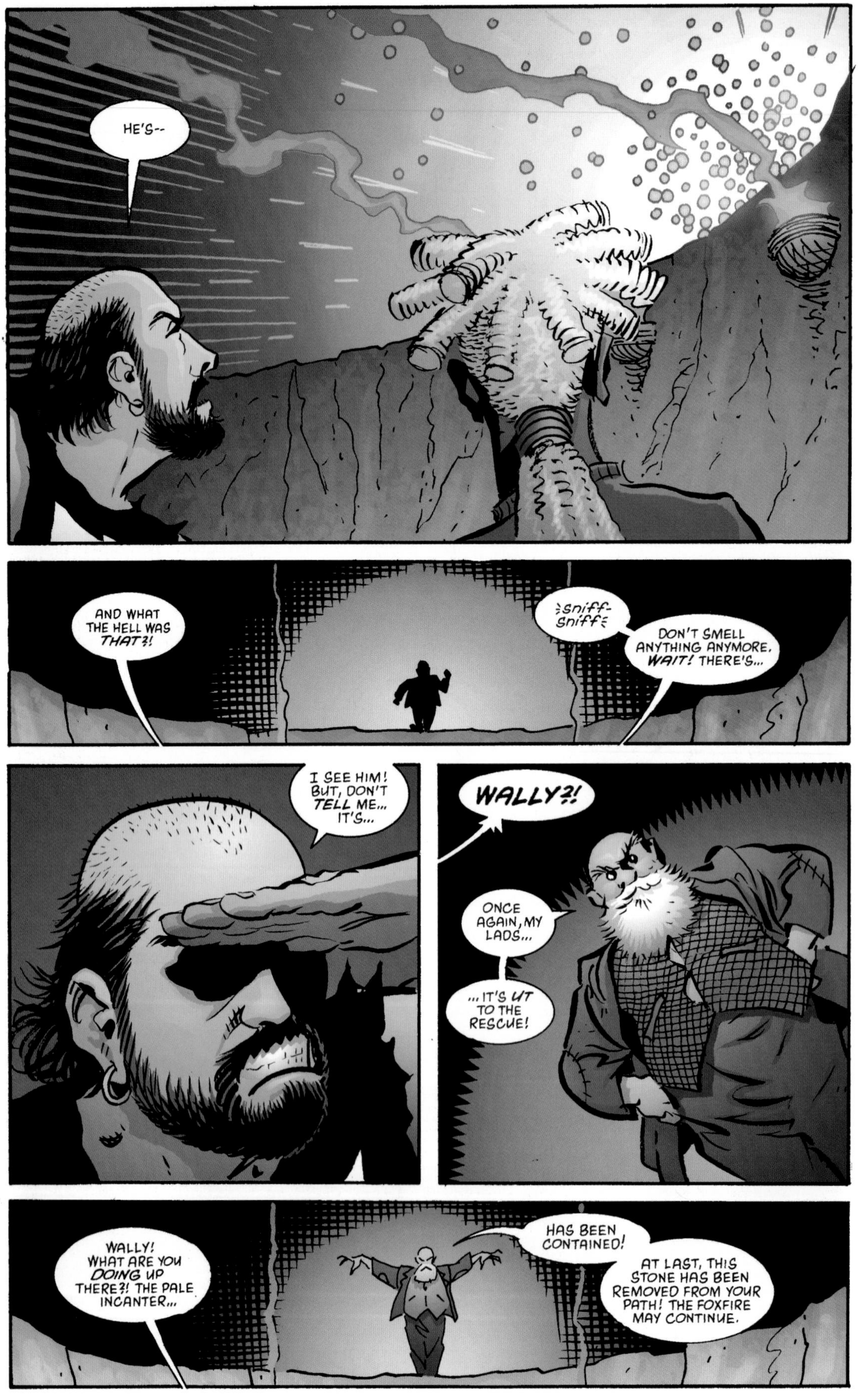
HE'S--
AND WHAT THE HELL WAS THAT?!
SNIFF-SNIFF
DON'T SMELL ANYTHING ANYMORE. WAIT! THERE'S...
I SEE HIM! BUT, DON'T TELL ME... IT'S...
WALLY?!
ONCE AGAIN, MY LADS...
...IT'S UT TO THE RESCUE!
WALLY! WHAT ARE YOU DOING UP THERE?! THE PALE INCANTER...
HAS BEEN CONTAINED!
AT LAST, THIS STONE HAS BEEN REMOVED FROM YOUR PATH! THE FOXFIRE MAY CONTINUE.

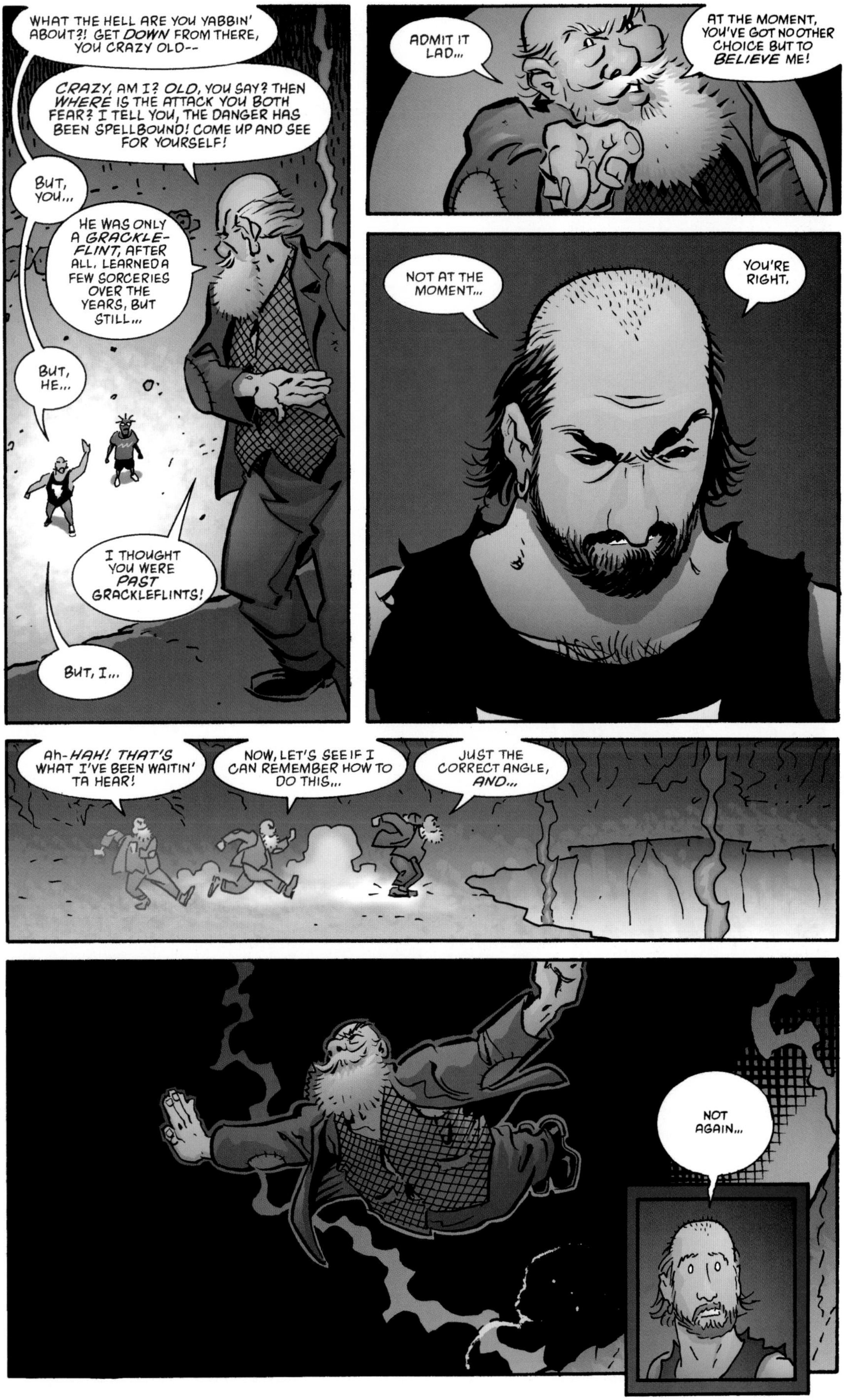
WHAT THE HELL ARE YOU YABBIN' ABOUT?! GET DOWN FROM THERE, YOU CRAZY OLD--
CRAZY, AM I? OLD, YOU SAY? THEN WHERE IS THE ATTACK YOU BOTH FEAR? I TELL YOU, THE DANGER HAS BEEN SPELLBOUND! COME UP AND SEE FOR YOURSELF!
BUT, YOU...
HE WAS ONLY A GRACKLE-FLINT, AFTER ALL. LEARNED A FEW SORCERIES OVER THE YEARS, BUT STILL...
BUT, HE...
I THOUGHT YOU WERE PAST GRACKLEFLINTS!
BUT, I...
ADMIT IT LAD...
AT THE MOMENT, YOU'VE GOT NO OTHER CHOICE BUT TO BELIEVE ME!
NOT AT THE MOMENT...
YOU'RE RIGHT.
Ah-HAH! THAT'S WHAT I'VE BEEN WAITIN' TA HEAR!
NOW, LET'S SEE IF I CAN REMEMBER HOW TO DO THIS...
JUST THE CORRECT ANGLE, AND...
NOT AGAIN...

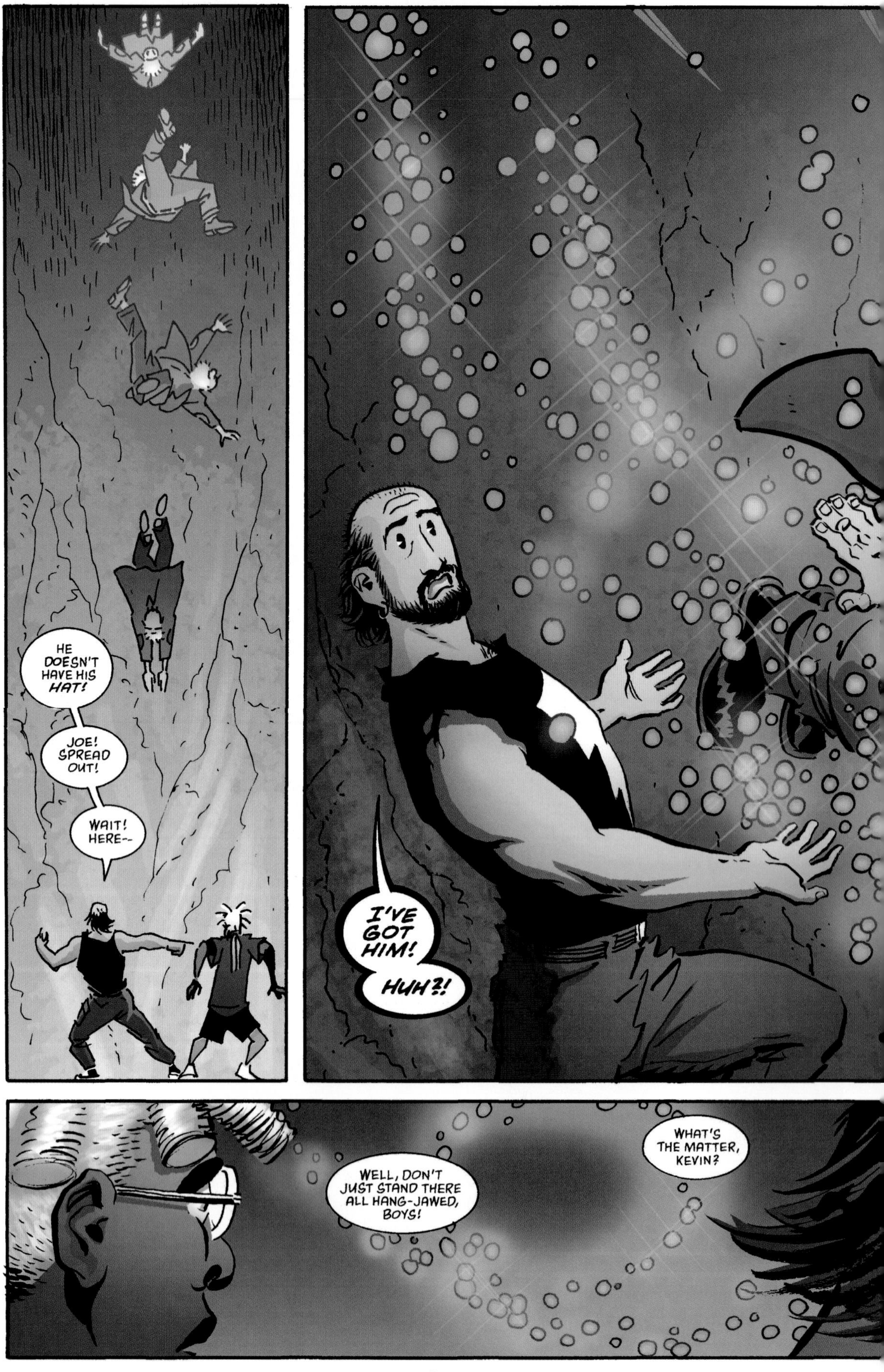
HE DOESN'T HAVE HIS HAT!
JOE! SPREAD OUT!
WAIT! HERE--
I'VE GOT HIM!
HUH?!
WELL, DON'T JUST STAND THERE ALL HANG-JAWED, BOYS!
WHAT'S THE MATTER, KEVIN?

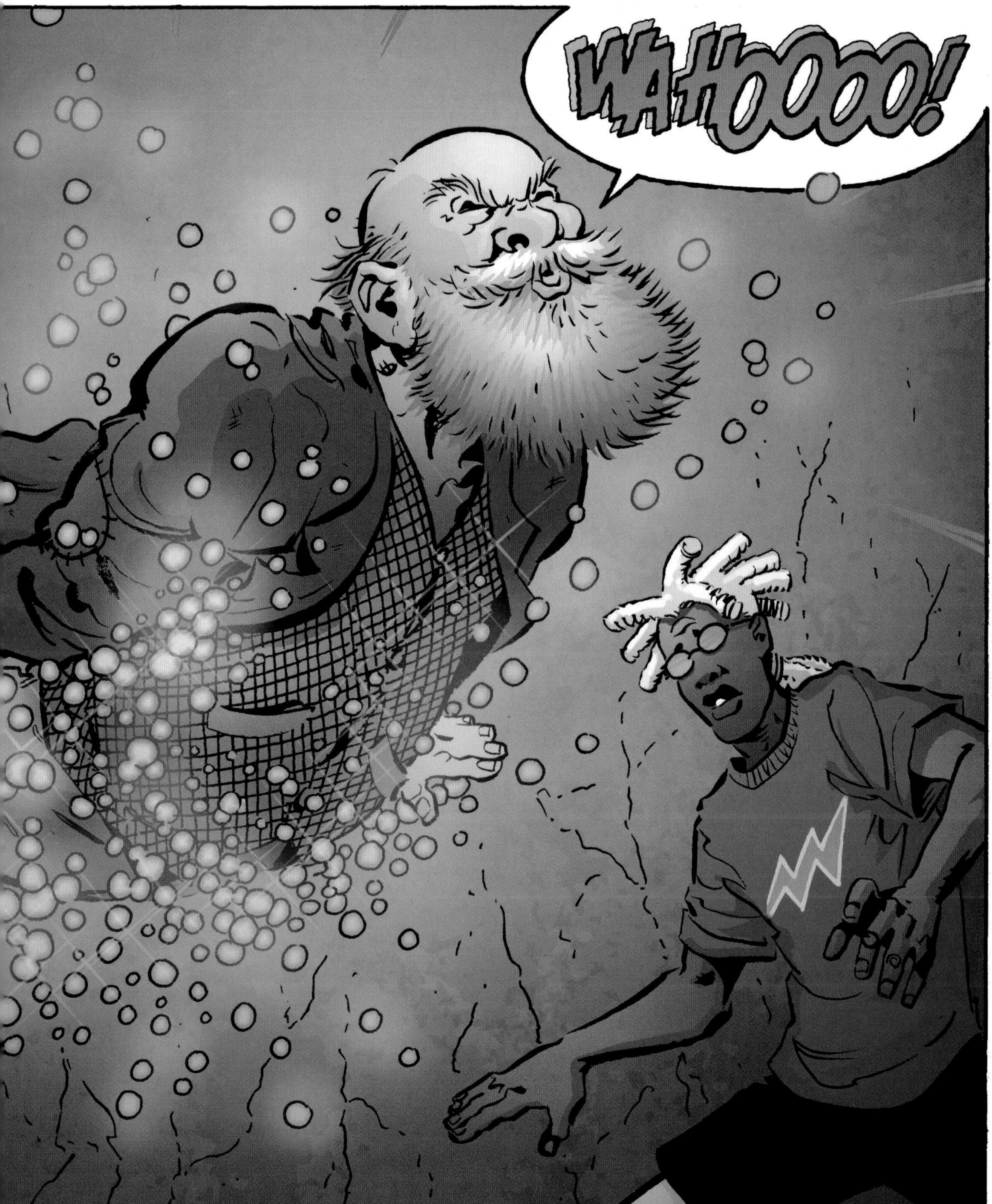
WAHOOOOO!

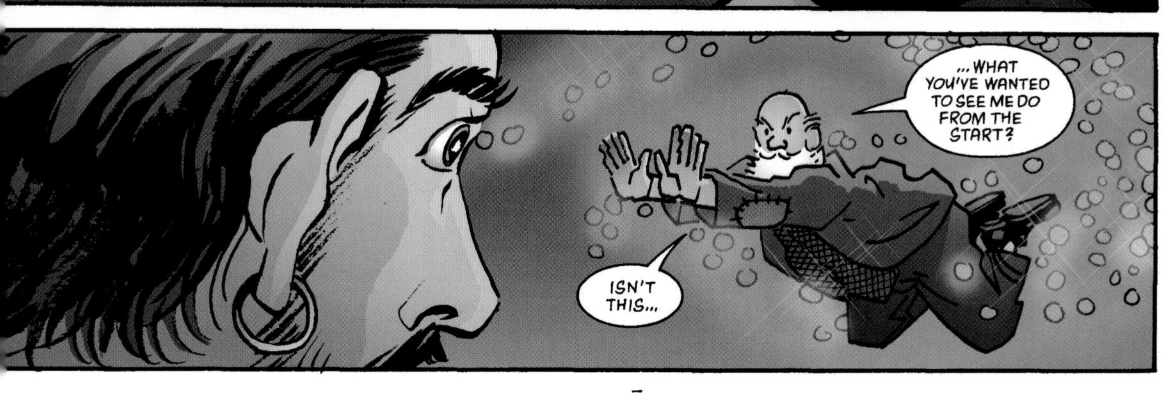
ISN'T THIS...
...WHAT YOU'VE WANTED TO SEE ME DO FROM THE START?

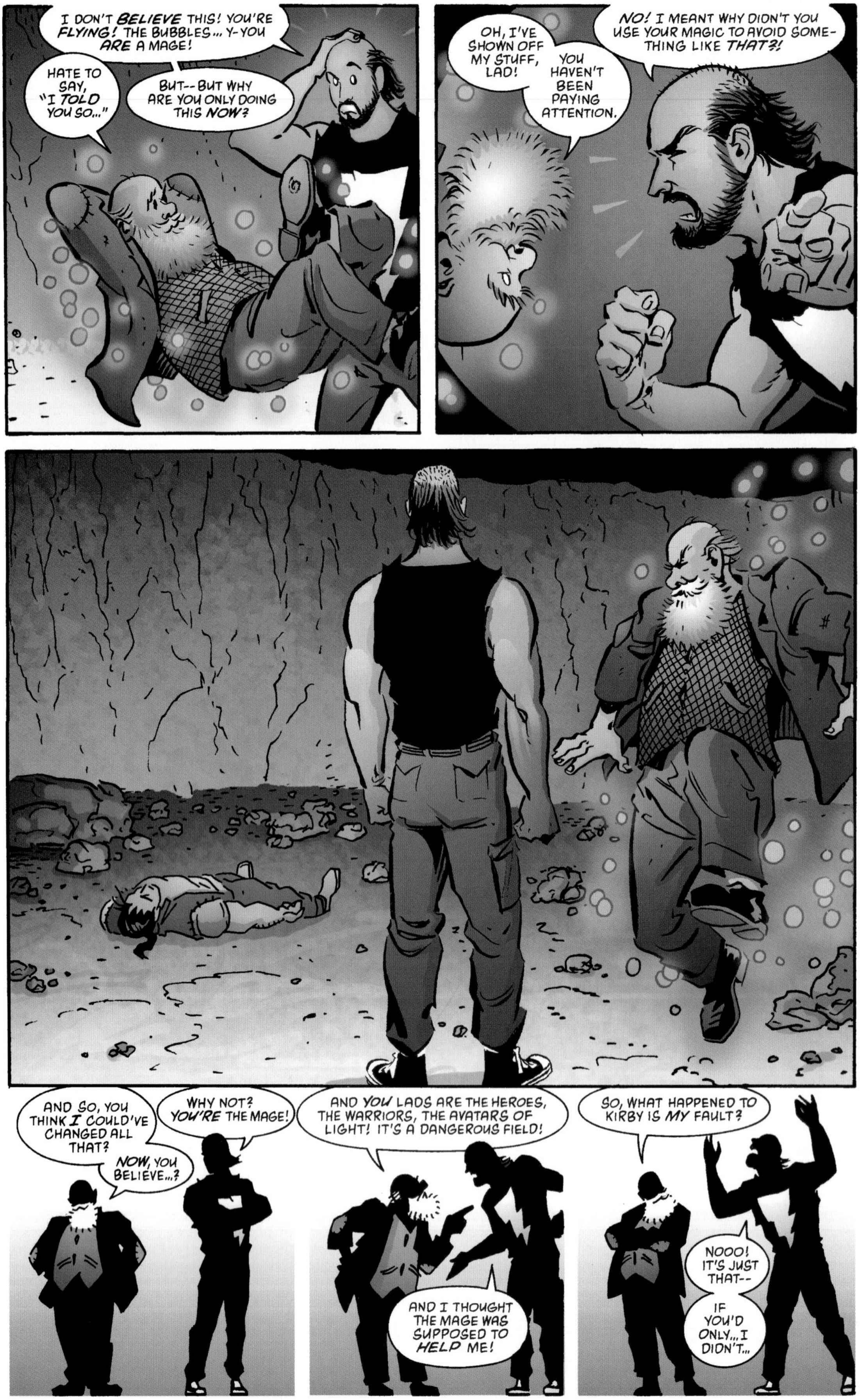
I DON'T BELIEVE THIS! YOU'RE FLYING! THE BUBBLES... Y-YOU ARE A MAGE!
HATE TO SAY, "I TOLD YOU SO..."
BUT--BUT WHY ARE YOU ONLY DOING THIS NOW?
OH, I'VE SHOWN OFF MY STUFF, LAD!
YOU HAVEN'T BEEN PAYING ATTENTION.
NO! I MEANT WHY DIDN'T YOU USE YOUR MAGIC TO AVOID SOMETHING LIKE THAT?!
AND SO, YOU THINK I COULD'VE CHANGED ALL THAT?
NOW, YOU BELIEVE...?
WHY NOT? YOU'RE THE MAGE!
AND YOU LADS ARE THE HEROES, THE WARRIORS, THE AVATARS OF LIGHT! IT'S A DANGEROUS FIELD!
AND I THOUGHT THE MAGE WAS SUPPOSED TO HELP ME!
SO, WHAT HAPPENED TO KIRBY IS MY FAULT?
NOOO! IT'S JUST THAT--
IF YOU'D ONLY... I DIDN'T...

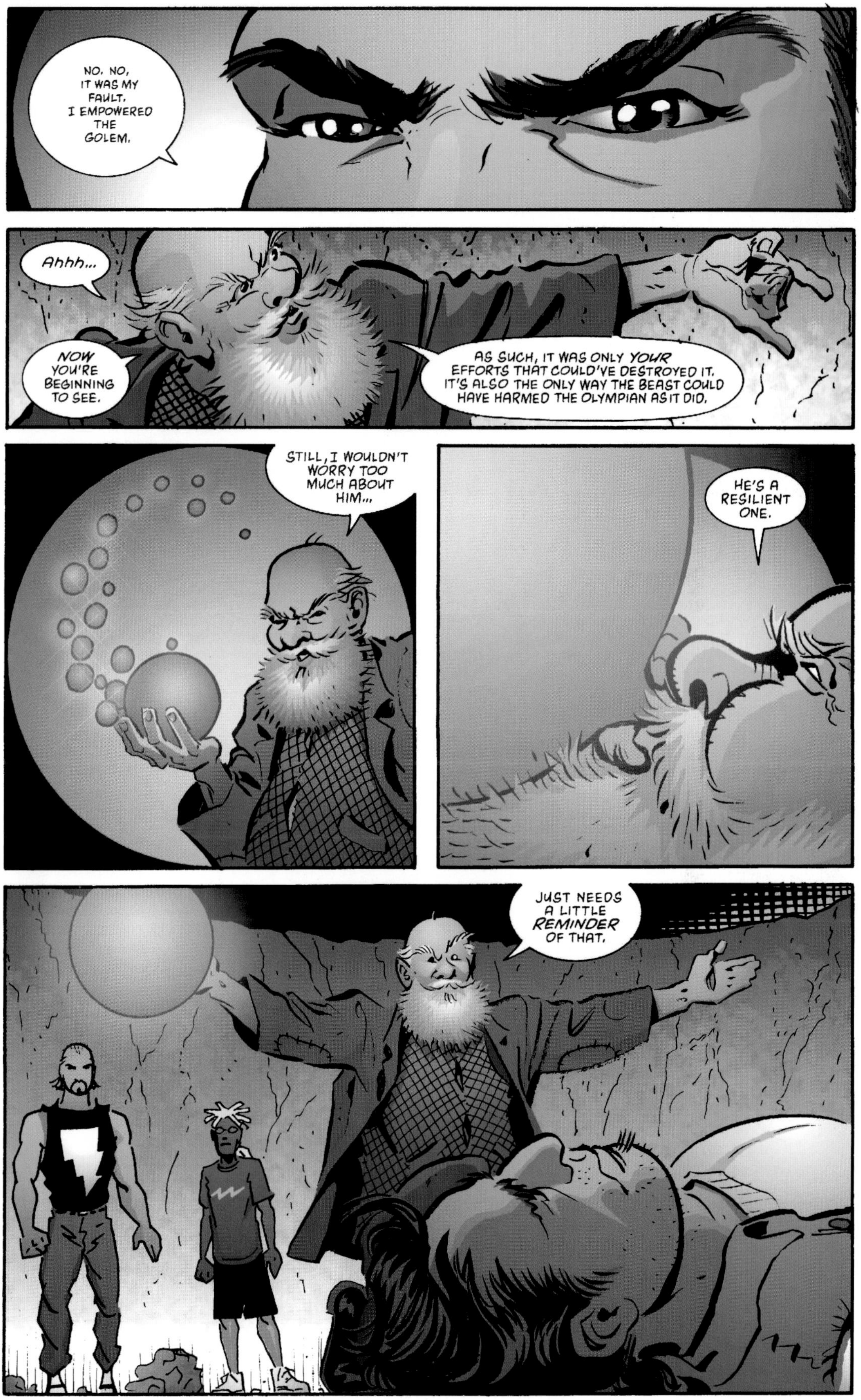

NO, NO, IT WAS MY FAULT. I EMPOWERED THE GOLEM.
Ahhh...
NOW YOU'RE BEGINNING TO SEE.
AS SUCH, IT WAS ONLY YOUR EFFORTS THAT COULD'VE DESTROYED IT. IT'S ALSO THE ONLY WAY THE BEAST COULD HAVE HARMED THE OLYMPIAN AS IT DID.
STILL, I WOULDN'T WORRY TOO MUCH ABOUT HIM...
HE'S A RESILIENT ONE.
JUST NEEDS A LITTLE REMINDER OF THAT.

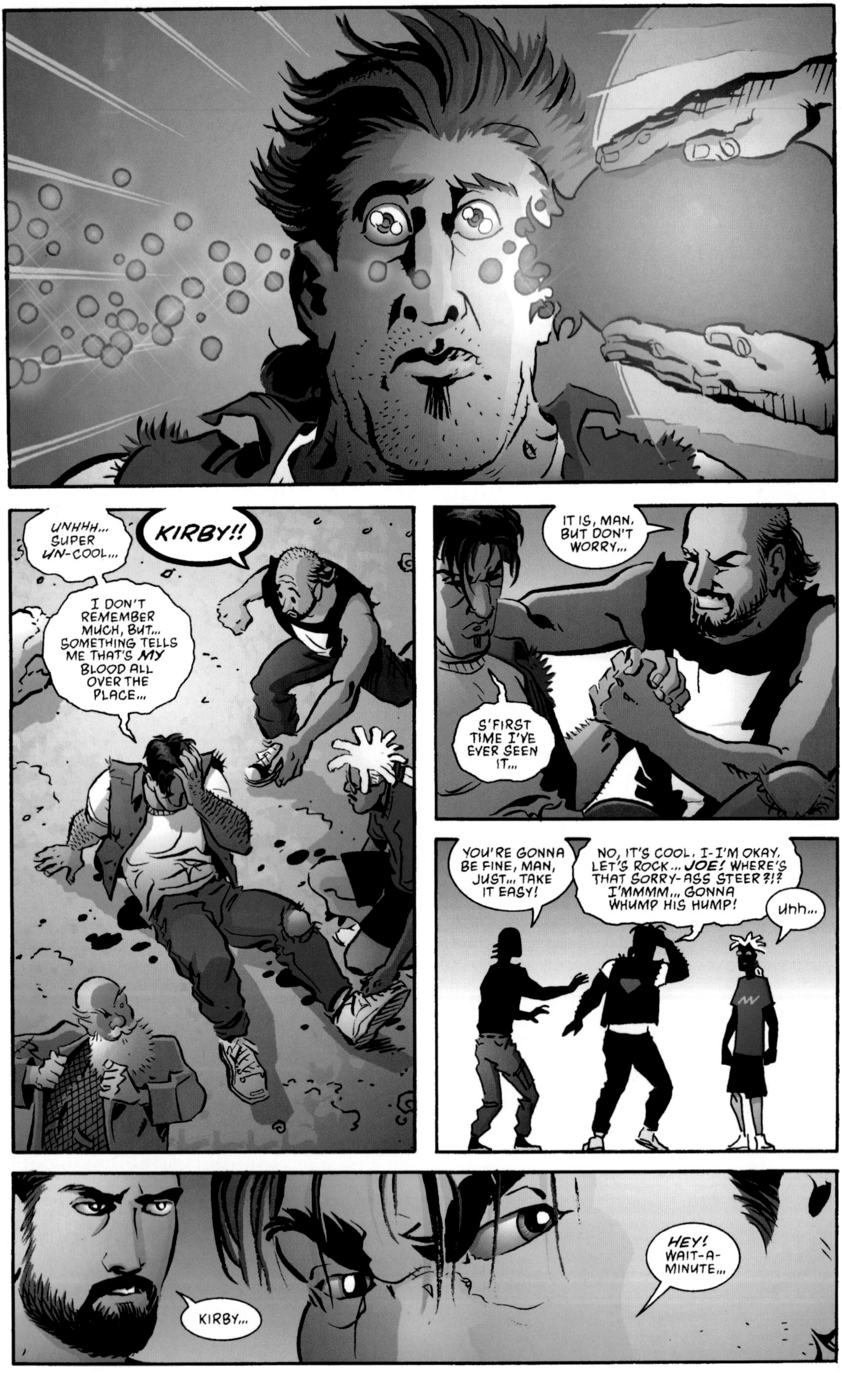
UNHHH... SUPER UN-COOL...
KIRBY!!
I DON'T REMEMBER MUCH, BUT... SOMETHING TELLS ME THAT'S MY BLOOD ALL OVER THE PLACE...
IT IS, MAN, BUT DON'T WORRY...
S'FIRST TIME I'VE EVER SEEN IT...
YOU'RE GONNA BE FINE, MAN, JUST... TAKE IT EASY!
NO, IT'S COOL. I-I'M OKAY. LET'S ROCK... JOE! WHERE'S THAT SORRY-ASS STEER?!? I'MMMM... GONNA WHUMP HIS HUMP!
Uhh...
KIRBY...
HEY! WAIT-A-MINUTE...

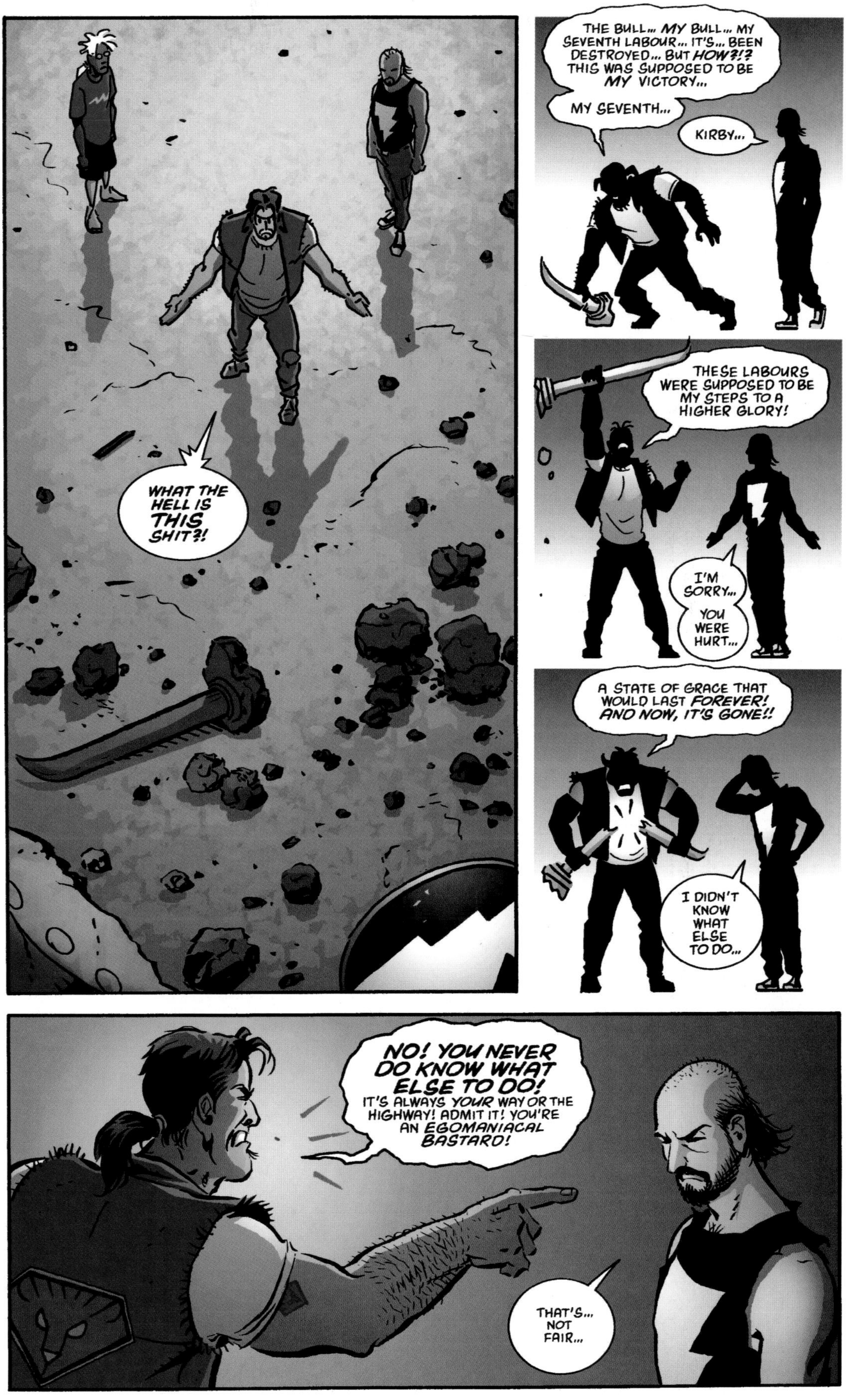
WHAT THE HELL IS THIS SHIT?!
THE BULL... MY BULL... MY SEVENTH LABOUR... IT'S... BEEN DESTROYED... BUT HOW?!? THIS WAS SUPPOSED TO BE MY VICTORY...
MY SEVENTH...
KIRBY...
THESE LABOURS WERE SUPPOSED TO BE MY STEPS TO A HIGHER GLORY!
I'M SORRY...
YOU WERE HURT...
A STATE OF GRACE THAT WOULD LAST FOREVER! AND NOW, IT'S GONE!!
I DIDN'T KNOW WHAT ELSE TO DO...
NO! YOU NEVER DO KNOW WHAT ELSE TO DO! IT'S ALWAYS YOUR WAY OR THE HIGHWAY! ADMIT IT! YOU'RE AN EGOMANIACAL BASTARD!
THAT'S... NOT FAIR...

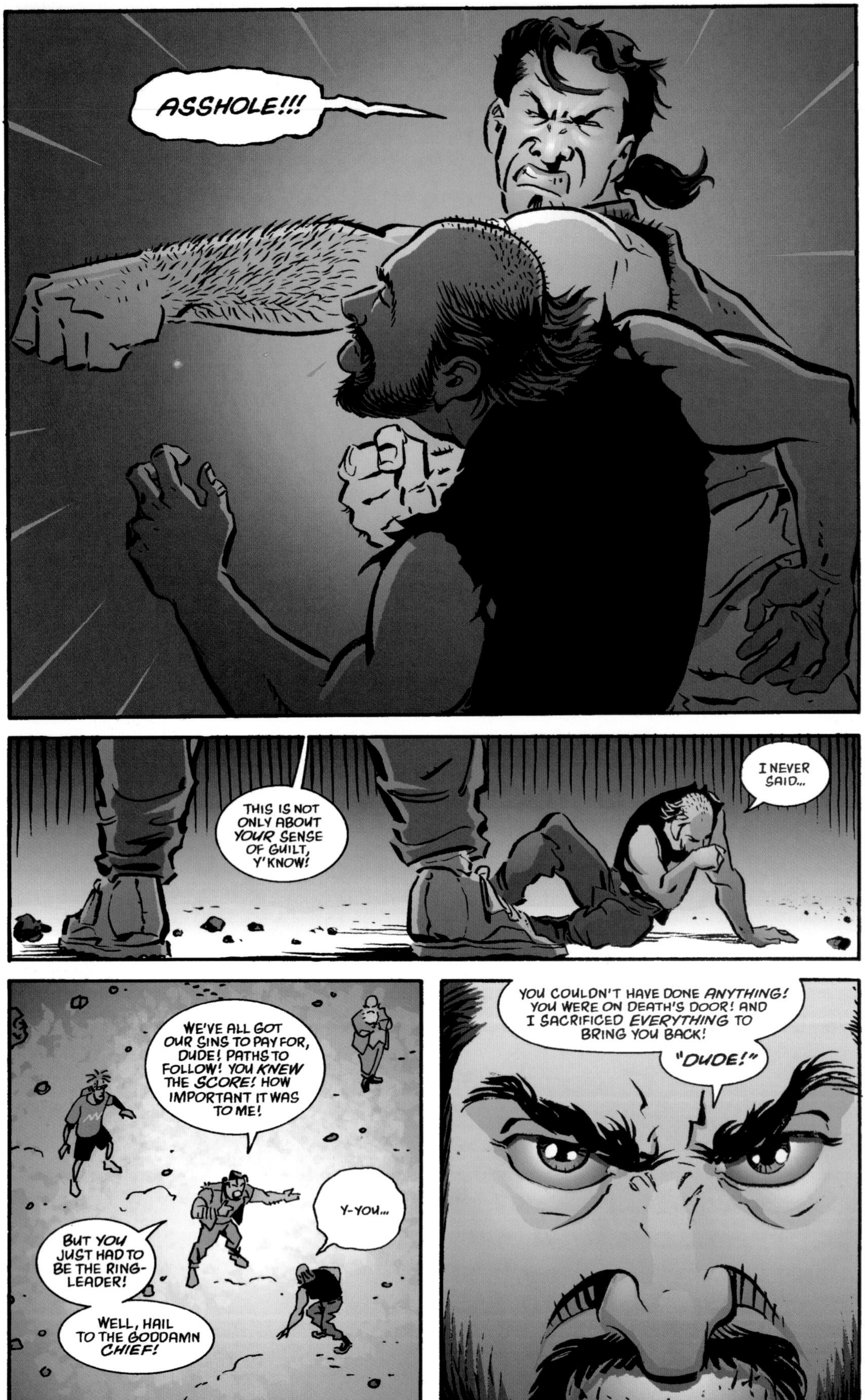
ASSHOLE!!!
THIS IS NOT ONLY ABOUT YOUR SENSE OF GUILT, Y'KNOW!
I NEVER SAID...
WE'VE ALL GOT OUR SINS TO PAY FOR, DUDE! PATHS TO FOLLOW! YOU KNEW THE SCORE! HOW IMPORTANT IT WAS TO ME!
Y-YOU...
BUT YOU JUST HAD TO BE THE RING-LEADER!
WELL, HAIL TO THE GODDAMN CHIEF!
YOU COULDN'T HAVE DONE ANYTHING! YOU WERE ON DEATH'S DOOR! AND I SACRIFICED EVERYTHING TO BRING YOU BACK!
"DUDE!"

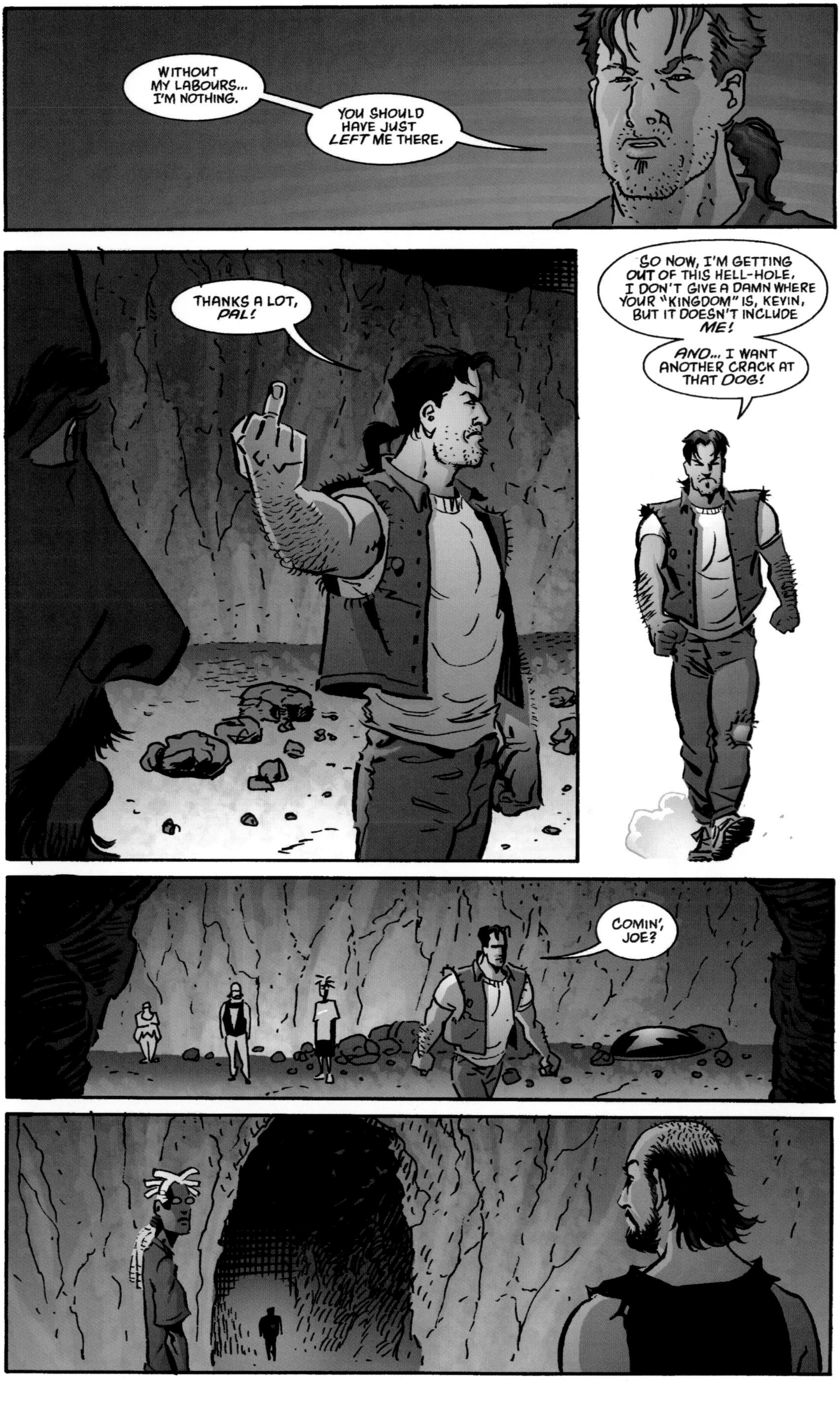
WITHOUT MY LABOURS... I'M NOTHING.
YOU SHOULD HAVE JUST LEFT ME THERE.
THANKS A LOT, PAL!
SO NOW, I'M GETTING OUT OF THIS HELL-HOLE. I DON'T GIVE A DAMN WHERE YOUR "KINGDOM" IS, KEVIN, BUT IT DOESN'T INCLUDE ME!
AND... I WANT ANOTHER CRACK AT THAT DOG!
COMIN', JOE?

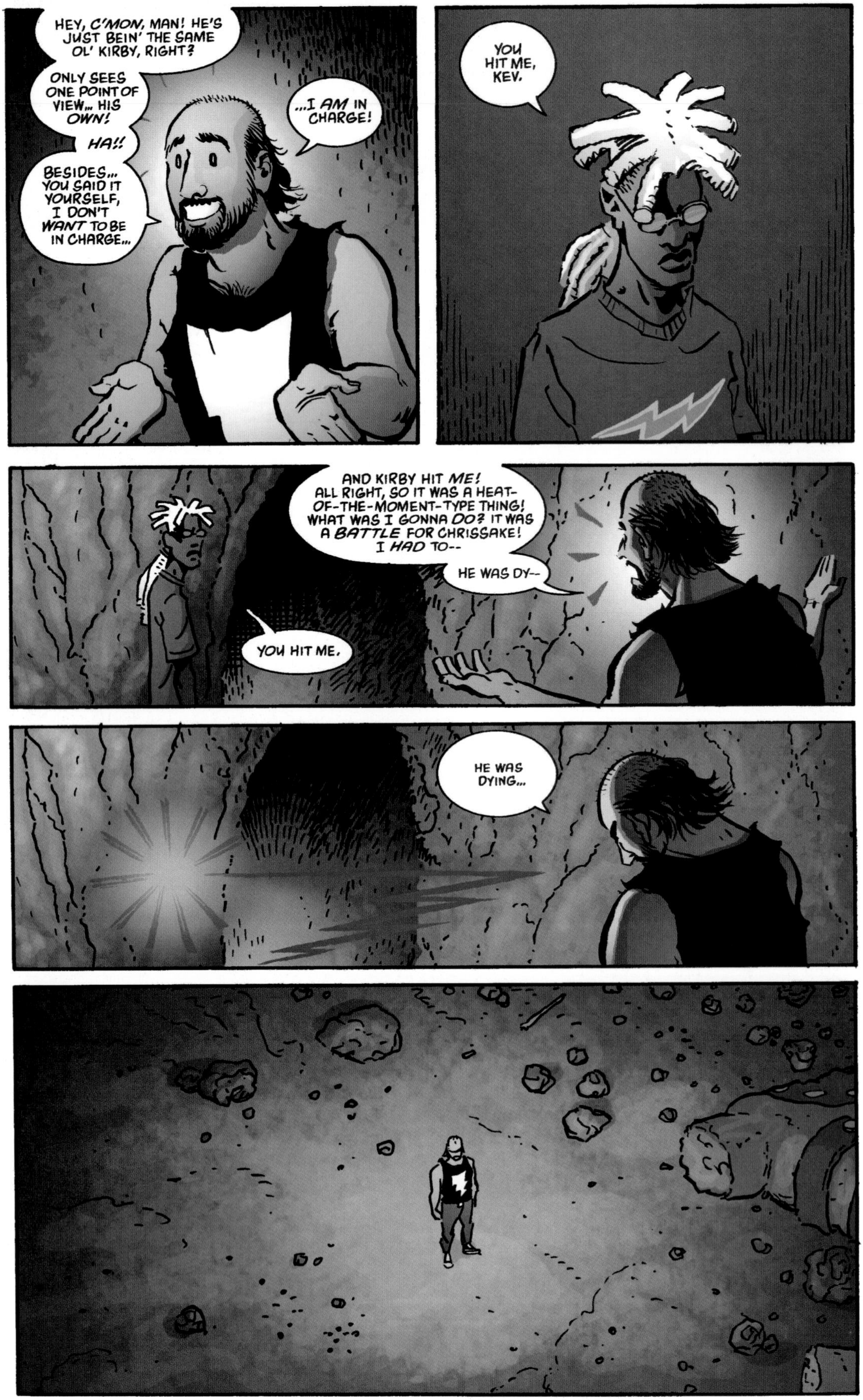
HEY, C'MON, MAN! HE'S JUST BEIN' THE SAME OL' KIRBY, RIGHT?
ONLY SEES ONE POINT OF VIEW... HIS OWN!
HA!!
BESIDES... YOU SAID IT YOURSELF, I DON'T WANT TO BE IN CHARGE...
...I AM IN CHARGE!
YOU HIT ME, KEV.
AND KIRBY HIT ME! ALL RIGHT, SO IT WAS A HEAT-OF-THE-MOMENT-TYPE THING! WHAT WAS I GONNA DO? IT WAS A BATTLE FOR CHRISSAKE! I HAD TO--
HE WAS DY--
YOU HIT ME.
HE WAS DYING...

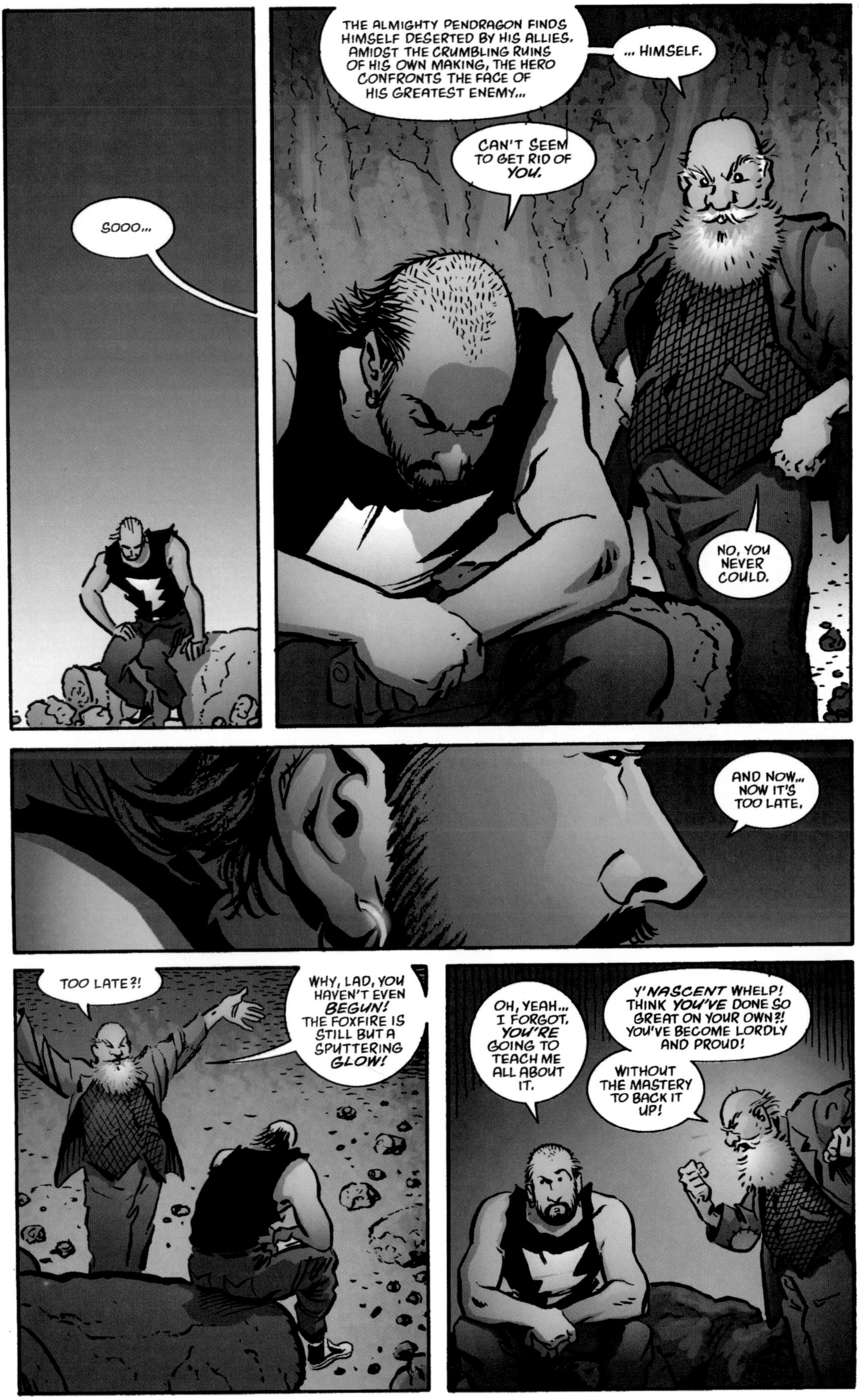
SOOO...
THE ALMIGHTY PENDRAGON FINDS HIMSELF DESERTED BY HIS ALLIES. AMIDST THE CRUMBLING RUINS OF HIS OWN MAKING, THE HERO CONFRONTS THE FACE OF HIS GREATEST ENEMY...
... HIMSELF.
CAN'T SEEM TO GET RID OF YOU.
NO, YOU NEVER COULD.
AND NOW... NOW IT'S TOO LATE.
TOO LATE?!
WHY, LAD, YOU HAVEN'T EVEN BEGUN! THE FOXFIRE IS STILL BUT A SPUTTERING GLOW!
OH, YEAH... I FORGOT, YOU'RE GOING TO TEACH ME ALL ABOUT IT.
Y'NASCENT WHELP! THINK YOU'VE DONE SO GREAT ON YOUR OWN?! YOU'VE BECOME LORDLY AND PROUD!
WITHOUT THE MASTERY TO BACK IT UP!

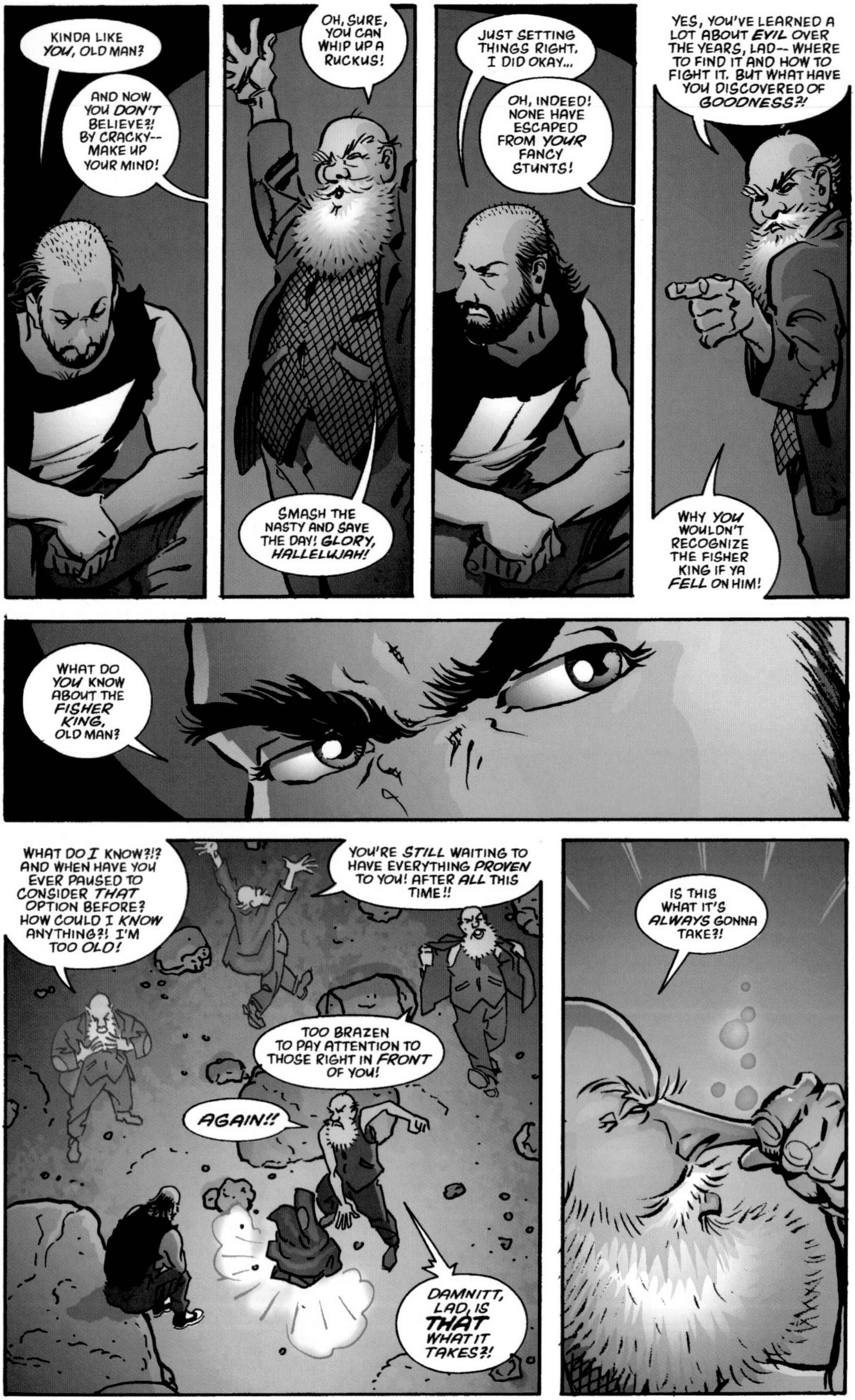
KINDA LIKE YOU, OLD MAN?
AND NOW YOU DON'T BELIEVE?! BY CRACKY-- MAKE UP YOUR MIND!
OH, SURE, YOU CAN WHIP UP A RUCKUS!
SMASH THE NASTY AND SAVE THE DAY! GLORY, HALLELUJAH!
JUST SETTING THINGS RIGHT. I DID OKAY...
OH, INDEED! NONE HAVE ESCAPED FROM YOUR FANCY STUNTS!
YES, YOU'VE LEARNED A LOT ABOUT EVIL OVER THE YEARS, LAD-- WHERE TO FIND IT AND HOW TO FIGHT IT. BUT WHAT HAVE YOU DISCOVERED OF GOODNESS?!
WHY YOU WOULDN'T RECOGNIZE THE FISHER KING IF YA FELL ON HIM!
WHAT DO YOU KNOW ABOUT THE FISHER KING, OLD MAN?
WHAT DO I KNOW?!? AND WHEN HAVE YOU EVER PAUSED TO CONSIDER THAT OPTION BEFORE? HOW COULD I KNOW ANYTHING?! I'M TOO OLD!
YOU'RE STILL WAITING TO HAVE EVERYTHING PROVEN TO YOU! AFTER ALL THIS TIME!!
TOO BRAZEN TO PAY ATTENTION TO THOSE RIGHT IN FRONT OF YOU!
AGAIN!!
DAMNITT, LAD, IS THAT WHAT IT TAKES?!
IS THIS WHAT IT'S ALWAYS GONNA TAKE?!

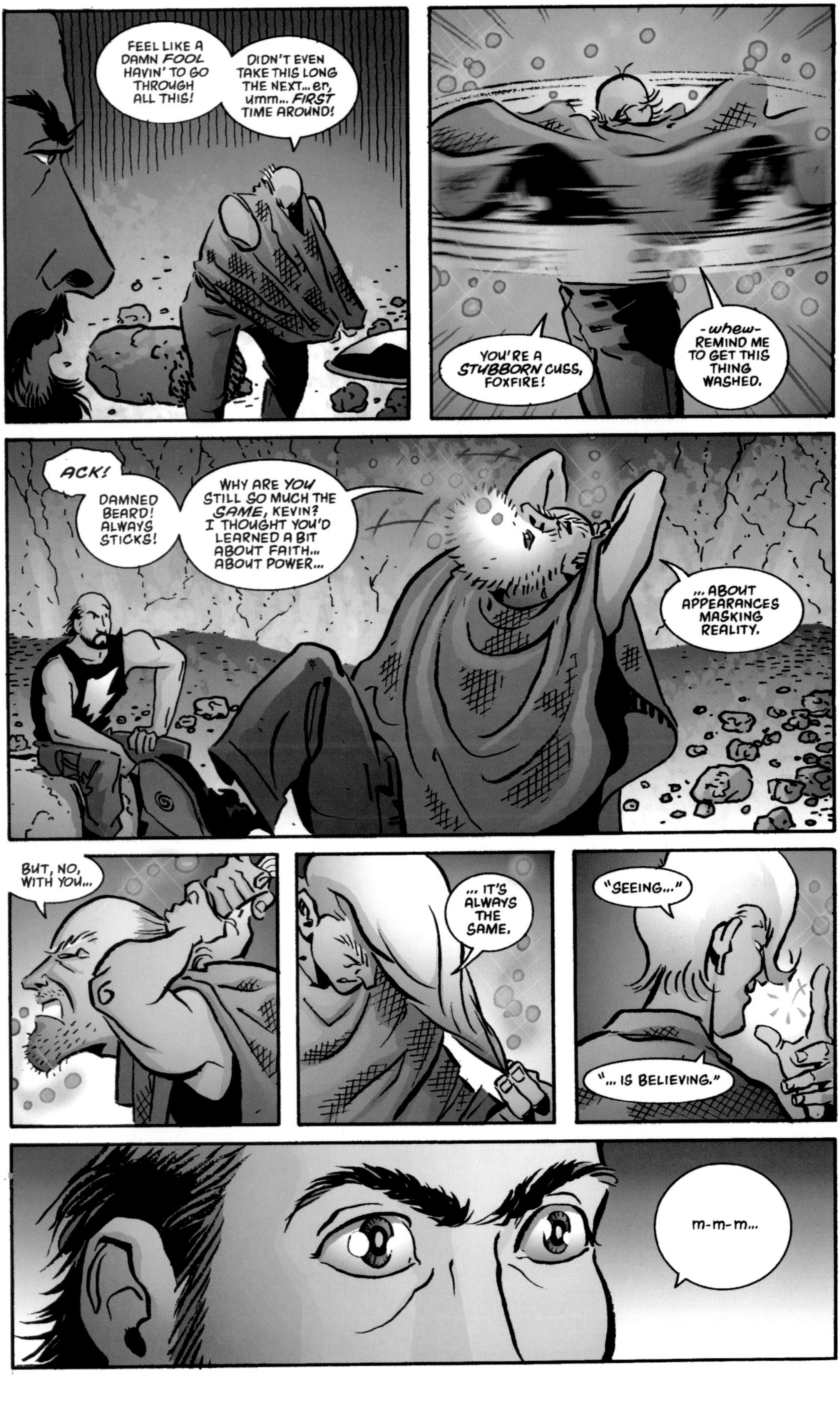
FEEL LIKE A DAMN *FOOL* HAVIN' TO GO THROUGH ALL THIS!
DIDN'T EVEN TAKE THIS LONG THE NEXT... er, umm... *FIRST* TIME AROUND!
YOU'RE A *STUBBORN* CUSS, FOXFIRE!
-*whew*- REMIND ME TO GET THIS THING WASHED.
ACK!
DAMNED BEARD! ALWAYS STICKS!
WHY ARE *YOU* STILL *SO* MUCH THE *SAME*, KEVIN? I THOUGHT YOU'D LEARNED A BIT ABOUT FAITH... ABOUT POWER...
...ABOUT APPEARANCES MASKING REALITY.
BUT, NO, WITH YOU...
... IT'S ALWAYS THE SAME.
"SEEING..."
"... IS BELIEVING."
m-m-m...

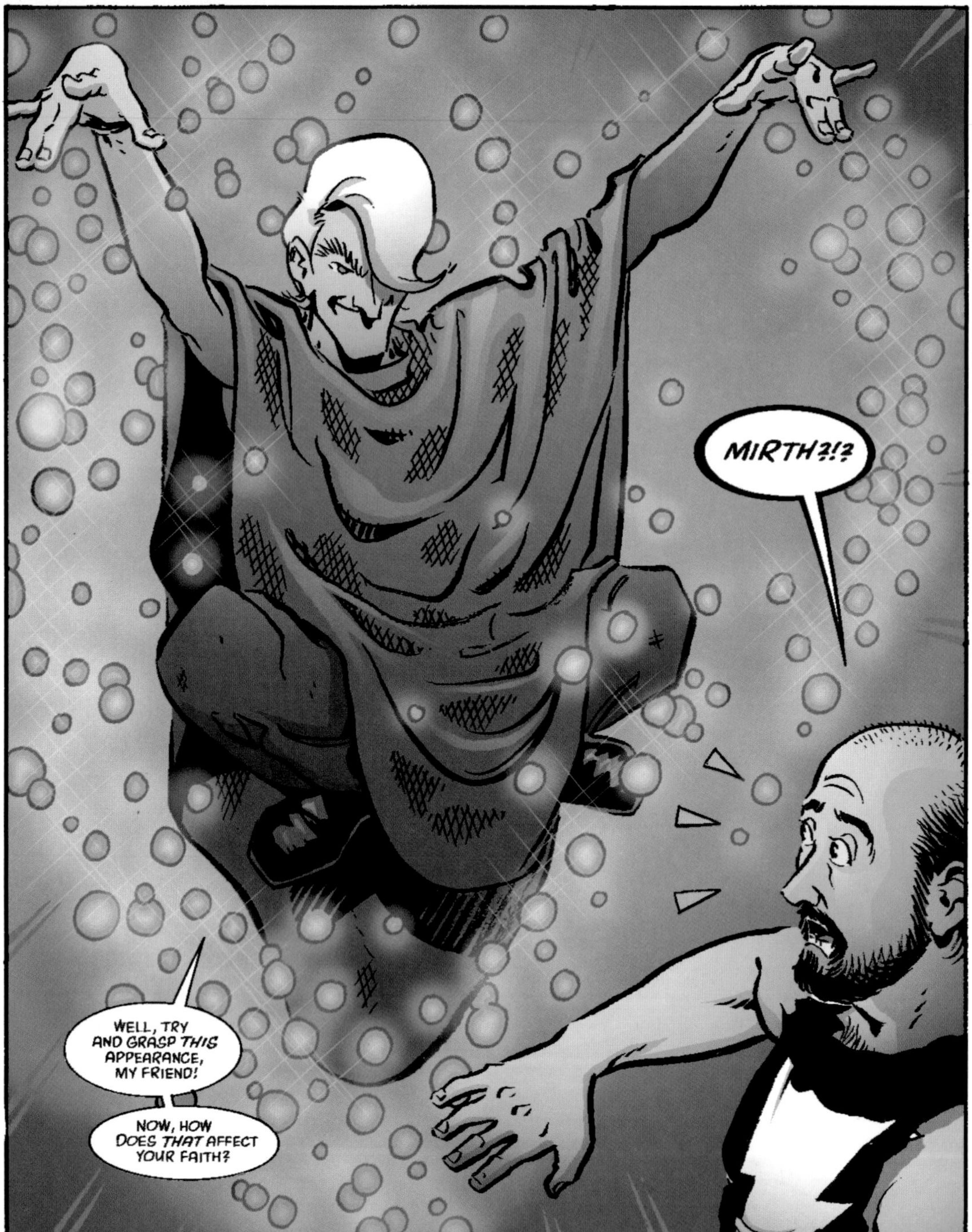
MIRTH?!?
WELL, TRY AND GRASP *THIS* APPEARANCE, MY FRIEND!
NOW, HOW DOES *THAT* AFFECT YOUR FAITH?

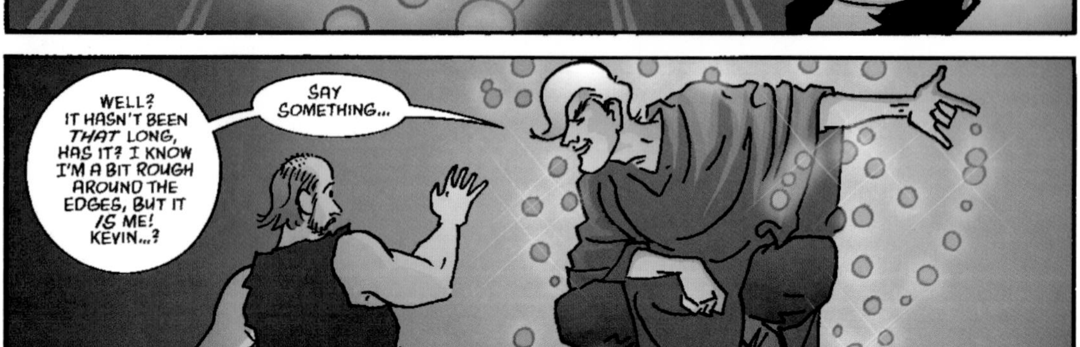
WELL? IT HASN'T BEEN *THAT* LONG, HAS IT? I KNOW I'M A BIT ROUGH AROUND THE EDGES, BUT IT *IS* ME! KEVIN...?
SAY SOMETHING...

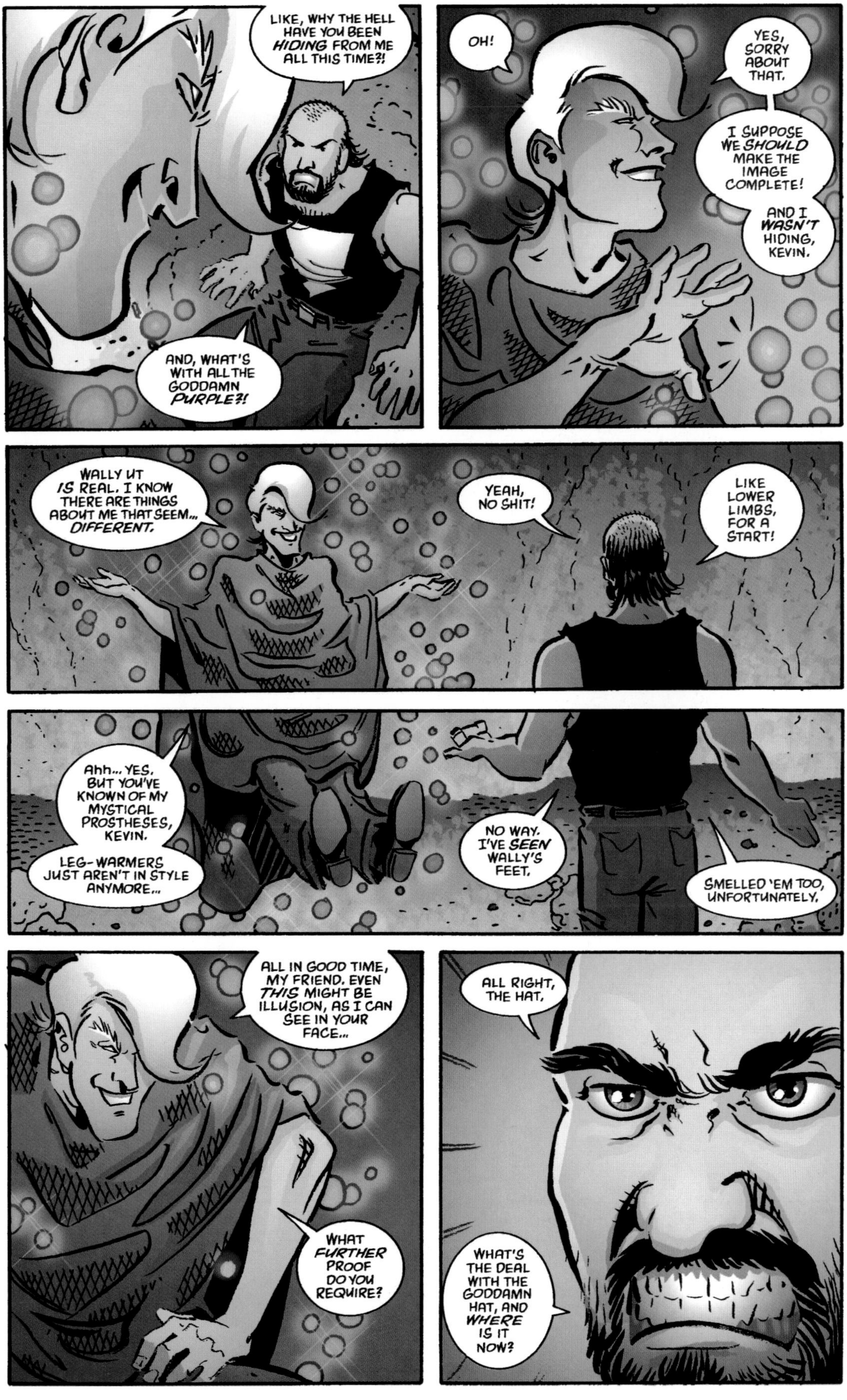
LIKE, WHY THE HELL HAVE YOU BEEN *HIDING* FROM ME ALL THIS TIME?!
AND, WHAT'S WITH ALL THE GODDAMN *PURPLE*?!
OH!
YES, SORRY ABOUT THAT.
I SUPPOSE WE *SHOULD* MAKE THE IMAGE COMPLETE!
AND I *WASN'T* HIDING, KEVIN.
WALLY UT *IS* REAL. I KNOW THERE ARE THINGS ABOUT ME THAT SEEM... *DIFFERENT.*
YEAH, NO SHIT!
LIKE LOWER LIMBS, FOR A START!
Ahh... YES, BUT YOU'VE KNOWN OF MY MYSTICAL PROSTHESES, KEVIN.
LEG-WARMERS JUST AREN'T IN STYLE ANYMORE...
NO WAY. I'VE *SEEN* WALLY'S FEET.
SMELLED 'EM TOO, UNFORTUNATELY.
ALL IN GOOD TIME, MY FRIEND. EVEN *THIS* MIGHT BE ILLUSION, AS I CAN SEE IN YOUR FACE...
WHAT *FURTHER* PROOF DO YOU REQUIRE?
ALL RIGHT, THE HAT.
WHAT'S THE DEAL WITH THE GODDAMN HAT, AND *WHERE* IS IT NOW?

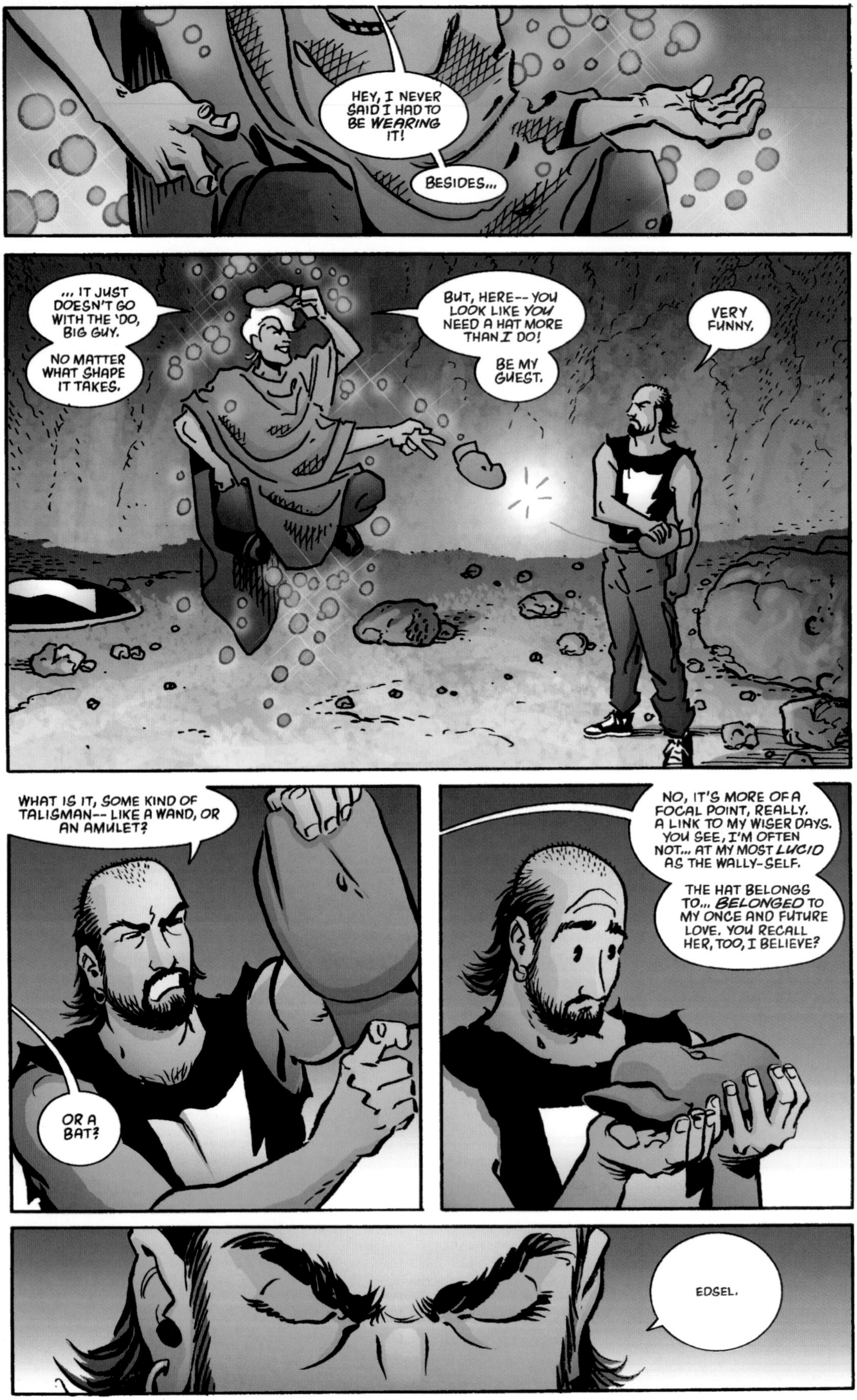

HEY, I NEVER SAID I HAD TO BE *WEARING* IT!
BESIDES...
... IT JUST DOESN'T GO WITH THE 'DO, BIG GUY.
NO MATTER WHAT SHAPE IT TAKES.
BUT, HERE-- YOU LOOK LIKE *YOU* NEED A HAT MORE THAN *I* DO!
BE MY GUEST.
VERY FUNNY.
WHAT IS IT, SOME KIND OF TALISMAN-- LIKE A WAND, OR AN AMULET?
OR A BAT?
NO, IT'S MORE OF A FOCAL POINT, REALLY. A LINK TO MY WISER DAYS. YOU SEE, I'M OFTEN NOT... AT MY MOST *LUCID* AS THE WALLY-SELF.
THE HAT BELONGS TO... *BELONGED* TO MY ONCE AND FUTURE LOVE. YOU RECALL HER, TOO, I BELIEVE?
EDSEL.

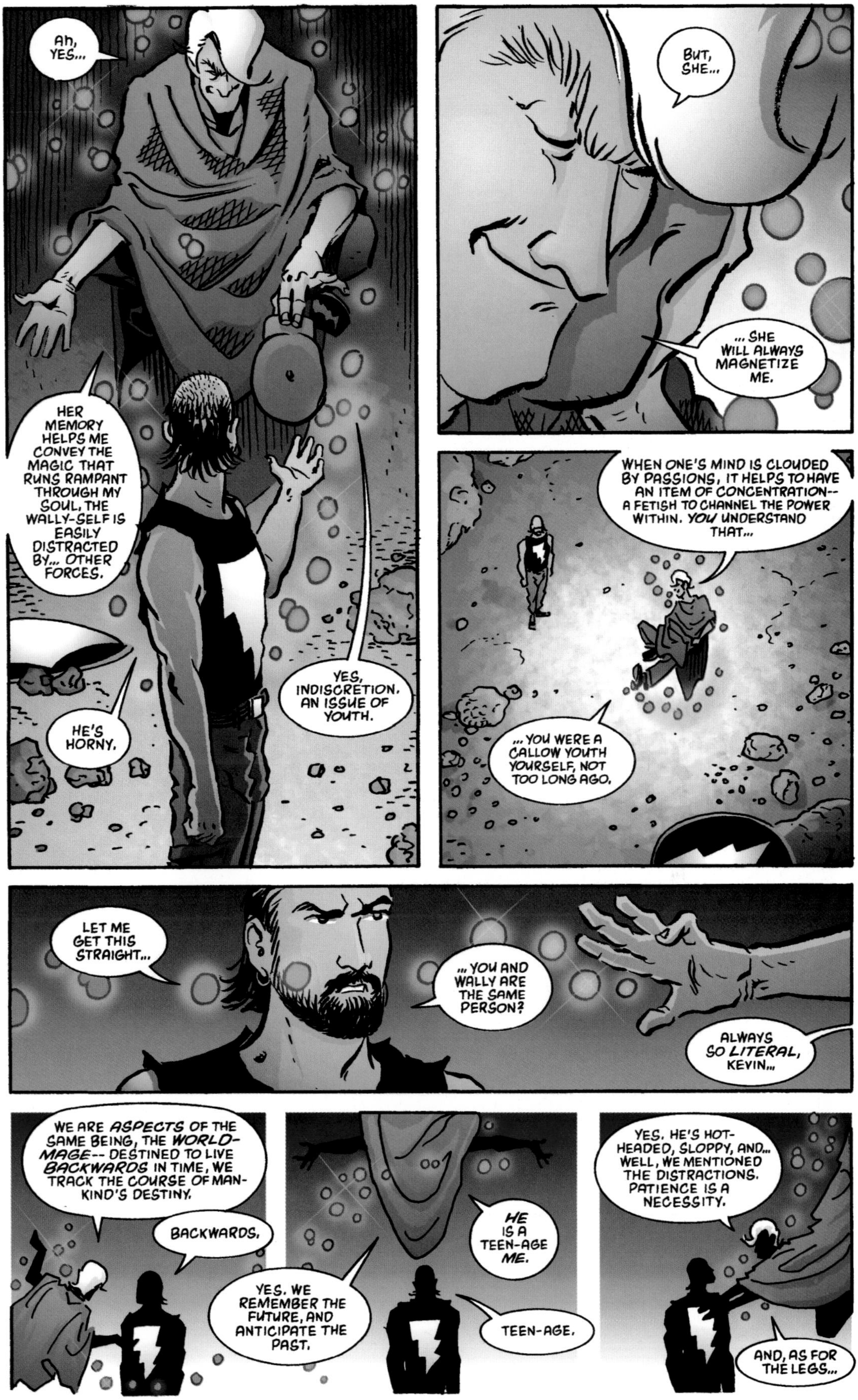

Ah, YES...
HER MEMORY HELPS ME CONVEY THE MAGIC THAT RUNS RAMPANT THROUGH MY SOUL, THE WALLY-SELF IS EASILY DISTRACTED BY... OTHER FORCES.
HE'S HORNY.
YES, INDISCRETION. AN ISSUE OF YOUTH.
BUT, SHE...
... SHE WILL ALWAYS MAGNETIZE ME.
WHEN ONE'S MIND IS CLOUDED BY PASSIONS, IT HELPS TO HAVE AN ITEM OF CONCENTRATION-- A FETISH TO CHANNEL THE POWER WITHIN. YOU UNDERSTAND THAT...
... YOU WERE A CALLOW YOUTH YOURSELF, NOT TOO LONG AGO.
LET ME GET THIS STRAIGHT...
... YOU AND WALLY ARE THE SAME PERSON?
ALWAYS SO LITERAL, KEVIN...
WE ARE ASPECTS OF THE SAME BEING, THE WORLD-MAGE-- DESTINED TO LIVE BACKWARDS IN TIME, WE TRACK THE COURSE OF MAN-KIND'S DESTINY.
BACKWARDS.
YES. WE REMEMBER THE FUTURE, AND ANTICIPATE THE PAST.
HE IS A TEEN-AGE ME.
TEEN-AGE.
YES. HE'S HOT-HEADED, SLOPPY, AND... WELL, WE MENTIONED THE DISTRACTIONS. PATIENCE IS A NECESSITY.
AND, AS FOR THE LEGS...

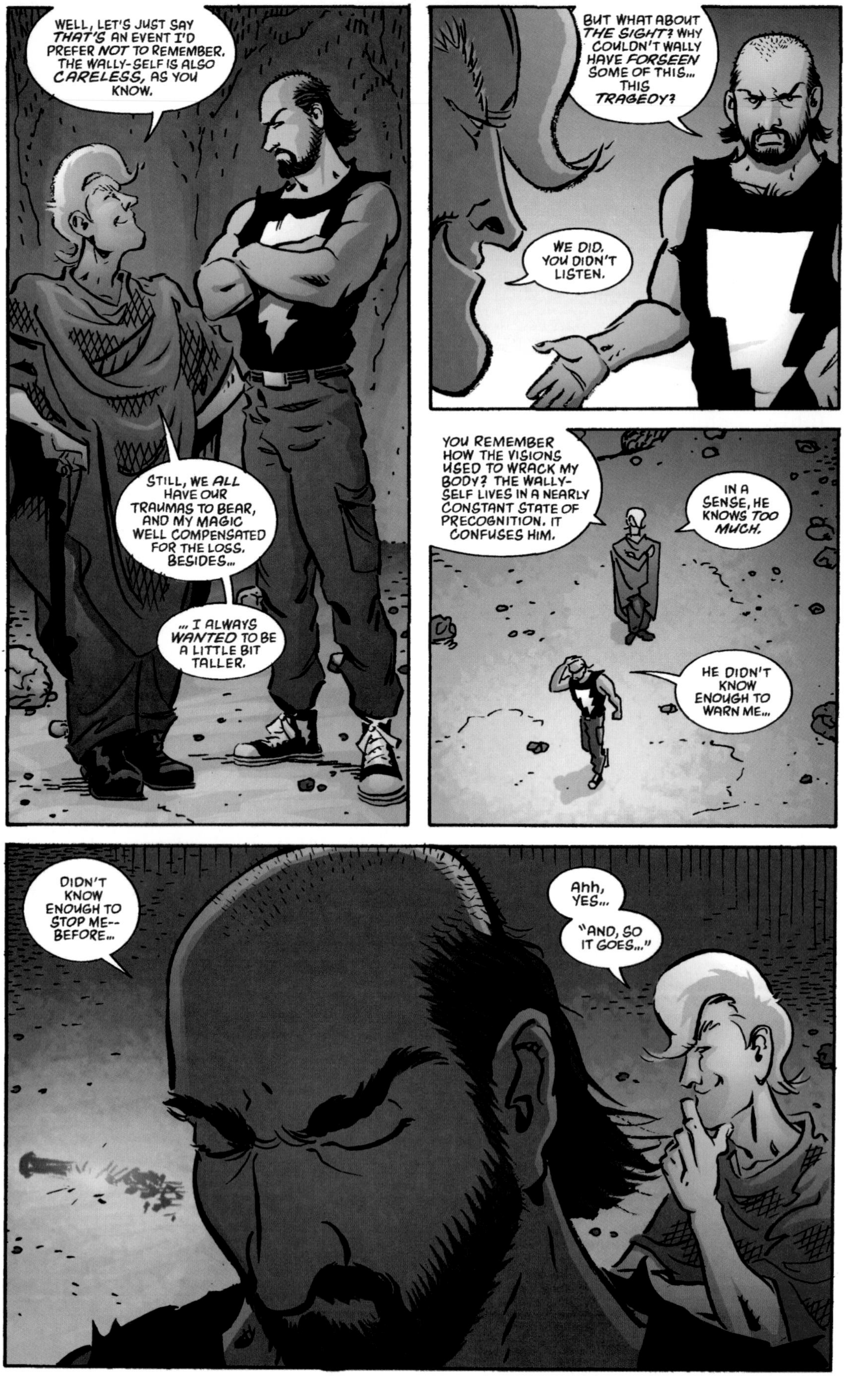
WELL, LET'S JUST SAY *THAT'S* AN EVENT I'D PREFER *NOT* TO REMEMBER. THE WALLY-SELF IS ALSO *CARELESS,* AS YOU KNOW.
STILL, WE *ALL* HAVE OUR TRAUMAS TO BEAR, AND MY MAGIC WELL COMPENSATED FOR THE LOSS. BESIDES...
...I ALWAYS *WANTED* TO BE A LITTLE BIT TALLER.
BUT WHAT ABOUT *THE SIGHT?* WHY COULDN'T WALLY HAVE *FORSEEN* SOME OF THIS... THIS *TRAGEDY?*
WE DID. YOU DIDN'T LISTEN.
YOU REMEMBER HOW THE VISIONS USED TO WRACK MY BODY? THE WALLY-SELF LIVES IN A NEARLY CONSTANT STATE OF PRECOGNITION. IT CONFUSES HIM.
IN A SENSE, HE KNOWS *TOO MUCH.*
HE DIDN'T KNOW ENOUGH TO WARN ME...
DIDN'T KNOW ENOUGH TO STOP ME-- BEFORE...
Ahh, YES...
"AND, SO IT GOES..."

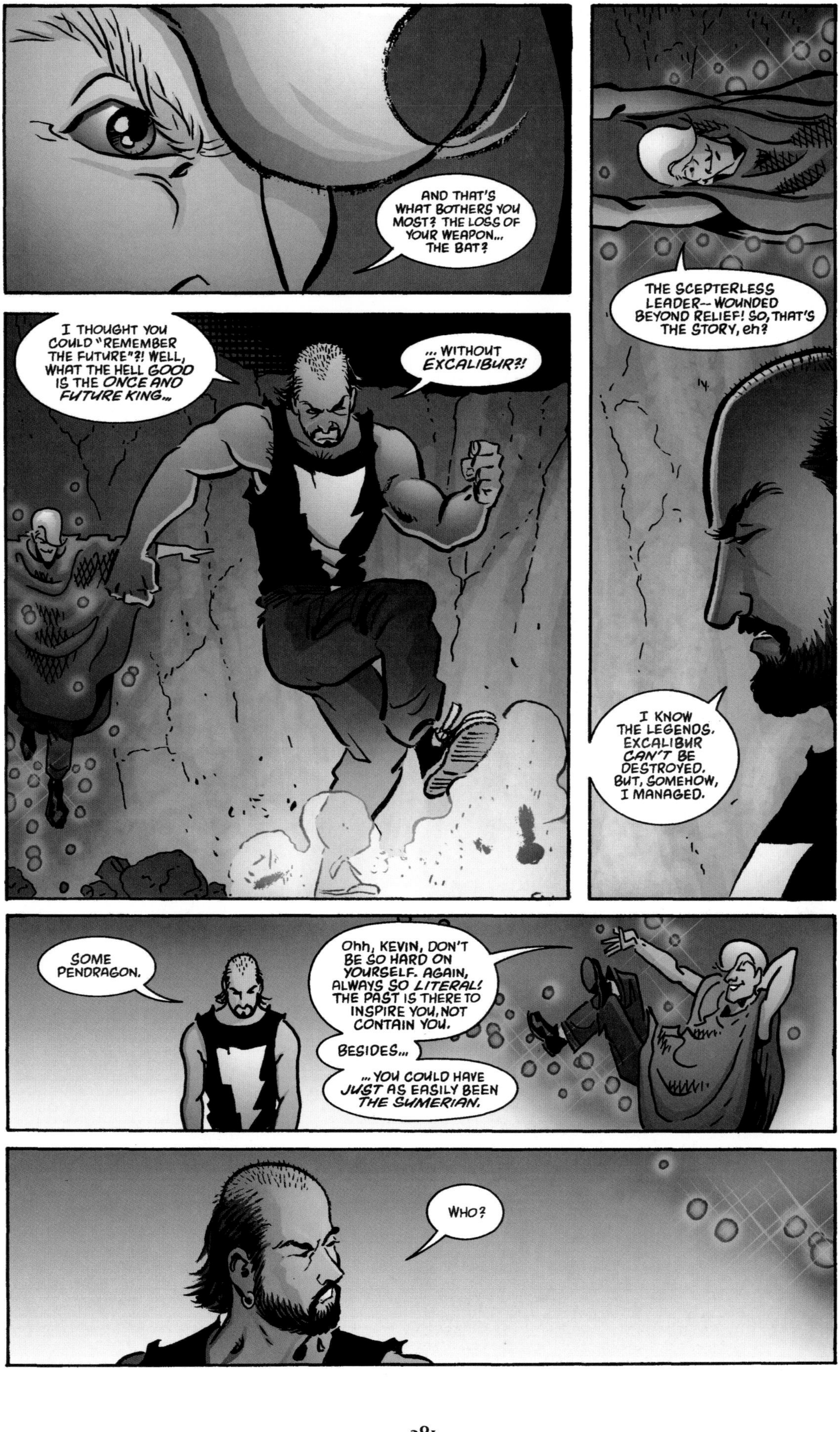
AND THAT'S WHAT BOTHERS YOU MOST? THE LOSS OF YOUR WEAPON... THE BAT?
I THOUGHT YOU COULD "REMEMBER THE FUTURE"?! WELL, WHAT THE HELL GOOD IS THE ONCE AND FUTURE KING...
...WITHOUT EXCALIBUR?!
THE SCEPTERLESS LEADER-- WOUNDED BEYOND RELIEF! SO, THAT'S THE STORY, eh?
I KNOW THE LEGENDS. EXCALIBUR CAN'T BE DESTROYED. BUT, SOMEHOW, I MANAGED.
SOME PENDRAGON.
Ohh, KEVIN, DON'T BE SO HARD ON YOURSELF. AGAIN, ALWAYS SO LITERAL! THE PAST IS THERE TO INSPIRE YOU, NOT CONTAIN YOU.
BESIDES...
...YOU COULD HAVE JUST AS EASILY BEEN THE SUMERIAN.
WHO?

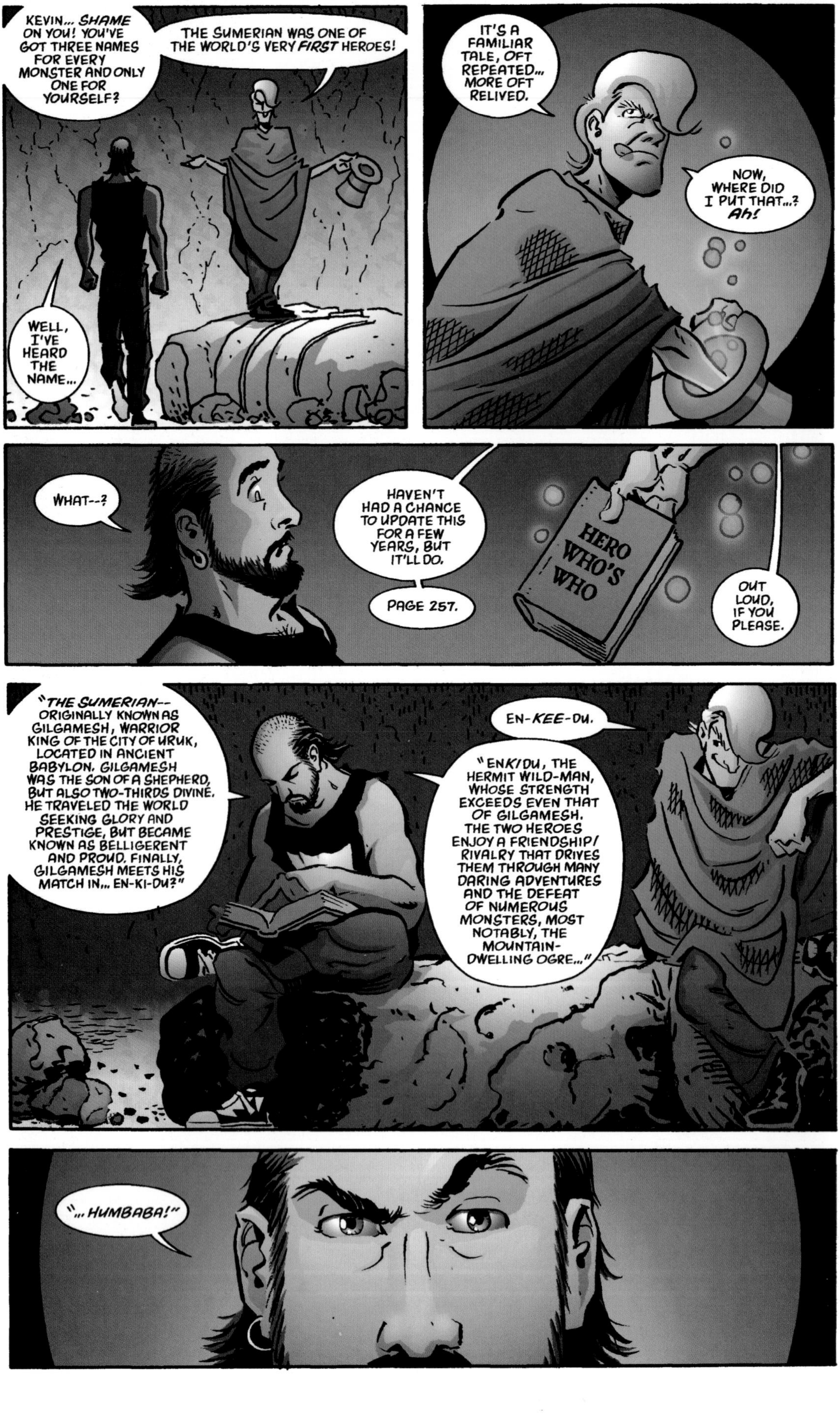
KEVIN... SHAME ON YOU! YOU'VE GOT THREE NAMES FOR EVERY MONSTER AND ONLY ONE FOR YOURSELF?
THE SUMERIAN WAS ONE OF THE WORLD'S VERY FIRST HEROES!
WELL, I'VE HEARD THE NAME...
IT'S A FAMILIAR TALE, OFT REPEATED... MORE OFT RELIVED.
NOW, WHERE DID I PUT THAT...? Ah!
WHAT--?
HAVEN'T HAD A CHANCE TO UPDATE THIS FOR A FEW YEARS, BUT IT'LL DO.
PAGE 257.
HERO WHO'S WHO
OUT LOUD, IF YOU PLEASE.
"THE SUMERIAN-- ORIGINALLY KNOWN AS GILGAMESH, WARRIOR KING OF THE CITY OF URUK, LOCATED IN ANCIENT BABYLON. GILGAMESH WAS THE SON OF A SHEPHERD, BUT ALSO TWO-THIRDS DIVINE. HE TRAVELED THE WORLD SEEKING GLORY AND PRESTIGE, BUT BECAME KNOWN AS BELLIGERENT AND PROUD. FINALLY, GILGAMESH MEETS HIS MATCH IN... EN-KI-DU?"
EN-KEE-DU.
"ENKIDU, THE HERMIT WILD-MAN, WHOSE STRENGTH EXCEEDS EVEN THAT OF GILGAMESH. THE TWO HEROES ENJOY A FRIENDSHIP/RIVALRY THAT DRIVES THEM THROUGH MANY DARING ADVENTURES AND THE DEFEAT OF NUMEROUS MONSTERS, MOST NOTABLY, THE MOUNTAIN-DWELLING OGRE..."
"...HUMBABA!"

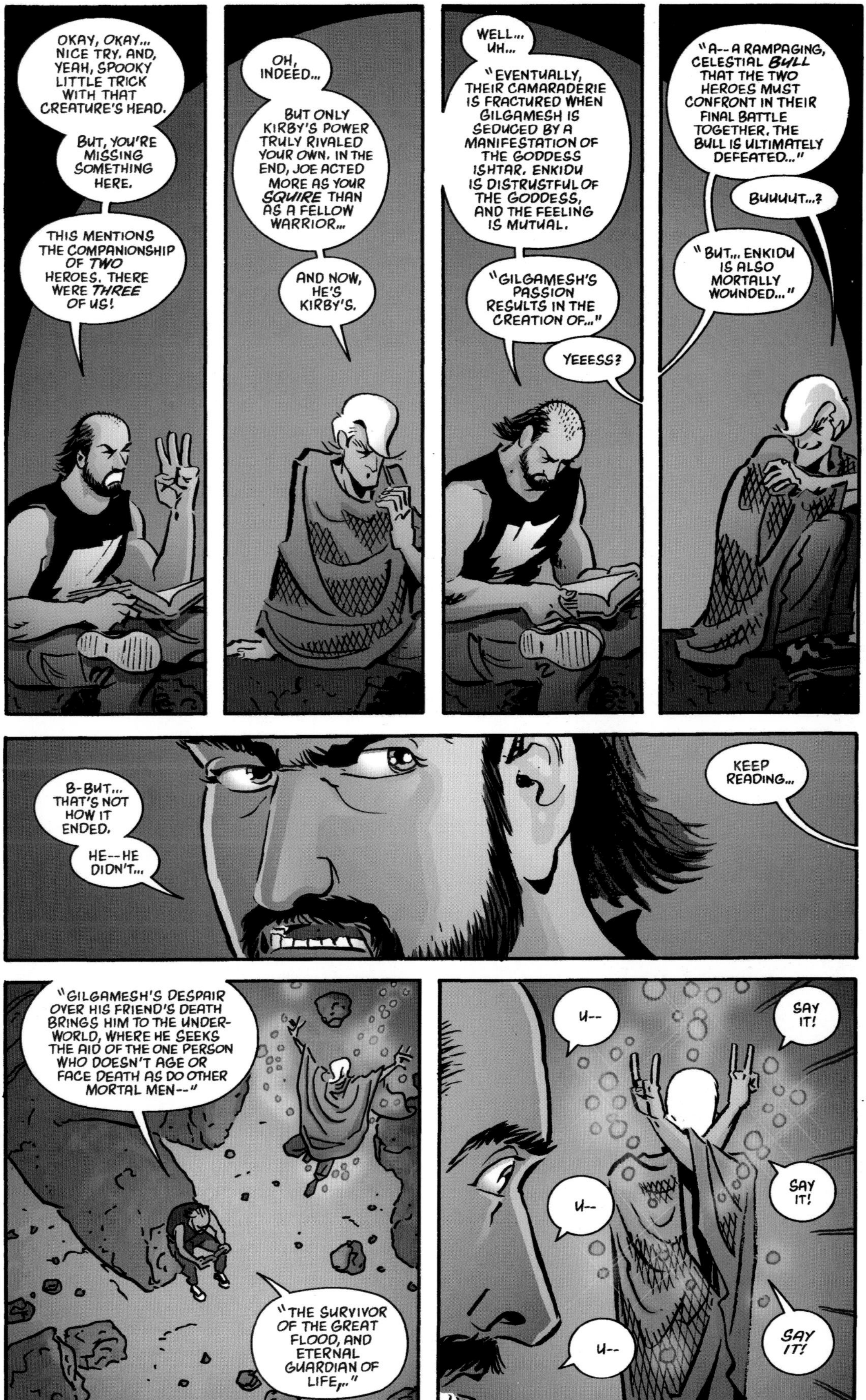
OKAY, OKAY... NICE TRY. AND, YEAH, SPOOKY LITTLE TRICK WITH THAT CREATURE'S HEAD.
BUT, YOU'RE MISSING SOMETHING HERE.
THIS MENTIONS THE COMPANIONSHIP OF TWO HEROES. THERE WERE THREE OF US!
OH, INDEED...
BUT ONLY KIRBY'S POWER TRULY RIVALED YOUR OWN. IN THE END, JOE ACTED MORE AS YOUR SQUIRE THAN AS A FELLOW WARRIOR...
AND NOW, HE'S KIRBY'S.
WELL... UH...
"EVENTUALLY, THEIR CAMARADERIE IS FRACTURED WHEN GILGAMESH IS SEDUCED BY A MANIFESTATION OF THE GODDESS ISHTAR. ENKIDU IS DISTRUSTFUL OF THE GODDESS, AND THE FEELING IS MUTUAL.
"GILGAMESH'S PASSION RESULTS IN THE CREATION OF..."
YEEESS?
"A-- A RAMPAGING, CELESTIAL BULL THAT THE TWO HEROES MUST CONFRONT IN THEIR FINAL BATTLE TOGETHER. THE BULL IS ULTIMATELY DEFEATED..."
BUUUUT...?
"BUT... ENKIDU IS ALSO MORTALLY WOUNDED..."
B-BUT... THAT'S NOT HOW IT ENDED.
HE--HE DIDN'T...
KEEP READING...
"GILGAMESH'S DESPAIR OVER HIS FRIEND'S DEATH BRINGS HIM TO THE UNDER-WORLD, WHERE HE SEEKS THE AID OF THE ONE PERSON WHO DOESN'T AGE OR FACE DEATH AS DO OTHER MORTAL MEN--"
"THE SURVIVOR OF THE GREAT FLOOD, AND ETERNAL GUARDIAN OF LIFE,..."
U--
SAY IT!
U--
SAY IT!
U--
SAY IT!

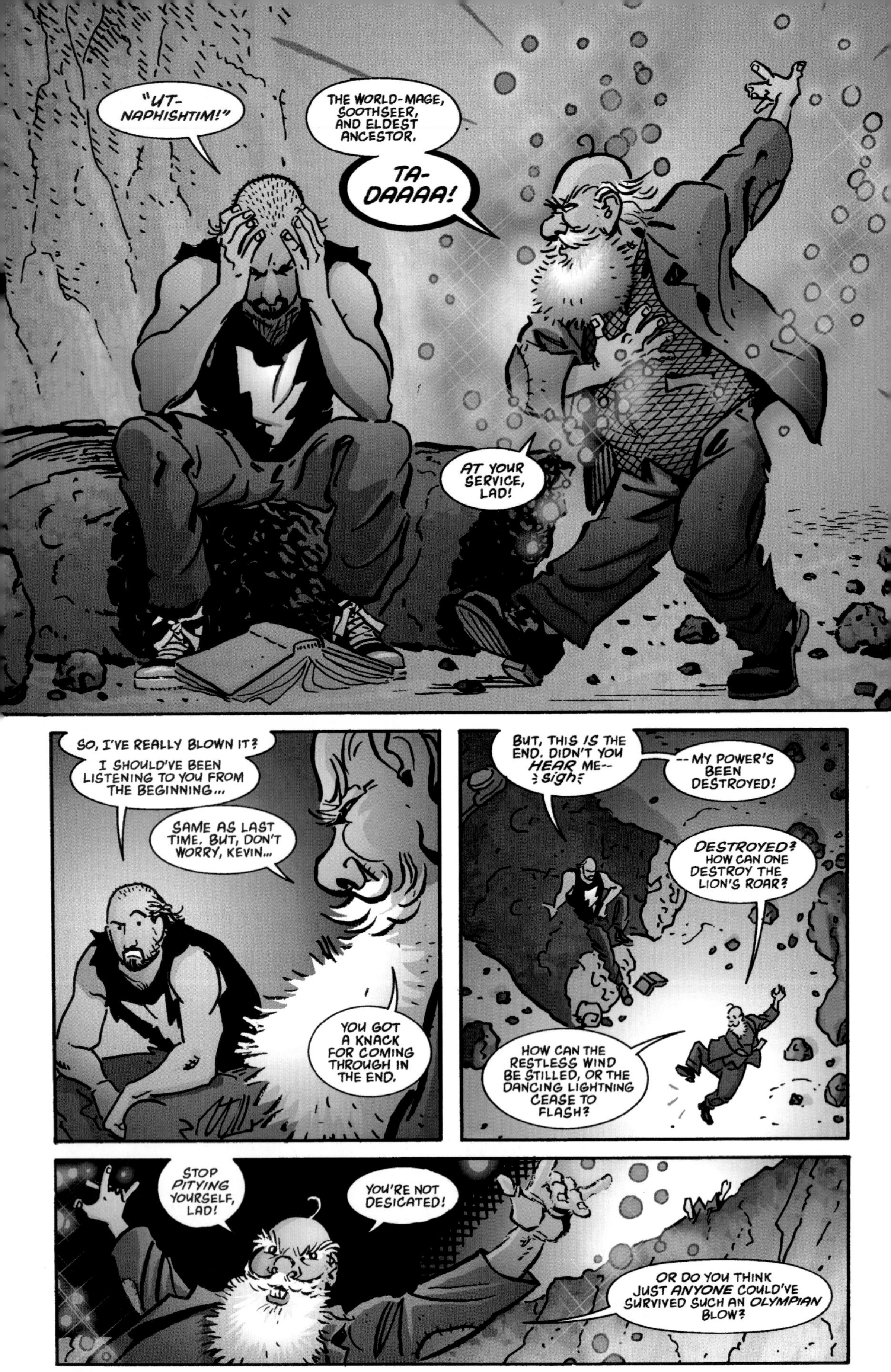
"UT-NAPHISHTIM!"
THE WORLD-MAGE, SOOTHSEER, AND ELDEST ANCESTOR.
TA-DAAAA!
AT YOUR SERVICE, LAD!
SO, I'VE REALLY BLOWN IT?
I SHOULD'VE BEEN LISTENING TO YOU FROM THE BEGINNING...
SAME AS LAST TIME. BUT, DON'T WORRY, KEVIN...
YOU GOT A KNACK FOR COMING THROUGH IN THE END.
BUT, THIS IS THE END. DIDN'T YOU HEAR ME-- *sigh*
--MY POWER'S BEEN DESTROYED!
DESTROYED? HOW CAN ONE DESTROY THE LION'S ROAR?
HOW CAN THE RESTLESS WIND BE STILLED, OR THE DANCING LIGHTNING CEASE TO FLASH?
STOP PITYING YOURSELF, LAD!
YOU'RE NOT DESICATED!
OR DO YOU THINK JUST ANYONE COULD'VE SURVIVED SUCH AN OLYMPIAN BLOW?

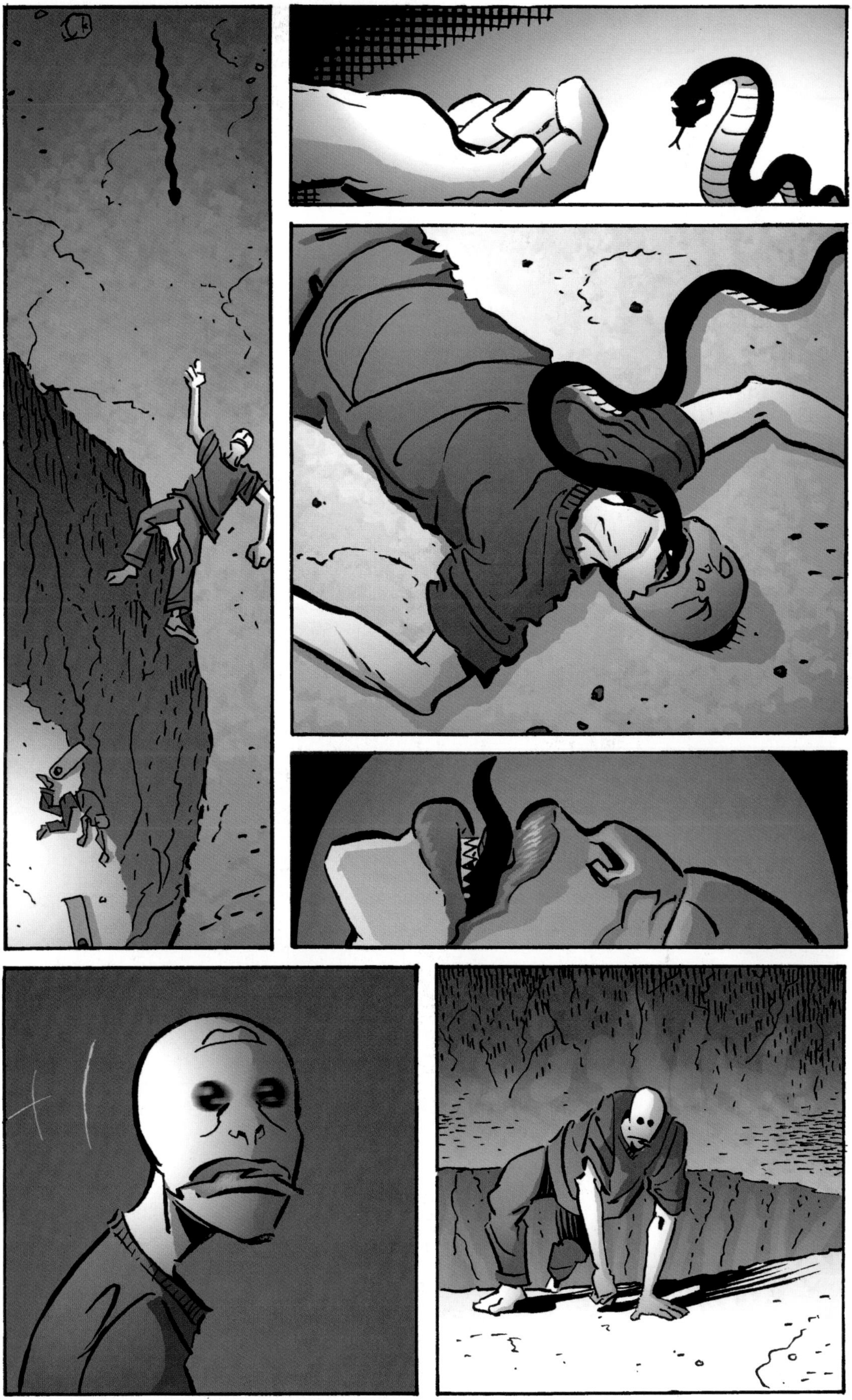

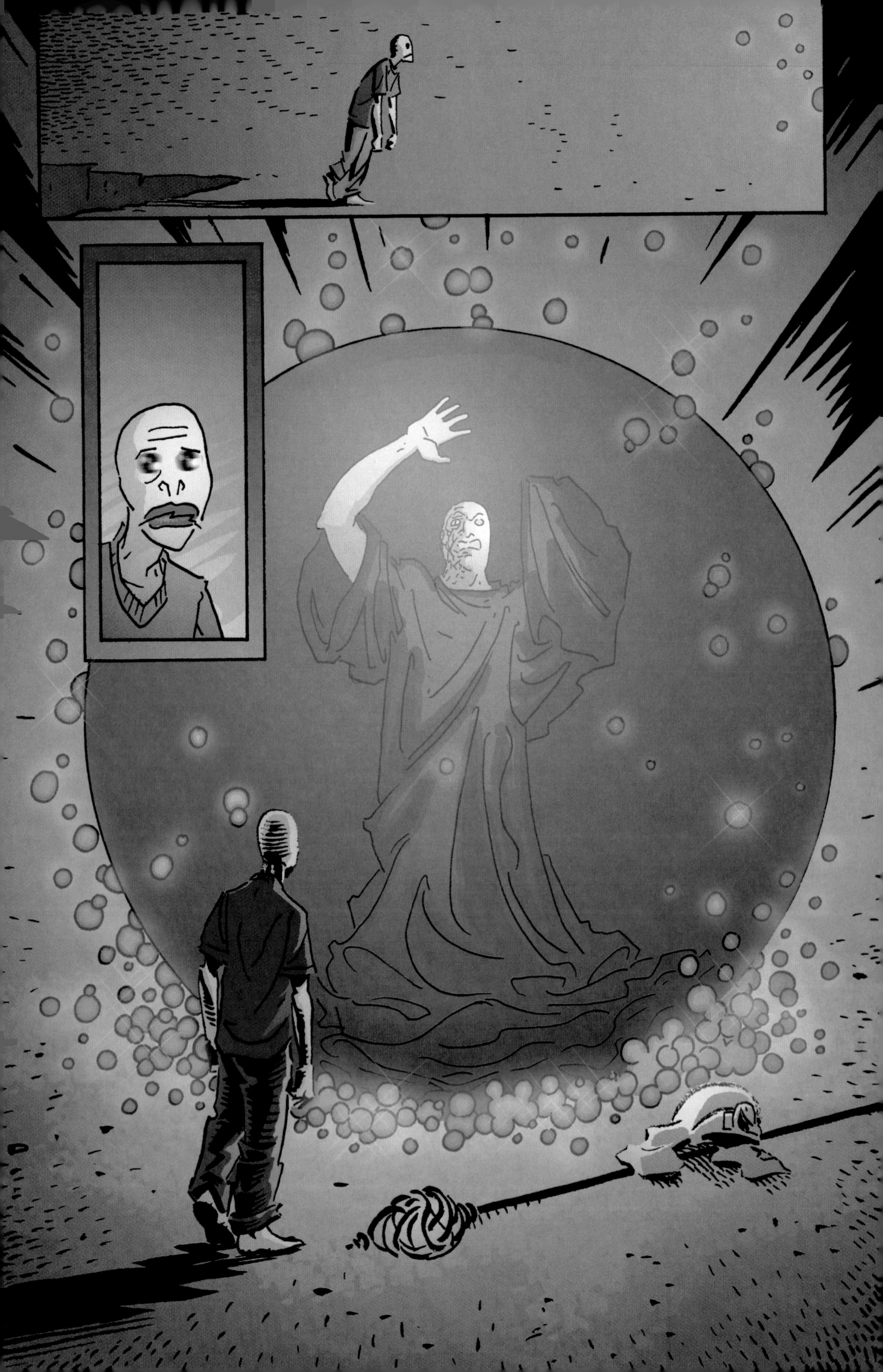

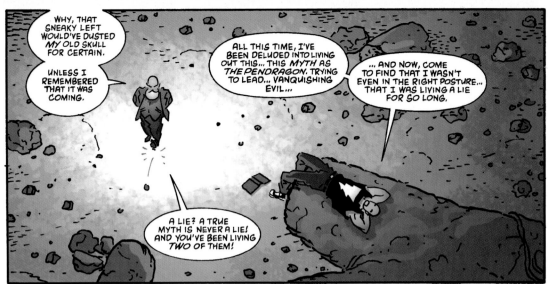

WHY, THAT SNEAKY LEFT WOULD'VE DUSTED *MY* OLD SKULL FOR CERTAIN.

UNLESS I REMEMBERED THAT IT WAS COMING.

ALL THIS TIME, I'VE BEEN DELUDED INTO LIVING OUT THIS... THIS *MYTH* AS *THE PENDRAGON.* TRYING TO LEAD... VANQUISHING EVIL...

... AND NOW, COME TO FIND THAT I WASN'T EVEN IN THE RIGHT POSTURE... THAT I WAS LIVING A LIE FOR SO LONG.

A LIE? A TRUE MYTH IS NEVER A LIE! AND YOU'VE BEEN LIVING *TWO* OF THEM!

AND MAGIC... JUST WHAT THE HELL COLOR *IS* MAGIC?

MAGIC ISN'T *A* COLOR, LAD! IT *IS* COLOR!

IT IS ARRANT SENSATION AND RAPTUROUS FRUITION! IT IS THE BLOOM OF TRANSFERAL AND THE PERSISTANCE OF WISHES.

IT IS THE OOZE THAT OILS THE GEARS OF EXISTENCE.

BUT, MIRTH SAID...

BAH! HE TOLD YOU WHAT YOU NEEDED TO *HEAR!*

FORGET IT!

THE NAME IS NOT AS IMPORTANT AS THE GAME!

ALL THIS TIME, YOU'VE BEEN TOO BUSY TRYING TO FIX THE MISTAKES OF YOUR ARROGANT RELUCTANCE. REMEMBER, FOXFIRE, THE POWER IS *YOU,* ALTHOUGH YOU ARE NOT *IT.*

THAT, AT LEAST, THE FIRST MAGE TAUGHT YOU TRUE.

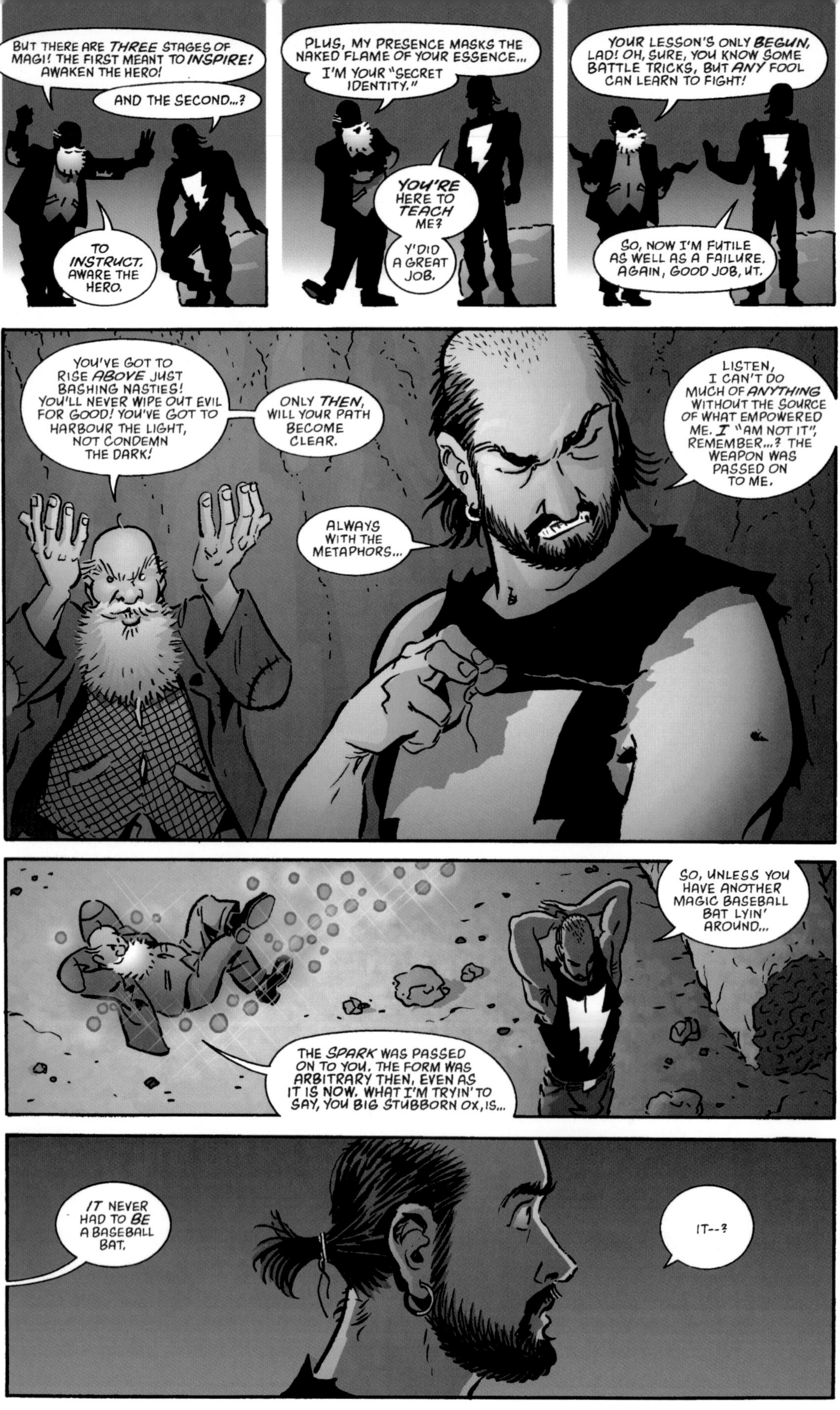

BUT THERE ARE THREE STAGES OF MAGI! THE FIRST MEANT TO INSPIRE! AWAKEN THE HERO!
AND THE SECOND...?
TO INSTRUCT. AWARE THE HERO.
PLUS, MY PRESENCE MASKS THE NAKED FLAME OF YOUR ESSENCE... I'M YOUR "SECRET IDENTITY."
YOU'RE HERE TO TEACH ME?
Y'DID A GREAT JOB.
YOUR LESSON'S ONLY BEGUN, LAD! OH, SURE, YOU KNOW SOME BATTLE TRICKS, BUT ANY FOOL CAN LEARN TO FIGHT!
SO, NOW I'M FUTILE AS WELL AS A FAILURE. AGAIN, GOOD JOB, UT.
YOU'VE GOT TO RISE ABOVE JUST BASHING NASTIES! YOU'LL NEVER WIPE OUT EVIL FOR GOOD! YOU'VE GOT TO HARBOUR THE LIGHT, NOT CONDEMN THE DARK!
ONLY THEN, WILL YOUR PATH BECOME CLEAR.
LISTEN, I CAN'T DO MUCH OF ANYTHING WITHOUT THE SOURCE OF WHAT EMPOWERED ME. I "AM NOT IT", REMEMBER...? THE WEAPON WAS PASSED ON TO ME.
ALWAYS WITH THE METAPHORS...
SO, UNLESS YOU HAVE ANOTHER MAGIC BASEBALL BAT LYIN' AROUND...
THE SPARK WAS PASSED ON TO YOU. THE FORM WAS ARBITRARY THEN, EVEN AS IT IS NOW. WHAT I'M TRYIN' TO SAY, YOU BIG STUBBORN OX, IS...
IT NEVER HAD TO BE A BASEBALL BAT.
IT--?

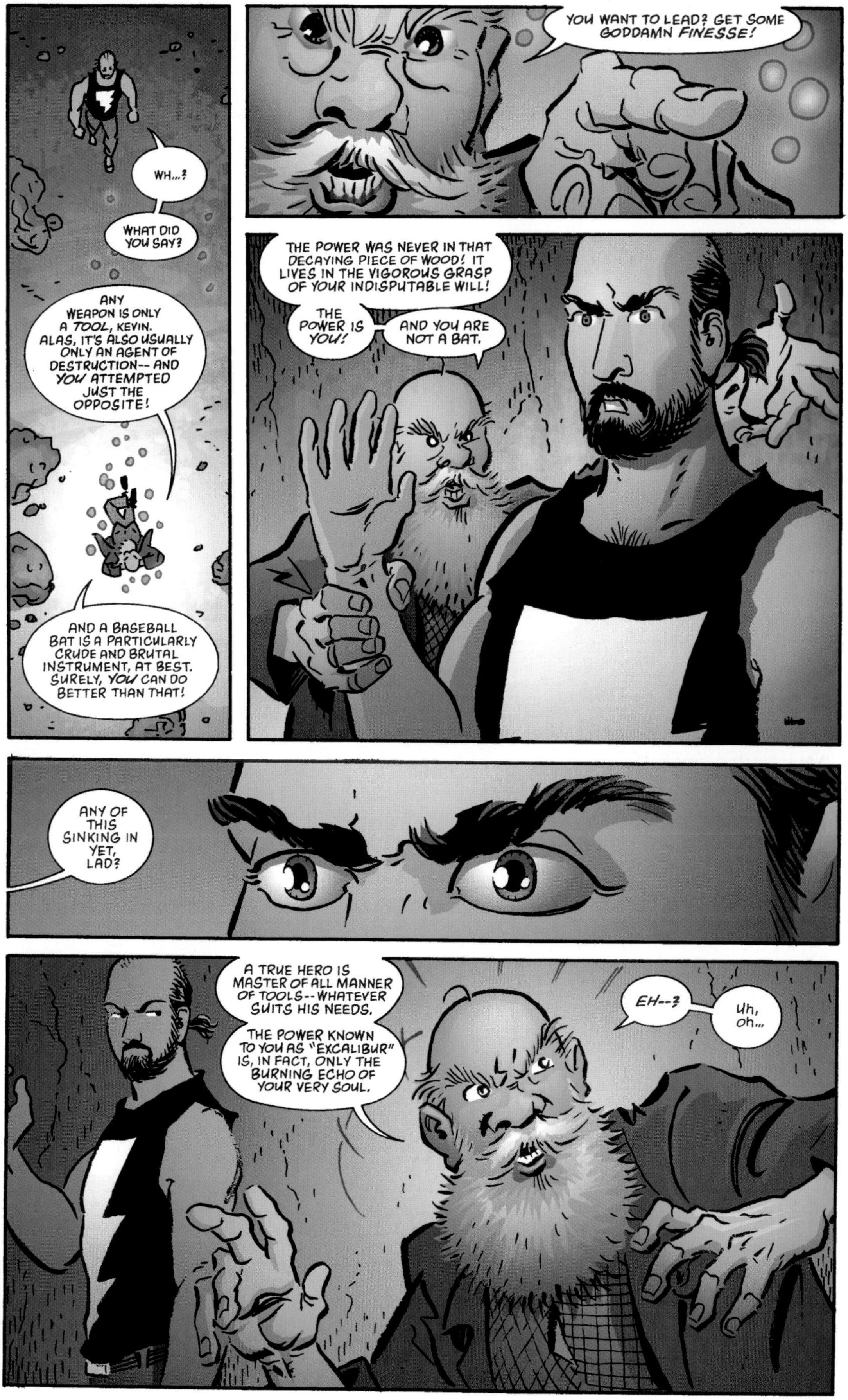
WH...?
WHAT DID YOU SAY?
ANY WEAPON IS ONLY A TOOL, KEVIN. ALAS, IT'S ALSO USUALLY ONLY AN AGENT OF DESTRUCTION-- AND YOU ATTEMPTED JUST THE OPPOSITE!
AND A BASEBALL BAT IS A PARTICULARLY CRUDE AND BRUTAL INSTRUMENT, AT BEST. SURELY, YOU CAN DO BETTER THAN THAT!
YOU WANT TO LEAD? GET SOME GODDAMN FINESSE!
THE POWER WAS NEVER IN THAT DECAYING PIECE OF WOOD! IT LIVES IN THE VIGOROUS GRASP OF YOUR INDISPUTABLE WILL!
THE POWER IS YOU!
AND YOU ARE NOT A BAT.
ANY OF THIS SINKING IN YET, LAD?
A TRUE HERO IS MASTER OF ALL MANNER OF TOOLS--WHATEVER SUITS HIS NEEDS.
THE POWER KNOWN TO YOU AS "EXCALIBUR" IS, IN FACT, ONLY THE BURNING ECHO OF YOUR VERY SOUL.
EH--?
Uh, oh...

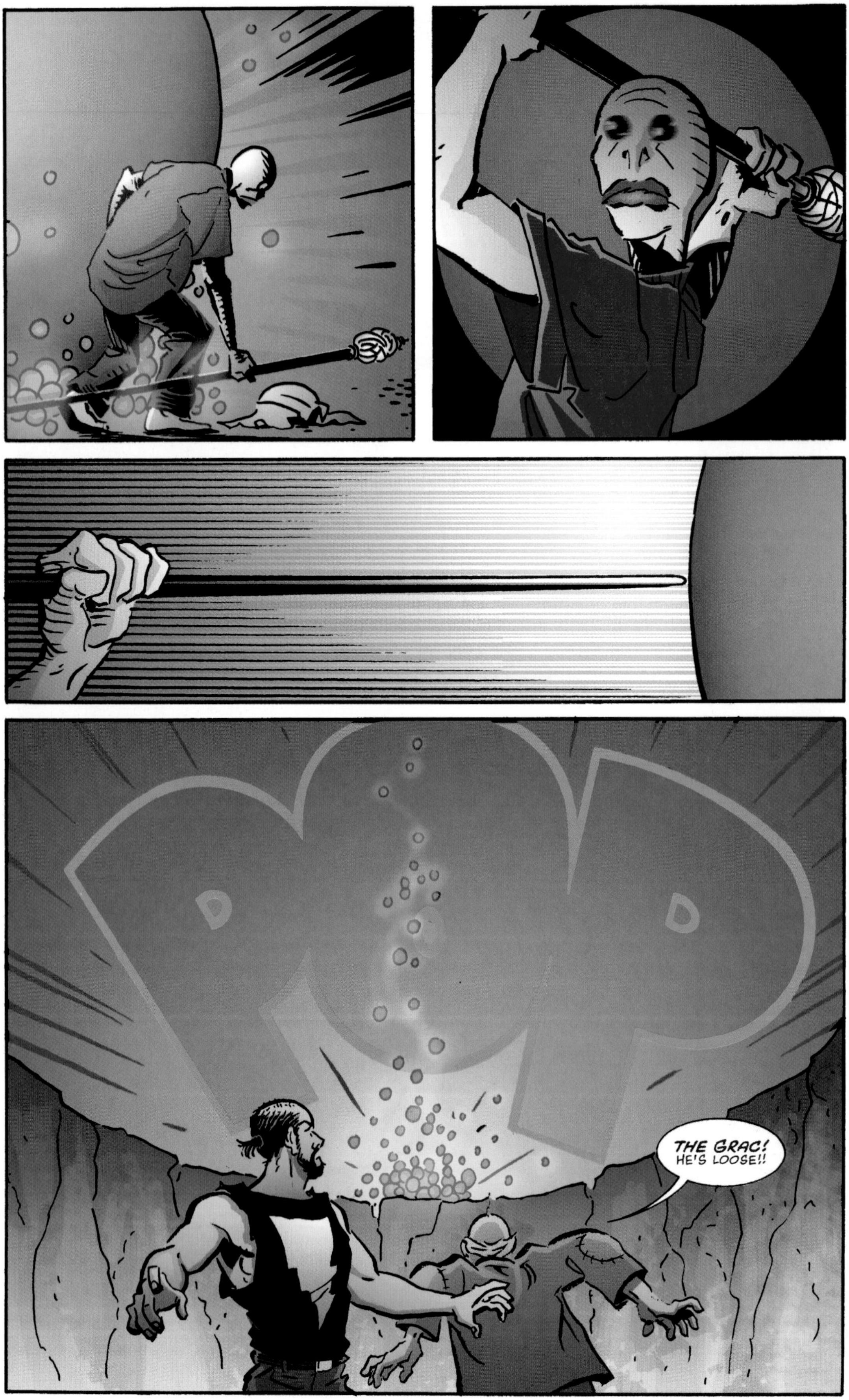
POP
THE GRAC! HE'S LOOSE!!

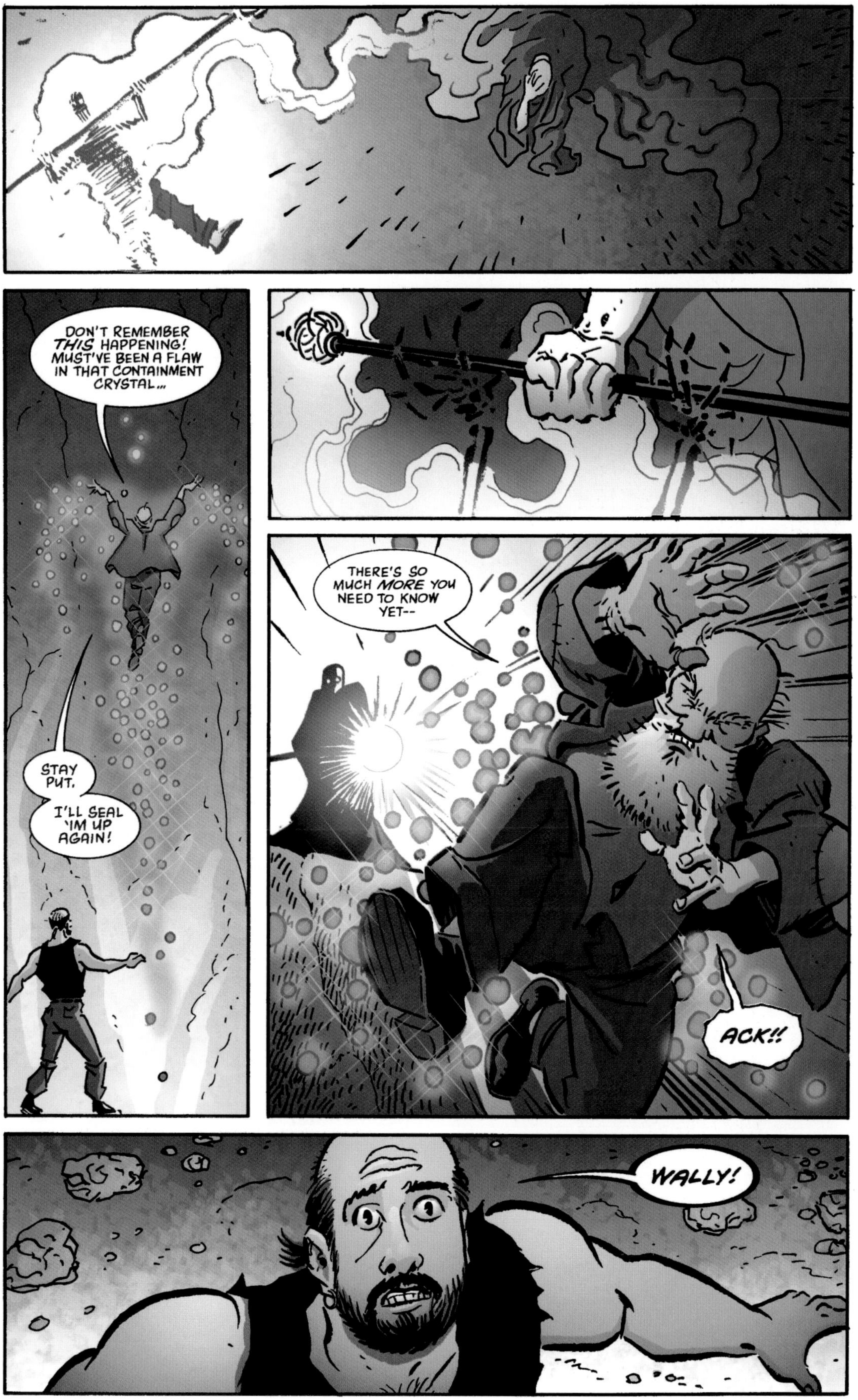
DON'T REMEMBER THIS HAPPENING! MUST'VE BEEN A FLAW IN THAT CONTAINMENT CRYSTAL...
STAY PUT.
I'LL SEAL 'IM UP AGAIN!
THERE'S SO MUCH MORE YOU NEED TO KNOW YET--
ACK!!
WALLY!

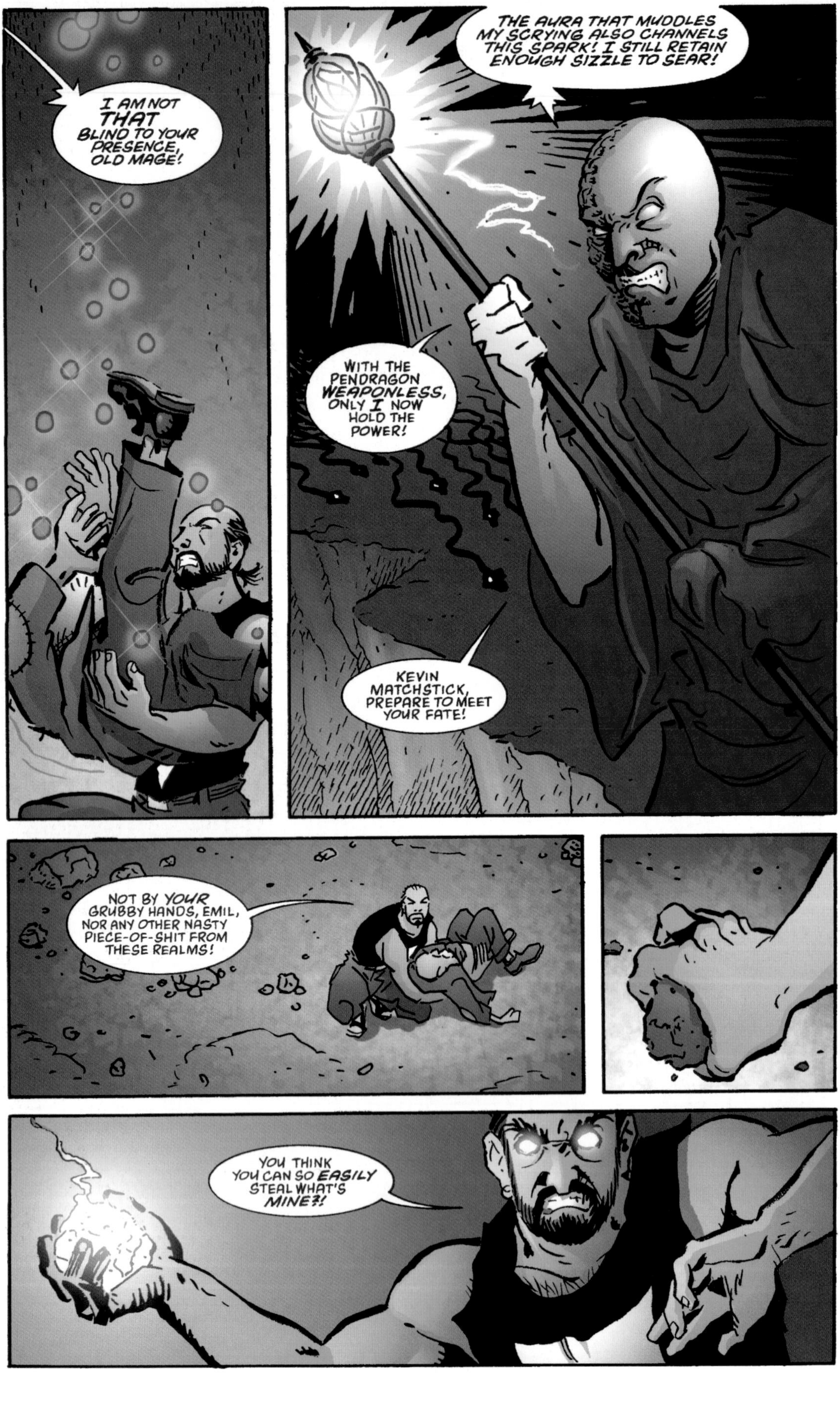
I AM NOT THAT BLIND TO YOUR PRESENCE, OLD MAGE!
THE AURA THAT MUDDLES MY SCRYING ALSO CHANNELS THIS SPARK! I STILL RETAIN ENOUGH SIZZLE TO SEAR!
WITH THE PENDRAGON WEAPONLESS, ONLY I NOW HOLD THE POWER!
KEVIN MATCHSTICK, PREPARE TO MEET YOUR FATE!
NOT BY YOUR GRUBBY HANDS, EMIL, NOR ANY OTHER NASTY PIECE-OF-SHIT FROM THESE REALMS!
YOU THINK YOU CAN SO EASILY STEAL WHAT'S MINE?!

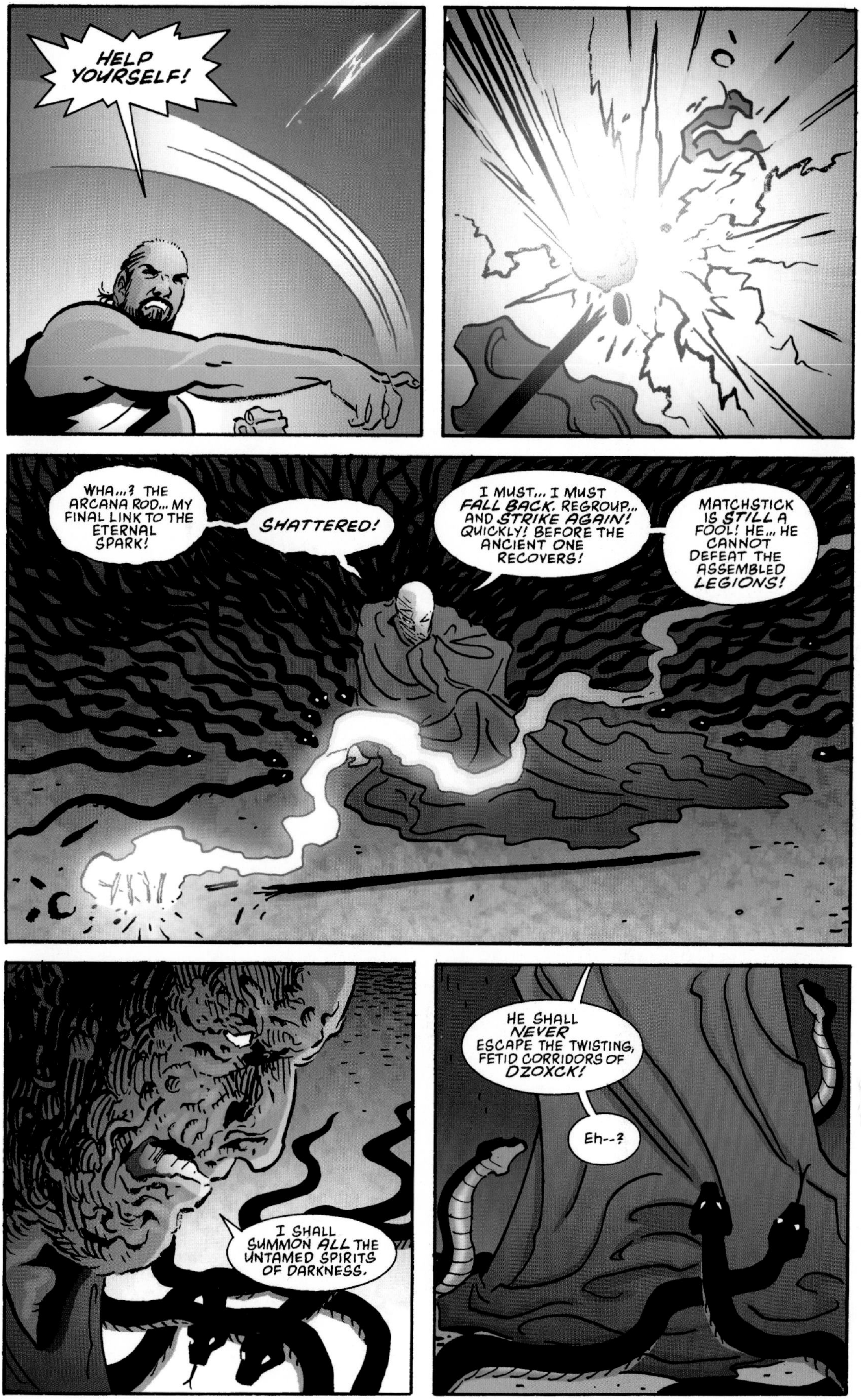
HELP YOURSELF!
WHA...? THE ARCANA ROD... MY FINAL LINK TO THE ETERNAL SPARK!
SHATTERED!
I MUST... I MUST FALL BACK. REGROUP... AND STRIKE AGAIN! QUICKLY! BEFORE THE ANCIENT ONE RECOVERS!
MATCHSTICK IS STILL A FOOL! HE... HE CANNOT DEFEAT THE ASSEMBLED LEGIONS!
I SHALL SUMMON ALL THE UNTAMED SPIRITS OF DARKNESS.
HE SHALL NEVER ESCAPE THE TWISTING, FETID CORRIDORS OF DZOXCK!
Eh--?

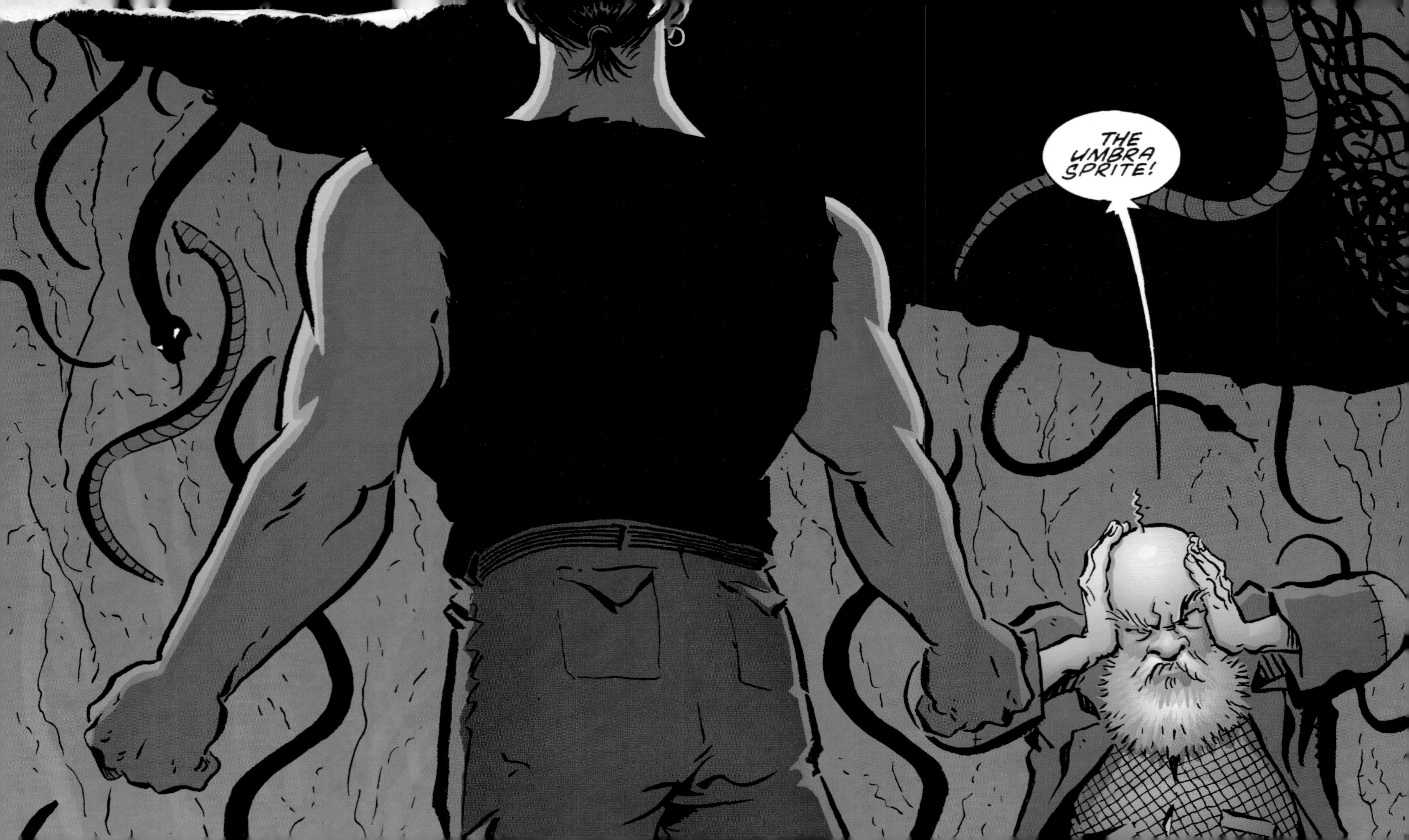
THE UMBRA SPRITE!

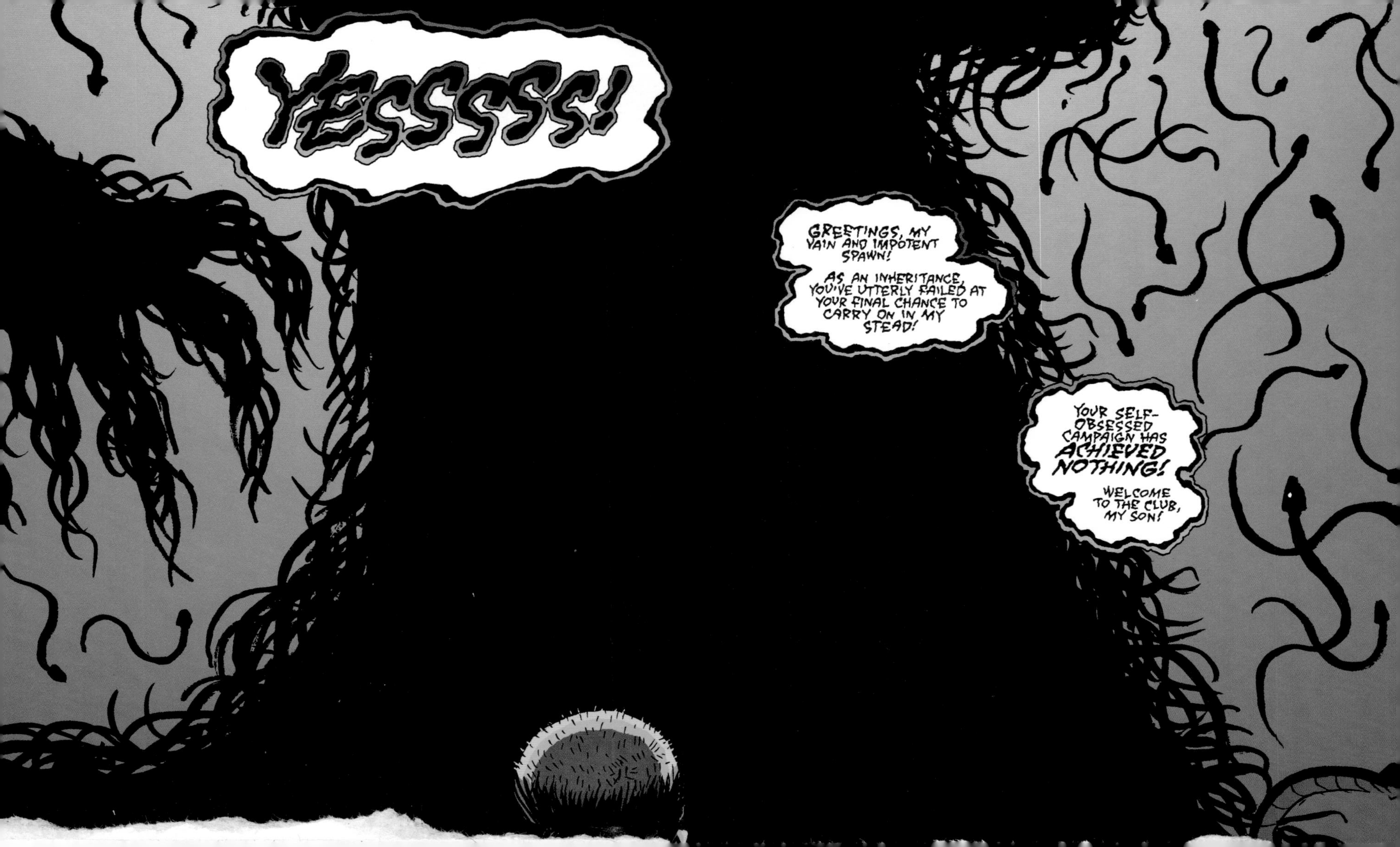
YESSSSS!
GREETINGS, MY VAIN AND IMPOTENT SPAWN!
AS AN INHERITANCE, YOU'VE UTTERLY FAILED AT YOUR FINAL CHANCE TO CARRY ON IN MY STEAD!
YOUR SELF-OBSESSED CAMPAIGN HAS ACHIEVED NOTHING!
WELCOME TO THE CLUB, MY SON!

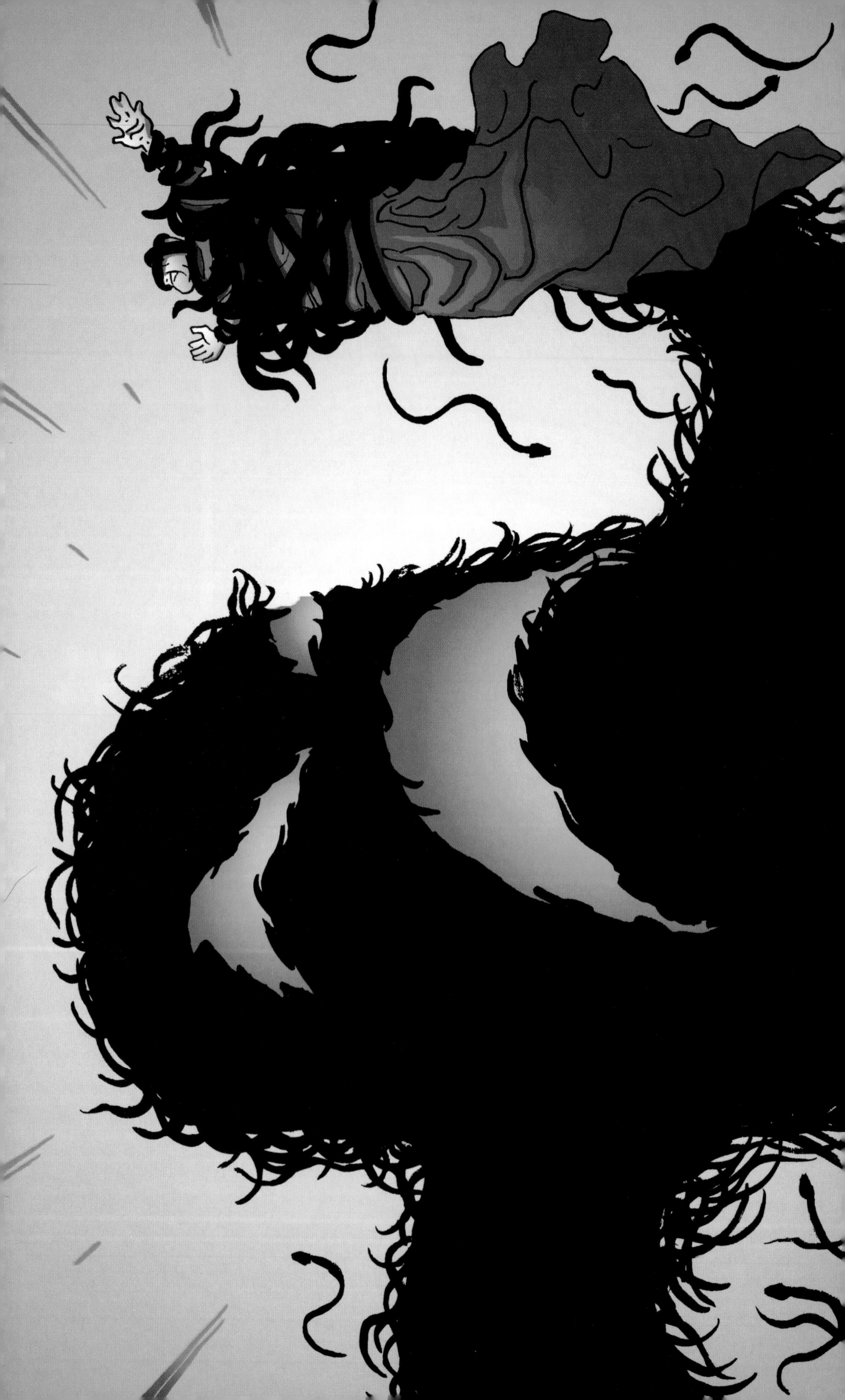

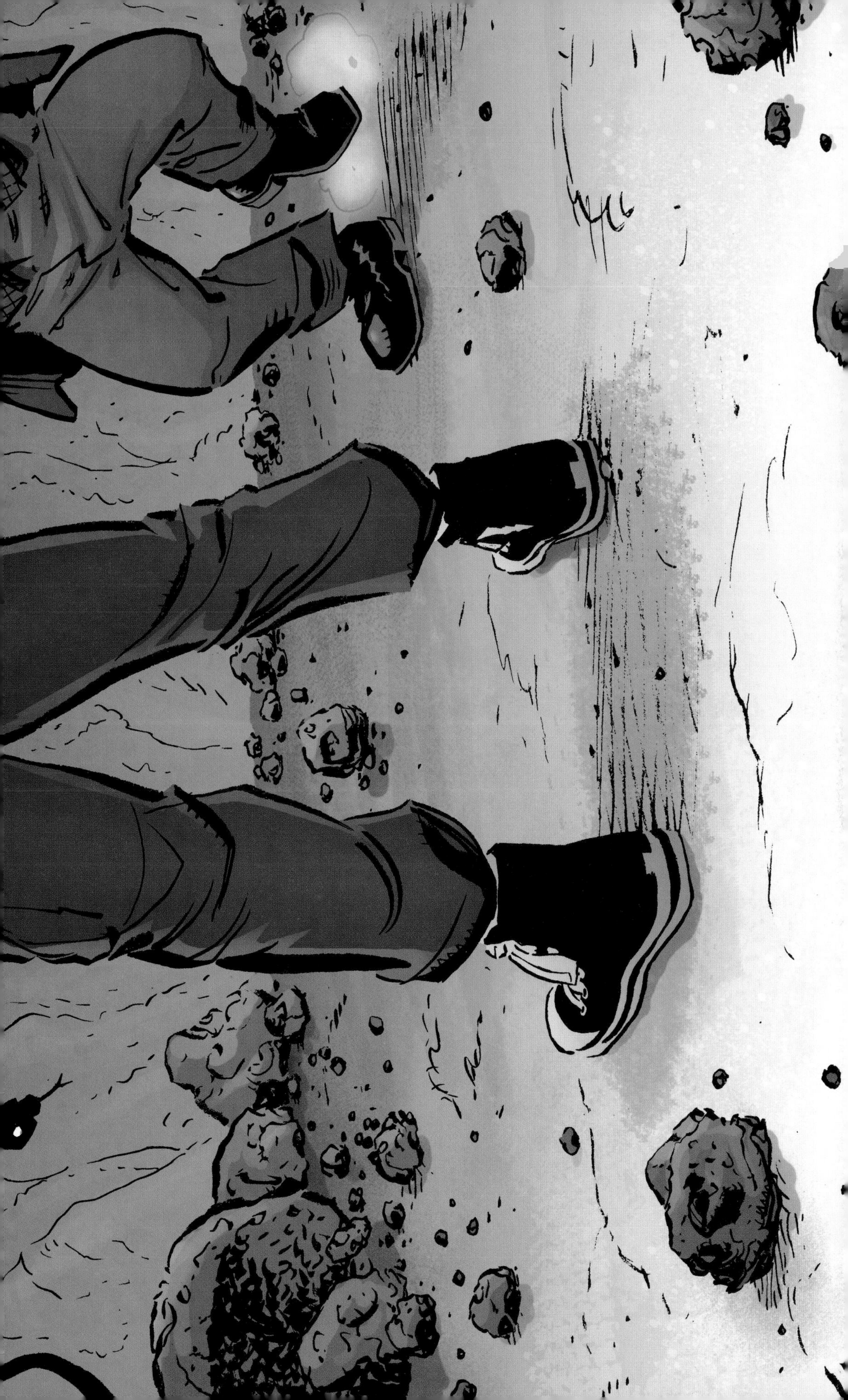

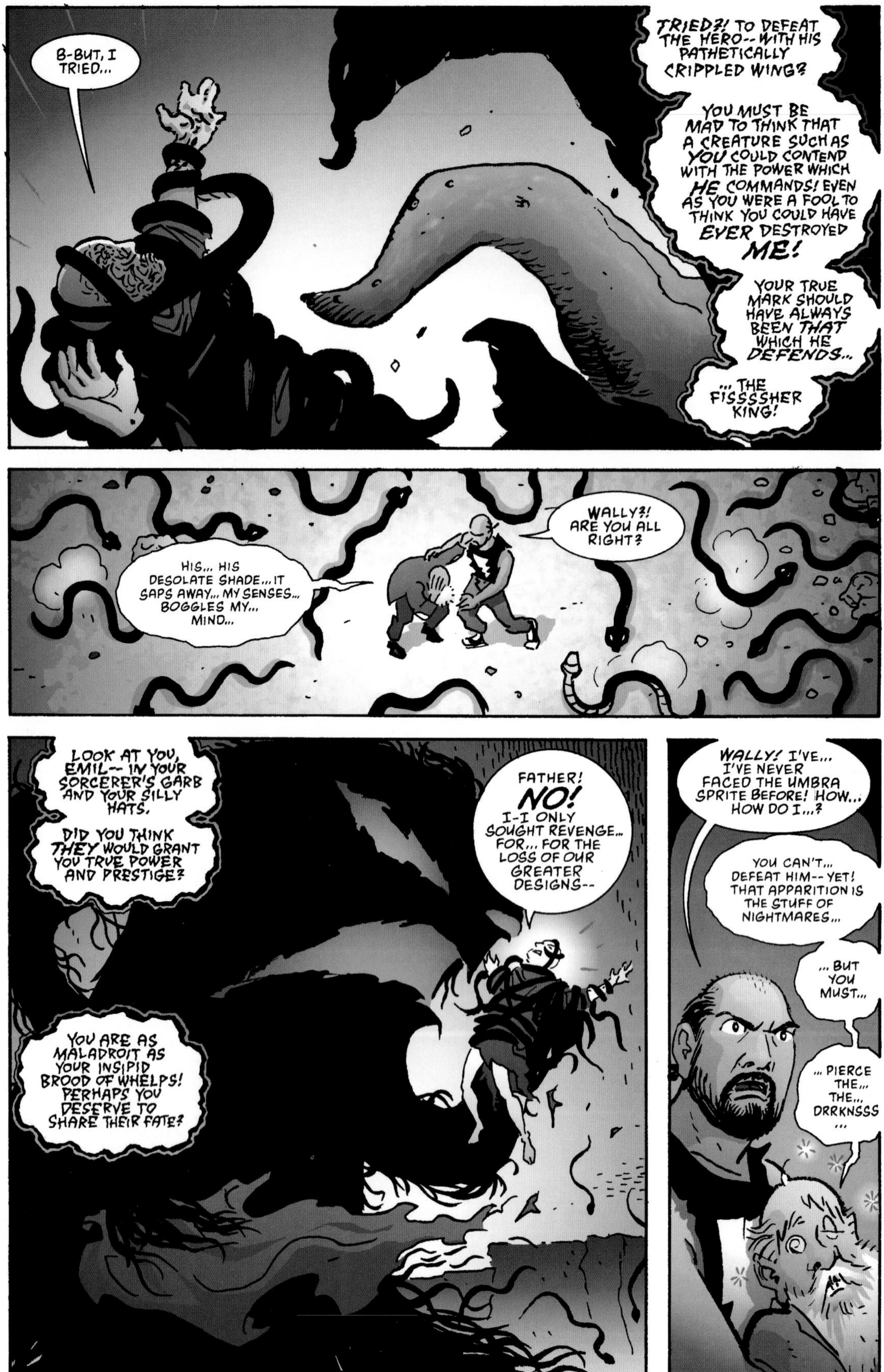
B-BUT, I TRIED...
TRIED?! TO DEFEAT THE HERO-- WITH HIS PATHETICALLY CRIPPLED WING?
YOU MUST BE MAD TO THINK THAT A CREATURE SUCH AS YOU COULD CONTEND WITH THE POWER WHICH HE COMMANDS! EVEN AS YOU WERE A FOOL TO THINK YOU COULD HAVE EVER DESTROYED ME!
YOUR TRUE MARK SHOULD HAVE ALWAYS BEEN THAT WHICH HE DEFENDS...
... THE FISSSSHER KING!
HIS... HIS DESOLATE SHADE... IT SAPS AWAY... MY SENSES... BOGGLES MY... MIND...
WALLY?! ARE YOU ALL RIGHT?
LOOK AT YOU, EMIL-- IN YOUR SORCERER'S GARB AND YOUR SILLY HATS.
DID YOU THINK THEY WOULD GRANT YOU TRUE POWER AND PRESTIGE?
FATHER! NO! I-I ONLY SOUGHT REVENGE... FOR... FOR THE LOSS OF OUR GREATER DESIGNS--
YOU ARE AS MALADROIT AS YOUR INSIPID BROOD OF WHELPS! PERHAPS YOU DESERVE TO SHARE THEIR FATE?
WALLY! I'VE... I'VE NEVER FACED THE UMBRA SPRITE BEFORE! HOW... HOW DO I...?
YOU CAN'T... DEFEAT HIM-- YET! THAT APPARITION IS THE STUFF OF NIGHTMARES...
... BUT YOU MUST...
... PIERCE THE... THE... DRRKNSSS ...

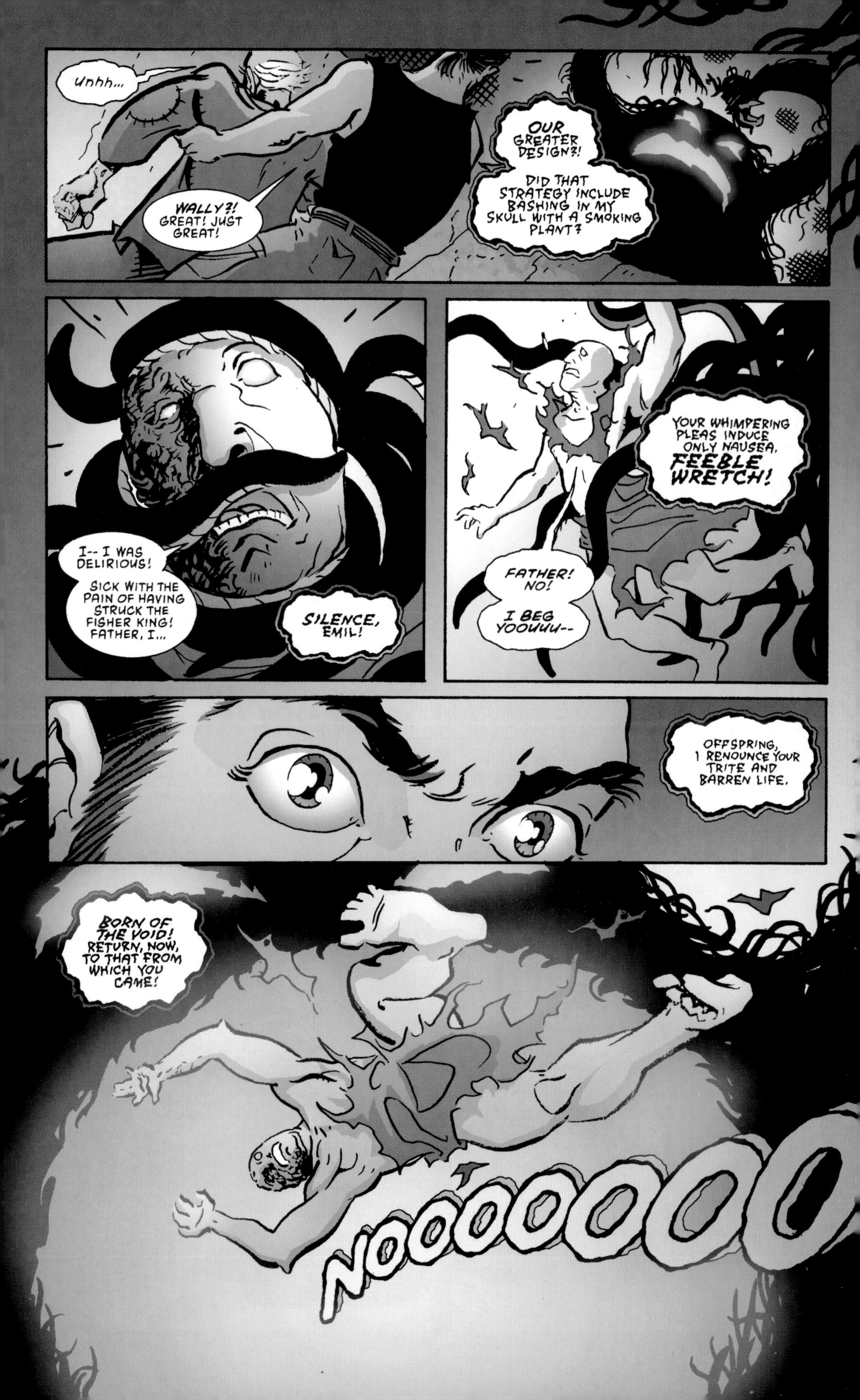

UNHH...
WALLY?! GREAT! JUST GREAT!
OUR GREATER DESIGN?!
DID THAT STRATEGY INCLUDE BASHING IN MY SKULL WITH A SMOKING PLANT?
I-- I WAS DELIRIOUS!
SICK WITH THE PAIN OF HAVING STRUCK THE FISHER KING! FATHER, I...
SILENCE, EMIL!
YOUR WHIMPERING PLEAS INDUCE ONLY NAUSEA. FEEBLE WRETCH!
FATHER! NO!
I BEG YOOUUU--
OFFSPRING, I RENOUNCE YOUR TRITE AND BARREN LIFE.
BORN OF THE VOID! RETURN, NOW, TO THAT FROM WHICH YOU CAME!
NOOOOOOOO

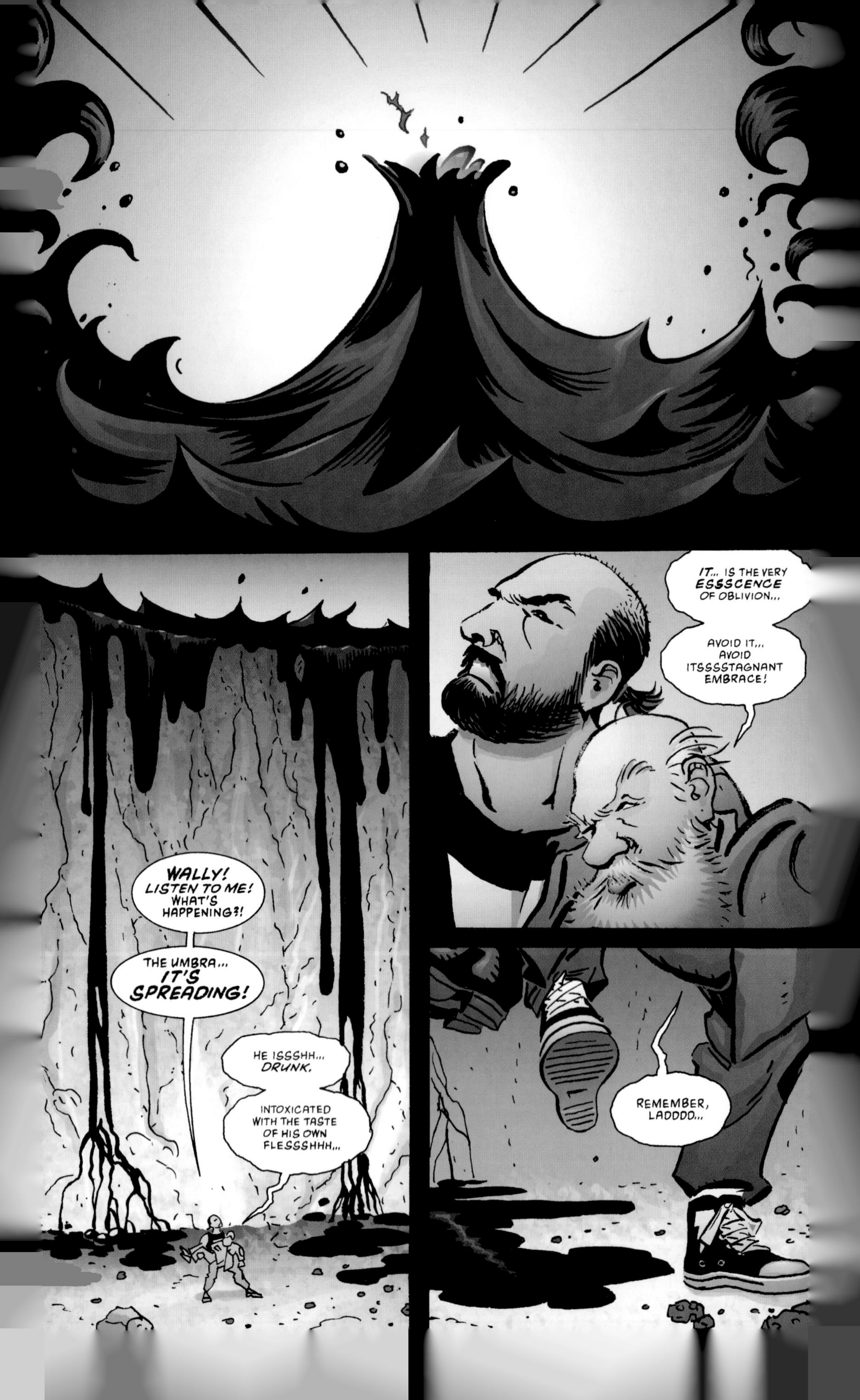
WALLY! LISTEN TO ME! WHAT'S HAPPENING?!
THE UMBRA... IT'S SPREADING!
HE ISSSHH... DRUNK.
INTOXICATED WITH THE TASTE OF HIS OWN FLESSSHHH...
IT... IS THE VERY ESSSCENCE OF OBLIVION...
AVOID IT... AVOID ITSSSSTAGNANT EMBRACE!
REMEMBER, LADDDD...

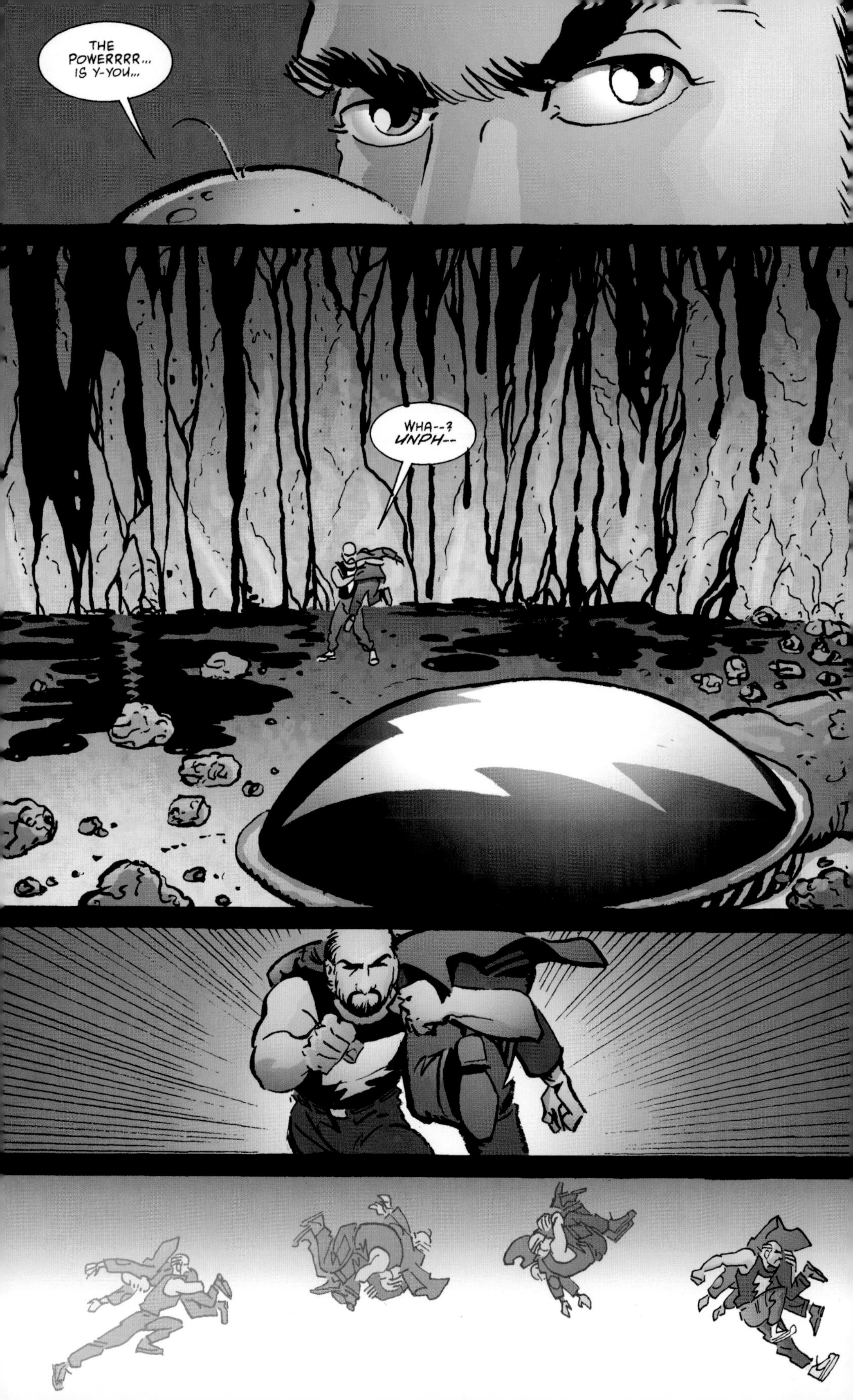
THE POWERRRR... IS Y-YOU...
WHA--? UNPH--

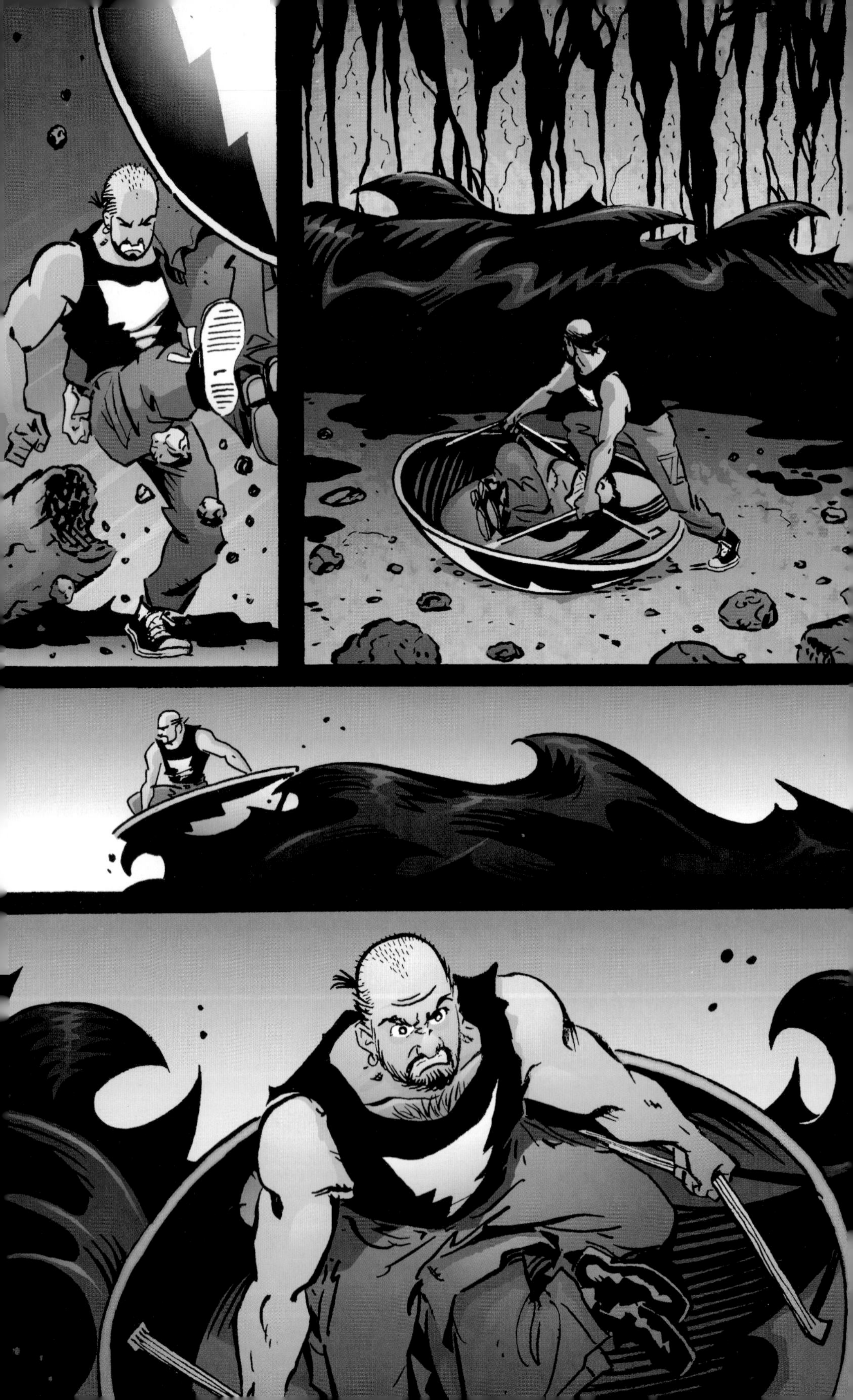

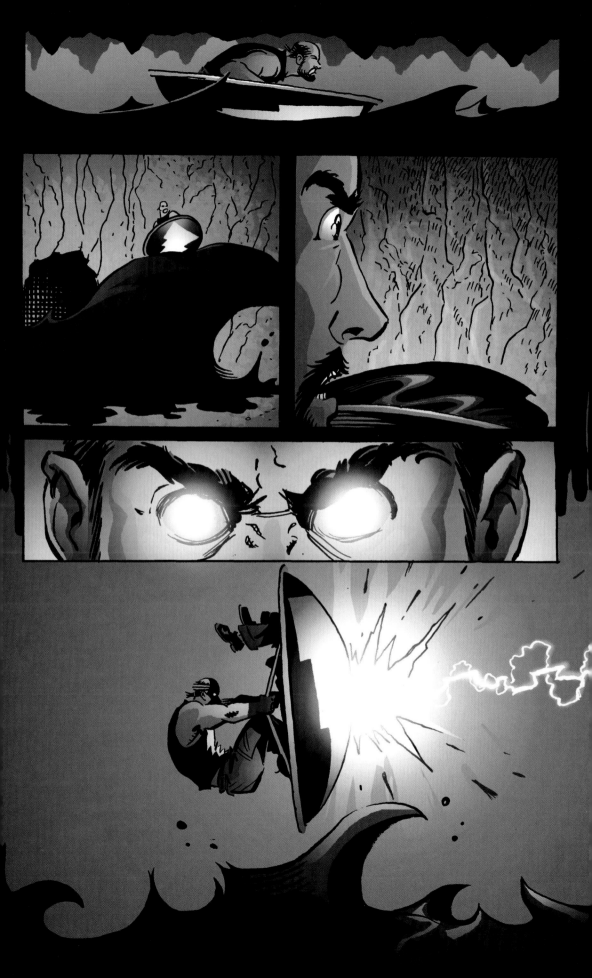

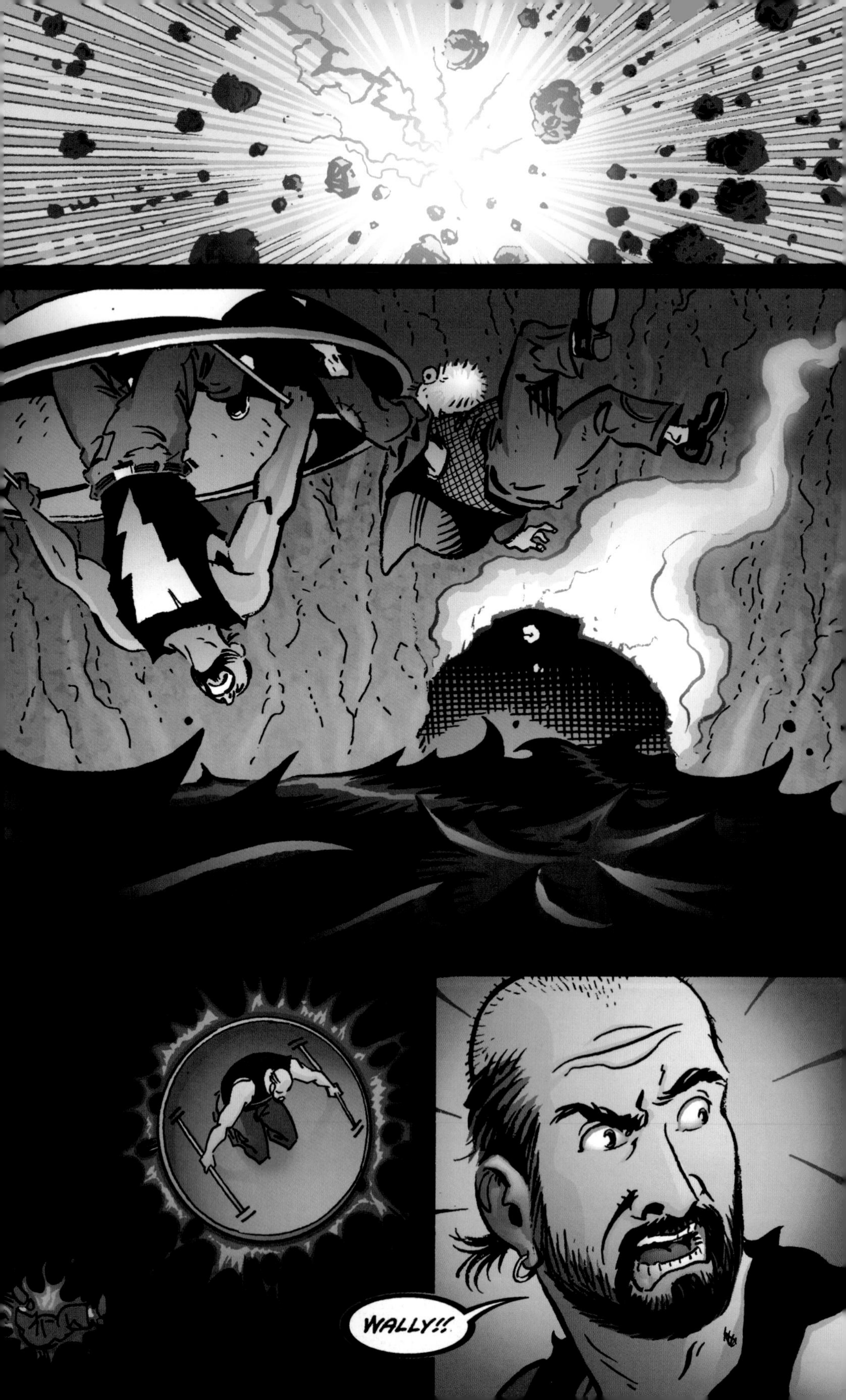
WALLY!!

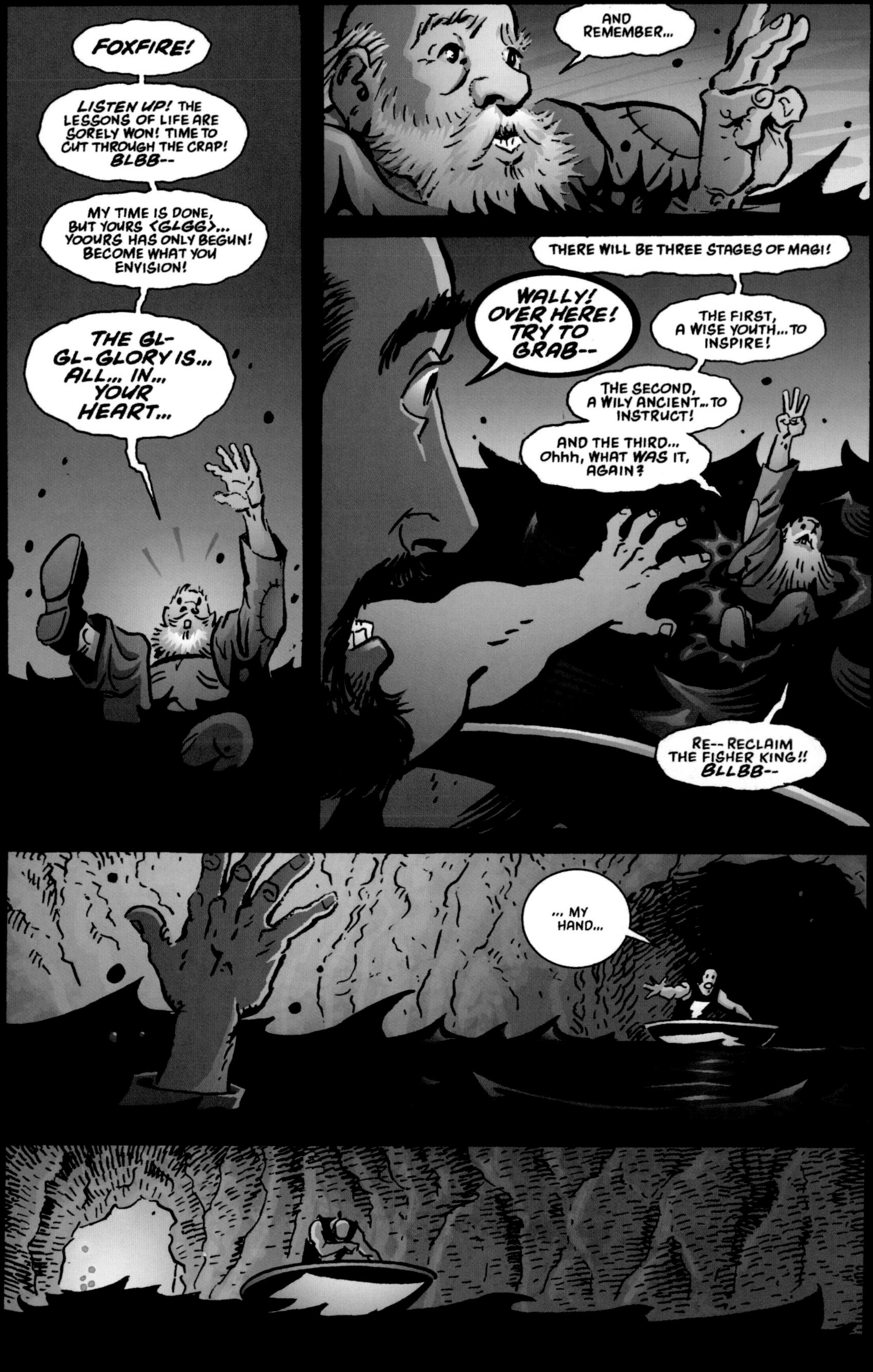
FOXFIRE!
LISTEN UP! THE LESSONS OF LIFE ARE SORELY WON! TIME TO CUT THROUGH THE CRAP! BLBB--
MY TIME IS DONE, BUT YOURS <GLGG>... YOOURS HAS ONLY BEGUN! BECOME WHAT YOU ENVISION!
THE GL-GL-GLORY IS... ALL... IN... YOUR HEART...
AND REMEMBER...
THERE WILL BE THREE STAGES OF MAGI!
WALLY! OVER HERE! TRY TO GRAB--
THE FIRST, A WISE YOUTH... TO INSPIRE!
THE SECOND, A WILY ANCIENT... TO INSTRUCT!
AND THE THIRD... Ohhh, WHAT WAS IT, AGAIN?
RE-- RECLAIM THE FISHER KING!! BLLBB--
... MY HAND...

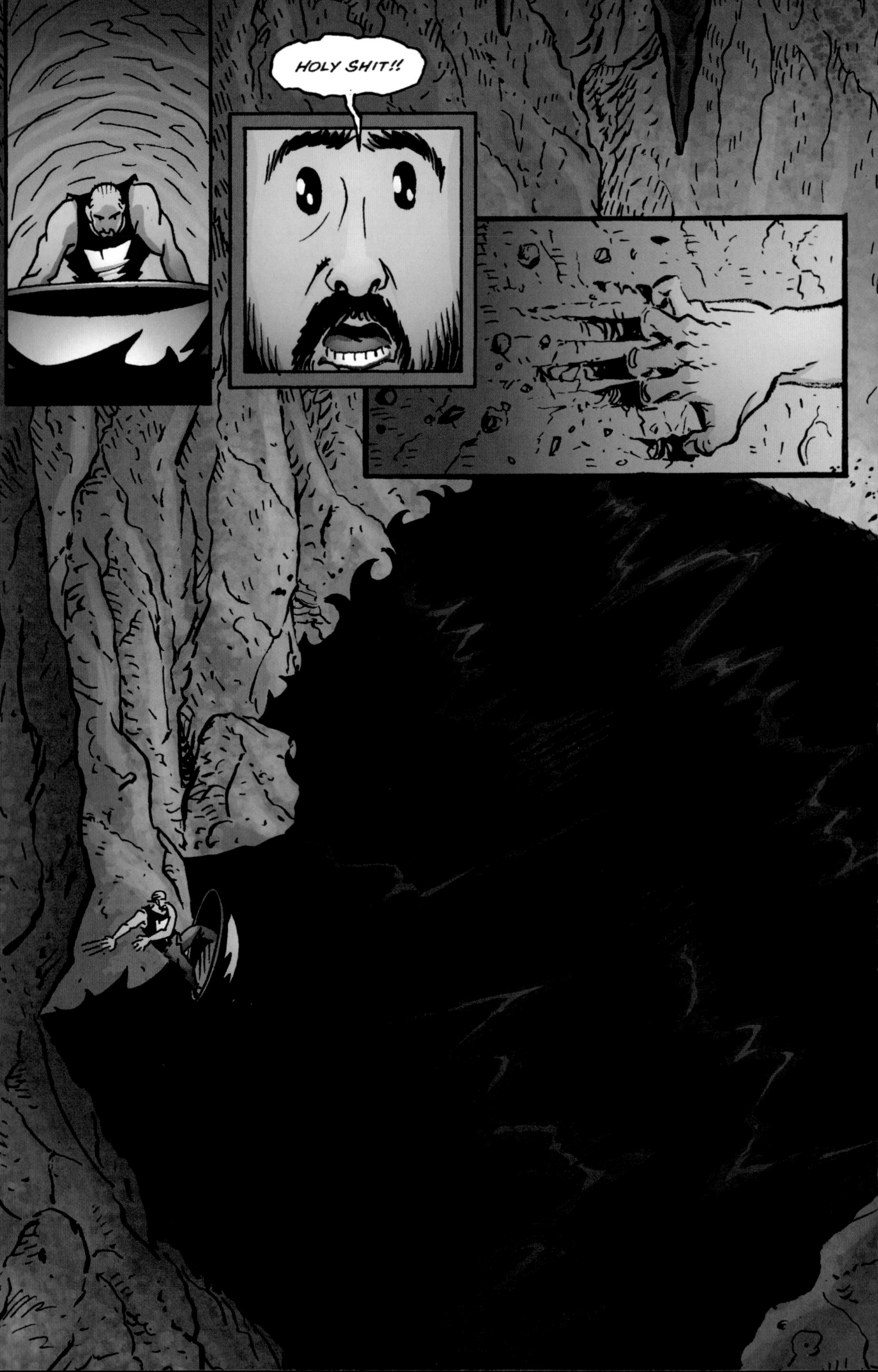
HOLY SHIT!!

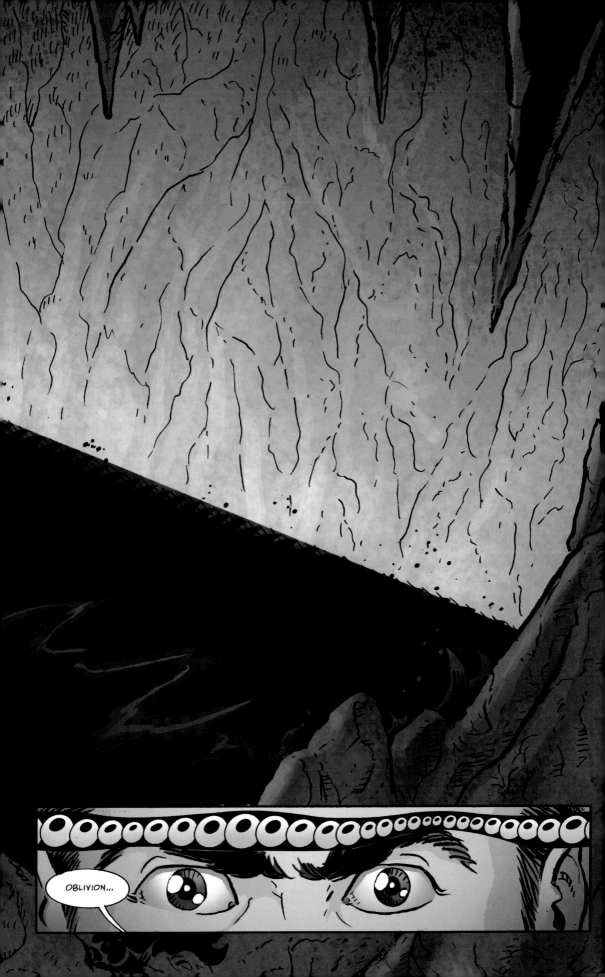

OBLIVION...

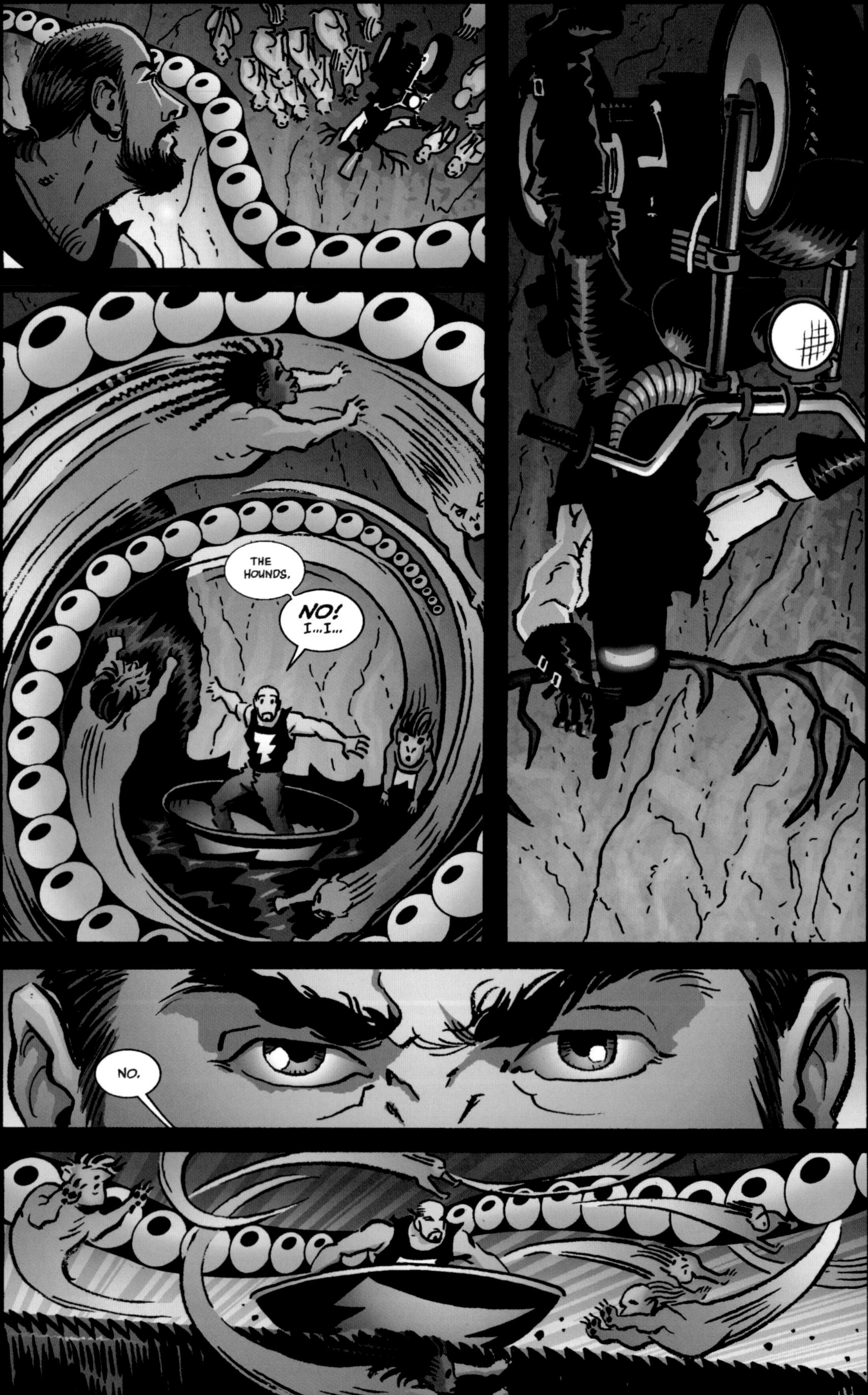
THE HOUNDS,
NO! I...I...
NO.

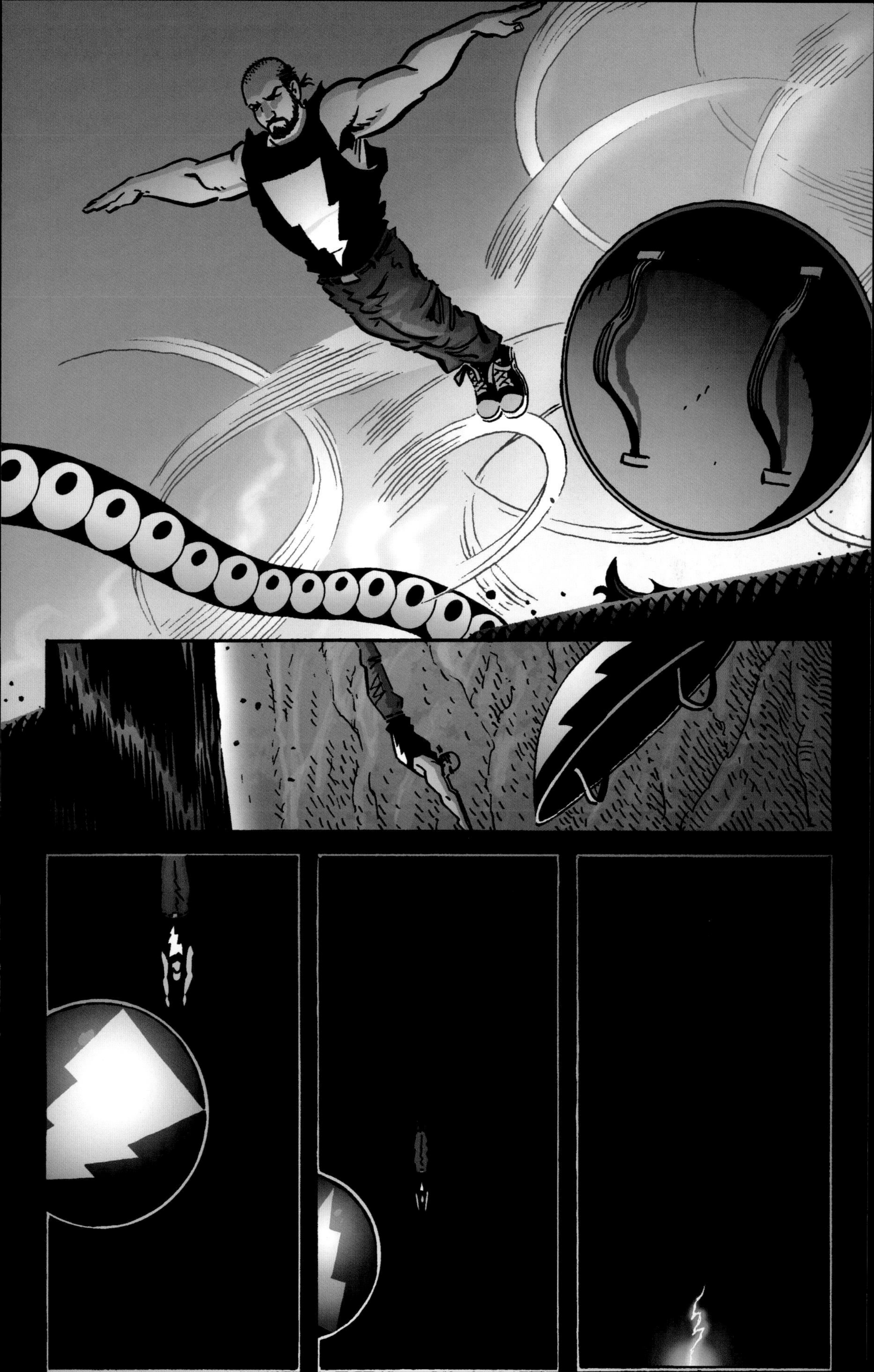

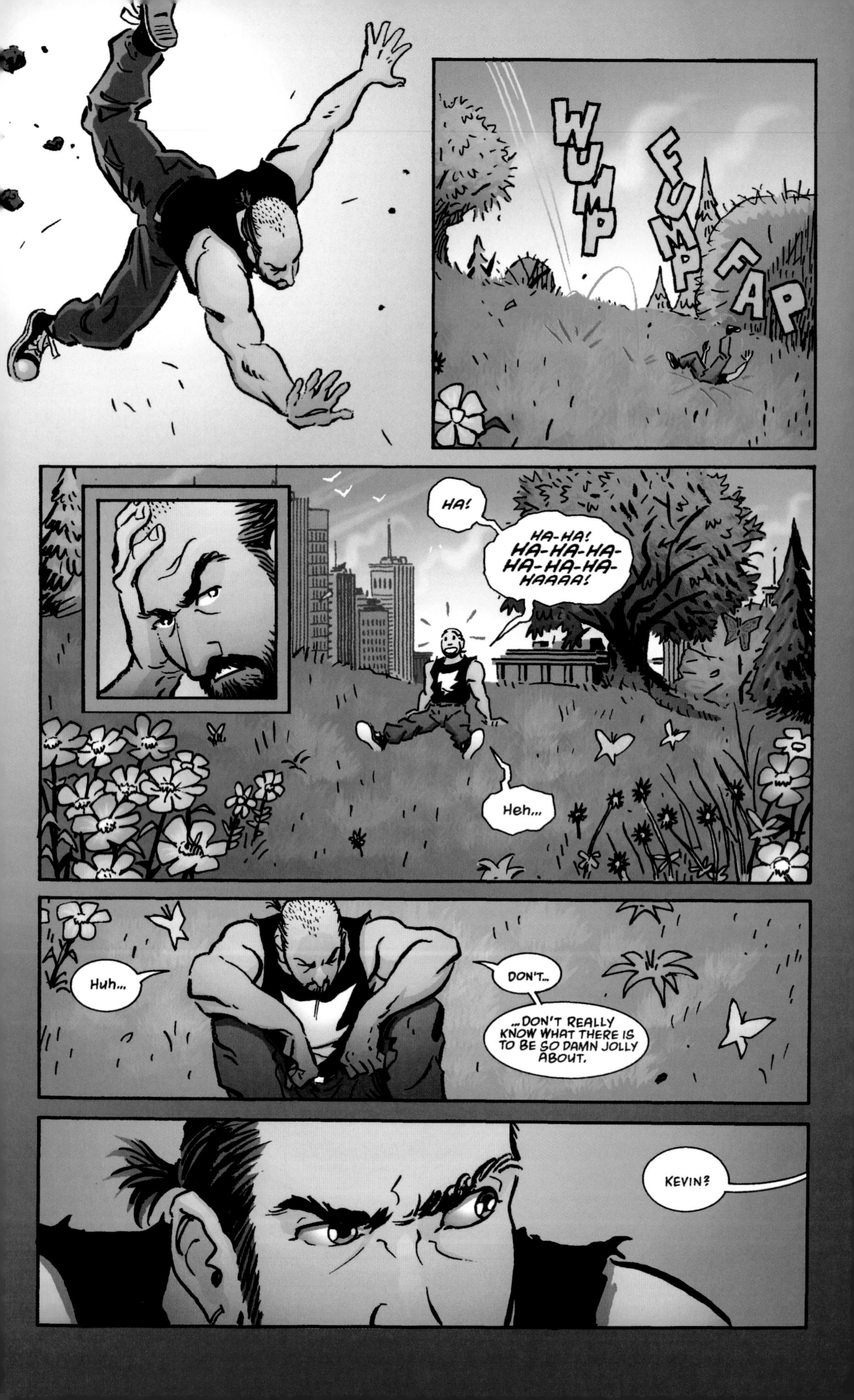

WUMP
FUMP
FAP
HA!
HA-HA! HA-HA-HA-HA-HA-HA-HAAAA!
Heh...
Huh...
DON'T...
...DON'T REALLY KNOW WHAT THERE IS TO BE SO DAMN JOLLY ABOUT.
KEVIN?

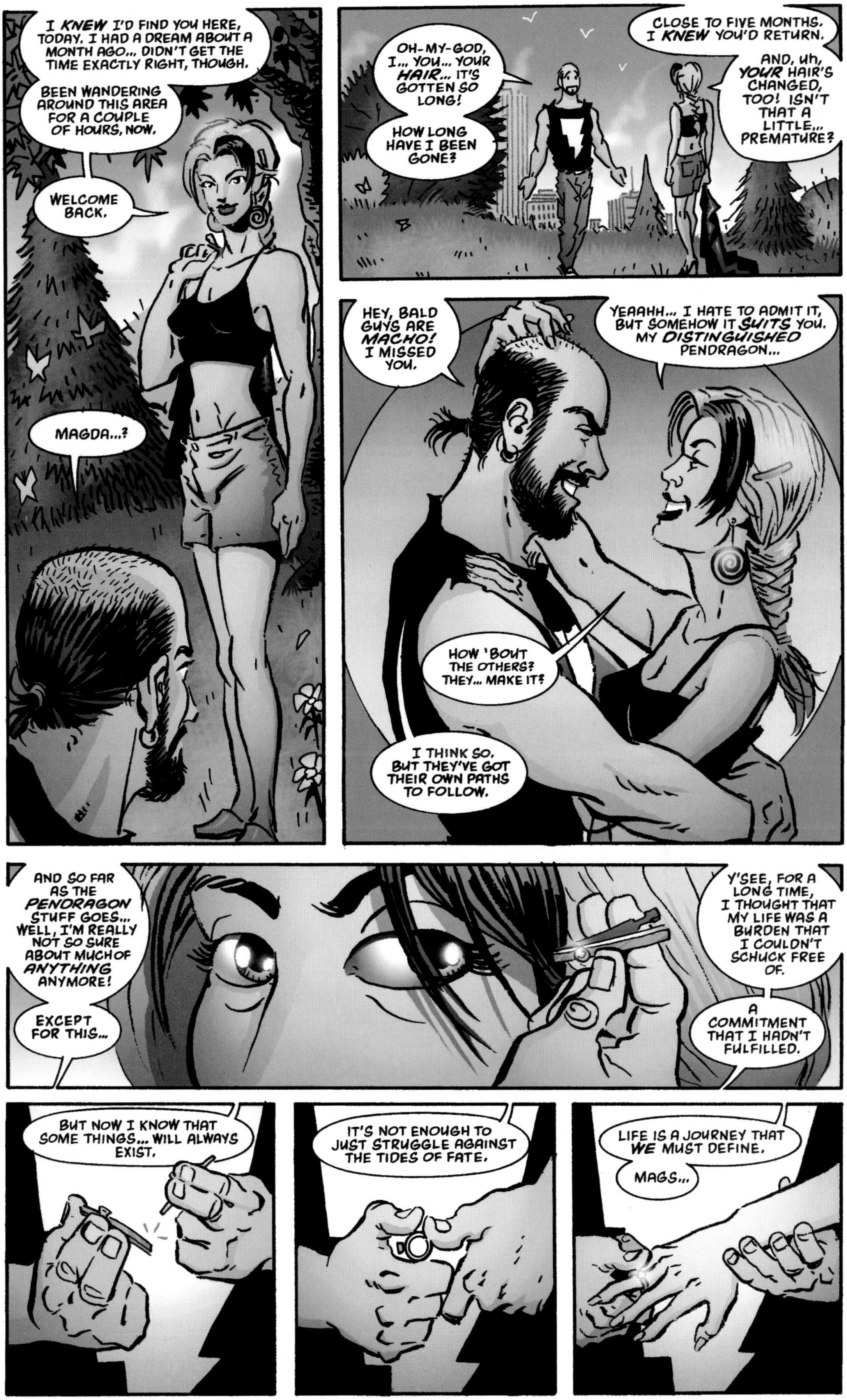

I KNEW I'D FIND YOU HERE, TODAY. I HAD A DREAM ABOUT A MONTH AGO... DIDN'T GET THE TIME EXACTLY RIGHT, THOUGH.
BEEN WANDERING AROUND THIS AREA FOR A COUPLE OF HOURS, NOW.
WELCOME BACK.
MAGDA...?
OH-MY-GOD, I... YOU... YOUR HAIR... IT'S GOTTEN SO LONG!
HOW LONG HAVE I BEEN GONE?
CLOSE TO FIVE MONTHS. I KNEW YOU'D RETURN.
AND, uh, YOUR HAIR'S CHANGED, TOO! ISN'T THAT A LITTLE... PREMATURE?
HEY, BALD GUYS ARE MACHO! I MISSED YOU.
YEAAHH... I HATE TO ADMIT IT, BUT SOMEHOW IT SUITS YOU. MY DISTINGUISHED PENDRAGON...
HOW 'BOUT THE OTHERS? THEY... MAKE IT?
I THINK SO, BUT THEY'VE GOT THEIR OWN PATHS TO FOLLOW.
AND SO FAR AS THE PENDRAGON STUFF GOES... WELL, I'M REALLY NOT SO SURE ABOUT MUCH OF ANYTHING ANYMORE!
EXCEPT FOR THIS...
Y'SEE, FOR A LONG TIME, I THOUGHT THAT MY LIFE WAS A BURDEN THAT I COULDN'T SCHUCK FREE OF.
A COMMITMENT THAT I HADN'T FULFILLED.
BUT NOW I KNOW THAT SOME THINGS... WILL ALWAYS EXIST.
IT'S NOT ENOUGH TO JUST STRUGGLE AGAINST THE TIDES OF FATE.
LIFE IS A JOURNEY THAT WE MUST DEFINE.
MAGS...

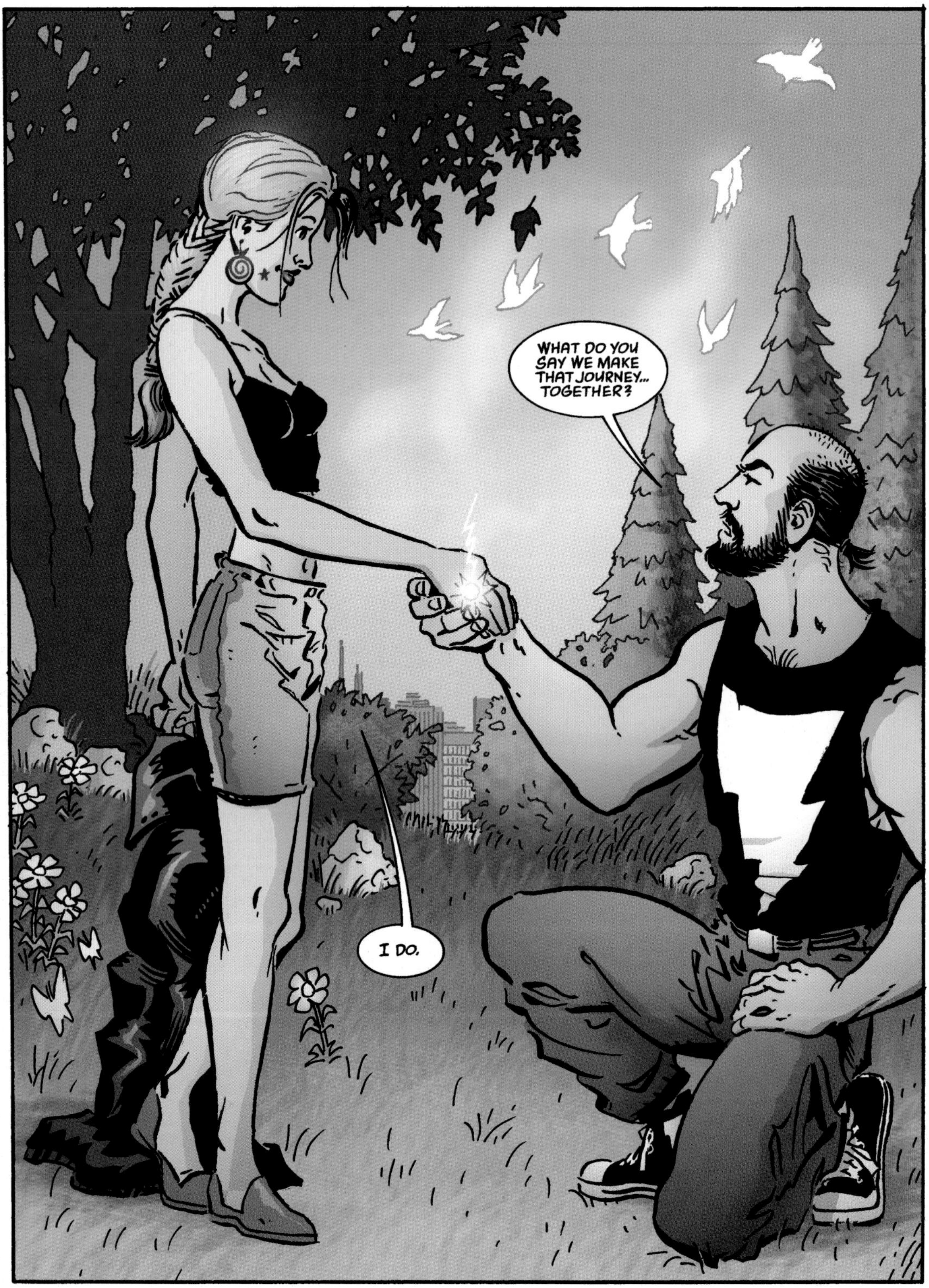
WHAT DO YOU SAY WE MAKE THAT JOURNEY... TOGETHER?
I DO.

THE
COVERS

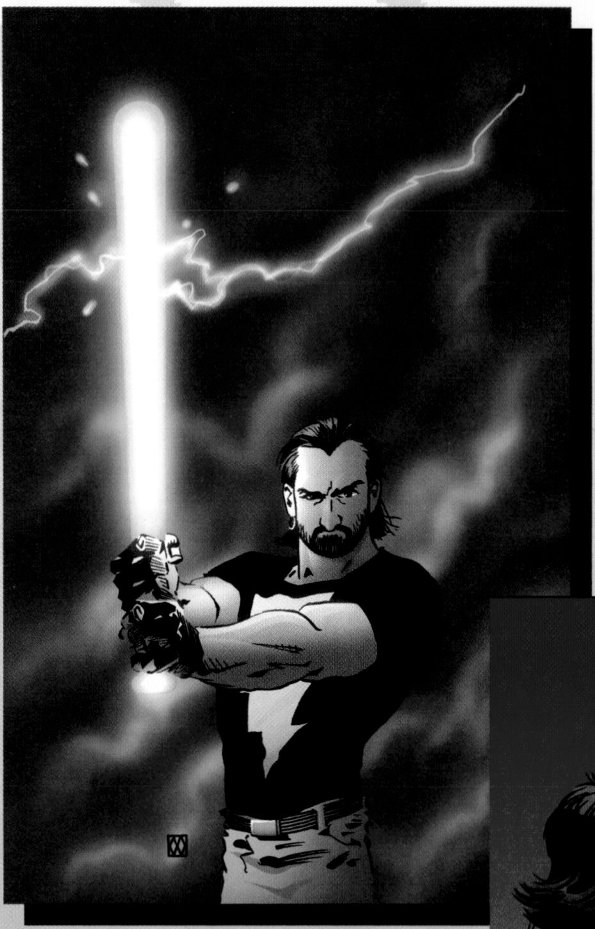

Similar to the first MAGE series, THE HERO DEFINED is divided into four acts. After the initial release of the individual issues, each act was then collected into trade editions in an attempt to appeal to those readers who need more than a single chapter at a time.

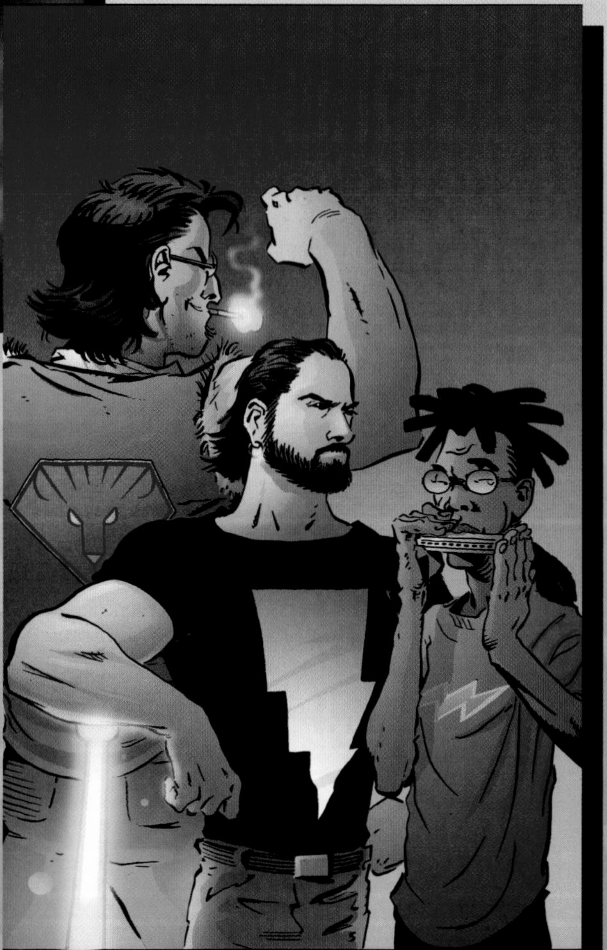

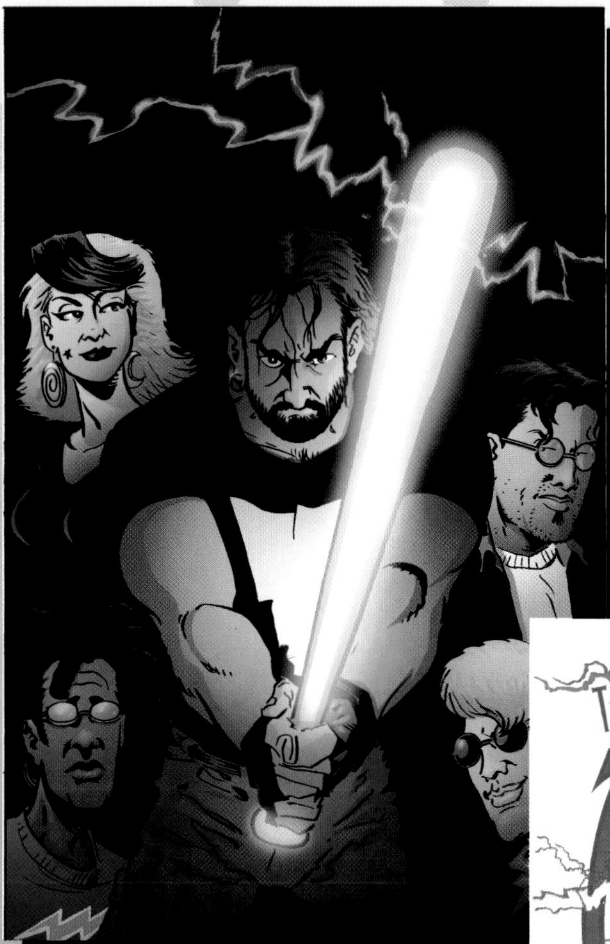

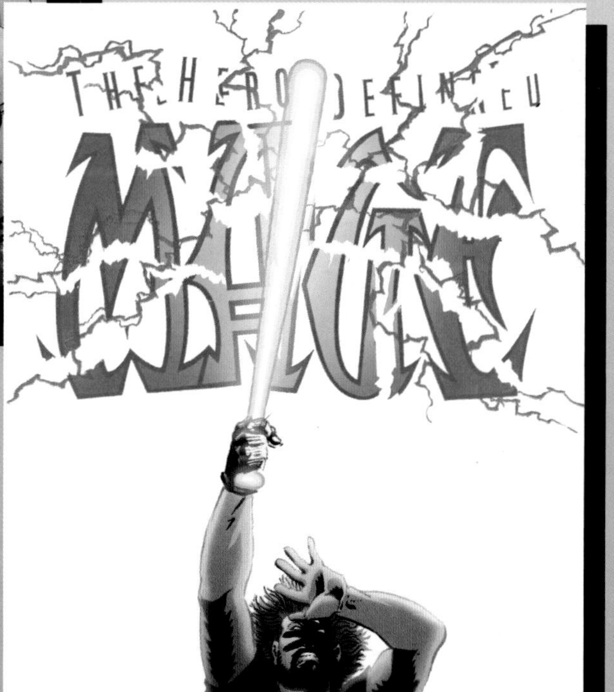

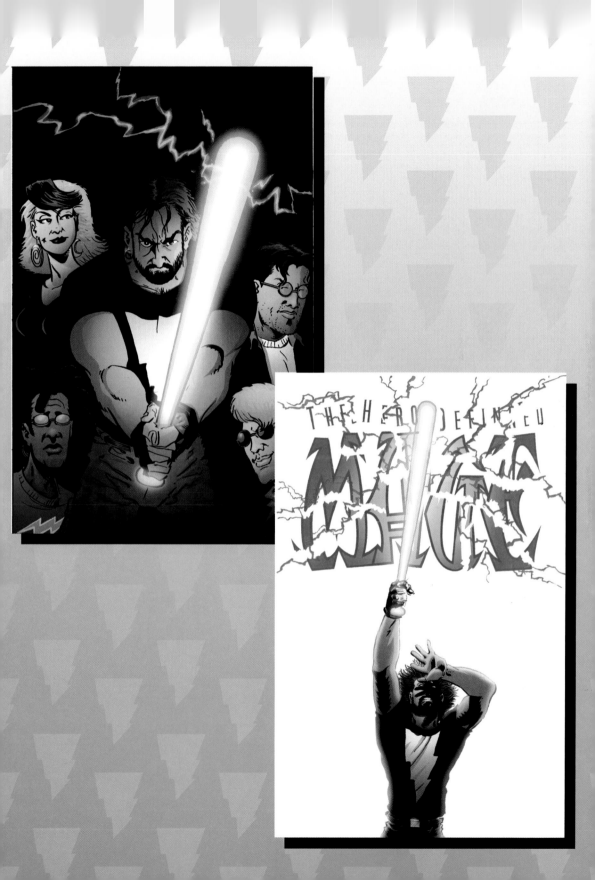

1

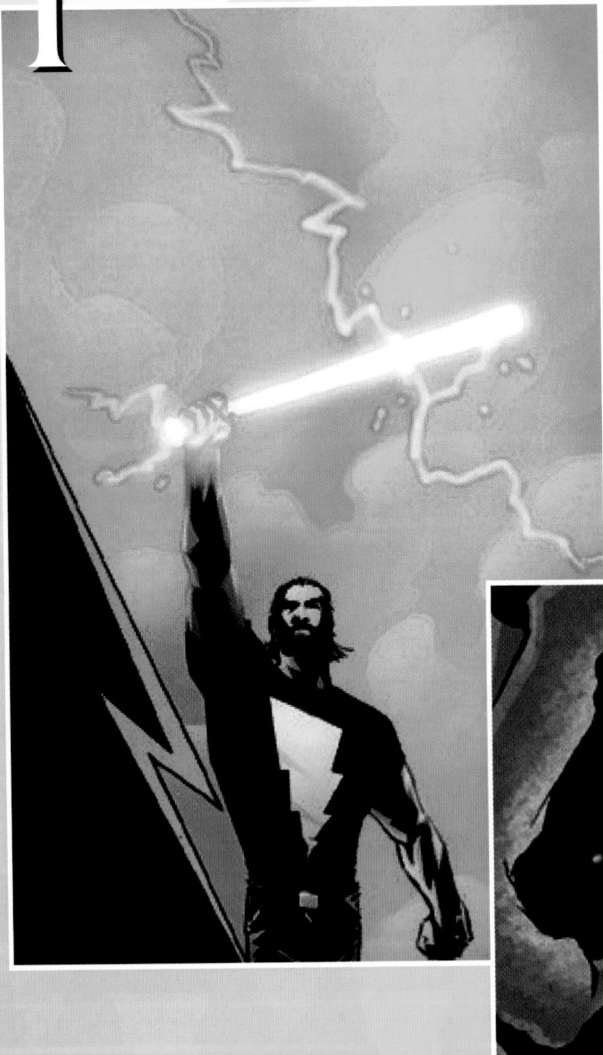

2

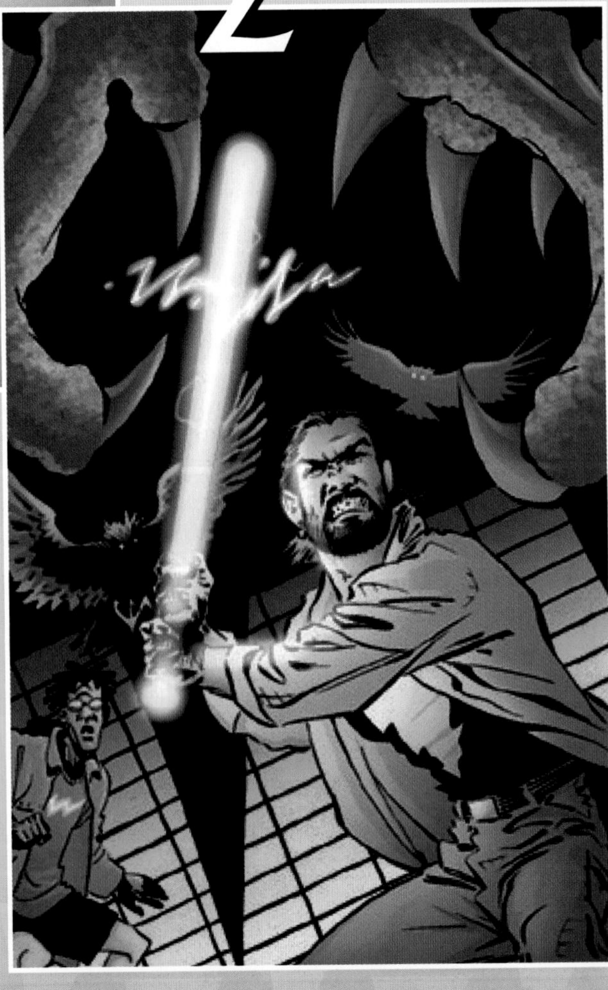

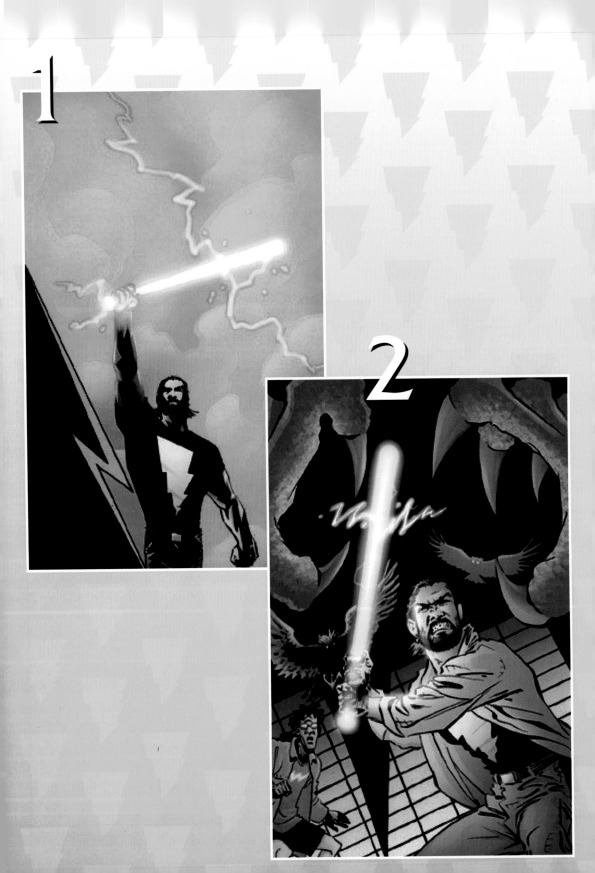

Single Issues

3

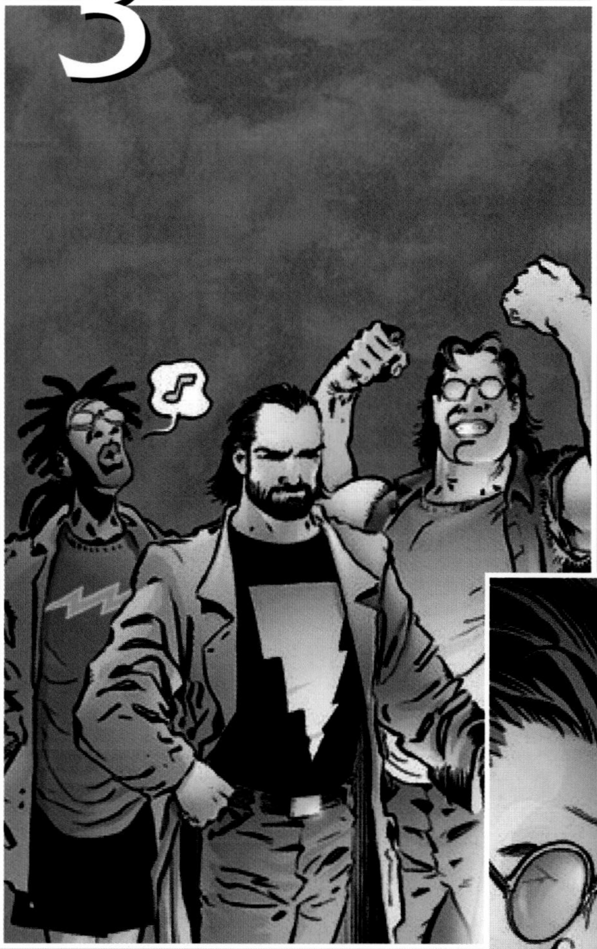

4

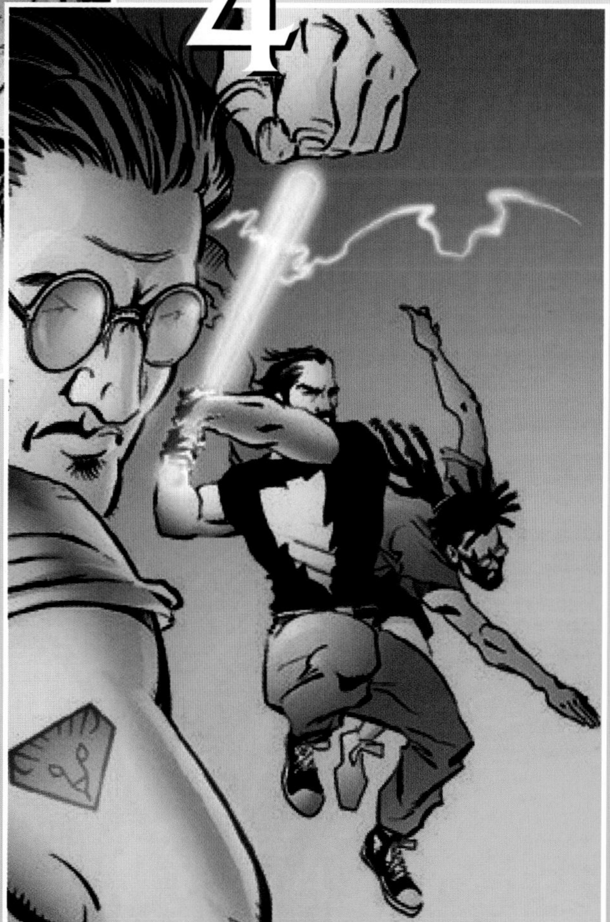

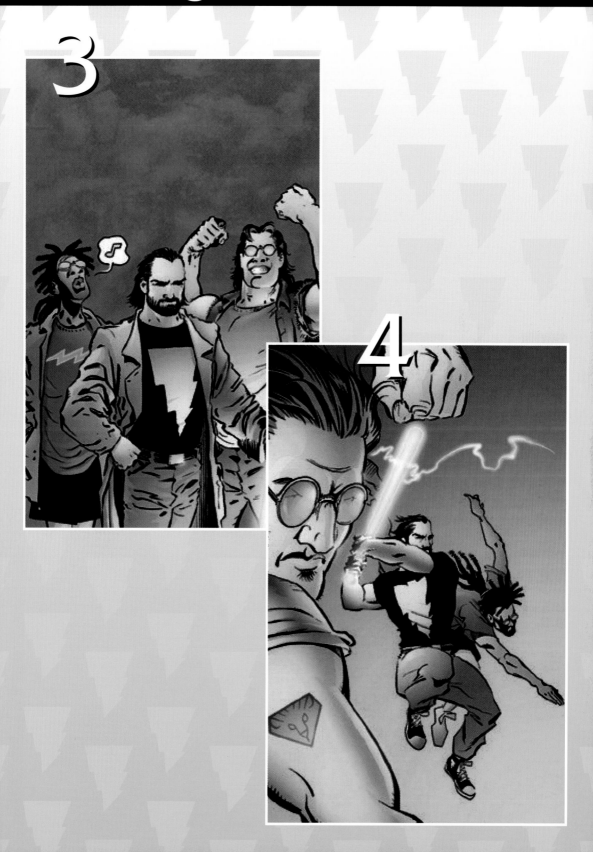

5

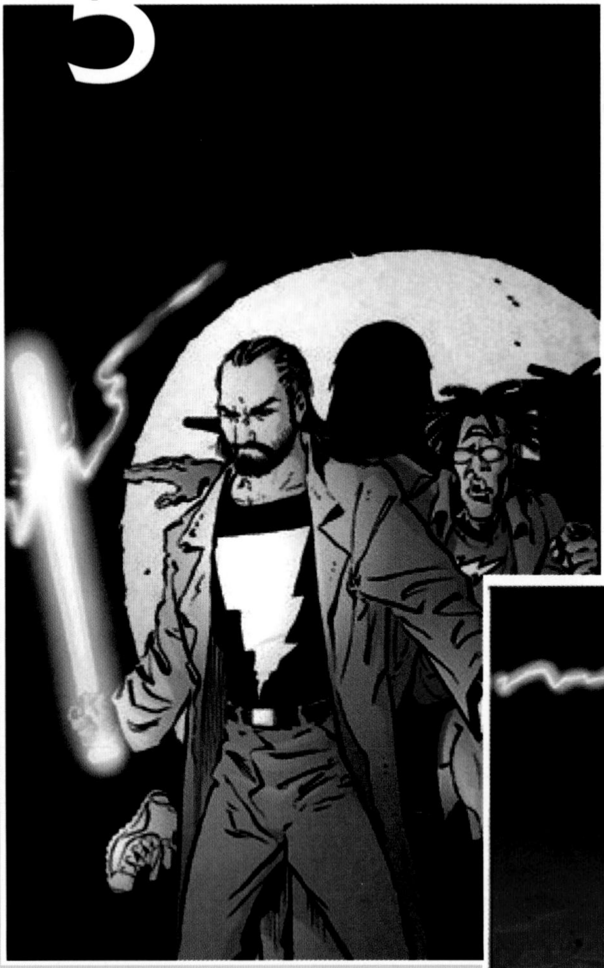

6

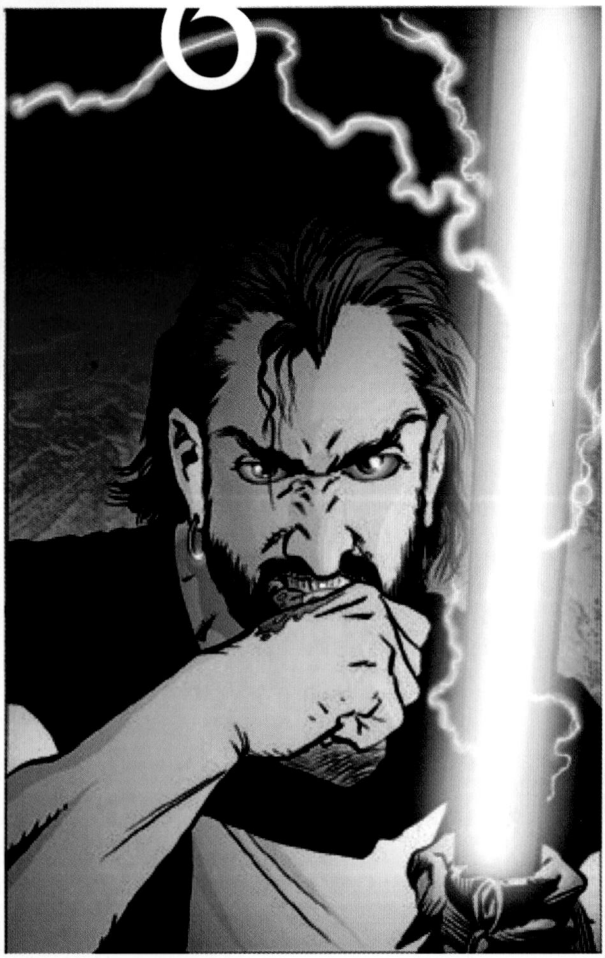

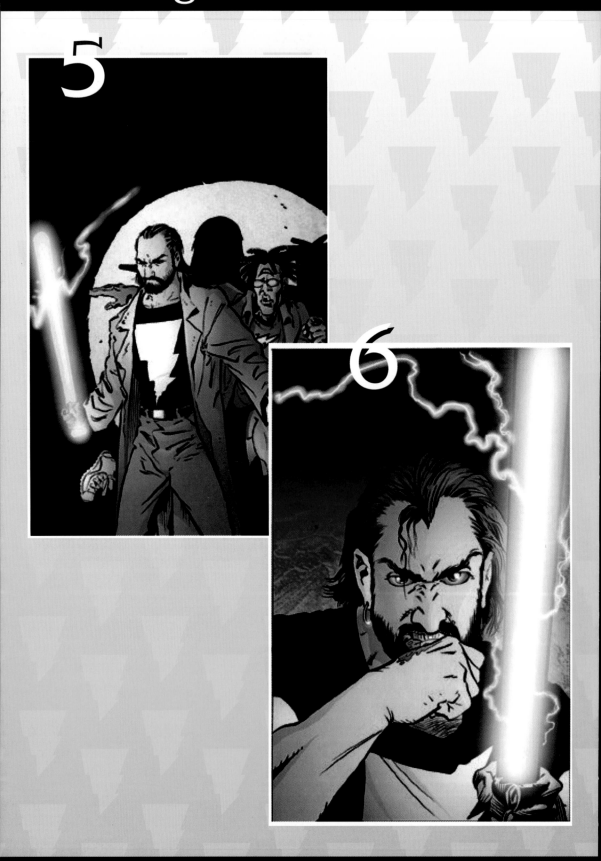

7

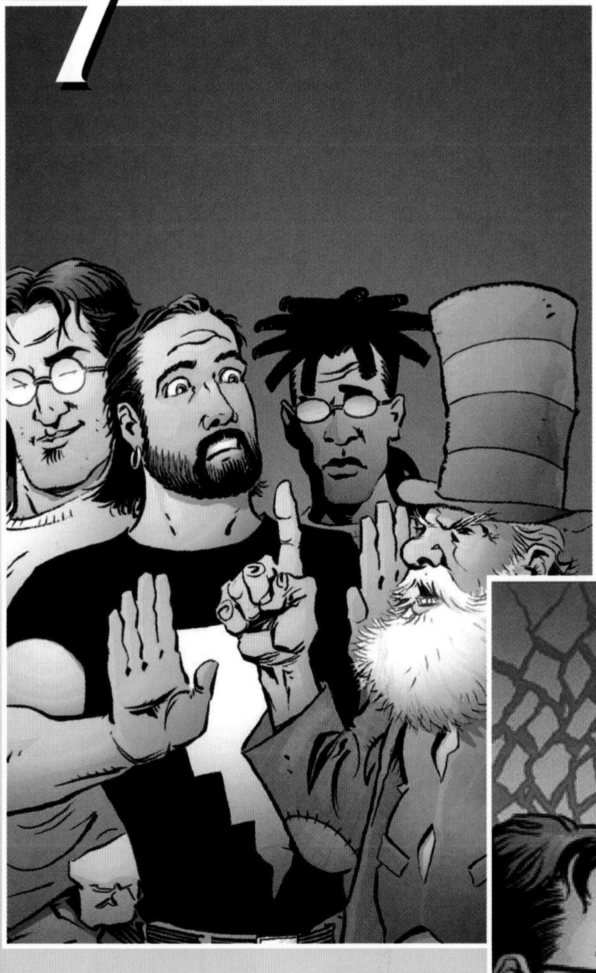

8

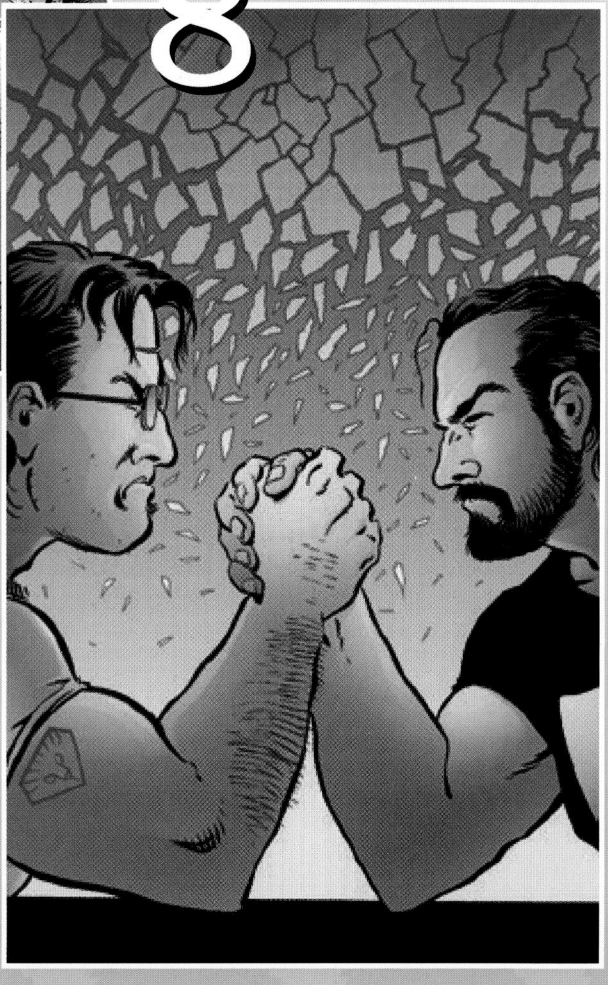

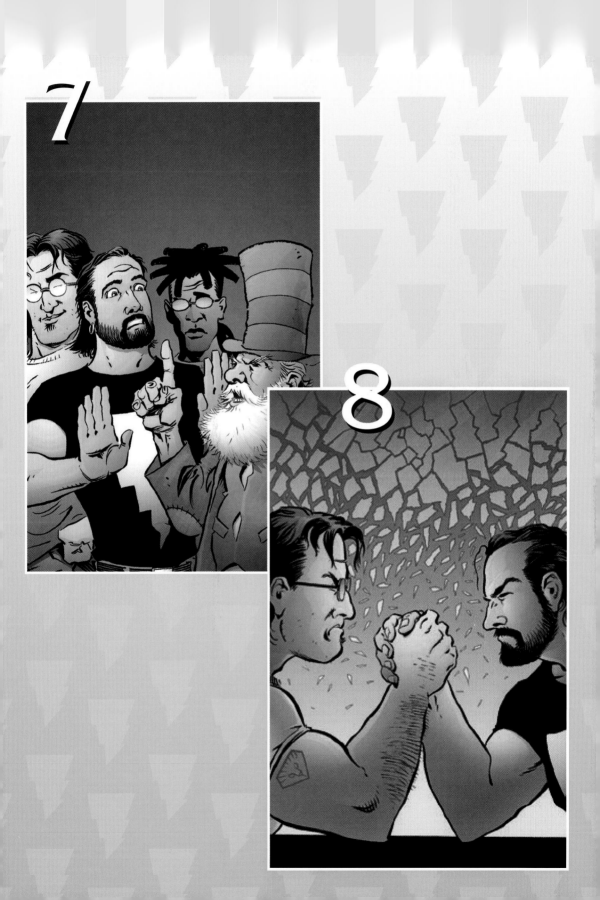

9

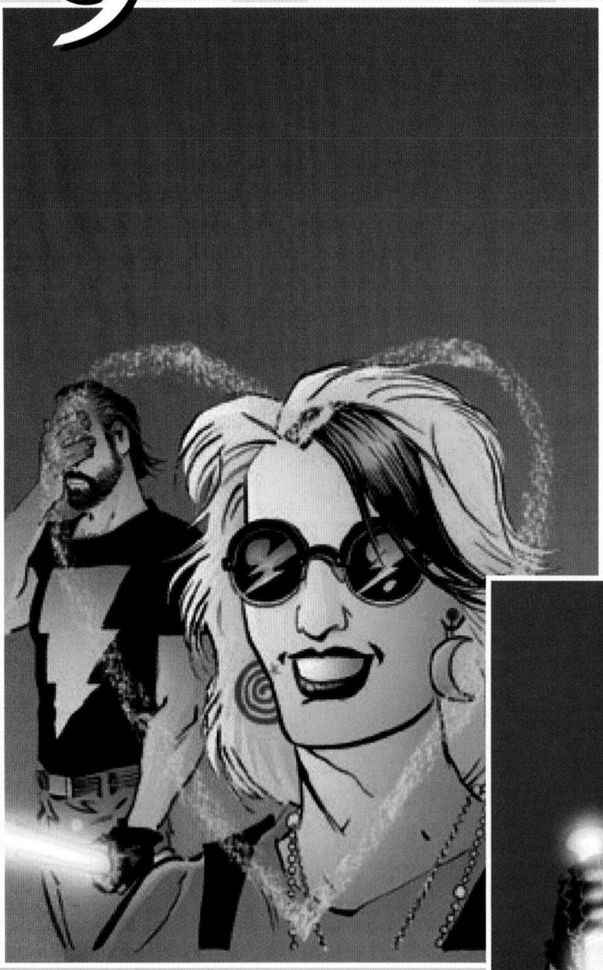

10

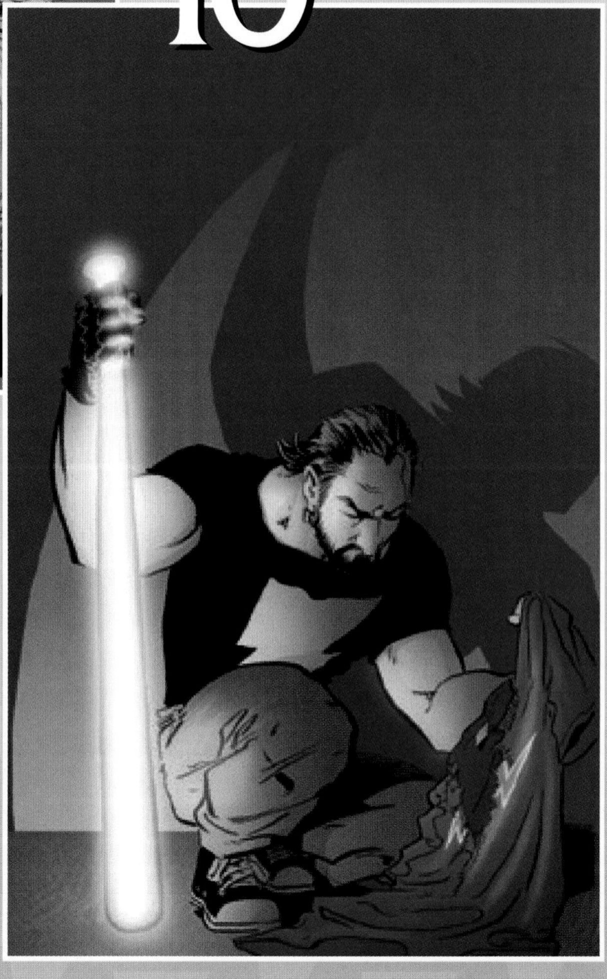

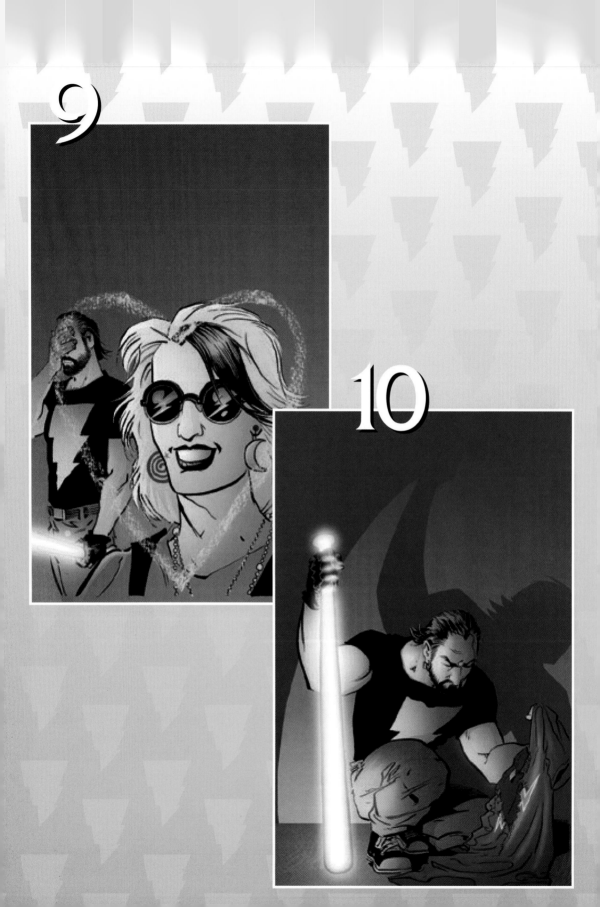

11

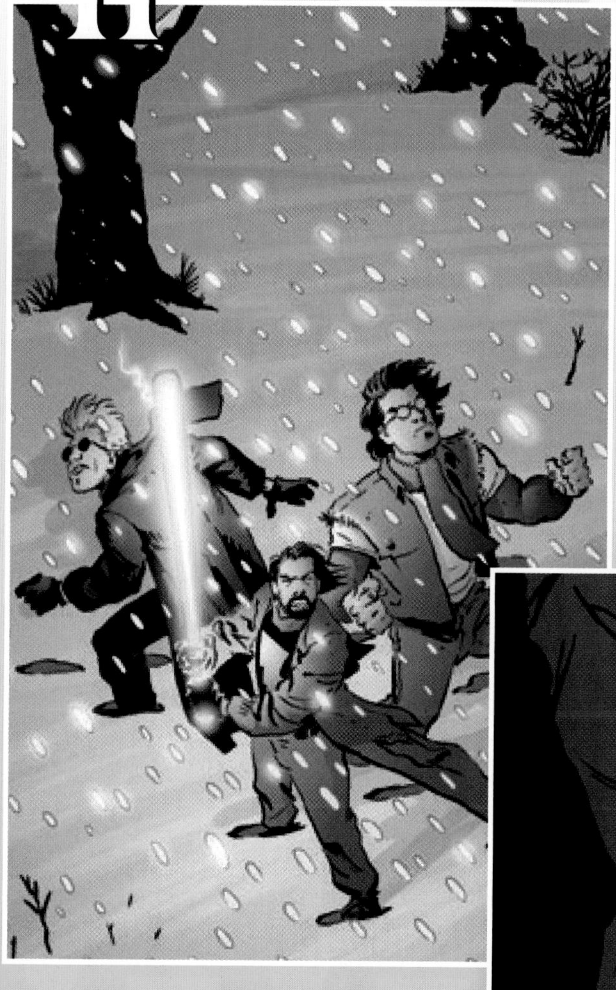

12

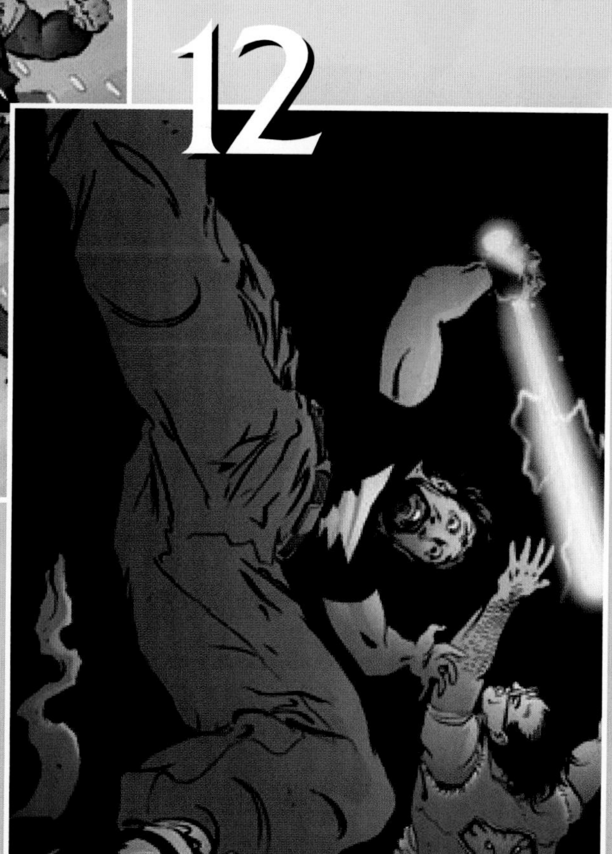

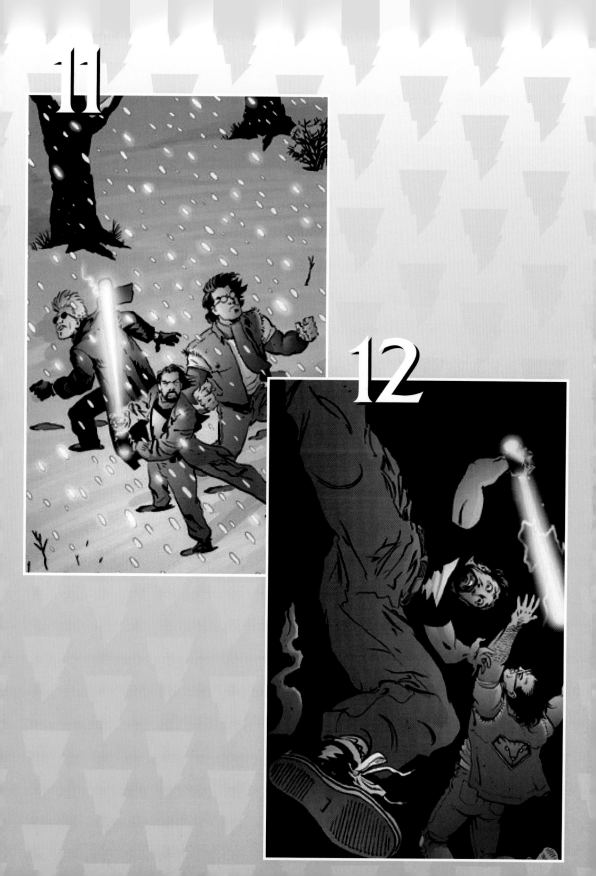

13

3 Varients

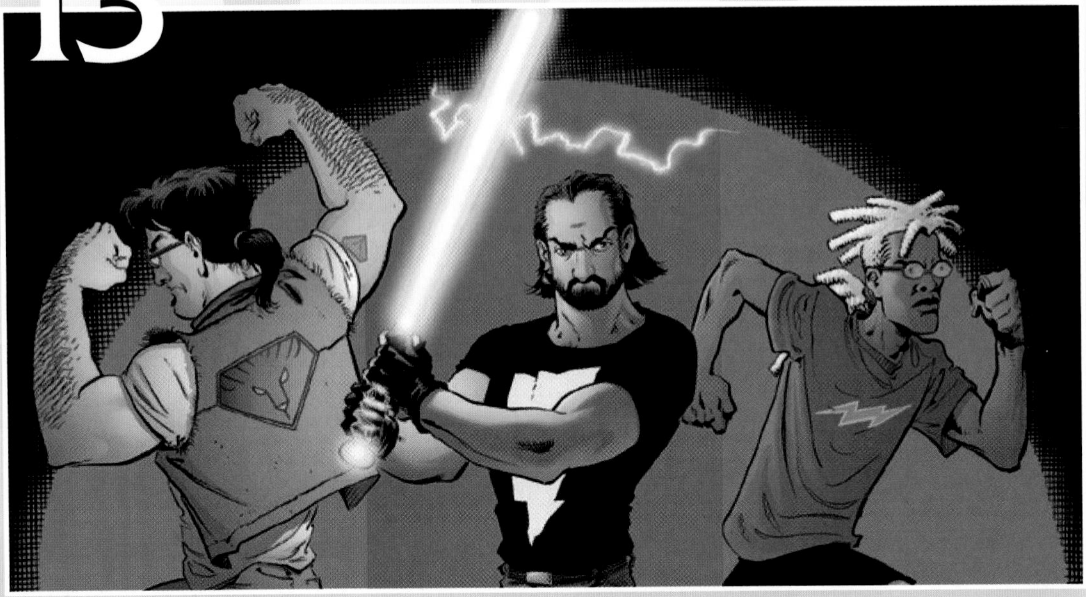

14

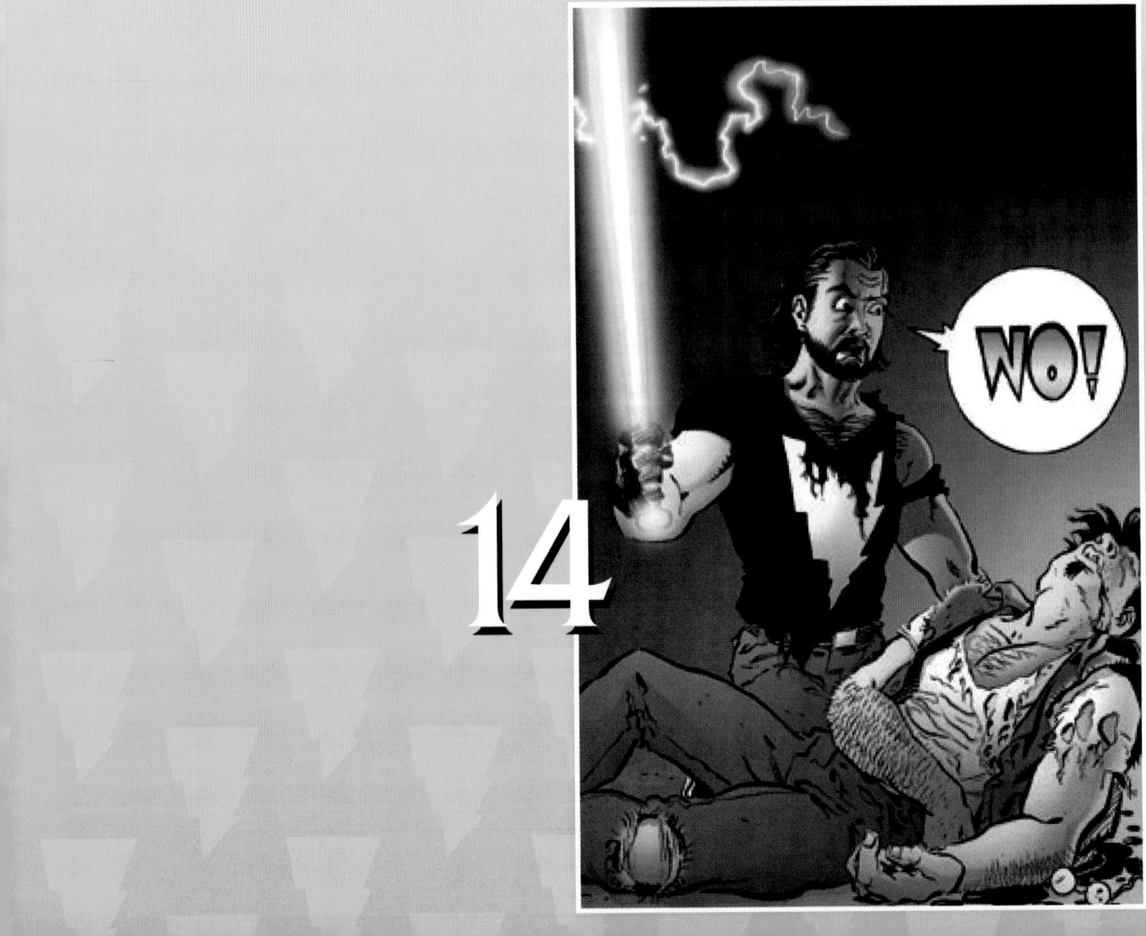
WO!

14 Alternate

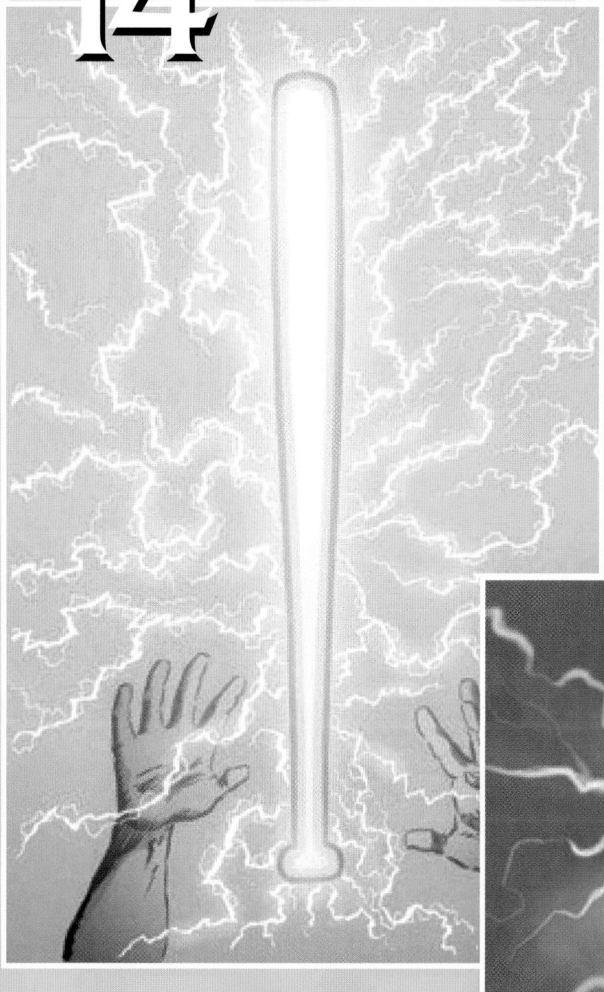

15

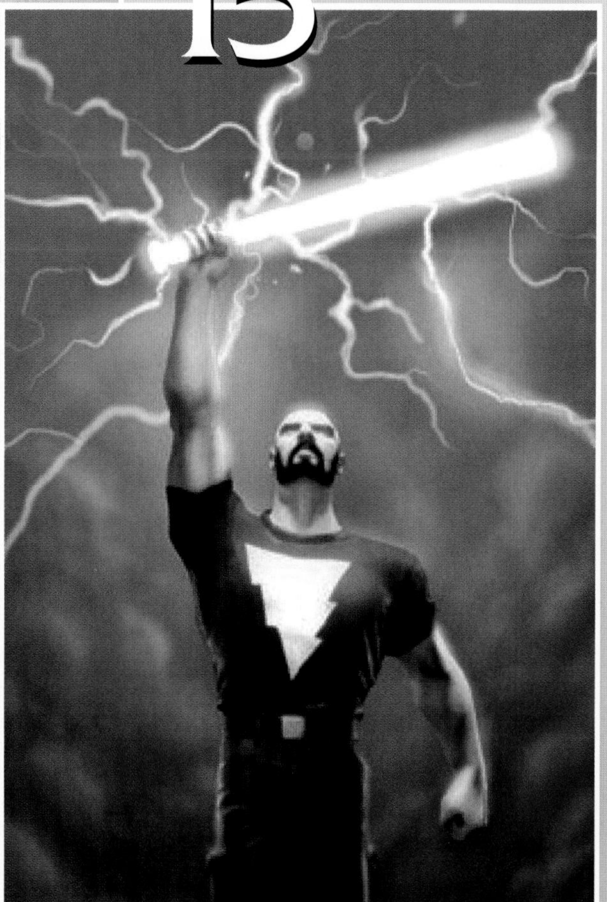

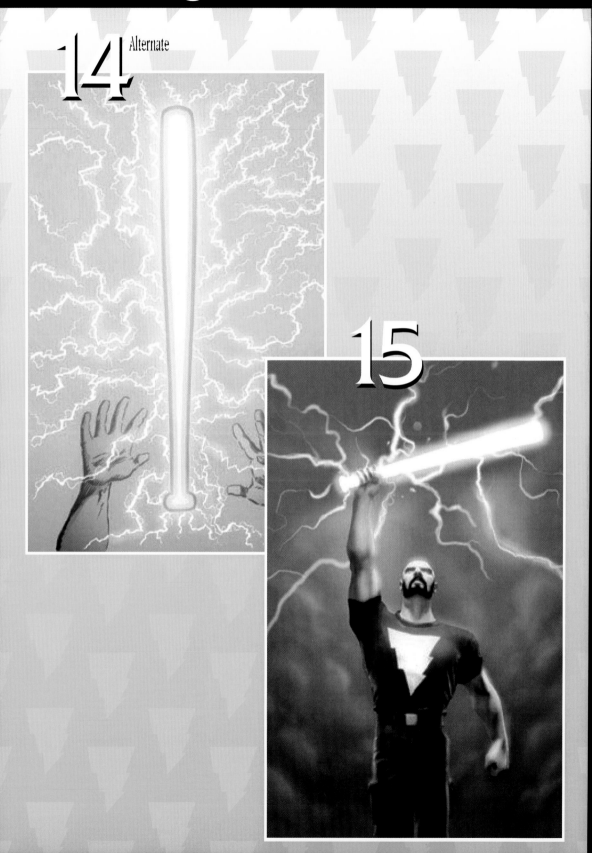

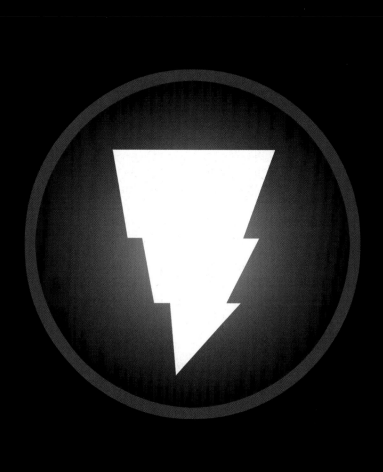

EXTRAS

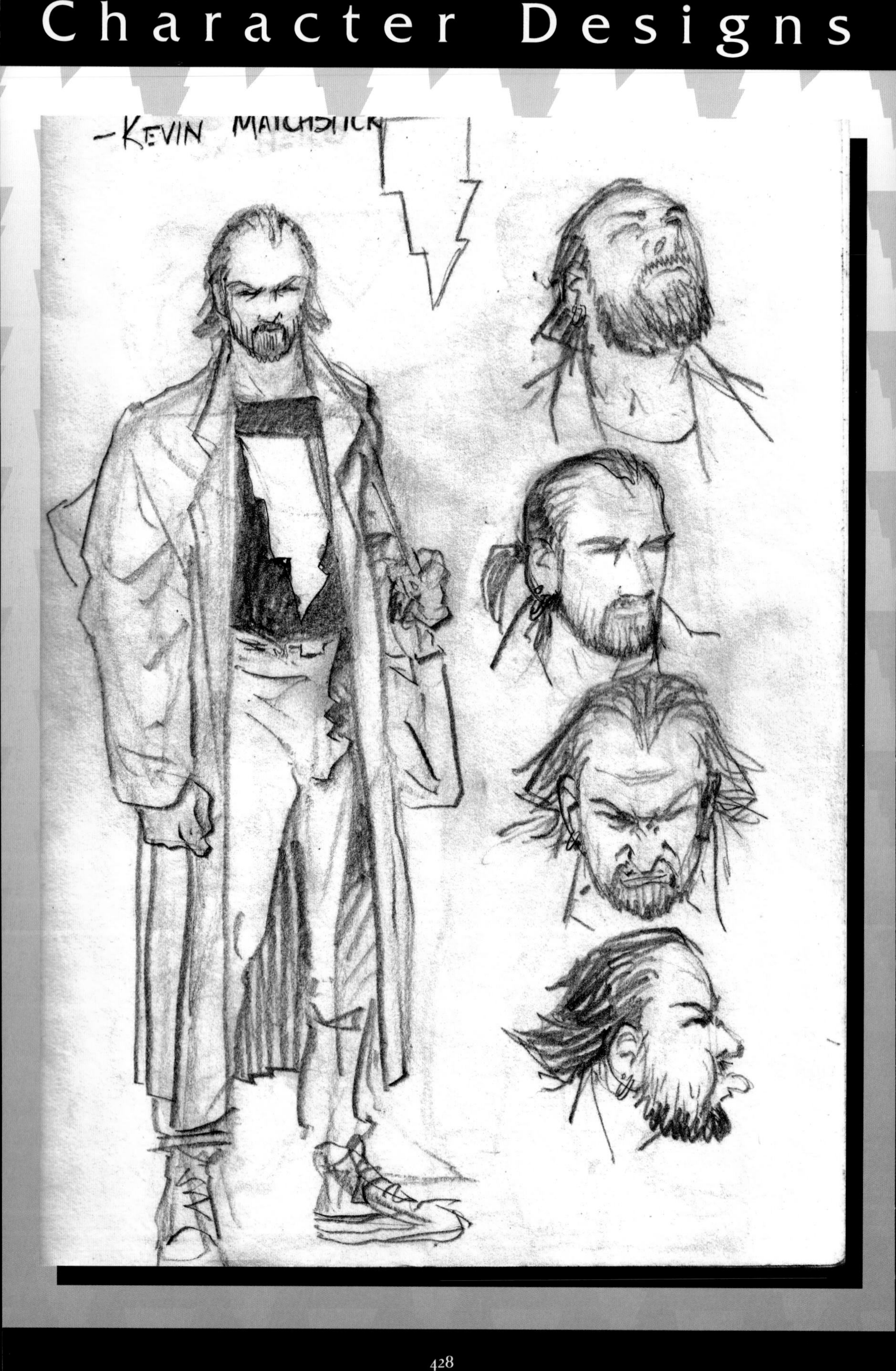
-KEVIN MATCHSTICK

Character Designs

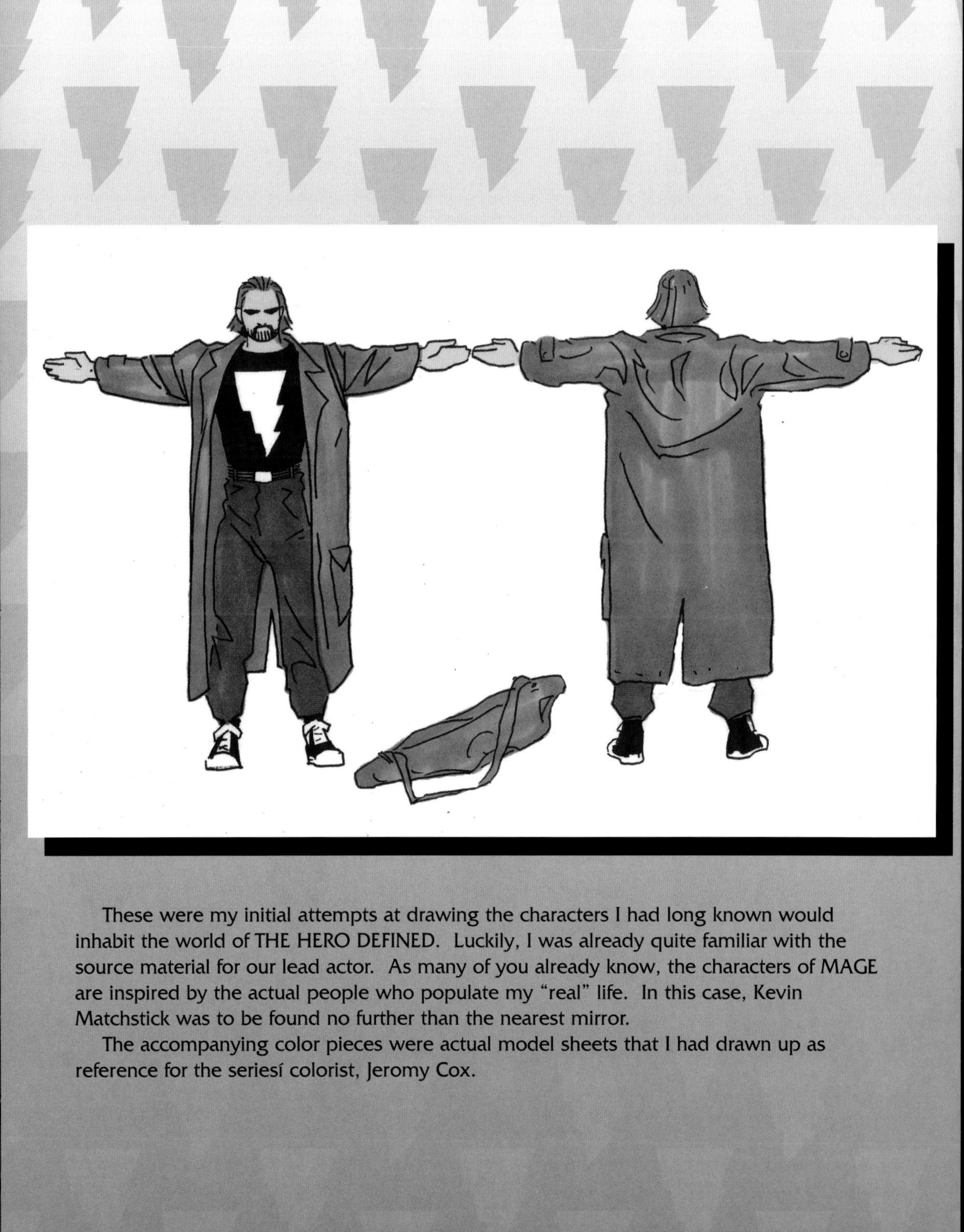

These were my initial attempts at drawing the characters I had long known would inhabit the world of THE HERO DEFINED. Luckily, I was already quite familiar with the source material for our lead actor. As many of you already know, the characters of MAGE are inspired by the actual people who populate my “real” life. In this case, Kevin Matchstick was to be found no further than the nearest mirror.

The accompanying color pieces were actual model sheets that I had drawn up as reference for the seriesí colorist, Jeromy Cox.

KIRBY HERO

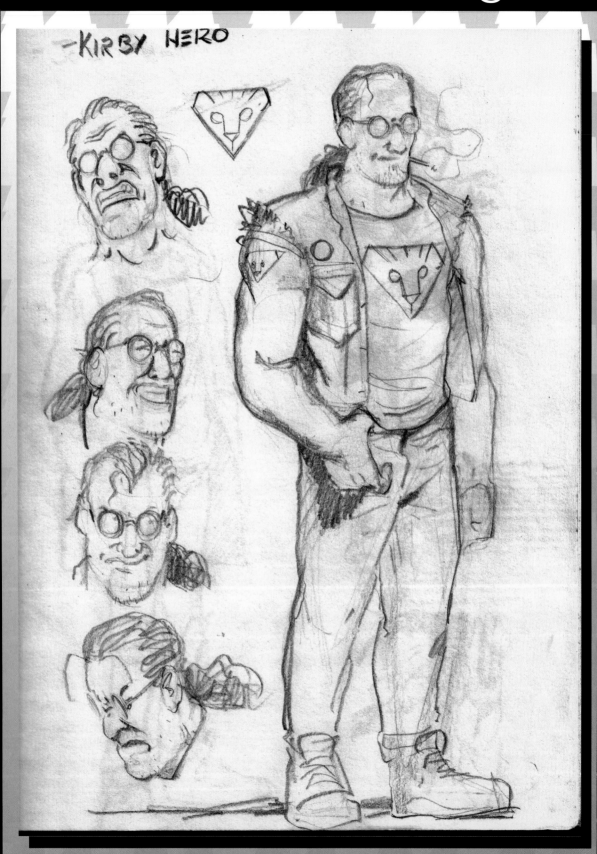

This fledgling version of Kirby isn't quite as refined as the final depiction that eventually saw print. For some reason, that I can't remember, the pony-tail was lost in transition and he appears a bit more chunky here, rather than brawny. I also bumped the lion symbol off the front of his t-shirt, opting instead to feature it on the back of his denim vest, further evidence of his stand-alone attitude. Still, I find these facial shots do capture the bombastic and mercurial nature of Kevin's on-again/off-again comrade.

-JOE PHAT   KIM SONG

Joe Phat seems to be suffering from a bit of premature balding in this first crack at his character design.   Many people knew that this (ultimately much hairier) Coyote was based on my old college chum, Joe Matt. I elected to make his MAGE incarnation black to distinguish my version from his already existing depiction as a comic book character in the pages of his own autobiographical book, PEEPSHOW. The bottom head-shot shows that I had originally intended Joe to have other hyper-senses in addition to his mystic sense of smell. Unfortunately, I found that an instance to show off this attribute just never arose over the course of my narrative.

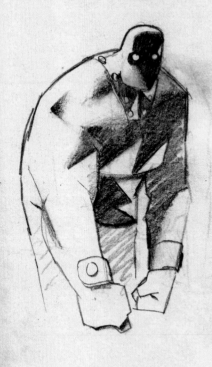

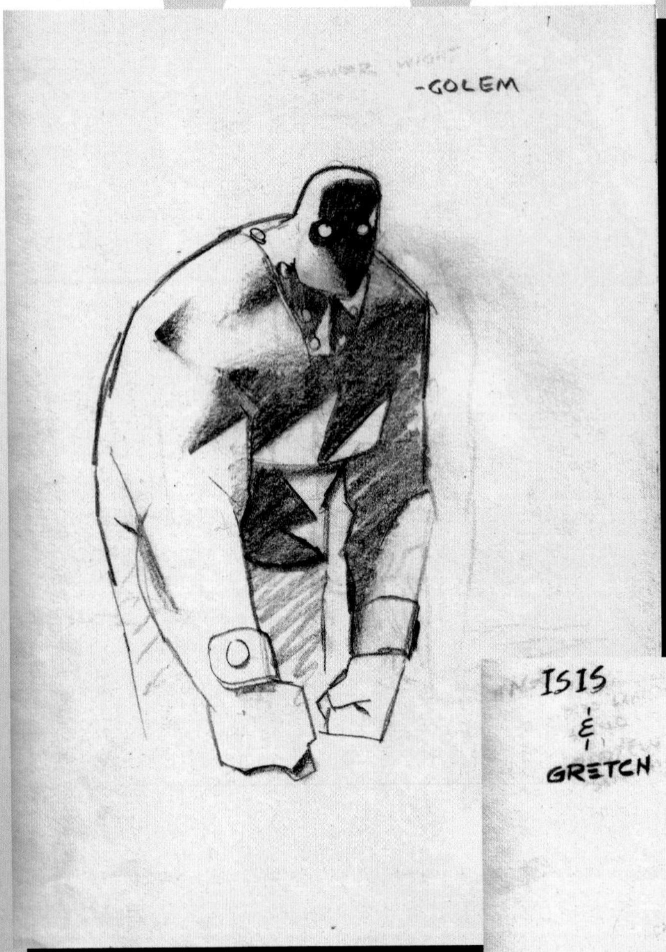

-GOLEM

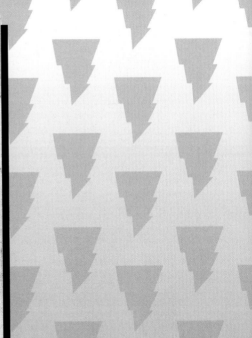

ISIS
&
GRETCN

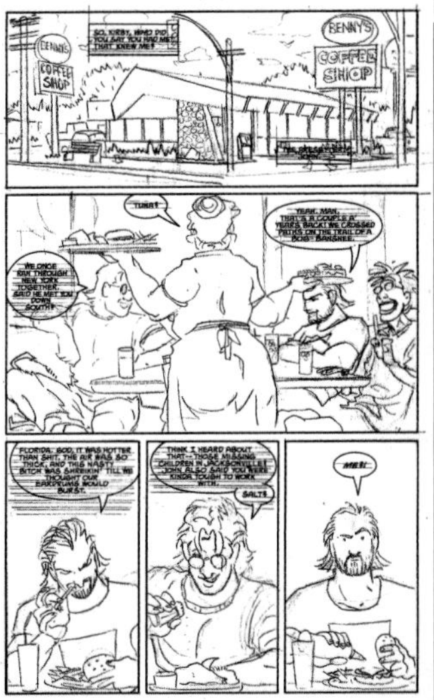
SO, KIRBY, WHO DID YOU SAY YOU HAD MET THAT KNEW ME?
BENNY'S COFFEE SHOP
BENNY'S COFFEE SHOP
TUNA?
ME?!

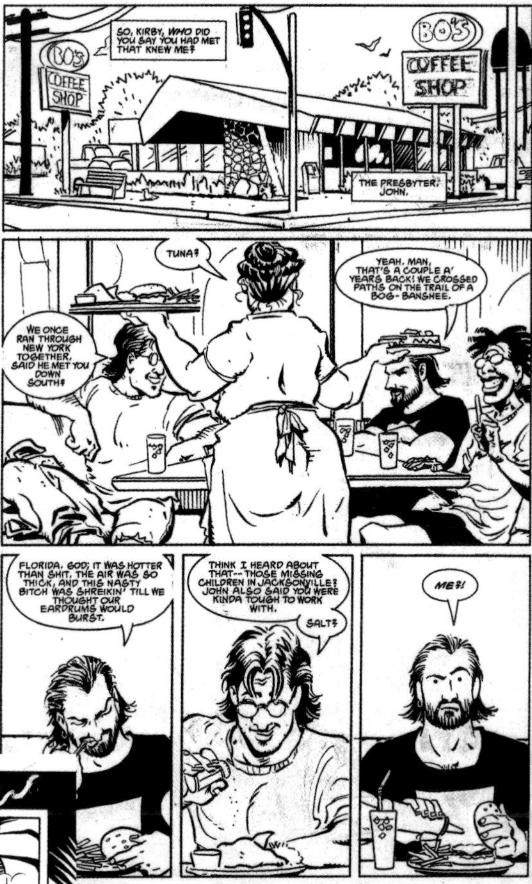
SO, KIRBY, WHO DID YOU SAY YOU HAD MET THAT KNEW ME?
BO'S COFFEE SHOP
BO'S COFFEE SHOP
THE PRESBYTER, JOHN.
TUNA?
WE ONCE RAN THROUGH NEW YORK TOGETHER. SAID HE MET YOU DOWN SOUTH?
YEAH, MAN, THAT'S A COUPLE A' YEARS BACK! WE CROSSED PATHS ON THE TRAIL OF A BOG-BANSHEE.
FLORIDA. GOD, IT WAS HOTTER THAN SHIT. THE AIR WAS SO THICK, AND THIS NASTY BITCH WAS SHREIKIN' TILL WE THOUGHT OUR EARDRUMS WOULD BURST.
THINK I HEARD ABOUT THAT-- THOSE MISSING CHILDREN IN JACKSONVILLE? JOHN ALSO SAID YOU WERE KINDA TOUGH TO WORK WITH.
SALT?
ME?!

I always produce very loose pencils before moving on to the finished version, rendered in ink. This is an effort to keep every stage of the artwork's creation

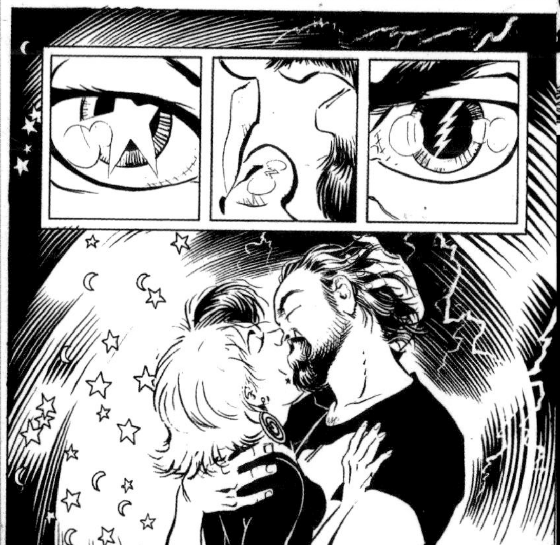

exciting and vital. God knows, I don't want anyone accusing me of being merely some kind of "tracer"!

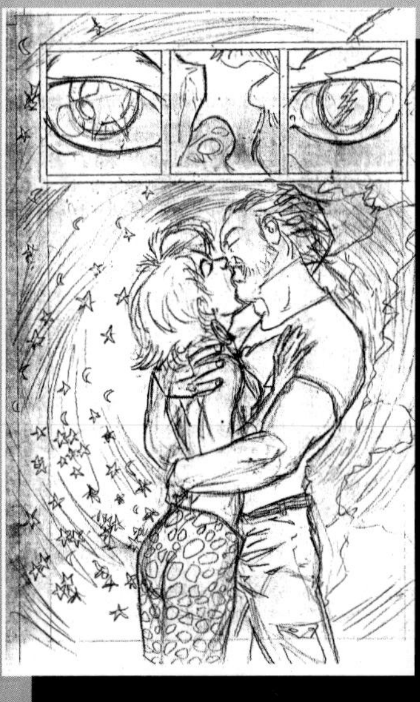

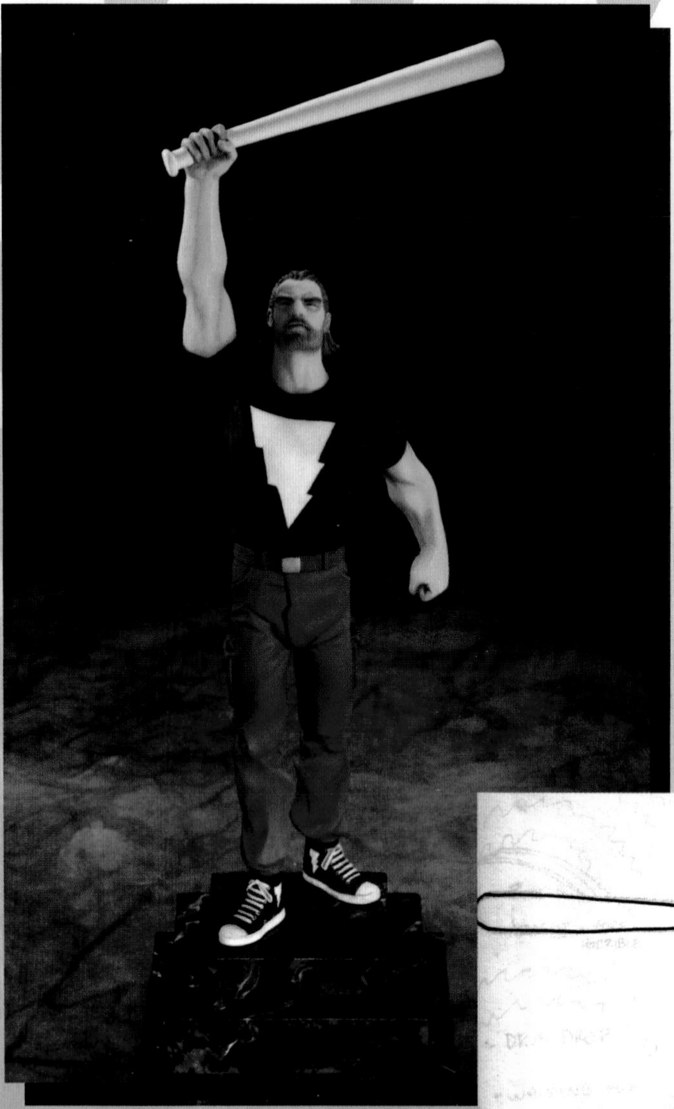

Considering my long-standing relationship with Bowen Designs, it seemed only natural that a MAGE statue would see the light of day. The initial plan, though, was to only produce a mini-bust of Kevin Matchstick. Still, sculptor Randy Bowen was unsatisfied with the "cropped" nature of the figure in such a piece, despite my attempts at lessening this effect by having the lightning bolt on the character's shirt extend onto the statue's base. In the end, a full-figure of Kevin emerged, still triumphantly brandishing his magic bat.

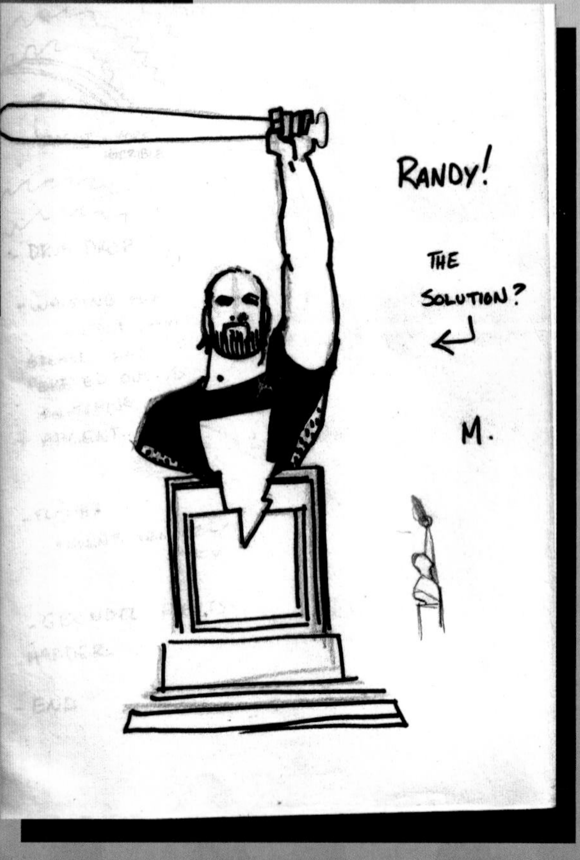
RANDY!
THE SOLUTION?
M.